THE
HUMAN PAST
ESSENTIALS

Edited by
Chris Scarre and
Tammy Stone

THE
HUMAN PAST
ESSENTIALS

395 illustrations

The Human Past Essentials © 2021 Thames & Hudson Ltd,
London

Edited by Chris Scarre and Tammy Stone

First published in 2021 in the United States of America
by Thames & Hudson Inc., 500 Fifth Avenue, New York,
New York 10110

Library of Congress Control Number 2021930604

ISBN 978-0-500-843864

Printed and bound in China by C & C Offset Printing Co. Ltd

Be the first to know about our new releases,
exclusive content and author events by visiting
thamesandhudson.com
thamesandhudsonusa.com
thamesandhudson.com.au

CONTENTS

Contributors 7

Preface 9

**1 INTRODUCTION: THE STUDY OF
THE HUMAN PAST** 12

Chris Scarre and Tammy Stone

What Is Archaeology? 14

The Current State of Archaeology 17

The Responsibilities of Archaeology 17

Enduring Themes in Archaeology 20

Approaches and Techniques 23

2 AFRICAN ORIGINS 30

Nicholas Toth and Kathy Schick

Evolution and Human Origins 32

Environments and Landscapes 35

The Rise of the Earliest Hominins 35

The First Stone Tools and the Oldowan 37

Food Procurement and Diet 42

The Behavior of Oldowan Hominins 44

3 HOMININ DISPERSALS 48

Richard Klein

African *Homo erectus* 52

The Acheulean 53

Peopling the Landscape: The Dispersal
  of *Homo erectus* 54

Asian *Homo erectus* 56

The Initial Occupation of Europe 59

Homo heidelbergensis 60

Neanderthals 62

Evidence for Early Human Behavior 62

4 THE RISE OF MODERN HUMANS 72

Paul Pettitt

Environments and Landscapes 76

The Rise of Modern Humans in Africa 76

The Neanderthals 79

The Peopling of East Asia and Australia 85

The Peopling of Europe and Russia 87

5 THE WORLD TRANSFORMED: FROM HUNTER-GATHERERS TO EARLY FARMERS 94

Chris Scarre

Environments and Landscapes, 13,000–9600 BCE 96

Hunter-Gatherer Trajectories 99

Transitions to Agriculture 100

Expansion of Domestication 105

The Consequences of Agriculture 106

6 SOUTHWEST ASIA: FROM MOBILE FORAGING TO SETTLED FARMING 110

Trevor Watkins

Environments and Landscapes, 20,000–9600 BCE 113

The Last Hunter-Gatherers: The Epipaleolithic in the Levant, 20,000–9600 BCE 115

The Transition to Farming: The Early Aceramic Neolithic, 9600–8800 BCE 121

Early Farming Communities: The Later Aceramic Neolithic, 8800–6500 BCE 125

The Expansion of Farming, 6500–6000 BCE 135

7 SOUTHWEST ASIA: CITIES AND STATES 138

Roger Matthews

Cities and States of the World 141

Transitions to States in Southwest Asia: The Halaf and Ubaid Periods, c. 6000–4200 BCE 145

Urban Communities: The Uruk Period, c. 4200–3000 BCE 149

City States, Kingdoms, and Empires in Southwest Asia: Early Bronze Age, c. 3000–2000 BCE 154

Cities and Empires in Southwest Asia: The Middle Bronze Age, c. 2000–1700 BCE 160

8 SOUTH ASIA 164

Robin Coningham

Environments and Landscapes 167

Hunter-Gatherer Trajectories: Early South Asia, c. 26,000–6500 BCE 167

Transitions to Agriculture, 6500–1000 BCE 168

Transitions to States: Early Harappan, Kot Diji, and Regionalization, c. 3000–2600 BCE 171

Urban Communities: The Indus River, c. 2600–1900 BCE 173

Collapse and Localization: The Eclipse of the Indus Cities, c. 1900 BCE 178

Expansion and Integration: Re-Emergence of Complexity, c. 1200–500 BCE 180

9 EAST ASIA: FROM MOBILE FORAGING TO SETTLED FARMING 182

Charles Higham

Environments and Landscapes 185

Agriculture in East Asia 185

Transitions to Agriculture: The Yangzi Valley, 12,000–6000 BCE 186

Early Farming Communities: The Yangzi Valley, 6000–2500 BCE 187

Transitions to Agriculture: Northern China and the Yellow River Valley, 9000–5000 BCE 191

Early Farming Communities: Northern China and the Yellow River Valley, c. 5000–2600 BCE 193

The Expansion of Farming: Southern China and Southeast Asia, 2000–1000 BCE 197

Complex Hunter-Gatherers: Jōmon Japan, 14,000–1000 BCE 202

Expansion of Domestication: Korea and Japan 203

10 EAST ASIA: CITIES AND STATES 208

Charles Higham

Transitions to States: China, c. 3500–200 BCE 210

Transitions to States: Korea, 108 BCE–900 CE 225

Transitions to States: Japan, 250–650 CE 228

Expansion and Integration: Early States in Southeast Asia 229

11 AUSTRALIA AND THE PACIFIC ISLANDS 236

Peter Bellwood and Peter Hiscock

Environments and Landscapes: Australia 240

Hunter-Gatherer Trajectories, c. 5000 BCE–1700 CE 242

Environments and Landscapes: The Islands of Southeast Asia 245

Transitions to Agriculture: New Guinea 245

Expansion of Domestication: The Austronesian Dispersal 247

Expansion of Domestication: Oceania
and Lapita **251**

Farming Communities: The Austronesian World
after Migration, 1100–1500 CE **255**

Seaborne Trade and Contact in Southeast Asia **261**

12 EUROPE **264**

Chris Scarre, with Susan E. Alcock and John F. Cherry

Environments and Landscapes **267**

Hunter-Gatherer Trajectories: Mesolithic
Communities in Europe, *c.* 9000–6000 BCE **268**

Early Farming Communities: Southeastern Europe,
c. 6900–3000 BCE **269**

Early Farming Communities: The Mediterranean
Zone, *c.* 6000–2500 BCE **274**

Early Farming Communities: Central Europe,
c. 5600–3000 BCE **275**

Early Farming Communities: Atlantic Europe,
c. 5000–2000 BCE **279**

Hunter-Gatherer Trajectories: Northern Europe,
9600–4000 BCE **281**

Early Farming Communities: Northern Europe,
4000–2000 BCE **284**

Later Farming Communities: Bronze Age Europe,
2300–800 BCE **285**

Transitions to States: The Aegean,
c. 3000–1000 BCE **290**

13 AFRICA **294**

Graham Connah

Environments and Landscapes **297**

Hunter-Gatherer Trajectories: Intensified Hunting,
Gathering, and Fishing, *c.* 9000–5000 BCE **297**

Transitions to Agriculture: From Cattle Domestication
to the Bantu Expansion, 7000 BCE–500 CE **301**

Early States: Ancient Egypt, 3500–1070 BCE **304**

Early States: Nubia and Ethiopia,
1500 BCE–700 CE **310**

Early Farming Communities: Ironworking Farmers
in Central, Western, and Southern Africa,
1000 BCE–1900 CE **313**

Early States: The Sahara and West Africa,
500–1500 CE **315**

Early States: Eastern, Southern, and Central Africa,
1000–1900 CE **316**

14 EARLY AMERICAS **322**

David J. Meltzer

Environments and Landscapes **324**

Peopling the Landscape: Earliest Occupation
in the Americas **327**

Hunter-Gatherer Trajectories: The Clovis Occupation
of North America, *c.* 11,400–10,600 BCE **334**

Regionalization: North America after Clovis **337**

Peopling the Landscape: The Earliest
South Americans **342**

15 NORTH AMERICA **346**

**George R. Milner and W. H. Wills, with David L. Browman,
Gayle J. Fritz, and BrieAnna S. Langlie**

Environments and Landscapes **349**

Hunter-Gatherer Trajectories: Eastern North America,
Archaic Period, *c.* 9500–1000 BCE **350**

Transitions to Agriculture: Eastern North America,
Early and Middle Woodland Periods,
c. 1000 BCE–400 CE **352**

Expansion of Domestication: Late Woodland Period,
c. 400–1000 CE **355**

Early Farming Communities: Mississippian Period,
c. 1000–1700 CE **356**

Transitions to Agriculture: Southwest North America,
2100–1100 BCE **359**

Early Farming Communities: Preclassic and
Classic Hohokam, *c.* 700–1450 CE **360**

Early Farming Communities: Pueblo Villages on
the Colorado Plateau **362**

Hunter-Gatherer Trajectories: Great Plains,
Archaic Period, 6500–1000 BCE **368**

Transitions to Agriculture: Great Plains **369**

Hunter-Gatherer Trajectories: Pacific Northwest **370**

Hunter-Gatherer Trajectories: Arctic and Subarctic **372**

Native Americans and European Colonialism **374**

16 MESOAMERICA **378**

David Webster and Susan Toby Evans

Environments and Landscapes **381**

Transitions to Agriculture **382**

Early Farming Communities **383**

The Olmecs and the Early to Middle Preclassic,
c. 1200–400 BCE **384**

Cities, States, and Empires: Late Preclassic
Mesoamerica, *c*. 400 BCE–250 CE **386**

Expansion and Integration: The Classic Period:
Teotihuacán and Its Neighbors, *c*. 100–550 CE **391**

Collapse and Reorganization: Epiclassic
Mesoamerica, *c*. 600–900 CE **396**

Cities, States, and Empires: The Classic Maya,
250–900 CE **396**

Collapse and Reorganization: Postclassic
Mesoamerica, 900–1521 CE **402**

Cities, States, and Empires: What the
Spaniards Found **403**

17 SOUTH AMERICA 410

Michael E. Moseley and Michael J. Heckenberger

Environments and Landscapes **413**

Hunter-Gatherer Trajectories **415**

Transitions to Agriculture, *c*. 9000–2000 BCE **416**

Urban Communities: Aceramic Communities,
c. 3000–1800 BCE **417**

Early Farming Communities: Initial Period and
the Early Horizon, *c*. 1800–200 BCE **419**

Collapse and Reorganization: The Early Intermediate
Period, *c*. 200 BCE–650 CE: Andean Confederacies
and States **421**

Cities, States, and Empires: The Rise and Fall
of the Andean Empires **425**

Amazonia **434**

Transitions to States: The Amazonian Formative
Period, *c*. 1000 BCE–500 CE **434**

Regionalization: Amazonia, *c*. 1–1500 CE **435**

18 THE HUMAN PAST: CURRENT HORIZONS 442

Tammy Stone and Chris Scarre

Migration **444**

Domestication and Population Increase **445**

Climate Change **447**

Urbanization **448**

Social Inequality **449**

Glossary **451**

Sources of Illustrations **454**

Index **456**

CONTRIBUTORS

Chris Scarre is Professor of Archaeology at Durham University. He is a specialist in European prehistory, but has broad interests in the archaeology of other regions of the world. His current research interests include the study of prehistoric burial, the development of world prehistory, and the origin and significance of the Neolithic monuments of western Europe.

Tammy Stone is Professor of Anthropology at the University of Colorado Denver. She has won four awards for Excellence in Teaching, and has been on the Society for American Archaeologists Curriculum Committee twice; 2012–14 and 2007–10. Her research specialty is the American Southwest.

Susan E. Alcock serves as Provost of the University of Michigan–Dearborn, and is Professor of Classical Archaeology and Classics at the University of Michigan–Ann Arbor. Her research interests include the Hellenistic and Roman East, landscape archaeology, archaeological survey, and archaeologies of memory and of imperialism.

Peter Bellwood is an Emeritus Professor in Archaeology at the Australian National University. He has carried out field research widely in Southeast Asia and many Polynesian islands, and has a special interest in archaeological and linguistic aspects of Austronesian prehistory in both Southeast Asia and Oceania, in the prehistories of early farming populations in all parts of the world, and in the global prehistory of human migration.

David L. Browman is Professor of Anthropology and Chair of the Interdisciplinary Program in Archaeology at Washington University, St. Louis. His research interests mainly concern the Americas, and include nomadic pastoralism, the development of economies based on domesticated species, the origins of prehistoric complex societies, Andean regional culture history, applied archaeology, historical archaeology, and, more recently, the intellectual history of archaeology.

John F. Cherry is Joukowsky Family Professor of Archaeology and Professor of Classics and Anthropology at Brown University. His research and fieldwork interests include Mediterranean prehistory, regional survey, island archaeology, lithic studies, and Caribbean archaeology.

Robin Coningham holds UNESCO's Chair in Archaeological Ethics and Practice in Cultural Heritage and is also Professor of Early Mediaeval Archaeology at Durham University. He has conducted fieldwork throughout South Asia, including directing major excavations at the city of Anuradhapura in Sri Lanka. Recent research projects have included surveys of the hinterland of Anuradhapura, survey and excavation within Iran's Central Plateau, excavation inside the temple of the Buddha's birth in Lumbini, Nepal, and post-earthquake excavations in the Kathmandu Valley.

Graham Connah is an Emeritus Professor of Archaeology at the University of New England, Armidale, New South Wales, and a former Visiting Fellow in the School of Archaeology and Anthropology at the Australian National University, Canberra. He has excavated and conducted archaeological fieldwork in Britain, Nigeria, Egypt, Uganda, and Australia.

Susan Toby Evans is Series Editor for *Occasional Papers in Anthropology* at the Pennsylvania State University. She has studied Mesoamerican cultural evolution in general and the Aztecs in particular, having excavated at the Aztec site of Cihuatecpan (Woman Palace), near Mexico City, and undertaken research into Aztec palace life.

Gayle J. Fritz is Professor Emerita of Anthropology at Washington University, St. Louis. Her research interests include paleoethnobotany, plant domestication, the origins and spread of agriculture, subsistence and social change, and the archaeology of North America before and after European contact.

Michael J. Heckenberger is Professor of Anthropology at the University of Florida. He has developed major research projects in the southern and central Amazon regions of Brazil and in Guyana, and has collaborated on archaeological research in the Caribbean and Eastern North America.

Charles Higham is an Emeritus Professor at the University of Otago in New Zealand. He studied Archaeology at Cambridge University, and was appointed in 1968 to the Foundation Chair of Anthropology at Otago. He currently directs the Origins of Angkor research project in Thailand, having undertaken fieldwork in Southeast Asia since 1969.

Peter Hiscock is a Research Associate of the Australian Museum, Sydney. He is a specialist in the prehistory of Australia. His research focus includes the interpretation of Paleolithic technology, combined with morphometric analyses. He also writes about the way archaeologists are represented in cinema.

Richard G. Klein is Anne T. and Robert M. Bass Professor in the School of Humanities and Sciences, Stanford University. In his research and writing he focuses on the co-evolution of human anatomy and behavior. He has done fieldwork in Spain and especially in South Africa, where he has excavated ancient sites and analyzed the excavated materials since 1969.

BrieAnna S. Langlie is an Assistant Professor in the Department of Anthropology at Binghamton University, New York. Her research focuses on the origins and long-term sustainability of agricultural systems and foodways in the Andes Mountains of South America. She specializes in paleoethnobotany and landscape archaeology.

Roger Matthews is Professor of Near Eastern Archaeology at the University of Reading and President of RASHID International, an organization dedicated to assisting with Iraq's heritage. He has directed excavation and survey projects in Iraq, Syria, Turkey, and Iran. His research focuses on early farming and sedentism, and early literate, urban societies of Mesopotamia.

David J. Meltzer is the Henderson-Morrison Professor of Prehistory in the Department of Anthropology, Southern Methodist University, Dallas, Texas. He has conducted archaeological fieldwork on Paleoindian sites across North America, and published extensively on the peopling of the Americas, Pleistocene environments and human adaptations, and the history of American archaeology. He is a member of the US National Academy of Sciences.

George R. Milner is Distinguished Professor of Anthropology at the Pennsylvania State University. His research interests cover human osteology and archaeology, with an emphasis on prehistoric Eastern North America. He has conducted field- and museum-based archaeological and skeletal research in several Midwestern states, Europe, Africa, Asia, and Micronesia.

Michael E. Moseley, member of the National Academies, directed the Chan Chan-Moche Valley Project while at Harvard. At the University of Florida his research has focused upon the far south of Peru, and ranged from the late Pleistocene arrival of the continent's first colonists through the region's conquest by Indigenous empires and into the Spanish subjugation.

Paul Pettitt is Professor of Archaeology at Durham University. His research focuses on the Middle and Upper Paleolithic of Europe. His specific interests are Neanderthal behavior and extinction, the origins of modern humans, mortuary activity, and the appearance and early development of art. In 2003 he co-discovered Britain's first examples of Upper Paleolithic cave art, and he researches cave art in Spain.

Kathy Schick is Professor of Anthropology and Cognitive Science and Adjunct Professor of Biology and of Earth and Atmospheric Sciences at Indiana University, Bloomington. She is also Co-Director of the Center for Research into the Anthropological Foundations of Technology (CRAFT) at Indiana University, and Co-Director of the Stone Age Institute. Her interests include paleoanthropology, geoarchaeology, and human evolutionary studies.

Nicholas Toth is Professor of Anthropology and Cognitive Science and Adjunct Professor of Biology and of Earth and Atmospheric Sciences at Indiana University, Bloomington. He is also Co-Director of the Center for Research into the Anthropological Foundations of Technology (CRAFT) at Indiana University, and Co-Director of the Stone Age Institute. His interests include paleoanthropology, lithic technology, and the evolution of human cognition.

Trevor Watkins is Emeritus Professor of Prehistoric Archaeology at the University of Edinburgh. He had directed fieldwork projects in Cyprus, Syria, Iraq, and Turkey, working on the Neolithic of Southwest Asia for most of his career. His current research concerns the demographic and social transformation represented by the change from small-scale forager bands to networks of large-scale permanent communities, and the cultural, ideological, and symbolic means that were devised to facilitate that transformation.

David Webster is Professor of Anthropology at the Pennsylvania State University. His main interests are the evolution of complex societies, human and political ecology, settlement and household archaeology, and ancient warfare. He has worked in Yugoslavia and Turkey, but his main research focus is Mesoamerica, and specifically Classic Maya civilization.

W. H. Wills is Professor of Anthropology at the University of New Mexico. His research interests include the transition from foraging to agriculture, village formation, and the role of religion in economic change. He has conducted field research in several parts of the American Southwest and is currently directing archaeological investigations at Chaco Canyon, New Mexico.

PREFACE

The first edition of *The Human Past* was groundbreaking in bringing together more than twenty authors, each a leading expert on the archaeology of a different region, to explain and illustrate the range and diversity of past human societies across the world. Since then, many instructors have asked for a concise version of *The Human Past,* one that is tailored to students studying at an introductory level, but maintains the book's broad geographical scope and big-picture narrative. At half the length of *The Human Past,* with a range of new features to help students understand the past from a global perspective, *The Human Past Essentials* is our answer.

The emphasis on exploring a wide range of societies remains, but *The Human Past Essentials* has also been updated and revised with the help of reviewers and specialist consultants to ensure the narrative is inclusive and that the language and coverage accurately reflect the current, postcolonial outlook of archaeology. The book also looks to the future of the field, embracing greater inclusion of women and scholars of color in archaeology, the active participation of descendant and Indigenous communities in archaeological research, and the exploration of social and environmental issues that still challenge us today, to support building a more just and sustainable future. All this is done while also making sure students understand some of the most influential developments in human prehistory.

Five themes unite the chapters and enable cross-referencing between different world regions:

Climate change: how modern humans have exploited natural resources, sometimes with devastating effects on the environment.

Domestication: how humans have domesticated plants and animals through selective breeding, and the consequences this has had for population increase, social change, and environmental impact.

Urbanization: how humans have adapted their environments to accommodate growing populations, living in increasingly crowded settlements.

Social inequality: how humans have interacted with one another in a variety of ways, often defining, challenging, and reinforcing or reinventing inequality in relationships, access to material goods, and political power.

Migration: how and why humans have migrated throughout the world.

How to Use this Book

The Human Past Essentials includes features that help students follow and compare the trajectories of human history across the world:

- **Chapters open with a list of Key Points** that highlight major events and themes covered in the chapter. These points then reference similar or contrasting events in other chapters, allowing students to see wider patterns in the past.

- **Broader regional chronologies are emphasized**, allowing students to focus on wider trends in history.

- **Similar headings across chapters**, including Environments and Landscapes, Transitions to Agriculture, and Hunter-Gatherer Trajectories, help students to compare more easily the history of each culture across the world and through time.

- **Timelines** at the beginning of each chapter allow students to identify easily the chronology and key events, peoples, sites, and artifacts for the region under discussion.

- **Glossary definitions** appear in the margin where specific terms first appear (in bold text) in the book, helping students to learn new vocabulary without interrupting their reading. In addition, a Glossary is provided at the end of the book for easy reference. Bold text is also used to draw attention to key sites and cultures within each chapter.

As with *The Human Past*, this book also includes key box features that highlight important debates and discoveries in archaeology, including significant discussions concerning ethics and social justice in archaeology (in cases where these box features have been written by us and not the chapter author(s), we have added our initials, CS and TS, to indicate this):

- **Key Sites** describe important individual sites or finds in greater detail than is possible within the main text.

- **Key Controversies** supplement the chapter texts by focusing on important areas of debate, for example, toolmaking and gender; genomic research and Indigenous communities; and Indigenous archaeology in Hawai'i.

- **Key Discoveries** include discussion of breakthroughs in long-standing archaeological enquiries, for example, the emergence of the Denisovans, or genetics and the First Americans, as well as descriptions of world-famous discoveries, such as the identification of Maya sites by use of LiDAR, and the *khipu* of Andean societies.

- **Key Themes** highlight issues that continue to be of critical relevance to the present day, presenting these within the context of one of the core themes of the book: migration, domestication and population increase, climate change, urbanization, and social inequality.

The introduction (**Chapter 1**) explains what archaeology is, how it is practiced (including the use of cutting-edge research based on DNA anlysis), and the responsibilities of the discipline today to challenge colonialist assumptions and to achieve diversity and inclusion by increasing the visibility and agency of previously marginalized groups in archaeological work and narratives. The next three chapters cover the Paleolithic period, beginning with human evolution and human origins in Africa (**Chapter 2**). **Chapter 3** describes the dispersal of early humans across much of Africa, Europe, and Asia, and looks at early human behavior. The emergence of modern humans and how they proliferated is the focus of **Chapter 4**, including evidence of inter-breeding between *Homo sapiens*, Neanderthals, and Denisovans. The period of global transformation as a result of the end of the last Ice Age is the subject of **Chapter 5**, which sets out the main themes of the postglacial period around the world: climate change; the origins of farming; the rise in human population density; and the development of the social complexity that in some regions underpinned the emergence of cities and states.

The arrangement of the following chapters (**Chapters 6–17**) enables a world focus, region by region, discussing how human societies adjusted to postglacial environments in each area, while presenting a broadly chronological narrative within each chapter. This tour of the globe covers:

- Southwest Asia (**Chapters 6–7**)
- South Asia (**Chapter 8**)
- East Asia (**Chapters 9–10**)
- Australia and the Pacific Islands (**Chapter 11**)
- Europe (**Chapter 12**)
- Africa (**Chapter 13**)
- Early Americas, including North America (**Chapters 14–15**)
- Mesoamerica (**Chapter 16**)
- South America (**Chapter 17**)

Chapter 18 Current Horizons emphasizes the unique viewpoint that studying the human past affords us in recognizing that the key themes of migration, domestication and population increase, climate change, urbanization, and social inequality have been important to all people, regardless of when or where they lived, and that they are still present today.

Instructor and Student Resources

The Human Past Essentials offers the most engaging range of digital resources available, developed and vetted by Tammy Stone. The following resources are available to qualified adopters in North America at digital.wwnorton.com/humanpastess. More limited resources are available outside of North America. Readers outside North America should email education@thameshudson.co.uk for more information.

FOR INSTRUCTORS. Our ancillary resources will help you to plan your course and teach whichever parts of the world and narratives of the past you choose. Go online to access:

Instructor's Manual, offering helpful and creative resources for lecture planning and classroom activities, including teaching ideas, chapter outlines and summaries, discussion prompts, and a curated list of web links to additional readings, videos, websites, and Google Earth coordinates.

Test Bank with more than 600 questions—including multiple choice, true/false, and essay questions—revised and evaluated by Tammy Stone. This Test Bank will be offered through Norton Testmaker, which will allow you to create assessments from anywhere with an Internet connection, without downloading files or installing specialized software. You will be able to search and filter test-bank questions by chapter, type, difficulty, learning objectives, and other criteria. You can also customize questions to fit your course. Easily export your tests to Microsoft Word or Common Cartridge files for import into your LMS.

PowerPoint Lecture Slides for each chapter, making it easy to develop your own classes; slides feature all images, and bullet points cover all major concepts.

Image slides in PowerPoint and JPEGs, featuring the photos, maps, and diagrams from the textbook in formats you can easily use for your lectures.

Archaeology Global Gallery, offering hundreds of captioned supplementary photos of archaeological sites, artifacts, landscapes, and diagrams, all available for you to use in your lecture. The Gallery is searchable by keyword and organized by chapter.

FOR STUDENTS. Our resources will help you prepare for in-class discussion and testing, and improve your overall performance in your world prehistory course. Go online to digital.wwnorton.com/humanpastess to access:

An **ebook** that provides you with an active reading experience, enabling you to take notes, bookmark, search, highlight, and even read the ebook offline. This ebook includes such features as tool-tip key terms and definitions, and clickable and zoomable maps and images.

InQuizitive. This easy-to-use online learning tool helps you to master—and retain—the key course concepts. Through a variety of question types, answer-specific feedback, and game-like elements, such as a confidence slider, you will be motivated to keep working until you've mastered the concepts and to be better prepared for class and examinations. (In a recent study, InQuizitive was found to increase quiz scores by more than a full letter grade—visit wwnorton.com/inquizitive for more information.)

Student Site. Accessed via the URL above, you'll find resources to help you learn and prepare for exams,

including chapter summaries, terminology flashcards, web links, and glossary terms.

Archaeology Videos. Watch in-the-field videos by Professor Joy McCorriston, key concept and laboratory videos by Professor Kelly Knudson, and introductory talks by Professor Colin Renfrew. These videos will introduce you to the methods and theories involved in understanding human history. Topics include ethics, protecting our cultural heritage, radiocarbon dating, isotopes, and Indigenous archaeology.

Acknowledgments

First and foremost, we would like to thank our authors for their continuing expertise and for working with us in editing their chapters. We are also grateful to Brenna Hassett (University College London, and TrowelBlazers) and Stephen Silliman (University of Massachusetts Boston) for important advice on inclusivity, and to John Gowlett (University of Liverpool) for assistance with updating several of the earlier chapters. We would like to thank Melissa Baltus (University of Toledo), Alison Carter (University of Oregon), Tiffany Collins (Salt Lake Community College), R. Alan Covey (University of Texas at Austin), Andrew Jones (University of Southampton), Amy Kowal (Florida State University), Susan Krook (Normandale Community College), Justin P. Lowry (SUNY Plattsburgh), Hannah Marsh (University of Central Missouri), Grant McCall (Tulane University), Mark McCoy (Southern Methodist University), Mark Schwartz (Grand Valley State University), David Small (Lehigh University), Joshua Wright (University of Aberdeen), and numerous additional anonymous reviewers who participated in the peer-review process. Their feedback was invaluable. Finally, our special thanks go to the editorial, design, and picture-research team at Thames & Hudson: Mark Sapwell, Katherine Wallis, Rowena Alsey, and Sally Nicholls.

Introduction: The Study of the Human Past

Chris Scarre and Tammy Stone

What Is Archaeology? 14

The Current State of Archaeology 17

The Responsibilities of Archaeology 17

Enduring Themes in Archaeology 20

Approaches and Techniques 23

Summary and Conclusions 29

Further Reading 29

A Skeetchestn First Nation archaeological team assesses a site near Battle Creek in British Columbia. The area was burned by wildfire in 2017, revealing many unrecorded archaeological sites.

Modern humans (*Homo sapiens*) have been living on the earth for at least 300,000 years, an immense span of time when compared to the length of written history. Human ancestors go back even further, to the first of those who made stone tools, at least 2.8 million years ago, or further still, to the earliest so-called hominins of Africa, 8–6 million years ago.

Little of this history is recorded in writing, and so archaeology is our main source of knowledge for the human past. Archaeology can illustrate the full diversity of human culture and society, and shows how humans have changed and adapted, both to external factors, such as climate and environment, and to new social circumstances and technologies. These issues remain pertinent today, and the study of archaeology gives us a unique opportunity to examine how societies have developed, using a long-term perspective. Before exploring the range of societies that makes up our shared history, this first chapter introduces the various methods archaeologists have used to reconstruct world prehistory and some important considerations this involves.

WHAT IS ARCHAEOLOGY?

Archaeology is the study of the human past from material remains. It is often considered (especially in North America) as a sub-field within the discipline of **anthropology**. Anthropology—the study of humans—includes a number of other sub-fields:

- **Cultural anthropology** (or social anthropology), the study of the diversity of living societies, often based on the work of researchers who live or spend considerable time with various societies and observe them firsthand. For example, a cultural anthropologist may study the lives of the Kalahari San in Namibia or the Dogon in Mali, or specific groups within North American or European societies, such as immigrant communities or inner-city groups.

- **Biological anthropology**, the study of human evolution and physiology, and the relationship between culture and the body. Biological anthropology includes the study of fossil and skeletal remains of early humans, which feature predominantly in Chapters 2–4. It also studies human adaptation to environment and disease, including patterns of nutrition, fertility, and genetics.

- **Linguistic anthropology**, the study of world languages, their development, and interrelationships. Studying the connections between languages can offer valuable insights into how groups have traveled across the globe, or interacted with one another. We will find excellent examples of this in the case of the Polynesians in Chapter 11.

Archaeology is the fourth of these sub-fields of anthropology. It is famous for discoveries such as the so-called royal tombs of Sipán in Peru (Chapter 17) or Qin Shi Huangdi's pottery army in China (Chapter 10) [1.1]. These catch the headlines but are only one small element of the story that archaeology tells us about the human past. What we can learn about the details of daily life is often equally intriguing and arguably more significant. One of the greatest advantages of archaeology is that it deals with rich and poor, literate and illiterate, the ordinary and the exceptional, dependent simply on the survival of evidence and the attentions of archaeologists themselves. The result is a rich and insightful account of human history.

archaeology the study of past human societies through their material remains

anthropology the study of humans, their evolution and culture

hominin species in human evolution that are more closely related to people than to chimpanzees

material culture the physical products of culture; culture is defined as socially transmitted rules for behavior and ways of thinking about the world, and the term is also used by archaeologists to describe a distinctive collection of archaeological remains, which might often be associated with an ancient population

species distinct populations of plants or animals that can and do interbreed and produce fertile offspring

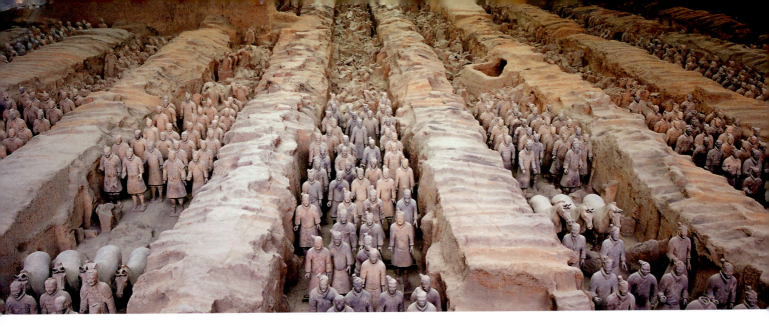

Many consider that archaeology begins when early **hominins** first began to create **material culture**, in this case stone tools, some 2.8 million years ago or more (Chapter 2). Such tools, and the technology used to produce them, are often presented as one of the hallmarks of humanness. Several other **species** use and modify objects (e.g. twigs, stones) to probe for food or to break open nuts, but no other animal creates objects at the same breadth or complexity as humans. The reliance on material culture is distinctively human and has given us a substantial advantage in coping with a wide range of environments. Without certain key items (e.g. clothing and shelter), humans would still be restricted in distribution to the tropical regions, where our closest primate relations, the gorillas and chimpanzees, live today. It is material culture that has allowed humans to populate the globe, and to develop large and complex settlements and societies.

But archaeology is not just about technology. The material remains form part of the broader category of human culture that also includes oral literature, dance, song, belief, myth, and ritual practices. And the remains of material culture are also rich in evidence about the social, economic, symbolic, and religious life of past human societies. Powerful structures of belief and understanding underpin the ways in which humans comprehend the world, and these can be seen in imagery or traces of ritual practice. Carvings and figurines may provide direct representations of mythical beings and religious ceremonies. Scenes in Egyptian temples and tombs, for example, show deities weighing the souls of the dead, while Angkor temples (Chapter 10) depict elements of the Khmer pantheon [**1.2**].

1.1 Terra-cotta army. Discovered by accident in 1974, the army of life-size terra-cotta warriors at Xian in China was intended to protect the tomb of the first emperor, Qin Shi Huangdi. Pit 1, shown here, contained 3,210 armored infantrymen, while a second pit held 1,400 cavalry, chariots, and crossbowmen.

1.2 The Churning of the Sea of Milk, from the eastern gallery of the twelfth-century CE temple-mausoleum of Angkor Wat in Cambodia. The scene is taken from the Hindu creation myth and depicts gods and demons pulling on the body of a giant snake in order to churn the cosmic sea and release the elixir of immortality.

prehistory the period of human history before the invention of writing

Burials, the ways in which people have disposed of their dead, show a growing concern with identity and the afterlife across thousands of years. Ancient art can throw light on social practices and political power; but popular beliefs and household rituals are as much a part of archaeology's domain as the lavish stage-managed cults of temples and priesthoods.

Prehistory vs. History

Archaeology has no upper chronological limit. It is not a method exclusively for the study of the *early* human story, but of the *whole* of the human past. It can as well be applied to contemporary societies as much as to those thousands of years ago. One particularly flourishing sub-field of the subject is devoted to industrial archaeology—the archaeology of the Industrial Revolution and later, focusing not only on factories and machines but also on the housing and living conditions of ordinary families of the time. There have also been projects on the archaeology of modern society, one example being the Arizona garbage project, which studied the contents of domestic trash cans from Tucson, Arizona. Another is the archaeological analysis of the twentieth-century Lovell radio telescope at Jodrell Bank Observatory in the UK.

Archaeology is essentially an approach to human societies based on the study of material culture, and so there is a methodological distinction between historic and prehistoric archaeology. History is the study of the human past from written records (or from recorded oral traditions). Since writing was first invented fewer than 5,500 years ago in Southwest Asia, the whole of the human story before that time falls within the period of **prehistory** [1.3]. As writing was adopted at different times in different places, however, so the transition from prehistoric to historic (text-based) archaeology occurs at diverse stages. In western Europe, for example, written history begins with the Greeks and Romans in the south, and with the Middle Ages in the north. It is important to stress that archaeologists do not stop their study through time once written records become available. Writing often records only particular histories (for example, of elite groups within society, or of incoming colonists), so giving writing primacy leads to a biased picture of the past. Prehistory is therefore a misleading word, as people with and without writing have often lived at the same time. One should not be prioritized over the other. In this book, the two terms are used in their methodological senses, where prehistory requires studying the past without only one of many sources of the past: writing.

1.3 Prehistoric and historical archaeology.
Writing was invented at different times in different parts of the world, but earliest of all in Southwest Asia around 5,500 years ago; prehistory, the period before written records, covers a vast time span, for which material remains form our only evidence. Because writing was adopted at differing times around the world, the transition from prehistory to history also varies. Non-written and oral histories continue today.

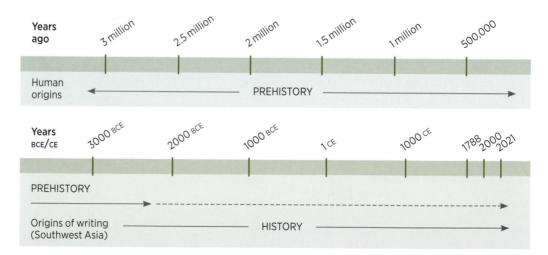

THE CURRENT STATE OF ARCHAEOLOGY

As well as redefining how the term prehistory is used, archaeologists are now seeking to broaden the range of people involved in the discipline. Film and television have traditionally portrayed archaeologists as white, male heroes out-running booby traps, but many people are working to increase the diversity of the archaeology profession. A 2015 survey of the Society for American Archaeology (SAA) showed 50.5 percent of membership to be male and 47.9 percent female. The survey also showed how the field remains predominantly white, at 77 percent, with 6.7 percent Latinx, 1.9 percent Asia/Pacific, 0.8 percent Native American, and 0.3 percent Black. In the face of these statistics, archaeologists are looking hard at academic and professional bodies to confront the existing barriers that block opportunities to join and succeed in the profession, and they are challenging practices that are rooted in colonialism and sexism, in order to make meaningful change that empowers everyone. There is a great deal more to do.

THE RESPONSIBILITIES OF ARCHAEOLOGY

Archaeology involves the study of the human past through material remains, but it is not only archaeologists who feel a responsibility toward archaeological materials. Archaeology was initially a subject of European and North American origin, which spread to other regions of the world often through colonialism. Archaeology has therefore frequently come into conflict with the values held by Indigenous and descendant communities and the views they have about their own pasts. Recent decades have witnessed a greater awareness among archaeologists about the communities they work in, and a growing number of members of Indigenous communities becoming involved in archaeology. This progress has led to the development and success of **Indigenous archaeology [1.4]**, which involves research that critiques and deconstructs colonial archaeological practices and interpretations, and works toward investigating Indigenous experiences and knowledge systems.

Archaeologists now do not claim to own the past that they explore, and excavations today are generally undertaken only with the consent of local communities. The **artifacts** uncovered do not in any way belong to the archaeologists who find them, and in best practice are handed to a competent regional authority. Consultation with local and descendant populations is of the utmost significance, and more projects now involve active collaboration with elders and specialists from Indigenous communities. This can lead to the inclusion of Indigenous interpretations, which can offer entirely new ways of looking at the archaeological evidence. It also brings to the fore questions of importance to local and descendant populations that archaeologists may not have thought to ask. Indigenous archaeology is therefore relevant not only to Indigenous communities but to all archaeologists, for whom methodologies of collaboration can provide new ways of exploring and stewarding the past. One example is the Narungga maritime project in South Australia, where the active collaboration of people of the Narungga community was formative in understanding

1.4 Indigenous archaeology. Zuni elders Octavius Seowtewa and John Bowannie, and archaeologist Sarah Herr, examine a shrine misidentified by archaeologists when excavating a site in the path of a new Arizona highway.

Native American Graves Protection and Repatriation Act (NAGPRA) the law (1990) that requires federally funded institutions and government agencies in the United States to assess the cultural affiliation of Native American and Native Hawaiian artifacts held in collections and, where cultural affiliation can be shown, to return the materials to the affiliated group or organization; also dictates how human burials encountered in the future will be treated

and preserving the history of a twentieth-century sunken vessel that archaeologists were attempting to rediscover.

Increasingly, members of Indigenous communities are entering the field of archaeology themselves, resulting in a more diverse discipline as well as opening new avenues of research and allowing a wider understanding of archaeology.

Efforts to decolonize archaeology, as with many academic disciplines, are becoming increasingly prominent and important. Decolonization means to untangle and remove colonial assumptions, ownerships, and agendas that North American and European practitioners have placed on the global past. This work is critical, especially as the colonial past continues to influence all aspects of our social, political, and economic life as well as the stewardship and interpretation of archaeology. Again, this requires the archaeologist to collaborate with Indigenous and descendant communities.

Repatriation

Awareness of Indigenous communities is never more important than when excavating and studying human remains. In the recent past, archaeologists often shipped excavated remains back to distant museums and other institutions. In many cases, their removal was a violation of long-held Indigenous religious beliefs. Many descendant communities understandably campaigned for the return of human remains, stressing that the memories of the deceased are deserving of respect. A great number of collections have now been repatriated to the descendant communities living in the places from which they were taken. In some cases, the practice is enforced by legislation, the result of Indigenous activists and archaeologist allies. In the USA, the **Native American Graves Protection and Repatriation Act** (1990) recognizes the rights of Indigenous American and Hawaiian groups over human remains and other cultural items and sacred objects to which they have a claim through ancestry.

Archaeologists planning excavations in an area where they may encounter findings of this nature must consult with descendant communities in advance to ensure the concerns and beliefs of those groups are respected. Indigenous communities determine the appropriate treatment when human remains and items of cultural patrimony are returned to them. Sometimes these are reburied, on other occasions they are maintained in curation facilities by the group, or the community may request that the bodies or objects continue to be held in a museum. Ceremonies may be conducted when reburial does not occur, depending on the religious beliefs held by a community. When burials are maintained in curatorial facilities, the descendant populations may request that no destructive analysis (such as **DNA** analysis or chemical analysis for diet) be conducted. Similar legislation applies in Australia.

Repatriation of archaeological materials extends far beyond human remains. Some of the most contentious issues concern iconic cultural relics, for example the Parthenon marbles in the British Museum, taken from the Athenian **Acropolis** in 1801, and the bust of Nefertiti, excavated from Amarna in Egypt in 1912, and now on display in the Neues Museum in Berlin [**1.5**]. The legitimacy of their acquisition has been contested and it has been urged that these and other selected cultural items and collections should be returned to their place of origin. Once again, the fundamental issue concerns ownership and control.

1.5 Bust of Egyptian queen Nefertiti. This famous sculpture was found during German-led excavations at Amarna in Egypt in 1912. The legitimacy of its removal to Germany the following year has been challenged and has continued to raise objections from the Egyptian antiquities authorities.

The monetary value of some archaeological remains raises a related and growing concern: the plundering of archaeological sites by looters seeking objects to sell. Numerous Maya sculptures and ceramics entered public and private collections through the activities of looters and an antiquities trade that failed to respect national legislations forbidding the export of such materials. In many other countries, ancient cemeteries have been systematically robbed, with little or no respect for the human remains.

Recent warfare and the breakdown of civil authority have led to looting and extensive damage to museums and archaeological sites from Afghanistan to Libya, either for profit or to eradicate an enemy's past, or both. The profits to be made from the theft and plundering of antiquities are considerable, especially for the dealers who purchase and resell the material. The results are alarming: satellite photos show famous Syrian sites—Mari, Dura Europos [1.6], and Apamea, among others—pockmarked by hundreds of small craters, each of them a looting pit. The marketable materials that are unearthed in this process may ultimately find their way onto the illicit antiquities market, illegally exported from their country of origin. Even if they are recovered, the archaeological damage has been done; there will be no record of the context in which they were found, and an intact burial, complete with human remains and a range of accompanying objects, might be reduced to a single decorated pot in a saleroom or personal collection in New York, Paris, London, or Tokyo.

The response of archaeologists and the international community has been to put pressure on governments, museums, and private collectors to prevent the sale of ancient cultural relics that have no secure provenance. Archaeologists are also discouraged from studying or publishing such items, since in doing so they may inadvertently be legitimizing the objects in question and increasing their market value.

The growing concern with professional ethics and responsibilities has been a welcome development within archaeology, and emphasizes wider social and political contexts. This includes an awareness of the various cultural lenses archaeologists inherently use to interpret

DNA deoxyribonucleic acid, the molecule that carries genetic instructions from parents to offspring

acropolis the upper part of a city; usually a group of fortified buildings atop of a hill

1.6 Damage at Dura-Europos (Syria). The left image, dated June 28, 2012, shows relatively little disturbance to the ground surface either within or beyond the walls of this Roman frontier city. The right image reveals that by April 2, 2014, however, high-density looting had damaged much of the walled area of the ancient city, while parts of the site beyond the city wall had been extensively pillaged with thousands of individual pits.

the past. Archaeologists must respect the beliefs and understanding of the people among whom they work and whose pasts they are recovering. Moreover, the results are frequently of great interest to local communities, who are encouraged to collaborate with archaeologists in the exploration of the past.

ENDURING THEMES IN ARCHAEOLOGY

We live today in a global age where cultures and ideologies meet in diverse, multi-ethnic societies. Archaeology is global in scope, and tells us about both literate and non-literate societies, redressing the imbalance of a document-based history. Striking examples of this can be found in Australia and southern Africa, both areas without any written historical record prior to the arrival of Europeans, and where archaeology now demonstrates a rich prehistoric past.

World prehistory is both enlightening and empowering. It is enlightening in that it offers a varied perspective, enabling local and regional developments to be understood better, and events and circumstances in the recent past to be set within the context of human developments stretching back over hundreds or thousands of years. It is empowering in that it documents the whole human past and is not restricted to dominant political players, but also details the lives of ordinary people—how they farmed or herded, what they ate and made, how they buried their dead—subjects about which conventional historical sources have relatively little to say. It is also increasingly enabling us to rectify the serious imbalance that has generally emphasized male histories and roles, by including all members of society and allowing us to build a narrative of the past for everyone.

The study of world prehistory also encourages us to view human development from a long-term perspective. This can be seen most obviously in the early stages of human evolution, where the gradual expansion in settlement and the ability to cope with varied and changing environments are major themes. In addition, it allows us to pose key questions about the origins of agriculture, the development of cities, and various other important cultural milestones that emerged in different parts of the world, often independently from one another. Archaeology also allows us to examine and learn from how people in the past reacted to migration as well as environmental and economic change. What worked in the past and what did not?

We highlight such key features of long-term change in thematic boxes throughout this volume. Our main themes have been chosen to capture some of the most important processes that have affected human communities in the past, and the consequences of which continue to have major impact on societies in the present day: climate change, **domestication**, urbanization, social inequality, and migration.

domestication the human propagation of selected species, generally involving change to their genetic makeup and physical characteristics as compared with their wild progenitors

Climate Change. Over many thousands of years, early humans became adept at adjusting to the cycle of warm and cold episodes, as ice sheets advanced and retreated in the north, deserts grew or diminished, and sea levels rose and fell [**1.7**]. Human groups prospered, shrank in size, or were forced to migrate in response to these changes. From around 11,600 years ago, the Ice Age ended, enabling people to move to new regions and develop new ways to exploit the environment. One of the most impactful of these was agriculture. Even small-scale shifts in climate could have damaging effects, however, disrupting these productive but fragile farming systems. In recent centuries, the process has taken a further twist, with

1.7 Global warming.
An ice island calved off Petermann glacier in northwestern Greenland in August 2010. One of the greatest challenges to human society during the twenty-first century is the break-up of the ice sheets, which could release sufficient meltwater to flood many coastal regions and cities. But the possibility that rising temperatures will disrupt world climate systems is an even greater threat. Adaptability to such changes has been one of the keys to human survival and success over the past 3 million years, but as archaeology shows, that survival has not been achieved without cost.

escalating human numbers impacting directly on climate itself, as global temperatures are raised through the burning of fossil fuels.

Domestication. For most of the human past, population size was limited by the ability of the natural environment to provide sufficient food. When social and environmental challenges changed, some communities developed agriculture, which allowed for substantially bigger populations. This occurred many times independently across the world. Farmers experimented with plants, animals, and farming systems, with more productive varieties of cereals and other crops being developed through selective breeding. Manuring was used to restore fertility to the fields, and in arid regions elaborate irrigation systems provided the all-important water. Plowing with draft animals enabled larger areas of land to be cultivated more efficiently. In the nineteenth century, mechanization took the process a step

1.8 Modern industrial agricultural systems are mechanized and specialized, growing a single crop on a large scale.

further [**1.8**], while recent tests in genetic engineering are, in a sense, only the latest stage in a long-term quest to improve the productivity of the plants and animals that sustain us. At the same time, the wilderness has shrunk. Today, the last surviving unclaimed wildernesses are the polar regions and the deep oceans. This process of human encroachment into untouched regions represents the latest stage in a long-term story of human manipulation of plants, animals, and the environment.

Urbanization. Recent UN figures indicate that more than half of the world's population of 7.5 billion people now live in cities. Around 40 percent and 48 percent of people respectively in Africa and Asia live in cities. This rises to 82 percent in North America, 80 percent in Latin America and

1.9 Early settlements. Israeli archaeologists work at the ancient site of En Esur, where a 5,000-year-old city was uncovered.

the Caribbean, and 73 percent in Europe (United Nations 2014). Among such urban centers are mega-cities, for example Tokyo with its 38 million inhabitants. These are settlements of a size never previously encountered, yet we can find the first examples in the earliest cities in southern Mesopotamia, around 6,000 years ago [**1.9**]. What these population centers of different sizes share is the bringing together of people in large communities, resulting in specialization in crafts and other activities, and a growing divorce between an urbanized population and the agricultural communities it depends on for food. As with agriculture, the development of cities is a strategy many societies have taken independently. But we will see that this is one of many possible choices and that cities do not last for ever. The rise and fall of urban centers in the past provides a cautionary narrative of considerable relevance to the modern world.

Social Inequality. Archaeology and **ethnography** together suggest that the earliest human societies were relatively egalitarian, without great distinctions in individual wealth. Among many past hunter-gatherer societies, the obligation to share put strict limits on the ability to accumulate resources. Today, by contrast, the growing level of inequality between rich and poor is one of the world's greatest concerns. It has been estimated, for example, that one-third of city dwellers in the developing world are living in urban slums, while the richest 1 percent of the world's population owns more than half of the world's wealth. Archaeology allows us to view these changes in long-term perspective, to understand how elite groups came to power. The pattern we see today is the result of processes stretching back several millennia.

Migration. Early humans were a migrating species, spreading from their African homeland to occupy every habitable continent of the globe. Movement is a strong feature of the human story, at both the individual level and for entire communities. Early farmers faced with expanding populations spread into new territories. Climatic fluctuations, too, have been a common driver of human resettlement. Migration has profoundly shaped the world that we

ethnography a branch of anthropology that studies an individual society, its people and customs inhabit. It is a powerful counterpoint to examples of xenophobia, racism and nationalism, which often assume ideas of origin and homeland that the archaeological evidence commonly disproves. Relocation can also be violent, with the displacement of existing societies by incursive groups, or the forceful migration of communities through enslavement. Archaeology is throwing new light on the many aspects of population movement by documenting its causes, contexts, and consequences.

APPROACHES AND TECHNIQUES

Archaeology draws on a range of disciplines, including physics, chemistry, biology, botany, geography, and geology, which are employed for the discovery and analysis of excavated materials, to understand human ways of life, and to reconstruct key features of the environments that previous human societies inhabited. Archaeologists today make extensive use of statistical and analytical techniques, using **GIS** and computer modeling. Most archaeologists will also be familiar with human and animal anatomy, and with the technologies used to make the ancient artifacts that they study. The dependence on such a wide range of other disciplines is a key feature of the archaeological approach.

Evolution

One of the key events underlying the development of archaeology as a discipline was the publication of *On the Origin of Species by Means of Natural Selection* by the English naturalist Charles Darwin in 1859, followed by his *Descent of Man* in 1871. In 1831, the young Darwin (1809–1882) had embarked on a voyage of survey and exploration in the *Beagle*, which was mapping the coast of South America. His observations of the diversity and interrelationships of the plants and animals he encountered and recorded led him, in the following decades, to recognize the key role of natural selection in shaping the development of single species over time (Chapter 2). Successful individuals would be more likely to reproduce and pass on their characteristics to their offspring, and so features that conferred an advantage—a longer beak, a different coloring—would spread through a population. Ultimately, a single species might be divided into sub-groups, each of which was increasingly specialized and successful within its particular environmental niche. This could lead eventually to the division of one species into two or more separate species, each of which would become increasingly different from the others as they underwent further adaptations to their environment. Darwin's theory was revolutionary in suggesting a mechanism behind the diversity of life; a theory that could also be applied to humans.

Darwin's views brought him into fierce conflict with others, who continued to maintain that the account of divine creation contained within the Bible was correct. Gradually, however, his theory succeeded in winning general acceptance as the most persuasive explanation for the development of the diversity of life. It came to be appreciated that humans, along with other species, are not fixed in their form or behavior, but are constantly changing in response to the pressures and circumstances around them. The model of evolution through natural selection was given further support by advances in genetics, beginning with the plant-breeding experiments of Gregor Mendel, the Austrian botanist, in the 1860s, which showed how particular characteristics are passed from parent to offspring. With the rapidly developing knowledge of DNA in the past fifty years, geneticists are now able to explain in detail how Darwinian natural selection operates at the level of the genetic code.

GIS Geographical Information Systems; software-based systems for the collection, storage, retrieval, analysis, and display of spatial data held in different layers, which can be combined or examined separately

morphology physical structure or form

Three Age System the classification system for the sequence of technological periods (Stone, Bronze, Iron) identified for the prehistory of Africa, Asia, and Europe

stratigraphy the successive deposition of superimposed layers of either natural or cultural material

relative chronology determination of chronological sequence without reference to a fixed time scale

absolute chronology determination of chronological sequence with reference to a fixed time scale or calendar date

radiocarbon dating an absolute dating method based on the radioactive decay of the isotope carbon-14

half-life the time it takes for half the quantity of a radioactive isotope in a sample to decay

AMS dating accelerator mass spectrometer dating, a highly accurate form of radiocarbon dating

dendrochronology an absolute dating method based on counting the growth rings in trees

For some, however, these new understandings are unwelcome, and a number of people continue to believe in a creationist view: that the world, and all the species within it, were created in the form we see them today by divine action. Archaeology allows us to demonstrate that creationist views, though deeply held, are incompatible with the evidence of the past that is available to us. The fossil record of human evolution, with its numerous and increasingly well-dated remains of earlier hominin species, indicates clearly the steady **morphological** and behavioral change that preceded the development of the first modern humans somewhere between 350,000 and 300,000 years ago. Nor did natural selection stop at that point: to this day we are still continuously (if almost imperceptibly) changing in response to selective pressures.

Darwin's thesis of human origins, coupled with the discovery of Neanderthal fossils and early stone tools, suggested that the human story went back much further than had previously been supposed, and could certainly not be accommodated within the 6,000 years offered by the biblical time frame. This new knowledge allowed for the study of human prehistory to begin in earnest.

Closely associated with biological evolution was the idea of human progress. It had long been recognized that the human story was one of social and technological change, with stone tools later replaced by metal, and villages by cities. In the early nineteenth century, archaeologists in northern Europe developed the **Three Age system** to classify their finds. The three successive ages of stone, bronze, and iron tools and weapons marked key changes in prehistoric technology. While many regions of the world have indeed witnessed transitions to different forms of technology and new ways of living, such as from hunting and gathering to farming, and to the urban complex societies to which most of us today belong, the notion of so-called progress fails to recognize the richness and diversity of early societies and their specific achievements, as well as the many forms complexity can take. Any attempts to elevate some past communities over others using such terms as civilization are judgmental and of little use in understanding the past. Change through time, however, remains one of the key features of the human story.

Dating

The construction of a reliable time frame has been an essential ingredient in building a secure knowledge of the human past. For more than a century, archaeologists have borrowed three basic principles from geology to provide backbones for time frames around the world. The first of these is the Principle of Superposition, which states that if a sequence of sediments is unmixed and undisturbed, the oldest layers will be at the bottom. These sedimentary layers are called strata, which together form **stratigraphy**. Although this relationship seems simple and even self-evident, its logic is fundamental in terms of positioning sedimentary layers to help build chronologies in all parts of the world.

Related to superposition is a second principle, the Principle of Association, which states that materials found close together tend to date to roughly the same period. Very different animals thrived in the past, but we can deduce that any human fossil or artifact found in the same layer as a fossil of that extinct animal must be of a similar age.

The third principle, related to the second, is the Principle of Identification of Strata by Fossils/Artifacts. As already noted, because different animals existed in the past, when fossils of certain extinct species occur together that can serve to indicate the age of those deposits. The same principle is useful in archaeology because different groups in the past used unique kinds of artifacts, which when they occur together provide a rough estimate of age.

These three principles provide the foundation of all archaeological dating techniques because practitioners use them to evaluate the context in which samples for absolute dates are obtained. With these principles in mind, archaeologists can provide a **relative chronology** of artifacts, and other methods may be used to assign an **absolute chronology**, or numerical ages for deposits and the materials they contain.

Radiocarbon Dating. In the late 1940s, a Chicago scientist, Willard Libby (1908–1980), developed the first absolute dating technique that could be used worldwide: **radiocarbon dating** (also known as carbon-14 or C14 dating). The method is widely applicable to organic archaeological materials—for example charcoal, bone, and shell. The resulting radiocarbon revolution brought about many surprises, not least of which was that the origins of agriculture occurred much earlier than originally thought.

Radiocarbon dating depends on the predictable decay of the unstable isotope carbon-14 (^{14}C). It remains the most important absolute dating method for the period after 40,000 years ago. Carbon is present in all living things, entering plants through photosynthesis, and then into animals through the consumption of plants, and up through the food chain [**1.10**]. Carbon occurs in three isotopes of similar chemical properties, each with a different atomic weight: ^{12}C, ^{13}C, and ^{14}C. Of these, ^{12}C and ^{13}C are stable, whereas ^{14}C is unstable, as it is radioactive. It takes around 5,730 years for half the amount of ^{14}C in a sample to decay, a period known as its **half-life**. As the ratio of ^{14}C to the stable isotopes ^{12}C and ^{13}C is known, the original amount of ^{14}C in the sample at death can be estimated.

Modern methods of detecting surviving amounts of ^{14}C in samples, which include accelerator mass spectrometers (**AMS dating**), are very accurate, and a precise estimate of the amount of ^{14}C that has decayed in a sample since that organism's death can be turned into a radiocarbon date using the half-life.

The major assumption required by radiocarbon dating, however, is that the production of ^{14}C in the upper atmosphere has remained constant. Comparisons of samples dated by the radiocarbon method and by other, independent, methods (e.g. **dendrochronology**) have demonstrated that this is not the case. The production of atmospheric ^{14}C has fluctuated over past millennia, being sometimes lower and sometimes higher than today. Radiocarbon dates are therefore calibrated against other dating methods to provide a true calendar date from the apparent radiocarbon age.

Other Dating Methods. There are other methods for dating archaeological material. Some are similar to radiocarbon dating in that they rely on the decay of one element into another. For instance, potassium-argon dating depends on the decay of the isotope potassium-40 into argon-40. This can provide an age for material that is millions of years old and is therefore useful in determining how old deposits containing early hominins are (Chapters 2 and 3). Similarly, uranium-series dating relies on the radioactive decay of uranium and is used to date cave deposits, such as stalagmites and stalactites, found with archaeological material.

A series of other dating methods rely on electrons that get trapped in material that has a crystalline structure, such as tooth enamel and igneous rock. By measuring the number of particles that are caught in the material, it is possible to determine when the crystalline structure was created or last modified. For example, electron-spin resonance examines tooth enamel and calculates when it first developed. Luminescence dating examines artifacts or features made of clay (pottery or hearths) and calculates the last time they were heated.

1.10 Radiocarbon decay. The basic principles of radiocarbon dating involve the creation of radiocarbon in the atmosphere through the bombardment of nitrogen atoms by cosmic rays (1). Plants and animals absorb ^{14}C while alive (2). At death, as radiocarbon decays it begins to disappear in organic material at a known rate (3). Counts of remaining radiocarbon provide the age estimate of the death of the sample (4).

ancient DNA (aDNA) extracted from ancient human remains—often many thousands of years old—these molecules provide scientists with the genetic code for long-dead individuals

nuclear DNA DNA present within the chromosomes in the nucleus of the cell

mitochondrial DNA (mtDNA) genetic material inherited through the maternal line

molecular clock the estimated rate of evolutionary change that can be measured through the study of fossil and modern DNA

haplogroup a collection of genetic markers shared by a group of people

1.11 The location of DNA in the cell. The majority of DNA is found in the nucleus of the cell. This is called nuclear DNA and replicates every time a new cell is produced. Mitochondria in the cell also contain DNA (called mtDNA) and these replicate separately from nuclear DNA. Both nuclear and mtDNA are important in archaeological genetic research.

Archaeologists also create master chronologies, built from placing a large number of dated materials together. The two most important dating methods using master chronologies are paleomagnetism and dendrochronology. Paleomagnetism compares the location of the magnetic pole evident in soils with high iron content to a master chronology to determine when a stratigraphic layer or an iron-rich feature (for example, a clay-lined hearth) was laid down. Dendrochronology uses the pattern of the annual growth rings of trees employed as building material or firewood and compares it to a master chronology of tree rings to determine when the tree was cut down.

DNA in Archaeology

DNA is the material that carries the instructions for the formation of all living organisms and is passed from parent to offspring. Segments of this DNA molecule that influence the growth and characteristics of any offspring are called genes. Genetics has revolutionized our understanding of the past. Molecular genetics involves two branches of analysis: studies of the genetic material of living populations, and those that rely on the extraction of DNA directly from ancient human remains. The former has demonstrated that modern human populations are much more genetically diverse in Africa than anywhere else in the world, a finding that supports the idea that modern humans (*Homo sapiens*) originated in Africa and spread outward from there (see Chapter 4). The second involves so-called **ancient DNA** (sometimes abbreviated to aDNA), which has the potential to document the genetic interrelationships of all hominins, living and dead. Studies in aDNA techniques have shown that modern humans interbred with our close relatives, the Neanderthals, and with another extinct group, the Denisovans, from Siberia. Ancient DNA has also been successfully applied to the study of the development and spread of domestic livestock since the end of the last Ice Age (Chapter 5).

DNA is found in the nucleus of the cell, tightly bound into chromosomes, or in structures called mitochondria, many of which exist in one cell [**1.11**]. Archaeologists study DNA in both the nucleus (**nuclear DNA**) and the mitochrondria (**mitochondrial DNA**) of both modern and ancient samples to answer questions about the past. Mitochondrial DNA (mtDNA) is inherited directly through the maternal line. Unlike nuclear DNA, mtDNA does not combine with other DNA during sexual reproduction, but instead replicates itself. The changes between two mitochrondial DNA samples are due only to mutation. By examining the number and types of mutations in mtDNA, it is therefore possible to trace changes and movements in ancient populations.

An important concept in using DNA to examine population change is the **molecular clock**. DNA is known to mutate at a predictable rate, so by counting and comparing the number of mutations between two DNA samples it is possible to estimate when two species diverged, or when two populations separated. Based on the number of accumulated mutations in mtDNA, researchers have concluded that *Homo sapiens* first appeared in southern Africa between 170,000 and 130,000 years ago. A similar genetic approach is examining the Y chromosome in nucleic DNA. This is inherited directly from the male line.

A distinctive group of DNA mutations is known as a **haplogroup**. Archaeologists can trace haplogroups in

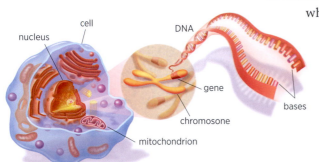

cell

nucleus

DNA

gene

chromosone

bases

mitochondrion

modern DNA to examine how vast migrations occurred in the past, such as the movement of farming populations in Europe, or the peopling of the Americas. DNA is also being used in archaeozoology to explore the origins of domesticated animals. Genetics in archaeology remains a fast-paced field and continues to reshape our understanding of the past.

Archaeological Fieldwork

Alongside laboratory techniques, fieldwork continues to play a central role in archaeology. Only excavation can provide direct access to the buried layers, revealing stratigraphies, recovering artifacts, and allowing first-hand study of *in-situ* remains [**1.12**]. Many excavations today are funded by developers in advance of quarrying or building work. Others are undertaken with specific research questions in mind. New techniques, such as laser scanning and 3D photo-modeling, are providing ever better records of the excavated deposits and are sometimes extended beyond the trench into the surrounding landscape.

Many field campaigns today do not involve digging, but instead the collection or recording of archaeological material lying on the ground surface. Off-site or survey archaeology enables broader patterns of human occupation to be explored, at the scale of cities, villages, and individual farmsteads. Here again, new technology in the field and in the laboratory is revolutionizing the process, with the help of **GPS** (Global Positioning System) to map sites and finds quickly and accurately in the landscape, and GIS to analyze their interrelationships.

Besides methods for reconstructing chronologies, archaeologists employ many techniques to recover, record, and reconstruct objects, landscapes, and environments. Some of these will be practiced during fieldwork: the planning and recording of layers and buildings (now generally using modern laser technology); the screening (sieving) of the excavated earth to ensure no finds are missed; and the collection and labeling of samples for dating or analysis. Technology will also have been important before fieldwork commenced: aerial photography or airborne **LiDAR** (Light Detection and Ranging) [**1.13**, p. 28] to locate sites, and geomagnetic prospection or resistivity to identify such below-ground features as pits

GPS Global Positioning System; a worldwide navigation system based on signals received from satellites orbiting Earth, enabling archaeologists to map quickly and accurately locations of sites in the landscape

LiDAR Light Detection and Ranging, an airborne remote-sensing technique that sends pulses of laser light to the ground and, by measuring the time it takes them to return to the instrument, calculates the distance with extreme accuracy; produces a detailed image of the ground surface, especially since forests and clouds can be filtered out

1.12 Excavations at Must Farm in eastern England, showing preserved timbers of collapsed prehistoric house roofs. Despite advances in remote-sensing techniques, excavation remains a key feature of archaeological research, providing direct access to the living floors, burials, and physical remains of early societies.

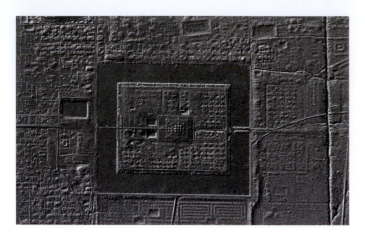

1.13 LiDAR imaging. This airborne imaging technique detects topographical detail by measuring laser pulses sent to the ground from equipment in an airplane or UAV. It is able to penetrate vegetation and often reveals unexpected features. At Angkor Wat in Cambodia, recent LiDAR survey showed that the enclosure around the temple that now appears empty was once filled with houses and ponds.

phytoliths minute particles of silica derived from the cells of plants, able to survive after the organism has decomposed or been burned; common in ash layers, pottery, and even on stone tools

oxygen isotope analysis analysis of the ratio of two oxygen isotopes (^{18}O and ^{16}O) in ancient materials; in sediments from the deep-sea floor, differences in oxygen isotope ratios correlate with glacial and interglacial intervals recorded on land, enabling archaeology to be dated by extrapolation from the deep-sea record

and hearths. Subsurface visualizations using LiDAR are among some of the most exciting developments in recent archaeology (see Chapter 16).

When the field season closes, further work follows in laboratories, where the samples that have been collected are analyzed for remains of **phytoliths** (minute particles of silica from plant cells), pollen, or seeds; for traces of manufacture and use-wear on stone and metal artifacts; for organic deposits surviving in the fabric of pottery vessels; and for faunal and human remains. As already noted, a recent addition to the range of techniques for the study of organic remains has been the means to locate and analyze fossil DNA— preserved segments of the genetic code recovered from bones or seeds and used to reconstruct the relationships between past and present species. This has been especially helpful to our understanding of the origin and spread of domesticated plants and animals, and has also been applied to the issue of modern human origins (Chapter 4).

Reconstructing Ancient Environments. A wide range of types of prehistoric evidence can be employed in attempts to reconstruct environments. One of the most commonly used is the study of deep-sea cores and the isotopes they contain (**oxygen isotope analysis**). The oxygen isotope ^{16}O is lighter than ^{18}O. When water from the ocean evaporates, ^{16}O is carried toward the poles on air currents and precipitates out as snow and ice. During warmer periods, as the polar ice and glaciers melt, sea levels rise, producing oceanic waters with a higher percentage of ^{16}O. In colder periods, much of the ocean water is locked up in the form of ice sheets and glaciers effectively storing massive quantities of the lighter ^{16}O and creating oceans with higher percentages of the heavier isotope ^{18}O. These periods of cooler and warmer global conditions are reflected in changes in the ratio of the oxygen isotopes ^{16}O and ^{18}O found in the shells of microscopic **foraminifera**, or forams, a type of shelled protozoa.

Cores taken from the seabed contain numerous layers that have accumulated continuously over many millennia, which can be dated using various methods. Examining the chemistry of forams found within particular layers of these deep-sea cores can provide information about **glacial** and **interglacial** stages going back tens of millions of years.

A key method for reconstructing ancient environments is **palynology**. Pollen preserved in lake beds, bogs, or dryland sediments can reveal changing patterns of vegetation through time. The technique typically involves coring in a wetland environment and the extraction of a continuous core of deposit that might be several meters in length. Sampling the absolute and relative frequencies of pollen at regular points along the core gives details of changing plant species in the area. That can serve as a proxy for climate change (temperature and rainfall) and can also reveal the impact of human activities, such as woodland clearance and cereal agriculture. A chronological scale can be provided by radiocarbon dating of organic materials within the core. Palynology is a key method for understanding human interaction with the environment and reveals the progressively invasive impact of human activity on the natural world over the past 10,000 years.

Other isotopes, notably those of strontium and oxygen, found in the soil are absorbed by plants, which humans then eat. These isotopes can be measured in human teeth and bones, and compared with the local environment. In cases where they do not match, it implies that the individual who has been sampled passed their earlier years (at the time when their teeth were forming) in a region of contrasting geology. The method can hence provide evidence of human mobility, and recent applications have shown how many more people in prehistoric Europe, for example, traveled significant distances during their lifetimes than had previously been believed.

SUMMARY AND CONCLUSIONS

In this chapter we have discussed the nature of archaeology and how it provides broad and fuller understandings of the human past. In the nineteenth century, with the discovery of fossil hominins and Darwin's theory of evolution by natural selection, the problem of chronology began to be resolved.

The long-term perspective that archaeology provides makes it possible to identify key features of the human story. These include climatic and environmental changes, demographic increase, and the development of symbolic behavior. Modern humans are a product of the Ice Ages, but also of the novel strategies and trajectories that have been adopted during the past 11,600 years, including agriculture and urbanization [**1.14**]. World prehistory sets all of these developments in the context of a human story stretching back more than 6 million years, to the appearance in Africa of the first recognizable hominin species.

foraminifera skeletons of shelled protozoa, also called forams, found in deep-sea cores

glacial an Ice Age

interglacial a period of warmer, wetter climate between two Ice Ages or glacials

palynology the study of pollen and spores

1.14 The Marib Dam in Yemen blocked the floodwaters of the Wadi Dhana and supplied irrigation water to 9,600 hectares (23,722 acres) of fields. The dam was built in the sixth century BCE and spanned 580 meters (1,902 feet) between impressive stone-built sluices at its northern and southern ends. The southern sluice shown here reached its final form in the sixth century CE.

FURTHER READING

Useful introductions to archaeology and the history of the discipline include:

Atalay, S. 2006. Indigenous Archaeology as Decolonizing Practice. *American Indian Quarterly* Vol. 30, No. 3/4, Special Issue: Decolonizing Archaeology: 280–310.

Bahn, P. G., ed. 1996. *The Cambridge Illustrated History of Archaeology.* Cambridge: Cambridge University Press.

Lydon, J. and Rizvi, U. Z. (eds.). 2010. *Handbook of Postcolonial Archaeology.* London: Routledge.

Stringer, C. 2011. *The Origin of Our Species.* London: Penguin Books.

https://www.saa.org Website of the Society for American Archaeology.

African Origins

2

Nicholas Toth and Kathy Schick

Evolution and Human Origins 32

Environments and Landscapes 35

The Rise of the Earliest Hominins 35

The First Stone Tools and the Oldowan 37

KEY DISCOVERY Hadar and Laetoli: Lucy, the First Family, and Fossil Footsteps 38

KEY SITE Olduvai Gorge: The Grand Canyon of Prehistory 40

KEY CONTROVERSY Toolmaking and Gender 42

Food Procurement and Diet 42

The Behavior of Oldowan Hominins 44

Summary and Conclusions 46

Further Reading 47

Olduvai Gorge in Tanzania is one of the oldest archaeological sites in the world. Its numerous layers of sediment provide a remarkable record of its environment and the activities that have taken place there over the past 3 million years, including early hominins and the stone tool tradition first found at the site (Oldowan tradition).

Where does the human story begin? In this chapter we consider the evidence for the earliest members of the human lineage. This requires some explanation of the human family tree, skeletal remains, and material culture and behaviors of our evolutionary ancestors.

We begin with some general observations on human evolution and the emergence of the hominin lineage from within the order of primates, which includes our closest living relatives, the gorillas and chimpanzees. The crucial role played by environmental change in the development, spread, and extinction of different hominin species lays the groundwork for understanding the first tool-using members of hominins in eastern and southern Africa, around 2.8 million years ago or possibly earlier.

- Based on genetic data, the human line split from other primates 8 to 6 million years ago (mya) in Africa. The earliest fossil material with evidence of bipedalism is 6 mya in Chad and Kenya.

- As with later evolutionary developments (Chapters 3 and 4), the early history of the family tree of humans included several branches resulting in many early human species living at the same time 3 to 2 mya.

- The earliest species in our genus (*Homo*) arose around 2.8 million years ago in Africa. The earliest tool tradition (Oldowan) also dates to 2.8 mya in Africa.

For a century and a half, prehistorians have conducted fieldwork throughout the world looking for **paleontological** (fossil-based) and archaeological (artifact-based) evidence of the emergence of the human lineage. For some time, it had been believed that the human evolutionary pathway involved a unique combination of traits that developed more or less at the same time. These characteristics are **bipedalism**, the making of stone tools, and a significant increase in brain size, which are considered some of the most important distinguishing features of humans. These traits did not evolve together, however, but were drawn out in a sequence over millions of years. Bipedal walking preceded the first evidence for stone tools by millions of years, and an increase in brain size is apparent only several hundreds of thousands of years after the beginnings of stone tools.

Bipedal hominins emerged in Africa from an ape ancestry by 6 million years ago. A number of different hominin species—possibly a dozen—are known to have existed between then and 1.5 million years ago; our own **genus**, *Homo*, appeared fairly recently, by perhaps as early as 2.8 million years ago. The fossil record suggests that at many periods during the span of this time more than one hominin species co-existed, indicating evolutionary complexity during this phase of our development, with different lineages focusing on different foods and habitats, rather than a single evolving hominin line. This chapter explores the rise of the first hominins, how they responded to changing climates, and how they gained the attributes we associate with being human.

EVOLUTION AND HUMAN ORIGINS

The path to modern *Homo sapiens* was not simple or direct. The human evolutionary record shows evidence of a number of major splits in the past several million years, sometimes producing multiple lineages of contemporary, related species. The genetically closest living

paleontology the study of fossils

bipedalism walking on two legs

genus (pl. genera) a group of closely related species

Ardipithecus extinct genus of a hominin that existed in East Africa between 5.8 and 4.4 million years ago

Australopithecus extinct genus of a bipedal hominin that existed in southern and eastern Africa between about 4.2 and 1 million years ago; probably the ancestor of the genus *Homo*, which includes modern humans

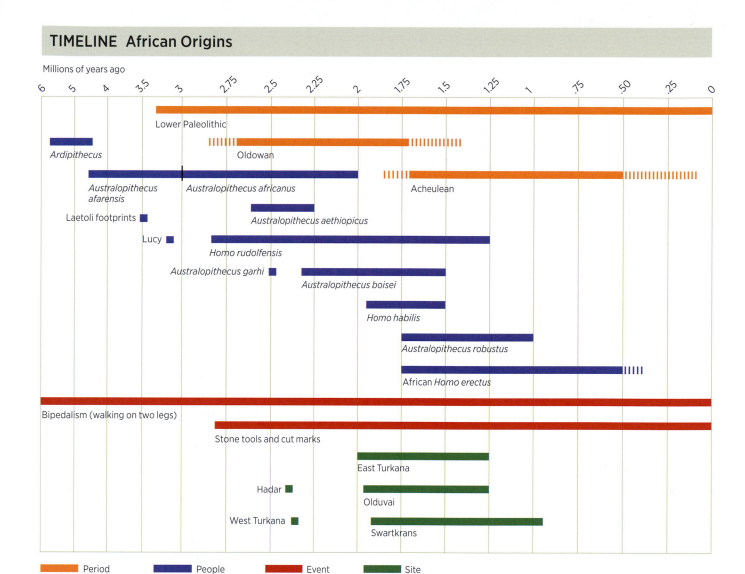

Millions of years ago

Period · People · Event · Site

IIIIIIIII Estimated · IIIIIIIII Estimated

relatives to *H. sapiens* today are chimpanzees, which share a common ancestor with humans that lived probably between 8 and 6 million years ago. Yet at many times during the past few million years we had much closer relatives, now known only from their fossil remains. Sometime after our split with the other apes, the ancestral human lineage apparently developed bipedal locomotion. This adaptation was shared by a number of contemporary cousin lineages, including the early species in the genus **Ardipithecus** and **Australopithecus**, before our own genus (*Homo*) developed.

Behavioral patterns, either instinctive or learned, may also be adopted because they confer an evolutionary advantage. It seems certain that in the human lineage two important behavioral traits, the early development of tool use and the probable later development of symbolic communication (language), were highly adaptive and ultimately selected for in the course of our evolution. Any genetic basis to help support and promote these behaviors (larger and more complex brains, changes in hand morphology—form or structure—changes in vocal tracts, etc.) would have been selected for very strongly if they conferred higher survivorship and reproductive success. Technological traditions, represented by stone tools in the early prehistoric record, may therefore have helped support the relatively rapid evolution of aspects of the brain and body, which in turn helped to develop and maintain more sophisticated tool traditions in a feedback loop.

Our Ape Ancestry: The Comparative Anatomical and Genetic Evidence

Somewhere between 8 and 6 million years ago we shared a common ancestor with other apes. It is more accurate to describe ourselves as apes, and to speak of our divergence from other apes, than to characterize our evolutionary pathway as some radical departure from that lineage. Many aspects of our anatomy, genetic makeup, and behavior are rooted in our shared ancestry. The strong morphological similarities between humans and the great apes, particularly chimpanzees and gorillas, have long been recognized and taken as evidence that they are our closest living relations. Now knowledge of the tremendous genetic similarity among the living apes corroborates this evidence, and further refines our understanding of the order and the timing of the evolutionary divergence of the diverse ape lineages.

Anatomical Evidence. Apes (including humans) are distinguished from their closest living relatives, the Old World monkeys, by a number of shared traits. Among them are a broadened nose, a widened palate, the lack of a tail, and an enlarged brain. As a group, apes have, in fact, carried the primate evolutionary trend toward larger brain size and greater intelligence to an extreme. Other morphological features shared by humans and the great apes are a relatively mobile shoulder joint and many aspects of the core part of the body, which are probably components of an adaptation to hanging from and moving about in trees. Human and ape hands, arms, legs, and feet also show many similarities, despite some major differences that have emerged since our common ancestor.

Prominent among these differences is human bipedal locomotion, involving numerous transformations in our spine, pelvis, legs, and feet [**2.1**]. Later differences that emerged in the evolving human lineage include smaller teeth, particularly the reduction in the size of the anterior teeth (canines and incisors), but an increase in body size, and a very significant expansion in brain size. Another important human trait that emerged is a finely manipulative hand, with a long and opposable thumb. In addition, body proportions have changed substantially in the evolution of our lineage, with the development of longer legs relative to arms in humans, whereas apes retain relatively long arms and short legs.

Genetic Evidence. The remarkable similarities between humans and apes is corroborated by analysis of the degree of similarity among their proteins and even their DNA. From the late 1960s onward, scientists began looking at protein differences among primates and other animals. These gave quantifiable results indicating that humans possess a very strong protein similarity with chimpanzees and gorillas, a somewhat lesser similarity with Asian apes, and successively less with Old World monkeys, New World monkeys, and prosimians. It was found that humans differ genetically from the chimpanzee by 1.5 percent, the gorilla by about 2 percent, the orangutan by

2.1 Anatomical evidence. The spines and lower limbs of bipedal humans (left), knuckle-walking chimpanzees (center), and quadrupedal (walking on four legs) baboons (right) show significant differences in posture for the different modes of locomotion.

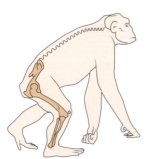

3 percent, the gibbon by 4 percent, Old World monkeys by 6 percent, New World monkeys by 12 percent, and prosimians by more than 20 percent.

Attempts made to quantify the rate of genetic change gave an estimated time of separation between humans and chimpanzees that was relatively recent, only around 8–6 million years ago. This was surprising, as decades ago it was believed that this split had taken place much earlier, perhaps 20–15 million years ago.

These genetic differences build a family tree, with our more immediate relatives (those that have branched off from our line more recently) classified closer together with us compared to relatives that branched off much earlier.

ENVIRONMENTS AND LANDSCAPES

There is growing evidence that changes in the earth's climate had profound effects on the African landmass, altering temperature and rainfall and, subsequently, flora and fauna. Some of these major changes appear to relate to those in human evolution as well. While there is a danger of becoming overly deterministic when trying to correlate environmental variations with evolutionary ones, such correlations that can be documented in the prehistoric record are nonetheless intriguing and warrant further investigation.

Global changes in climate greatly influenced the African continent and its environments during the time of the evolution of the African apes and the emergence and development of bipedal hominins. In addition, the mountain ranges of the African Rift created by tectonic uplift caused by movements of the earth's plates gave rise to a rain shadow in much of East Africa, gradually leading to drier, more open environments, particularly around 14 million years ago. This trend continued, apparently also part of a global swing toward cooler and drier conditions, ultimately leading to pronounced cold glacial periods interspersed with numerous warmer interglacial periods.

This pattern of repeatedly oscillating climatic conditions, and the associated changes in plant and animal communities, was the environmental context in which our protohuman ancestors evolved and must have had a significant effect on the course of ape evolution and, ultimately, on the human lineage.

Early in the evolution of the African apes, around 22 million years ago, the African continent was quite different from how it is at present. Lush tropical forests and woodlands covered much of the landmass in tropical and subtropical Africa, and the Sahara Desert had not yet developed. As the drier, more open habitats started spreading, the abundance of apes that had flourished and diversified in the wetter, more forested conditions dwindled dramatically.

THE RISE OF THE EARLIEST HOMININS

Identifying the early hominins that branched off since the last common ancestor of humans and chimpanzees and gorillas is usually based on one of two criteria: either cranial (the skull), where differences in skull size and form as well as dental characteristics can distinguish hominins from non-hominins, and postcranial (the skeleton below the skull), which can show evidence of bipedality. The hominin fossil record becomes much better represented at around 4 million years ago with the appearance of the early australopithecines, with fossils attributed to the genus *Homo* appearing as early as 2.8 million years ago, slightly before the beginning of the Ice Age [**2.2**, p. 36].

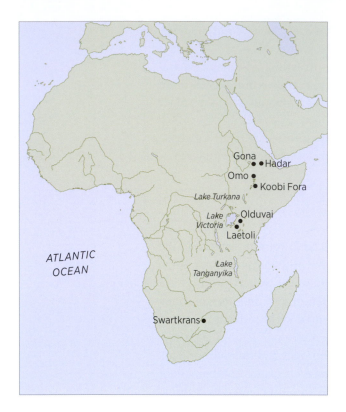

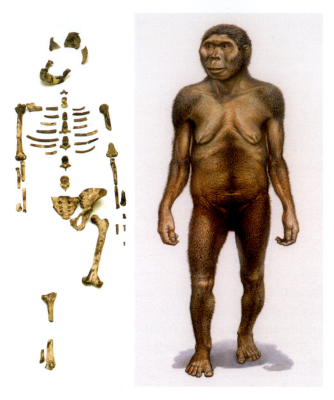

The Ardipithecenes

Although there are hints of changing morphology that suggest bipedalism occurred earlier, ardipithecenes are often seen as the earliest hominins. Species of *Ardipithecus* existed in Ethiopia, Chad, and Kenya between 5.8 and 4.4 million years ago, and demonstrate attributes of both great apes and later hominins. Their hip features, level with where the backbone and pelvis join, suggest bipedalism, similar to the later australopithecines, and the hands lack the wrist-stabilizing features and long metacarpals of an ape that knuckle-walks. But *Ardipithecus* also has a grasping big toe more in keeping with great apes and does not have adaptations to heavy chewing found in later hominins. It is this combination of traits of both great apes and the australopithecines it preceded that marks *Ardipithecus* as the first hominin.

The Australopithecines

Earlier forms of *Australopithecus,* including *Australopithecus (A.) anamensis* (4.2 million years ago) and *A. afarensis* (3.9 million years ago)—represented by the famous partial skeleton that has become known as Lucy [**2.3**, **2.4**]—were characterized as bipedal, had shorter legs and longer arms than modern humans, and had skulls with large **dentition** (see Key Discovery box: Hadar and Laetoli: Lucy, the First Family, and Fossil Footsteps, p. 38). Some **paleoanthropologists** suggest that the proportionately long arms and ape-like curved **phalanges** indicate that these creatures were still spending a significant amount of time (perhaps most of the time) in the trees. Other researchers contest this, arguing that the fossil evidence of a broad and short pelvis, long femur neck, angled knee joint, and arched foot indicates they were predominately bipedal. There is no definitive evidence for the creation of artifacts during this early stage of human evolution. It is possible that the material culture of these early bipeds was on a scale comparable to that seen in modern chimpanzees (such as the use of twigs to extract termites, or stones as hammers to crack open nuts).

The later australopithecines include, in South Africa, *Australopithecus africanus* between 3 and 2 million years ago and, by 2 million years ago, *A. sediba* [**2.5**], as well as, in East Africa by 2.5 million years ago, *A. garhi. A. sediba*, represented by partial remains from at least four individuals from the cave at Malapa, South Africa, has been suggested by some to represent a possible transition form between *A. africanus* and *Homo*, while others contend that it probably represents a later evolution of *A. africanus* that coexisted with early evolving *Homo*.

Between 3 and 1.8 million years ago, two new trajectories in hominin evolution occurred alongside the continuation of these forms of *Australopithecus*. The first was the emergence of the *Homo* line (below) and the second was the appearance of other forms of australopithecines—*A. aethiopicus* and *A. boisei* in East Africa, and *A. robustus* in South Africa—sometimes referred to as *Paranthropus*, with a modest increase in brain size and the development of massive jaws and cheek teeth (molars), occurring as an adaption to a diet of nuts and seeds, which required strong jaw muscles. Already, the story of human evolution shows many branches of human species living in various regions of the African continent.

2.5 Australopithecine. The cranium of MH1, the juvenile skeleton of *Australopithecus sediba* found at Malapa Cave, South Africa.

Homo rudolfensis, Homo habilis, *and* Homo erectus

Following the appearance of the australopithecines, the second major development in hominin evolution was the emergence of early forms of the genus *Homo*—*H. rudolfensis, H. habilis*, and African *H. erectus* (also called *Homo ergaster*) between 2.8 and 2 million years ago. They probably evolved during this period from one of the australopithecines. Larger brains and, usually, smaller jaws and teeth characterize these early *Homo* forms and define the species, although *H. rudolfensis*, the earliest of these three, still retains large, australopithecine-like premolars and molars. The overall architecture of the skulls of some of these larger-brained forms seems to foreshadow many modern human cranial features. It is just before this time, around 2.8 million years ago, that the first stone tools are found, establishing the earliest known archaeological record.

THE FIRST STONE TOOLS AND THE OLDOWAN

A significant step in the human story is the first appearance of stone tools. The earliest recognizable objects modified by hominins are found approximately 2.8 to 2.5 million years ago in the form of flaked and battered stone artifacts from the Middle Awash Valley in Ethiopia. Further finds from Dikika in Ethiopia and Lomekwi in Kenya may push this date back to 3.3 million years, and while these estimates remain controversial, no paleoanthropologists would be surprised, given our increased knowledge of toolmaking by other species.

Most anthropologists assume that prior to this, hominins may have produced and employed simple technologies that would leave little visibility in ancient deposits, either being made of perishable organic material or being so little modified as to be unrecognizable as an artifact. The uses of material culture by wild chimpanzees in East and West Africa give some possible clues into such rudimentary technologies.

The earliest archaeological sites found have been assigned to the Oldowan industry, first found at **Olduvai Gorge** in Tanzania (see Key Site box: Olduvai Gorge: The Grand Canyon

dentition teeth: incisors, canines, and molars

paleoanthropology the study of earliest humans from fossil remains

phalange a finger or toe bone

KEY DISCOVERY Hadar and Laetoli: Lucy, the First Family, and Fossil Footsteps

The species named *Australopithecus afarensis* (after the Afar region of Ethiopia) is well represented from several sites, notably **Hadar**, in the Ethiopian Rift Valley, and **Laetoli**, about 50 kilometers (30 miles) south of the main gorge at Olduvai in Tanzania (see Key Site box: Olduvai Gorge: The Grand Canyon of Prehistory, p. 40). The Hadar finds included the partial skeleton of a 1-meter-tall (3.3 feet) female now known as Lucy; the remains of at least thirteen adult and juvenile individuals (the so-called First Family); and a nearly complete male skull.

The celebrated Lucy skeleton is approximately 60 percent complete, with body parts that include cranial fragments, a mandible with teeth, vertebrae, ribs, partial scapula (shoulder blade), humeri (upper arm bones), radii and ulnae (the two types of lower arm bones), a pelvis, femur (thigh bone), tibia (shin bone) and fibula (smaller lower leg bone), and some foot and hand bones. This find was critical in providing an earlier date for bipedalism.

The wealth of fossil specimens of *A. afarensis*, and the great diversity within the First Family collection of fossils, has also given anthropologists a much better appreciation of the variability of this species.

Footsteps in Time

The Laetoli area was the site of an amazing discovery made in the 1970s by the paleoanthropologist Mary Leakey. It consisted of a layer of compacted volcanic ash, or tuff, that preserved a number of sets of animal tracks, including those of mammals, birds, and insects—as well as those of three hominins [**2.6**]. The distinctive carbonatite chemistry of the tuff (highly alkaline; essentially a volcanic limestone) meant that, after a brief wetting with rain, it solidified into a concrete-like consistency that retained the prints of the animals that had walked across its surface.

The tracks chronicle the footmarks of animals from insect to elephant size, including the famous set of footprints of three bipedal hominins that were all walking in the same direction. These hominin prints have become an icon of paleoanthropological research and remain one of the most remarkable and unexpected finds. The Laetoli fauna, with grazing animals well represented, and the footmarks showing linear and uninterrupted animal tracks, suggest fairly open grasslands, possibly with forest along stream channels.

2.6 Excavation of the Laetoli footprints in northern Tanzania. These footprints, believed to be the product of three hominins (the larger tracks are the result of superimposition of the prints of two individuals), are dated to 3.5 million years ago.

of Prehistory, p. 40). The Oldowan industry involves taking and shaping a piece of rock by removing flakes from its surface. These were created from river-worn cobbles or angular blocks and are often called **cores**. Other large tools were not flaked in this way, but rather battered, possibly used as hammerstones. The removed flakes from cores were often sharp-edged and angular, and were occasionally **retouched** by striking off tiny chips to reshape or sharpen the edge [**2.7**]. Mary Leakey grouped cores and some battered stones into the category heavy-duty tools, and most of the retouched forms into light-duty tools. Combined, these are referred to as the Oldowan industrial **complex**.

Oldowan tools continued to be used for a long time but after about 1.5 million years ago these sites existed alongside the newer Acheulean **handaxe** and cleaver industries (see Chapter 3). While the definition, distribution, and dating of the Oldowan industry are constantly being refined by archaeologists, the Oldowan is commonly considered the first recognizable stone-tool industry in the human story.

Technology

Experimentation has shown that many of the artifacts that characterize the Oldowan industry can be explained by least-effort flaking strategies, reducing stone to produce cores that could be used for chopping or hacking and flakes with sharp-cutting edges [**2.8**, **2.9**]. Much of the variation seen in the Oldowan tools can probably be explained by differences in the nature of the raw materials available at different sites (the size, shape, and flaking quality of stones used for tools), as well as how heavily the cores had been flaked. Retouched flakes, however, suggest intentional modification to resharpen or shape the edges.

At some sites in South Africa, polished and striated bone and horn core fragments associated with Oldowan artifacts have been interpreted as digging implements.

Who Made the Oldowan Tools?

The Oldowan industry is known from about 2.8–2.5 million years ago until new forms of tool are introduced from around 1.5 million years ago, notably handaxes, cleavers, and picks.

2.7 Oldowan artifacts. First discovered at Olduvai Gorge in Tanzania, Oldowan artifacts have been recovered from several localities in eastern, central, and southern Africa, the oldest of which is a site at Gona, Ethiopia.

---

core the parent piece of rock from which flakes are detached

retouched where the edges of stone flakes have been further modified by the striking off of tiny chips to reshape or sharpen the edge

complex a recurring group of artifacts and activities that appear together at a particular time and place and are presumed to represent an archaeological culture

handaxe a flat cobble flaked over both surfaces to produce a sharp edge around the entire periphery; also called a biface

2.8, 2.9 Oldowan toolmaking. Examples of Oldowan artifacts and a diagram to show the method of manufacture of an Oldowan bifacial chopper using a hammerstone.

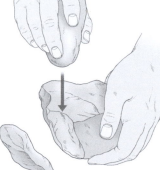

KEY SITE   Olduvai Gorge: The Grand Canyon of Prehistory

Olduvai Gorge, a 100-meter-deep (330 feet), 50-kilometer-long (31 miles) gash in the Serengeti Plain of northern Tanzania, is one of the most famous prehistoric sites in the world, and the closest we have to a time machine to take us back over the past 2 million years to document the biological and technological evolution of the human lineage. One can literally walk through deep prehistory here, with layer upon layer of ancient sediments documenting an unparalleled sequence of ancient environments, animal communities, stone technologies, and prehistoric hominins during earlier (and later) periods of the Stone Age.

This impressive gorge was first described by the entomologist Wilhelm Kattwinkel, who was chasing butterflies across the Serengeti in 1911 when, in pursuit of an especially interesting specimen, he nearly fell into it. The German prehistorian Hans Reck led expeditions here beginning in 1913, and from their many years of fieldwork at Olduvai (the type site of the Oldowan industry, meaning that it is considered definitively characteristic of that particular culture), Louis and Mary Leakey gained an international reputation in paleoanthropology and a level of celebrity. The Leakeys were able to establish a prehistoric sequence with chronological control that began about 1.85 million years ago in the lowest level, Bed I, with Oldowan sites and hominin fossils that included the type specimens of *Homo habilis* and *Australopithecus boisei* (originally called *Zinjanthropus*).

The *Zinjanthropus* site (FLK Zinj) is one of the richest Oldowan sites ever excavated [**2.10**], containing more than 2,000 stone artifacts and more than 3,500 fossil animal bone specimens, with at least 1,000 of the bones identifiable to taxon (unit of zoological classification, for example species, genus, or family) or body part; more than 90 percent of these belong to larger mammals. Bed II begins around 1.7 million years ago and contains Oldowan sites, some of which have relatively high proportions of retouched pieces and spheroids.

By about 1.7 million years ago, the first early Acheulean industries appear in the sequence here, characterized by handaxes, picks, and cleavers. Bed II has also yielded fossils of *Homo erectus* (see Chapter 3). Beds III and IV, and the overlying Masek Beds, have produced a number of Acheulean and Developed Oldowan sites, and the topmost beds, Ndutu and Naisiusu, contain Middle Stone Age and Later Stone Age sites. The site therefore offers a long sequence that traces the prior dominance of the Oldowan industry before it is overlapped by the development of early Acheulean industries.

Olduvai Gorge holds a special place in the history of paleoanthropology because it established a long sequence of biological and cultural evolution in East Africa. It also set a number of standards for the varieties of evidence that could be gathered and the diverse multidisciplinary investigations that could fruitfully be focused on such a rich paleoanthropological record.

A range of studies has been focused on Olduvai Gorge's geology and paleoenvironmental setting, its archaeological record of technological change, landscape archaeology, paleontological record, and its hominin fossils.

It is also a major tourist attraction for the Tanzanian government, being a UNESCO World Heritage Site with a field museum and tours to many of the famous prehistoric sites in the gorge. As such, it is not only one of the foremost locations for primary research into human origins but also an important destination for public archaeology and education in human prehistory.

2.10 The FLK Zinj site at Olduvai Gorge, dated to *c.* 1.84 million years ago.

Between 2.8 and 1.5 million years ago, a number of hominin species (perhaps eight) are found in Africa, including the large and robust, cheek-toothed australopithecines, as well as more gracile (slender) forms, and *Homo rudolfensis, H. habilis,* and *H. erectus*. Which species made these early stone tools? There are three lines of evidence that are often followed to address this question: zoological studies of modern apes, evidence for increased brain size in hominins, and the archaeological contexts of the artifacts themselves.

Experiments with present-day chimpanzees and gorillas suggest that they have the cognitive and biomechanical capacity to flake stone and use stone tools, and therefore early bipedal hominins had at least the same ability. It is possible that all of these prehistoric species used technology to different degrees, some (or perhaps all) with flaked stone [**Table 2.1**].

The genus *Homo* is characterized by larger absolute brain size and greater brain-to-body ratio than the australopithecines. It also exhibits a reduction in the size of jaws and cheek teeth. For many paleoanthropologists, these two changes would seem a logical consequence of hominins becoming more technological, slowly replacing their biology with tools, and expanding their diet breadth to include higher-quality foods procured and processed with the use of manufactured implements.

The Oldowan period established the critical biological and behavioral foundations for the later emergence of *Homo erectus*, and the Acheulean industrial complex, which is discussed more thoroughly in the next chapter.

The Nature of Oldowan Sites

At present, there is no clear evidence for architectural features in the Oldowan or of any complex behaviors. Rather, archaeological sites during this time tend to be relatively small and low density, with stone artifacts and (preservation permitting) the fossil remains of animals. The majority of locations are found in sedimentary environments that include riverine floodplains and channels, lake margins, river deltas, and—in South Africa—**karstic** (limestone) cave infillings. Plant communities range from closed woodlands, often along stream courses, to more open or wooded grasslands. At some sites, substantial quantities of fossil bone are associated with Oldowan artifacts, yielding valuable evidence of the environmental context of these places, as well as information about the possible procurement and processing of animal carcasses by ancient hominins. In general, raw materials for stone tool manufacture (see Key Controversy box: Toolmaking and Gender, p. 42) were transported short distances, usually less than a few kilometers.

There has been considerable debate as to how the prehistoric accumulations of flaked and battered stones and fossil bones formed. Some archaeologists suggested that these sites were home bases, similar to modern hunter-gatherer camps. Glynn Isaac, an archaeologist

Table 2.1 Hominin Species and their Association with the Oldowan

Million years ago	Species	Archaeological association
4.0–3.0	*Australopithecus afarensis* *Australopithecus africanus*	None
3.0–2.5	*Australopithecus africanus* *Australopithecus aethiopicus* *Australopithecus garhi* *Australopithecus sediba* *Early Homo* sp. indet.	Oldowan
2.5–1.8	*Homo habilis* *Homo rudolfensis* *Australopithecus boisei* *Australopithecus robustus*	Oldowan
1.8–1.5	*Homo habilis* *Homo erectus (ergaster)* *Australopithecus boisei* *Australopithecus robustus*	Oldowan and Acheulean

karstic region a limestone region with sinkholes, underground streams, and caverns

The development of stone tools is often closely associated with the evolution of hominins and the definition of what it is to be human, so the assigning of gender to this form of activity has important connotations. For a number of years, archaeologists have challenged an enduring assumption that stone toolmaking was a male activity. How did this assumption come about, and is there evidence that tools were made by both sexes?

Joan Gero was an American archaeologist who tackled these questions, and looked first to her colleagues, arguing that male bias is imposed on archaeological interpretations of stone toolmaking. For example, while many women archaeologists have learned to knap flint, traditionally flint-knapping is considered male territory, undertaken by male experimental archaeologists. Gero contended that the reconstructed tools are more often spear points, knives, or those used to fulfil tasks associated with modern maleness, especially hunting. Gero contrasted this with research on tool use, which is a topic studied by a greater proportion of women.

Often ethnography has been used to form a case that stone toolmaking is a male activity. Again, Gero looked at the researchers themselves, especially those in the mid-twentieth century, noting that male ethnographers were more likely to note male activity, and even highlighted examples where ethnographic observations of women making stone tools was made but never incorporated into wider studies.

Accounts of Indigenous Australian women making flake and core tools, such as Tiwi women in Australia creating stone axes, are enough to reason that attributing a single gender to such a wide-ranging category of material culture is deeply problematic.

from South Africa, later used the more neutral term central-place foraging to describe how these concentrations may have formed, with hominins radiating out on foraging rounds and returning for food processing and consumption. Others proposed that these sites were simply carnivore leftovers that were scavenged by early hominins, primarily through marrow processing.

A further argument still was that the concentrations at Olduvai Gorge were stone caches, where hominins created stores of raw stone material in areas where it did not occur naturally, and in proximity to areas where they would be foraging.

It is probable that these Oldowan sites formed through more than one behavioral mode. The more substantial ones may well represent favored places, where stones and bones were carried to an area that afforded amenities, such as shade, protection, water, animal carcasses, or other resources. In this model, stone may have been characteristically carried around by hominins for potential use, and sites developed where stone imports significantly exceeded their subsequent export when leaving the spot, possibly because transport of foods took on a greater priority.

FOOD PROCUREMENT AND DIET

Hunters or Scavengers?

Where bone preservation is good, Oldowan sites are often associated with fossil animal bones that are usually broken up and sometimes show distinctive grooves or scratches characteristic of cut marks from a sharp-edged stone tool. This demonstrates a functional relationship between the bones and the stone tools. Since the beginning of the 1980s, there has been an ongoing debate about the significance of these co-occurrences. Did early hominins intentionally bring parts of animal carcasses back to a central place to process and consume? If so, were these obtained through hunting, scavenging, or a combination of these two strategies? The African Early Stone Age has proved to be a good testing ground to address these questions.

For instance, early researchers argued that Oldowan sites were the remains of carnivore kills and accumulations that were subsequently scavenged by hominins, who had access only to marrow and limb bones, and leftover scraps of meat on bones. The scavenging model contends that the body-part representation and cut-mark location and frequency are most consistent with hominins that were opportunistic scavengers exploiting the remnants of carcasses killed and eaten by big carnivores.

More recent research indicates that Oldowan sites were either the product of hominin hunters who could bring down game, or the product of hominin scavengers who were able to drive predators off kills and had access to complete or nearly complete carcasses. This Early Access model is also based upon empirical studies, body-part representation, and cut-mark patterns [2.11]. In this interpretation, the bones at sites often represent the most nutritious parts of an animal, notably upper limbs and crania, and the cut marks indicate removal of large, meaty muscle units. According to this theory, then, early hominins were capable and efficient foragers with early or primary access to animal carcasses, rather than scavengers with late or secondary access to already ravaged kills.

As new Oldowan sites are located, excavated, and analyzed, a clearer picture of early hominin adaptive behavior will emerge. The answers will probably be complex, showing a range of different patterns and indicating that the Oldowan is not some monolithic form of adaptation, but involves diverse behavior patterns in varying circumstances.

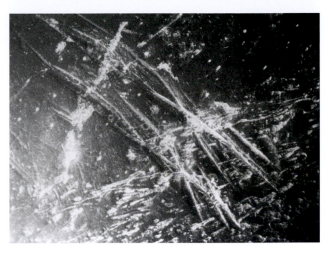

2.11 Cut-mark analysis. These cut marks (magnified) on a 1-million-year-old fossil animal limb bone were made by a stone knife with an irregular edge.

Food for Thought: Diet and Encephalization

The human brain is a voracious organ: although it makes up only 2 percent of our body weight, it demands 18 percent of our metabolic energy. No other primate has evolved such a high brain-to-body ratio as the human species, and this unusually large organ has clearly given us the neurological foundation that is responsible for our complex technologies, food-procurement strategies, symbolic and linguistic behavior, and culture. Since the time of Darwin, scientists have presented different explanations for brain enlargement (**encephalization**), suggesting driving forces, such as tool use, hunting, gathering, food sharing, and increased socialization.

In 1995, the anthropologists Leslie Aiello and Peter Wheeler published an article titled "The Expensive-Tissue Hypothesis." They noted that animals with diets that include great amounts of plant foods with lower nutrient content tend to have more complex digestive tracts and need to devote more metabolic energy to digesting and detoxifying these foods. Animals (for example, carnivores and omnivores) with diets characterized by better-quality foods (in that they are high in protein and calories), such as meat and fat, tend to have simpler, more streamlined digestive tracts and need substantially less energy for digestion. Aiello and Wheeler argued that hominin groups that could process greater amounts of meat and fat (with the assistance of technology) would need to consume fewer vegetable foods that require more metabolic energy to digest and detoxify. A more omnivorous diet would allow more metabolic energy to be devoted to a larger brain. Therefore, tool use, meat or marrow consumption, and brain expansion all evolved in tandem.

encephalization enlargement of the brain

We have evidence in *Homo habilis*, which emerged between 2 and 1.8 million years ago, of a significant brain enlargement (increasing to 510–687 cc) from the australopithecine condition; this occurred within a half million years of the first appearance of stone tools and cut-marked bones, if not sooner. While this is not proof that Aiello and Wheeler's hypothesis is correct, many anthropologists think that the close timing of the Oldowan and encephalization is more than coincidence.

The expensive-tissue hypothesis is potentially testable by examining strontium–calcium ratios in fossil hominin bones and teeth to determine the degree of animal foods in the diet. The prediction would be that hominin species with larger brains would have more meat and marrow in their diet, and therefore lower strontium-to-calcium ratios. Robust australopithecines, for example, might be expected to have higher ratios than their contemporary early *Homo* counterparts (but see below). And later forms of *Homo*, being larger-brained, should have lower ratios than early *Homo*. This chemical approach to hominin evolution is still in its infancy, with small sample sizes, but nonetheless it suggests that a significant inclusion of animal protein in hominin diet, accomplished through the use of tools, may have provided a critical impetus to the rapid evolutionary expansion of brain size in the hominin lineage.

Another hypothesis (the social brain hypothesis) sees the increasing challenges and benefits of larger social groups as a driver of cognitive development. This is based on observations of living primates, where species with larger brains tend to exist in bigger and more complex social groups.

THE BEHAVIOR OF OLDOWAN HOMININS

We know that early hominin populations must have had distinctive patterns of social behavior, mating systems, vocal and non-vocal communication, dietary preferences and food-procurement strategies, land use and ranging behaviors, and a wealth of other characteristics that did not involve stone tools and material culture. Many of these would leave little, if any, prehistoric visibility, but others can leave hard evidence behind.

Social Organization

Barring a Pompeii-like burial of toolmakers at an Oldowan site, our information about social organization of hominin groups is centered on studies of modern primates and comparing the morphology of their bodies to the biological clues from hominin fossils. Primates with similar morphology suggest hominins may have typically lived in a social group of perhaps thirty individuals; individuals banded together into big groups or broke up into smaller groups at different seasons of the year, according to the availability of food and water resources. We do not know the nature of the relationships between the individuals in these groups. Furthermore, we do not know if they divided up the tasks needed for survival and shared resources beyond parent–child groupings or if each individual or family was autonomous and they came together only for protection and companionship.

Diet

Based on modern primate models, it is probable that plant foods formed the bulk of the early hominin diet, with animal foods an important but smaller portion of their food intake. The large molars and premolars of the robust australopithecines, and the microscopic striations and pitting that characterize their chewing surfaces, suggest that their diet was dominated by hard, gritty foods, such as seeds or roots and tubers. The more gracile australopithecines and the early *Homo* forms may have had a more generalized diet including a variety of plants and some meat. As mentioned, chemical studies of hominin bones (discussed in more detail opposite) may provide further evidence of dietary patterns, particularly the proportion of animal foods and the general types of plant foods consumed by different species.

Cut marks and fracture patterns on long bones show that Oldowan hominins processed massive mammal carcasses (weighing several hundred pounds on the hoof) and therefore incorporated some animal protein and fat in their diet. How much, how frequently, and by what means of procurement are highly debated issues. In any case, the size of the animals these early hominins processed far exceeds the small body sizes of prey seen in the predatory behavior of chimpanzees and baboons, and may have been much larger than the hominins themselves. This implies a new and unique adaptive pattern within the primate order, one achieved by hominins through the use of stone tools (and, presumably, other material culture), and one that would have pitted them in a competition for resources against predators and scavengers on the landscape.

Fire

Controlled use of fire by early Oldowan hominins is a subject of some debate and controversy. There is evidence for thermal alteration of sediments and prehistoric materials at some Oldowan sites. At Swartkrans in South Africa, burned bones are found in layers associated with stone tools and cut-marked bones. At other places, for example Koobi Fora in Kenya, several patches of discolored, apparently baked sediment have been found, which have been interpreted as possible fire locations [**2.12**, **2.13**]. At these sites, some artifacts also have been found that show evident heating in a fire, producing discoloration, fine surface

2.12, 2.13 Controlled use of fire. Excavation at the site of FxJj 20 at Koobi Fora, Kenya (left), and a closeup of the baked sediments at FxJj 20 (below). This evidence, along with thermally altered stone artifacts, demonstrates the presence of a high-temperature fire at the site, but whether this represents a natural brushfire or hominin control of fire cannot be established with certainty.

cracking, or heat-induced fractures. In the absence of a discrete hearth structure, however, or spatially concentrated burned artifacts or bones, indicating contolled use of fire as a part of the behavioral repertoire of early hominins cannot be demonstrated and the possibility that these features resulted from natural fires remains. (See also Chapter 3 for further consideration of fire use by early hominins.)

Art, Ritual, and Language

At present, there is minimal or no direct evidence for symbolic or ritualistic behavior among Oldowan primates. In fact, little sign of features, such as representative or abstract art, intentional burials with grave goods, or the collection of exotic stones or shells, is seen until much more recent times, primarily only in the past 100,000 years. Others have argued that the encephalization and expansion of the prefrontal cortex of *Homo habilis* shortly after 2 million years ago indicate the beginnings of a more symbolic communication system with consistent use of consonants indicating rudimentary language.

SUMMARY AND CONCLUSIONS

The first bipedal hominins appear to have emerged in Africa from an ape ancestry. The earliest known is *Ardipithecus*, dated to between 5.8 and 4.4 million years ago. Between 5 and 2 million years ago, bipedal hominins (*Australopithecus/Paranthropus*) are characterized by having relatively small brains and large jaws and teeth, especially cheek teeth, in comparison to *Homo*. The first archaeological sites, dated to around 2.8 million years ago, are found in Ethiopia, characterized by flaked-stone technologies assigned to the Oldowan industry.

Between 2 million and 1.8–1.7 million years ago, the first hominins that appear to show marked encephalization are found. These forms are usually assigned to the genus *Homo* and a number of species are present at this time. It cannot be demonstrated with certainty which of these species made Oldowan tools. It is possible that all hominin species contemporaneous with the Oldowan made stone tools, but the fact that the genus *Homo* exhibits encephalization and tooth reduction over time, and continues after the extinction of the robust australopithecines, suggests that they were major players in flaked-stone technology.

The Oldowan industry is characterized by simple core forms, battered stones, flakes, and retouched forms. Experimentation has shown that much of the variability in the Oldowan can be explained in terms of least-effort strategies to produce sharp flakes and chopping edges from cobbles and chunks of rock. Cut marks on bones, as well as functional experiments, show that Oldowan flakes were excellent knives for animal butchery. Such uses would have expanded the breadth of the hominin diet, incorporating greater quantities of high-quality foods. This change in diet would reduce gut size and allow encephalization over time.

The earliest archaeological sites tend to be situated in depositional environments, such as river floodplains, river channels, deltas, and lake margins. Faunal remains are found associated with stone artifacts at some sites, notably at Olduvai Gorge. Bones of larger and smaller mammals are often present, usually heavily fragmented and sometimes exhibiting cut marks, suggesting that Oldowan hominins processed meat and marrow from animal carcasses. **Zooarchaeologists** argue whether this pattern represents hunting/primary access scavenging or more marginal scavenging, and a consensus has not yet been reached.

A wealth of evidence has now been uncovered regarding these early phases of human biological, technological, and cultural evolution. The hominin fossil record has now bushed

zooarchaeology a branch of archaeology specializing in the analysis of animal bones and shells; also called archaeozoology

and burgeoned into a multiplicity of different fossil forms, which evolved over a substantial amount of time and spread geographically over considerable distances and varying environments. Tighter chronological controls have allowed us to assign more precise dates to many sites and evolutionary events, to document the pattern of these emerging biological and cultural traits, and to try to explain them. What, therefore, was once thought to be a monolithic package of bipedality, tools, and encephalization, is now observed to have evolved not all at once but rather in sequence. Africa was clearly the cradle of humankind, witnessing the emergence of the earliest humans and the first archaeological record.

FURTHER READING

Useful general introductions to human origins and the archaeological evidence for them include:

Aiello, L. C. and Wheeler, P. 1995. The expensive-tissue hypothesis: the brain and digestive system in human and primate evolution. *Current Anthropology* 36(2), 199–221.

Delson, E. *et al.* (eds.). 2000. *Encyclopedia of Human Evolution and Prehistory.* 2nd edn. New York: Garland.

Hovers, E. and Braun, D. (eds.). 2009. *Interdisciplinary Approaches to the Oldowan.* Dordrecht: Springer.

Isaac, G. Ll. 1984. The archaeology of human origins: studies of the Lower Pleistocene in East Africa 1971–1981. *Advances in World Archaeology* 3, 1–87.

Johanson, D. and Edgar, B. 2006. *From Lucy to Language.* Revised edition. New York: Simon & Schuster.

Klein, R. G. 2009. *The Human Career: Human Biological and Cultural Origins.* 3rd edn. Chicago: University of Chicago Press.

Pickering, T. R. *et al.* 2007. *Breathing Life into Fossils: Taphonomic Studies in Honor of C. K. (Bob) Brain.* Gosport, IN: Stone Age Institute Press.

Schick, K. and Toth, N. 2018. An overview of the cognitive implications of the Oldowan Industrial Complex. *Azania: Archaeological Research in Africa* 53(1), 3–39.

Stollhofen, H. *et al.* 2021. Olduvai's oldest Oldowan. *Journal of Human Evolution* 150 102910.

Stringer, C. and Andrews, P. 2011. *The Complete World of Human Evolution.* Revised edition. London and New York: Thames & Hudson.

Toth, N. and Schick, K. 2009. The Oldowan: The Tool Making of Early Hominins and Chimpanzees Compared. *Annual Review of Anthropology* 38, 289–305.

Hominin Dispersals

Richard Klein

3

African *Homo erectus* 52

The Acheulean 53

Peopling the Landscape: The Dispersal of *Homo erectus* 54

KEY THEME: CLIMATE CHANGE Human Evolution and Adaptability 55

Asian *Homo erectus* 56

KEY CONTROVERSY The Hobbit: *Homo floresiensis*—A Unique Species? 57

The Initial Occupation of Europe 59

Homo heidelbergensis 60

KEY THEME: MIGRATION *Homo erectus* as the First Afro-Eurasian Hominin 61

Neanderthals 62

Evidence for Early Human Behavior 62

KEY SITE The Mystery of Dinaledi Cave and *Homo naledi* 66

Summary and Conclusions 70

Further Reading 71

Excavations in Liang Bua Cave on the island of Flores in Indonesia, where fossils of the species *Homo floresiensis* have been discovered.

The course of human evolution can be described as a sequence of short, abrupt steps, separated by long periods of stasis. One of the most important steps occurred around 2.5–2 million years ago and resulted in a species that was similar to living people in every major respect of anatomy and behavior, save mainly for its smaller brain. Their species is most commonly called *Homo erectus*, but early African members are often also called *Homo ergaster*. Here we follow the success of *Homo erectus*, its movement across Africa and Eurasia, and its subsequent diversification into other species, including *Homo heidelbergensis*.

- *Homo erectus* was the first hominin species whose anatomy and behavior fully justify the label human.

- *H. erectus* probably invented the Acheulean (handaxe) industry, which was adopted across much of Africa and Eurasia and remained in use for over one million years. Besides the handaxes themselves, some Acheulean examples that could imply art, such as incised bones and pigment, date to 600,000–270,000 years ago.

- *H. erectus* was in all probability the first hominin species to expand out of Africa, into Europe and Asia. Its descendants then began to diversify into a variety of human types.

- Other species of *Homo* evolved from *H. erectus* and are found in Africa, Europe, and Asia. These ultimately were replaced by *H. sapiens*, which evolved in Africa.

3.1 Map showing the major sites and regions mentioned in this chapter.

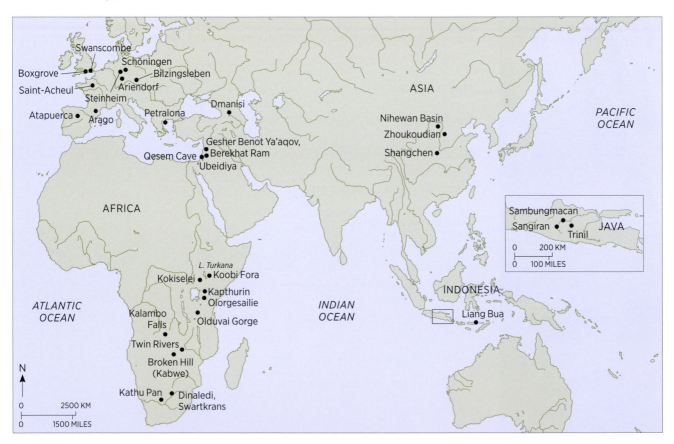

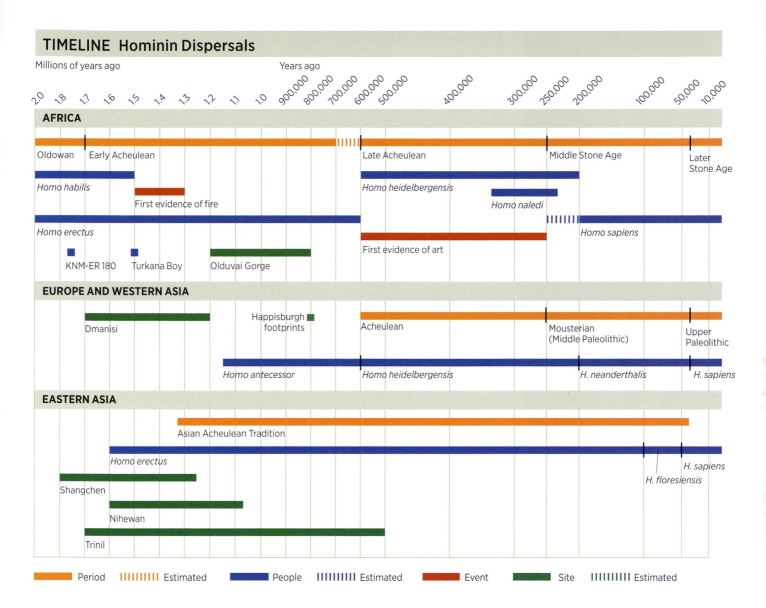

TIMELINE Hominin Dispersals

Millions of years ago   Years ago

2.0 1.8 1.7 1.6 1.5 1.4 1.3 1.2 1.1 1.0 900,000 800,000 700,000 600,000 500,000 400,000 300,000 250,000 200,000 100,000 50,000 10,000

AFRICA

Oldowan   Early Acheulean   Late Acheulean   Middle Stone Age   Later Stone Age

Homo habilis   *Homo heidelbergensis*

First evidence of fire   *Homo naledi*

Homo erectus   *Homo sapiens*

First evidence of art

KNM-ER 180   Turkana Boy   Olduvai Gorge

EUROPE AND WESTERN ASIA

Dmanisi   Happisburgh footprints   Acheulean   Mousterian (Middle Paleolithic)   Upper Paleolithic

Homo antecessor   *Homo heidelbergensis*   *H. neanderthalis*   *H. sapiens*

EASTERN ASIA

Asian Acheulean Tradition

Homo erectus   *H. sapiens*

Shangchen   *H. floresiensis*

Nihewan

Trinil

▬ Period   ‖‖‖‖‖ Estimated   ▬ People   ‖‖‖‖‖ Estimated   ▬ Event   ▬ Site   ‖‖‖‖‖ Estimated

The first hominin species with the anatomy and behavior that fully justifies the label human appeared 2.5 to 2 million years ago in Africa, and is called African *Homo erectus* (also known as *Homo ergaster*). It coexisted with a number of other *Homo* species, including *H. habilis* around 1.8–1.7 million years ago, and a third species, *Homo rudolfensis*. *H. rudolfensis* may have disappeared shortly after 1.7 million years ago and *H. habilis* 1.4 million years ago. Some archaeologists prefer to make a clear distinction between African and Asian *H. erectus,* calling the African branch *H. ergaster*.

The Acheulean (handaxe) industry first appeared shortly after *H. erectus* evolved in Africa, suggesting that this species created a new tool tradition. Anatomical changes, more sophisticated technology, and other probable behavioral advances allowed this new hominin to expand into new landscapes, including drier, more seasonal African environments, where surface water and shade were relatively scarce. In an even more momentous development, *H. erectus* became the first hominin species to expand out of Africa [**3.1**]. Its far-flung descendants then began to diversify into a variety of human types.

AFRICAN *HOMO ERECTUS*

Homo erectus was a well-established African species that flourished 1.9–1.8 million years ago and so must have evolved some time earlier (2.5–2 million years ago). It quickly replaced earlier *Homo* species (*H. habilis* and *H. rudolfensis* discussed in Chapter 2), and survived until perhaps 700,000 years ago. Its behavioral complexity, movement into diverse environments, and postcranial changes make it human. Our understanding is based mostly on remains from deposits on the eastern and western shores of **Lake Turkana** in northern Kenya, which date to 1.8–1.5 million years ago. One of the most important is the Turkana Boy.

The Turkana Boy. Discovered in the Turkana Basin, the Turkana Boy is an important skull and skeleton that has contributed to an understanding of the early African *Homo erectus* [**3.2**]. The robustness of the skull and the shape of the sciatic notch (which permits passage of the sciatic nerve to the legs) on the pelvis indicate that the owner was male, while dental eruption (the appearance of teeth in pre-adults) and limb-bone formation show that he was immature. It is for this reason his discoverers dubbed him the Turkana Boy.

Modern Characteristics of Turkana Boy. The shortness of the Turkana Boy's arms relative to his legs points to the final abandonment of any ape-like reliance on trees for feeding or refuge. A greater commitment to life on the ground meant even more emphasis on bipedalism, and this could explain the narrowing of the pelvis and the development of a barrel-like chest. The reduced pelvis increased the efficiency of the muscles that operated the legs in bipedal movement, and it would have forced the lower part of the ribcage to narrow correspondingly. To maintain chest volume and lung function, the upper part of the ribcage would have had to expand, and the modern barrel shape would have followed. In females, the narrowing of the pelvis also constricted the birth canal, and this may have forced a reduction in the proportion of brain growth that occurred before birth. This may have prolonged infant dependency, foreshadowing the uniquely long dependency period that marks living humans.

Homo erectus was the first human species to occupy hot, truly arid, highly seasonal environments in Africa, and this may partly explain why Turkana Boy's body below the skull was built like a modern equatorial East African person, with a slim body and long limbs. As the body thins, its volume decreases more rapidly than skin area, and greater skin area promotes heat dissipation. Long limbs provide the same benefit. Adaptation to hot, dry conditions can also explain why *H. erectus* was the first human species to have a forwardly projecting, external nose. In living humans, the external nose is usually cooler than the central body, and it therefore tends to condense moisture that would otherwise be exhaled and so lost during periods of heightened activity. Finally, given that *H. erectus* was shaped for a hot, dry climate, we can speculate that it was also the first human species to possess a nearly hairless, naked skin. If it had an ape-like covering of body hair it could not have sweated efficiently, and sweating is the primary means by which humans prevent their bodies (and their brains) from overheating.

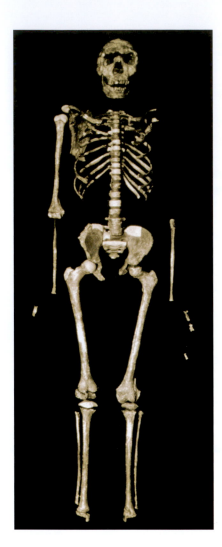

3.2 Skeleton of Turkana Boy (African *Homo erectus*). Turkana Boy's near-complete skeleton shows both similarities and differences to modern humans.

THE ACHEULEAN

A small brain surely means that *Homo erectus* was less intelligent than people living today, and if brain size was all we had to go by, we might wonder if it differed cognitively from earlier hominins. We have artifacts that show that it did. These demonstrate a level of behavioral advancement that helps us to understand how *H. erectus* was able to move into more arid, seasonal environments, and how it became the first human species to expand widely out of Africa.

The Acheulean Handaxe

Homo erectus began a new kind of stone toolmaking in which core forms of stone were often deliberately, even meticulously fashioned, where shape obviously mattered a lot, unlike the Oldowan industry. The characteristic artifact of the new tradition was the handaxe or **biface**—a large flat piece of stone that was more or less completely flaked over both surfaces to produce a sharp edge around the entire periphery [**3.3**, **3.4**]. Many handaxes resemble teardrops, as they narrow from a broad base or butt at one end to a rounded point at the other. Ovals, triangles, and other forms are also common, and in some places, handaxe makers produced pieces with a straight, sharp, guillotine-like edge opposite the butt. Archaeologists often call such pieces cleavers, to distinguish them from handaxes, on which one end tends to be more pointed. Together, handaxes, cleavers, and similar large bifacial tools define the Acheulean cultural tradition, which spanned more than a million years and three continents.

The oldest-known Acheulean tools are dated to 1.76 million years ago at the Kokiselei locality, northern Kenya. The Acheulean industry surely developed from the previous Oldowan industry (Chapter 2), and the oldest Acheulean **assemblages** often contain numerous Oldowan-style core forms and flakes alongside Acheulean handaxes. The earliest Acheulean toolmakers made one other noteworthy discovery that was often tied to biface manufacture: they learned how to strike big flakes, sometimes 30 centimeters (1 foot) or more in length, from boulders, and it was from these that they often made handaxes and cleavers.

Handaxe Use and Development

The term handaxe implies that each piece was handheld and used for chopping. Nonetheless, many handaxes are far too large and unwieldy for this, and their precise use remains a source of debate. The puzzle is heightened at sites where handaxes occur by the hundreds, often crowded close together and with no obvious signs of use. Since the tools come in a wide variety of sizes and shapes, the probability is that they served multiple utilitarian functions. Some of the more carefully shaped, symmetric examples may have been hurled at game (prey) in the manner of a discus; other, more casually made pieces, may have served simply as portable sources of sharp-edged flakes; and yet others could have been used to chop or scrape wood. Experiments have also shown that handaxes make effective butchering tools, particularly for dismembering the carcasses of elephants or other large animals. The truth is that handaxes may have been used for every imaginable purpose, and the type probably had much in common with a Swiss Army knife.

Once in place, the Acheulean tradition was remarkably conservative, and it is often said that it persisted mostly unchanged from its inception roughly 1.76 million years ago until its end about 250,000 years ago. Still, despite the apparent sameness over long periods,

3.3, **3.4 The Acheulean handaxe.** The diagram (top) shows the method of manufacture of an Acheulean handaxe, with a finished example (above) from Saint-Acheul, France, the site that gave the tradition its name. Handaxes were almost completely flaked over both surfaces, hence the term biface, to produce deliberately and meticulously shaped forms.

biface a flat cobble flaked over both surfaces to produce a sharp edge around the entire periphery; the earliest example is the Acheulean handaxe

assemblage a group of artifacts recurring together at a particular time and place, representing the sum of human activities in that respect

early and late Acheulean artifact assemblages do differ in some important respects. Early Acheulean handaxes tend to be much thicker, less extensively trimmed, and less symmetrical. Late Acheulean handaxes are often remarkably thin and extensively trimmed, and they are highly symmetric not just in plan form, but also when viewed edge on.

Late Acheulean handaxes are often accompanied by more refined flake tools that foreshadow those of the Mousterian people who came after the Acheuleans (Chapter 4). Late Acheuleans knew how to prepare a core so that it would provide a flake of predetermined size and shape. Archaeologists call such deliberate core preparation the **Levallois technique** [**3.5**, **3.6**], named for a western suburb of Paris where prepared cores were found and recognized in the later nineteenth century. The term Levallois refers strictly to a method of stone flaking, not to a culture or tradition, and Levallois flaking was practiced by various societies.

3.5, 3.6 The Levallois technique. In this method of stone flaking, a core was deliberately prepared (left) so that a flake of predetermined size and shape could be removed with a single blow. The Levallois technique was practiced by people of various cultures and traditions, including the late Acheuleans.

PEOPLING THE LANDSCAPE: The Dispersal of *Homo erectus*

What routes did *Homo erectus* take soon after the species evolved? Simultaneously, it expanded throughout the continent of Africa itself, moving into new and different environments not previously occupied: for example, by 1.5 million years ago, the drier peripheries of lake basins on the floor of the Great Rift Valley. By 1 million years ago, *H. erectus* had settled the extreme northern and southern margins of Africa. The Sahara Desert might seem an impenetrable barrier to movement northward, but during the long currency of the Acheulean, there were numerous periods when it was somewhat moister and more hospitable, and Acheulean people entered it readily (see Key Theme box: Climate Change—Human Evolution and Adaptability).

As to how and why people expanded through Africa and beyond, they almost certainly did so simply because their physiology and technology enabled them to for the first time. A group on the edge of the human range would periodically outgrow its resource base, and a splinter party would then establish itself in empty territory next door. Such a party probably rarely moved far but, given time, the splintering process would inevitably have brought humans to the northeastern corner of Africa. From there, members of a breakaway group would have moved into the southwestern corner of Asia without even knowing that they had left Africa. From southwestern Asia, the same process of population budding would inevitably lead other groups eastward toward China and Indonesia or northward and westward toward Europe. Could this primeval human dispersal have been achieved partly by boat? Apart from the still-debated evidence from the Indonesian island of Flores (see Key Controversy box: The Hobbit: *Homo floresiensis*—A Unique Species?, p. 57), there is no evidence for such boats before perhaps 45,000 or 50,000 years ago, when modern humans must have used them to island hop from Southeast Asia to Australia.

As *H. erectus* moved from Africa, many would have brought Acheulean tools with them. The earliest Acheulean tools outside of Africa are found in India and Israel. Those in India, from Attirampakka, have been dated to between 1.51 and 1.07 million years ago, and those in Israel, from **'Ubeidiya** in the Jordan Rift Valley, are dated to between 1.4 and 1 million years ago.

Levallois technique the method of stone flaking associated with Mousterian societies, in which the core was shaped in advance so that when knapped it would provide a flake of predetermined size and shape

KEY THEME: CLIMATE CHANGE Human Evolution and Adaptability

Beginning roughly 3.2 million years ago, the planet's climate oscillated between cold glacial periods and warmer interglacial periods. Glacial/interglacial alternation became especially marked after 2.5 million years ago. The glacial intervals became longer and more intense beginning about 1 million years ago, and they would have placed significant pressures on hominins. The growth of glaciers in North America and Europe drained water from the oceans, resulting in lower sea levels. The world ocean was cooler, which meant reduced evaporation and generally drier conditions on the continents. During interglacial intervals, the climate was more like the present.

Some scientists see climate and environmental change as the driving force behind human evolution. The palaeo-anthropologist Rick Potts has argued that environmental variability (not a particular environment) propelled our evolution, producing the adaptability that made it possible for hominins to expand from Africa and to cope with the challenges of colder climates and fluctuating resources. Climate continued to play a role in evolution: human populations will have responded to the cycle of glacial and interglacial phases by expanding or contracting their range. Individual populations may have become extinct along the way, but new populations from the warmer regions took their place once temperatures rose again. The ability to adapt to climatic change was probably a powerful driver in human prehistory, until humans themselves became a main agent of that environmental change.

The Expansion of Homo erectus *to Eurasia: Shangchen and Dmanisi*

The dispersal of *Homo erectus* occurred by at least 2.1 million years ago [**3.7**]. Widespread, lasting occupation of Europe happened from only around 800,000 years ago. The earliest remains outside Africa are found at Shangchen on China's **loess** plateau, dated through paleomagnetism to 2.12 million years old. These are a collection of flake tools and cores found in a continuous sequence. The next earliest are found at **Dmanisi**, Republic of Georgia, a site that has produced more than 1,000 artifacts and 3,000 bones, including five partial human skulls, four mandibles (three linked to skulls), and at least sixteen isolated teeth

loess fine, wind-blown silt

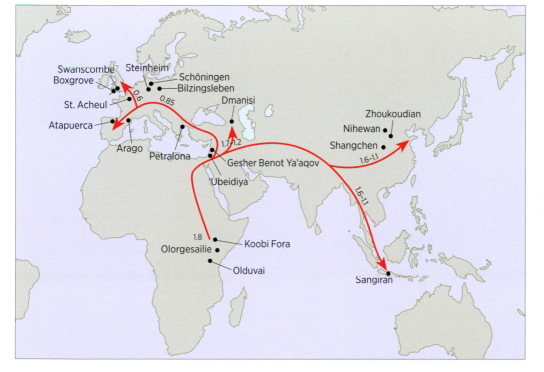

3.7 The expansion of *Homo*. A map showing the possible routes by which early *Homo* may have dispersed from Africa westward to Europe and eastward to China, with dates given in millions of years ago. The map also shows some of the principal sites that are thought to reflect this dispersal.

and twenty-four elements from the skeleton below the head. Based on paleomagnetism and detailed stratigraphy of the human and fauna remains, they could date from any time between 1.85 million and 780,000 years ago.

The dates of the material at Shangchen in central China are somewhat controversial because the soil dates provide a wide span of 2.12 to 1.26 million years ago. The oldest skeletal remains (two incisors) date to 1.7 million years ago. Further research is underway to build more conclusive evidence for setting the date for the first hominin outside Africa to before 1.85 million years.

Both the Shangchen and Dmanisi artifacts include only flakes and flaked pebbles. There are no handaxes, and this could mean that these sites formed before Africans invented handaxes roughly 1.8–1.7 million years ago. Even long after this time, however, not all sites in Africa and Europe contain handaxes, for reasons that are obscure. In short, not all *H. erectus* sites include Acheulean tools, possibly because suitable raw material was not always available.

ASIAN *HOMO ERECTUS*

Remains of *Homo erectus* have been found also in both Java (Indonesia) and China, and are dated at around 1.6–1.3 million years ago [**3.8**].

The discovery of *H. erectus* in China stems from the age-old Chinese custom of pulverizing fossils for medicinal use. In 1899, a European doctor found a probable human tooth among fossils in a Beijing (then Peking) drugstore, and the search for its origin led paleontologists to

3.8 Indonesian and Zhoukoudian *Homo erectus*. Restorations of *H. erectus* skulls from Sangiran in Java and Zhoukoudian Locality 1 in China, by the German anatomist and anthropologist Franz Weidenreich. The features that unite the Sangiran and Zhoukoudian skulls include a thick, forwardly projecting, shelf-like brow ridge; a large face with pronounced forward projection of the jaws; a long, low, flat braincase; a keel or gable along the top of the skull; and a highly angulated rear with a prominent occipital bar (torus) at the back of the skull.

Indonesian *Homo erectus*

Zhoukoudian *Homo erectus*

KEY CONTROVERSY   The Hobbit: *Homo floresiensis*—A Unique Species?

In 2003–4, distinctive human remains were discovered in **Liang Bua Cave** on the island of Flores in eastern Indonesia. The principal find was the skull and partial skeleton of a diminutive individual called Liang Bua (LB) 1, but elements from at least two and perhaps as many as eight additional individuals were also found [**3.9**, **3.10**].

The dentition of LB1 shows it was a full adult, but its femoral length implies it stood only about 1 meter (a little more than 3 feet) tall, and its body mass has been estimated at between 16 and 29 kilograms (35 and 64 pounds). The remains of other individuals imply comparably small size, and the endocranial capacity of LB1 has been estimated at about 417 cc, just above the lower limit for adult australopithecines.

In some features, including the long, low shape of the LB1 braincase and the absence of a chin on both mandibles, the fossils suggest a miniature *Homo erectus*. In others, including the great length of the arms relative to the legs, LB1 was arguably more australopithecine-like, while in still others, including the size and proportions of the teeth, it could pass for *H. sapiens*.

The mix of primitive, derived, and unique features led the discoverers to create a new species, *Homo floresiensis*, nicknamed the Hobbit after the mythical creature of short stature in J. R. R. Tolkien's epic fantasies. They suggested that *H. floresiensis* descended from *H. erectus*, which arrived on Flores and then dwarfed in response to the small available living area.

Flores was always separated from other islands to the west and so from mainland Southeast Asia by at least 19 kilometers (12 miles) of open water, which suggests the seemingly unlikely conclusion that *Homo erectus* had boats. Alternatively, it is possible that future research will show there was a transient, now-submerged land bridge to the west.

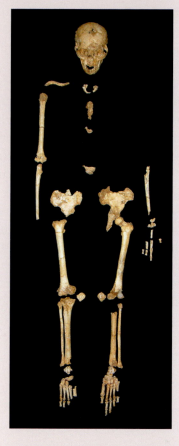

3.9, 3.10 The partial skeleton known as Liang Bua (LB) 1 or the Hobbit (left). A view of the excavation in the Liang Bua cave (below left).

Radiocarbon, uranium-series, electron-spin resonance (ESR), and luminescence dates initially suggested that the cave deposits spanned the interval between roughly 95,000 and 12,000 years ago. LB1 was thought to date from near the end of this time, about 18,000 years ago. More recent research suggests that the Hobbit remains actually date from between 100,000 and 50,000 years ago. Flores lies on the probable route that *H. sapiens* took from Southeast Asia to Greater Australia (across Sahul, the continuous landmass formed by Australia and New Guinea in periods of low sea level) perhaps 45,000 years ago, and the revised dating removes the need to explain how the Hobbit and *H. sapiens* managed to coexist on Flores for thousands of years.

Flaked stone artifacts from surrounding deposits consist mostly of simple shards, but include points, perforators, blades, and bladelets that are said to imply technological convergence on *H. sapiens*. Animal bones come mainly from two large species of monitor lizard (*Varanus*) and a dwarf form of *Stegodon* (an extinct East Asian relative of the elephants). They include pieces that were cut or charred, suggesting butchery and cooking.

braincase the part
of the skull that encases
the brain

a rich complex of remains-bearing limestone caves and fissures on the slopes of Longgushan (Dragon Bone Hill), about 40 kilometers (24 miles) southwest of Beijing, near the village of **Zhoukoudian**. In 1921, the Swedish geologist J. G. Andersson (1874–1960) began excavating in a collapsed cave at Zhoukoudian that was particularly intriguing, not only for its bone remains but also for quartz fragments that prehistoric people must have introduced.

Through the 1930s, excavations produced 5 more or less complete human **braincases**, 9 large braincase fragments, 6 facial fragments, 14 partial mandibles, 149 isolated teeth, and 11 limb bones. The specimens represented more than forty individuals of both sexes and various ages. The Chinese *H. erectus* fossils have been dated to between 800,000 and 400,000 years ago, through paleomagnetism, associated mammal species, and climatic shifts recorded in the enclosing deposits.

China has also provided numerous stone artifacts produced by local *H. erectus* populations. Some of the oldest known come from the Nihewan Basin, about 150 kilometers (90 miles) west of Beijing. The basin once housed a huge lake, and the artifacts accumulated with fragmentary animal bones at sites on the lake margins. Paleomagnetic analysis, combined with the estimated rate at which the lake sediments accumulated, suggest that the oldest-known artifact occurrences date between 1.6 and 1.3 million years ago. They comprise crudely flaked stones, the human (versus natural) origin of which depends as much on their occurrence in fine-grained lake deposits as it does on their form. If these objects are genuinely artifactual and their age has been correctly assessed, they imply that human occupation of northeast Asia occurred at a remarkably early date. Research of excavations at Shangchen published in 2018 (see above) may push this date earlier still, to 2.1 million years ago.

The Chinese *H. erectus* fossils differ from the Indonesian ones in some details, and the differences appear to grow with decreasing age. This may mean that the Chinese and Indonesian specimens (see Key Controversy box: The Hobbit: *Homo floresiensis*–A Unique Species?, p. 57) represent two divergent East Asian evolutionary lineages, but the basic point remains the same: *Homo erectus* or its variants followed a separate evolutionary trajectory from similarly aged populations in Africa and Europe.

The Fate of Homo erectus

Archaeological evidence from Java suggests *Homo erectus* persisted in parts of Indonesia until between 300,000 and 106,000 years ago. The most telling late *H. erectus* remains come from the site of **Ngandong** on the Solo River near Trinil in central Java, where excavations between 1931 and 1980 have uncovered more than 26,200 fossil bones, including twelve partial human skulls and two incomplete human tibiae (shin bones). Between 2000 and 2005, Indonesian scientists announced two skulls from Sambungmacan, and a similar skull from the nearby location of Ngawi. The Ngandong, Sambungmacan, and Ngawi skulls tend to be larger than those of classic Indonesian *H. erectus*, but they exhibit the same basic characteristics, including a massive, shelf-like brow ridge, a flat, receding forehead, thick skull walls, a tendency for the walls to slope inward from a broad base, and substantial angularity at the rear. Based on these features, the Ngandong, Sambungmacan, and Ngawi hominins are commonly assigned to an evolved variant of *H. erectus*. Associated animal species suggest the Sambungmachan late *H. erectus* remains are between 300,000 and 143,000 years old, and a uranium-series date directly on one of the Ngandong skulls puts them at between 117,000 and 106,000 years ago.

The next chapter includes discussion of the archaeological evidence for the expansion of modern humans from Africa after 50,000 years ago to replace the Neanderthals in Europe.

But what then of *H. erectus*, which was firmly entrenched in eastern Asia long before the Neanderthal and modern human lines diverged from each other? The issue is difficult to address, because relevant East Asian fossils and artifacts are much sparser and more poorly dated than European ones. Still, the available evidence indicates that *H. erectus* continued on its own evolutionary trajectory after 500,000 years ago, when Neanderthals and modern humans had separated in Europe and Africa. Eventually, *H. erectus* suffered the same fate as the Neanderthals and was replaced by modern humans expanding from Africa.

THE INITIAL OCCUPATION OF EUROPE

By 1 million years ago, humans had spread to the northern and southern margins of Africa and had moved into eastern Asia as far east as China and Java. But what about Europe? The Dmanisi site puts people on the southern flank of the Caucasus Mountains in modern Georgia, at the so-called Gates of Europe, by 1 million years ago, and perhaps as much as 1.85 million years ago. Yet, despite searches that began in the 1830s, the antiquity of human presence in Europe remains debatable, particularly in northern Europe, north of the Alps and Pyrenees.

The contrast with Africa and southern Asia is stark, and it implies that Europe posed special obstacles to early human settlement, particularly during glacial intervals. The first permanent occupants of Europe were late Acheulean handaxe makers. The earliest evidence of hominins in Europe comes from Sima del Elefante and Atapuerca in Spain, and Happisburgh in the UK. At Gran Dolina cave at Atapuerca, at least eighty fossil human bone fragments have been found that range in date from 850,000 to 750,000 years old. Spanish investigators have assigned the Gran Dolina fossils to *Homo antecessor*, a hominin that may have evolved from a population of *H. erectus* living in Africa that then migrated to Europe.

At Happisburgh, preserved footprints that date to more than 800,000 years ago were discovered in ancient estuary mud [**3.11**]. Such remains suggest that these hominins resembled their African contemporaries in gait and morphology, and probably descended from an expanding African population. Again, the most probable makers of the footprints are argued to be *H. antecessor*, though as yet no human fossils have been found.

3.11 Early human footprints revealed in recent erosions of laminated silts at Happisburgh, UK.

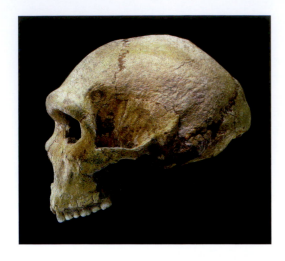

3.12 The Petralona skull, discovered in Petralona Cave in Greece. Probably dating to between 500,000 and 250,000 years ago, it anticipates Neanderthal skulls in the forward projection of the face along the midline. On the other hand, its braincase differs from Neanderthals and is more like that of *Homo erectus*, in the angle of the occipital or rear region. The skull is assigned to *Homo heidelbergensis*, which was ancestral to the Neanderthals in Europe.

HOMO HEIDELBERGENSIS

One of the closest ancestors of *Homo sapiens* and Neanderthals is *Homo heidelbergensis*, named for a lower jaw found near Heidelberg, Germany, dated by associated animal species to around 500,000 years ago. *H. heidelbergensis* was dispersed throughout eastern and southern Africa as well as Europe though its exact relation to the earlier African *H. erectus*, and to later lineages, is unclear.

H. heidelbergensis shared many features with *H. erectus*, including a large, forwardly projecting face, a massive, chinless lower jaw with big teeth, big brow ridges, a low, flattened frontal bone (forehead), great breadth across the skull base, and thick skull walls [**3.12**]. At the same time, it differed from *H. erectus* in its much enlarged brain, which averaged more than 1,200 cc (compared to about 900–1,000 cc for *H. erectus*). *H. heidelbergensis* probably evolved from the African *H. erectus*, and in its anatomy and its geographic distribution it is a plausible common ancestor for the Neanderthals (*Homo neanderthalensis*), who appeared subsequently in Europe, and for modern humans (*Homo sapiens*), who evolved later in Africa.

Brain Expansion and Change within the Handaxe Tradition

Beginning roughly 500,000 years ago, the makers of late Acheulean handaxes were not only able to hang on in Europe through thick and thin (or warm and cold), but also they occupied more northerly regions that *Homo antecessor* or other earlier Europeans may not have been able to reach. The reason was probably that late Acheulean Europeans benefited from technological advances that occurred roughly 700,000 years ago in the African source land.

It has been argued that the early Acheulean ability to impose two-dimensional symmetry on a handaxe probably signals a cognitive advance over preceding Oldowan toolmakers. If so, then the wonderful three-dimensional symmetry of many late Acheulean handaxes may mark an equally important advance, which now allowed their creators to rotate the final tool in their minds while it was still encased in the raw rock. The nature and timing of the shift from the early to the late Acheulean remain to be firmly established, but if the transition turns out to have occurred abruptly about 700,000 years ago, it could have coincided with a rapid expansion in brain size that may have happened about the same time. Careful analysis of human remains suggests that between 1.8 million and 700,000–600,000 years ago, brain capacity remained remarkably stable at roughly 65 percent of the modern average; not long afterward, it increased to about 90 percent of the modern value. If a jump in brain size and associated changes in skull form sparked the appearance of *H. heidelbergensis*, its emergence 700,000–600,000 years ago [**3.13**] would signal a significant evolutionary shift similar to the one that may have introduced *H. erectus* more than 1 million years earlier (see Key Theme box: Migration—*Homo erectus* as the First Afro-Eurasian hominin).

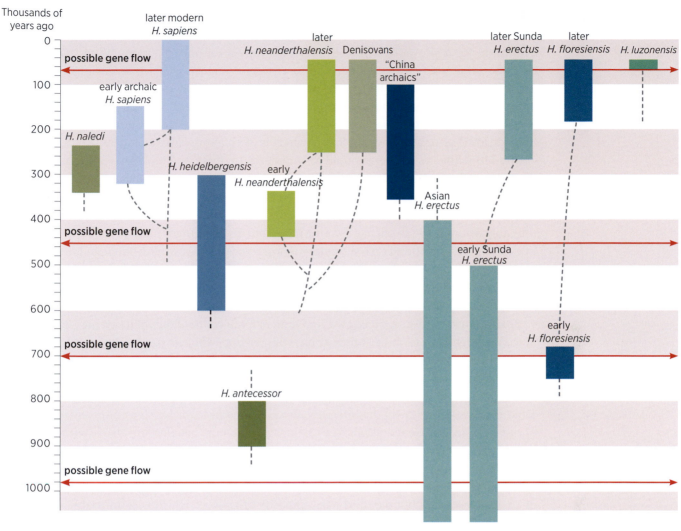

3.13 Human evolution over 1 million years, showing the relationship of various species.

KEY THEME: MIGRATION *Homo erectus* as the First Afro-Eurasian Hominin

A significant part of understanding the human story is realizing how and why we spread across the globe. The rich history of migration began with the first movement of hominins from Africa to Eurasia, and it was our ancestor *Homo erectus* that can be given the title of the first hominin to have succeeded in such expansion, evolving in Africa before 1.9 million years ago and occupying parts of eastern Asia no later than 1.8 million years ago and southern Europe by 800,000 years ago.

This dispersal was not a singular exodus, but probably a sequential splintering and budding of groups to occupy new territories. It was made possible through a suite of both cultural and anatomical adaptations, including larger body size, increased brain size, and the development of technologies, such as the use of fire and the production of more sophisticated tools. The occupation of colder, more northerly latitudes would have posed particular challenges, yet already by 800,000 years ago hominin ancestors may have occupied southeastern Britain. For a species of tropical origin to survive in such a different setting would have demanded a range of further adaptations, including the ability to keep warm and to cope with the lower primary productivity of shorter summers. These adaptations allowed *H. erectus* to occupy new environments and exploit new food resources, contributing to a wider picture of flexibility that characterizes human evolution.

NEANDERTHALS

The European record after 500,000 years ago is critical to a full understanding of human evolution, for it shows that the Neanderthals were a European phenomenon, evolving over the same interval that modern humans were doing so in Africa. Occasional proto-Neanderthal remains have long been known from sites between 400,000 and 200,000 years old, for example Swanscombe, England, and Steinheim, Germany. The certainty with which we can now reconstruct Neanderthal roots stems mainly from one site—the extraordinary Sima de los Huesos at Atapuerca, Spain, which is often abbreviated to the Sima.

The site at Sima was never exposed by commercial activity, and its original entrance long ago collapsed. It is a tiny chamber with a floor area of about 17 square meters (185 square feet), which can be reached today only via a 13-meter (43 feet) vertical shaft located about half a kilometer (a third of a mile) from the entrance to the cave system. The chamber would probably be unknown to science if young men from nearby Burgos had not been interested in exploring underground cave systems with torches and ropes. Graffiti show that they had entered the Sima system by the late thirteenth century CE, and in the mid-1970s an exploratory group told a paleontology student that the Sima was plentiful in bear bones. These were so striking and abundant that the Sima took its full name (Pit of the Bones) from them.

Spanish investigators retrieved the first human fossil—a mandible, or lower jaw—in 1976. Since 1982, yearly excavation at the site has resulted in 17 whole or partial skulls and a great number of postcranial fragments.

Uranium-series analysis shows that a fragment of cave **flowstone** that was deposited directly on one of the human skulls formed about 434,000 years ago. This would place the Sima fossils somewhere in the interval between *Homo heidelbergensis* and the emergence of the fully-fledged Neanderthals (see Chapter 4). The Sima people were also intermediate between these two species in key anatomical respects. Neanderthal skulls were remarkably big, with an average internal skull volume of about 1,520 cc. This compares to perhaps 1,400 cc in living humans. Two of the Sima skulls are relatively small, with endocranial capacities of 1,125 and 1,220 cc, but the third has a capacity of 1,390 cc, which is comfortably within the Neanderthal range. It is, in fact, the largest skull yet recovered from any site older than 150,000 years.

In their retention of primitive skull features, the Sima people were not Neanderthals, but they were surely on or near the line that produced them. Mitochondrial DNA extracted from two of the Sima fossils confirms this conclusion. It is so far the oldest DNA to have been extracted from any human fossil.

EVIDENCE FOR EARLY HUMAN BEHAVIOR

The behavior of Acheulean people and their contemporaries must be inferred from fewer than fifty reasonably well-excavated archaeological sites. These are widely scattered in time and space, and the time dimension is poorly controlled, particularly outside Africa. Compounding these problems of small sample size and poor temporal control, the behavioral implications of excavated materials are often highly ambiguous, but some inferences remain possible.

Using Raw Materials Other than Stone

Stone artifacts dominate the Paleolithic record because of their durability, but early humans surely used other raw materials, including bone and more perishable substances, such as

wood, reeds, and hide. Animal bones survive at many sites that Acheulean people or their contemporaries occupied in Africa, Europe, and Asia, and striking marks or cut marks sometimes suggest that the people used individual bones as hammers, stone-tool retouchers, anvils, or cutting boards. A few, mainly European, sites have also produced bones that were percussion-flaked the same way as stone.

Artifacts in the most perishable raw materials are scarce by definition. Bamboo makes edges that rival or exceed those of stone for sharpness and durability, and it is especially likely to have been used in the eastern regions of Asia, where bamboo roughly mirrors the distribution of non-handaxe assemblages. An emphasis on bamboo could explain why East Asian stone artifact assemblages generally appear to contain a smaller range of stone artifact types than contemporaneous Acheulean assemblages from Africa, western Asia, and Europe, but actual bamboo artifacts remain unknown.

Reed and skin artifacts are also lacking, and indisputable shaped wooden artifacts have been found at only four African, West Asian, and European Acheulean or Acheulean-age sites dated variously to between 790,000 and 300,000 years ago. The pieces are mainly nondescript and of uncertain function. At Schöningen, Germany, however, deposits that are about 320,000 years old have produced three complete, indisputable wooden spears [**3.14, 3.15**]. Each was more than 2 meters (6.5 feet) long, and the only debate is whether they were thrust or thrown. All three are heaviest and thickest near the pointed ends, similar to modern javelins, but they probably could not have been projected hard enough to penetrate an animal from a distance, and they are therefore more likely to have been used as thrusting spears at close quarters. They provide the oldest, most compelling evidence for human hunting.

refitting reassembling stone flakes or blades to recreate the original core, in order to determine the sequence in which the flakes had been removed, and give insight into knapping technology

biostratigraphy a dating method that allows the relative placement of a site or strata based on the presence of animal species found at sites of known age

Shelter

Early humans almost surely required shelters of some kind, particularly after they began to people Eurasia, but the surviving evidence is remarkably sparse and ambiguous. At Ariendorf 1, Germany, several hefty quartz and quartzite blocks (measuring up to 60 × 30 × 30 centimeters, or 24 × 12 × 12 inches) occur in a fine-grained, sandy-silty deposit, where they could have been introduced only by people. Conceivably, they mark the base of a structure, and they partly surround a scatter of artifacts and fragmentary bones. **Refittable** artifacts (which can be rejoined to reveal the original core from which they were struck) and conjoinable bone fragments imply that many pieces were deposited at more or less the same time.

The evidence for substantial shelters before 130,000 years ago is remarkably sparse, and only becomes abundant and unambiguous between 50,000 and 40,000 years ago, after the advent of fully modern humans. People before 50,000 years ago must have built shelters, particularly at open-air sites in mid-latitude Europe and Asia, but the constructions were apparently too flimsy to leave unmistakable archaeological traces. The more substantial structures that appeared after 50,000–40,000 years ago help to explain how fully modern humans were able to occupy the most continental parts of Eurasia, where no people had lived before.

Fire

Homo erectus may have had to master fire for warmth and cooking before it could move into Eurasia, but direct archaeological support is tenuous. Swartkrans Cave in South Africa, with burned animal bones, may provide the strongest case, because the bones appear only high in the strata. They are absent in older layers where they might also be expected if natural burning were responsible. Swartkrans has produced a partial skull and other craniodental elements of *H. erectus*, dated by associated mammal species (**biostratigraphy**) to about 1.5 million years ago.

Spreads of burned sediment, ash, and charcoal that almost certainly signal fireplaces are conspicuous in many sites occupied by the European Neanderthals and their near-modern African contemporaries after 130,000 years ago, and it is generally assumed that people everywhere after 130,000 years ago could make fire when they needed it. The question, then, is when this ability evolved, or perhaps more precisely, whether a stage of full control followed one when fire use was sporadic and opportunistic. This issue is difficult to address since sites older than 130,000 years ago are relatively rare and they are mostly open-air localities.

In the deeply stratified cave fill at the Caune de l'Arago, France, where natural burning is less probable, burned objects appear only in layers provisionally dated to about 400,000 years ago. They are absent in layers dated to between 700,000 and 400,000 years ago. The implication may be that Europeans began to control fire only about 400,000 years ago, and that little or no control before this explains why they were apparently confined to southern Europe during glacial periods prior to 300,000 years ago.

Sites younger than 130,000 years ago are not only more abundant, but evidence of occupation occurs much more often in caves. This increase may be due to the life span of caves themselves and older sites may be buried under collapsed cave roofs (noted again on p. 69), and it is crucial, because caves are far more likely to preserve fossil fireplaces. The difficulty of separating natural from human burning at open-air sites, and the rarity of equally ancient cave sites, means that reconstructing the history of human fire use may always depend more on speculation than on archaeological discovery.

3.16 Early art? An elephant tibia shaft fragment from Bilzingsleben, Germany, with a partial fan-like pattern of incised lines. The regular spacing of the incisions, their near-equal lengths, and V-like cross-sections suggest that they were created at the same time with a single stone tool. The fragment is 350,000 to 400,000 years old, and it is one of only a handful of potential art objects from before 40,000 years ago.

Art

The late Acheulean people, who lived after 700,000–600,000 years ago, often produced handaxes that appeal to the modern eye for their remarkable symmetry in both plan form and edge view. The makers shaped these handaxes extensively and meticulously, and there is the possibility that they were guided by an evolving aesthetic sensibility. Alternatively, they might have been driven by the need to produce a piece that was finely balanced; the possibilities cannot be separated, since, as we have already seen, handaxe function remains largely speculative.

Besides the Acheulean handaxes themselves, artifacts that can be described as art objects are sparse, but include the use of mineral pigments, and the geometric incision of bones, shells, and the modification of pebbles. Four examples stand out. Fragments of humanly introduced pigment have been found associated with Acheulean artifacts and animal bones at sites such as Kapthurin in Kenya (285,00 years ago), at Kathu Pan in South Africa (600,000 years ago), and with similar-aged non-Acheulean artifacts and bones at Twin Rivers, Zambia (270,000 years ago). The Twin Rivers fragments are notable for their abundance and variety of colors, and for indications that some were modified by grinding or rubbing.

An elephant tibia shaft (shinbone) fragment from Bilzingsleben, Germany (400,000–350,000 years ago) has a fanlike set of lines incised on its surface. The incised marks on the tibia fragment are noteworthy for their even spacing [**3.16**], and for the extent to which they replicate each other in length and especially in cross-section. The strong similarity in form suggests that they were made in quick succession by a single stone tool. Their meaning is obviously debatable, but neither their placement nor their form suggests butchery marks.

Finally, a 35-millimeter-long (1.4 inches) modified lava (tuff) pebble from Berekhat Ram on the Syrian/Israeli border dated between 702,000 and 232,000 years ago may represent a crude human figurine [**3.17**]. The pebble is remarkable for three distinct grooves: a deep one that encircles the narrower, more rounded end, setting off the putative head and neck, and two shallow, curved incisions that run down the sides and that could delineate the arms. The deep groove and, to a lesser extent, the shallower ones closely match marks produced by sharp-edged flakes on the same material, and they are distinguishable from natural lines. The Berekhat Ram pebble seems, therefore, to have been

3.17 Early art? A proposed human figurine from the Acheulean site of Berekhat Ram, Golan Heights. The base object is a lava (tuff) pebble on which at least three grooves have been incised with a sharp-edged stone tool. If the object was intended to replicate a human figure, it would be the oldest known example of representational art in the world.

KEY SITE The Mystery of Dinaledi Cave and *Homo naledi*

In 2015, an international group of researchers announced the discovery of hominin fossils in **Dinaledi Cave** within the boundaries of the so-called Cradle of Humankind, around 60 kilometers (37 miles) northwest of Johannesburg, South Africa. In 1999, UNESCO designated the Cradle a World Heritage Site for its wealth of hominin—mostly australopithecine—fossils. The Swartkrans Cave, with its famous australopithecine fossils, lies about 800 meters (0.5 miles) northeast of Dinaledi.

At other Cradle sites, the fossils are mainly encased within rock-hard breccias—sand grains, rocks, and fossils cemented together by limey glue—and erosion of the cave roofs has exposed the breccias at the present surface. In contrast, at Dinaledi, the fossils occur on and in a fine clay on the floor of a chamber 80 meters (250 feet) from the present entrance and about 30 meters (100 feet) down a steep slope. Entry requires passage through a narrow shaft that only researchers of small stature can navigate. The fossils come exclusively from hominins, except for occasional bones of birds and small rodents that do not seem to have been associated with the hominin fossils. The hominin sample so far includes

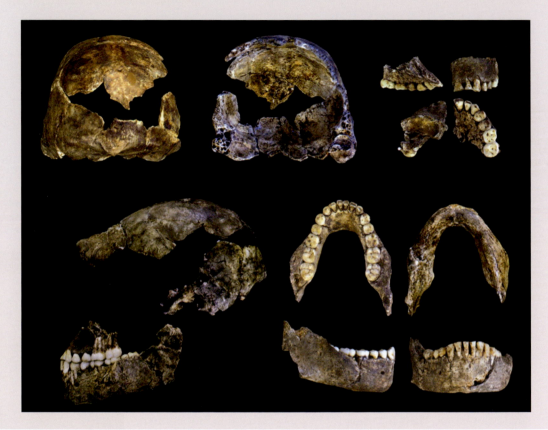

3.18 A skull and mandibles of *Homo naledi* from the Dinaledi Cave, South Africa. The skull recalls an australopithecine's in its small size, but that of early *Homo* in its form.

humanly modified, even if its final form resembles only dimly the finely crafted, aesthetically attractive human figurines that appear in Europe and elsewhere after 40,000 years ago.

The finds at these early art sites anticipate those that occur commonly at succeeding Middle Stone Age and Mousterian sites dated between 250,000 and 50,000 years ago in Africa, western Asia, and Europe. People before 50,000 years ago may have employed pigments in tanning hides, medication, and perhaps especially as an ingredient in the mastic or glue used to fix stone bits to wooden handles. In the absence of hard evidence, body painting or

1,550 elements from at least fifteen individuals. Nearly all parts of the skeleton occur, often in multiple copies. Stone artifacts are absent.

The large bone sample reveals a small-bodied hominin (adult stature under 1.5 meters, or 5 feet) with a small australopithecine-size brain (average female and male endocranial capacities near 465 and 560 cc respectively) [**3.18–3.20**]. The hands and feet resemble those of living humans, but the shoulder, body, and pelvis are more primitive, recalling those of the australopithecines. The peculiar mix of primitive and derived (advanced) features suggests a new species, which the researchers named *Homo naledi*. The limestone that includes the cave is part of the Rising Star Formation and its caverns, and *naledi* is the local Sotho word for star.

Some of the apparently distinctive features of *H. naledi* depend on skeletal parts that are rare or absent in samples of primitive *Homo* elsewhere, and the skull suggests that *H. naledi* may ultimately be considered a small-brained version of *H. erectus*. Uranium-series and electron-spin resonance dating suggest the *H. naledi* fossils were deposited between 335,000 and 236,000 years ago. There are no associated mammal fossils that might serve as a cross-check, but if the age estimate is valid, it implies that *H. naledi* overlapped with evolving *H. sapiens* in southern Africa. Perhaps most intriguing is the question of how the hominin bones reached the Dinaledi chamber. The bone surfaces are mostly poorly preserved, but where they are intact, they exhibit no stone tool or carnivore tooth marks. The investigators have therefore suggested Dinaledi was a kind of cemetery in which *H. naledi* disposed of the dead. Mortuary behavior seems unlikely for such a small-brained and presumably ancient hominin, but at the moment there is no more compelling alternative explanation.

Future work at Dinaledi Cave will produce hundreds, perhaps thousands, of additional hominin fossils, and perhaps too a compelling explanation for how they were introduced to the site. DNA could also inform on the relationship of *H. naledi* to other species of *Homo*.

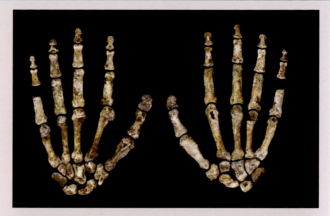

3.19, **3.20** *Homo naledi* hand (top) and foot bones (above). In these, it looks like *H. sapiens*, but in its shoulder, body, and pelvis, it more closely resembles the australopithecines.

some other broadly artistic behavior cannot be ruled out either. Objects that exhibit the same degree of possible artistic intent also occur sporadically in sites occupied by the Neanderthals and their near-modern African contemporaries between roughly 130,000 and 50,000 years ago. Far clearer evidence of art becomes more common only after 50,000 years ago, when art objects are associated with the origins and spread of fully modern humans from Africa. Figurative art, or art that resembles objects from the real world, appears abruptly about 40,000 years ago in the western and eastern margins of Eurasia, Europe, and Indonesia.

Diet

Plant Foods: Foraging. As with control over fire, advances in the ability to obtain food could help explain how *Homo erectus* and its descendants managed to migrate into new regions. The evidence for such advances, however, is limited. Both logic and observations of historic hunter-gatherers suggest that, in general, early people everywhere depended more on plants than on animals. Tubers may have been especially important, since they were staples among historic low- and mid-latitude hunter-gatherers. It may not be coincidental that *H. erectus* emerged at a time—around 2 million years ago—when tubers had probably become more abundant, following a shift to a drier, more seasonally variable climate over much of Africa. Key features of *H. erectus* anatomy and behavior suggest that the species was well adapted for foraging in arid, highly seasonal environments.

Unfortunately, plant tissues that could illuminate the importance of tubers or other plants in early human diets survive at only a handful of Acheulean and Acheulean-age sites. In addition, at the few very early sites where remnants of edible plants do occur, they cannot be unequivocally linked to human activity. The case for human consumption is strongest at Gesher Benot Ya'aqov (GBY), because the plant remains include specimens from seven different nut-bearing species, and the accompanying artifacts include pitted stones that could have been used to crack nut shells. A human origin for the pitting is indisputable, and if nut cracking was even partly responsible, similar pitted stones at other Acheulean sites may imply nut eating even though plant fossils are absent.

Given the failure of plant tissues to be preserved at the vast majority of relevant sites, dietary reconstruction for early *Homo* depends on an unusual partial skeleton, KNM-ER 1808, from Koobi Fora, Kenya; on the stable carbon isotope analysis of fossils; on dental **microwear**; and, above all, on the animal bones found at many sites. KNM-ER 1808 is dated to roughly 1.7–1.6 million years ago, and it comes from *H. erectus*. Its long bone shafts are covered by a layer of abnormal, coarse-woven bone up to 7 millimeters (0.25 inches) thick. A toxic excess of vitamin A (hypervitaminosis A) could be responsible and, if so, it might reflect an overindulgence on carnivore livers or on honeybee eggs, pupae, and larvae. Alternatively, it might mark the oldest known case of yaws, an infectious disease related to syphilis, which induces similar bone growth in its final stage.

Molar microwear analysis indicates that *H. erectus* consumed relatively substantial quantities of tough fibrous foods that could have included tubers, meat, or both. The results lack specificity, but the importance of flaked-stone technology to *H. erectus* and its immediate descendants and their ability to exploit diverse environments, including remarkably arid ones, suggest that they usually depended to some extent on animals, particularly large mammals.

Animal Foods: Hunting and Scavenging. Mammal bones accompany the artifacts of *Homo erectus* and its descendants at numerous sites, including Duinefontein [**3.21**] in South Africa; Olduvai Gorge in Tanzania; Olorgesailie in Kenya; and Boxgrove in England. Assessing human ability to obtain animals, whether by hunting or scavenging, requires, at minimum, a site where people were the only, or at least the principal, bone accumulators. In this regard, caves are generally more promising than open-air sites, because the main game animals available to early people do not, for the most part, enter caves voluntarily. In most instances, therefore, it is safe to assume that their bones were introduced by a human predator or scavenger. Where the cave fill contains numerous artifacts, hearths, and so on, and little or no evidence for carnivore activity (coprolites or fossil feces, chewed bones, etc.), then people

microwear minute patterns of wear or damage on teeth or on stone tools, which can reveal how they were used

are clearly implicated as the principal bone accumulators. Caves to which Neanderthals and their modern or near-modern African contemporaries surely brought most bones are well known after 130,000 years ago.

Unfortunately, caves have a limited lifespan, and most of those that existed in Acheulean times have either collapsed or were long ago flushed of their deposits.

A layer that formed at Qesem Cave, Israel, sometime between 380,000 and 200,000 years ago, perhaps provides the best case for frequent hunting by Acheulean-age people, followed by butchery. The artifacts and bones in this layer are unusually fresh looking (chemically and physically unaltered) for a cave occupation of such antiquity, and it means that many exhibit unambiguous traces of wear from use. The principal application appears to have been butchery, and the abundance of tools for this task coincides with an unusually high proportion of tool-marked bones.

Qesem Cave demonstrates the importance of meat to at least some late Acheulean people, and it foreshadows abundant evidence for butchery by Neanderthals and their African Middle Stone Age contemporaries after 130,000 years ago. These species commonly introduced great numbers of bones to cave sites, and numerous cut or percussion marks prove that the bones represent food debris. In both Europe and Africa, the ages of animals when killed sometimes imply that they were driven to their death by people, but authorities have disagreed

3.21 Hunting and scavenging? A spread of buffalo bones at the Duinefontein 2 Acheulean site, South Africa. Few of the bones exhibit tool marks, and they may have accumulated naturally near a waterhole to which people were repeatedly attracted. At present, no Acheulean site shows that people routinely obtained buffalos or other large ungulates.

Evidence for Early Human Behavior **69**

vigorously on how important hunting was relative to scavenging. Stable isotope analysis of protein residues preserved in Neanderthal bones imply that meat dominated the diet, and it is difficult to imagine that scavenging alone could have met their requirements. The issue, then, is not whether they actively hunted, which they must have, but how successful they were. Analyses of animal bone assemblages imply that their southern African contemporaries obtained large ungulates relatively infrequently, whatever their hunting methods.

SUMMARY AND CONCLUSIONS

The emergence of *Homo erectus* in Africa marked a watershed, for it was the first hominin species whose anatomy and behavior fully justify the label human. Unlike the australopithecines and *H. habilis*, in which body form and proportions retained ape-like features, *H. erectus* achieved essentially modern form, proportions and increased stature. It was larger brained than earlier hominins, and this was probably linked to the nearly simultaneous appearance of handaxes and other relatively sophisticated artifacts of the Acheulean industrial tradition.

The anatomical and behavioral advances that mark *H. erectus* help explain how it became the first hominin species to invade arid, highly seasonal environments in Africa, and how it became the first to move into Eurasia. The eventual result was the emergence of at least three geographically distinct human lineages: *H. erectus* in East Asia, *H. sapiens* in Africa, and *H. neanderthalensis* in Europe.

Fossils and artifacts indicate that *H. sapiens* and *H. neanderthalensis* shared a common ancestor as recently as 600,000 years ago, and their morphological differentiation is manifest only after 500,000 years ago.

The obstacles to earlier long-lasting European occupation remain obscure, but it is probably pertinent that the first permanent populations arrived with the more sophisticated tools of the late Acheulean cultural tradition that probably appeared in Africa around 700,000 years ago, and that they may have been immediate descendants of the first Africans whose average brain size significantly exceeded that of *H. erectus*. To begin with, the earliest permanent Europeans looked very much like their African contemporaries, and they are often lumped with them in the species *Homo heidelbergensis*. By 430,000 years ago, however, European skulls and faces had already begun to anticipate those of the Classic Neanderthals.

It is impossible to say whether brain size in these species increased in sudden spurts or gradually over time, but the archaeological record associated with each lineage nowhere reveals a striking behavioral advance that might reflect abrupt brain enlargement. Instead, even between 500,000 and 250,000 years ago, when average brain size was everywhere within the modern range, humans in both Africa and Eurasia produced a relatively small range of stone artifact types; their artifact assemblages varied remarkably little over long time spans and vast areas; they rarely, if ever, produced formal (standardized) artifacts from bone, ivory, antler, or similar organic materials; they left little or no evidence for art; and they failed to build structures that would leave an unambiguous archaeological trace. In all these respects, the people differed little from their immediate successors between 250,000 and 50,000 years ago, and if there were differences, they were that the people between 250,000 and 50,000 years ago may have hunted more effectively than their predecessors, and may have been the first to gain full control over fire. Both contrasts, however, may reflect only the much smaller number of sites older than 250,000 years ago where evidence for hunting and especially for fire may be firmly detected.

Archaeologists agree that the pattern changed sharply after 50,000 years ago, when formal bone artifacts, art, housing remnants, and other items associated with historic hunter-gatherers appeared widely for the first time. It is therefore only after 50,000 years ago that fully modern behavior became firmly established. Archaeologists disagree, however, whether completely modern behavior developed abruptly about 50,000 years ago or more gradually over the preceding 30,000–20,000 years. The next chapter outlines the evidence and the continuing debate.

FURTHER READING

Useful general introductions to human evolution and the archaeological evidence for it include:

Cartmill, M. and Smith, F. H. 2009. *The Human Lineage*. Hoboken: Wiley-Blackwell.

Gamble, C. 1999. *The Palaeolithic Societies of Europe*. Cambridge: Cambridge University Press.

Howell, F. C. 1965. *Early Man*. New York: Time-Life; London: Penguin Books.

Johanson, D. and Edgar, B. 2006. *From Lucy to Language*. Revised edition. New York: Simon & Schuster.

Klein, R. G. 2009. *The Human Career: Human Biological and Cultural Origins*. 3rd edn. Chicago: University of Chicago Press.

Norton, C. and Braun, D. R. 2011. *Asian Paleoanthropology*. New York: Springer.

Potts, R. 1998. Variability selection in hominid evolution. *Evolutionary Anthropology: Issues, News, and Reviews* 7(3), 81–96.

Stringer, C. 2006. *Homo britannicus: The Incredible Story of Human Life in Britain*. London: Allen Lane.

Tattersall, I. and Schwartz, J. H. 2000. *Extinct Humans*. Boulder: Westview Press.

Zhu, Z. *et al.* 2018. Hominin occupation of the Chinese Loess Plateau since about 2.1 million years ago. *Nature* 559: 608–12.

http://www.becominghuman.org The site of the Institute of Human Origins at Arizona State University, a multidisciplinary research institute dedicated to the recovery and analysis of the fossil evidence for human evolution.

http://humanorigins.si.edu The Smithsonian Institution Human Origins Program.

http://leakeyfoundation.org The site of the Leakey Foundation (San Francisco), an organization devoted to funding research on human evolution.

The Rise of Modern Humans

4

Paul Pettitt

Environments and Landscapes 76

The Rise of Modern Humans in Africa 76

The Neanderthals 79

KEY CONTROVERSY The Evolution of Language 80

KEY SITE Blombos Cave and the Origins of Symbolism 81

KEY DISCOVERY The Denisovans 83

The Peopling of East Asia and Australia 85

KEY THEME: MIGRATION Changing Pleistocene Environments Drove Human Dispersals 87

The Peopling of Europe and Russia 87

KEY SITES Three Sites with Upper Paleolithic Art 88

KEY CONTROVERSY The Meaning of Female Figurines 91

Summary and Conclusions 92

Further Reading 93

Cave painting on the island of Sulawesi in Indonesia includes hand stencils and a representation of a babirusa (pig-deer). Some of the island's art appears to be older than 40,000 years.

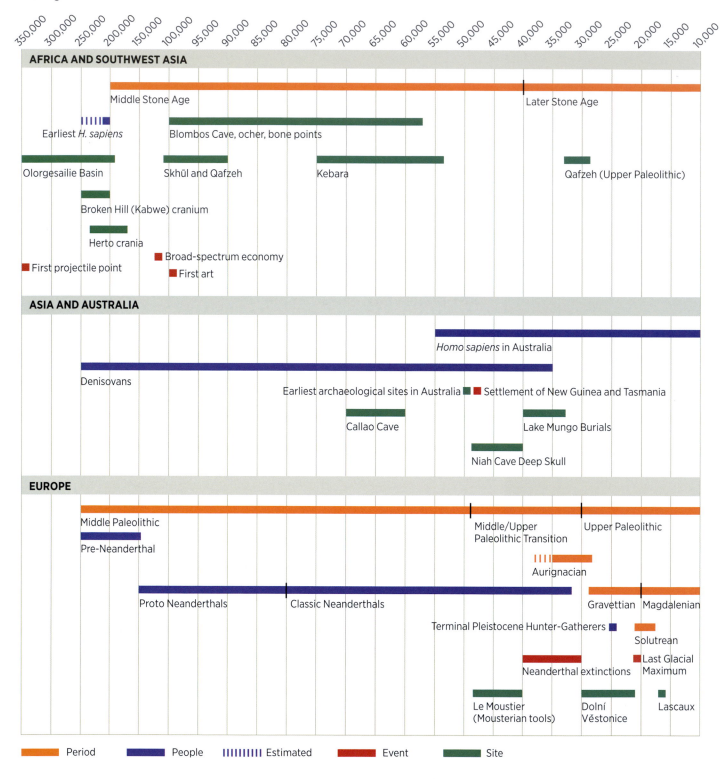

TIMELINE The Rise of Modern Humans

Years ago

AFRICA AND SOUTHWEST ASIA

Middle Stone Age

Later Stone Age

Earliest *H. sapiens*

Blombos Cave, ocher, bone points

Olorgesailie Basin

Skhūl and Qafzeh

Kebara

Qafzeh (Upper Paleolithic)

Broken Hill (Kabwe) cranium

Herto crania

First projectile point

Broad-spectrum economy

First art

ASIA AND AUSTRALIA

Homo sapiens in Australia

Denisovans

Earliest archaeological sites in Australia ▪ ▪ Settlement of New Guinea and Tasmania

Callao Cave

Lake Mungo Burials

Niah Cave Deep Skull

EUROPE

Middle Paleolithic

Middle/Upper Paleolithic Transition

Upper Paleolithic

Pre-Neanderthal

Aurignacian

Proto Neanderthals

Classic Neanderthals

Gravettian Magdalenian

Terminal Pleistocene Hunter-Gatherers

Solutrean

Neanderthal extinctions

Last Glacial Maximum

Le Moustier (Mousterian tools)

Dolní Věstonice

Lascaux

| ▬ Period | ▬ People | ‖‖‖‖ Estimated | ▬ Event | ▬ Site |

In the previous chapter, we traced the dispersal of hominins from Africa to Asia and Europe, and saw the emergence of new species: *Homo erectus*, *H. antecessor*, and *H. heidelbergensis*. Some time after 400,000 years ago, two more new species arose: the Neanderthals in western Eurasia, and *H. sapiens*, modern humans, in Africa. Recent genetic research has also uncovered a new hominin, the Denisovan, which shared a common ancestor with both *H. sapiens* and *H. neanderthalensis*. Eventually, *H. sapiens* spread out of Africa and replaced earlier species elsewhere. In this chapter we focus on these three humans, their behavior, and their expansion.

- *H. sapiens* throughout the known world replaced several human species, such as *H. erectus* in eastern Asia and the Neanderthals in western Europe.

- From 200,000 years ago in Kenya, the archaeological record reveals evidence for a number of new behaviors: the shaping of materials and the making of art, treating the dead, new methods of procuring food, and new ways of modifying living sites and organizing space. Archaeologists call these behaviors modern, associated with anatomically modern *H. sapiens*.

- *H. sapiens* spread to Australia and New Guinea between 60,000 and 50,000 years ago.

- An explosion of artistic expression occurred throughout the world around 40,000 years ago.

This chapter covers the end of the Lower Paleolithic (*c.* 250,000 years ago) and spans the Middle and Upper Paleolithic (to *c.* 12,000 years ago). The period includes the expansion of *Homo sapiens* and the demise of other hominin species, such as *H. erectus* and the Neanderthals [**4.1**]. For the greater part of the Pleistocene, a number of different hominin species had coexisted, such as *H. heidelbergensis* and *H. erectus* half a million years ago. By around 30,000 years ago, the last communities of *H. neanderthalensis* and *H. erectus* were replaced by *H. sapiens*—anatomically modern humans—the sole surviving hominin species on the planet, with the possible exception of *H. floresiensis* (the Hobbit). It is from this moment that we define the Upper Paleolithic, which also sees the emergence of modern human behavior, such as the earliest demonstrable art-making, and modern humans spreading to continents apparently unoccupied by earlier hominin species.

Research of this period involves some crucial questions about our understanding of human prehistory. These include whether anatomically modern humans evolved in Africa or in multiple regions across the globe, and how and to what degree Neanderthals and *H. sapiens* were in contact.

4.1 Map showing the extents reached by *Homo sapiens*, Neanderthals, Denisovans, and *Homo erectus*.

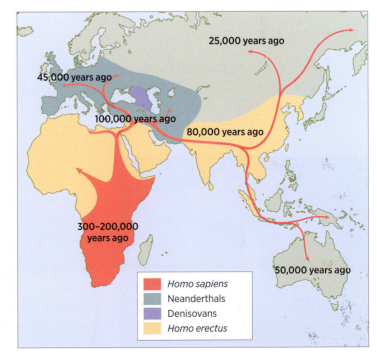

25,000 years ago

45,000 years ago

100,000 years ago

80,000 years ago

300–200,000 years ago

50,000 years ago

🟥	*Homo sapiens*
⬛	Neanderthals
🟪	Denisovans
🟨	*Homo erectus*

Attempts to address these questions have recently been revolutionized through the application of DNA research, and studies outside of Europe where much investigation has historically taken place. In addition, discoveries of other early human species, such as the Denisovans and *H. floresiensis,* remind us that the study of human origins is a fast-changing field of research.

ENVIRONMENTS AND LANDSCAPES

Remarkably unstable climatic change forms the backdrop to the evolution and dispersals of modern humans. Climate change seems to have affected different regions of Africa at different times, causing regional environmental change that would stimulate distributions of *Homo sapiens* around the continent. In Africa, the climate cycled between arid and wetter periods, when major geographical features, such as the Sahara, would expand and contract. In some periods, the region of North Africa now covered by the Sahara supported rich, well-watered, varied settings where human populations may have been widespread. The contraction of these environments and the growth of desert may have forced small groups of anatomically modern humans out of Africa to the north or east.

In eastern Asia, by contrast, climate appears to have remained relatively stable, perhaps explaining in part the lack of any major biological and behavioral evolution from *H. erectus* and Lower Paleolithic variants of this species established there by at least 1 million years ago.

THE RISE OF MODERN HUMANS IN AFRICA

A key event of this period is the origin and spread of modern humans, our own species, which occurred during the Middle Stone Age (Middle Paleolithic) in Africa from around 350,000–300,000 years ago. To understand how *Homo sapiens* evolved in Africa, we must look not only at changes in the skeleton through time, but also at alterations in genetics and the behaviors that we associate with fully modern humans. Following their evolution, *H. sapiens* expanded into other parts of the world, replacing and interbreeding with earlier human species.

Skeletal Evidence

The skeletal record for the emergence of modern humans in Africa is still relatively poor, but enough has been recovered from secure contexts to reveal that the essential skeletal form of *Homo sapiens* existed as early as 300,000 years ago, and could be found in pockets from the extreme south to northwest of the continent. Several cranial remains are known from Jebel Irhoud (Morocco), although most examples date to 100,000 years ago or after, possibly due to the fact that burial of the dead was not practiced until much later and, therefore, that earlier skeletons were not protected from erosion. Fossils dating to 300,000 to 100,000 years ago, such as the remarkably complete cranium from Kabwe [**4.2**] display clear *Homo sapiens* traits (such as its nasal aperture and the form of the back of the cranium) but retain a number of features of earlier (archaic) hominins such as *Homo erectus*. Such retentions lessen after 250,000 years ago (such as in the crania from two adults and one child from **Herto**, Ethiopia), leaving distinctly anatomically modern humans after 125,000 years ago.

4.2 Kabwe cranium. It was once classified as *Homo rhodesiensis,* but is now thought to be *H. heidelbergensis,* which possesses a mixture of both *H. erectus* and *H. sapiens* traits.

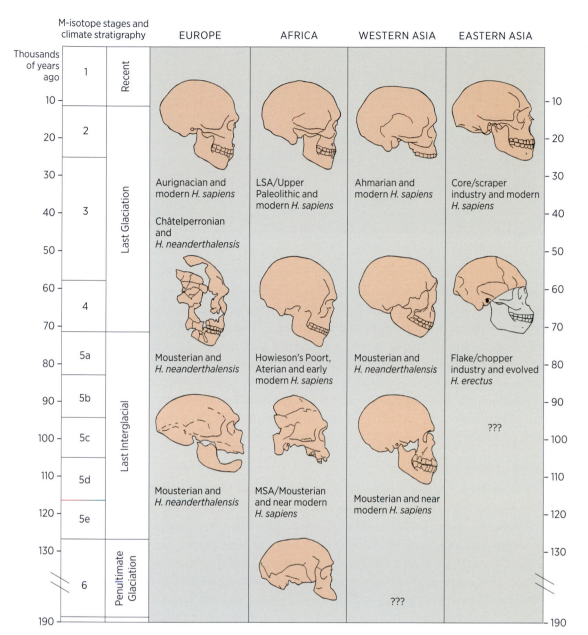

M-isotope stages and climate stratigraphy			EUROPE	AFRICA	WESTERN ASIA	EASTERN ASIA

Thousands of years ago

EUROPE: Aurignacian and modern *H. sapiens*; Châtelperronian and *H. neanderthalensis*

AFRICA: LSA/Upper Paleolithic and modern *H. sapiens*

WESTERN ASIA: Ahmarian and modern *H. sapiens*

EASTERN ASIA: Core/scraper industry and modern *H. sapiens*

EUROPE: Mousterian and *H. neanderthalensis*

AFRICA: Howieson's Poort, Aterian and early modern *H. sapiens*

WESTERN ASIA: Mousterian and *H. neanderthalensis*

EASTERN ASIA: Flake/chopper industry and evolved *H. erectus*

???

EUROPE: Mousterian and *H. neanderthalensis*

AFRICA: MSA/Mousterian and near modern *H. sapiens*

WESTERN ASIA: Mousterian and near modern *H. sapiens*

???

The crania of these modern *H. sapiens* skeletons show facial projection, and the size of the brow and teeth have decreased [**4.3**]. Some of the most famous skeletons dating to this time are from the Israeli caves of the **Mugharet es-Skhūl** and **Jebel Qafzeh**. Between them, Skhūl and Qafzeh have yielded the remains of more than twenty individuals, many of whom seem to have been buried in simple graves [**4.4**, p. 78], dating to between 110,000 and 90,000 years ago. At Qafzeh, the burials were covered in red **ocher**.

Genetic Evidence

Genetics play a critical role in our understanding of human evolution, including establishing the primacy of Africa in modern human origins, the phasing of their earliest dispersals out of that continent, and the genetic relationships between *Homo sapiens,* Neanderthals, and other

ocher the iron oxide minerals hematite (for red ocher), limonite and goethite (for brown, yellow, and black ochers), used as pigments for painting and pottery slips

4.4 Qafzeh burials.
Qafzeh 9 (adult, interpreted as female) and Qafzeh 10 (infant) were apparently buried in the same grave, on the terrace of Jebel Qafzeh near Nazareth, Israel. Dating to between 110,000 and 90,000 years ago, the numerous burials at Qafzeh are in many respects anatomically modern.

archaic humans. Genetic research historically first involved mitochondrial DNA (mtDNA, Chapter 1), but the ability to code the entire genomes of *H. sapiens* and archaic humans has opened up completely new questions about the relatedness of different hominin species.

In 1997, mtDNA was successfully sequenced from Neanderthal fossils. This, together with the recent publication of the entire Neanderthal **genome** (see pp. 80 and 82), clarified the evolutionary position of Neanderthals relative to modern humans. The Neanderthal mtDNA sequenced so far suggests that a long period of evolutionary divergence—in the order of 400,000 years—separated them from modern humans. The results also suggest that there was restricted mtDNA diversity among Neanderthals, indicating they were an isolated offshoot, probably evolving from *H. heidelbergensis* in Europe.

Evidence of Modern Behavior

Aside from skeletal evidence and genetics, evidence of new behaviors can be used to trace the evolution of modern humans. These behaviors [**Table 4.1**] mark the beginning of the Middle Stone Age from as early as 350,000 years ago, with the increasing appearance of smaller retouched tools, including projectile points and bone points. The rise and spread of the Middle Stone Age corresponds with an environmental shift to a more arid and open grassland, allowing grazing animals to spread, and warmer lake and river temperatures, enabling the success of new fish and shellfish. In response, the large cutting tools and bifaces associated with the Acheulean traditions were abandoned in favour of these smaller artifacts. Associated with these transformations in tool shape are other changes in lithic technology, including the **heat treating** of raw material to improve the **knapping** quality, and the importation of raw material from distant sources. Examples of art also appear in the form of beads, complexly carved geometric designs, and the use of pigment. Combined, these changes represent an increasingly sophisticated system of symbolic expression, planning and learning. These behaviors are usually seen as modern and are associated with anatomically modern *Homo sapiens*.

An important aspect of behavioral modernity is the development of **broad-spectrum economies**, or the ability to invest in multiple food strategies. Those first evident in the Olorgesailie Basin in southern Kenya spread throughout the basin starting 120,000 years ago. Freshwater fish remains have been found at White Paintings Shelter in Botswana, and extensive shell **middens** occur at several sites in South Africa dating to between 120,000 and 40,000 years ago. The ability to predict the temporary availability of great quantities

genome complete genetic component of a cell; nuclear DNA and mitochondrial DNA each comprise a single genome

heat treating the heating of stone in a controlled manner to facilitate the process of tool knapping

knapping to work a piece of stone using percussion or pressure to remove flakes

broad-spectrum economy a subsistence system that includes multiple food sources rather than a narrow range of resources

midden a concentration of cultural debris (artifacts and food remains); in places where marine resources are a primary element in subsistence middens are often made up predominantly of shells

of shellfish, which requires a knowledge of lunar cycles as well as tides, may have been particularly important in providing fatty acids, iron, and other nutrients vital for brain growth and for supporting relatively big populations on the South African coast. The recovery of plant residues and even grinding stones on sites in savanna environments adds to the picture of a broad-spectrum economy, and small, gatherable animals, such as tortoises, also provided important nutrients.

Another major hallmark of modern human behavior is the making of imagery, or art, which can be anything from initial markings or piercings of shell to large-scale cave paintings. Evidence of this appears earlier in Africa and Southwest Asia than in Europe, Southeast Asia, and Australia. Red ocher, often in some abundance, is ubiquitous on sites in Africa dating to 100,000 years ago and younger. Although ocher can often have a practical function, for example, for weatherproofing hides or repelling insects, its clear selection for its saturated red hues, and the use of ocher crayons (artificially shaped by use), suggest that it was primarily used to create two-dimensional symbols. Shell jewelry and ocher fragments found at Blombos Cave in South Africa are possibly some of the earliest convincing examples of art objects in the world and attest to symbolic activity at 100,000 years ago (see Key Site box: Blombos Cave and the Origins of Symbolism, p. 81). This activity is not restricted to Africa. As early as 50,000 years ago, and possibly 60,000 years ago, there are ocher crayons in northern Australia. Well-defined cave art is dated to 40,000 years ago at the sites in Southeast Asia in the form of hand stencils and paintings of animals from 35,000 years ago. Similarly, both carved figures and rock art are identified in Europe at around 40,000 years ago.

It is important to note that many examples of ancient art now exist that through their early dates could be assigned to Neanderthals. This raises the question of exactly what modern behavior is, and whether it was restricted to *Homo sapiens* alone. Does the use of pigments denote modernity? If so, then it would have to be concluded that the Neanderthals were modern in at least some of their behaviors. In fact, the notion that living humans can be distinguished from Neanderthals by the behavioral modernity of the former may not be an altogether useful concept because of the danger that we will focus on elements familiar from our own behavior rather than considering ancestral behaviors in their own terms.

Table 4.1 Archaeological Evidence for Modern Human Behavior after 100,000 Years Ago

- Increased typological diversity and standardization of artifacts
- Greater frequencies of artifact/assemblage change over time
- Shaping of organic materials such as bone, antler, and ivory, by carving into formal categories of such implements as needles, awls, and harpoons
- Jewelry of pierced shells and carved organics, often transported in the landscape
- Incontrovertible figurative and non-figurative art
- Clear organization of space, including dwelling structures and elaborate hearths
- Transport of lithic raw materials over longer distances, occurring more frequently
- Broad-spectrum economies incorporating small terrestrial animals; marine resources; vegetal resources; and often requiring trapping and processing technologies, such as grindstones
- Storage
- Prey selectivity in large mammal hunting
- Occupation of more difficult environments
- Growth in population density

THE NEANDERTHALS

Anatomical change in the African *Homo sapiens* lineage differed markedly from that in European *H. neanderthalensis*. In Africa, most development occurred in the shape of the cranial vault, with relatively little change in the facial area. By contrast, in Europe the Neanderthals retained the vault structure characteristic of *H. heidelbergensis*, but there was a great degree of modification of the facial area that occurred during fetal and early postnatal development.

coalesce the appearance of specific genotypes in mitochondrial DNA

This may reflect responses to using their teeth as tools, resulting from large biting forces that were employed habitually, or a degree of adaptation to cold conditions that maximized sinus tracts through which air could be warmed and moistened, but there is little conclusive indication that these explain the Neanderthal face.

The Neanderthals kept the basic cranial and large postcranial body of *H. heidelbergensis* and adapted it to the cold, dry environments that they encountered in the northern tundra and to a lifestyle that was physically demanding. Short in stature and wide-chested, their bodies are well suited to colder regions, and they probably had considerable energetic needs due to cold temperatures. In particular, the selection for a big brain—on average greater than that of *H. sapiens*—also occurred, although its growth occurred in significantly different ways to that of *H. sapiens*. Genetic data indicates that many Neanderthal traits had **coalesced** by at least 250,000 years ago, and European fossils demonstrate that characteristic cranial features began to appear as early as 450,000 years ago on specimens classed as *H. heidelbergensis*.

The Neanderthals nevertheless demonstrate strong regional variation in anatomy and behavior compared to hominins in lower latitudes. Study of the last Neanderthals also raises the possibility of anatomically modern humans living alongside another hominin, which in turn presses questions of how the Neanderthals became extinct, and whether *H. sapiens* and *H. neanderthalensis* procreated and produced fertile offspring.

Neanderthal DNA

The publication of the draft Neanderthal genome in 2010 must rank among the greatest achievements of science, as it is now possible to define an extinct human species on the basis of genetics [**4.8**, p. 82]. The study was undertaken using fragmentary DNA from the fossils

---

KEY CONTROVERSY The Evolution of Language

In a process almost unprecedented in the biological world, *Homo sapiens* has become the only species of human on the planet and has moved into an extreme variety of environments over much of its surface. How has this been possible? Archaeologists are drawn to the notion that one event or evolutionary mutation has marked us out as special.

To many, this is the evolution of sophisticated language, which differs from simple speech in that it has syntax—organized ways of stringing words together to give variable meanings—as well as tenses to allow communication about things not necessarily in the present. Language facilitates considerable storage and communication of information, freeing the mind from the present and opening up a vast amount of adaptive potential.

Evidence from the Brain

The limited endocranial evidence that is available suggests that some language faculties developed gradually over the evolution of the genus *Homo*. Strong lateral asymmetry of the brain is connected both to handedness and speech. Handedness can be traced back to the earliest stone tools,

which display evidence of a clear dominance of right-handedness from the late Pliocene, around 2.8 million years ago. Although the two hemispheres of the brain interact in language production, the right hemisphere, which has grown larger in *Homo sapiens* at the expense of the left, actively interprets linguistic information in a very distinct way.

It is debatable as to whether any premodern hominins, such as the Neanderthals, possessed linguistic abilities approaching our own, although it is generally agreed that a certain linguistic ability arose slowly through the hominin lineage since the divergence from other hominoids in the group Hominoidea, which comprises humans and apes and their fossil ancestors.

Debate currently exists as to whether our own capacity for complex language evolved bit by bit, perhaps in parallel with a gradual unfolding of modern behavior as discussed above, or whether it was a sudden, and possibly quite recent, critical event. Linguists have demonstrated that the first split between language families separated the !Kung of southern Africa and the Hadza of Tanzania, supporting the notion that the evolution of speech as we know it occurred in Africa.

KEY SITE   Blombos Cave and the Origins of Symbolism

4.5 Excavations in progress at Blombos Cave, South Africa. Caves on the Cape coast of South Africa contain deep sequences representing long time spans, covering the period over which modern human behavior was developing. Blombos continues to reveal increasing evidence of an early emergence of such behavior, including plausible indication of symbolism.

It is the evidence of shell jewelry and pigment that makes Blombos so important in the story of the emergence of modern human behavior and the origins of symbolism [**4.5**]. The recovery of forty-nine shell beads pierced for suspension from levels dating to 75,000 years ago can be accepted as clear evidence of symbolic activity. Ocher fragments or crayons—many of which bear engraved motifs—attest similarly to symbolism going back to 100,000 years ago.

On one piece, both flat sides and one thin edge are worn by scraping and grinding, and one side bears a number of cross-hatched lines. A second piece also carries a row of cross-hatched lines, in addition to long lines across the top, center, and bottom of the cross-hatching [**4.6**]. These were clearly deliberate, and the similarity of the two objects suggests that these lines represent a deliberate design template.

The recovery of two sets of pigment-processing equipment, including quartzite grinding stones, shell containers [**4.7**], and evidence for the deliberate mixing of fatty trabecular (spongy) bone with ocher in layers of the cave dating to 100,000 years ago demonstrates unambiguously the careful attention to paint production at that time, and that this was a deliberate and important activity at the site. It is difficult to see this as anything else but symbolic activity, and because engraved ocher fragments have been recovered from other South African Middle Stone Age sites the practice may well have been widespread if not habitual in nature.

4.6 A red ocher crayon bearing engraved diagonal lines from Blombos Cave, South Africa. At least 65,000 years old, this and other examples found at the site represent some of the earliest credible evidence of art objects in the world.

4.7 A shell container, part of one of the sets of pigment-processing equipment, which bore evidence for the deliberate mixing of fatty, spongy bone with ocher.

of three female Neanderthals from Vindija Cave, Croatia, and smaller sequences of DNA from Neanderthal bones found in Spain, Germany, and Russia that have been sequenced since 1997. This research led to the finding that the modern human genome of those not indigenous to sub-Sahara Africa include on average 2 percent Neanderthal DNA, a result that has been taken to suggest a small degree of admixture between the two species.

In 2016, genetic evidence from Neanderthal remains found in Altai Cave in Siberia, as well as Croatia and Spain, offered new information on interbreeding between *Homo sapiens* and Neanderthals, supporting the claim that the two interbred as early as 100,000 years ago.

If *H. sapiens* and Neanderthals did interbreed, why is the amount of DNA remaining in some modern humans so small? Some researchers suggest that interbreeding was exceptionally rare, perhaps even restricted socially. Others have argued that male offspring produced from interbreeding between Neanderthal and *H. sapiens* were far more likely to be infertile, creating a selection pressure that chose against human–Neanderthal hybrids.

A further surprise came with the sequencing of DNA from a human finger bone excavated from Denisova Cave in southern Siberia (see Key Discovery box: The Denisovans). The results showed that it shared a common origin with Neanderthals but had an evolutionary history distinct from both them and *H. sapiens*. Although this has not yet been formally defined as a new human species, it has been informally termed Denisovan, a distinct group with a long ancestry in the region. Two crania from Lingjing in China—Xuchang 1 and 2—may also represent this species. Their characteristics indicate a degree of regional continuity distinct from the contemporary Neanderthals, while retaining broader traits observable across Europe and Asia.

Research into the story of interbreeding continues to expand and change, remaining a fertile field of new discoveries and debate.

4.8 Neanderthal genome sequencing. A researcher collecting samples for DNA analysis from Neanderthal remains in El Sidrón Cave, Spain.

Hunting, Gathering, and Scavenging

Neanderthals seem to have lived relatively short lives, and physical trauma was a common event. The aging of Neanderthal remains suggests that most individuals died by their early forties, although it is conceivable that some lived into their fifties. Substantial samples of early pre-Neanderthal and proto-Neanderthal remains, such as those from the Sima de los Huesos at Atapuerca in Spain and Krapina in Croatia, reveal mortality peaks in infancy (possibly connected to weaning) and in adolescence (potentially connected to childbirth and behavioral changes upon reaching adulthood, such as joining the hunt).

Recent excavations, with improved recovery techniques, have revealed that plant resources played an important role in Neanderthal diet when available. The charred remains of legumes, including wild pea, and of grasses, acorns, and pistachio nuts recovered from

Kebara Cave, Israel, hackberry from Dederiyeh Cave, Syria, and pine nuts from Gorham's Cave, Gibraltar, indicate a diverse diet. Microscopic traces of plants preserved in calculus on Neanderthal teeth show that food was often cooked.

Animal resources, though, were critical for survival in the north, and a number of studies suggest that Neanderthals employed both scavenging and hunting strategies to obtain these. Stable-isotope analyses of Neanderthal bones suggest that up to 90 percent of their dietary protein came from meat, which is not surprising given its importance among high-latitude populations today. Despite this, they may still have been malnourished, as their routine breaking of the phalanges of their prey for marrow might suggest. Scavenging might account for the association of lithic assemblages with large pachyderms, such as mammoth at Pagnolo d'Asolo, Italy, and straight-tusked elephant at Gröbern, Germany. Numerous sites, however, attest to the hunting of medium-sized and, on occasion, large herbivores by Neanderthals, probably with hand-thrust spears of sharpened wood or with **hafted** stone points. A fragment of such a stone point was embedded in the neck vertebra of a steppe ass from Umm el Tlel, Syria, dating to more than 50,000 years ago.

The nature of faunal assemblages, only rarely dominated by one species, implies that Neanderthals employed opportunistic hunting methods—animals were hunted as they were encountered in the landscape, for example, reindeer and horse in colder environments and bovids and deer in more forested ones. In many cases, the hunters brought down a number of species and then used the carcasses relatively wastefully, a strategy one might refer to as shoot first, ask questions later. Some evidence points to a more specific choice of animal. Mammoth and woolly rhinoceros were possibly driven over a fissure at La Cotte de St. Brelade on the island of Jersey as early as 200,000 years ago. As Sabine Gaudzinski, an archaeologist from Germany, notes, however, faunal assemblages overwhelmingly dominated by one species become prominent only after 150,000 years ago, and often involve the targeting of prime adult bison and **aurochs**. It is probable that Neanderthals utilized a range of hunting methods that varied in space and time. According to the anthropologist

hafted furnished with a handle (refers to a tool or a weapon)

aurochs a Paleolithic species of wild bovine

denticulate a stone flake or blade retouched to produce a saw-tooth edge

notch a denticulate tool with a single indentation

pseudomorphs the spaces left by decayed organic objects within brecciated sediments

Mary Stiner, they may have become more predatory after around 55,000 years ago; she noted that around that time Neanderthals in coastal Italy replaced scavenging with a variety of hunting-based foraging strategies.

The Mousterian Lithic Industry

Neanderthals produced a lithic industry generally referred to as the Mousterian [**4.9**]. Within the Mousterian tradition, there is considerable variability, resulting in a highly flexible and adaptable toolkit. Raw materials were overwhelmingly local, although on occasion a range of cores and tools were transported up to 100 kilometers (62 miles). A number of Levallois flaking techniques were common, allowing a certain degree of control to be exercised over the shape and size of resulting flakes and blades (see **3.5** and **3.6**, p. 54); simpler techniques were also employed, such as the discoidal method, which produced as many flakes as possible in varying sizes and shapes. Flakes and blades were either used unmodified or were altered into a small number of simple tool forms, such as scrapers, **denticulates**, **notches**, points, and bifaces. Technological strategies and dominant tool forms vary over time.

Neanderthal Behavior

In addition to producing a Mousterian lithic industry, Neanderthals were also skilled workers of organic materials, such as antler and bone, some of which were specialized tools. While they seem not to have possessed the carving skills of modern humans from the Upper Paleolithic and Late Stone Age, the shaping of such materials into points and other forms was probably common. The recovery of **pseudomorphs** of flat wooden items with rounded profiles, for example from the Abric Romaní rock shelter in Spain, and a preserved wooden spear from Lehringen in Germany, remind us that woodworking was probably a habitual Neanderthal activity, at least where tree cover was plentiful.

Neanderthals commonly constructed simple hearths for warmth, light, and cooking. Where wood was scarce, it seems that they transported coal up to 15 kilometers (9.4 miles) from outcrops, as at Les Canalettes, France. Beyond the organization of activities around such hearths, and the paving of wet floors with stones, Neanderthal use of space seems to have been fairly simple, with certain areas reserved for disposal and messy tasks, and others for eating, resting, and maintenance. Some Neanderthal groups buried certain of their dead, at least on occasion, and most scholars agree that there are at least twenty clear examples of interment in shallow graves. A number of sites, for example Shanidar Cave in Iraq and La Ferrassie rock shelter in France, were used over long periods of time and contain multiple burials. This suggests that particular sites may have been known as mortuary centers, although the majority of burials, from children to adults, are isolated.

Neanderthals were clearly using pigments from time to time. Fragments of manganese dioxide have been found on several western European Mousterian sites, and shells stained with red ocher—presumably utilized as containers or mixing palettes—have been found in 50,000-year-old deposits in two Spanish caves and modified for use as jewelry in Fumane Cave in Italy. Cut-marked bones of vultures, eagles, and other birds from this latter cave [**4.10**] indicate the deliberate removal of feathers, and eagle claws were modified for use as jewelry at Krapina in Croatia as early as 130,000 years ago.

4.9 Mousterian tools. Typical Mousterian tool types, which probably served as weapon tips and pointed implements. Wear traces and remains of sticky materials, such as bitumen, show that some of these were, on occasion, hafted.

No convincing evidence of figurative art or decorated objects has yet been recovered, suggesting that it was not a common practice in Neanderthal society.

An examination of the faunal remains, lithics, and placement of sites helps us to understand how Neanderthals moved across the landscape. The paleoanthropologists, Daniel Lieberman and John Shea, suggest that those in Southwest Asia practiced a locally intensive radiating mobility strategy. Large, multipurpose sites formed cores from which activities were organized, resulting in the creation of more specialized peripheral sites. In such a strategy, the Neanderthals were highly predatory within fairly small, circumscribed areas, producing relatively high numbers of weapon tips, and hunting throughout the year. By contrast, modern humans in the area seem to have practiced a strategy of residential circulating mobility, organized around seasonal change. Movement would take them between several seasonal camps located in different environments, at which activities would vary according to season. This broader strategy, in which the hunting of gazelle and other ungulates (hoofed mammals) was the focus of activity during only one season, put less demand on the production of weapon tips and presumably incorporated several other exploitation strategies, including gathering. Such differing strategies and their associated nutritional demands and returns may have had evolutionary significance.

4.10 Cut-marked bones. A close-up image of a bone of a Eurasian black vulture with cut marks produced during its disarticulation, indicating the deliberate removal of feathers. From the Mousterian site of Fumane Cave, Italy.

THE PEOPLING OF EAST ASIA AND AUSTRALIA

By 50,000 years ago, *Homo sapiens* was clearly established throughout all of Africa, and expanded into Southeast Asia and Australia, northeastward into the Caucasus and southeast Siberia, and northward into Europe. Although archaeological data for the modern human peopling of southern Asia by *H. sapiens* is very sparse, it seems that they were present in China by 80,000 years ago [**4.11**], and in Laos, **Sundaland** and Sarawak, Borneo [**4.12**, p. 86] by *at least* 40,000 years ago. Some sites, such as Callao Cave, Philippines, suggest dates as early as 70,000–60,000 years ago, but these are imprecise. Sundaland, however, was always separated from **Sahul** by the deep waters of the Wallacea Strait, so would have required sea crossings to reach [**4.13**, p. 86].

The human peopling of Australia, New Guinea, and Tasmania during the Ice Age is well established. MtDNA suggests that this had occurred by 50,000 years ago and perhaps as early as 60,000 years ago. Existing radiocarbon dates, taken at face value, tail off before 40,000 years ago, although this probably reflects the limitations of the technique rather than the earliest signs of human incursion, which many hold to have occurred much earlier. After 40,000 years ago, the number of sites in Australia rises considerably. Recent dating using luminesence and electron-spin methods consistently date early finds to 50,000 years ago. Early sites, including the Madjedebe rock shelter in northern Australia, and burials at Lake Mungo near the Darling River in southeast Australia, have been held to suggest that people moved here before this watershed. Furthermore, a number of distinct and differing peopling events may have occurred.

Sundaland the continuous landmass formed by island Indonesia and Borneo during periods of low sea level

Sahul the continuous landmass formed by Australia and New Guinea in periods of low sea level

4.11 The Dali cranium from China. Approximately 200,000 years old, it was originally classified as *Homo erectus*, but with some derived characteristics. The cranium is, however, highly distorted through post-depositional weight loading, and recent analyses have weakened this notion; its classification is currently unclear.

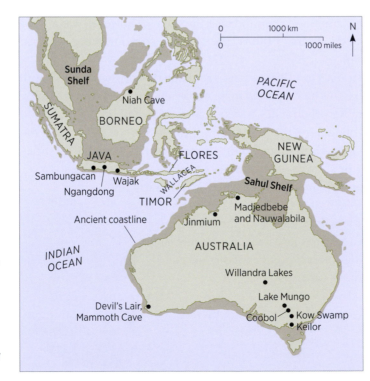

4.12 The Niah Great Cave, Borneo, which was in use by humans from around 45,000 years ago. Excavations in the 1950s just to the right of this image yielded the Deep Skull, the 40,000-year-old remains of a fourteen- to fifteen-year-old, probably female, *Homo sapiens*.

Early Australian sites demonstrate a complex and rich symbolic life. At Lake Mungo, there is evidence of cemeteries associated with camp sites. At Carpenter's Gap in the Kimberley region of northwest Australia, painted stones and paint-grinding slabs are dated to 41,000 years ago. Pictures of extant animals are present in rock art of the Arnhem Land region, in the north of the continent, from 40,000 years ago. Ocher crayons are common throughout this time.

4.13 Island Southeast Asia. At times of low sea levels in the Pleistocene, island Southeast Asia formed a large landmass from the Sunda shelf, while New Guinea, Australia, and Tasmania were linked as the Sahul landmass. The deep waters of Wallacea would still have provided a barrier between the two. The map shows major early modern human sites.

Variations in the earth's orbital axis affected the climate and therefore the location of plant and animal communities. This, combined with frequent climatic shifts during the Upper Pleistocene, acted as a main driver of the dispersal of humans across the world [**4.14**]. In northern latitudes, the distribution of Neanderthals fluctuated in response to brief stadials (a colder period within one of the Ice Ages) and interstadials (a warmer period within an Ice Age), and their scattering from northwestern Europe to Uzbekistan probably reflects this displacement over time, rather than their presence across this vast range at any one point in time. In Africa, climate change in the period 150,000 to 30,000 years ago affected the carrying capacity of regions, such as the deserts of the north or the forests of the central (tropical) regions, and the early movements of *Homo sapiens* seem to have occurred as responses to opportunities when they arose in warm interglacials and interstadials. The spread of resource-laden environments—particularly coastal—facilitated the first journeys out of Africa in the warm conditions at times in the period between 180,000 and 90,000 years ago. This was particularly the case along the rich ecosystem of the Nile Valley, Africa's dispersal highway. These migrations were probably numerous; humans seem to have been present in the Arabian Peninsula, for example, around 125,000 years ago and again around 110,000 years ago.

Following the initial dispersal, several bursts of migration occurred in the warm interstadials as conditions allowed. It was during these that *Homo sapiens* moved as far east as India, China, Sundaland (the continuous landmass formed by the Indonesian islands and Borneo during low sea levels) and Sahul (the landmass formed by Australia and New Guinea in periods of low sea level), and north up into Europe and Siberia.

4.14 Map showing the major trends in the dispersal of modern humans around the world, with very approximate dates given as years ago.

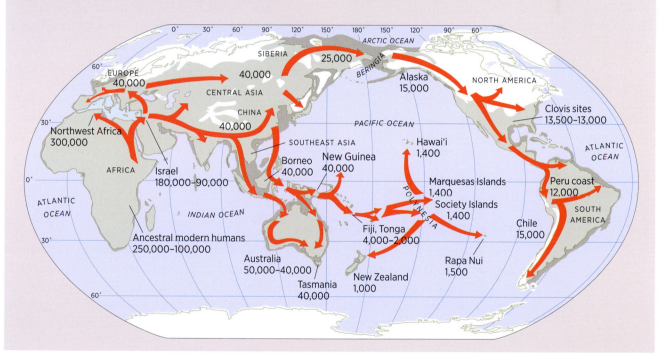

THE PEOPLING OF EUROPE AND RUSSIA

We know a great deal more about the expansion of modern *Homo sapiens* into Europe and Russia than we do other areas of the world. This is not because it was, in some way, more spectacular or of greater achievement. Rather, it is because there has been more research concentrated in this area for a very long time. The movement of *H. sapiens* into Europe is marked by the appearance of the Aurignacian industry, followed by the Gravettian.

In the 1990s, three major discoveries changed our perceptions of Upper Paleolithic cave art. The French prehistorian Jean Clottes has named these the Three Cs: the **Cosquer** and **Chauvet** caves in southeast France, and the open-air engravings in Portugal's **Côa Valley**.

Cosquer Cave

The discovery of Cosquer Cave, which can be entered only underwater, extended the geographical range of French decorated caves (in this case to within 200 kilometers, or 125 miles, of Italy), as well as the range of certain motifs, such as hand stencils, and the depiction of sea creatures, for example seals. As it is in part flooded by the Mediterranean, this cave reminds us that many sites have probably been lost due to the erosive processes of the sea.

Côa Valley

The petroglyphs pecked and engraved along at least 16 kilometers (10 miles) of the deep Côa Valley and in neighboring Spanish open-air locations, such as at Domingo Garcia, are indications that Upper Paleolithic art was probably very widespread in the landscape, and the tendency for art to survive in caves is probably due to very lucky preservation.

Chauvet Cave

Chauvet Cave, discovered in 1994, is located in southeast France. It is a complex system containing large galleries, one of which was used by bears. In addition to a rich bear paleontology, and evidence for the arrangement of some of the bear remains by humans, abundant art appears on its walls, and numerous traces of human activity remain on its floors.

Chauvet was immediately hailed as a new Lascaux, due to the abundance of its engravings and its black (charcoal) and red (ocher) paintings, and to the number of sophisticated techniques and styles that were employed. Compositional groupings of grazing herbivores and predatory carnivores are probably scenes from life [**4.15**]. The cave wall was often prepared by scraping it clean prior to the creation of several panels, spatial perspective was created by a number of means, the natural relief of the cave's walls was used to enhance dynamism, and shading by spreading pigments around (stump drawing) is common in the black animals.

A number of species are depicted at Chauvet that are rare in caves elsewhere, for example rhino and lion, and some animals—such as the long-eared owl, a panther, and a possible hyena—appear for the first time. Although differences exist between the red and black paintings as to the animals depicted and where the compositions are placed, stylistic similarities point to a degree of artistic unity in the works.

This having been said, radiocarbon dates, both directly on the black series art and on numerous charcoal fragments from hearths lit on the cave's floor, indicate that at least two periods of activity are reflected in the cave. A number of hearth charcoal fragments and two depictions (the confronting rhinos, and a bison and an aurochs) have been dated to between 33,000 and 30,000 years ago. Because of this, the Chauvet drawings have been seen

The Aurignacian and the Gravettian

The Aurignacian, dating from around 35,000 years ago, included sophisticated stone and organic technologies, organized production of personal ornamentation, and art. Aurignacian lithic and organic tools appear fairly generalized and functionally flexible, probably an important requisite for a dispersing pioneer population. From the outset, the Aurignacian reflects the employment of considerably more efficient and varied tools than those used by the Neanderthals.

By 35,000 years ago, the Aurignacian was well established throughout much of Europe. From this time, evidence of the manufacture of beads and other jewelry from teeth and mammoth ivory, and the circulation of these and marine shells over several hundred kilometers, attest to the presence of established exchange networks. Blade technology (blades were struck off from the top of a core around its periphery, leaving it prismlike) was widely employed, and a variety of bone and antler tools, such as points, awls, needles, and more enigmatic pieces indicate the fashioning of elaborate clothing and use of sophisticated weaponry. Tailored clothing, for example leggings and coats, would have been far more effective in dealing with

as possibly the earliest evidence of painted art in Europe, although some scholars have questioned these dates based on stylistic, other dating, and archaeological grounds. If these are the earliest known examples of European art, the sophistication of techniques and style make them crucial to our understanding of how art emerged, at least on this continent.

4.15 An Upper Paleolithic carnivore hunting scene? The left wall of the end chamber of Chauvet Cave in southeast France contains a masterpiece of composition. A group of lions appears to be advancing toward a herd of bison. Note the shading (the technique is known as stump drawing) and perspective.

severe climates than the simpler furs and hides probably worn by the Neanderthals, and may have been a significant factor in the expansion of Upper Paleolithic populations into northern regions, such as Siberia.

Art is present in the form of engraved ivory and bone, as well as painted and engraved cave walls. Examples of such Aurignacian art [**4.16–4.19**, p. 90] include figurines in mammoth ivory from Hohle Fels Cave in southwest Germany; animal carvings from the Vogelherd Cave in southern Germany; the lion–anthropomorph carvings on mammoth ivory, for instance that come from nearby Hohlenstein-Stadel Cave; anthropoid painting from Fumane Cave in northern Italy; engravings of vulvae (especially common in France); and possibly some of the paintings of Chauvet Cave (see Key Site box: Three Sites with Upper Paleolithic Art). On the other hand, there are no convincing indications of burial of the dead or sophisticated dwelling structures, which suggests that although something of a behavioral revolution had taken place, this process was ongoing and far from complete at this time.

Aurignacian material culture came to an end in all areas of Europe by around 28,000 years ago. It was succeeded across most of the continent by more regionally distinct groups that

4.16–4.19 Aurignacian art. The enigmatic lion–anthropomorph mammoth-tusk carving, with a human body and a lion's head (far left), is from the site of Hohlenstein-Stadel in southern Germany. A curious anthropomorphic figure painted on a stone block (center) is one of several simple paintings from Fumane Cave, northern Italy. The carvings of a horse and mammoth on mammoth ivory from Vogelherd Cave, also in southern Germany (left, above and below), form some of the earliest traces of modern humans in Europe.

shared general characteristics over a wide area. This general **technocomplex** is referred to as the Gravettian; it lasted from at least 29,000 years ago to 21,000 years ago in some areas, and much later in southern and eastern regions of Europe, where the late stage, down to around 14,000 years ago, is usually referred to as the Epigravettian (see p. 92). Similarly to the Aurignacian, its origins are unclear, although unlike that industry, which may have originated outside Europe and spread with modern human populations, the Gravettian most probably originated within the indigenous later Aurignacian, possibly in Central Europe.

The Gravettian represents innovations in subsistence, mortuary activity, organization in the landscape and on site, artistic endeavor, projectile technology, and other non-utilitarian aspects of behavior. Technologically, the Gravettian employed prismatic blade technology and a variety of points, often bearing steep backing (blunting) to facilitate hafting. A number of **burins** and endscrapers attest to the working of skins and organic materials, such as wood, bone, and antler. Of the latter, a profusion of distinctive weapon tips can be used to divide the period chronologically, resulting in a number of discrete phases. The small dimensions of some of these weapon tips suggest that the bow and arrow may have been invented at this time, although this is unproven, alongside the javelin thrown with the aid of a spearthrower or **atlatl**. On the Dyje River in Moravia (in the Czech Republic), site complexes, such as Pavlov and Dolní Věstonice I and II, have yielded hundreds of mammoth, bison, and reindeer bones, and complex patterning of artifacts is suggestive of highly organized campsites. At another camp, Předmostí, three crania have been identified as domesticated wolves (dogs) [**4.20**], which have also been found on Russian sites of broadly similar age. At Paglicci Cave in Italy, wild oats were ground into flour, a reminder of the continued importance of plant foods. Clearly, a highly complex hunter-gatherer-fisher subsistence had emerged by at least 27,000 years ago.

More than forty burials, generally single but with some double and two triple examples, and the ubiquity of human remains amid settlement sites, attest to the development of Gravettian mortuary activity from France to Siberia. The high degree of ornamentation of many burials, and the inclusion of grave offerings with most, suggests considerable social complexity. Two children buried head to head around 24,000 years ago at Sungir', Russia, for example, wore mammoth-ivory pendants and were highly colored with red ocher; their shallow grave contained thousands of fox teeth and numerous items of mammoth ivory and bone.

technocomplex a group of cultures that share a similar technology or technologies

burin a stone flake or blade with chisel-like edges

atlatl a spearthrower

4.20 Domesticated wolf. A skull identified as domesticated wolf (dog) from the Gravettian of Předmostí, Moravia (Czech Republic).

KEY CONTROVERSY   The Meaning of Female Figurines

Female figurines (sometimes called Venus figurines) are present throughout the European Upper Paleolithic. Only a small number of depictions are known from the Aurignacian, such as the green serpentine Dancing Venus of the Galgenberg, Austria, and a mammoth-ivory bas-relief (low-relief sculpture with a carved background to leave the design slightly raised) from Geissenklösterle Cave in southern Germany, both dating to around 33,000–31,000 years ago. In the late Upper Paleolithic, stylized carvings of the female form are known from Magdalenian sites and contemporary cultures elsewhere. It was during the mid-Upper Paleolithic (Gravettian), however, that the creation of female figurines flourished, one or two millennia either side of 25,000 years ago. Since their discovery in the late nineteenth century, the figurines have been the subject of much speculation, and some, such as the Black Venus of Dolní Věstonice in the Czech Republic, the Venus of Willendorf in Austria, and the Dame à la Capuche (Lady with the Hood) from the Grotte du Pape at Brassempouy, in southwest France, have become icons of the European Paleolithic.

Form and Function

Figurines were carved from mammoth ivory, soft stones, such as steatite, and even limestone in the case of Willendorf [**4.21–4.23**].

Some have seen them as especially linked to pregnancy, although the anthropologist Patricia Rice suggested, using ethnographic analogy, that they represented females at all stages of life, not just fertile and pregnant individuals, and speculated that they may have been a general symbol of womanhood. Clive Gamble, the British archaeologist, noted that their flowering coincided with a climatic downturn, and argued they may represent shared symbols that are used to reinforce alliances between groups. The art historian LeRoy McDermott suggested that some relate to self-expression among pregnant women, who were communicating their personal experience of their own bodies through the figurines.

Since many were excavated in the infancy of archaeology, contextual information is often lacking. French figurines seem to have been tucked away in caves; in Moravia, some were found in domestic refuse; and at such sites as Kostenki and Avdeevo in Russia, they were placed in pits, which may indicate that they were goddesses protecting stores, or were even buried accompanied by grave offerings.

The figurines are often colored with ocher, which depicts items of clothing, such as simple hats, or textile adornments, such as belts and bands. There are several regional variants across Europe, from France to the Russian Plain. Some may have been hidden or short-lived, others put on display.

It may be too simplistic to view the figurines as having one function, and perhaps it is best to see them as having a variety of meanings, with regional variations, within a general theme. Whatever their purpose, they contrast markedly with actual mid-Upper Paleolithic burials, which are overwhelmingly male, and they may be at least a shadowy reflection of complex social dynamics from around 26,000 to 23,000 years ago.

4.21–4.23 Three female carvings from the European earlier Upper Paleolithic. From left to right: bas-relief on serpentine from the Galgenberg hill in Austria (Aurignacian); figurine from Hohle Fells (Aurignacian); and the limestone Venus from Willendorf, Austria (Gravettian).

type site an archaeological site considered definitively characteristic of a particular culture; the name of the site is often applied to that culture

Portable art, particularly carving on mammoth ivory, is abundant across Europe, and may reflect the social importance of art and symbolic activity in the context of climatic deterioration toward the Last Glacial Maximum. The iconic Venus figurines (see Key Controversy box: The Meaning of Venus Figurines, p. 91) are part of this Gravettian artistic flowering. Cave painting and engraving continued, with handprints, stencils, and human figurines alongside herbivores, as well as complex, multiphased panels, for example the dappled horses and associated hand stencils of Pech Merle, France, which have been dated directly by radiocarbon to 25,000–24,000 years ago.

Later Upper Paleolithic: 21,000 to 14,000 Years Ago

As the climatic downturn reached its severest point during the Last Glacial Maximum around 21,000 years ago, people abandoned northern Europe and high-altitude areas, moving to southern European refuges. Here they underwent marked regionalization, probably due to their isolation from neighboring regions. While some areas show continuity with the Gravettian, such as the Italian Epigravettian, in other areas new cultures emerged, such as the French and Iberian Solutrean. In this culture, flints were often heat-treated to improve their fracture mechanics, and pressure flaking was employed to create a variety of leaf-shaped weapon tips. These seem to have been produced to tight design specifications in terms of size and weight, probably reflecting the demands of hafting and aerodynamic efficiency of javelins. Some of the weapon tips are so small and light it is conceivable that the bow and arrow was in use by this time.

With the climatic improvements from 18,000 years ago, depopulated regions of Europe were rapidly occupied, and the late Upper Paleolithic Magdalenian technocomplex (named after La Madeleine rock shelter in the Dordogne, France, the **type site** for the industry) was soon established from its early roots in Iberia and southern France eastward to Russia and across southern Europe. From around 17,000 years ago, the improvement of the glacial environments of the northern European plain allowed the Magdalenian technocomplex to spread into this region, reaching Britain by 14,000 years ago.

Cave art is mainly known from southwest France and northern Spain, although examples exist in Italy, Germany, and Britain, suggesting that it was probably a widespread phenomenon in caves and also in open locations. Portable art is remarkably abundant and diverse across Europe in this period, and includes exquisitely carved animal heads and engraved and notated bones from the Pyrenees and southern France, stylized female carvings from Germany, atlatl crooks for throwing javelins, and a host of other highly worked pieces. It is difficult to escape the conclusion that the Magdalenian world was a very decorative one.

SUMMARY AND CONCLUSIONS

This chapter has described the evidence for human behavior and development during the last 400,000 years of the Pleistocene, up to the end of the last Ice Age some 11,600 years ago. The key theme of this time period is the origin and spread of modern humans, and the extinction of all other hominin species. The demise around 30,000 years ago of the last communities of *Homo neanderthalensis* and *H. erectus* left *H. sapiens*—anatomically modern humans—the sole surviving hominin species on the planet, with the possible exception of *H. floresiensis*.

Chapter 4 has also discussed the new behaviors developed by modern humans. Their brains were no larger than those of the Neanderthals, but they engaged in a much richer repertoire of cognitive and symbolic activity, which is manifest archaeologically in the evidence for cave art, personal adornment, and burial.

The last half million years of the Pleistocene saw two distinct evolutionary and behavioral trajectories. In Eurasia, Middle Paleolithic populations evolved as a biological response to the often cold environments of northern latitudes, resulting in the Neanderthals, whose characteristics coalesced by 250,000 years ago and persisted until around 30,000 years ago. By contrast, in the southern latitudes of Africa (and perhaps including Southwest Asia), anatomically modern humans of the Middle Stone Age evolved as a response to very different selective pressures, possibly accompanied by complex social organization and language. There is ongoing debate as to whether the development of modern behavior occurred rapidly and was connected to the emergence of sophisticated language and symbolic systems, or more gradually in Africa over a considerable period. Nevertheless, it is agreed that by the Upper Paleolithic or Late Stone Age, modern humans were clearly behaving very differently from their predecessors and from contemporary Neanderthals.

New behavioral innovations by modern humans facilitated for the first time the inhabitation of hostile areas, such as Siberia and the crossing of relatively short stretches of sea. These permitted the peopling of Australia and New Guinea by 60,000 to 50,000 years ago. In northern latitudes, the development of the Eurasian Upper Paleolithic reveals a number of modern behavioral patterns that developed over time, such as semi-sedentism, elaborate dwelling structures and settlement layouts, and multi-component weaponry, including altatl-driven javelins and the bow and arrow. Collectively, these innovations indicate that the modern hunter-gatherer had evolved by at least 27,000 years ago, and perhaps considerably earlier.

FURTHER READING

Good introductions to early modern human behavior and the Neanderthals include:

Clottes, J. 1998. The 'three Cs': fresh avenues towards European Paleolithic art, in *The Archaeology of Rock Art*. Chippendale, C. and Tacon, P. S. C. (eds.). Cambridge: Cambridge University Press.

Cummings, V. *et al.* (eds.). 2014. *The Oxford Handbook of the Archaeology of Hunter-Gatherers.* Oxford: Oxford University Press.

Dennell, R. and Porr, M. 2014. *Southern Asia, Australia and the Search for Human Origins.* Cambridge: Cambridge University Press.

Hovers, E. and Kuhn, S. (eds.). 2006. *Transitions before the Transition: Evolution and Stability in the Middle Paleolithic and Middle Stone Age.* New York: Springer.

Pääbo, S. 2014. *Neanderthal Man: In Search of Lost Genomes.* New York: Basic Books.

Reich, D. 2018. *Who We Are and How We Got Here.* Oxford: Oxford University Press.

Rice, P. 1981. Prehistoric Venuses: symbols of motherhood or womanhood? *Journal of Anthropological Research* 37, 402–14.

Shreeve, J. 1995. *The Neandertal Enigma: Solving the Mystery of Modern Human Origins.* New York: Morrow; London: Viking.

Stiner, M. C. 1994. *Honor among Thieves: A Zooarchaeological Study of Neandertal Ecology.* Princeton: Princeton University Press.

Stringer, C. 2011. *The Origin of Our Species.* London: Allen Lane.

Stringer, C. and Gamble, C. 1993. *In Search of the Neanderthals.* London and New York: Thames & Hudson.

Stringer, C. and McKie, R. 1996. *African Exodus.* London: Pimlico.

www.neanderthal.de Official website of the Neanderthal Museum, Germany, with general information pertaining to the Neanderthals and the museum, and excellent related links.

The World Transformed: From Hunter-Gatherers to Early Farmers

Chris Scarre

Environments and Landscapes: 13,000–9600 BCE 96

Hunter-Gatherer Trajectories 99

Transitions to Agriculture 100

Expansion of Domestication 105

The Consequences of Agriculture 106

Summary and Conclusions 109

Further Reading 109

Rock paintings at Tassili n'Ajjeri in Algeria were made by cattle pastoralists who were able to occupy this region of the central Sahara during the fifth millennium BCE, when winter rains allowed grasslands to flourish.

In this chapter we cover the global transformation that followed the end of the last Ice Age, at around 9600 BCE (11,600 years ago). This involved massive environmental change. The warmer climate caused the ice sheets to retreat and the sea level to rise, drowning formerly extensive coastal lowlands. At the same time, plant and animal species were able to expand into new environments. Human societies responded to this warmer climate in several ways, one of the most significant being the development and spread of agriculture.

The domestication of plants and animals resulted in a growth in world population to far higher levels than were sustainable by hunting and gathering alone. Food production and demographic increase were accompanied by other changes, notably larger and more permanent settlements, more complex social organization, growing social inequality, and new technologies. But change was not restricted to farming cultures, and many hunter-gatherer societies also developed larger settlements, greater symbolic complexity, and more intensive subsistence practices as the postglacial period progressed.

- The beginning of the postglacial epoch saw rising sea levels caused by the retreat of the glaciers, which submerged land masses, such as the Bering land bridge between North America and Eurasia, Doggerland in Europe, and Sundaland in Southeast Asia.

- The warming climate allowed new forms of social and economic activity, including more intensive forms of hunting and gathering, and eventually agriculture, which arose independently in at least seven regions of the world.

- The reasons for the adoption of agriculture were diverse, including social competition and longer-term pressures toward food production imposed by demographic growth. Agriculture enabled much greater populations to be supported but involved more work and had many health disadvantages for individuals.

- Social complexity often accompanied the development of agriculture, but there are many examples of socially complex hunter-gather communities.

ENVIRONMENTS AND LANDSCAPES: 13,000–9600 BCE

At the end of the last Ice Age, around 11,600 years ago (c. 9600 BCE), temperatures began to increase. This warming process was not constant, but included intervals of temperature reversal and cooling. By around 13,000 BCE, summer temperatures had reached almost their present levels, but then temperatures went into dramatic reverse, and cold conditions returned for a further 1,000 years during the Younger Dryas phase (c. 10,800–9600 BCE). This was probably caused by the melting of the northern ice sheets, which released immense quantities of cold meltwater into the North Atlantic and weakened or stopped the warm conveyor belt North Atlantic current known as the Gulf Stream, which brings water north from the tropics. We will see in following chapters how human populations across the world reacted to this period of cold climate. At around 9600 BCE, warm conditions re-established themselves, with temperatures rising by 7°C (12.6°F) in only fifty years, ushering in what we call the postglacial epoch or the Holocene.

5.1 Rising sea levels at the end of the last Ice Age drowned significant areas of low-lying land (shown here in a darker shade), especially in East and Southeast Asia and northwest Europe. One outcome was the formation of new islands: the Japanese archipelago; New Guinea; Borneo, Sumatra and Indonesia; Britain and Ireland. At the same time, the loss of productive lowlands must have had major regional impacts on human and animal populations.

The Early Postglacial Environment

The first 2,000 years of the postglacial period were a time of especially rapid change. Though summer temperatures had reached modern levels very early in this epoch (by *c.* 9000 BCE), the ice sheets took many centuries to melt, and sea levels were still more than 50 meters (165 feet) below those of the present. The melting of the ice sheets led to a rise in sea level, which drowned low-lying areas at a speed that must at times have been perceptible to human communities on a year-by-year basis [**5.1**].

In high northern latitudes, the melting of the ice sheets had a reverse effect. The removal of the weight of the ice caused land areas to rebound in a process known as **isostatic uplift**, which far outstripped the rise in sea level. In previously glaciated areas, early postglacial shorelines and coastal settlement sites of the period are now to be found well above sea level and far inland, whereas throughout most of the world, where there were no glaciers, the rising sea level drowned out coastal areas. As a result, in most regions, save where isostatic uplift has preserved early shorelines, the history of human coastal exploitation can be traced back only to some 5,000 years ago.

One notable effect of early sea-level rise was the creation of islands. The Japanese islands were separated from the Asian mainland, Tasmania from Australia, and Britain from continental Europe. East Asia and North America became divided by the flooding of the Bering Strait around 8500 BCE. In terms of geographical extent, however, the most dramatic of all late Pleistocene and early postglacial coastal losses occurred in Southeast Asia. Here the Pleistocene landmass known as Sundaland lost more than half of its land area to rising sea levels between 15,000 and 5000 BCE, resulting in the creation of the Southeast Asian islands [**5.2**].

By the time that sea-level rise began to slow appreciably (around 5000 BCE), the shapes of continents and islands were very much the same as in the present day. Although some former mainland communities now

isostatic uplift the rising of landmasses once the weight of the ice sheets has been removed

5.2 Islands of Indonesia created by rising sea levels during the postglacial period.

5.3 Rock art in the Sahara. During the early postglacial period, North Africa experienced a wetter climate than today and much of what is now the Sahara Desert became dry grassland, punctuated in the south by extensive lakes. Rock art of the period depicts crocodile, elephant, and other animals now restricted to the sub-Saharan region. These are joined by images of herds of domestic cattle from the fifth millennium BCE (see pp. 94–95).

5.4 Postglacial climatic change. Evidence for the changing intensity of human occupation in the Sahara, reflecting variations in rainfall. The wetter Saharan climate of the early postglacial was reflected in growing density of settlement in the African Humid Phase *c.* 9000–3000 BCE, which ended with the reversion to arid conditions that have continued up to the present day.

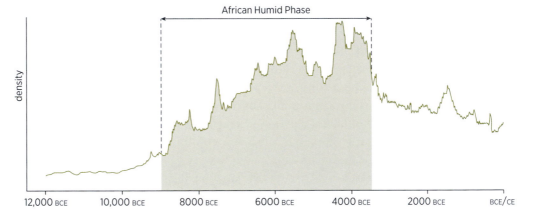

found themselves living on islands, that only rarely resulted in cultural isolation. The human response to changes in sea level and island formation was usually more innovative, resulting in new strategies of marine exploitation and highly developed navigational skills. It was these that enabled Polynesian seafarers to discover and settle far-flung and often tiny islands of the Pacific during the first and early second millennia CE, as discussed in Chapter 11.

Tropical areas were also affected by postglacial warming. During the earlier postglacial period, the Inter-Tropical Convergence Zone, which carries rains through tropical Africa and via the monsoon systems across the Indian Ocean, moved farther north to pass over the Sahara. The southern Sahara became a region of lakes within an extensive savanna grassland, rather than the desert familiar to us today. By 9000 BCE, pottery-using fishers and hunters had settled this region. Only from 3000 BCE did climate patterns change and the Sahara begin to take on the desert-like character it has today [**5.3**, **5.4**].

HUNTER-GATHERER TRAJECTORIES

During the last Ice Age, human populations had been concentrated in tropical and sub-tropical zones, and those living in more marginal areas were severely constrained by the harsh glacial environment. The postglacial world, by contrast, offered enormous opportunities, especially to communities occupying or migrating into the temperate zones of North America, Europe, and Asia.

The technology and material culture of early postglacial groups were directly developed from that of their late Paleolithic forebears. **Microliths** were used to make composite tools, with flint or chert cutting edges inserted into wooden or bone hafts. In Europe, microliths are a distinguishing feature of the Mesolithic, the period between the end of the Paleolithic (the end of the last Ice Age) and the beginning of the Neolithic (characterized by the adoption of farming), although they had been used much earlier in Africa, where quartz and other fine-grained rocks formed the raw material.

Stone was far from being the only material worked and used by hunter-gatherers, although it is prominent in the archaeological record because it has survived so well. Where waterlogging or aridity allow the preservation of organic remains, wooden tools and implements and basketry containers are also found. Some hunter-gatherer communities also produced pottery vessels. The earliest known pottery vessels were made by hunter-gatherers of East Asia around 16,000 years ago [**5.5**]. Analysis of organic residues within the pots has shown that these vessels were used for processing marine resources. In an independent development, pottery was also invented by hunter-gatherer communities of the southern Sahara in the tenth millennium BCE, long before farming, where they may have been used for processing both freshwater resources and wild seeds.

Like their Paleolithic predecessors, early postglacial communities exploited resources by moving around their landscapes, generally in small groups, occasionally coming together in larger seasonal gatherings at places of abundant productivity. The geographical and seasonal distribution of resources dictated the size and spread of these human communities and set a limit to their numbers.

Generally, early postglacial communities gathered plant foods using stone reaping knives, or dug up tubers with digging sticks, and hunted with spears and bows. Yet already during the final stages of the last Ice Age, certain groups of hunters and gatherers had begun to exploit their environment in a new way, moving beyond collecting to the intentional management of some plant species. Among these were the Jōmon of Japan, who developed successful methods of exploiting wild plants and marine resources, which they maintained until past 1000 BCE, long after farming had become established in mainland China. In southwest Asia, Natufian hunter-gatherers (c. 12,500 to 10,200 years ago) used a strategy that exploited a wide range of resources and supported communities that, similar to the Jōmon, developed complex symbolism and ceremonial sites. The Natufians paid special attention to the wild cereals that grew in the hilly flanks of the Fertile Crescent, which were easy to harvest when they became ripe. They began to manipulate the wild wheat and barley, favoring those with larger seed heads, and those with seeds that remained attached to the seed head rather than shattering and scattering in the natural way. These were the first steps towards domestication

5.5 Pottery. Pottery vessels are fragile and heavy to transport, and in most regions appear only with sedentary farmers. The oldest, however, were produced by hunter-gatherer societies in East Asia, as illustrated by this example from the Initial Jōmon period from Shimoda shironaya in Aomori Prefecture, Japan.

microlith a small, standardized stone blade, originally set into a composite tool or weapon

and cultivation in southwest Asia, and similar developments occurred independently in other parts of the world, including China, where the main cereal species were rice and millet. Spreading from its origins in a number of separate regions, the shift from food collection to food production dramatically increased the human-carrying capacity of the planet. In the process, the landscape was transformed, as modest clearings gave way to fields, and forests were felled to provide farmland for ever-increasing human numbers.

The cultural and social complexity of hunter-gatherers should not be underestimated. The Jōmon of Japan, who carefully managed their food resources but never domesticated them, developed long-lived settlements comprising significant numbers of houses. Excavations at Sannai-Maruyama have uncovered remains of more than 650 houses, a huge post-built structure, a large cemetery, and some 1,800 clay figurines, although these remains span a period of 1,500 years (3500–2000 BCE) and only a few of the houses would have been in occupation at any one time. Other hunter-gatherers in productive environments, such as the societies of the northwest coast of North America, moved only once or twice during the year and had villages of substantial timber houses. Communities supported by hunting and gathering were also capable of major cooperative undertakings, such as the construction of the massive Poverty Point and Watson Brake mounds in Southeast North America. Poverty Point, involving the movement of 750,000 cubic metres of earth, is one of the largest prehistoric monuments in the world. Complex hunter-gatherers were therefore an important feature of the human past in both Eurasia and the Americas. Ultimately, however, agriculture became established in almost every region where conditions of climate and soils allowed, whether through indigenous domestication of local species, through the adoption of domesticated animals and plants from neighboring farming communities, or through the expansion of the farmers themselves.

TRANSITIONS TO AGRICULTURE
What Is Agriculture?

Agriculture is the system in which selected species of plants and animals are cultivated and reared by humans. It has two basic features. First is the selection of some plants and animals over others by humans. This leads to the second feature, which is the isolation of those selected species from their wild relatives. That ongoing process causes changes (intended and unintended) in the morphology of the selected plants and animals, and they often end up relying on humans for reproductive success. Agriculture also involves dramatic changes in human behavior and society, where humans become equally dependent on their domesticated plants and animals, most especially to feed and maintain the new population numbers that agriculture can provide. When describing early food production, a number of terms are used that have different, if overlapping, meanings.

• **Domestication** is a process that involves genetic changes in plants and animals as they become dependent on humans for reproductive success. Domestication may often be unintentional, resulting from continuing interaction between humans and wild species.

• **Cultivation** is a cultural phenomenon that involves intentionally preparing fields, and sowing, harvesting, and storing seeds or other plant parts. Cultivation required significant and deliberate changes in human technology, subsistence, and perspectives.

- **Herding**, similarly to cultivation, requires intentional changes in the relationship between humans and animals. It can take varying forms: herding close to a permanent settlement, as part of a mixed economy combining livestock and cultivation, or transhumant herding, where animals are moved between pastures on a seasonal basis (for example from summer uplands to sheltered lowlands for the winter). There are also **pastoral** communities where the emphasis is on livestock herding and plant cultivation plays only a minor role.

- **Agriculture** is a commitment to this relationship between humans and plants and animals. It ultimately involves changes in the human use of the earth and in the structure and organization of human society, including the extensive clearance of forest, the cultivation of hard-shelled cereals or root crops that can be stored for long periods of time, and the invention and adoption of new technologies for farming and/or herding (plows, field systems, irrigation).

The adoption of agriculture required solutions to new problems, such as assigning greater investments of time and energy to clearing forests and constructing and managing storage facilities to keep the annual harvest. These solutions usually involved forms of **sedentism**: permanent, year-round settlement. The relationship between agriculture and sedentism may be too simplistic, however, as certain non-farming communities in favorable locations, such as the Jōmon mentioned above, already had relatively permanent settlements.

Hunter-gatherers often develop close relationships with key plant species that lead to practices verging on domestication. Aboriginal communities in Australia, for example, often replant parts of the yams that they dig up, and the Owens Valley Paiute of eastern California diverted streams so as to irrigate natural fields of water-meadow root crops. Hunter-gatherers were not simply passive bystanders in the history of plant and animal exploitation, but modified those species on which they relied, both intentionally and unintentionally. Furthermore, close relationships between humans and animals did not begin abruptly with the development of agriculture in the early postglacial period, but have a much longer history, stretching back into the Paleolithic. The first species to be domesticated was the dog. Remains of domestic dog that are more than 12,000 years old have been found at archaeological sites in Europe and East Asia. This animal, however, was a hunting aid rather than a food animal, and the development of fully fledged farming communities, where it occurred, marked a significant break with what had gone before.

Domestication

Domesticated animals and plants are predominantly subject to selection by humans. Farmers may, for example, prefer smaller and more docile individuals in a herd, or may breed new forms that have specially valued characteristics, such as thick wool or short horns.

In cereals such as wheat, rice, and millet, the first stages in domestication involved changes in the shape and size of the grains. For wheat and barley in Southwest Asia, grain size began to increase in the ninth millennium BCE. This stage could be described as semi-domestication, where human selection changes the plant's form, though the plant itself is not dependent on humans for reproduction.

Full domestication of plants involved morphological changes that meant the plants could no longer survive in the wild without human intervention. The most important change to cereals was in how the plants' seeds dispersed, or shattered [**5.6**, p. 102]. Grains that shattered

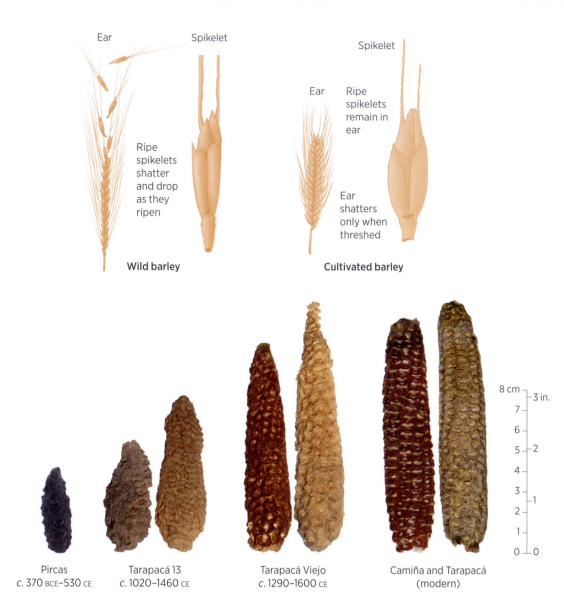

5.6 Wild and cultivated barley. The differences are slight, and the difficulty of identification is compounded by the fact that the archaeobotanist sees only fragments, never the complete ear, and the carbonized fragments have been distorted by being burned. The domesticated grains are a little fatter, and the rachis of the wild form is usually complete, while the tough rachis of the domesticated species of wild barley has to be broken by threshing.

Ear   Spikelet

Ripe spikelets shatter and drop as they ripen

Wild barley

Spikelet

Ear   Ripe spikelets remain in ear

Ear shatters only when threshed

Cultivated barley

5.7 Preserved maize cobs from prehistoric sites in the Atacama Desert of northern Chile. Early domesticated varieties were still small in size but had the advantage of kernels that remained attached to the cob when harvested. Over subsequent millennia, farmers developed larger maize cobs with more rows that steadily increased in size, first in the Americas before European contact, then later both in the Americas and beyond, eventually giving rise to modern varieties (far right, from Camiña and Tarapacá).

Pircas
c. 370 BCE–530 CE

Tarapacá 13
c. 1020–1460 CE

Tarapacá Viejo
c. 1290–1600 CE

Camiña and Tarapacá
(modern)

from the plants too soon (at the point of each plant called the **rachis**) would not be gathered by humans and sown the following season. Seeds of plants that tended to keep hold of their grains for longer were more likely to be gathered and planted by people, and this trait was therefore selected for in future generations. The eventual result of these changes was the emergence of distinct domesticated species. In Southwest Asia this process took a further 1,000 years to appear. It can have been only at that stage that sickles came systematically into use for harvesting the cereal heads. Full domestication is therefore the end result of a prolonged period of human–plant interaction and adaptation. In the Americas, the impact of selective breeding on grain size can be charted through time in preserved maize cobs from prehistoric sites in the Atacama Desert of northern Chile [**5.7**].

The success of the new food-producing economy, based on effective combinations, or packages, of domestic plants and animals, led to its relatively rapid expansion at the expense of hunting and gathering. As a consequence, plant and animal species were carried by humans to areas far beyond the geographical range of their wild ancestors.

rachis the tiny stalk that connects the cereal grain to the ear in plants, such as maize, wheat, and other cereals

Aside from the domesticated species themselves, cultivation, herding, and agriculture leave a range of other archaeological traces. We see combinations of technologies of cultivation (grindstones, sickles, storage facilities, and plows), and technologies of the landscape (field systems, forest clearances, terracing, and irrigation).

The Geography of Domestication

Only certain species of plants and animals are capable of successful domestication and of being combined into a full farming economy. Such animal domesticates include a few large terrestrial herbivores, notably sheep, goat, cattle, pig, horse, camel, water buffalo, and llama, and a few smaller herbivore and bird species, including chicken, turkey, rabbit, and guinea pig. These represent only a tiny percentage of the total available species, and it has been argued that of the 148 available big terrestrial herbivorous mammals, only fourteen have been successfully domesticated. Others do not breed readily in captivity or are very difficult to herd and manage.

Domesticated plant species are more numerous. Especially important among these plants are the large-seeded grasses: wheat and barley in Southwest Asia (Chapter 7); millet and rice in East Asia (Chapter 9); maize in Mesoamerica (Chapter 16); and pearl millet in Africa (Chapter 13). Along with root crops, such as manioc, yams, and potatoes, these constitute the staples that have proved an excellent source of carbohydrate and are grown in many parts of the world today. Successful farming economies, however, needed to combine these carbohydrate-yielding staples with sources of protein from pulses (beans, peas, and lentils) or animal products.

Research in recent decades has confirmed that agriculture arose independently during the postglacial epoch in at least seven different regions of the world—Southwest Asia, East Asia, the New Guinea highlands, sub-Saharan Africa, Andean South America, Central Mexico, and the eastern United States—at different times. Why should this have occurred?

Why Agriculture?

Early writers assumed that agriculture brought such clear advantages that the only obstacle to its development had been lack of knowledge: the earliest human societies did not have sufficient understanding of the plants and animals around them to undertake their domestication. It was envisaged that once invented, agriculture spread rapidly among prehistoric human communities, its progress stalling only where hostile environmental conditions intervened. This theory condemned hunter-gatherers to a marginal existence.

The assumption that hunter-gatherers were constantly threatened by starvation was emphatically refuted by a number of ethnographic studies. In one famous example, the anthropologist Richard Lee showed that among the Kalahari San of southwest Africa, population levels were kept well within the capacity of the available food supply. For the most part, the San had copious wild resources on which to rely and enjoyed far more leisure time than peasant agriculturalists or, indeed, than working adults in industrialized societies. The Danish economist Ester Boserup demonstrated the increasing amounts of labor that farmers needed to invest in order to increase the productivity of their fields. More intensive agriculture can feed more people, but at a cost of much greater labor input per person, since if a plot of land is planted more frequently, with shorter and shorter fallow intervals between, it is necessary to devote an increasing amount of agricultural labor to weeding, fertilizing, and irrigating the crop. This contested the widely held view put forward by Thomas Malthus,

5.8 Dental cavities in an adult found at Çatalhöyük, *c.* 7100 BCE. The increased consumption of carbohydrates from a cereal diet led to more cavities in teeth.

the English economist and demographer, in the eighteenth century, by showing that the threat of starvation does not necessarily cause people to limit their population growth; they can choose to increase the amount of food that is produced by increasing their labor.

The development of agriculturally based societies also had an adverse impact on human health. The reliance on a narrow range of cultivated plants in particular led to an increased incidence of dental decay [**5.8**] and nutritional deficiencies, and a decrease in average stature.

Such studies presented agriculture as an undesirable strategy that demanded greater labor input, so scholars began to look at factors that might have *forced* communities to adopt it. The two most frequently cited have been demographic increase and environmental change, or a combination of the two. Alternatively, it may have been that competition within societies played a significant role in the development of agriculture. Ethnography shows that social status and power are frequently achieved through establishing relations of indebtedness or dependency via principles of reciprocity. One of the most common ways that ambitious individuals seek to gain power and status is by throwing feasts, which create indebtedness among those who attend but cannot reciprocate. Feasting is a conspicuous public display of wealth and status, and generates a powerful incentive for ambitious individuals to increase their food resources. Many of the first **cultigens** may have been chosen for their value as luxury foods, and some, such as the chili peppers that are among the earliest domesticates in highland Mesoamerica, can hardly have played a role in fending off starvation, for they are flavorings or additives. Cultivation may, therefore, have been adopted in part in order to provide the specially valued kinds of food and drink deployed in competitive strategies.

Agriculture was possible only during the postglacial period. Ice Age climates were both too cold and too climatically unstable (with short-term oscillations) for the development of agricultural economies, even in warmer regions, such as Central Africa. Postglacial climates, by contrast, were sufficiently stable to allow the evolution of agriculture in vast areas that benefited from relatively warm, wet climates, or access to irrigation. Whatever the mechanism, more food allowed for population growth, which must quickly have passed the threshold of what could be supported by hunting and gathering.

The reasons for the adoption of agriculture were likely diverse, and probably included both strategies of social competition and longer-term pressures toward food production imposed by demographic growth that occurred in the postglacial world. Once the severe environmental constraints of the last Ice Age had relaxed, the intensification of relationships between human communities and their plant and animal food sources might be regarded as both inevitable and unsurprising.

Not all communities adopted agriculture, though, even when successful domestic species were easily within reach. We return again to the Jōmon hunter-gatherer populations in Japan, who maintained a sophisticated non-agricultural lifestyle long after farming had become established in Korea and China. That does not mean that they did not manipulate and manage their environment and food resources. On the contrary, there is clear evidence that they did. One striking illustration is the intentional transport of wild boar to such islands as Hachijō and Hokkaido, where they were not native. These interventions did not amount to domestication, however, and the agricultural transition came only in the fourth century BCE, at the end of the Jōmon period, when wet rice cultivation was introduced from the adjacent mainland.

cultigen a plant or crop cultivated by humans, as opposed to wild species

EXPANSION OF DOMESTICATION

Archaeology has shown that agriculture was developed independently in a few geographically dispersed centers of origin throughout the world [**5.9**]. While there are important regional variations, the dominant pattern during the postglacial is of the spread of domestication and the reduction of hunting and gathering, so much so that within the last few centuries hunting and gathering has mostly been restricted to marginal areas where farming is impossible, such as arid deserts or the frozen Arctic. The expansion of domesticates was particularly rapid across Eurasia, where east–west similarities in climate and day length imposed few constraints on the successful transfer of cultivated plants to new areas. Farming spread much more slowly north and south through the Americas and sub-Saharan Africa, where tropical forests and greater climatic variations intervened.

The two major causes of farming spread were its adoption by hunter-gatherers from their neighbors and the displacement of hunter-gatherers by expanding farmers. It is generally difficult to distinguish between these alternatives from archaeological evidence alone. Farming holds a demographic advantage over hunting and gathering, since it is able to support many more people per unit area, and where farmers and hunter-gatherers came into conflict over land, it was the former who usually prevailed.

Attempts have been made to associate the distributions of language families with demographic expansions that might be the consequence of farming. It is argued that the geographical patterning of related groups of languages, or language families, around the world might reflect the expansion of the initially small farming communities that spoke the ancestral forms of those languages. This approach has been applied with varying degrees of success in different regions of the world.

Such broad-scale models of farming spread have become popular in recent years, but evidence exists in many areas that farming may have been preceded or accompanied by

5.9 The origins and spread of agriculture. Agriculture was developed independently in several regions of the world at different times during the postglacial period. From these core areas, the productive new economy spread eventually to adjacent regions, allowing the development of more populous societies and leading ultimately to the demise of hunting and gathering in most of the world.

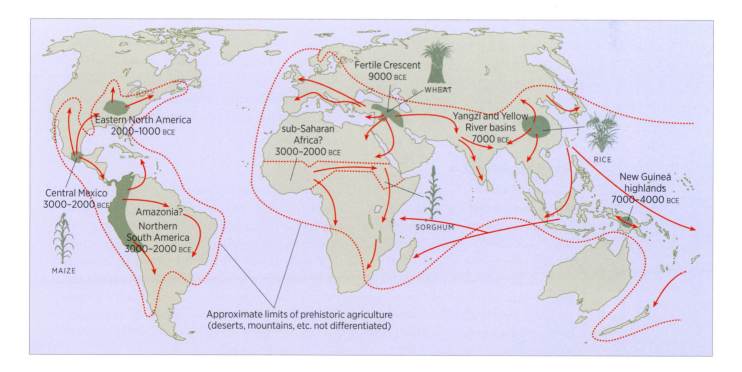

small-scale local adjustments through which postglacial communities responded to their changing environments. The pattern of subsistence change, therefore, may have been much more mosaic-like in character than is sometimes supposed. Nonetheless, a growing body of DNA analysis indicates that in many parts of the world, farming was introduced by colonist farmers and involved substantial movements of population. Genetic studies also confirm the rapid increase of human populations following the introduction of agriculture. Analysis of skeletal evidence at a global scale supports that, revealing what has been termed a Neolithic Demographic Transition, with much higher percentages of juvenile individuals represented among the dead than in previous hunter-gatherer populations. This indicates an increase in fertility and birth rate among early farming populations.

THE CONSEQUENCES OF AGRICULTURE

The consequences of agriculture were more than simply increased populations. Farming communities often involved different ways of living, which manifested in various ways, including settlement, material culture, and social stratification. It is important to mention here again that settled life and social stratification were not exclusive to farming communities but became more common with the development of farming.

Settlement

Most farming communities are distinguished by being sedentary, their members living in permanent farmsteads or villages that are occupied year-round. This required a shift from traveling between food sources to collecting food and bringing it back to a central place. The ability to store food is an important part of this change, and storage pits and ceramic containers are prominent features of both farming societies and sedentary hunter-gatherers.

The permanence of farming settlements encouraged greater investment in individual houses, which might be substantial structures built of timber, stone, mud brick, **pisé**, or wattle and daub. These, in turn, revolutionized human experience of daily life. Households took on greater importance, their affairs hidden from the community at large, while allowing the discreet accumulation of household wealth. There is a constant tension between the well-being of the community or village and the success of the individual household. Sedentary settlements also provide fixed points within the landscape and become a focus of identity (the place where you live), ethnicity (the community you belong to), and ancestry (where you and your forebears were born and buried).

Social Stratification

The development of larger communities also involved changes in social complexity. As group size increased with the adoption of agriculture, new types of social organization emerged.

Small-scale hunter-gatherer societies have flexible group membership, and disputes may often be resolved by one or other party leaving to join another group. Kinship remained the key structuring principle, but questions of authority and differences in status and possessions became more contentious. Prestige goods began to play an ever more prominent part in both signaling and creating social distinctions. Status that may at first have been based on individual achievement (for example, personal prowess as a hunter or war leader) became transferred to particular lineages or families. In many parts of the world, systems of hereditary leadership arose through processes such as these.

---

pisé rammed earth

But social complexity is not restricted to hereditary leadership. Rather, it takes many forms and is not the exclusive preserve of farmers, and evidence shows that cultural and ritual changes sometimes preceded the adoption of agriculture. A key site is Göbekli Tepe in southeast Turkey (see Chapter 6), where carved and decorated T-shaped pillars were set up in so-called shrines in the tenth millennium BCE by people who had begun cultivating cereals, though at this early stage they were more wild than domesticated in form. It has been argued that the new ideologies or religious beliefs represented here may have facilitated the gradual transition to an agricultural lifestyle. Recent discoveries in Southwest Asia more generally suggest that, in a reversal of the usual sequence, it was hunter-gatherers that came together in the first big, permanent communities to form extensive settlements, which only later needed to be fed by farming.

It is nonetheless clear that the higher population densities that agriculture could support, and the greater potential for generating a storable surplus, led in many regions to increasing inequalities in social status. These differences become manifest in the archaeological record through the evidence from graves and houses. Powerful and prosperous families may build grander houses than their neighbours, while differences in wealth and status can be expressed by the size and elaboration of a grave or burial monument, and by the objects that are placed with the dead. Underlying these more unequal societies are higher densities of populations and levels of food production, all stemming ultimately from the adoption of agriculture in different regions of the world.

Material Culture

Changes in material culture were an integral part of the transformation of human societies that involved the adoption of agriculture. Sedentism in itself allowed the accumulation of material goods, and the increasing adoption of containers made of pottery—heavy and fragile to transport—was a part of this trend. Yet many of the most conspicuous items of material culture were designed to be worn or carried on or around the body: beads and necklaces, polished stone axes, bracelets, and amulets. Textiles, too, are attested, albeit most often indirectly through spinning and weaving equipment, or from the designs on pottery or other objects that may reflect patterned cloth.

Technological change must also be viewed in social terms. The development of metallurgy, similarly to agriculture, was independently discovered in a number of different regions, and it too appears to have been driven by social rather than economic or technical need. It is significant that in Europe, for example, gold was worked alongside copper from the very inception of metallurgy (around 7,000 years ago), yet gold had little practical application, and the earliest copper objects took the form of personal ornaments. Metal tools replaced stone for everyday use in Europe only in the late second or first millennium BCE, 4,000 years after the first exploitation of copper and gold.

Agricultural Intensification

The success of the new agricultural economies led to an increase in human populations to levels far beyond those that had previously been sustainable by hunting and gathering. Where populations continued to grow, however, early farming communities sought new ways of increasing productivity, almost inevitably at the cost of ever greater labor input. Technologies of intensification took a number of forms, three of the most significant being irrigation, plowing, and terracing.

5.10 Plow agriculture.
The development of the plow from the fifth millennium BCE was restricted to areas of Africa and Eurasia where domestic cattle provided a suitable source of traction (indicated by the darker shading). Elsewhere—in southern Africa beyond the tsetse fly belt, and in the Americas where there were no suitable traction animals—cultivation continued to rely on human labor and the hoe.

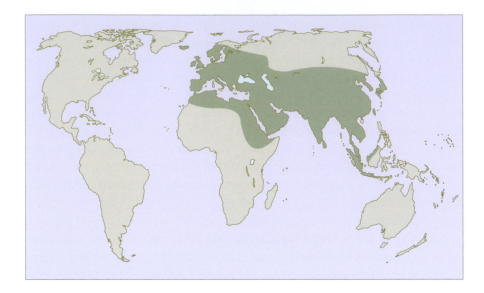

5.11 Agricultural terraces
cut into the steep sides of the mountains of Banau province in northern Luzon, the Philippines, increase the area of land available for cultivating rice.

Irrigation is a means of overcoming seasonal deficiencies in rainfall. It takes two primary forms: a) the storage of rainwater or floodwater in tanks and basins, and its release to the fields by a system of canals (for example, the traditional receding flood agriculture of the Nile Valley in Egypt); or b) the distribution of river water to the fields via canals (such as the irrigation agriculture of early Mesopotamia or coastal Peru). The cost implications of irrigation agriculture lie in the heavy labor input needed for the construction of channels, banks, sluices, and reservoirs, and the need for constant cleaning and repair.

Plowing generally requires animal traction (although humanly pulled plows have sometimes been used). As a result, plow agriculture developed only in areas where suitable animals were available, and traditional systems can accordingly be divided into two types: hoe agriculture and plow agriculture. The latter covers the greater part of Eurasia and North and northeast Africa; the former, whereby people work the fields by hand, unaided by animal traction, is characteristic of southern Africa and the Americas before European colonization [5.10].

Terracing is designed to increase the area of cultivable land in rough or mountainous terrain by the construction of tiers of dry-stone walling to support fertile but often narrow and restricted fields; terraces also stabilize slopes and limit erosion. Agricultural terraces are sometimes combined with irrigation canals, and spectacular landscapes of terraced fields are found in Andean South America and the Philippines (Luzon) [5.11]; they were also a regular feature of Greek and Roman farming in the Mediterranean region. Much earlier agricultural terraces, however, have been discovered at Dhra', in Jordan, where terrace walls were built to conserve soil and control water around 6000 BCE.

SUMMARY AND CONCLUSIONS

As the ice sheets melted, temperatures and sea level rose, and human communities took advantage of the new opportunities, growing rapidly in numbers where conditions allowed that. In several regions, population increase and the availability of suitable local plants and animals led to new patterns of exploitation, which resulted in the development of agriculture. In several other regions, hunter-gatherers, too, developed larger settlements and social complexity.

The greater productivity made possible by food production, however, ensured the further growth of farming communities and the extension of farming (and in many cases colonist farmers) to wider and wider areas. It came to dominate the world far beyond the confines of the original habitats of the domesticated plants and animals. In favored regions, notably lowland river valleys, the potential for high agricultural yields was linked to the development of the first state societies.

FURTHER READING

Barker, G. 2006. *The Agricultural Revolution in Prehistory: Why Did Foragers Become Farmers?* Oxford: Oxford University Press.

Bellwood, P. 2005. *The First Farmers: Origins of Agricultural Societies.* Oxford: Blackwell.

Finlayson, B. and Warren, G. M. 2010. *Changing Nature: Hunter-Gatherers, First Farmers and the Modern World.* London: Duckworth.

Mithen, S. 2003. *After the Ice: A Global Human History, 20,000–5000 BC.* London: Weidenfeld & Nicolson; Cambridge: Harvard University Press (2004).

Roberts, N. 1998. *The Holocene: An Environmental History.* 2nd edn. Oxford: Blackwell.

Southwest Asia: From Mobile Foraging to Settled Farming

6

Trevor Watkins

Environments and Landscapes, 20,000–9600 BCE 113

KEY THEME: CLIMATE CHANGE Environmental Shocks in Southwest Asia BCE 114

The Last Hunter-Gatherers: The Epipaleolithic in the Levant, 20,000–9600 BCE 115

KEY CONTROVERSY Explaining the Neolithic Revolution 119

KEY SITE Abu Hureyra: The Transition from Foraging to Farming 120

The Transition to Farming: The Early Aceramic Neolithic, 9600–8800 BCE 121

KEY SITE Jerf el Ahmar: A Neolithic Village 122

Early Farming Communities: The Later Aceramic Neolithic, 8800–6500 BCE 125

KEY SITE Göbekli Tepe: Religious Structures at a Central Place 126

KEY SITE Çatalhöyük 130

KEY THEME: DOMESTICATION A Story of Unintended Consequences 135

The Expansion of Farming, 6500–6000 BCE 135

Summary and Conclusions 136

Further Reading 13

One of the ceremonial buildings with carved stone pillars at the Early Neolithic site of Göbekli Tepe in southeastern Turkey, Enclosure D is the largest of a cluster of four, still under excavation.

TIMELINE Southwest Asia–From Mobile Foraging to Settled Farming

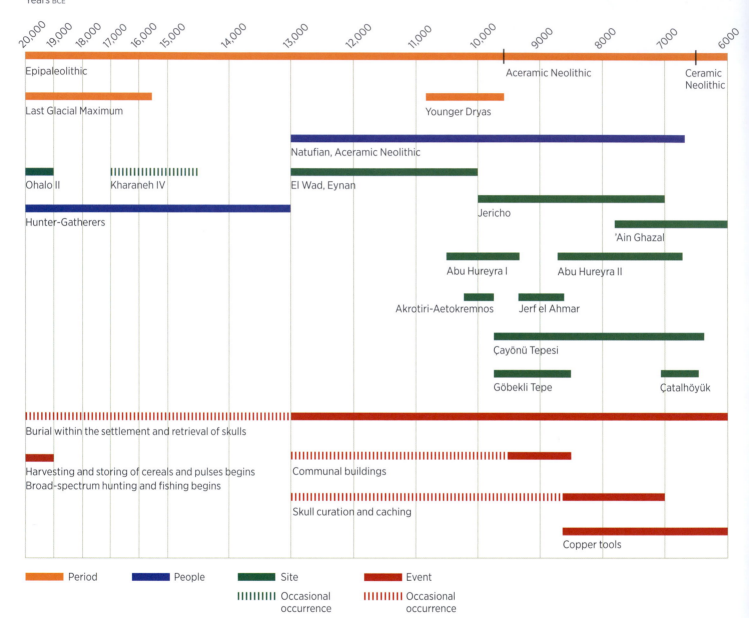

Years BCE

20,000	19,000	18,000	17,000	16,000	15,000	14,000	13,000	12,000	11,000	10,000	9,000	8,000	7,000	6,000

Epipaleolithic

Aceramic Neolithic

Ceramic Neolithic

Last Glacial Maximum

Younger Dryas

Natufian, Aceramic Neolithic

Ohalo II

Kharaneh IV

El Wad, Eynan

Hunter-Gatherers

Jericho

'Ain Ghazal

Abu Hureyra I

Abu Hureyra II

Akrotiri-Aetokremnos

Jerf el Ahmar

Çayönü Tepesi

Göbekli Tepe

Çatalhöyük

Burial within the settlement and retrieval of skulls

Harvesting and storing of cereals and pulses begins
Broad-spectrum hunting and fishing begins

Communal buildings

Skull curation and caching

Copper tools

Legend:
- Period
- People
- Site
- Event
- Occasional occurrence
- Occasional occurrence

In this chapter we turn to communities in Southwest Asia, which were the very first human societies to become settled and to have developed agriculture. We have divided this process into three phases. The first, lasting more than 15,000 years, saw the move from living in small mobile groups to relatively large, permanently settled communities, and the beginnings of cereal cultivation. The second phase involved a cascade of cultural, social, and economic changes associated with the development of agriculture: the cultivation of wheat and barley, followed by the domestication of sheep, goat, cattle, and pigs. The new economy allowed population density to accelerate, and settlements increased in size. These changes were unsustainable, however, and at the end of this period, around 6500 BCE, the biggest settlements declined dramatically. Consolidation came in the third phase, when smaller settlements of farmers appeared in parts of Southwest Asia beyond the core area. The expansion of smaller farming communities across a wider landscape may indicate that these settlements offered a more viable way of life. It may also have been a response to a period of rapid climate change and aridification at the end of the seventh millennium BCE.

- The Natufian societies who occupied the Levant during the final stages of the last Ice Age show how complex hunters and gatherers could develop permanent settlements without agriculture.

- Göbekli Tepe in Turkey demonstrates how the last of these hunter-gatherer communities began to build monuments and ceremonial centers for large-scale seasonal gatherings.

- In Southwest Asia, the transition to a fully agricultural economy took place over a period of several millennia, leading eventually to the establishment of a mixed farming economy of domesticated plants and animals late in the Pre-Pottery Neolithic period, around 7000 BCE.

- The substantial early farming settlements that developed in Southwest Asia later collapsed, and smaller farming communities expanded out into new regions. We can compare this to the collapse of great centers in Mesoamerica (Chapter 16).

ENVIRONMENTS AND LANDSCAPES, 20,000–9600 BCE

Within Southwest Asia [6.1, p. 114] there is a great variety of landscapes and climates. In the 1940s, the American archaeologist Robert Braidwood set out to find sites where he could investigate the transition from hunting and gathering to farming. It was well known that the earliest cities had developed in the Mesopotamian lowlands, but the wild plants and animals that were first domesticated would not have been found there in the early postglacial period, rather in the mountainous zones to the north and east: the Taurus and Zagros ranges. Braidwood called this arc "the hilly flanks of the Fertile Crescent." Around that arc there is sufficient rainfall to sustain open woodland of oak and pistachio, with plenty of space for wild wheat and barley, a variety of pulses—peas, beans, lentils, and chickpeas—and a range of fruits and nuts. These hilly flanks as well as parts of Central Anatolia constitute the core area of transformation that occurred from the end of the Paleolithic. This must have been where farming in Southwest Asia first began.

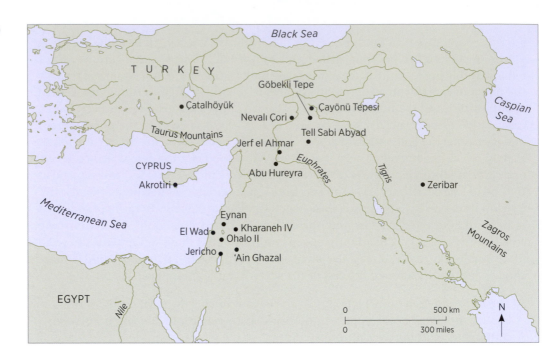

6.1 Southwest Asia. Map showing major physical features and sites discussed in the text.

The period from 20,000 years ago saw significant changes in climate (see Key Theme box: Environmental Shocks in Southwest Asia), environments, and the natural distribution of key plant and animal species [**6.2**]. After the recovery from the Last Glacial Maximum, there was a relatively short but quite sharp return to colder conditions, known as the Younger Dryas phase, between about 10,800 and 9600 BCE. Following the Younger Dryas, there was a rapid recovery of temperature, coinciding with the flourishing of the early **aceramic** Neolithic period. But in the seventh millennium BCE, when permanent settlements begin to appear, the climate in Southwest Asia became both cooler and drier.

aceramic a time or place in which pottery was not created, traded, or used; also known as preceramic, and prepottery

---

KEY THEME: CLIMATE CHANGE Environmental Shocks in Southwest Asia

Within the time range of this chapter there were three periods of rapid climate cooling. The first was the Last Glacial Maximum (LGM), between about 21,000 and 15,500 BCE, in Southwest Asia coinciding with the earliest part of the Epipaleolithic period (20,000 to 9600 BCE). The second was the Younger Dryas in the last millennium of the Pleistocene, 10,800–9600 BCE, and the third was between 6600 and 6000 BCE. These periods involved returns to colder conditions but affected different regions in different ways.

For example, while the Younger Dryas was thought to have caused a serious environmental deterioration all around the hilly flanks of the Fertile Crescent, adding to the difficulties of the late Epipaleolithic community at **Abu Hureyra**, in some other places, the cooler temperatures meant that less moisture was lost through solar evaporation. In southeast Turkey, where the Younger Dryas was believed to have instigated the loss of wild grasses and cereals, we now know of permanent settlements that were established at the height

of this cold period. This reminds us that climatic changes have diverse effects. It has been suggested, for instance, that the reduction in woodland seen in the pollen diagrams of the Younger Dryas phase may have made more space for grasses, cereals, and legumes.

While varied, the effects of these periods of cooling had huge consequences for human life. The rapid climate change between 6600 and 6000 BCE coincided with the end of the aceramic Neolithic, the implosion of the South Levantine mega-sites and the dispersal of population into smaller settlements, and the switch to wide-ranging pastoralist economies in the ceramic Neolithic. The large communities of the late aceramic Neolithic, dependent on intensive mixed farming, may indeed have been pushed over the edge by the onset of the rapid climate change event, resolving the social pressures by forming new, smaller communities, and the economic pressures by revised, flexible farming and pastoralist strategies.

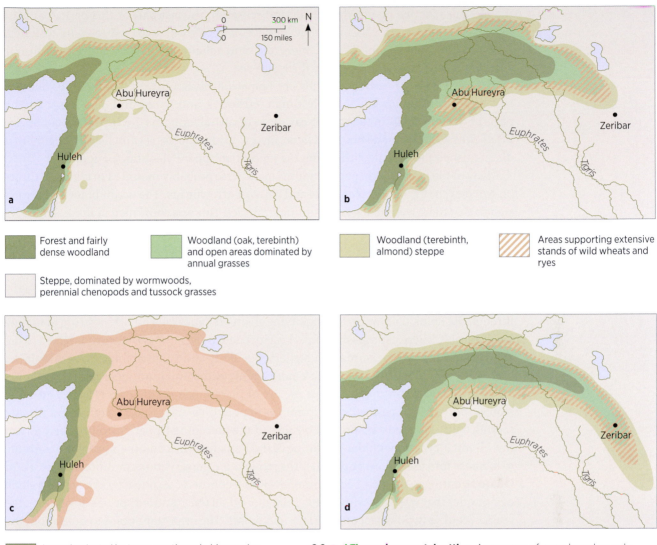

Forest and fairly dense woodland

Woodland (oak, terebinth) and open areas dominated by annual grasses

Woodland (terebinth, almond) steppe

Areas supporting extensive stands of wild wheats and ryes

Steppe, dominated by wormwoods, perennial chenopods and tussock grasses

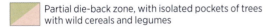

Areas dominated by trees, mostly probably growing as thin scatters

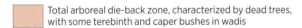

Partial die-back zone, with isolated pockets of trees with wild cereals and legumes

Total arboreal die-back zone, characterized by dead trees, with some terebinth and caper bushes in wadis

6.2 a–d The environmental setting. A sequence of maps based on only three sources of environmental data: Lake Huleh, the settlement of Abu Hureyra, and Lake Zeribar, in a high intermontane valley in the Zagros Mountains. **a**) the Last Glacial Maximum (*c.* 21,000–15,500 BCE): the woodland zone maps the restricted zone where wild cereals and pulses would have been found; **b**) recovery of the open woodland (and therefore cereals and pulses) by around 14,000 BCE; **c**) the cooler, drier Younger Dryas phase may have seen a return to Last Glacial Maximum conditions in some regions (*c.* 10,800 BCE); and **d**) the recovery in the early postglacial period (from 9600 BCE).

THE LAST HUNTER-GATHERERS: THE EPIPALEOLITHIC IN THE LEVANT, 20,000–9600 BCE

The story of the major transformation in how people lived their lives starts in the **Epipaleolithic** and the beginning of the Neolithic. People changed from living in small, mobile forager groups to living together in substantially higher numbers in permanent settlements. They began by putting more and more emphasis on harvesting and storing the seeds of a wide range of wild plant species. As the period progressed, they moved to concentrating on

Epipaleolithic a period between the Upper Paleolithic and Neolithic, often marked by the production of small stone bladelets

the most productive plants: the cereals and pulses. In the last part of this period, at least in some sections of the core area, they had begun to cultivate two or three types of cereal and some pulses. As people became more and more reliant on mixed farming, the cultural, social, and economic changes came thick and fast.

The most widely researched regions of Epipaleolithic Southwest Asia are the southern Levant, specifically Jordan, the Palestinian territories, and Israel, and, to a lesser extent, parts of western Syria. In the early excavations of cave sites, it was the appearance of microliths—tiny, skillfully made flint bladelets only 25–50 millimeters (1–2 inches) in length—that distinguished the Epipaleolithic from the preceding Upper Paleolithic period.

Many of the precisely shaped microliths made were probably mounted in twos and threes on wooden shafts to form the points and barbs of arrowheads. The use of bows and arrows signals that there were changes in hunting strategies. This was confirmed in the assemblages of animal bones found at sites in the southern Levant: the ratio of bones from large herd species, such as wild cattle (which are relatively rare finds), red deer, and fallow deer, decreases relative to the increasing numbers of small animals, such as tortoise, hare, fox, and birds. The major source of meat was the hunting of gazelle, which are lean and agile animals, about the size of sheep or goats. These ratios between larger and smaller animals continue to fluctuate through the Epipaleolithic period, signifying greater reliance on a broad spectrum of mainly small species. These changes may have been needed as big animals became depleted in the area around their more permanent settlements. Birds and small mammals, such as hares and foxes, reproduce quickly and can more readily withstand hunting pressure.

We also have indirect evidence of the use of plant foods in the form of heavy grinding stones, mortars, and pestles. Some examples of pounding and grinding equipment for processing hard, dry seeds are present on sites of the preceding Upper Paleolithic period, but their frequency rises with the beginning of the Epipaleolithic, and their numbers continue to increase into the following periods. The remarkable preservation conditions at the site of **Ohalo II**, dating to the very beginning of the Epipaleolithic (*c.* 20,000 BCE), document a small community that was harvesting seeds from more than one hundred species of large-seeded grasses, cereals (wild wheat and barley), and pulses. The important point to note about the trend toward using such species is that they were harvested annually and were then storable food resources. These stores meant that groups could stay in one place for longer periods of time, while they processed and consumed their stockpiled harvests. A well-chosen location at the interface of complementary ecological zones meant that different resources could be accessed from a single place.

Through the Epipaleolithic, there was a distinct trend toward seasonal settlement and then toward sedentism. From the early Epipaleolithic there are several substantial sites, which were probably places of seasonal aggregation where groups from around the region came together for a time. Kharaneh IV, in an oasis area of pools and wetlands in the north of Jordan, for example, became a low mound covering 2.2 hectares (5.4 acres), its surface covered with millions of discarded flints. Preliminary indications suggest that it was occupied over long seasons. A few of these large aggregation sites have also produced ceremonial burials. We should think of them as supporting a variety of social and symbolic activities that held the wider community together. The groups who met at aggregation sites, such as Kharaneh IV, were also engaged in social relationships with other, more distant groups, as is demonstrated by the frequency of finds of marine shell beads from both the Mediterranean, around 200 kilometers (125 miles) away, and the Red Sea, around 400 kilometers (250 miles) away.

The Natufians in the Late Epipaleolithic Levant

In the Late Epipaleolithic in the southern Levant, the Natufian culture, dated between 13,000 and 9600 BCE, represents a major change. Natufians began to live in permanent settlements before the wholesale development of agriculture, although they invested more in the processing of stored cereals and pulses. They are well known for their sickle blades, used to cut cereal stems, and for being at the cusp between hunter-gatherers and agriculturalists.

Some Natufian occupations are cave sites, most already in use for many tens of thousands of years but demonstrating significant differences from those of previous Paleolithic occupations. The cave of **el Wad**, in a dry valley in the Mount Carmel hills in the north of Israel, is a good example. Natufian groups were larger and needed more space than the cave could offer. They terraced the slope outside, and built small, circular, stone-built huts with paved floors both inside and out. There were also two series of burials at el Wad cave. In the early excavations at the site in the 1920s, the English archaeologist Dorothy Garrod found both single and multiple interments. Some of the bodies had been wearing elaborate head coverings, cloaks, or other clothes onto which were sewn hundreds of small, cylindrical dentalium seashells. Shells, pierced animal teeth, and bird bones were also found as parts of bracelets, armlets, belts, or necklaces. Recent excavations and research have shown that Garrod's cluster of burials belong early in the Natufian period. The investigations have discovered a second cluster of later Natufian burials outside the cave.

Similar cemeteries have been found at several other Natufian base-camp type settlements. In a few burials the skull is missing, and the careful observations made during excavation indicate that the grave had been reopened in order to remove the skull from the buried body. At Hilazon Tachtit, another cave site in Israel, a number of burials accumulated in the late Natufian period. One of them, that of an elderly, disabled female, is remarkable. She was buried at one side of a burial pit that was much bigger than usual, and around her were laid at least fifty complete tortoise shells, the foreleg of a wild boar, a wing bone of a golden eagle, the tail bones of a wild cow, the pelvis of a leopard, and the skulls of two martens, as well as a complete human foot. The fill of the grave above the body included a mass of animal bone, mostly of gazelle, that seems to represent the remains of feasting events that had accompanied and followed the burial rituals. Because of the peculiarity of the burial, the excavators suggest the female individual was a shaman.

Mortars and pestles have been found at all the larger, and some of the smaller, Natufian sites. Heavy ground-stone equipment for the pounding and grinding of hard seeds was present at some sites from the beginning of the Upper Paleolithic. But the numbers of such implements on Natufian sites represent a big step up in their use. There are small, cup-shaped mortars carved in the rock surface, others cut into boulders, and beautifully shaped, smaller mortars made from black basalt. In parallel with the increase in the frequency of pounding and grinding equipment, there is a marked increase in the occurrence of sickle gloss (a polishing of the surface through use in cutting the silica-rich stems of cereals) on microlithic blades [**6.3**, **6.4**, p. 118]. The implication is that these late Epipaleolithic groups invested more in the processing of stored cereals and pulses. A recent study of Natufian sickle flints has concluded that they were used to harvest cultivated wild cereals, and a site in northeast Jordan has produced charred remains that have been identified as having been accidentally burned.

In parallel with the intensification in the productivity of wild crops, the analysis of the animal bones from el Wad shows a distinct change from earlier Epipaleolithic sites. As the

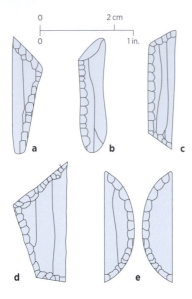

6.3 ABOVE LEFT **Microliths** are tiny, carefully shaped tools made on bladelets struck from small cores. These examples are all from the southern Levant; **a**, **b**, **c**, and **d** were probably parts of arrowheads in the early Epipaleolithic, while **e** is a lunate (crescent-shaped microlith), characteristic of the Natufian, the late Epipaleolithic of the region.

6.4 ABOVE RIGHT **Natufian stone implements.** Artifact Cluster 11, from Phase 1 of the Natufian site of Wadi Hammeh 27, including a fine basalt mortar and two pestles, one of which is carefully shaped.

group living there was permanently resident, their hunting and trapping of animals for meat were necessarily focused on the immediate catchment area: while they still relied on the hunting of gazelle, they invested much more than their predecessors in snakes, lizards, tortoises, and birds.

In order to sustain their permanently settled communities, Natufian groups were adept at locating their settlements within the landscape so that several different and complementary ecological zones were accessible. The site of **Eynan** in the far north of Israel illustrates this very well. The village was established in the open, and its circular stone houses were built and rebuilt throughout the three millennia of the late Epipaleolithic period (c. 13,000–10,000 BCE) [**6.5**]. The settlement was located at the foot of the hills of a basin, which at that time had a shallow lake at its center. The Eynan community could fish in the lake, take amphibians and waterfowl from its margins, and hunt and gather around the basin and up into the hills above the site.

Whether open sites, such as Eynan, or cave-mouth settlements, such as el Wad, Natufian living spaces represent a step change: in the size and permanence of the groups that occupied them, in the intensification of the use of cereals and pulses, and in their attention to ritual and symbolism. The Natufian sites show an important transformation, where people began to develop plant cultivation alongside increased sedentism and the use of a rich material culture to distinguish their dead.

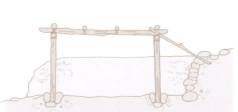

6.5 Eynan. Structure 131 was an open, D-shaped building with a complex timber roof. All sorts of materials were found on the floor, but as if deliberately deposited when the building was buried, rather than as a result of everyday use.

Archaeologists have long sought to explain the process of the Neolithic transformation. In the 1960s, leading processual archaeologists—who asserted an explicitly scientific framework of archaeological method and theory, with hypotheses rigorously tested, and promoted an emphasis on culture process, understanding how and why change occurred, rather than simple description—argued for an ecological–evolutionary underpinning. For example, Kent Flannery argued that the process began in the Epipaleolithic period as an adaptation to the environmental pressure of population growth as people began to live more sedentary lives. His broad-spectrum revolution hypothesis involved the broadening of the range of hunted and trapped species and the harvesting of storable plant foods, leading to the further intensification of productivity by cultivating crops and herding selected species of domesticated animals.

Since the middle of the twentieth century, more information has been accumulated, more sophisticated methods of investigation and analysis have been developed, and new techniques of investigation have been applied, such as stable-isotope analysis of strontium, calcium, and nitrogen in human and animal teeth and bones. Perhaps more significantly, different theoretical perspectives have been proposed. The debate was widened by two influential thinkers and authors in particular, Ian Hodder and Jacques Cauvin. Both Hodder and Cauvin rejected the ecological–evolutionary, processualist approach. They encouraged more focus on the great cultural and social changes, and the very evident symbolism in material representation and in symbolic rituals. Researchers today come from many disciplinary backgrounds, but all would agree that the transformation process was more complex than simply a series of economic adaptations to external environmental pressures. Human communities changed most aspects of their way of life, making individually small innovations here or there, or adjusting to many kinds of pressures. Over a period of some 15,000 years, human society, its cultural modes, as well as the technology and economics of subsistence, were transformed at a pace, and to a degree, without precedent in all the tens and hundreds of millennia of previous human history.

The Epipaleolithic beyond the Southern Levant

Dorothy Garrod, the excavator of el-Wad, also ventured into the Zagros Mountain valleys of northeast Iraq. Her expeditions identified a cultural sequence that broadly parallels that of the Levant: following a classic Upper Paleolithic, there is an Epipaleolithic, typified by its microlithic chipped-stone industry. The climate in the Zagros Mountain region during the Last Glacial Maximum cold phase was harsh, and it seems that the area was scarcely populated for several thousand years.

In southeast Turkey we have very little knowledge of the Epipaleolithic period in general. The best documented site is Abu Hureyra in northern Syria (see Key Site box: Abu Hureyra: The Transition from Foraging to Farming, p. 120), which was occupied from the end of the Epipaleolithic to the early Neolithic, and was excavated in the early 1970s as part of a salvage archaeology project in the Euphrates Valley. The first settlers had to contend with the onset of the Younger Dryas on their somewhat marginal environment by extending the range of plant species that they exploited and by beginning to cultivate wild rye.

Further west, we have only isolated glimpses of the presence of Epipaleolithic groups. At Pınarbaşı in Central Anatolia, a small sounding below the Neolithic levels found an Epipaleolithic occupation with burials containing bodies accompanied by red ocher, tortoise carapaces, and many dentalium shell decorations, closely reminiscent of—and contemporary with—Natufian burials in the southern Levant.

In Cyprus, the earliest evidence for human occupation dates to end of the Epipaleolithic, around 10,000 BCE, at the rock-shelter site of **Akrotiri-Aetokremnos** on the south coast of the island. In the uppermost layer there are hearths, some chipped-stone tools and, among the animal bones, a handful from wild boar. Zoologists agree that there were no indigenous wild boar on Cyprus, so the wild pig must have been intentionally introduced. It seems, then,

KEY SITE Abu Hureyra: The Transition from Foraging to Farming

A cherished aim of archaeologists studying the origins of agriculture in Southwest Asia has been to excavate a site where the transition from foraging to farming could be directly observed. Abu Hureyra, a prehistoric settlement on a bluff at the edge of the Euphrates Valley in northern Syria seemed to be just such a site [**6.6**]. Only two seasons of salvage excavation were possible before the site was drowned, but intensive wet sieving and flotation produced tons of floral and faunal data that fueled a quarter of a century of investigation and research on the environment, the plant foods, and the exploitation of animals.

The Epipaleolithic Settlement

The remains of a small Epipaleolithic settlement were found under the center of the later aceramic Neolithic village of Abu Hureyra. This earlier settlement consisted of round houses sunk into the ground, their thatched roofs supported on wooden poles [**6.7**]. The villagers hunted gazelle, a few wild cattle, sheep, and a now-extinct species of zebra-sized ass

(*Equus hemionus*). They gathered a great range of plants from a variety of different ecological zones, including wild cereals and grasses. The location of the village was well chosen to allow the exploitation of the complementary resources of the river, the floodplain, seasonal watercourse valleys in the semi-arid zone, and the moist steppe.

The settlement was established about 1,000 years before the end of the Epipaleolithic period, around 11,000 BCE, just before the Younger Dryas cold phase. It was situated at a critically marginal location, and the effect of the cooler, drier climate is evident in the plant foods collected. As cereals and trees, such as plum and almond, began to decline, people extended the range of small-seeded grasses and other plants that they gathered. These were harder to collect, required more processing, and were less nutritious. As conditions continued to deteriorate, the inhabitants turned to the intensive cultivation of wild rye, a cereal that could tolerate the harsh conditions. Nevertheless, the community's efforts were not enough: the settlement was abandoned before the

6.6 The site of Abu Hureyra. The Neolithic settlement covered a limestone promontory jutting into the floodplain of the Euphrates (in the foreground).

that hunter-gatherers established a breeding stock of a wild species in order to make up for the island's impoverished fauna. And that suggests that these were not short visits, but that there was an organized colonization of the island, making it economically habitable for hunter-gatherers.

Epipaleolithic sites outside the southern Levant, therefore, offer another picture of transition, this time in more marginal environments. At Abu Hureyra, occupants began to cultivate wild rye to supplement their diets during the onset of the Younger Dryas. This was also a time of exploration and expansion, as the island of Cyprus was occupied by hunter-gatherer communities for the first time.

6.7 At the bottom of Trench E, the excavators dug through more than 1 meter (3 feet) of Epipaleolithic occupation to reveal the circular sunken floors of some of the earliest houses The black holes are the cavities left where wooden roof-supporting posts had decayed. Beyond, at a higher level, is part of a rectangular mud-brick house of the aceramic Neolithic period.

end of the Younger Dryas. The site of Abu Hureyra, however, was reoccupied several centuries later, around 8800 BCE, in the later aceramic Neolithic period.

The Aceramic Neolithic Settlement

After re-occupation, the aceramic Neolithic settlement rapidly grew to become a large village, the remains of which were found wherever the archaeologists dug around the modern houses and village cemetery. The population was substantial, probably numbering in the thousands, making Abu Hureyra one of the largest settlements of the aceramic Neolithic period. It was also long-lived, having been abandoned only early in the ceramic Neolithic period, when pottery was coming into use, stretching over some 2,000 years.

The mud-brick buildings of Abu Hureyra were rectangular and seem to have consisted of storage rooms at ground-floor level, with living accommodation on an upper floor. The ground-floor rooms were closed cells, and must have been reached from above by trapdoors and ladders. These upper stories were more lightly built. As buildings became decrepit and were replaced time and again, the whole settlement gradually accumulated several meters of stratified building remains and occupation debris.

The first inhabitants of the aceramic Neolithic settlement brought with them domesticated wheat, barley, and pulses. They relied for much of their meat on the hunting of gazelle (and smaller amounts of wild ass and cattle), much as their Epipaleolithic predecessors had done. There were also relatively small numbers of sheep bones, representing a population in the early stages of domestication. The sheep were morphologically wild, but the age and sex profiles suggest that the population was being managed. Then, quite suddenly, the high percentage of gazelle bones drops to a very low figure, while the small numbers of sheep rise sharply to become the dominant component among the animal bones. Sheep herding became a major element in the economy, and the hunting of gazelle in particular became an activity of minor economic significance.

This range of information provided by Abu Hureyra gives a unique insight into the changes affecting a community at the transition from foraging to farming. The excavations reveal that the process was not sudden, but a more gradual shift extending over several centuries.

THE TRANSITION TO FARMING: THE EARLY ACERAMIC NEOLITHIC, 9600–8800 BCE

The beginning of the Neolithic period (from 9600 BCE) marked significant changes. The smooth progress that can be traced in chipped-stone toolmaking [**6.12**, p. 124] is not mirrored by the settlements. There is an almost complete disruption of settlement location; in the southern Levant, none of the early aceramic Neolithic sites had been occupied in the previous late Epipaleolithic period. The number of these, their size, and the solidity of their architecture point to continued growth in general population density throughout the hilly flanks of the Fertile Crescent, and to a significant increase in the size of communities.

At some sites, such as Jerf el Ahmar in northern Syria (see Key Site box: Jerf el Ahmar: A Neolithic Village, p. 122), we can see that the settlement was organized to a plan, with communal buildings and activity areas at the center. When in the 1950s Kathleen Kenyon,

KEY SITE Jerf el Ahmar: A Neolithic Village

How were early Neolithic villages in Southwest Asia organized? What did their houses look like? And did they have other buildings, such as shrines or storage facilities? For an answer to these questions we can look to **Jerf el Ahmar**, a small village in northern Syria on the west bank of the Euphrates, occupied during the early aceramic Neolithic period (9600–8800 BCE).

Because Jerf el Ahmar was not inhabited after the aceramic Neolithic, archaeologists were able to explore the settlement extensively, seeing how the buildings related to one another. Houses of the early village, dating to the first centuries of the aceramic Neolithic period, had quite diverse plans. Some were simple, small, circular structures built from cut lumps of soft limestone and mud mortar. If more space was needed, another circular structure was stuck against the first.

Over the many centuries that the settlement was occupied, it was rebuilt a number of times. On each occasion, it followed a similar general plan, although the village center shifted from time to time. The location that was chosen was a low, rounded hill at the edge of the floodplain. In order to cope with the sloping terrain, the villagers terraced the hillside with stone walls to provide level space for their houses. There was a broad formula to the village, and the implication of the repetitions of this formula is that, even if the ordinary houses were the work of their owners, the overall layout and the construction of the terraces and the central buildings were carried out by all the villagers together.

An Enigmatic Communal Building

Whenever the village was rebuilt, space was made for an open central area. One example contained a massive, circular, subterranean structure, 8–9 meters (26–30 feet) in diameter, much larger than any of the individual houses; its floor was fully 2 meters (6.6 feet) below the ground level [**6.8**]. Two-thirds of the building was divided by mud-brick walls into large, doorless cells. These stored lentils and barley, with some

6.8 This large subterranean structure existed at the center of the earliest village at the site of Jerf el Ahmar and was originally roofed. At the end of its life, the roof was dismantled and the supporting posts were pulled out.

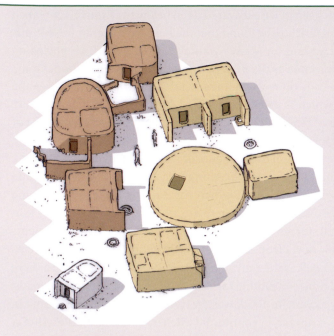

6.9 LEFT Several buildings clustered around the large, communal storage structure with its circular roof close to ground level and trapdoor access. These buildings were larger than the ordinary houses, and were equipped with multiple sets of quernstones, basins, kneading slabs, and ovens.

6.10 BELOW LEFT A room in one of the communal kitchen buildings beside the communal storage structure. In the foreground there are large limestone basins; in the middle of the room are three grinding slabs in stone settings; against the rear wall are two large, flat limestone slabs (more than 60 centimeters, 24 inches, in diameter), the surfaces of which were polished smooth by kneading. A large oven was built against the outside wall of the kitchen, which was supplemented by a small hearth, perhaps for keeping food warm, that lay against an internal wall.

traces of rye, too. Their capacity was so large that the building probably served as a communal storage facility shared by the whole village: a storage space as well as a special place for community ceremonies.

Around the subterranean circular structure, there were rectangular, multi-roomed buildings that were larger and a good deal more formal than the ordinary houses [**6.9**, **6.10**]. They contained heavy quernstones (coarse stone blocks used for hand-grinding cereals and other materials) set into the floor. If there was communal storage of cereals, it seems that there was also communal milling of the grain in preparation

for cooking. There were large fireplaces in spaces among the small houses, suggesting that groups of households cooked together.

Among the small objects found within the settlement were two flat stone plaques that have motifs or signs incised on both surfaces [**6.11**]. We now know of similar plaques, and identical signs, from a number of contemporary sites in northern Syria, and two examples from Göbekli Tepe. It is thought that these may have been a non-textual prototype of written communication (similar to mathematical symbols representing ideas rather than specific words).

6.11 ABOVE Small enough to fit in the palm of the hand, one of the stone plaques with incised signs on each face. Snakes with triangular heads resemble those carved in relief on monoliths at Göbekli Tepe. There is also a schematic quadruped with a long tail.

6.12 Projectile points of the early aceramic Neolithic. These one-piece arrowheads replaced the microlithic technology of the Epipaleolithic. The points of the later aceramic Neolithic are generally much larger, and indicate a switch from bow and arrow to thrown spears.

the British archaeologist, excavated deep below the Bronze Age walled city of ancient Jericho, she found that the long-lived aceramic Neolithic settlement had had a massive wall and a rock-cut ditch enclosing much the same area as the Bronze Age city walls. At one point, on the inside of the wall, there was a huge, solid, cylindrical stone tower, the purpose of which is difficult to define [**6.13**]. Around its base there was a cluster of large, doorless **cells**, which perhaps were some sort of communal storage facility.

One of the earliest of the sequence of sizable, circular, subterranean, communal buildings at Jerf el Ahmar was designed also to include generous storage cells, from which the excavators recovered some traces of cereals in one cell and lentils in another. There are small, circular structures that have been interpreted as communal storage cells also at Wadi Feynan and other settlements in southern Jordan. Such sites show how life in early aceramic Neolithic settlements seems to have been lived communally. As well as the centralized storage of harvested crops, there is evidence that the laborious and time-consuming tasks of grinding and pounding cereals, and even of the preparation and cooking of food, was carried out by groups of people in public areas or, in the case of Jerf el Ahmar, in communal kitchen buildings. Jerf el Ahmar was not unique in possessing large, subterranean, communal buildings at the heart of the community; at two other contemporary settlements on the same stretch of the River Euphrates there were similar, but not identical, structures.

The most striking discovery of the last thirty years, however, must be the site of **Göbekli Tepe** (see Key Site box: Göbekli Tepe: Religious Structures at a Central Place, p. 126). Its

cell in a dwelling, a walled space without a doorway; a common example is storage cells under the floor of a building

6.13 The early aceramic Neolithic tower at Jericho. The tower was built of solid stone set in mud mortar and was attached to the inside of the wall of the settlement, rather than the outside, as would be expected if it had a defensive role.

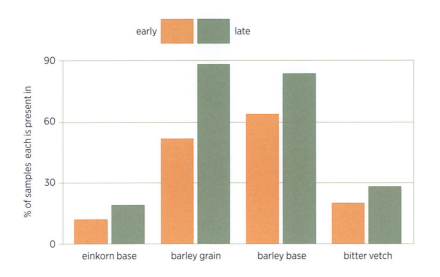

early late

6.14 Trend toward cultivation. Jerf el Ahmar was occupied during the early aceramic Neolithic, and over the centuries the presence of einkorn spikelet base, barley grain, barley spikelet base, and bitter vetch seeds increased, which researchers interpret as suggesting a trend toward cultivation. Base refers to the base of the spikelet, which connects the grain to the stalk.

massive, circular, subterranean enclosures repeat the pattern of the communal buildings of the settlements in the Euphrates Valley. It demonstrates once again how ritual and ceremony at a communal level played a key role in enabling greater numbers of people to live together.

Pre-Domestic Cultivation

During this earlier phase of the aceramic Neolithic period, cereal grains become more and more abundant in archaeological samples through time, suggesting that cereals increased in importance. All around the arc of the hilly flanks zone, communities were focusing their efforts on a smaller range of more productive species, especially the cereals einkorn wheat, emmer, and barley [**6.14**], and legumes, such as lentils, peas, beans, and chickpeas. It is now becoming clear that there were different specializations in different regions, depending on which species were locally available.

George Willcox, an archaeobotanist, has identified five regions around the hilly flanks zone where cultivation of a somewhat different suite of crops had begun in this period.

EARLY FARMING COMMUNITIES: THE LATER ACERAMIC NEOLITHIC, 8800–6500 BCE

Once we cross from the earlier into the later aceramic Neolithic, the tempo of demographic, social, cultural, and economic change increases sharply. By the beginning of the later aceramic Neolithic, the earlier centuries and millennia of pre-domestic cultivation had begun to produce changes in shape, size, and structure that mark the domesticated forms of wheat and barley. Shortly afterwards, we encounter the earliest examples of domesticated sheep and goat across the northern and eastern parts of the hilly flanks zone [**6.18**, p. 128]. The first domesticated pig and domesticated cattle are almost as early.

The point in time when domesticated animals can be recognized, however, tells us only that communities were controlling the breeding of their livestock. At this stage, they continued to hunt, but over the following centuries they gradually came to rely more on their flocks and herds, and less and less on hunting. It is only from about 7500 BCE that communities seem to have been more or less completely reliant on a developed and effective mixed

KEY SITE Göbekli Tepe: Religious Structures at a Central Place

Göbekli Tepe sits on a bare limestone ridge northeast of Urfa, in southeast Turkey [**6.15**]. It commands an extraordinary panorama: south toward the rolling Mesopotamian plains, east to the broad, fertile basin at the headwaters of the Balikh river, and northeast toward the basalt plateau that is Karaca Dağ, where einkorn wheat still grows wild. But although the 300-meter-diameter (1,000 feet) mound is formed of at least 15 meters (48 feet) of cultural debris of human origin, it is not a normal settlement mound.

What the excavators have found are large ceremonial buildings and extraordinary sculpted monoliths. The cultural debris and the radiocarbon dates fix the site in the early aceramic Neolithic and just into the beginning of the later aceramic Neolithic (9600–8000 BCE). Whoever built and used these structures, and carved the vividly decorated monoliths, lived by hunting wild animals, but we also know that wild cereals were being harvested in the region around Göbekli Tepe, and many grindstones were found at the site that must have been used to process them.

The people who came to build the structures and carve and erect the monoliths probably lived in the surrounding region. It may have been a place of seasonal ceremonial activity and feasting. The symbolism of the architecture and of the carved motifs at Göbekli Tepe echoes other sites in southeast Turkey and north Syria, for example at Jerf el Ahmar. To date, five large circular enclosures have been almost completely excavated, and several more structures partially explored. Excavation and geophysical prospection have also revealed residential structures elsewhere on the site: this was not purely a ceremonial complex.

6.15 The large mound of Göbekli Tepe sits on top of a hill northeast of Urfa in southeast Turkey, making it a landmark clearly visible from the surrounding plains.

The Enclosures and Monoliths

The large enclosures that have been excavated each had a stone bench around the base of the circular retaining wall. Two of the enclosures (C and D) had a floor made by smoothing the rock surface of the hilltop. Two stone pedestals were formed in the rock floor, and a pair of limestone monoliths was set upright in them; ten or twelve more monoliths were set radially in the circular wall and the stone bench. The central ones were taller than the peripheral stones; the pair in Enclosure D were the tallest, and still stand 5.5 meters (18 feet) tall (see pp. 110–11).

Many believe that the site served as a central place for the ceremonies of many communities across the wider region. The tall, T-shaped monoliths [**6.16**] are not unique to Göbekli Tepe. Similar ones were found in a special-purpose, rectangular subterranean building at Nevalı Çori. Some of the Göbekli Tepe monoliths, like the smaller Nevalı Çori pillars, have arms shown in low relief; the arms are bent at the elbows, and the fingertips of the hands meet on the figures' stomach areas. The monoliths were conceived as human in form but, most significantly, their heads lack any human feature: they are inscrutable figures from another world [**6.17a**, **b**]. Many of the monoliths carry raised-relief depictions of wild animals (lions, bulls, wild boar, foxes), birds (cranes, storks, swans), snakes, spiders, and scorpions.

The five excavated enclosures have concentric rings of walls, and some of the outer rings have some radially set monoliths. The excavators believe that these enclosures were reshaped, each time being made into a smaller-diameter structures. They also think that the enclosures were roofed. None of them has any means of access at ground level, but the excavators have found huge portal stones with rectangular openings, which they think may have been set into the flat roofs of the enclosures.

Unanswered Questions

The site is a paradox: its construction required a very large labor force but the internal spaces could accommodate only a small number of people. If the enclosures were roofed, activities inside would not be visible to those outside the structure. And what do the T-monoliths represent: are they gods, ancestors, or a council of elders? Why are so many of the small sculptures broken human heads?

6.16, 6.17a, b The enclosures contain pairs of T-shaped central monoliths of limestone, decorated with low-relief carvings with various motifs (below left). The narrow side of Pillar 18 (below), from Enclosure D, is carved with hands (above), revealing that these stones are highly schematized human forms, and the edge is in fact the front, with the top of the T-shape a head (the wooden brace is for temporary stabilization). Beneath the hands, a belt with a clasp encircles the body and a fox skin is suspended below.

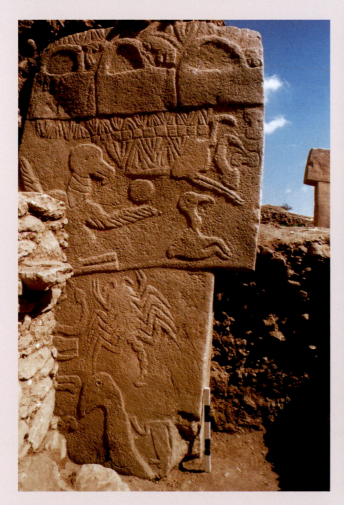

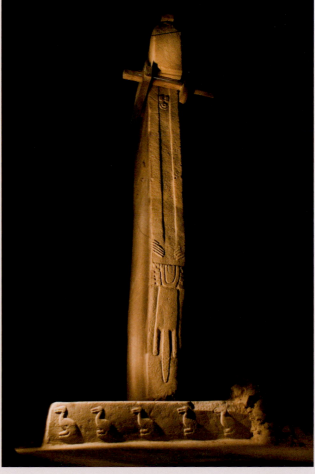

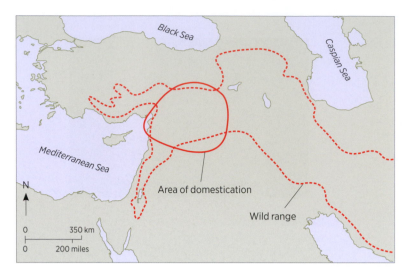

6.18 The domestication of sheep. Wild sheep were widely distributed in mountainous, hilly, and piedmont landscapes in final Pleistocene times, as shown by the more extensive, dotted outline on the map. The area of southeast Turkey and northern Syria where sheep were probably first domesticated is enclosed by a solid red outline.

farming economy. Different crops were grown in different regions, and there were local or regional herding traditions. In addition to their meat, sheep and goat can provide milk that can be made into yoghurt and cheese, and their hair or wool can be spun and woven into textiles. While sheep and goat became the norm, they were not dominant everywhere. Cattle were kept in southeast Turkey and northern Syria, but were not significant in many other parts of the region. At the **tell** settlement of **Çatalhöyük**, the community preferred to retain their traditional and deeply embedded practices of hunting wild cattle, feasting on the meat (one kill might provide several hundred kilograms of meat), and setting the massive spreads of wild bull horns in their houses until around 6500 BCE, when they turned to herding domesticated cattle. The presence or absence of domesticated pig at later aceramic Neolithic settlements follows no observable pattern; just as earlier communities had hunted or not hunted wild boar, some of the farming communities kept pigs, while others simply refrained from pork.

Settlements and Communities

With the improving efficiency of farming, population levels rose steeply over the later aceramic Neolithic. It is in the southern Levant that we have the best evidence, accumulated over many years of fieldwork. The number of settlements increased, and their average size grew sharply. In the last millennium of the aceramic Neolithic period, a number of villages, mostly east of the Jordan Valley, expanded rapidly to be more than 10 hectares (25 acres) in area. The best-documented example is **'Ain Ghazal**, where the growth of population is estimated to have been so fast that we must assume that many people were arriving here from elsewhere. At the same time, other long-lived settlements west of the Jordan seem to have been abandoned one by one. Those of the later aceramic Neolithic had a much higher density of buildings than those of the early aceramic Neolithic. In a settlement of the latter period, there was more open space between buildings than roofed space; in many of the later aceramic Neolithic settlements, there was very little open space between buildings, which were packed closely together (see **6.20**, p. 130, for example). Such a settlement as Jerf el Ahmar (see Key Site box: Jerf el Ahmar: A Neolithic Village, p. 122) may have had a population of one hundred or so—three or four times larger than the typical mobile forager band—while a settlement of the later aceramic Neolithic might have housed several thousand inhabitants, some fifty times greater than the earliest aceramic Neolithic villages.

Within those settlements, houses were generally bigger than in the preceding period, were rectilinear in plan, and often had internal subdivisions into rooms with different uses. They were built in distinct local or regional styles. In the southern Levant, for example, the mud-brick houses in a settlement might conform to pier house design, a rectangular footprint within which access was through an anteroom into a square living room. The two rooms were separated by mud-brick piers projecting from the side walls. The interior walls and floors were finished with lime plaster, which required the burning of limestone to produce

tell an artificial mound created by the accumulation of centuries of disintegrated mud-brick walls and domestic debris; characteristic of early cities in Southwest Asia

the lime. The floor plaster was often colored with a red ocher wash. The whole process of plastering the interior had been repeated multiple times.

In general, houses in later aceramic Neolithic settlements show strong evidence of having been constantly and carefully maintained and renewed. In this period, too, we increasingly see the management of the farming economy at household level. Individual households each had their own facilities for storage, food preparation, and cooking.

Special Buildings for Special Purposes

The massive circular enclosures at Göbekli Tepe belong to the early aceramic Neolithic. Near the top of the mound there is a cluster of much smaller, rectangular buildings that date to the beginning of the later aceramic Neolithic. One of them has been fully excavated. Its floor was somewhat lower than the outside ground level, and it had a pair of T-shaped monoliths that are smaller versions of the huge stones in the earlier circular enclosures. It is strikingly similar to a special building at the settlement of Nevalı Çori, which stood on a terrace beside a stream that flowed into the Euphrates, not far to the northwest of Göbekli Tepe. The Nevalı Çori building also had a pair of central T-shaped monolithic pillars [**6.19**] and a stone bench. It is rectangular in shape, its plastered floor set two or three steps below the outside ground level. Fixed into the bench were more stone monoliths.

Another site with communal special purpose buildings is Çayönü Tepesi. Houses formed an arc that left a wide, open, public space at the center of the settlement. The excavators found three buildings in the central plaza, and several tall standing stones. All the special buildings were different, and all quite unlike the domestic structures. They probably did not all exist at the same time, but their relationship to one another and to the stratified remains of the houses has proved difficult to establish. The first of the three, the so-called Skull Building, was repeatedly modified and rebuilt. Under one end of the structure were three

6.19 Nevalı Çori.
The stone walls of the almost square central building at Nevalı Çori are revetments, for the plaster floor was well below ground level. Behind the revetment walls (to the top and to the right) are traces of similar walls for an earlier, larger version of the building. The surviving pillar is partnered by a gaping hole where another pillar once stood. At intervals in the stone bench around the building there were other stone pillars, but they were broken when the building was destroyed, leaving only stumps.

KEY SITE Çatalhöyük

Çatalhöyük is one of the largest Neolithic settlements in Southwest Asia. This extraordinary site was discovered in 1958 by the British archaeologist James Mellaart, who showed that it was both very large (13 hectares, or 32 acres) and very long-lived, and spectacular in its decorated architecture and many subfloor burials. Mellaart's dramatic descriptions and vivid interpretation of the site caught the popular imagination and made the images of Çatalhöyük famous worldwide. In 1993, Ian Hodder resumed work at the site with a twenty-five-year research plan and a determination to make Çatalhöyük accessible and comprehensible to the thousands who visit it. We are now seeing the fruits of that intensive program.

The settlement was founded around 7100 BCE, toward the end of the aceramic Neolithic period, when several small communities living in the area came together.

Location

Çatalhöyük sits on the dry bed of a huge Pleistocene lake, lying in the middle of the Anatolian Plateau at an elevation of just over 1,000 meters (3,300 feet). The area has the lowest rainfall in Turkey, only 200–250 millimeters (8–10 inches) annually, marginal for dry farming, which relies on normal rainfall for cultivation and does not use irrigation. The rivers that once fed the former lake have formed alluvial fan shapes around the margins of the plain, and Çatalhöyük was established in the middle of the largest of those fans. Braided streams provided the essential water, and the combination of alluvial soils, reed marshes, and seasonal swamps made the location potentially very productive.

Archaeological survey has shown that there is a scatter of settlements earlier than Çatalhöyük, and a few more dating to the period after the Neolithic mound was abandoned, but no other site of the same date on the alluvial fan. It seems that Çatalhöyük represents the coming together of a number of pre-existing communities at a new location beside the main stream running across the fan. The whole area of the settlement was packed tight with housing; there must have been almost 10,000 people in the new super-community.

Architecture and Art

The architecture of the settlement is strikingly unusual. Houses were built like rectangular boxes pushed together, the four walls of one touching the walls of the four adjacent houses. There are almost no lanes or other approaches at ground level [**6.20**]. Rather, the flat rooftops served as the means of circulation and access. Each house consisted of a rectangular main room, usually with a secondary, smaller room opening off it, which was used for storage [**6.21**]. The walls and floors were repeatedly covered with a mud plaster made from the white marl of the Pleistocene lake bed. Floors were often painted red, and the same color was also used to paint patterns, motifs, or whole scenes on the walls. The floor of the main room had a series of low platforms of different heights around a square central area [**6.22**].

A clay oven was usually sited below the access ladder and the hatch in the roof. Most of the activities associated with food preparation and other everyday tasks were concentrated at that side of the room. The opposite side of the room was

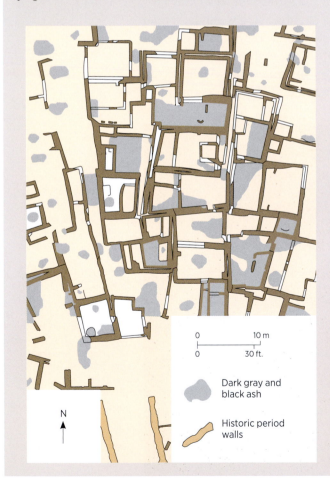

0   10 m
0   30 ft.

Dark gray and black ash

Historic period walls

N

6.20 Mellaart's original excavations were in the southwest part of the east mound of Çatalhöyük (there is also a smaller, later, Chalcolithic-period mound immediately to the west). It is Neolithic from top to bottom, with a depth of more than 21 m (69 ft.) of accumulated building debris extending over 13 ha (32 acres). When the new research project explored another area near the north end of the site (left), they found similar architecture—the rectangular houses built against each other, with few lanes or alleys for ground-level access.

kept clean, and that is where elaborate wall decoration and subfloor burials would be found.

When houses needed to be replaced, the precious wooden roof-support posts and main beams were withdrawn, and the mud roof was collapsed. The upper part of the walls was thrown down into the interior until the area was level; the new house could then be built with its walls sitting on the top of the stumps of the old. Sometimes, when a house fell out of use, the roof would be removed so that neighboring households could use the considerable space for disposing of refuse. ▶

6.21 LEFT A typical house interior. The main room was entered by a ladder from a trapdoor in the roof. A smaller room, accessed by a low doorway from the main room, was used for storage. Under the trapdoor and ladder, there was a clay oven and an open hearth for cooking. The floor of the main room was arranged in a series of plastered platforms at different levels.

6.22 BELOW Part of the main living area of a house. To the right, a diagonal scar in the wall plaster marks where the ladder that gave access from the flat roof was fixed. The cooking fire and oven were placed in that corner of the house to allow the smoke to escape through the trapdoor in the roof. One corner of the room is fitted with the horn-cores of two wild bulls, and there is also an animal head sculpted on the wall above.

Any of the accumulated coats of whitewash on the interior walls of a house might have been decorated with red designs. Some of the surviving wall paintings consist of geometric patterns, while others are figurative [**6.23**]. The scenes depicted include one with human figures engaged in a variety of activities, all centered around a colossal wild bull. Another painting shows schematically represented human figures lacking heads, surrounded by vultures. In addition to paintings, a number of houses had three-dimensional sculptures attached to the walls. These might take the form of a bull's head, modeled in mud plaster around the actual cranium and horns of a bull. There are also sculpted goats' heads, and large, leopard-like felines. Finally, there are examples of human figures schematically rendered in female form. Over the centuries, the settlement grew in size and the buildings became more elaborately decorated, reaching a climax around 6500 BCE.

Burials

Mellaart found many burials below the plastered platforms of the houses, and the renewed excavations under Ian Hodder have shown that, while some houses have no burials, others may have as many as sixty-eight bodies buried under the floor (including infants interred during the construction of the house) [**6.24**]. Given the life of a mud-brick house is perhaps seventy years, it is inconceivable that a family group living in a single-roomed house could have suffered on average one death per year. Some houses seem to have been special, and to have attracted many burials, perhaps functioning as the focal household in a lineage, or something similar. Hodder and

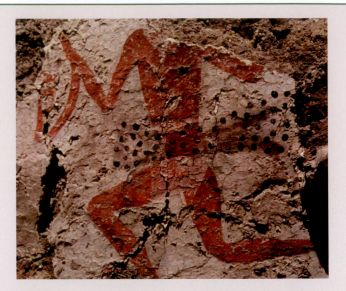

6.23 Detail from a painted plaster wall panel in a house, Çatalhöyük. The scene shows many human figures around a massive wild bull. Here, a man, painted in brick red, runs or dances. He carries a bow and wears a strange (possibly leopardskin) costume around his waist.

his team have found that the buildings where most burials were concentrated tended to be larger than average, and had the most elaborate symbolism. They tended to be rebuilt again and again in exactly the same spot, retaining their concentration of symbolic activities. Hodder has called them "history houses."

square, stone-built cells full of human bones. One contained a heap of human skulls—hence the building's nickname—and analysis has shown that non-human blood was poured over them. Another of the public buildings was almost square; it was built with a terrazzo floor (made of small pieces of stone set into plaster) below ground level, which had two upright tall stone monoliths set into it (very similar to the semi-subterranean building at Nevalı Çori).

Ritual Cycles of Burial, Skull Retrieval, and Curation

Ceremonial burial was practiced by Natufian societies in southwest Asia during the Epipaleolithic, and it continued to be a prominent feature of later societies in the same region. As before, there was particular focus on the treatment of the head. This became especially elaborate in the southern Levant. In the 1950s, Kathleen Kenyon found the first modeled skulls in her excavations at Tell es-Sultan, ancient Jericho. Since then, archaeologists have been fascinated by the burials that have been found in among the houses of many later aceramic Neolithic settlements. Careful excavation began to show that many of the burial pits had been reopened, and the cranium, or the complete skull and jawbone, had been

Economy

The community relied on the farming of domesticated crops of cereals and legumes, and the herding of large flocks of sheep. The rich alluvium of the fan would seem to have been ideal for productive farming, but environmental research has shown that the locality of the settlement was prone to seasonal flooding. At some times of year, the sheep must have been taken away to graze beyond the alluvial fan.

Exploitation of resources over a wide area is just one more of the peculiarities of Çatalhöyük. Its chipped stone was almost entirely made from obsidian, a volcanic glass, the geological origin of which was in the mountains of Cappadocia, about 125 kilometers (78 miles) away. The timbers used in the houses were pines and slow-growing junipers brought from the mountains to the south and west. The people of Çatalhöyük also acquired venison from deer, which would have been found only in the forested mountains.

Climax and Resolution

Around 6500 BCE, when the settlement was most densely occupied with a population of as many as 10,000, and the houses were most densely filled with frequently repainted decoration, three-dimensional installations, and subfloor burials, things suddenly changed. Many people left Çatalhöyük, establishing new, smaller settlements elsewhere in the alluvial fan and beyond. Those who remained built their houses with space all around them. They had begun to manage domesticated cattle, and gave up the old traditions of hunting wild cattle, feasting, and installing the skulls and horns in their houses. There was much less decoration painted on the wall plaster, and many fewer burials under the floors.

6.24 The tightly contracted burial of a young female beneath the floor of a house at Çatalhöyük. Some time after the initial burial, the grave was reopened and the complete cranium and mandible were removed (scattering a couple of the cervical vertebrae, at top left). Just visible below her ribs are the tiny ribs of the full-term fetus that she was carrying when she died.

removed. The removal of skulls was confirmed by the discovery of small clutches of skulls buried together. And, very occasionally, skulls have been found with facial features modeled in clay, and sometimes also colored. At no settlement were there enough burials to account for the whole population. Males and females of all ages, including children, can be identified, but we have no idea why certain people were given special treatment. The archaeologist Ian Kuijt has teased apart the sequential cycles of ritual that would have accompanied the different stages, reflecting on their role in the social construction of identity and memory.

As more settlements of the later aceramic Neolithic have been investigated, we have learned that there was not one single canon of ritual practices. While most settlements have revealed intramural burials, under house floors or between the houses, and in many cases the skulls are often missing from some or most burials, the particular ritual practices vary from one settlement to another. At Tell Haloula, a settlement beside the Euphrates in north Syria, for example, the bodies of the dead were bundled into a tightly crouched position and placed sitting up in narrow cylindrical pits below the plaster floors of houses. At **Tell Aswad**, near Damascus in southern Syria, the bodies were placed in a fetal position on the floor against

6.25 Skull caching.
A cluster of plastered skulls found at Tell Aswad, northern Syria. After removal from the original burial, facial features were modeled in plaster and these skulls circulated for a while in that form, before finally becoming the primary deposit in a new burial place in an area of settlement specially cleared for the purpose.

the wall of the house, sometimes within the house and sometimes on the outside. The bodies were then covered with clay and the conspicuous lump was finished with a plaster surface. But here there was a further twist in the story. For some time some of the dead had been placed against the walls of houses, when the custom suddenly changed: at the edge of the settlement the excavators found two wide shallow pits. Into each of these a clutch of skulls with features carefully modeled in painted plaster had first been placed [**6.25**]. Then, bodies were given shallow burial in the pits, one after another, apparently in quite rapid succession. And, to start the next cycle, almost all of the skeletons had been revisited in order to remove the skull. The frequency of intramural burials and of the rituals concerned with skull retrieval, curation, and occasional modeling of the facial features increased in the later aceramic Neolithic.

Regional and Supra-Regional Networks of Sharing and Exchange

Each Neolithic settlement represented an autonomous community, responsible for its own affairs; yet all of these were locked into local and regional networks, exchanging goods and materials, and sharing innovations and ideas. Social exchange systems had operated long before the Neolithic, but the extent and the intensity of networking at local and regional scales grew through the Epipaleolithic and the Neolithic to reach an unprecedented peak in the later aceramic Neolithic period.

The first studies of Neolithic networking were carried out on obsidian, a black volcanic glass that can be worked like flint. Almost all of the obsidian found on early Neolithic sites proved to come either from two sources in Central Turkey or two in the far east of Turkey. While settlements within 200–300 kilometers (125–185 miles) of these locations could supply themselves with the material and use obsidian for their everyday chipped-stone tools, settlements further from the sources relied on contacts from whom they could obtain obsidian in exchange for something else. The British archaeologist Colin Renfrew found that amounts of obsidian on sites declined sharply with distance, until, at the southern extremes—in southern Israel and Jordan, or in southwest Iran, around 900 kilometers (560 miles) from the sources—only one piece of chipped stone in a hundred, or one in a thousand, was obsidian. Clearly, the tiny amounts of obsidian that were obtained in these trades do not represent essential raw materials, but were part of social exchanges. There were other sorts of materials that were also exchanged extensively, such as marine shells from the Mediterranean and the Red Sea, beads of malachite (a vivid green copper oxide) and other greenstone beads, and marble bracelets.

Recent simulation studies have shown that some people traveled to exchange with partners in societies living some distance away, bypassing their near neighbor communities. This is called a small-world or distant link network; while most exchanged with their nearest neighbor communities, a small number had direct links with distant partners, which became hubs.

Why was it so important for someone in a community somewhere in the Levant, or in southeast Turkey, or in the valleys of the Zagros Mountains in western Iran, to have a small blade of obsidian, some seashells, or a greenstone bead? In part, possession of such exotic items showed that the owners belonged in the prestigious system of far-flung contacts; at the same time, these special objects of exotic materials ensured the good social relations that were enjoyed between those who had exchanged them with one another. For people to be able to feel that they were part of an extended, networked super-community it was necessary to emphasize what they had in common. It has been argued that communities benefited from their investment in these networks because such interaction facilitated the rapid spread of useful knowledge and innovations, and ensured that separate groups recognized each other as partners rather than as strangers and rivals.

Some exchanged items, such as pieces of Anatolian obsidian at settlements in the far south of the Levant, were special because they were exotic. Others, for example the green malachite beads, because they were very rare. From early in the aceramic Neolithic period, small tools and beads of worked copper began to be made. Bright, shiny pieces of hot-worked copper were another kind of rare and exotic material that was fed into the extensive social exchange networks.

THE EXPANSION OF FARMING, 6500–6000 BCE

What Was the Cause of Dispersal and Expansion?

From 6500 BCE, there were major changes throughout Southwest Asia that saw the dispersal of populations and the replacement of the large, densely peopled late aceramic Neolithic settlements with new, smaller communities that had different strategies of farming and herding. Were the stresses of living by farming while abiding together in great numbers simply unsustainable in the long term? Social inequality would have arisen from differences in land productivity and in access (some families would have had to cope with farming land that was several kilometers from the settlement), and such economic differences would have been magnified as land and resources were inherited down the generations. For societies that valued their egalitarian community life, dispersal into smaller communities might have been a solution. Alternatively, were the dispersals driven by environmental degradation and soil erosion brought about by over-extraction of timber and over-grazing by goats and sheep, as has been argued for 'Ain Ghazal? Or was this a series of regional responses to climate change and environmental pressures? There was rapid climate change, beginning around 6500 BCE and worsening between 6200 and 6000 BCE, which coincides with these dispersals and changes in settlement and subsistence strategies. New research in the Dead Sea area combined with intensive examination of the 'Ain Ghazal evidence indicates that there was significant aridification in the region.

As settlements were abandoned, some people shifted to nomadic pastoralism, and others to a combination of this and limited cultivation. Still others colonized new territories. They were realizing the potential portability of a mixed farming economy and, ultimately, its potential to fuel major colonizing movements. As well as dispersal within Southwest Asia, around 6500 BCE or a couple of centuries earlier small farming communities began to spread in all directions, notably to the west coast of Anatolia and the islands of the Aegean. Around 6000 BCE, farming villages began to move onto the lowland plains of southern Mesopotamia, leading eventually to the rise of the first cities.

SUMMARY AND CONCLUSIONS

Robert Braidwood asked why people who had lived successfully for hundreds of thousands of years in small, mobile, hunter-gatherer bands turned to village-farming, cultivating crops, herding animals, and living in permanent settlements of mud-brick houses. Kent Flannery's answer was the broad-spectrum revolution theory, which in the Epipaleolithic period involved a positive feedback loop. Changes in subsistence strategy (increasing reliance on small game and stored harvests) were connected to changes in settlement strategy (reducing mobility, increase toward sedentism). More food and the ability to stay in one place allowed for the raising of more offspring. This led to an increase in population, which in turn demanded an increase in food supply and motivated innovations in intensified food production.

The question of *how* remains energetically debated, as archaeologists work to reconcile ecological, economic, social, cultural, and symbolic processes into one narrative. The chapters that follow describe the transition from hunting and gathering to farming in the other key regions of the world. These conversions to agriculture depended on a different range of plant and animal species in each of the regions where they occurred, and must therefore be considered as independent from one another. Nevertheless, there are striking parallels among the early farming communities of these different regions, in particular the close association between sedentary settlement, rapidly increasing population, and food production. By the late aceramic Neolithic, communities seem to have experienced severe stress, as some settlements were abandoned as people shifted to nomadic pastoralism, and others to a combination of limited cultivation and seasonal nomadic pastoralism. Still others moved into new territories, realizing the potential offered to them by the mixed farming economy. Farming spread, and farming villages, became larger and more complex, leading ultimately to the first cities of southern Mesopotamia.

FURTHER READING

Useful introductions to Epipaleolithic and Neolithic culture, and early agriculture, include:

Bar-Yosef, O. and Valla, F. R. (eds.). 1991. *The Natufian Culture in the Levant*. International Monographs in Prehistory, Archaeological Series 1. Ann Arbor: University of Michigan Press.

Cauvin, J. 2000. *The Birth of the Gods and the Origins of Agriculture*. Cambridge: Cambridge University Press.

Garrod, D. A. E. and Bate, D. M. A. 1937. *The Stone Age of Mount Carmel: Joint Expedition of the British School of Archaeology in Jerusalem and the American School of Prehistoric Research (1929–1934)*. Oxford: The Clarendon Press.

Hodder, I. 2006. *Çatalhöyük: The Leopard's Tale—Revealing the Mysteries of Turkey's Ancient Town*. London and New York: Thames & Hudson.

Hodder, I. 2014. Çatalhöyük: the leopard changes its spots. A summary of recent work. *Anatolian Studies* 64, 1–22.

Kuijt, I., ed. 2000. *Life in Neolithic Farming Communities: Social Organization, Identity, and Differentiation*. New York: Kluwer Academic.

Kuijt, I. 2008. The regeneration of life: Neolithic structures of symbolic remembering and forgetting. *Current Anthropology* 49 (2), 171–97.

Mellart, J. 1967. *Çatal Hüyük: A Neolithic Town in Anatolia*. London: Thames & Hudson.

Moore, A. M. T., Hillman, G. C., and Legge, A. J. 2001. *Village on the Euphrates*. Oxford and New York: Oxford University Press.

Watkins, T. 2010. New light on Neolithic revolution in south-west Asia. *Antiquity* 84 (325), 621–34.

Zeder, M. A. 2011. The origins of agriculture in the Near East. *Current Anthropology* 52 (S4), S221–S335.

www.catalhoyuk.com Website of the *Çatalhöyük Research Project*, with information about the project and all aspects of the research being carried out.

https://www.dainst.blog/the-tepe-telegrams Blog written by members of the Göbekli Tepe research team, with short pieces about various aspects of the research, and excellent color pictures; hosted by the German Archaeological Institute.

Southwest Asia: Cities and States

7

Roger Matthews

Cities and States of the World 141

Transitions to States in Southwest Asia: The Halaf and Ubaid Periods, *c.* **6000–4200** BCE 145

KEY DISCOVERY Early Steps toward Social Complexity on the Iranian Plateau 148

Urban Communities: The Uruk Period, *c.* **4200–3000** BCE 149

KEY THEME: URBANIZATION The World's First True Cities 151

City States, Kingdoms, and Empires in Southwest Asia: Early Bronze Age, *c.* **3000–2000** BCE 154

KEY SITE Ebla 157

Cities and Empires in Southwest Asia: The Middle Bronze Age, *c.* **2000–1700** BCE 160

KEY THEME: MIGRATION Small and Large Movements across Southwest Asia 161

Summary and Conclusions 162

Further Reading 163

Detail of the Standard of Ur, excavated in the Royal Cemetery at the ancient Sumerian city state of Ur in southern Iraq, dated to *c.* 2500 BCE.

TIMELINE Southwest Asia: Cities and States

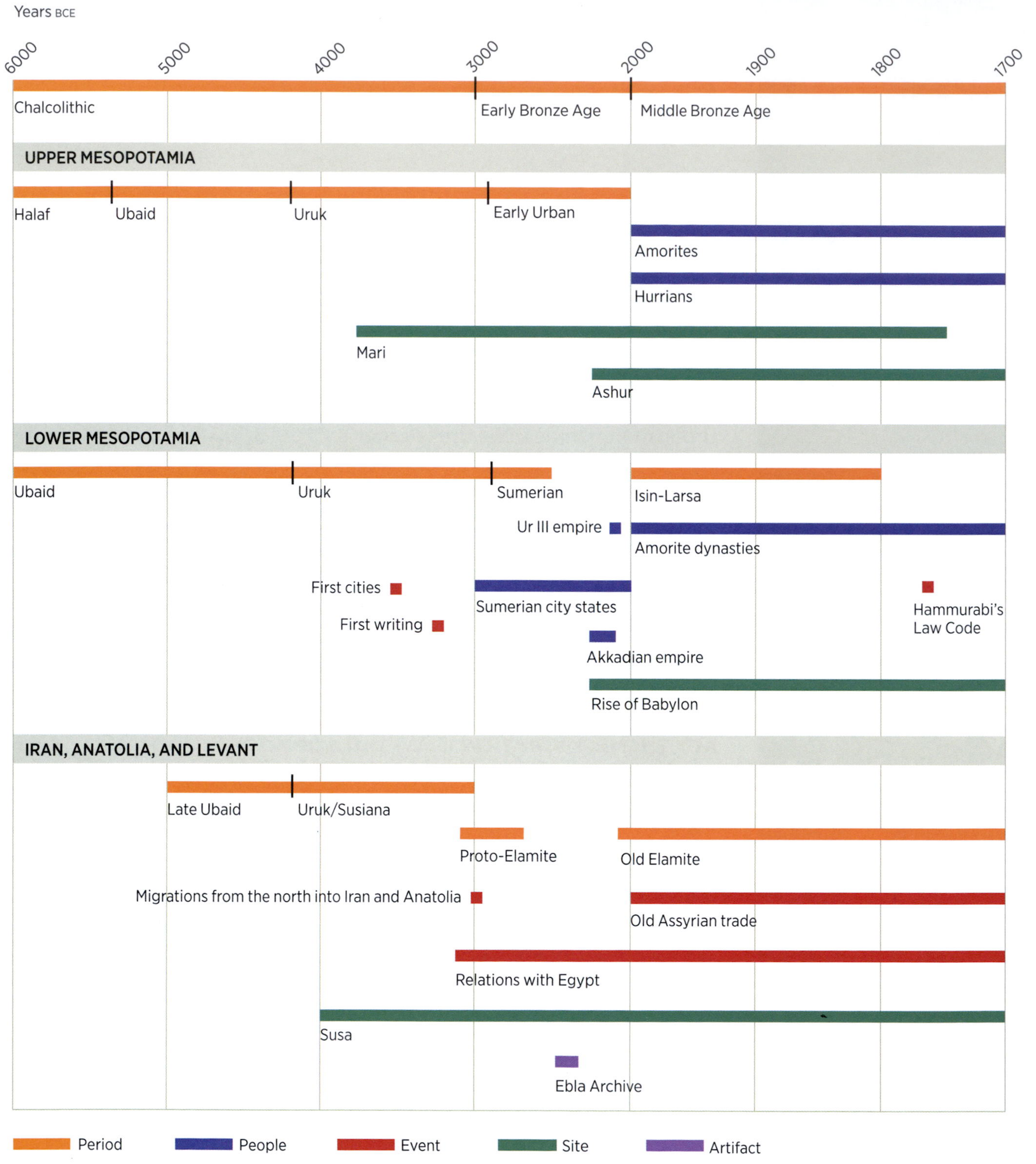

Years BCE

6000	5000	4000	3000	2000	1900	1800	1700

Chalcolithic — Early Bronze Age — Middle Bronze Age

UPPER MESOPOTAMIA

Halaf — Ubaid — Uruk — Early Urban

Amorites

Hurrians

Mari

Ashur

LOWER MESOPOTAMIA

Ubaid — Uruk — Sumerian

Isin-Larsa

Ur III empire

Amorite dynasties

First cities

First writing

Sumerian city states

Akkadian empire

Hammurabi's Law Code

Rise of Babylon

IRAN, ANATOLIA, AND LEVANT

Late Ubaid — Uruk/Susiana

Proto-Elamite

Old Elamite

Migrations from the north into Iran and Anatolia

Old Assyrian trade

Relations with Egypt

Susa

Ebla Archive

Legend:
- ▬ Period
- ▬ People
- ▬ Event
- ▬ Site
- ▬ Artifact

From *c.* 10,000 BCE, communities in Southwest Asia took the first steps in the development of a settled way of life supported by farming and animal husbandry (Chapter 6). Demographic and social changes made for large and increasingly complex societies, until, between 4000 and 3000 BCE, Southwest Asia became the scene for the emergence of a new kind of society: the first city states. Urban life arose in Southwest Asia in close association with the development of mechanisms of social control, including early writing and bureaucracy, social hierarchy, elite ideology, and the formation of states and empires. This chapter will follow the story over 4,000 years, from the expansion of farming settlements around 6000 BCE to the first empires around 2300–1650 BCE.

- States are centralized political institutions in which ruling elites exercise control over large populations. They developed independently across the world.

- Cities are substantial settlements—sometimes walled—with structured spaces for the execution of a broad range of social functions.

- Southwest Asia saw the emergence of the first city, Uruk, in modern-day southern Iraq, around 3500 BCE.

- Southwest Asia's history involved city states that were regions of centralized control that cover only a city and its territories.

- The first signs of centralized administration occur in the Halaf period in circular stamp seals, *c.* 6000–5400 BCE.

- The development of writing in 3500–3000 BCE also primarily had an administrative function.

- The first recorded dynasties in Southwest Asia are Sumerian, dating to the period *c.* 2900–2350 BCE (the Early Dynastic period).

- The period of city states was followed by the rise and fall of a succession of empires between 2300 and 1700 BCE.

CITIES AND STATES OF THE WORLD

A traditional narrative of the development of cities and states around the world features two stages. First, the development of agriculture allowed the growth of denser populations. Then, in certain regions, these populations became still larger, giving rise to cities and states.

This two-stage description has the advantage of simplicity, but the reality is more complex. Cities and states are not a specific pattern-book response to rising population levels. They are only one form of solution to environmental and social challenges, and themselves encompass diverse types of society—the differences between them are as significant as the similarities.

Too great an emphasis on the transition to states can easily obscure the fact that early examples were very limited in geographical extent. It is true that some had impacts far beyond their borders, through trade or cultural exchange, but it is nonetheless important to acknowledge that between 2000 and 1000 BCE, when early states had emerged in several regions, a majority of the human population worldwide still lived in non-state societies, including not only farmers but also significant numbers of hunter-gatherers.

Simplistic descriptions of the transition to states run the risk of creating a progressivist view of human history, which considers state societies as somehow more worthy than early farming societies or hunter-gatherers. While state societies receive a great deal of attention, they must be considered as only one alternative among a mosaic of human social forms extending far back into the past.

The Development of Cities and States

The reasons why cities arose varied from region to region and from period to period. Some were important centers for trade and exchange, located on major travel routes or natural harbors that drew traders and craftspeople together. Others were important religious centers: **Teotihuacán** in Mexico, with its sacred cave below the Pyramid of the Sun, and **Uruk** in Iraq, with its major Eanna and Kullaba temple complexes. Many were places of political power, growing in size and importance as their resident elites extended control over surrounding areas. A few, indeed, were political foundations, built and planned on pristine sites, to provide new seats of government or to project political and military power. In all cases, a fundamental requirement was the availability of sufficient food to support the growing urban populace. Hence many cities grew up in fertile lowlands, or in hill country transformed by terracing and irrigation. All of them offered also new opportunities for craftspeople, merchants, bureaucrats, and religious elites.

By the term city we mean a large agglomeration of people, probably tens of thousands, living in a well-defined place that contained designated structures and spaces for the execution of a broad range of social functions. Yet there is considerable variation [**7.1**]. A dispersed or low-density urban pattern characterized Angkor in Cambodia (Chapter 10). The Maya cities of Mesoamerica likewise consisted of dispersed populations focused around a ritual and ceremonial core, with pyramid temples, palaces, and ball courts (Chapter 16). This low-density urbanization is typical of tropical environments, where control of seasonally variable water

7.1 Ancient cities come in many forms. Chan Chan in Peru is one of the largest mud-brick city complexes in the world.

resources was all-important. Once climate change disrupted the fragile ecological balance, the power of the ruling elites dissolved and the low-density cities themselves collapsed as their inhabitants were forced to seek their livelihood elsewhere.

The first cities are generally believed to have developed in Mesopotamia around 3500 BCE. The origins of the Egyptian state may be placed at around the same period or very slightly later. Exact chronologies are sometimes difficult to establish, since the earliest layers of many cities lie deeply buried beneath the remains left by later generations. In the Indus Valley, the build-up of sediment and the high water table have hindered attempts by archaeologists to study the origins of the Indus cities, which are known to date from around 2500–2000 BCE but could have had still earlier origins. In China, cities appear from around 2000 BCE.

All these developments are generally regarded as independent of one another, in the same way that agriculture was an independent development in different regions. The possibility that trade contacts led to imitation cannot be excluded, however, since links between Egypt and Mesopotamia, and later between Mesopotamia and the Indus Valley, have been documented.

States may be defined as centralized political institutions in which ruling elites exercise control over a population [**7.2**]. The size of the population can vary between several thousand and several million, with most early states toward the smaller end of this range. State institutions gather revenues from their subject people, whether as agricultural produce, craft items, raw materials, or in labor dues. In return they offer protection and support in times of famine or warfare. State institutions usually reserve for themselves the right to use force, either in external warfare or for internal control. There has been some debate as to whether states should be considered beneficent institutions, operating for the good of all, or whether they are essentially exploitative, with governing elites gaining wealth and power at the expense of the majority. For most documented examples, the latter seems closer to reality. In terms of scale, however, it is only with the benefit of centralized state control that large populations can be integrated and supported; the collapse of states (as for instance the Classic Maya collapse, see Chapter 16) is inevitably followed by population decline.

The variability between the different kinds of state and city that we encounter in the archaeological record demonstrates a wide range of social formations that do not really belong together. It is very clear that there is no single package of characteristics that can be applied cross-culturally, and equally clear that it is difficult to determine exactly when a population center becomes a city and a society becomes a state. Nonetheless, as the Meso-american specialist Joyce Marcus has argued, "For the study of social evolution to advance, the field of anthropology must be willing to generalize; to compare and contrast cultures from different parts of the world; and to search for common patterns in the ways human societies responded to similar challenges."

The Geography of State Formation. Early states across the world developed in areas of high primary agricultural productivity, where sufficient food was available to feed sizable, concentrated populations [**7.3**]. In this way, the Egyptian state depended on the Nile, Mesopotamian **city states** on the Tigris and Euphrates, and Indus cities on the Indus and the Ghaggar-Hakra rivers. In China, the first cities developed in the valley of the Yangzi and the basin of the Yellow River (the Huang He), while in the Americas, the city state of Teotihuacán developed in the Basin of Mexico, and in coastal Peru states formed within the river valleys running through the desert from the Andes to the Pacific. Most of these were in warm environments, where exceptional crop yields were possible provided that sufficient water could be brought to the fields. This was perhaps only to be expected, since several of the key staples (maize, wheat, and barley) had originated as species of large-seeded grasses that flourished in hot climates. Forms of irrigation were essential to support many early state societies, which might rely on receding flood agriculture (Egypt, Indus Valley) or canal irrigation (Peru, Mesopotamia, highland Mexico).

States developed independently in the Andean zone and in highland Mexico during the second millennium BCE, where contacts between these and neighboring regions may have stimulated social change and state formation. One powerful mechanism was the threat of war: smaller communities adjacent to burgeoning states sought safety by transforming themselves into states as well, in order to have greater resources of military manpower to resist their now threatening neighbors.

Archaeological Features of States. Though states clearly interacted with one another, and sometimes played a role in one another's rise and fall, each was the product of its own specific circumstances. That is not to deny that they share many archaeological features, and it is these that allow us to label them as states. The key element for both cities and states is scale, and the level of resources and human labor that were available. Cities may cover hundreds of hectares with houses, temples, storerooms, and palaces, and are often enclosed within a defensive wall. Monumentality is a consistent feature: public buildings are usually big and elaborate. States also usually include the propaganda of the ruling elite, seen in statues, palaces, and tombs, or in architectural settings where the rulers played their role in carefully stage-managed public performances.

Mediterranean
c. 3200 BCE

Mesopotamia
c. 3500 BCE

Northern China
c. 2000 BCE

Mesoamerica
c. 1500 BCE

ATLANTIC OCEAN

Egypt
c. 3000 BCE

Indus Valley
c. 2500 BCE

PACIFIC OCEAN

Andes
c. 1500 BCE

INDIAN OCEAN

Spectacular diversities and inequalities of wealth and power are also seen, exemplified by luxury objects, which employ both elaborate craft skill and materials brought from far afield. Royal graves, such as Pakal's at Palenque in Mexico (seventh century CE) or Tutankhamun's in Egypt (late fourteenth century BCE), are justly famous for their richness and the insight they provide into craftsmanship, ideology, and trade. Nor is it only the contents that testify to the new levels in inequality that states relied upon. Excessively sized tomb structures, for example, the Giza pyramids in Egypt or the keyhole-shaped tombs of Japan, illustrate the immense resources that early rulers must have been able to command.

TRANSITIONS TO STATES IN SOUTHWEST ASIA: THE HALAF AND UBAID PERIODS, *c.* 6000–4200 BCE

The development of farming in central and southern Iraq was set in the alluvial plains of the Euphrates and Tigris rivers and their tributaries. These rivers formed the lifeblood of the region, enabling irrigation in an area where agriculture was not otherwise possible. It is in this flat, featureless landscape, flanked by desert to the west and southwest, that we can detect the origins of urban life and writing, and it is on this region, known as Mesopotamia (meaning between the rivers), that this chapter will principally focus [**7.4**, p. 146].

By *c.* 6000 BCE, the early farming societies of Southwest Asia had developed into fully agricultural communities, living permanently in small villages and providing for themselves

7.3 State formation.
State societies, in the same way as agriculture (see 5.9, p. 105), developed independently in different parts of the world at different periods. Common features of these state societies are the reliance on high primary productivity from successful and often intensive agriculture, and the development of complex social organization that is frequently associated with the stylized or idealized portrayal of leaders and deities.

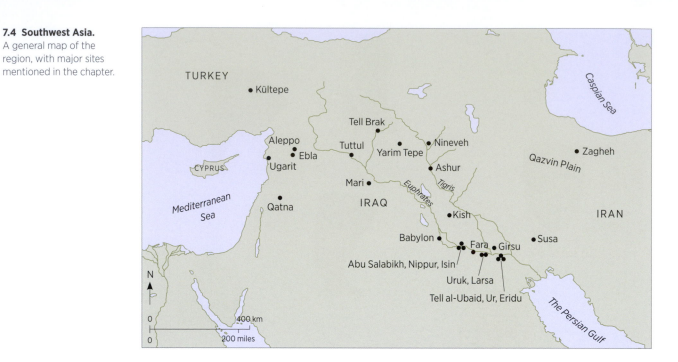

7.4 Southwest Asia.
A general map of the region, with major sites mentioned in the chapter.

Chalcolithic the period between the Neolithic and the Bronze Age in Europe and West Asia, marked by the widespread use of copper metallurgy, which probably developed in northern Mesopotamia

dry farming farming without the use of irrigation, in areas where normal rainfall is sufficient for cultivation

seal a stone object carved with a design that is impressed into a lump of clay to form a sealing; the design might be carved into the flattened surface of the stone (a stamp seal) or around the surface of a cylindrical stone to be rolled over the clay (a cylinder seal)

sealing a lump of clay impressed with a seal, used for administrative purposes to seal jars, documents, and other objects

through animal husbandry, principally of sheep, goat, pigs, and cattle, as well as rain-fed crops (Chapter 6). Around this time, a major breakthrough came with the development of irrigation agriculture—the systematic use of constructed canals and channels to bring water from rivers to otherwise dry land, enabling new areas of fertile soils to be brought under cultivation. This single step opened up the broad plains of southern Mesopotamia for extensive settlement throughout the **Chalcolithic** period. These early societies are called Halaf and Ubaid, after the sites in Syria and Iraq where their remains were first excavated.

The Halaf Period, c. 6000–5400 BCE: The Marking of Property

The remains of Halaf communities are found in a broad arc from western Iran across northern Iraq and Syria to southern Turkey and south into the Lebanon, in hilly country with sufficient rainfall for **dry farming** [7.5]. These sites often include circular buildings, high-quality painted pottery, female figurines, obsidian artifacts, and clay sling bullets. During the Halaf period, we also see the first development of administrative technology in

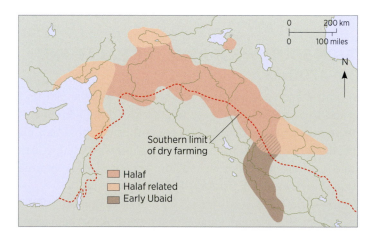

7.5 Map of the distribution of sites of the Halaf and Ubaid periods.

the form of **seals**. The most common are small square or circular stone stamp seals incised with geometric designs on one face. They were pressed into soft clay and used to seal doors or as the stoppers of pottery vessels, perhaps to indicate contents or ownership.

Halaf settlements were generally small, occupied by groups of perhaps 20 to 150 people. A few sites were much larger, and there is some evidence for trade among and beyond communities. Analysis of the distinctive painted pottery found at all Halaf sites suggests that some sites functioned as pottery-production centers.

Our understanding of Halaf religious beliefs is minimal. There are no clear ritual buildings, and human burials are treated in a variety of ways, including single inhumation, multiple interments, skull burials, and cremations. A possible clue to religious belief are painted female figurines found at various sites [**7.6**].

There is little evidence for social stratification within Halaf communities, but there are signs of early forms of administration. The presence of stone stamp seals, and pieces of clay impressed by these seals (called **sealings**), are the earliest extensive evidence for the use of these objects in Mesopotamia. Clay sealings were used to secure portable containers, such as baskets and pots, and this suggests a need by some people to exercise control over their possessions and to mark property as their own.

The Ubaid Period, c. 5900–4200 BCE: Temple Platforms in the South

Contemporary with the Halaf in Upper Mesopotamia, human communities began to settle on the plains of Lower Mesopotamia in southern Iraq (see **7.5**, p. 146). Modern alluvial deposits brought by the Euphrates and Tigris rivers have blanketed the earliest settlements under deep silt, making archaeological detection difficult, but some have been located and excavated. It is here that we see the early use of irrigation agriculture, the systematic exploitation of the waters of the Euphrates and Tigris to cultivate cereals.

In the early postglacial period, when sea levels were lower, much of the present-day Persian Gulf was marshy lowland, but as sea levels rose the shoreline moved northward, separating Iran from the Arabian Peninsula. The Gulf was to develop into an important maritime artery in the centuries that followed.

Eridu and the Persian Gulf. Eridu in southern Iraq is one of the most important Ubaid sites, where a sequence of temples dedicated to Enki, the water god, has been excavated. These mud-brick structures are built one on top of the other in a sequence spanning almost all of the Ubaid period [**7.7**]. From a small, single-roomed construction in the first phase, the temples were built on an increasingly grand scale, culminating in edifices with buttresses, altars and offering tables, the whole building set on a raised platform. Large amounts of ash

7.6 Female figurine.
A painted vessel in the shape of a woman, from Yarim Tepe II in north Iraq. Height 21 cm (8 in.).

7.7 Successive temples of the Ubaid period at Eridu, south Iraq. Temples of increasing size and elaboration were built atop one another over a period of several centuries, culminating in the grand structure of level VII. This architectural sequence is good evidence for the continuity of cult in a specific location.

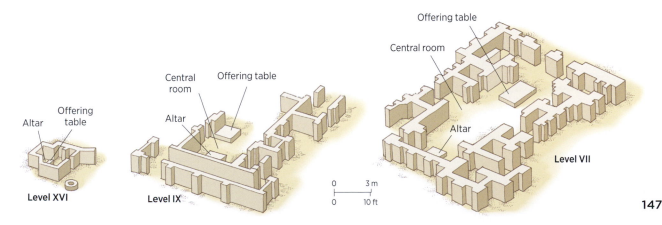

Offering table

Central room

Offering table

Central room

Offering table

Altar

Altar

Altar

Altar

Offering table

Level XVI

Level IX

Level VII

0   3 m

0   10 ft

147

KEY DISCOVERY Early Steps toward Social Complexity on the Iranian Plateau

Much research has focused on the development of complex societies in the Chalcolithic period (Halaf–Ubaid–Uruk) of Mesopotamia, but what kinds of society were developing on the Iranian Plateau to the east? This question is important because throughout the Chalcolithic and Bronze Age, the communities of the Mesopotamian lowlands looked to the highland zone, including Iran, for cherished raw materials and products, including timber, metals (copper and silver above all), and semi-precious stones, such as carnelian, turquoise, and lapis lazuli.

On the Qazvin Plain, west of Tehran, renewed excavations are taking place at the site of **Zagheh**, dated to 5200–4600 BCE. Excavations in the 1970s revealed a unique mud-brick building, the Painted Building, with red, black, and white designs on its walls, an array of eighteen skulls of wild male goats set into the wall faces, and plastered benches and bins. New research is uncovering more about this unusual structure.

Striking features include about forty clay figurines, many of which appear to represent pregnant women, one bearing a child, found scattered around the outside of the Painted Building. To the south of the structure, a group of eight adult females, aged twenty-five to thirty, had been individually buried, facing toward the Painted Building and with their arms outstretched toward it in a classic pose of cultic devotion. Their bodies were decorated with necklaces, armlets, and belts of multiple stone beads. The building appears to have been a special cultic structure, and the presence of female figurines and burials, along with the male goat skulls, strongly suggests a connection with fertility and childbirth.

Elsewhere at Zagheh, new excavations have explored areas of craft production, including kilns and debris from pottery-making. Associated with these features are large numbers of clay tokens—deliberately shaped pieces of clay in the form of cones, spheres, disks, and double cones [**7.8**]. These objects seem to be connected with counting, and we interpret them as basic administrative devices used to keep account of movements of raw materials and products in and out of the ceramic production area.

Taken together, the Painted Building and the evidence for specialized craft production and basic accounting at Zagheh all point toward significant levels of social complexity among communities of the Iranian Plateau by 5000 BCE.

7.8 Clay tokens from the Zagheh craft-production area, which seem to be connected with keeping account of the movements of raw materials and finished products.

and fish bones found in the upper temples suggest offerings of fish to the god. Temples were highly significant elements in the origins of complex society in the region, their priests and administrators overseeing many aspects of daily life, including land and labor management, distribution of food and, above all, the correct procedures for religious rites and rituals.

Excavation of an Ubaid cemetery at Eridu recovered some 200 graves of individuals buried in brick-lined pits, many interred with goods in the form of pots, jewelry, and food offerings. Distinctive to Ubaid sites are figurines, some of which have lizard-like heads, found in these graves and elsewhere [**7.9, 7.10**]. In general, however, there are relatively few luxury goods at Ubaid sites, by contrast with those of later periods. The focus of power was the control of local agricultural surpluses, rather than long-distance trade.

7.9, 7.10 Eridu figurines. Clay figurines, some with lizard-shaped heads (far left) and decoration in the form of painted spots and applied blobs of clay. The figurines are found in burials at Eridu and other sites of the Ubaid period. Height 10–15 cm (4–6 in.).

The Ubaid period witnessed the institution of the temple as a community focus. Stamp seals with images of snakes, birds, animals, and people came into use for economic and cult administration. One of the most striking manifestations of the Ubaid phenomenon is the existence of some fifty sites in the Persian Gulf region, each with Ubaid pottery and other typical artifacts. These occur along eastern Saudi Arabia, on the island of Bahrain, in Qatar, and on the western shores of the Oman peninsula, far from southern Iraq. Analysis of the clays used to make the pottery suggests that the vessels were made in Lower Mesopotamia and then transported several hundred kilometers down the Persian Gulf. This spread shows how there existed inter-community exchange of goods over long distances, and the sharing of material culture attributes over a region totaling several thousand square kilometers.

URBAN COMMUNITIES: THE URUK PERIOD, *c.* 4200–3000 BCE

From 4200 BCE, the alluvial plains of Lower Mesopotamia hosted large-scale societies that experimented with new modes of living, warfare, craft production, and administration. By 3200 BCE, people in this region were living in urban and literate communities.

By careful irrigation and farming of the alluvial soils of the Lower Mesopotamian plains, communities were able to produce significant levels of surplus in staple commodities, such as cereals, flour, fish, wool, and textiles. The temples acted as consumers of surplus wealth, accepting the produce of the land as offerings to divinities, as well as serving as clearing houses, collecting the surplus on behalf of the gods and then redistributing it in the form of rations to temple workers, or as capital advanced to entrepreneurs who might then engage in commerce and long-distance trade. These developments soon began to merge with the actions of highly ranked social groups, and by 2900 BCE these elites can be designated as rulers of dynasties.

Similar developments occurred in Upper Mesopotamia to the north. Yet the evidence here also suggests that the route to urbanization was fraught with violence and instability between 4000 and 3000 BCE. At Tell Brak, a discovery of several mass graves of hundreds of young adults, many of them showing evidence of disarticulation, provides vivid evidence for major conflict between or within communities at this time [**7.11**].

Uruk: The First City

From around 3200 BCE, developments in Lower Mesopotamia are best seen at the great site of Uruk itself, from which the period takes its name [**7.12**, p. 150]. Uruk's modern name is Warka, and it appears in the Bible as the city of Erech. It was a major location by about 5000 BCE, becoming the dominant settlement from 3500 BCE. Its temples would have been visible from great distances across the level plains, and the city was sustained by the participation of large segments of the urban and rural population.

It is fair to claim Uruk as the first genuine city. It included large-scale temples and associated administrative and residential buildings for priests and officials, open spaces for gatherings or worship, specialized craft production zones for pottery-making, stoneworking, and metalworking, and areas of housing.

7.11 Conflict on the route to urbanization. A mass burial of more than sixty individuals excavated at Tell Brak, northeast Syria, dating to *c.* 3800 BCE, provides evidence of conflict between or within communities at this time.

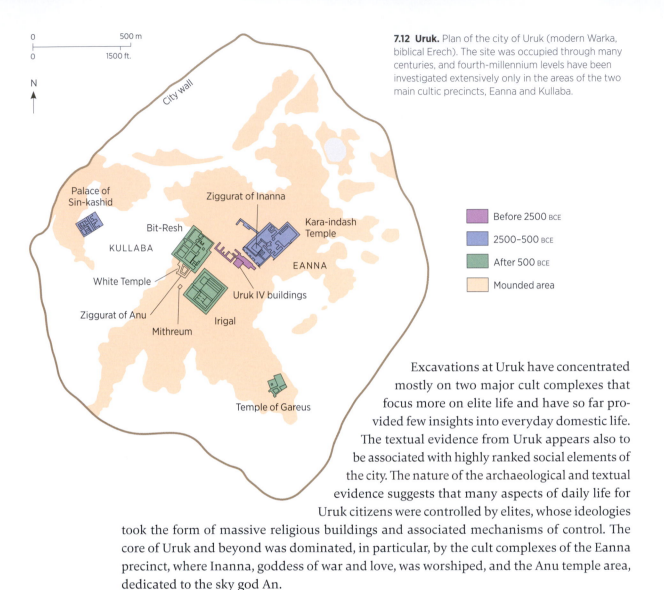

0   500 m
0   1500 ft.

N

City wall

7.12 Uruk. Plan of the city of Uruk (modern Warka, biblical Erech). The site was occupied through many centuries, and fourth-millennium levels have been investigated extensively only in the areas of the two main cultic precincts, Eanna and Kullaba.

Palace of Sin-kashid

Ziggurat of Inanna

Kara-indash Temple

Bit-Resh

KULLABA

EANNA

White Temple

Uruk IV buildings

Ziggurat of Anu

Irigal

Mithreum

Temple of Gareus

Before 2500 BCE

2500–500 BCE

After 500 BCE

Mounded area

Excavations at Uruk have concentrated mostly on two major cult complexes that focus more on elite life and have so far provided few insights into everyday domestic life. The textual evidence from Uruk appears also to be associated with highly ranked social elements of the city. The nature of the archaeological and textual evidence suggests that many aspects of daily life for Uruk citizens were controlled by elites, whose ideologies took the form of massive religious buildings and associated mechanisms of control. The core of Uruk and beyond was dominated, in particular, by the cult complexes of the Eanna precinct, where Inanna, goddess of war and love, was worshiped, and the Anu temple area, dedicated to the sky god An.

Several massive structures have been excavated in the Eanna precinct, built principally of mud brick. Decorative use of baked-clay cones with colored heads, set into wall faces, typifies many of these buildings throughout Uruk-period Mesopotamia. The size and layout of a number of the Eanna-precinct buildings suggest their use as temples, but some of the buildings may have served more as communal meeting houses or as residences of priests and officials.

In the Anu temple area, to the west of Eanna, a series of successive temples was built on terraces. The best preserved is the White Temple, smaller in scale than the Eanna precinct structures but in an imposing location, set on a platform 13 meters (42.7 feet) high, a precursor of the **ziggurats** that would in subsequent centuries feature so prominently on the Mesopotamian horizon. Within the White Temple, deliberate burial of a leopard and a lion cub may be traces of a foundation ritual. Close parallels in temple plans, orientation, and the location of fixtures, such as altars and niches for holding cult statues, all support the idea that across all of Lower Mesopotamia there were common patterns of cult and ritual activity, even though multiple deities, male and female, were worshiped.

ziggurat in Southwest Asia, a high platform surmounted by a small temple

cuneiform a form of script used in Southwest Asia during the Bronze Age and Early Iron Age; literally meaning wedge-shaped, from the impressions made in the originally damp clay

Some scholars claim that large prehistoric sites, such as Neolithic Çatalhöyük in central Turkey, were the first towns or cities, but we lack any evidence from these sites for the wide differentiation of function that marks a city. At Çatalhöyük we have no evidence for specialized areas for craft production, public meetings, markets, large temples, or special residences for elite rulers or priests, nor for a bureaucratic means of controlling sectors of society.

Since the rise of Uruk as the first true city, almost all modes of large-scale human political enterprise have been urban-based, with major core cities serving as focal points for control of hinterlands and trade routes. The model of urban structure defined and refined by the citizens of Uruk in the late fourth millennium BCE stands as a template of social, political, and cultural interaction that persists throughout history right up to today's global, highly urbanized world.

The Invention of Writing

Among the most significant of the many objects excavated at Uruk are the more than 5,000 clay tablets bearing evidence of early writing [**7.13**]. This takes the form of incised or impressed signs made by a stylus on carefully prepared soft clay tablets in the script known as proto-**cuneiform** [**7.14**]. This is the earliest known writing anywhere in the world, but it was not a unique invention, since writing was subsequently developed independently in other regions, such as China and Mesoamerica. It is a practice that was employed by a number of early states, for a variety of purposes.

7.13 The development of the cuneiform script.
The general trend is for symbols to become less pictorially representative through time as writing speed and familiarity with signs developed. The cuneiform script, similarly to modern scripts, such as Arabic or Latin, was used to write a host of often unrelated languages throughout its 3,000-year history in Southwest Asia, including Sumerian, Akkadian (and its many dialects), Ugaritic, Hittite, Hurrian, Elamite, and Urartian.

Pictographic sign c. 3100 BCE							
Interpretation	Star	?Stream	Ear of barley	Bull's head	Bowl	Head and bowl	Lower leg
Cuneiform sign c. 2400 BCE							
Cuneiform sign c. 700 BCE, turned 90°							
Meaning	God, sky	Water, seed, sun	Barley	Ox	Food, bread	To eat	To walk, to stand

Tablet turned 90 degrees to match later orientation

Quantity of the product:

c. 135,000 liters

Accounting period:

37 months

Name of the responsible official:

Kushim

Type of the product:

barley

Function of the document (?):

Final account? (inscribed over a partially erased sign)

Use of barley (?):

exchange

7.14 Proto-cuneiform.
Clay tablet with proto-cuneiform (wedge-shaped) script, dating to about 3000 BCE. These texts are hard to interpret as there are no obvious grammatical elements, but generally appear to relate to administration on the part of large public organizations, such as temples. In this case, the text accounts for the use of an enormous quantity of barley grain over a period of thirty-seven months.

Uruk writing often employed pictographic signs, the superficial meaning of which, at least, can be readily seen. Grain was represented by a drawing of an ear of grain. Additionally, most tablets have numerical signs as well as calendrical symbols, with months comprising three weeks, each of ten days.

The majority of the texts are of an administrative nature, relating to concerns such as the distribution of quotas of grain to laborers, the counting of flocks of animals, and the measurement and cultivation of fields belonging to officials. Other texts comprise lists of professions, city or place names, and types of animals. The very earliest texts date to the Late Uruk period (c. 3500–3000 BCE) and have so far been found only at Uruk itself, suggesting that the script originated there. The invention of a new means of recording detailed information, although rooted in previous systems of regulatory control involving tokens, seals, and pieces of clay, constituted a quantum leap in administrative and organizational capability. From this time onward, cuneiform writing on clay tablets would delineate and police the internal boundaries of Mesopotamian society for three millennia.

Cylinder Seals. Closely associated with early writing was another tool in the mechanism of administrative control, the cylinder seal. This was used to make an impression, in clay, that would be seen and understood by officials working within the administration. The depiction of apparently cultic scenes on many of the seals reinforces the picture of temple involvement in these early stages of bureaucratic control [**7.15**]. Although early examples of cylinder seals have been found in Upper Mesopotamia and Iran, it is with the rise of urban society in Lower Mesopotamia that these objects came to the fore. They were ideal for rolling over soft clay tablets, serving as both validation and identification of the participants involved in administrative activity. Additionally, they were employed to control access to containers and storerooms by means of sealings fixed to lids, door pegs, and jar covers.

The scenes depicted in cylinder seals tell us something about Uruk society. Especially frequent are bound captives brought before a skirted figure carrying a bow or spear, often identified as a priest-king, a ruler with both political and religious power. Other scenes show rows of offerings—animal, vegetable, and mineral—paraded before temples and high-status

7.15 Cylinder seals. This cylinder seal scene is from Uruk, dating to *c.* 3200 BCE. It depicts a procession of three nude figures advancing towards a temple (shown schematically on the left). The figure leading the procession pours liquid from a vessel; the central figure is damaged; the figure at the back holds up an object perhaps destined as a temple offering.

individuals. Such a scene is also depicted in low relief on the famous Warka Vase [**7.16**, **7.17**], a stone vessel found at Uruk depicting figures bearing tribute into the presence of the patron divinity of the city, the goddess Inanna. The atmosphere in all these scenes is of control, order, and hierarchy.

Uruk Expansion and Trade

The impact of these momentous social, political, and cultural developments in Lower Mesopotamia was felt in regions far from the city of Uruk itself; indeed, one of the characteristics of this period was the degree to which Uruk Mesopotamia interacted with its neighbors. To the east, on the alluvial plains of southwest Iran, was the city of Susa, which thoroughly adopted the Uruk style in its artifacts and architecture in the Late Uruk period. Further to the north, in the Zagros Mountains, Mesopotamian colonists settled and were well situated to exercise control over routes of communication from the lowlands into the hills and high plateaus. The early development of sophisticated copper metallurgy on the Iranian Plateau is likely to have been an important stimulant to these interactions.

On the upper Euphrates in Turkey, local communities maintained a strong sense of identity in the face of contact with Uruk-period Mesopotamia. There is good evidence that a considerable degree of political sophistication had been achieved prior to Uruk contact. Missing from these sites, however, and from all other contemporary sites outside Uruk, are tablets with proto-cuneiform script.

7.16, **7.17 The Warka Vase.** This famous vase, discovered at Warka (an alternative name for Uruk) is carved with scenes (illustrated above left) showing a cultic procession bearing offerings to a shrine, probably of the goddess Inanna. The vessel is made of alabaster and went missing from the Iraq Museum in Baghdad in April 2003, although it was later recovered. Height 100 cm (39 in.).

world system an economic system articulated by trade networks extending beyond the boundaries of individual political units and linking them together in a larger functioning unit

The engine for the expansion of the Uruk world in the later fourth millennium BCE is seen by most scholars as the desire by powerful elite groups of Lower Mesopotamia to acquire commodities from surrounding regions, thus spreading Uruk influence and cultural innovation far beyond the south Mesopotamian heartland of cities. Resources, such as stone and metals, were lacking on the alluvial plains of southern Mesopotamia but abundant in surrounding regions. Tapping into centuries-old prehistoric modes and routes of exchange, it seems that the Uruk people of Lower Mesopotamia attempted to settle, domesticate, and exploit an entire landscape of several thousand square kilometers and all its resources, on an imperial scale, solely to enhance the power and status of the elite groups now established at Uruk and other major centers of the south. The occurrence at many sites across the region of typically Uruk temples and administrative technology, suggests that highly ranked Uruk people successfully married politics with religion in their expansionist endeavors.

The Uruk **world system** collapsed around 3100 BCE, for unclear reasons, although there are suggestions that the climate became more arid at this time. Uruk society was maintained at Uruk itself and at a range of other sites where the use of proto-cuneiform tablets and cylinder seals shows the determination of local elites to maintain their identities after the collapse. Seal impressions with names of Mesopotamian cities, including **Ur**, Larsa, Uruk, and Kesh, may demonstrate a need for cities to act in collaborative ways. Outside the Lower Mesopotamian heartland, however, the communities of the peripheries cast off the Uruk mantle and over the following centuries developed distinct local and regional traditions.

CITY STATES, KINGDOMS, AND EMPIRES IN SOUTHWEST ASIA: EARLY BRONZE AGE, *c.* 3000–2000 BCE

Cultural and political developments of the Uruk period were consolidated through the centuries of the Early Bronze Age, from around 3000 BCE. Urbanization, literacy, religious administration, and interregional trade continued to characterize societies between 3000 and 2000 BCE, following the collapse of the Uruk world system. Increasingly abundant and rich textual evidence complements the wealth of archaeological material in defining a host of distinctive communities across the area. With varying access to sources of tin and copper—the ingredients of bronze—the societies of the region continued to develop their material and technological capabilities, engaging in both peaceful and hostile interactions through time.

Sumerian City States

The period *c.* 2900–2350 BCE is called the Early Dynastic period because, for the first time, written sources provide a list of kings and dynasties who controlled cities or groups of cities in Mesopotamia [**7.18**]. It is at this time that we call this region Sumer, an Akkadian (see below) word meaning Land of the Civilized Kings. Numerous cuneiform texts in the Sumerian language relate mainly to economic activity, but often also to religious, literary, and lexical matters.

Sumerian city states depended on irrigation farming, and the digging and maintenance of canals feeding off the Euphrates and Tigris rivers was a major social responsibility for urban authorities. These city states had independent political status, though they show remarkable similarities in their material culture, with such elements as pottery, jewelry, statuary, seals, and even mud-brick shapes and sizes being uniform across the entire southern alluvium. This points to consistent interaction between each of them, their craftworkers, farmers, soldiers, architects, and builders, throughout the Early Dynastic period.

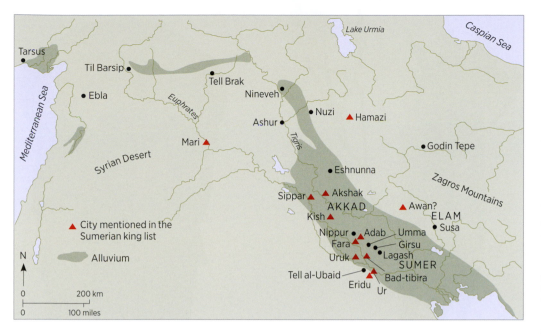

7.18 Map of Sumerian city states. In the Early Dynastic period, a large number of independent city states were dotted over the alluvial landscape of Mesopotamia, each controlling its own hinterland of agricultural and pastoral territory.

7.19 BELOW LEFT **Standard of Ur.** An enigmatic wooden box found, like the Ram in a Thicket sculpture (see **7.20**, p. 156), in one of the largest graves in the Royal Cemetery of Ur. The mosaic decoration in shell and red limestone against a blue lapis lazuli background was attached to the box by bitumen, and depicts a feasting scene in the upper register, with attendants bringing animals and sacks of food below. The opposite face of the Standard depicts scenes of war chariots and soldiers. The narrative may be one of a successful military campaign led by the king of Ur, followed by a celebratory feast. Height 21.6 cm (8.5 in.).

Farmers grew barley, wheat, pulses, fruits, and vegetables, and they herded cattle, sheep, goat, and pigs. Interactions between city dwellers and pastoral nomads are hinted at in the sources. Metals, semi-precious stones, and woods were the principal imports to Lower Mesopotamia, arriving from Iran, Anatolia, the Levant, and via the Persian Gulf. These luxury items were often only available to high-ranked people, embodied by the palace and the temple. A ruler existed for each city state, combining secular and religious authority, and ensuring their city's devotion to its principal deity. In addition to gods worshiped at specific cities, all Sumerian city states recognized a pantheon of supreme divinities headed by Enlil, whose temple at Nippur was the holiest shrine of the land.

The famous Royal Cemetery of Ur, with its spectacular artifacts of gold, lapis lazuli, and silver [**7.19** and **7.20**, p. 156], epitomizes the ability of city elites to accumulate wealth. In this

7.20 RIGHT **Sculpture from the Royal Cemetery of Ur.** Dating from the Early Dynastic III period, *c.* 2500 BCE, this is the so-called Ram in a Thicket sculpture, although it more probably depicts a goat. It is made of gold, silver, lapis lazuli, and shell over a shaped wooden core, and it formed part of an elaborate piece of furniture deposited in the tomb.

7.21 FAR RIGHT **Sargon.** Life-sized copper head, thought to be of the Akkadian king Sargon, found at Nineveh in northern Iraq.

cemetery, sixteen tombs stand out through lavish quantities of spectacular grave goods, as well as evidence of human sacrifice. These tombs may contain the bodies of either kings or high priests of Ur. At other sites, such as Tell Fara (ancient Shuruppak) and Tell Abu Salabikh, both dating to around 2500 BCE, the evidence from archaeology and texts suggests that a significant element of city states comprised a well-to-do middle class, occupying spacious houses, burying wealth with their dead, and conducting economic and administrative business, sometimes on an ambitious scale, within their own homes.

Kingdoms and Empires, c. 2300–2000 BCE

The centuries from 2300 BCE saw the rise of empires, large-scale political entities composed of a core state and areas subject to that core. Earliest of these was the Akkadian empire, initiated by Sargon (2334–2279 BCE) [**7.21**]. Sargon's capital city of Akkad has not been located archaeologically but is believed to lie somewhere in northern Sumer, probably in the region of **Babylon** and Kish. Under Sargon's influence, an increased emphasis on Semitic aspects of language and society can be detected through the 150 years of the empire's existence, indicated by the preference for Akkadian soldiers as elite troops and the dominance of the Semitic Akkadian language (supplanting Sumerian) in all forms of inscriptions.

The Akkadian empire began with Sargon's conquest of the cities of Sumer, and expanded into the world beyond, echoing the interregional connections of the Late Uruk period a millennium earlier. Akkadian influence is witnessed by archaeological and/or textual finds in Upper Mesopotamia, southeast Anatolia, and southwest Iran. The great city state of **Ebla** (in Syria) was conquered by Sargon (see Key Site box: Ebla), and in his inscriptions he boasts

KEY SITE Ebla

One of the most dramatic archaeological discoveries in Upper Mesopotamia took place at Ebla, near Aleppo in Syria, when Palace G, which was burned down sometime between 2400 and 2350 BCE, was discovered in the late twentieth century.

Within a suite of two rooms was found an archive of some 2,100 clay tablets that had once been neatly stacked and filed on wooden shelves as a reference collection of working documents. With the burning of the shelves at the palace's destruction, the tablets had fallen onto the floor, but careful excavation and recording procedures enabled the reconstruction of precisely how the texts had been arranged on the original shelves [**7.22**, **7.23**].

The texts show close links with Sumerian literate administration, as well as the local Semitic language, Eblaite. Not surprisingly, given its location, the archive indicates the important role played by the palace in the administration and economy of Ebla.

Up to 20,000 people were involved in some capacity in palace activities, and the palace owned large tracts of land around Ebla, including entire villages. In the direct remit of the palace was control over animal husbandry, with herds of up to 67,000 sheep, and associated wool and textile processing and production. Textile workshops were organized at an intensive level, and employed large numbers of female personnel.

Texts also reveal that Ebla participated in regional trade and commerce, particularly with the city of Mari and other towns of the Euphrates region, as well as engaging in political alliances and conflicts with neighboring states.

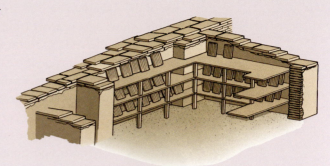

7.22 Reconstruction of the storage of clay tablets in the archive room of Palace G at Ebla. This was a working palace archive, where administrators could consult tablets for information relevant to a range of bureaucratic concerns; the tablets therefore needed to be carefully classified and arranged, just as the books in a modern library, to facilitate consultation.

By 2400 BCE, Ebla covered an area of 56 hectares (138 acres) and, with Mari on the Euphrates River, dominated the political scene of Upper Mesopotamia. The city's regional power base was the agricultural and grazing steppes of its large hinterland. Palace G and other buildings on the acropolis of Ebla, as well as the extent of the lower town, epitomize a local Upper Mesopotamian tradition of urban development and intensified rural settlement that accompanied, and certainly interacted with, the peak of Sumerian urban society on the Lower Mesopotamian plains at around 2600–2400 BCE.

7.23 Archive room of Palace G at Ebla, north Syria, c. 2400 BCE. The clay tablets lay where they had fallen from the wooden shelves; the texts provide important insights into the administration and economy of the city.

7.24 The Victory Stela of Naram-Sin, c. 2250 BCE, showing the Akkadian ruler Naram-Sin leading his army to victory over people of the Zagros Mountains. The mountainous terrain is clearly depicted, and the king is wearing a horned helmet, indicating his claim to divine status. Height 2 m (6 ft. 6 in.).

of reaching the Mediterranean coast in southern Turkey. To the south, there is evidence for Akkadian connections with Bahrain, Oman, and the Indus Valley.

Art of the Akkadian empire displays a marked sense of naturalism and restrained composition, which sets it apart from its Sumerian antecedents and successors. A particular masterpiece is the **stela** of Naram-Sin (2254–2218 BCE), depicting that king in triumphant conquest over an enemy on the eastern frontier [**7.24**].

In northern Mesopotamia, analysis of satellite imagery has revealed how the settlements of the period were connected together and to their hinterlands by a system of roads. These appear on satellite images as linear depressions or hollow ways, radiating out from the major city sites into the surrounding landscapes. The earliest roads date from the period 2600–2000 BCE.

The Akkadian empire collapsed around 2200 BCE in a flood of invading forces from the east, but there are also some indications of a major episode of aridification and the abandonment of agricultural land, which may have undermined the economic basis of the empire and other contemporary states of Southwest Asia.

Women in Mesopotamia

In both texts and **iconography**, women are under-represented in early Sumerian and Akkadian periods. They are most commonly mentioned in economic writings that detail transactions, such as the distribution of rations, and receipts of goods. These note how women formed a sizeable portion of the labor force, often through households, and mention textile production, cooking, agriculture, and herding as tasks undertaken by women. The texts also suggest women were paid less in rations than men.

One of the main avenues to an official position for a woman was through the temple hierarchy, though this would have been a path available only to the elite. Daughters and sisters of rulers were often made high priestesses, such as Enheduanna, daughter of Sargon. We know far more about Enheduanna than many other women in Mesopotamia due to the sheer quantity of inscriptions we have of her, some credited to herself. One example is "The Exaltation of Inanna," where Enheduanna describes how she was driven out of office at Ur, presumably during a rebellion against Sargon. She appeals to the goddess Inanna to reinstate her, which the inscription says the deity does.

When relying on textual evidence for the representation of women, it is important to acknowledge that many inscriptions do not mention the gender of the person they describe. In many cases, scholars have assumed male genders to these texts, so the relative scarcity of women in Sumerian texts may at least be partially due to our own preconceptions.

Third Dynasty of Ur

Following a period of regionalism, a grand return to imperial modes of power occurs with the empire of the Third Dynasty of Ur, or Ur III, which held sway from 2112 to 2004 BCE. Centered on the city of Ur in Lower Mesopotamia and covering much of the territory of the Akkadian empire, the Ur III empire oversaw a revival of the Sumerian language and culture, including a return to pre-Akkadian concepts of art. At this time, the city of Ur was completely rebuilt, with a massive ziggurat [7.25], magnificent temples, and large royal tombs. The Ur III kings ruled over significant tracts of Mesopotamia and western Iran through a system of provincial governors, each in control of an extraordinarily rigorous bureaucratic administration, which is bountifully recorded in thousands of clay tablets from this period. These texts, written in Sumerian, show a concern on the part of administrators and clerks to record every detail of the activities of empire, from labor devoted to canal-digging, to the animals that were provided as tax and tribute to the major shrine of the Sumerian god Enlil, located at the city of Nippur.

The Ur III empire disintegrated at the end of the third millennium BCE, according to the texts due to major military incursions from the east, including armies from the land of Elam. In this region, which is today southwest Iran, a dynamic dynasty of local origin had evolved at least partly in response to Mesopotamian stimulus. Centered on the site of Susa, where monumental building programs were pursued and inscriptions were written in the Elamite language, the kings of Elam maintained their control over Ur and its hinterland for some decades after the collapse of the Ur III empire.

In the Levant to the west, a serious decline in urban settlement is also detectable from around 2070 BCE. The collapse of the Egyptian Old Kingdom c. 2150 BCE (Chapter 13), and of the Indus Valley not long after (Chapter 8), adds to the picture of regional disintegration visible in the dramatic end to political entities across the entire area of Southwest Asia and beyond.

stela (pl. stelae) a freestanding carved stone monument

iconography a set of artistic representations that have overt religious or ceremonial significance; the study of such images

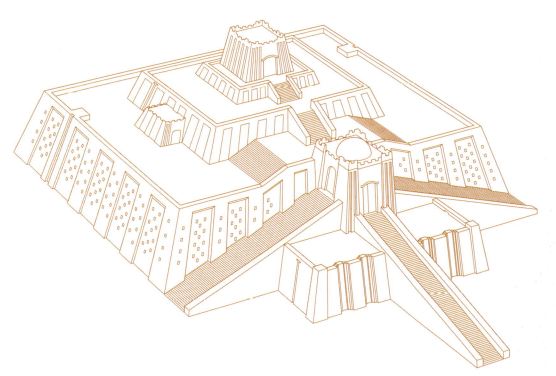

7.25 Reconstruction of the ziggurat of Ur, c. 2100 BCE. Ziggurats were staged towers, surmounted by shrines, with access by a series of staircases. In the flat and level landscape of Lower Mesopotamia, these shrines would have been visible for many miles around. Kings of the Ur III dynasty invested a great deal of effort and labor in building ziggurats and temples.

CITIES AND EMPIRES IN SOUTHWEST ASIA:
THE MIDDLE BRONZE AGE, *c.* 2000–1700 BCE

From 2000 BCE, new populations appeared in Southwest Asia: the Amorites and the Hurrians. This period is characterized by shifting alliances of cities, states, and societies across all Southwest Asia. From contemporary documents, including royal correspondence, we know that several major kings each had a following of minor kings in train.

The Amorite Ascendancy and the Age of Hammurabi

The Amorites founded the cities of Isin and Larsa, in the former heartland of the Akkadian and Ur III empires. The Isin kings saw themselves as successors to the Ur III empire. They purged the Elamites of southwest Iran from Ur and established control of southern Mesopotamia, but power alternated between Isin and its main rival, Larsa. Both cities maintained trade connections via the Persian Gulf, already well established in the Akkadian period. This trade involved the import of copper, timber, and precious stones, and the export of wool, cloth, oil, barley, and silver. Excavations at sites in Bahrain have investigated the settlements of local communities thriving on the profits of international trade at this time. Private entrepreneurs appear to have played the major role in organizing and executing this trade, although often with the participation of large urban institutions in the form of royal palaces and temples. With the increasing use of bronze for tools and weaponry, the import of copper from Oman was especially important. Evidence for these regional contacts includes the widespread occurrence of stamp seals throughout Mesopotamia, Iran, Anatolia, the Persian Gulf, and even the Indus Valley.

Within Lower Mesopotamia, the increasing dominance of Amorite dynasties is notable, with their kings established at many major cities, including Babylon, Kish, and Uruk. For a period of a century from 1865 BCE, the city of Larsa assumed dominance over Lower Mesopotamia, its kings carrying out massive programs of temple construction at many of the cities of the plains.

Hammurabi of Babylon (r. 1792–1750 BCE) was the most famous Mesopotamian king of the second millennium BCE. Of Amorite origin, he created a state that almost transcended traditional city-state rivalries. Throughout the 1780s BCE, he increased his power base through conquest. Hammurabi is famous today for his Law Code, one of the best-known documents from ancient Southwest Asia [**7.26**]. This text is inscribed on a stone stela, excavated at Susa in Elam, where it had been taken by eastern invaders long after Hammurabi's reign. The document commences by listing the gods and their cities that supported Hammurabi, including Tuttul, **Ashur**, Nineveh, Ur, Eridu, and Girsu. Similarly to all Mesopotamian kings, Hammurabi saw his rule as divinely sanctioned. The king is shown

7.26 The Stela of Hammurabi. Dating to *c.* 1770 BCE, the scene at the top depicts Hammurabi receiving the symbols of justice from the deity Shamash, below which the Law Code is inscribed. Similarly to the stela of Naram-Sin (see **7.24**, p. 158), this monument was found at Susa, where it had been taken by Elamite raiders of Mesopotamia in the late second millennium BCE. Many of the provisions in the Law Code threaten offenders with severe punishments. Law 53, for example, declares that anyone who through negligence allows his irrigation dam to collapse, flooding adjacent fields, shall be sold into enslavement and the proceeds of the sale used to compensate the farmers whose crops have been destroyed. Height 2.25 m (7 ft. 7 in.).

KEY THEME: MIGRATION Small and Large Movements across Southwest Asia

One of the striking features of ancient Southwest Asia is the high levels of human mobility attested at multiple times and places in its past. For the prehistoric period, when by definition we lack written records, we attempt to trace the movements of people through the distribution of their materials and artifacts. Modern scientific analysis of ancient DNA and of carbon, oxygen, and nitrogen isotopes can also provide rich data with which to study ancient population movements. Analysis of obsidian tools reveals that at least small-scale mobility was taking place, often over distances of hundreds of kilometers. Occasionally we can postulate much larger-scale migrations of human populations, as appears to happen at around 3000 BCE. In that case we can see the spread of a complex of material culture attributes—pottery, tools, architecture—which travels intact across large stretches of the landscape, suggesting migration of entire populations into Iran and Anatolia from the north.

as totally dominant in all aspects of the legal and social system addressed in the code, with the right to make decisions in any field of his society's affairs. Below the king were three social classes, the *awilum* or freemen, the *mushkenum*, of unclear dependent status, and the *wardum* or enslaved people.

In addition to his position at the apex of the Law Code, Hammurabi boasts of his public works: the construction and restoration of irrigation canals, temples, and fortifications. An associated boom in private-sector commerce and industry accompanied the rise of palace power, evident in numerous cuneiform texts of the time. In archaeological terms, however, we know little of the Babylon of Hammurabi's time, for much of it lies beneath the remains of later periods.

Upper Mesopotamia: Mari and Ebla

In Upper Mesopotamia and the Levant, a main focus of this period is the city of Mari in modern Syria, located on the Euphrates River at a key point where east–west and north–south trade routes met. Trade in tin, in particular, seems to have underlain the prosperity of the city at this period. The main architectural feature of the site is the great palace of Zimri-Lim (r. 1775–1761 BCE). The building was multi-storied, with more than 260 rooms at ground level, and covered an area of about 2.5 hectares (6.2 acres).

The walls of the palace still stand 4 meters (13 feet) high in places, built of sun-dried mud brick, with some use of baked brick and timber. Some rooms feature elaborate drainage systems, suggesting the presence of washing facilities. The main entrance was at the north, leading to a series of courtyards with surrounding rooms. The largest court covered a huge area (48 × 32.5 meters, or 158 × 107 feet) and provided access to a room where wall paintings depicted mythological scenes. A second court to the west gave access to the official focus of the palace: a throne room constructed with monumentally thick walls. Elsewhere, other official rooms were decorated with wall paintings including an investiture scene of Zimri-Lim receiving power from the goddess Ishtar in the presence of other deities [**7.27**, p. 162]. A fringed border around this scene suggests that textiles may have been hung on the walls. Other areas of the palace comprise shrines, administrative sections, and residences for the royal family and senior officials, as well as craft quarters, storerooms, and kitchens.

Within the palace, an archive of 20,000 cuneiform texts has been recovered. Some 30 percent of these texts are letters, the remainder being economic, legal, and administrative documents. They are mostly written in Akkadian, by this time the common language of

7.27 Mari, the palace of Zimri-Lim. Wall painting showing a scene of investiture. In the center, the goddess Ishtar hands a rod and a ring to the king; other elements include mythical animals, birds, and trees; *c.* 1775 BCE.

Southwest Asia, and they reveal a great deal about the role of Mari within the eighteenth-century BCE world of politics, diplomacy, and conflict.

For the Levant in the Middle Bronze Age, much of our information comes from these Mari archives. It is clear that the city participated keenly in the politics of the region. Zimri-Lim was married to a daughter of Yarim-Lim, king of Yamhad, a powerful kingdom centered on modern Aleppo. Zimri-Lim's predecessor, Yasmah-Adad, was married to a daughter of the king of **Qatna**, another powerful state of western Syria. There were also intimate connections with Ebla (see Key Site box: Ebla, p. 157), and a range of interactions with the major and minor states of Upper and Lower Mesopotamia and the Levant. The texts also tell of the important relations between the settled community at Mari and the pastoral nomads of the region—the Amorite tribes, such as those claimed as ancestors by the rulers themselves at Mari, Babylon, and elsewhere. These nomads might occasionally be conscripted into the army or employed for public projects, such as irrigation works, as well as seasonally tending to animals belonging to city dwellers.

SUMMARY AND CONCLUSIONS

In terms of political and cultural development, a number of clear threads run through the discussion of Southwest Asia. During the early centuries we see a steady trend toward increasing size and complexity in human communities. The Halaf societies of *c.* 6000–5400 BCE were characterized by small-scale settlements, their inhabitants engaged in farming the land and hunting. During the Ubaid period, *c.* 5900–4200 BCE, partly overlapping with the Halaf, there is good evidence for increasing social differentiation, with the first clear temples, as at Eridu, and some indications of long-distance trade, for example in the Persian Gulf region. A general lack of luxury goods on Ubaid sites, however, suggests that the social hierarchy of important Ubaid settlements may have been rooted in a concern to control surpluses of domestic staple commodities rather than in the trading of high-status materials or artifacts.

This concern comes to the fore around 4200–3000 BCE, when the first cities of the Mesopotamian plain, Uruk above all, show an ability to master the gathering, redistribution, and exchange of massive quantities of domestic surplus in foodstuffs and secondary products, such as milk and wool. Achieving this mastery is itself the step that creates a fleshed-out society with all its trappings, including a highly divided social hierarchy, an administrative system employing written records, a system of divine beliefs, rites, and rituals, and a hugely increased concern with trade in exotic, status-enhancing materials for use by elite groups.

Indeed, a consistent element in Southwest Asia during these millennia was the importance of trade and exchange. Marked by an irregular distribution of raw materials, particularly metals, timber, and stone, as well as of arable land and rainfall, the region hosted societies whose specific geographical location created needs and opportunities for engaging in commerce and interaction with neighbors. Furthermore, rivalry across Southwest Asia over access to trade routes and cherished commodities underpinned a dynamic of competition and conflict between the cities and states of the entire region, vividly attested in the historical records.

At all levels of society, the story of Southwest Asia is one of consistency and continuity. Structures of power persisted as templates of social control, even while individual instances of kingdoms, city states, and empires rose and fell with often spectacular speed. Even the specifics of elite ideologies show considerable continuity across thousands of years, delineating the ruler as a divinely sanctioned source of all power—legal, religious, social, and military.

FURTHER READING

The following offer a good introduction to ancient Southwest Asia:

Aruz, J., ed. 2003. *Art of the First Cities: The Third Millennium B.C. from the Mediterranean to the Indus*. New York: The Metropolitan Museum of Art.

Kuhrt, A. 1995. *The Ancient Near East, c. 3000–330 BC*. London: Routledge.

Liverani, M. 2006. *Uruk: The First City*. London: Equinox.

Liverani, M. 2014. *The Ancient Near East: History, Society and Economy*. London: Routledge.

Marcus, J. 2008. The Archaeological Evidence for Social Evolution. *Annual Review of Anthropology* 37, 251–66.

Matthews, R. 2003. *The Archaeology of Mesopotamia: Theories and Approaches*. London: Routledge.

Pollock, S. 1991. Women in a Man's World: Images of Sumerian Women, in Gero, J. M. and Conkey, M. *Engendering Archaeology*. Oxford and Cambridge: Blackwell. 366–87.

Potts, D. T. 1997. *Mesopotamian Civilization: The Material Foundations*. London: Athlone Press.

Potts, D. T., ed. 2012. *A Companion to the Archaeology of the Ancient Near East*. Oxford: Wiley-Blackwell.

Roaf, M. 1990. *Cultural Atlas of Mesopotamia and the Ancient Near East*. Oxford: Facts on File.

Sagona, A. and Zimansky, P. 2009. *Ancient Turkey*. London: Routledge.

Steiner, M. L. and Killebrew, A. (eds.). 2014. *The Oxford Handbook of the Archaeology of the Levant*. Oxford: Oxford University Press.

Van De Mieroop, M. 2015. *A History of the Ancient Near East c. 3000–323 BC*. 3rd edn. Oxford: Blackwell.

www.mesopotamia.co.uk British Museum site; good introduction to ancient Mesopotamia, including Sumer, Babylon, and Assyria.

www.etana.org Excellent resource covering all aspects of ancient Southwest Asia.

South Asia

Robin Coningham

8

Environments and Landscapes 167

Hunter-Gatherer Trajectories: Early South Asia, *c.* 26,000–6500 BCE 167

Transitions to Agriculture: 6500–1000 BCE 168

KEY SITE Mehrgarh: An Early Farming Community 170

Transitions to States: Early Harappan, Kot Diji, and Regionalization, *c.* 3000–2600 BCE 171

KEY CONTROVERSY The Decipherment of the Indus Script 173

Urban Communities: The Indus River, *c.* 2600–1900 BCE 173

KEY THEME: SOCIAL INEQUALITY Uniformity within the Indus Cities 174

KEY CONTROVERSY Origin of the Indus Cities: Indigenous or External? 175

Collapse and Localization: The Eclipse of the Indus Cities, *c.* 1900 BCE 178

KEY THEME: MIGRATION Migration and the End of the Indus Cities 179

Expansion and Integration: Re-Emergence of Complexity, *c.* 1200–500 BCE 180

Summary and Conclusions 181

Further Reading 181

The city of Mohenjo-daro, located in present-day Pakistan, was built *c.* 2500 BCE and became one of the largest settlements of the ancient Indus Valley.

TIMELINE South Asia

Years BCE

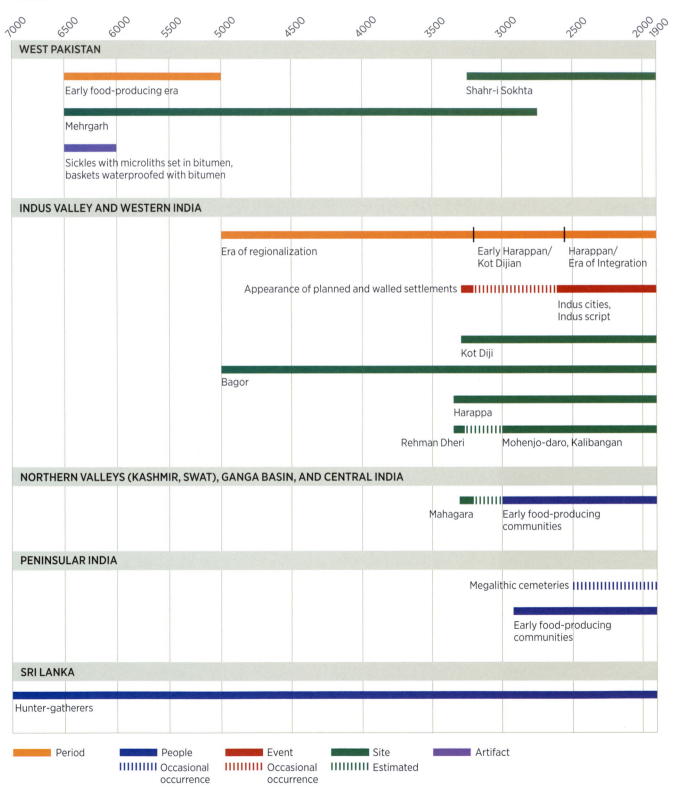

South Asia includes the modern nations of India, Bangladesh, Nepal, Bhutan, Pakistan, the Maldives, and Sri Lanka. The region provides another example of widespread changes occurring after the Ice Age, including agriculture and urbanization, which developed locally. The focus of this chapter is the period between 6500 and 1900 BCE, when South Asia witnessed dramatic transformations to the social and economic organization of its inhabitants. These involved the spread of early village-based communities from 6500 BCE and the emergence of the Indus cities between 3000 and 2000 BCE. These are the two key themes of this chapter. The Indus cities were in decline by 1900 BCE, but several areas of South Asia saw the emergence of a new series of cities and states in the first millennium BCE.

- The development of agriculture and pastoralism in South Asia occurred in multiple regions separately, and in some regions was not immediately followed by the significant increase in the number and size of settlements that we see in many other regions of the world.

- Farming began at very different periods in different regions: first in the northwest, and later in the east and south.

- The Indus Valley cities show no clear archaeological evidence of the social elites that must have governed them, and it is not yet clear whether they were autonomous city states or belonged to a larger political unit.

- The decline of the Indus Valley cities was followed by increased localization, until new cities and states formed during the first millennium BCE, associated with historical kingdoms and the rise of Buddhism.

ENVIRONMENTS AND LANDSCAPES

Similarly to Southwest Asia (Chapter 6), South Asia [8.1, p. 168] exhibits extremes of environment, stretching from the glaciers of its northern barrier, with ninety-five peaks higher than 7,500 meters (24,600 feet), to the 1,009 coral atolls of the Maldive Islands in the Arabian Sea, none of which is more than 2 meters (6.6 feet) above sea level. The key features within the northern half of this landmass are two great river basins, the Indus to the northwest and the Ganga (Ganges) to the northeast. To the south is the Deccan plateau and beyond that, off the southeastern tip of India, is the island of Sri Lanka.

Societies adapted to these striking variations in climate and environment by developing a wide range of subsistence practices, including floodplain farming in some regions, pastoralism and **transhumance** in others, or, for some societies, mobile lifestyles that have persisted up to the present day.

HUNTER-GATHERER TRAJECTORIES: EARLY SOUTH ASIA, c. 26,000–6500 BCE

The various regions of South Asia—Sri Lanka, western India, the Ganga plain, and Central India—are diverse, but share evidence of seasonal mobility (movement of human groups) shortly after the end of the Ice Age. In the Ganga plain, for example, game moved from the plains to the hills in the temperate winter season and were followed by hunter-gatherers,

transhumance the seasonal movement of human groups with their livestock, such as sheep, between mountain and lowland pastures

8.1 Map of South Asia
showing sites mentioned
in the text.

who camped in caves and shelters. As the year became hotter and drier, there was a general exodus of animals down to the perennial lakes in the plains, and people again followed, supplementing their diet with plant and aquatic resources. People began to become increasingly reliant on plants for their food supply, which is indicated by querns and perforated and polished stone rings, perhaps used as weights for the ends of digging sticks. Evidence of teeth worn by grit suggests a diet with as much as 60 percent plant content. Seasonal mobility can also be seen in western India and Sri Lanka, inferred from the appearance of materials from distant locations, such as a semi-precious stone called chalcedony found at Bagor, sourced more than 100 kilometers (60 miles) to the southeast, and marine shell in Sri Lanka transported 80 kilometers (50 miles) inland.

This pattern of mobility may have been accompanied by territoriality, where individual groups laid claim an area and its resources. This is suggested by the presence of human remains within camping sites, which may have linked ancestors with material resources in the surrounding region.

TRANSITIONS TO AGRICULTURE, 6500–1000 BCE

The pathway to domestication was varied across South Asia. Researchers have identified four distinct clusters of Neolithic communities (in western Pakistan, Kashmir and the Swat Valley, the Ganga basin, and peninsular India) that practiced pastoralism and agriculture. The first of these dates to as early as 7000–6000 BCE, but it is clear that the adoption of agriculture in South Asia was not immediately followed by the significant increase in the number and size of settlements that we see in many other regions of the world.

Western Pakistan

South Asia's earliest known Neolithic communities were located in western Pakistan in Baluchistan. There, between 7000 and 6000 BCE, small agricultural villages were established near the Bolan River and its pass, which links the uplands with the Indus plain (see Key Site box: Mehrgarh: An Early Farming Community, p. 170). Built of mud brick, the villages all shared a dependence on domesticated sheep or goat, cattle, wheat, and barley [**8.2**]. There is evidence for trade networks that brought turquoise, marine shell, and steatite beads from communities to the north, south, and west. How far these villages extended to the west and east is unknown, as few have surveyed on the Iranian border.

Scholars had assumed that Neolithic communities from Southwest Asia gradually diffused eastward, bringing the tradition of settled villages, ceramics, wheat, barley, and sheep or goat into South Asia. Early livestock herding in western Pakistan, however, did not imitate the Southwest Asian Neolithic practices of sheep and goat domesticates, but relied on native cattle. This suggests that the earliest of South Asia's Neolithic complexes developed locally.

Kashmir and the Swat Valley

Another cluster of early farming communities, the Northern or Kashmir–Swat Neolithic, was located across the southern valleys of the Karakoram and Himalayan ranges, and emerged in around 3000 BCE. In Kashmir, coarse, thick-walled ceramics only appeared at about 2850 BCE. Settlements are characterized by bell-shaped pits, the largest of them measuring 4.6 meters (15 feet) in diameter and 4 meters (13 feet) deep. Some were plastered with clay, and contained ceramics and faunal remains. The pits may represent underground dwellings, offering insulation from cold winters. No further pits were cut after 2250 BCE, when they were succeeded by mud-brick and timber structures on the surface.

The Swat Valley of Pakistan has similar evidence, although later in date, between *c.* 1700 and 1400 BCE. One village, **Kalako-deray**, is once again characterized by pits of various sizes. Some were stone-paved, and some had evidence of burning. They contained terra-cotta figurines in human and animal forms, pottery vessels, polished stone objects, rectangular stone sickles, hammerstones, grinding stones, bone objects, and jade beads. Here the pit-dwellings were also succeeded by rectangular mud-brick structures, erected on the surface.

The presence of jade beads and underground pit dwellings has led some scholars to suggest contact with Neolithic communities in Central and East Asia. Others have questioned the function of the pits as dwellings, and interpret their apparent domestic features as midden (cultural debris) fills accumulated after disuse. Such pits may be better interpreted as grain stores for the bitter winter months, when the transhumant communities who lived there moved south toward the plains before returning to the valleys in the spring for sowing. They may therefore have been seasonal rather than year-round occupations.

The Ganga Basin

The third Neolithic cluster is loosely centered on the Ganga basin. Some sites were established close to the earlier hunter-gatherer settlements and may have developed from them. This is not entirely surprising, as many of those earlier sites, associated with microlithic tools and broad-spectrum subsistence, relied heavily on the gathering of plant resources. They had stone querns for grinding cereals and perforated and polished stone rings that may have been digging-stick weights. Hence here, as in many other regions of the world, farming may have begun through the intensive use of locally available plant species by hunter-gatherer communities.

The earliest farming settlements of the Ganga basin appear several millennia later than those in regions to the west, highlighting the mosaic-like development of agriculture through South Asia as a whole. Sites such as Mahagara near the Belan River offer evidence of the transition to a Neolithic way of life. The Neolithic phase, from the mid-second millennium BCE, culminates in a settlement of at least eighteen huts centered on a stockade or pen. The huts may have been grouped into eight households, with a total population of 250 individuals and a degree of specialization among the inhabitants suggested by uneven distributions of querns and stone tools. In the later phases, inhabitants of Mahagara also consumed domesticated cattle, horse, and sheep or goat, and used cord-impressed ceramics, polished stone axes, and stone blades.

Despite the apparent continuity from hunting and gathering to agriculture in the Ganga Valley, there is controversy surrounding the identification and dating of domesticated rice at Mahagara. Some scholars argue that rice was introduced into this region from East and Southeast Asia in around 1500 BCE. Other archaeologists argue that rice domestication in

8.2 The first Neolithic farmers. Remains from the site of Mehrgarh provide evidence not only for the domestication of zebu cattle, but also for the cultivation of barley and wheat. These crops were harvested with sickles made of geometric stone blades set with bitumen into a wooden haft.

KEY SITE Mehrgarh: An Early Farming Community

Until the discovery of Mehrgarh, the earliest agricultural site known on the Indian subcontinent was dated to *c.* 4000 BCE, leading archaeologists to assume that agriculture in South Asia had its origins to the west. The discovery of Mehrgarh changed this, providing the earliest undisputed evidence of the formation of farming and pastoral communities in South Asia [**8.3**]. The settlement's plant and animal remains provide clear support for ongoing domestication and, most importantly, a distinct South Asian Neolithic subsistence package based upon local zebu cattle.

The earliest occupation at Mehrgarh dates to around 6500–6000 BCE, where the settlement consisted of rectangular mud-brick structures internally subdivided into small compartments. As some of the later compartments measure little more than 1 square meter (*c.* 11 square feet), they probably functioned as storage silos rather than residences.

Many of the finds from this period were recovered from burials and included exotic materials, such as turquoise, marine shell, steatite beads, and even a single copper bead. In the absence of ceramics, baskets lined with bitumen were utilized as waterproof containers; this material was also used to fix short stone blades in sickles (see **8.2**, p. 169).

Rich plant remains, including barley and wheat, have been recovered from within bricks, where they were used as temper (material added to clay to improve its firing qualities, preventing excessive shrinking and cracking). According to the archaeobotanist Lorenzo Constantini, although the wheat already appears to have undergone intensive domestication prior to arrival at the site, barley seems not to have been completely domesticated. These cereals were augmented with dates and jujube fruit, and wild animal species, such as gazelle, deer, and zebu cattle.

This pattern changed in around 6000–5500 BCE, which marks a phase characterized by the appearance of ceramics. It is in this period that the presence of many wild species declined and a subsistence strategy focused on cattle emerged. As this occurred at the same time that cattle declined in size, the zooarchaeologist Richard Meadow has suggested that this is evidence of a localized domestication of zebu cattle.

The size of cattle continued to decrease from *c.* 5500–4800 BCE. A copper ingot was discovered from this period as well as a tantalizing discovery of cotton, possibly providing the earliest evidence of its domestication in the world.

8.3 Prepottery Neolithic Mehrgarh, in western Pakistan, where evidence of the earliest farming community in South Asia was found.

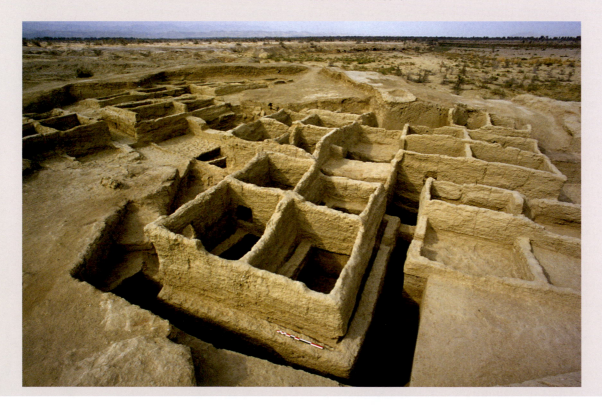

South Asia was indigenous, the result of a steady local development of food-producing communities. Only further investigation will resolve this debate.

Peninsular India

The final Neolithic cluster is broadly limited to peninsular India, and dated to between 4000 and 1000 BCE. It includes two types of sites: ash mounds and bigger open-area settlements. More than fifty ash mounds are recorded, the most massive being Kudatini, 130 meters (427 feet) in diameter and 10 meters (33 feet) high. They were formed by the burning of successive sets of stockades or pens. The presence of cattle hoof prints within stockades suggest that cattle were brought to these sites during the dry season and may have been augmented by wild cattle, which were then tamed.

Polished stone axes, stone blades, and coarse ceramics link these mound sites with larger settlements in the granite hills of the Deccan plateau. Less is known of these, as they are frequently covered by later occupations, but they appear to have been villages of circular structures built of boulders and stakes. Paleobotanical sampling indicates the presence of indigenous domesticated plants, including pulses, millets, and even tubers, suggesting that here again agriculture was a regional development.

TRANSITIONS TO STATES: EARLY HARAPPAN, KOT DIJI, AND REGIONALIZATION, *c.* 3000–2600 BCE

During the Early Neolithic, village communities were first established in western Pakistan in the intersection of the Indo-Iranian Plateau and the Indus plain. Dating to at least 7000 to 6000 BCE, they relied on domesticated species and stored surpluses, and traded with other communities for exotic materials. By 4000 to 3000 BCE, they had successfully colonized the Indus floodplain, and by 3000 to 2000 BCE they had created fortified, planned settlements. This later period is one of dynamic experimentation, culminating in the formation of a uniform cultural complex from *c.* 3200 BCE often called the Early Harappan period, or Kot Diji phase. This stretched from the west bank of the Indus to the bed of the Ghaggar in the east, with more than 300 identified sites. In describing this period, the archaeologist Jim Shaffer uses the phrase "era of regionalization" to designate the process by which a variety of distinct regional traditions emerged before coalescing. Some of the best-known Indus cities were established during this time, most notably **Harappa**.

Mehrgarh in western Pakistan (see Key Site box: Mehrgarh: An Early Farming Community) continued to grow steadily and emerged as a regional center of ceramic production. Indeed, pottery manufacture is a characteristic of communities of this region and period. In addition to monochrome, bichrome, and even polychrome wheel-thrown ceramics, these communities also manufactured copper, shell, and stone artifacts; they followed subsistence strategies dominated by domesticated cattle and sheep or goat, and buried their dead in formal cemeteries.

These communities were also in contact with populations to the west, who were gathering together in large, permanent settlements on the Indo-Iranian Plateau. The earliest evidence for the colonization of the lower Indus region dates to the fourth millennium BCE, perhaps because earlier sites are covered by alluvium. The key site is **Balakot**, where inhabitants built houses on mud-brick platforms, made distinctive decorated wheel-thrown ceramics, and lived on domesticated cattle and sheep or goat, wild gazelle, shellfish, and cultivated barley. Balakot's later ceramics are similar to those from more than twenty neighboring settlements.

Kot Diji and Early Pointers toward the Indus

Out of this mosaic of regional centers and traditions emerged the first indicator of cultural convergence within the Indus Valley. This was the Kot Diji phase, named after a site occupied from *c.* 3200 BCE, and distinguished by its pottery: wheel-thrown globular jars of red ware with geometric decorations including fish-scale patterns and intersecting circles, as well as depictions of bulls' heads, fish, and pipal leaves (a type of Indian fig). One of the most striking features of the Kot Diji phase, however, is not the pottery but the presence of formally planned settlements constructed with standardized mud bricks. Many of these features are also found later within the Indus area (see p. 176), suggesting degrees of continuity.

A prime example of a Kot Diji phase settlement is Rehman Dheri on the western bank of the Indus. Established around 3300 BCE, its final, Kot Diji phase shows evidence of a rectangular settlement with massive mud-brick walls. Erosion seen on aerial photographs reveals a rigid grid-iron street plan, even detailing individual structures and a kiln cluster. Formal planning is also found to the east of the Indus at **Kalibangan**. There, under the later Harappan citadel mound, the Indian archaeologist B. B. Lal identified a settlement enclosed by a 1.9-meter-thick (6 feet) wall. The parallelogram-shaped site includes mud-brick structures oriented to the cardinal directions and laid out in courtyard fashion [**8.4**].

Important continuities with the subsequent Indus cities range from the formal planning of settlements and cardinal orientation of structures to the use of ceramic motifs [**8.5**]. A cubic stone weight and a sealing bearing a unicorn motif from this period was discovered at Harappa, which stress progression between Kot Diji and the Indus era. The broad cultural convergence among the agricultural communities of the plains is further underlined by shared symbols, such as the bull. Some scholars have suggested that this indicates a common ideology, enabling further convergence and the eventual formation of the Indus cities.

8.4 Continuity at Kalibangan. Nowhere is the continuity between the formative proto-urban stage and the integrated era of the Indus Valley clearer than at Kalibangan in Rajasthan. The Bronze Age city is well represented by a citadel mound to the west and a lower town compound to the east, but archaeologists have also identified an earlier settlement under the citadel mound, indicating that the proto-urban town followed exactly the same plan.

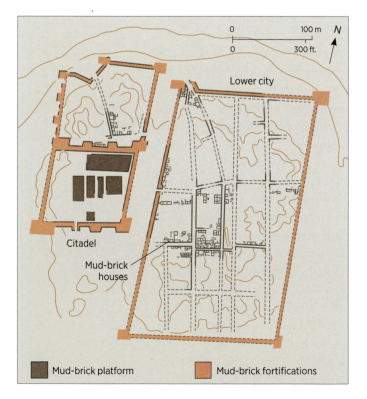

8.5 Cultural and ideological convergences. Anticipating the broad cultural integration of the Indus, the proto-urban settlements of the Indus basin began to display a number of common features including pottery of the Kot Diji style.

Since the first publication of a seal bearing the writing of the Indus in 1873, the script's meaning, and even its language, has been debated. From that date, the corpus of inscriptions has expanded to more than 2,700, and find sites range from the Oxus to the Indus and from South Asia along the Persian Gulf to the Euphrates. Composed of 170–220 simple signs and 170–200 composite signs, inscriptions are found on steatite, marble, ivory, silver, terra-cotta, shell, bone, and ceramic artifacts, including seals, axes, vessels, bangles, ladles, and sealings (the impression of a sealstone in clay). In addition to the signs, many inscriptions include a single standing animal [**8.6**], and a smaller number appear to depict a narrative scene. While some of the animals, such as tiger, elephant, and rhinoceros, are recognizable as native to South Asia, others appear to be hybrid or mythical.

Translation of the writings faces a number of obstacles. First, there are no bilingual inscriptions allowing a decipherment based on the comparison of a known and unknown script (such as the Rosetta Stone, which aided Jean-François Champollion in his decipherment of Egyptian hieroglyphs). Second, no single inscription is longer than twenty-six signs. Finally, there is no consensus as to the identification of the language, or languages, used in the inscriptions.

Despite this controversy, there is some common ground between the twenty or so attempts to decipher the Indus script. It is agreed that it was written from right to left. Second, most scholars accept that numerical value signs

8.6 The Indus script, as seen on this seal, has defied decipherment for more than one hundred years and will probably continue to do so until the discovery of a bilingual or trilingual inscription. The most we can advance now is that it probably represents a logo-syllabic script, with both word signs and phonetic syllables.

for single units are indicated by a simple downward stroke, and units of ten by semicircles. Finally, it is acknowledged that the script was probably logo-syllabic, possessing both word signs and phonetic syllables. Beyond this, decipherment is unlikely unless a bilingual inscription or a series of longer inscriptions is discovered; until then, the Indus cities will remain prehistoric.

URBAN COMMUNITIES: THE INDUS RIVER, *c.* 2600–1900 BCE

The Indus, or Harappan, community owes its names to the river basin where the culture was discovered, and to the site—Harappa—where it was first identified. Its developed, urbanized phase is dated to *c.* 2600–1900 BCE, when it covered an area of 500,000 square kilometers (193,000 square miles).

The period of the Indus cities was termed an era of integration by Shaffer and is typically identified at archaeological sites that show evidence of urbanization, artifact standardization, four-tier settlement hierarchy, writing (see Key Controversy box: The Decipherment of the Indus Script), long-distance trade, urban planning, craft and settlement specialization, and monumental public works. The Indus cities are often seen as including very little evidence of social hierarchy; no palaces or elite burials (see Key Theme box: Social Inequality—Uniformity within the Indus Cities, p. 174), which are a distinctive feature of Southwest Asia, East Asia, and the Americas. Settlements on the Indus River do, however, show elements of regional differentiation.

Regions on the Indus River integrated different levels of settlement. The largest were urban sites, the five best known being **Mohenjo-daro**, Harappa, Dholavira, Rakhigarhi,

KEY THEME: SOCIAL INEQUALITY Uniformity within the Indus Cities

Since its identification in the 1920s, scholars have been struck by the uniformity and standardization of the Indus region. These features are stressed by common urban plans, uniform script, shared weight and measure series, and even by standardized artifact forms and decorative motifs. This commonality is all the more striking as the majority of its urban centers were located in the Indus floodplain, an area devoid of raw materials, necessitating a supply chain of networks of procurement, manufacture, and distribution. As these features of uniformity and standardization stretched across an area of half a million square kilometers (193,000 square miles) and over a period of some 600 years, most scholars since the time of the researcher Stuart Piggott around the 1950s, have assumed they were enforced by the presence of a rigid state-level organization managed by elites [**8.7**].

Nevertheless, none of the characteristics of social inequality has been found within the Indus cities. Indeed, the analysis by the archaeologist Anna Sarcina of space at Mohenjo-daro failed to distinguish a single elite residence within the city, while the separate studies of grave goods by the anthropologists Danny Miller and Paul Rissman failed to differentiate elite higher-ranking communities. The absence of prestigious objects, hoards, and seals within the citadel mounds further undermines the concept of a visible elite.

Indeed, Miller has argued that the artifactual uniformity of Harappa stressed the scorning of material wealth and indicated that its inhabitants sought equality, while Rissman advanced this concept by observing that little wealth differentiation was visible in public burials, but that hoarded wealth was present, suggesting that a conscious masking

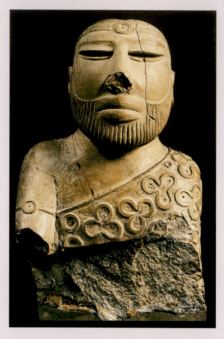

8.7 This sculpture, found in Mohenjo-daro in 1927, is known as the Priest-King statue.

or hiding of wealth was followed by the society's elites. Recent analysis of skeletal remains from Cemetery H at Harappa by the bioarchaeologist Gwen Robbins Schug and colleagues has found disturbing patterns of interpersonal trauma among women and children. This new evidence indicates that inequality was present.

and Ganweriwala. Each of these cities was located some 320 kilometers (200 miles) from its nearest neighbour. Although the political structure of the Indus area is impossible to determine from the evidence currently available, it is possible that the territory of the Indus River was divided into five separate domains, each centered on one of these major cities.

Character of the Indus Cities

The Indus Valley has commonly been considered inherently peaceful, from the absence of upper-class martial grave goods and representations of war or warriors. There is little evidence of any social differentiation within Indus settlements (see Key Theme box: Social Inequality—Uniformity within the Indus Cities), so conspicuous elite military displays should not be expected. Representations of war may have been made on materials unlikely to survive in the archaeological record. The presence of massive mud-brick walls in both the early and mature Harappan stages appears to indicate a substantial investment in conspicuous defenses, although these structures may have had multiple symbolic, ritual, or utilitarian functions (for example as flood defenses). It is probable that the Indus experienced as much violence as its neighbors, although it did not necessarily celebrate or ritualize warfare in the same way.

The political and economic basis of the Indus cities was very different from that of the rice-farming kingdoms that developed in later periods in the Ganga Valley and the south. The majority of the Indus settlements were located within the floodplains of the Indus and Ghaggar-Hakra rivers. Just as for the cities of Mesopotamia and Egypt, these locations allowed the establishment of large accumulations of people close to stretches of fertile land that were annually refreshed by seasonal floods. Zooarchaeological and archaeobotanical research has allowed the identification of the staples of the Indus cities. They included seasonal crops of wheat and barley, pulses, and millets, with limited evidence for fibers/oilseed, melons, cucumbers, squashes, and rice. For meat, milk, hides, and wool, people relied heavily on cattle and water buffalo, with goat and sheep, augmented by hunted species. The presence of regional networks of food has been postulated by the archaeologist William Belcher, with dried or salted fish traded and moved inland more than 850 kilometers (528 miles) from the coast.

Locations close to river basins had the advantage of silt, good for cultivating crops, and easy access to communications via boats, but they also had the disadvantage of the poor availability of raw material resources, such as lapis lazuli, carnelian, chert, tin, shell, copper, and gold. Urban economies nevertheless provided the core surplus necessary to function as a unit through exchange.

Finds of copper tools and drilled beads within such hunter-gatherer settlements as Bagor suggest exchange of semi-precious stone nodules for finished goods. These Indus materials, once processed to a highly standardized format, were redistributed among the settlements, and the surplus was traded across the Persian Gulf as well as through plateau hubs as far west as Elam and Mesopotamia. Indus weights, and ceramics bearing Indus characters in Oman, Bahrain, and the UAE, may even attest to the seasonal movement of Indus traders across the Arabian Sea and into the Persian Gulf.

KEY CONTROVERSY Origin of the Indus Cities: Indigenous or External?

Many early researchers thought the development of the Indus cities may have been a result of diffusion from Mesopotamia. This changed in the 1970s with the identification of a distinctive proto-urban phase that occurred in the Indus basin. This was of significance, as it demonstrated that the planned cities of the mature Indus phase were not suddenly imposed, but were built after an earlier phase of settlements, such as Rehman Dheri, with its grid city plan. With dates of c. 3200 BCE, Kot Diji appears very similar to the contemporary foundations of Shahr-i Sokhta on the Indo-Iranian Plateau and Mundigak in southwest Afghanistan, further weakening the diffusionist theory.

The nature of this sequence is also illustrated by excavations beneath the Indus cities of Harappa and Kalibangan. At the latter, the proto-urban walled compound becomes the mature-phase citadel, while at Harappa the walled compound is later augmented by a number of adjoining walled enclosures.

Even though there is a long developmental sequence for the Indus basin, it should be recognized that there remains a gulf between the 20-hectare (49 acres) Early Harappan settlement of Rehman Dheri and the mature Indus metropolis of Mohenjo-daro of 200 hectares (494 acres); a similar divide exists between the non-scriptural graffiti of the proto-urban phase and the Indus script. It should also be noted that the settlements of the two periods occupied slightly different areas, and while Kot Diji-phase settlements thrived in parts of Pakistan's Khyber Pakhtunkhwa Province to the west of the Indus, this region was never fully integrated into the Indus system.

Mohenjo-daro

Mohenjo-daro is by far the largest of the Indus cities at 120 hectares (296 acres) and with a population of perhaps 40,000 to 80,000 inhabitants. The lower town was arranged around a gridded street plan, the widest of the streets 9 meters (30 feet) across and paved in brick. The bigger houses consisted of rooms arranged around a central courtyard, and stairways indicate the existence of an upper floor. Brick sizes were standardized and the city was served by an extensive system of wells and drains.

Dominating the lower town was the fortified citadel, which rose 10 meters (33 feet) above the surrounding floodplain on a mud-brick podium. Surrounding the citadel are public buildings, including a great brick tank (perhaps for ritual purification). Built of fired brick set in bitumen to provide waterproofing, this structure, known as the Great Bath, is surrounded by a colonnade and individual chambers, and would have held more than 160 cubic meters (5,650 cubic feet) of water. It is immediately adjacent to the 6-meter-high (20 feet) granary, measuring 50 × 27 meters (164 × 89 feet), of which nothing above its mud-brick foundation survives. The final monument is a pillared hall covering 30 × 30 meters (100 × 100 feet) at the southern edge of the citadel, indicated by the presence of four rows of five brick pillars. The use of these structures remains unclear but the bath recalls the importance of lustration in later South Asian religions.

To the east of the citadel, the lower town lies on a 9-meter-high (30 feet) mound covering some 190 hectares (469 acres) [**8.8**]. It was unfortified and was subdivided into six or seven blocks by the broad brick-paved main streets; the blocks are further subdivided by smaller streets and lanes. Hundreds of individual houses are then grouped around their own court-yards within these smaller divisions and are entered from the lesser streets and lanes rather than directly from the main thoroughfares. The presence of bathrooms within most house compounds is very striking, as is the complex network of drains associated with them.

8.8 The citadel of Mohenjo-daro. The key monuments include the most recent, a Buddhist stupa (a solid dome often containing Buddhist relics) dating to the first or second century BCE, covering the Bronze Age buildings on the eastern side. To its west is the Great Bath and colonnade, abutting the mud-brick podiums of the granary. There is a pillared hall to the south of the mound, close to a surviving portion of the mud-brick retaining wall.

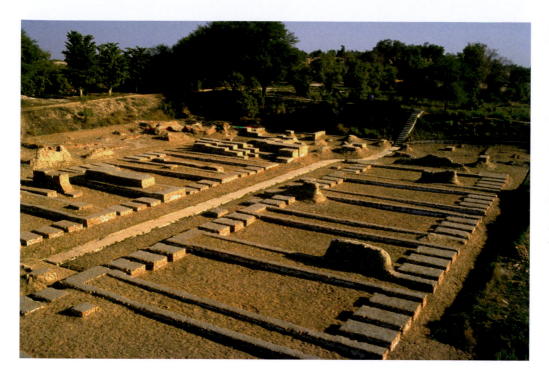

8.9 Harappa. Recently it has become apparent that the city has a different urban plan from Mohenjo-daro. While the latter has a citadel mound in the west and lower town in the east, Harappa has at least four separate walled mounds centered on a central depression. Other differences are also apparent between the square podiums of Mohenjo-daro's granaries and the rectangular units at Harappa.

Harappa

Harappa covers an area of more than 150 hectares (371 acres) and is located to the south of an old course of the Ravi River. Excavations indicated four walled mounds clustering around a central depression that may have held water. Each mound was entered through narrow gates and appears to have had little differentiation, offering the same array of craft manufacture and finished goods [**8.9**]. Archaeologists have extended Harappa's sequence to around 3000 BCE, and have helped challenge many of the preconceptions associated with Indus cities.

Harappa's urban plan was once thought to be identical to that of Mohenjo-daro, with the Indus having two twin capitals. Research has demonstrated, however, that in addition to Harappa's citadel mound, each of the settlement's other mounds was also fortified. The granaries of the two cities are also different, and even the concept of twin capitals is challenged by the discovery of the cities of Ganweriwala and Dholavira, the latter of which has an urban plan unlike any encountered previously.

Dholavira, Rakhigarhi, Ganweriwala, and Other Centers

The city of Dholavira was a later discovery [**8.10**, p. 178] and its plan is different from any other. Defined by a wall, enclosing a complex of further walled rectangular and square compounds, the city was built of mud brick and local sandstone. The lower or outer town, with its evidence for craft activities, is subdivided by cardinal streets. Located on Khadir Island in the marginal environment of Kutch, it has to be assumed that the Dholavira community was supported by the trade facilitated by its location close to the coast.

Little is known of the plans of Rakhigarhi and Ganweriwala, as they were identified by survey and have not been significantly excavated. Beyond the five larger centers, the next group of settlements includes some thirty-two sites that were smaller, covering areas of less than 20 hectares (49 acres). They vary but were formally walled and planned. Kalibangan, for example, is beside a former course of the Ghaggar-Hakra River in Rajasthan and shared

8.10 Dholavira. One of the most recently discovered Bronze Age cities in the region, Dholavira possesses a unique plan and, unlike the better-known sites of Mohenjo-daro and Harappa, was largely built of locally available stone. This reconstruction drawing illustrates the courtyard houses and gardens within the outer wall, and the heavily fortified citadel (top left) with its double rampart. Located in the Gulf of Kutch, the discovery of Dholavira demonstrates that western India was an integral part of the Indus.

a plan with Mohenjo-daro. Its rectangular citadel was located to the west of the walled lower town. The town was subdivided by cardinally oriented roads, and the citadel was split into two by a large internal bastioned wall.

A next level of settlements are small walled sites of 2 to 4 hectares (5 to 10 acres), some of which have been identified in western India. At the base of the settlement hierarchy are more than 15,000 sites under 1 hectare (2.5 acres), representing agricultural villages or highly specialized settlements.

The Western Borderlands

In western Pakistan, the Baluchistan borderlands were never absorbed into either the Early Harappan or the Indus. Southern Baluchistan did, however, become integrated. In contact with the Indus cities to the east, these communities built public complexes of boulders and mud brick. These may have been attempts by the communities of the borderlands to compete with, or imitate, the cultural experiment to the east.

COLLAPSE AND LOCALIZATION: THE ECLIPSE OF THE INDUS CITIES, *c.* 1900 BCE

From around 1900 BCE, much of the core of the Indus urban system underwent decline. The controversy concerning its eclipse is ongoing, but explanations based on single dramatic events effecting the entirety of the whole, such as migrations or floods, are no longer supported by evidence. Instead, scholars prefer a combination of factors contributing to the gradual loosening of the character of the Indus, as individual communities and regions opted for less extended and demanding political, social, and economic integration and favored new trading partners and materials. The physical manifestations associated with the loss of integrated traits include the disappearance of urban forms, monumental public buildings, and written script. These are associated with the appearance of new, localized cultural traits with links to western and Central Asia, as well as the reconfirmation of local, pre-urban cultural traditions within the greater Indus system. Although these changes are generally dated to *c.* 1900 BCE, the regional patterns differ.

The Core Cities

In this period, core cities were abandoned, sites became fewer, smaller, and less specialized and old traditions were replaced. For example, the Indus tradition of extended burial was replaced by disarticulated remains found within funerary jars with very characteristic black paint on red slip decoration. Smaller, specialized sites, such as Balakot, declined and the cities of Mohenjo-daro and Chanhu-daro were mostly abandoned. Evidence from this post-urban phase—such as stamp seals, as well as exotic items, for example copper pins and shaft-hole axes, often of western or Central Asian affinity—suggest that a level of administration continued at these sites.

In Gujarat, smaller settlements actually increase in frequency. A number of cultural styles and traditions, which had characterized this region prior to urbanization, also re-emerged and there is evidence to suggest continued investment in communal monuments at certain sites. Decline in some areas was therefore accompanied by development in others.

Peripheral Areas

While one might expect the peripheries of the Indus to be negatively impacted, many of these areas demonstrate the opposite. Mundigak in Afghanistan is a particularly good example. There, on the remains of an enormous palace structure, a new monumental stepped brick building was erected and painted red and white, indicating a continued success in the mobilization of surplus, but now with exchange directed north toward Central Asia.

A number of settlements in Baluchistan, to the south of Mundigak, were abandoned around 1900 BCE, although we still find rich objects, such as gold bull pendants, a gold chalice with lion frieze, and stone scepters of the Quetta Hoard, as well as the copper shaft-hole axes from the Sibri cemetery.

cist a box-like container made of stone slabs, often used for burials

Not all sites refocused on Central Asia. **Pirak**, occupied between *c.* 1700 and 700 BCE, demonstrates continuity and evidences trade and exchange networks that brought ivory from the Ganga plain, shell from the Arabian Sea, lapis from Afghanistan, and carnelian from western India.

EXPANSION AND INTEGRATION: RE-EMERGENCE OF COMPLEXITY *c.* 1200–500 BCE

The era between the end of the Indus cities and the emergence of what is known as the Early Historic period around 500 BCE was once referred to as a dark age. Now scholars cite evidence for some degree of continuity with the previous period, making this time less "dark" than was once thought.

These centuries between *c.* 1200 and 500 BCE eventually saw the re-establishment of fortified settlements, the emergence of states, the use of seals for administration, the creation of planned cities, the reintroduction of writing, and the standardized production of ceramics and other artifacts. Another important feature was the appearance of iron tools. It was a period of increasing complexity and witnessed the emergence of religious teachers, such as the Buddha and Mahavira, and the growth of Jainism, offering the new mercantile elite an escape from low Brahmanical status. A period of dynamic change, it was brought to a close with the integration of the western parts of the subcontinent into the Persian empire in the late sixth century BCE.

Southern India and Sri Lanka

In contrast with developments on the Indus plain, southern India and much of the Deccan Plateau pursued an alternative pattern of complexity. A number of the Neolithic settlements were continuously occupied from 3000 BCE into the Early Historic period. Their subsistence strategies appear to have remained principally unchanged. Continuity is also found within mortuary practices. From these early beginnings, experimentation with stone increased; stone circles surrounding pit burials gave way by 800 BCE to the creation of huge complexes of central stone **cists**, complete with portholes [**8.11**].

The south Indian sequence is in stark contrast to that of Sri Lanka, as revealed by chronological data from **Anuradhapura**. Excavations indicate that the settlement was established around 900 BCE. Initially a simple community with circular structures, reliant on a mixture of cultivation, pastoralism, and hunting, it had grown to an area of some 26 hectares (64 acres) by 450 BCE. Manufacturing debris suggests the working of iron, copper, bone, ivory, and semi-precious stone, while the presence of horse bones, a non-endemic species, indicates maritime links. Most striking is the identification of sherds scratched with inscriptions of Early Brahmi, implying the reappearance of a written script by 400 BCE. The inscriptions are part of the paraphernalia for managing trade and exchange.

8.11 Megalithic cist burial at Brahmagiri. While urban forms began emerging to the north and south, the Iron Age communities of the Deccan invested in funerary monuments of stone. These are often grouped into large cemeteries: there are more than 300 stone cists at Brahmagiri.

SUMMARY AND CONCLUSIONS

The archaeology of South Asia is by no means fully understood, and some of the debates concern fundamental issues, such as the nature of the Indus script, its social organization, and even the causes of its demise.

This chapter has concentrated on the development of the Indus cities through stages of regionalization, integration, and localization. The sequence is becoming better understood as a result of pioneering research at Mehrgarh and the proto-urban settlements of the Early Harappan period. The exact processes that transformed settlements, such as Rehman Dheri and Kalibangan, into centers of the enormous proportions of Harappa, Mohenjo-daro, and Dholavira are still uncertain, but the phasing and morphology of that change are now clearer.

Similarly, the abandonment of the concept of a post-Indus dark age has simplified our understanding of the emergence of the second, Iron Age, urbanization of South Asia. Rather than relying on a series of migrations and invasions, archaeologists are concentrating on the regional sequence and have identified the presence of proto-urban settlements predating evidence of foreign contact. Again, we may not be certain of the exact nature of the dynamics involved, but the characteristics of the resultant changes are now well understood on an intra- and extra-settlement basis. Only further research will enable us to comprehend fully these transformations, but the increasing use of high-quality excavation and survey and science-based analysis bodes well.

FURTHER READING

Useful introductions to ancient South Asia include:

Coningham, R. A. E. and Young, R. L. 2015. *The Archaeology of South Asia: From the Indus to Asoka c. 6500 BCE to 200 CE*. Cambridge: Cambridge University Press.

Dani, A. H. and Masson, V. M. (eds.). 1992. *History of Civilisations of Central Asia, Volume I: The Dawn of Civilisation: Earliest Times to 700 BC*. Paris: UNESCO.

Harmatta, J., ed. 1994. *History of Civilisations of Central Asia, Volume II: The Development of Sedentary and Nomadic Civilisations: 700 BC to AD 250*. Paris: UNESCO.

Harmatta, J., ed. 1996. *History of Civilisations of Central Asia, Volume III: The Crossroads of Civilisations: AD 250–750*. Paris: UNESCO.

Kenoyer, J. M. 1998. *Ancient Cities of the Indus Valley Civilisation*. Karachi: Oxford University Press.

Piggott, S. 1950. *Prehistoric India to 1000 BC*. Harmondsworth: Penguin.

Sarcina, A. 1979. The Private House at Mohenjo-daro, in *South Asian Archaeology 1977*. Taddei, M., ed. 433–62. Naples: Istituto Universitario Orientale, Seminario di Studi Asiatici.

Shug, G. W. *et al.* 2012. A peaceful realm? Trauma and social differentiation at Harappa. *American Journal of Physical Anthropology* 143 (1), 149–50.

Settar, S. and Korisettar, R. (eds.). 2002. *Indian Archaeology in Retrospect, Volume I: Prehistory: Archaeology of South Asia; Volume II: Archaeology of the Harappan Civilisation*. New Delhi: Indian Council of Historical Research.

Singh, U. 2008. *A History of Ancient and Early Medieval India*. New Delhi: Pearson Longman.

Wright, R. P. 2010. *The Ancient Indus: Urbanism, Economy and Society*. Cambridge and New Delhi: Cambridge University Press.

http://www.harappa.com/indus2/harpframe.html Website of the Harappa Archaeological Research Project.

http://www.dur.ac.uk/arch.projects/anuradhapura Website of the Anuradhapura (Sri Lanka) Project.

平台
Platform

灶坑
Fireplace

门坎
Threshold

门道
Gateway

East Asia: From Mobile Foraging to Settled Farming

9

Charles Higham

Environments and Landscapes 185

Agriculture in East Asia 185

Transitions to Agriculture: The Yangzi Valley, 12,000–6000 BCE 186

Early Farming Communities: The Yangzi Valley, 6000–2500 BCE 187

KEY CONTROVERSY The Origins of Rice Cultivation 188

Transitions to Agriculture: Northern China and the Yellow River Valley, 9000–5000 BCE 191

KEY SITE Jiahu: The Transition to Agriculture in the Huai River Valley 192

Early Farming Communities: Northern China and the Yellow River Valley, *c.* 5000–2600 BCE 193

KEY THEME: DOMESTICATION The Consequences and Significance of Agriculture 195

KEY SITE Tianluoshan 196

The Expansion of Farming: Southern China and Southeast Asia, 2000–1000 BCE 197

KEY SITE Man Bac 199

Complex Hunter-Gatherers: Jōmon Japan, 14,000–1000 BCE 202

Expansion of Domestication: Korea and Japan 203

KEY THEME: SOCIAL INEQUALITY The Role of Agriculture and Metallurgy 205

Summary and Conclusions 206

Further Reading 207

Excavations at Banpo, near present-day Xi'an in China, an early farming village of the Yangshao culture (5000–3000 BCE), showing the sunken floor of a rectangular house.

TIMELINE East Asia: From Mobile Foraging to Settled Farming

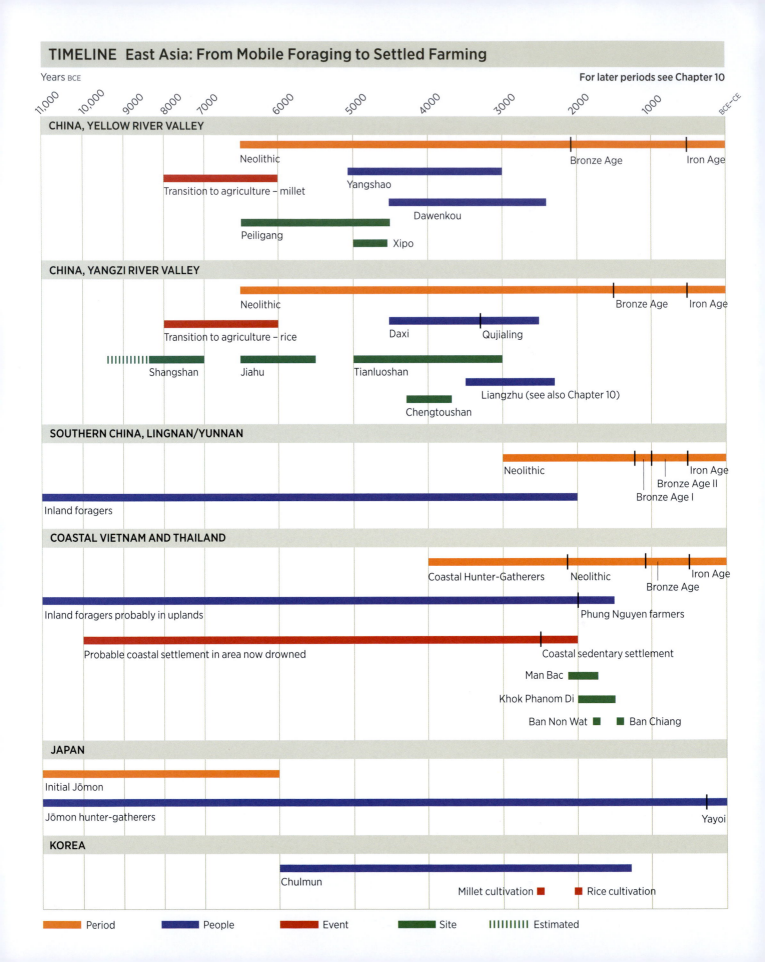

Years BCE

For later periods see Chapter 10

11,000   10,000   9000   8000   7000   6000   5000   4000   3000   2000   1000   BCE–CE

CHINA, YELLOW RIVER VALLEY

Neolithic

Bronze Age   Iron Age

Transition to agriculture – millet

Yangshao

Dawenkou

Peiligang

Xipo

CHINA, YANGZI RIVER VALLEY

Neolithic

Bronze Age   Iron Age

Transition to agriculture – rice

Daxi   Qujialing

Shangshan   Jiahu   Tianluoshan

Liangzhu (see also Chapter 10)

Chengtoushan

SOUTHERN CHINA, LINGNAN/YUNNAN

Neolithic

Iron Age

Bronze Age II

Bronze Age I

Inland foragers

COASTAL VIETNAM AND THAILAND

Coastal Hunter-Gatherers   Neolithic   Iron Age

Bronze Age

Inland foragers probably in uplands

Phung Nguyen farmers

Probable coastal settlement in area now drowned

Coastal sedentary settlement

Man Bac

Khok Phanom Di

Ban Non Wat   Ban Chiang

JAPAN

Initial Jōmon

Jōmon hunter-gatherers

Yayoi

KOREA

Chulmun

Millet cultivation   Rice cultivation

Period   People   Event   Site   Estimated

In East Asia, as in other regions of the world, the end of the last Ice Age opened up new opportunities for hunter-gatherer communities, who began to exploit in new ways the plants and animals on which they depended, ultimately domesticating key species and moving to a predominantly agricultural way of life. In some areas, notably the Yellow and Yangzi river valleys, this process began early in the postglacial, with people focusing in particular on millet in the north and rice further south. The development of agriculture was accompanied by the appearance of permanent villages, population growth, evidence of trade, and the first archaeologically visible signs of social inequality in China, which would set the stage for the later development of cities and states.

In Japan, by contrast, Jōmon hunter-gatherers did not adopt agriculture but developed sophisticated and intensive patterns of resource exploitation that enabled the growth of permanent village communities supported by wild resources alone.

- The process of domestication in East Asia is one of indigenous development by hunter-gatherer communities drawing upon local plant and animal species.

- In the Yangzi Valley, hunter-gatherers gradually cultivated and domesticated rice.

- In the Yellow River Valley, hunter-gatherers gradually domesticated millet.

- Animal domestication and crop cultivation later spread into southern China and Southeast Asia through the migration of farming communities.

- Jōmon societies of Japan continued to depend on wild resources, although they exploited these in novel and more intensive ways.

ENVIRONMENTS AND LANDSCAPES

The development of agriculture in mainland East Asia [**9.1**, p. 186] involved two plant species from two distinct regions. Millet was domesticated in the northern Yellow River Valley, and rice in the southern Yangzi Valley. Today, the southeastern monsoon brings moist and warm air to southern China, but its strength and influence wanes north of the Yangzi River. This benign climate favors the growth of wild rice. The drier conditions on the Yellow River and the loess plateau to the east, however, are suited to the growth of millet.

Climate change was a vital factor in the development and spread of domesticated plants and animals in East Asia. Periods of relative warmth saw the expansion northward of conditions that suited rice, while colder phases involved a contraction southward again. In the Yellow River region, increased temperature and rainfall (although still less than in the Yangzi) favored the proliferation of other wild grasses, including millet. It was under these conditions that domestication took place, which was commonly accompanied by major changes in social organization.

AGRICULTURE IN EAST ASIA

Domestication and food production developed in East Asia independently and in parallel with that of Southwest Asia (see Chapter 6), relying on different species, though with remarkable similarities in settlements, material culture, and social change.

Cultivation by humans began to apply new selective pressures on the reproduction of rice and millet. Grains that shattered from their plant too soon (at the point of the plant called

9.1 Map of China and surrounding countries, showing the location of the main rivers and other geographical features, and the major sites mentioned in the text.

the rachis, similar to wheat and barley in Southwest Asia) would not be gathered and sown the next season. Seeds of plants that tended to keep hold of their grains for longer, therefore, were more likely to be planted by people and propagate. Human lifestyles changed in turn, as dependence on rice and millet increased, with gradual but significant transformations including sedentism, population increase, and new opportunities for social inequality. As such, East Asia offers a powerful parallel to similar trajectories in Southwest Asia, Mesoamerica, India, and other regions where domestication developed independently. The consequences of farming for population numbers and social status meant that here, as elsewhere, the transition from hunter-gatherer to agricultural economies was irreversible.

Besides the independent development of agriculture in East Asia, migration was also a major cause behind the spread of domestication, as farming populations moved into new land, often already occupied by existing hunter-gatherer communities. We will see this in other parts of the world, such as Europe.

TRANSITIONS TO AGRICULTURE: THE YANGZI VALLEY, 12,000–6000 BCE

Rice is second only to maize in terms of world grain production today, and a significant amount of the latter is fed to animals. Rice is the dominant crop of much of East and Southeast Asia, and sustains hundreds of millions of people worldwide. Its origins are therefore a vital chapter in the human past. In the wild, it is a grass adapted to wet conditions and, being reliant on sufficient warmth and water to mature, rather than on soil fertility, it can be successfully grown in the same fields annually without crop rotation or years of fallow. When first tracing how humans adapted and exploited rice, archaeologists initially reconstructed the climatic changes that took place alongside the global warming that followed the last Ice Age, as rice requires specific conditions to thrive. With the development of archaeobotany techniques, archaeologists were later able to recover the rice remains themselves from prehistoric sites (see Key Controversy box: The Origins of Rice Cultivation, p. 188). These analyses have shown that domestication took place in the valley of the Yangzi River.

Hunter-Gatherer Communities in the Yangzi Valley

The story of rice cultivation in the Yangzi Valley begins with hunter-gatherer communities. Several sites reveal the presence of late Pleistocene hunter-gatherers, for example at the cave site of **Yuchanyang** in Hunan Province. Yuchanyang was occupied between 16,000 and 12,000 BCE, and overlooks low-lying, swampy terrain. Excavations have unearthed many hearths associated with the remains of wild pig, deer, tortoises, fish, birds, forty species of seeds, and the phytoliths (minute remains of plant tissue) and husks of rice that have all the characteristics of a wild variety.

Another cave, called **Diaotonghuan**, shows an increasing use of rice over time, and the adoption by hunter-gatherers of more sedentary lifestyles. Deposits dating to about 23,000–20,000 BCE yielded few rice phytoliths, but the number surged by a factor of ten in finds dated to the brief warm phase that began around 11,200 BCE. It appears that, at this time, hunters and gatherers of Diaotonghuan were collecting wild rice.

The collection of rice in the Yangzi Valley was affected by the rises and falls in temperature and humidity from the changing climate. During the Younger Dryas (c. 10,800–9600 BCE), a time of cooling climates, rice phytolith numbers show that far less rice was collected by hunter-gatherer communities. The return of cold temperatures during this period would have probably made rice available only in the warmer south. Its remains were back in force during the long period of warming between 8000 and 6000 BCE, and it is at this time that the first pottery **sherds** are found, which is significant because ceramic vessels often reflect a more sedentary lifestyle.

From the long warming period that followed the cold Younger Dryas, the cultivation of rice became possible. Communities adopted cultivation slowly, often in combination with established hunter-gatherer strategies. When cultivated rice appeared, it did so in conjunction with early evidence for ceramics and the adoption of more sedentary ways of living.

EARLY FARMING COMMUNITIES: THE YANGZI VALLEY, 6000–2500 BCE

The Development of Permanent Villages, c. 6000–5000 BCE

The sequel to the trend toward rice cultivation is a new form of settlement where houses, cemeteries, pits, and the remains of domestic activity accumulated in low mounds on the plains surrounding the major lakes of the Yangzi Valley. Material culture in these settlements took on a new aspect as spades and sickles appeared, more pottery was made from clay **tempered** with rice chaff, cloth was woven, and the dead were interred in permanent cemeteries. It is suggested that, having become increasingly familiar with rice manipulation

sherd a fragment, usually of pottery

temper the material added to clay to improve the firing qualities of pottery, preventing excessive shrinking and cracking

KEY CONTROVERSY The Origins of Rice Cultivation

Rice is so adaptive, and there are so many varieties, that it is grown today in upland fields, in irrigated plains, on hill terraces, and along the margins of lakes [**9.2**]. It is essentially a marsh plant that relies more on sufficient warmth and the nourishing qualities of water than on the fertility of the soil, and harvests are possible even on poor and sandy soils provided there is enough rainfall. In this way, rice has supported a greater number of people for a longer period of time than any other cultivated crop.

The increasingly widespread technique of flotation (the use of water to process soil samples and recover tiny artifacts) to recover plant remains from sites in the Yangzi Valley has now allowed specialists to examine the detailed changes in the structure and shape of the rice. This shows that it took thousands of years of human intervention before rice became a fully domesticated crop. Simply finding rice at a site is, therefore, not enough to establish that its cultivation has taken place. One must observe the shape and structure of the rice itself. Another issue is the important distinction between cultivation, which involves human intervention in the life cycle of the plant, and domestication, which reflects morphological changes in the plant resulting from human selection and manipulation. Cultivation of rice can occur before morphological alterations in the plant (domestication) are visible. These challenges make pinpointing the date of rice cultivation and domestication a difficult issue.

Many excavations have been conducted in the valley of the Yangzi River and its tributaries. The site of **Shangshan**, located about 150 kilometers (93 miles) southwest of Hemudu and dating as early as 9400–8400 BCE, is central to this issue of dating when rice was cultivated and domesticated. The occupants of the permanent houses there made ceramic vessels of clay tempered with rice chaff and stalks. The key question at Shangshan is whether or not this rice temper was domesticated. The archaeologist and botanist Dorian Fuller and colleagues have stressed that the presence of rice in such contexts does not necessarily constitute evidence of plant cultivation. They claim that the permanent village communities that developed between 9000 and 4000 BCE went through various phases of cultivation and domestication. The first, represented at Shangshan, involved tending and gathering a range of plants for consumption. This did not involve active cultivation. This was followed by the production of rice through tillage and some physical changes in the plant at Hemudu by about 5000 BCE. Cultivation through land clearance and the creation of dedicated rice fields was first seen from about 4500 BCE.

Fuller's model of early rice domestication involved a lengthy period of exploitation before it was finally established as the dominant source of food, and is supported by excavations at Diaotonghuan Cave, where a long sequence of rice use spanning the period from the late Pleistocene into the early postglacial period has been documented.

9.2 For at least 2,000 years, peasant farmers in China have created marshy conditions for rice to flourish by building low banks to retain rainwater. Much bigger returns can be obtained by carefully transplanting rice seedlings at some distance apart, rather than simply scattering seeds into the fields.

during the long warm phase, people withstood the next cold phase through a commitment to the cultivation of domestic rice (see Key Controversy box: The Origins of Rice Cultivation).

From an early date, sedentary village communities appeared in the lower Yangzi Valley. **Kuahuqiao** (*c.* 6200–5200 BCE) in Zhejiang Province is a site that suggests a settled lifestyle. The village included rectangular wooden house foundations and numerous storage pits. It commanded low-lying coastal marshland, a rich habitat for hunting and gathering. The faunal remains reflect this in the presence of numerous deer bones, as well as the remains of water buffaloes, serows, turtles, and fish. Dolphins, too, were hunted, probably by boat, known through the discovery of a 5.6-meter-long (18.4 feet) canoe during the excavations. Rice remains were of a cultivated variety, but were not found in significantly large quantities. Instead, acorns and other plants dominated numerically, suggesting that Kuahuqiao remained essentially a hunter-gatherer village community.

Settlements in the Middle Yangzi Valley. The middle Yangzi Valley contains many important sites that demonstrate both the foundation of permanently occupied village communities and evidence of rice cultivation. One of the most significant sites is **Bashidang** in Hunan Province, because of organic remains that survived there. Excavations revealed a ditch, perhaps to facilitate drainage away from the settlement, and an old riverbed that preserved more than 15,000 grains of rice claimed to have been of a cultivated variety. Other plants also survived, as well as wooden spades, which could have been used in agriculture, vestiges of houses raised on piles, pottery tempered with rice added to the clay to improve its firing qualities, and the bones of cattle, pigs, deer and chicken. A cemetery containing at least one hundred inhumation graves suggests a long-term, constantly occupied village.

Another important site is **Pengtoushan**, 20 kilometers (12 miles) southwest of Bashidang, where excavations revealed the remains of houses. It also demonstrated a flourishing ceramic industry in which rice husks, straw, and grains were used to temper the clay, and an inhumation cemetery where the dead were accompanied by siltstone ornaments and pottery vessels. The radiocarbon determinations derived from the rice used as a ceramic temper lie within the period 7000–6000 BCE. We do not know if the rice came from wild or domestic plants, and no tools that could have been used for cultivation been found here, but it is an important site for evidence of early permanent settlement and cultivation.

The Daxi Culture, c. 4500–3300 BCE

From 4500 BCE, the number of village sites in the middle Yangzi basin increased. These sites are generally described as the Daxi culture, distinctive for its type of pottery and for increasing intensification of agriculture. Rectangular, multi-roomed houses were constructed of clay, and strengthened with bamboo, reeds, and rice husks. Wetlands were chosen for settlement, and this swampy terrain would presumably have been suited to the establishment of rice fields. Early evidence of plowing has also been identified at Daxi sites. Domestic cattle and pigs were maintained, but not to the exclusion of hunting and fishing.

Chengtoushan is the most important Daxi site [**9.3**, p. 190]. Extensive investigations in the 1990s revealed an early walled town dating to around 4000 BCE. Modifications to the walls took place on at least three occasions. Inside, 700 burials have been excavated, most of them poor in terms of items placed with the bodies, though some are richly endowed with grave goods. The Daxi culture also shows some of the earliest signs of the presence of an elite social group. One individual, wearing two jade pendants, was buried with fifty

9.3 Chengtoushan is a major site occupied by rice farmers in the Yangzi River basin. It was once surrounded by a moat, beyond which lay the rice fields fed by irrigation ditches.

pottery vessels, and four individuals were interred in a crouched position in the corners of the tomb. The 10-meter-wide (33 feet) moat contained the remains of wooden agricultural tools, bamboo and reed basketry, linen cloth, and even paddles and rudders for boats, which would have been in regular use in this flood-prone terrain. The importance of rice can be judged from the discovery of the earliest known rice fields near the eastern wall, complete with ridges to retain water and irrigation ditches. From Kuahuqiao to the Daxi culture, the Yangzi Valley therefore witnessed the development from the first villages to a walled center over a period of a little more than 2,000 years.

The Songze Culture, c. 3800–3300 BCE

In the lower reaches of the Yangzi, the Songze culture demonstrates a pattern similar to that of the Daxi and Qujialing (see below) to the west: an established rice farming way of life, permanent village settlements, and the rise of an elite.

The site of Songze was first occupied in *c.* 3800 BCE. Its cemetery reveals an increase in mortuary offerings. Women were often buried wearing jade ornaments, with pieces of jade placed in their mouths. Some individuals were also given markedly richer offerings than others, suggesting distinct social differences within a settlement. For example, at Beiyinyanying in Nanjing, a cemetery site where 225 burials have been uncovered, some individuals wore fine jade and agate ornaments, while pottery vessels [**9.4**] and stone axes lay beyond the head and feet. The Songze settlements represent a long and important phase that culminated in the Liangzhu culture sites (discussed further in Chapter 10), where the quantity of jade and the ritual component of aristocratic graves signaled the path to later state formation.

The Qujialing Culture, c. 3300–2500 BCE

From 3300 BCE, the low-lying plains north and south of the middle Yangzi River witnessed a dramatic population increase, and the sites from this time are described as the **Qujialing** culture. Settlements varied in size, but one of the largest is the massive site of Qujialing itself, which covered at least 236 hectares (583 acres).

Within these growing communities, houses were comprised of a series of buildings set round a central courtyard, often associated with a cemetery. Some houses had multiple rooms for different functions. A room in one such house at **Shijiahe** contained the remains of a bamboo mattress, a hearth, stone axes, pottery vessels, and a spindle whorl. Pottery vessels were now crafted by specialists and fired in technologically advanced kilns. The cemeteries of this period reveal that some individuals were richly endowed with mortuary offerings while the majority of graves held a handful of pottery vessels.

But increasing populations did not just involve the development of new technologies and cultural innovations. Higher concentrations of people, probably measured in the tens of thousands for the biggest settlements, would have brought new health risks. The survival of dung beetles, fly pupae, and whip and round worms attests to the lack of sanitation and food hygiene as settlements grew.

9.4 Earthenware jar.
Lidded jar (*guan*) with incised pattern of interlaced leaves on its dark-faced upper body and lid. Height 26.2 cm (10.3 in.). Excavated from a site of the Songze culture (*c.* 3800–3300 BCE) in Qingpu district, Shanghai. Shanghai Museum. The Songze culture marks the beginning of increased social differentiation in the later Neolithic of the lower Yangzi Valley.

TRANSITIONS TO AGRICULTURE: NORTHERN CHINA AND THE YELLOW RIVER VALLEY, 9000–5000 BCE

North of the Yangzi Valley is the second important valley in early China, that of the Yellow River. From at least 26,000 BCE a broad swath of territory along the course of the Yellow River was occupied by mobile hunter-gatherers. Their dwelling sites contain small stone blades, struck from a core and then retouched to form scrapers, longer blades, and awls. Just as the hunter-gatherers in the Yangzi were familiar with harvesting wild rice, people in northern China harvested another wild plant that would later become a domesticated staple: millet.

The transition into millet-farming communities from the hunter-gatherer tradition is a missing link that has been partially explained. A pattern of hunting linked with plant collection and processing is seen at Nanzhuangtou and Donghulin. Nanzhuangtou has been dated to 9500–9000 BCE, while Donghulin has two phases, the first dated 9150–8500 BCE, and the second 8500–7500 BCE. Both sites contained numerous grinding stones that had been used to process plants. Microscopic examination of one of these from Nanzhuangtou recovered more than 400 starch grains. Nearly 40 percent of the grains are of wild form, while almost half are larger grains typical of domestic millet. The results suggest that foxtail millet was being ground on stone mortars and cooked in pottery vessels, and that during the period between approximately 9000 and 7500 BCE, foxtail millet was undergoing domestication.

KEY SITE Jiahu: The Transition to Agriculture in the Huai River Valley

Jiahu is a key site in tracing the impact of agriculture on the way of life of early Neolithic communities. Jiahu was located near a large lake and two rivers, in the upper reaches of the Huai River, China. Occupation dates between 7000 and 5500 BCE. This was a period of marked climatic warming and increased rainfall; an ideal habitat for hunting, gathering, and fishing. The bones of sika deer, muntjac, and pig dominate the faunal remains, and fish bones were abundant in the many rubbish pits within the settlement.

Cooking vessels, grinding stones, spades, and axes in the human burials and within the houses suggest cultivation practices. The presence of kilns for firing pots, and the large amount of debris from stone toolmaking, indicate vigorous manufacturing in the settlement.

Much social information has come from detailed studies of the 396 human burials. During the initial occupation, single and multiple burials were found adjacent to the semi-subterranean small houses, while the later residents interred their dead in tightly nucleated cemeteries within the settlement. The size and contents of the graves suggest an absence of any major social ranking within the Jiahu community. Some graves, however, contained ritual objects. These included bird-bone flutes [**9.5**] and turtle skeletons, each containing pebbles that might have been used as rattles. The few individuals interred with these remarkable offerings were probably leaders within the community, with shamanistic powers. Some of the turtle bones also bore incised symbols, which were to play such a dominant role in the divinations of the later Shang rulers (see Chapter 10).

With a population of probably fewer than 260 people at its height, the village continued to rely on wild resources supplemented by rice. Some of the women buried in the cemetery were incomers from other areas, and contact with other communities up to 100 kilometers (62 miles) away brought desirable supplies of stone to the site. Toward the end of its occupation the climate cooled, and the site was abandoned, it seems, when struck by a flood.

9.5 Music was clearly a significant aspect of life at Neolithic Jiahu. Bird-bone flutes were occasionally found in the human graves.

The Development of Permanent Villages, c. 7000–5000 BCE

What accompanied the domestication of millet? As with rice in the Yangzi Valley, the answer is clearly seen in people beginning to live in concentrations of permanent villages and to bury their dead in ancestral cemeteries. Among those settlements in the central plains are **Jiahu** (see Key Site box: Jiahu: The Transition to Agriculture in the Huai River Valley) and **Peiligang**. Excavations at Peiligang have uncovered semi-subterranean houses and 116 inhumation burials, together with many stone and pottery artifacts dating between 6000 and 5400 BCE [**9.6, 9.7**]. Most graves also contained two or three ceramic vessels, but the offerings with the burials do not single out any person or group as having an elevated social status. The mortuary remains instead indicate the importance attached to the tools associated with agriculture, which were buried with individuals, in particular stone spades and notched curved sickles.

As subsistence changed, so did material culture. Bone arrowheads and harpoons were used for hunting or fishing, and the presence of bone shuttles and needles suggests that nets

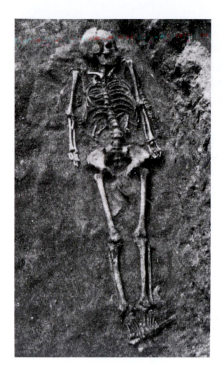

9.6, **9.7 Peiligang.** Cemeteries, such as this example from the early settlement of Peiligang, are a hallmark of early agricultural communities in China. The burials at this site occurred in three separate clusters, which may represent distinct clan groups within the community.

were also made. Some of the pottery vessels bear the imprints of cordage, further evidence for the manufacture of nets and cloth. Harvesting and processing millet was undertaken with stone pestles and mortars. These early permanent settlements therefore illuminate a key point in the development of agriculture in China, where a stable subsistence base contains a mixture of both domestic and wild food resources.

In addition to underwriting the establishment of permanent village communities, the development of agriculture in northern China involved expansion east and west into sparsely occupied new lands. Populations increased, and farmers spread into new territory.

EARLY FARMING COMMUNITIES: NORTHERN CHINA AND THE YELLOW RIVER VALLEY, *c.* 5000–2600 BCE

In Northern and Central China, agricultural settlements based on millet cultivation proliferated. Fed on this new staple, two major cultures developed: the **Yangshao** on the loess plateau and the central plains of Qinghai, Gansu, and Shaanxi provinces, and the **Dawenkou**, found further east, in Shandong Province. Both show the growth of social inequality, and the emergence of elite families or lineages in these early farming societies.

The Yangshao Culture, c. 5000–3000 BCE

The Yangshao culture lasted around 2,000 years, and during this time there was a rising tide of social stratification, seen in particular in the grave goods placed with the dead [**9.8**, **9.9**, p. 194]. There are many regional aspects to this culture, but common characteristics are its semi-subterranean houses with storage pits for the millet harvest and kiln-fired ceramic vessels bearing distinctive geometric painted designs and images.

Profound social changes took place with the middle Yangshao phase, *c.* 4000–3500 BCE. Settlements enlarged, accompanied by the development of ceremonial structures and the

visible ranking of individuals through the evidence of living space, diet, and burial rituals. Some of these locations might well have been regional centers. The settlement and cemetery site of **Xipo** is particularly important, as it offers insight into emerging social distinctions. People here lived in semi-subterranean houses, and were intensive pig farmers; even the pigs were fed on millet. Xipo is distinctive for two large buildings that would have required a considerable labor force to construct. The walls and floors were decorated with red pigment and, when abandoned, the interior fittings were removed. They were probably ceremonial structures that involved feasting, since great quantities of pig bones were found in their vicinity.

Mortuary rituals often reflect an individual's place in society. At Xipo, a handful of the thirty-four excavated graves are outstandingly wealthy [**9.10**]. One burial (Burial 27) stood out for its size, and includes a chamber beyond the feet of the skeleton that contained fine pottery vessels.

The body had been wrapped in fabric, and the grave covered by wooden planks and a filling of mud. The dried mud still bore the impressions of the flowers buried with the individual, which included wild jasmine. Another penetrating insight into Xipo society comes from the concentration of parasitic worms' eggs in the stomach area of the rich individuals; these were associated with eating pork.

9.8, **9.9** ABOVE AND BELOW **Yangshao pottery vessels.** (Above) The Neolithic Machang culture, part of the Yangshao complex, produced this extraordinary wine vessel standing 33.5 centimeters (13 inches) high and found at Liuwan. It was embellished with the image of a hermaphrodite human. It is highly likely that this figure was a shaman, a person believed to link humans on earth with the mysterious world of the gods. Perhaps the wine was drunk during rituals. (Below) The Yangshao pottery vessels are rightly famous for their spectacular decoration. This vessel from Banpo, 40 centimeters (16 inches) across, bears the image of a shaman with two fish as earrings.

9.10 RIGHT **The Middle Yangshao site of Xipo** contains some very rich burials, the most elaborate of which have an enlarged area beyond the feet to accommodate mortuary offerings.

KEY THEME: DOMESTICATION The Consequences and Significance of Agriculture

Where an environment is unusually bountiful in producing a regular supply of food, human communities can live permanently in one place. Prime examples are seen in the rich fishing grounds of Northwest America and the warm coastal habitat of Florida. The Kwakiutl of British Columbia relied on the massive harvest of migratory salmon to maintain their chiefly lineages, their workers, and the people they enslaved. The resource base, however, is too fragile and unpredictable to support urban life. Food production, by contrast, has the capacity to sustain very large populations, and if those populations remain in one place it is necessary to develop new forms of administration and social structure to manage those numbers. In East Asia, tracing the origins of food production is the first chapter in explaining how early states arose. Several plants were cultivated, and ultimately domesticated, in particular rice and millet. The significance of both comes readily to mind when reading the written records of the Shang kings. They regularly asked their oracles to reassure them that there would be sufficient rainfall for a good harvest (see pp. 215–16).

What we have found is that the domestication of millet and rice took several thousand years. One of the fascinating aspects of tracing the course of these developments is to identify how human societies adapted and changed. We find, for example, that the climate had a major impact. As it warmed, wild rice expanded its range, and hunter-gatherers began to show increasing interest in harvesting it. The weapons that were needed for hunting became increasingly rare, and those suited to processing plants, such as milling stones, sickles, and spades, made their appearance. No society can simply scatter seeds, and then go away with the hope that, months later, they will return to find an abundant harvest. Pests—weeds and wild animals—can destroy a field of millet in no time. So at least some members of a community had to live permanently in one location; that is, they became sedentary. They had to protect their growing crops, and care for their domestic animals. Hence, we find in the Yangzi and the Yellow river valleys the foundation of long-term settlements. There, they had to bury their dead in village cemeteries and open up trade relations to obtain their high-quality stone, or the jade and marine shell that they converted into prestigious display ornaments.

Wherever this process has been identified, be it in East Asia, Southwest Asia, or Mesoamerica, we find that population pressure encouraged farming communities to expand their range. In East Asia, this took place as the key lands that witnessed domestication filled up. Millet and rice farmers began to move northeast into the Korean peninsula and on to the Japanese islands. There was a parallel series of migrations into Southeast Asia. In both, the intrusive farmers encountered hunter-gatherers adapted over thousands of years to their respective homelands. If there is one constant in such interaction, it is genetic admixture. In East and Southeast Asia, although many of the modern inhabitants have genes that can be traced back to their hunter-gatherer ancestors, farming is now universal, save for small and scattered bands who survive in the remote forests of peninsular Thailand and Malaysia.

The Dawenkou Culture, c. 4150–2600 BCE

The history of the Dawenkou culture in the lower Yellow River Valley tells another story of a hierarchy of individuals, this time through their food and living space, and the increasing division of labor. People belonging to this culture subsisted on millet, supplemented by lesser quantities of rice, with pigs being the dominant domestic animal. Over time populations grew, social ranking intensified, and the study of isotopes in the teeth suggests that rice was the preferred food of the upper class.

From around 3550 BCE the potter's wheel was invented, and at Dawenkou itself, mortuary offerings [9.11] rose sharply in quantity and quality. Jade ornaments increased in number, along with stone adzes and stone beads. By 3050 BCE, there were specialists in the manufacture of jades and ceramic

9.11 RIGHT **Animal figurines** were regularly placed in elite Dawenkou graves to indicate the high status of the person buried. This representation of a pig emphasizes the importance of this animal in the Dawenkou culture.

KEY SITE Tianluoshan

Tianluoshan is located on a flat plain barely 1 meter (3.3 feet) above sea level, in the lower valley of the Hangzhou River, and dates to around 5000–3000 BCE. The site illustrates how rice farmers, who probably expanded out onto the flat, low-lying plains from earlier settlements inland, attained a high level of technological skill. Their economy, based on the cultivation of aquatic plants and widespread hunting, fishing, gathering, and raising of domestic animals, was adaptive to a process of rapid and relatively risk-free growth. The great advantage of Tianluoshan is that it has been excavated not only on a monumental scale but also using the latest techniques for the recovery of organic material and artifacts. It is a deeply waterlogged site, which has led to the preservation of the wooden foundations of houses, boats, paddles, and even a bridge crossing a stream flowing through the settlement [**9.12**]. Moreover, excavations adjacent to the site itself have revealed the remains of the village rice fields.

Tianluoshan was an impressive place, comprising stoutly constructed wooden houses that featured advanced joinery techniques. Their remains suggest that the site was home to hundreds of people. Among the artifacts are spades made from the shoulder-blade bones of bovids, animals that would have been used to cultivate the soft soil. Rice and plant-harvesting and processing of other crops was undertaken with knives, pestles, and mortars. The many ceramic vessels come in a wide variety of shapes and styles. It is evident that some were used for cooking, for the remains of cooked rice were found still adhering to the inside of a rectangular vessel known as a *fu*.

The very large number and variety of animal bones reveals intensive hunting as well as a varied environment within reach of the site. Remains of deer, water buffalo, tigers, and bears have been found, and also small arboreal animals, such as the macaque and civet; there is also evidence for the raising of domestic dogs and pigs.

Wooden oars stress the importance of water transport, and net sinkers and fishing spears, associated with the remains of sharks and whales, crocodiles and turtles, attest to the exploitation of marine resources. This site, similarly to Hemudu, also lies at the threshold of the movement of groups across the Taiwan Strait to the island of Taiwan. The presence of oars and strong rope at the site, together with carpentry skills, is compatible with deep-water transport, which may well have stood at the origin of the expansion of Austronesian-speaking people (see Chapter 11).

9.12 The excavations at Tianluoshan are protected by a massive roof. In the foreground, a wooden bridge crosses an ancient stream, with house foundations seen beyond.

vessels, supported by the rise of social elites. Social division may also be seen in housing, such as the site at **Yuchisi**, where extensive excavations within the moated enclosure have uncovered long rows of linked houses. The groups of houses revealed a differentiation between richer and poorer families, based on the number of food vessels found there. Each house cluster was also the focus for the surrounding human graves, divided into a majority of poorer individuals, and a small minority of rich men and women distinguished by their jade ornaments and numerous pig jawbones. Wealth might have been generated through the manufacture and exchange of fine kiln-fired ceramic vessels, for at this central site the tools were found for fashioning pots, whereas smaller settlements in the area had none.

The production of surpluses, be they measured in exotic ornaments or in millet harvests and domestic stock, would have been instrumental in the provision of the competitive feasts and display that are reflected in elite houses and burials. It is with these societies that we can identify a seamless development into the succeeding formation of early states.

The Hongshan Culture, c. 4500–3000 BCE

Partially contemporary to the Dawenkou is the Hongshan culture. This culture is marked by important ritual sites. For example, at Niuheliang, a cruciform structure 25 meters (82 feet) long was discovered that contained multiple subterranean chambers. Fragments found of gigantic over-life-size clay figurines have led to this being labeled the Goddess Temple, and its importance is emphasized by earthen platforms in the surrounding area that cover burials furnished with ritual jades. Carefully fashioned jade artifacts, many of highly standardized forms, became an important feature of Chinese symbolism and ceremony in the centuries that followed (see Chapter 10).

THE EXPANSION OF FARMING: SOUTHERN CHINA AND SOUTHEAST ASIA, 2000–1000 BCE

In the Yangzi and Yellow river valleys, domestication developed independently, which can be seen through the slow transition from wild plant to domesticated varieties of rice and millet. In the early agricultural villages of Southeast Asia (Vietnam, Thailand), there is no slow transition. Instead, all early village sites of this region reveal fully developed agriculture. Fine pottery vessels were manufactured with broadly similar decorative patterns; weaving was undertaken; houses were built on piles and, in some regions, at ground level; people were buried in permanent cemeteries; and domestic cattle, pigs, and dogs were raised. It appears, therefore, that communities with knowledge in agriculture, probably from the Yangzi Valley, moved into these regions of southern China and Southeast Asia as an example of the spread of domestication through migration.

Initial Dispersal into Southern China

The expansion of intrusive agriculturalists from the Yangzi Valley into the extensive region of warm lowlands has left an indelible archaeological signature. For example, the third-millennium BCE settlement of Shixia includes a cemetery where graves contained jade *cong*, bracelets, pendants, and split rings. Objects associated with increasing social difference are therefore found at the very foundational phases of settlements in this region.

From Southern China into Vietnam

Traveling by boat along the Red River, one can move from Yunnan Province to the lowlands of northern Vietnam. In this region, a hunter-gatherer tradition that stretched back tens of thousands of years was broken by the arrival of the new rice farmers. Settlers came in the form of the Neolithic **Phung Nguyen** culture, named after one important site, with initial settlements dating from about 2000 BCE. **Man Bac** is a second important site, dated from 1900 BCE (see Key Site box: Man Bac, p. 199).

The material culture of the Phung Nguyen society represents a complete break in the cultural sequence of this region. New to the region are pottery vessels decorated with complex incised patterns [**9.13**, p. 198], and spindle whorls, which attest to a weaving industry.

cong a Chinese ceremonial jade tube with a square or circular cross-section, often elaborately carved

9.13 Phung Nguyen pottery decoration. The pottery vessels at Phung Nguyen follow a widespread Neolithic preference for incised and impressed designs of considerable complexity. These examples probably date to between 2000 and 1500 BCE. Their appearance is widely paralleled among early farming sites in Southeast Asia and southern China.

The form and decoration of these spindle whorls here bear close parallels with sites in southeast China. More than 1,000 stone adzes in a variety of forms have also been found at Phung Nguyen, as well as small stone chisels and whetstones.

The introduction of craft skills for working nephrite and jadeite ornaments at late Phung Nguyen sites in Vietnam represents a key link with the Chinese Neolithic. One *ge* is particularly interesting, because it matches examples found in southern China and further north into the early urban states at Sanxingdui and Erlitou, discussed in Chapter 10. The *yazhang* is also a central feature of the latter two assemblages, and specimens have been recovered from Phung Nguyen. It is clear that the intrusive Neolithic groups in Vietnam remained in contact with their ancestors in the Yangzi Valley.

Early Rice Farmers in Northeast Thailand and Southern Vietnam

About 300 years after the arrival of the people of the Phung Nguyen culture in Vietnam, the first Neolithic rice farmers appeared in northeast Thailand from around 1700 to 1000 BCE. The Mekong River route provides the direct link between the headwaters of the Yangzi River and the extensive lowlands of the Khorat Plateau in northeast Thailand. These agriculturalists introduced inhumation burial: the dead were interred on their backs with mortuary offerings that included pottery vessels, animal bones, and personal ornaments. From evidence obtained from these sites, we know that early settlers brought with them weaving techniques and domestic stock, and that they chose to live near gently flooded terrain suited to rice cultivation. They also intensively hunted, fished, and collected shellfish.

The archaeological evidence for early rice farmers on the Khorat Plateau comes from several sites, although none has been extensively excavated. **Ban Chiang** began with Neolithic settlement with no sign of earlier hunter-gatherer occupation. The site was occupied by rice farmers by about 1500 BCE, slightly later than sites in northern Vietnam and Yunnan Province in China.

A site survey along these river courses in 1990–91 revealed many small settlement mounds, which provided samples of the same pattern-incised pottery as was found in the Phung Nguyen sites. An increasing number of Neolithic contexts are now coming to light in this region, often deeply stratified beneath later Bronze and Iron Age deposits. The faunal

ge a Chinese ceremonial jade halberd, an axe-like weapon

yazhang a Chinese ceremonial jade blade

Man Bac is an early farming site in northern Vietnam, which has provided new evidence of not only the subsistence and burial practices but also the human biology of its inhabitants [**9.14**]. Man Bac includes a large cemetery containing extended inhumation burials associated with ceramic containers, some of which were incised and impressed with complex motifs, dated to the period 1800–1500 BCE. Burial practices at the site differed from those of the indigenous hunter-gatherers. They involved placing the body on its back, usually accompanied by a small number of pottery vessels. Other offerings included clusters of cowrie shells, a grinding stone, stone adzes, and nephrite bracelets and beads.

The settlers of Man Bac lived in a favorable habitat that gave access to the forested uplands behind the site, grasslands suited to deer, and a mangrove-fringed shore punctuated by at least one river. The cultural deposits contained rice phytoliths, but rice by no means dominated subsistence. People were able to take marine and brackish water fish and also caught the barramundi, sharks, and rays. Among the mammalian fauna, we find that young pigs dominated. There were also deer, otters, rhinoceros, and a few bovines.

The population biology of Man Bac has been assessed in several complementary studies. The demographic profile shows that the number of people grew quickly. There are two skull forms present in the population: one had a narrow and flat face, while the other was lower and wider. Nine of the Man Bac males cluster in the results of the statistical analyses with the inhabitants of Weidun, an earlier agricultural community located in the Yangzi Valley. Five individuals, however, cluster with the earlier hunter-gatherers of this region. This suggests that incoming farmers met and integrated with the indigenous hunter-gatherers.

Mitochondrial DNA shows that there was a southward movement of immigrants, and a local admixture with the indigenous hunter-gatherers. The importance of the Man Bac site lies in the consistent indication that the population incorporated immigrants from southern China who encountered and integrated with the native inhabitants.

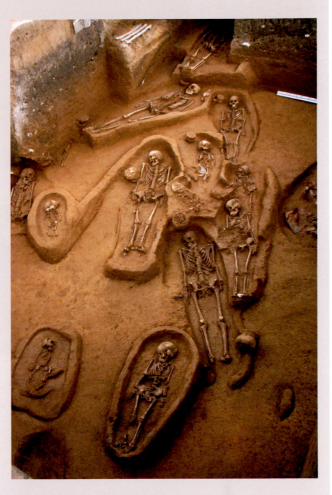

9.14 The cemetery at Man Bac in northern Vietnam is unique in demonstrating the presence of intrusive rice farmers and indigenous hunter-gatherers. The two groups differ on the basis of their skull shape and DNA.

remains of these sites indicate that the first farmers also hunted the local herds of deer and cattle. They collected shellfish and exploited the abundant local fish resources. The dead were interred with a range of mortuary offerings, such as black ceramic vessels decorated with incised, burnished, and painted motifs. Radiocarbon determinations date these initial occupations to the eighteenth century BCE.

Any expansionary movement of rice farmers southward down the coast of Vietnam would have found a fertile and strategic area for settlement in the broad floodplain of the Dong Nai River. Our knowledge of the Neolithic occupation has been greatly enlarged by

9.15 Opening one of the graves at the site of An Son. This site is located in the Dong Nai valley of southern Vietnam, and was occupied by early rice farmers whose ancestors came from the Yangzi River basin.

excavations at **An Son**, located on a terrace overlooking the river floodplain. The radiocarbon determinations indicate that the site was occupied from the start of the second millennium BCE, being abandoned by about 1000 BCE. Artifacts include many broken potsherds, stone adzes, grinding and whetstones, and clay pellets that to this day are used with a sling to hunt birds and small game. The dearth of quality stone in the river valley means that the stone for adzes had to be imported.

The thirty-five burials include pottery vessels placed with a corpse laid extended on its back [**9.15**]. Some of these pots were decorated with incised and impressed patterns, and there were also distinctive open bowls with a wavy rim. Other mortuary offerings included stone adzes, bivalve shells, and shell beads.

The first of the four phases identified provided pottery vessels with no rice chaff temper, but this was incorporated with the clay in the subsequent phases, and an analysis of the rice DNA shows it to have been from the same type as was grown in the Yangzi sites in northern China. No domestic cattle bones were recovered, however; the people of An Son consumed immature pigs, turtles, and dogs.

The Bangkok Plain

The Gulf of Thailand and the Bangkok Plain present in microcosm a drama that must have unfolded in virtually every part of East and Southeast Asia where intrusive farmers met indigenous hunter-gatherers. The Bangkok Plain was settled by migrant rice farmers by about 2000 BCE. Settlements and cemeteries contain impressed and incised ceramic vessels similar to those seen at An Son. The hunter-gatherer groups with whom these farmers interacted should not be identified as small and mobile groups of relative insignificance, for in southeast China many communities were large and complex.

Khok Phanom Di. At around 2000 BCE, evidence for marine hunting and gathering is found at the site of **Khok Phanom Di**, located near the Gulf of Thailand. The settlement was established when a group of marine hunter-gatherers settled near the mouth of a major estuary, which was fringed with a dense belt of mangroves. There, they exploited the wealth of marine food, collecting shellfish from the mudflats, fishing, and hunting. They made their pottery vessels from the good-quality local clay, and imported stone adzes. By this date, rice farmers were already established upstream, and it is likely that these coastal hunters were in contact with them.

The occupation layers at Khok Phanom Di accumulated so rapidly between 2000 and 1500 BCE that graves of members of descent groups were found superimposed over the ancestors [**9.16**]. It is possible to trace the history of this community through seven mortuary phases and about eighteen human generations. What is clear, from the analysis of the human remains, is that intrusive rice farmers occupied the site, but due to the inhospitable environment for growing rice, they concentrated on hunting, fishing, and gathering rich estuarine resources.

During the third phase, there is strong evidence for a fall in the sea level and the establishment of fresh water habitats. The people were now cultivating rice—seen in the evidence of the rice itself, harvesting knives, and stone hoes. In the fifth mortuary phase, rice cultivation ceased in favor again of marine hunting and gathering. Five burials from this phase were fabulously wealthy in terms of grave goods, one woman being found with more than 120,000 shell beads [**9.17**]. By the following phase, people were being interred in elaborate mortuary buildings with clay walls.

9.16 BELOW LEFT **Burials at Khok Phanom Di** were laid out in family groups, distributed in clusters. They were accompanied by fine ceramic vessels and bone and shell jewelry.

9.17 BELOW RIGHT **The richest burial at Khok Phanom Di** comes from Mortuary Phase 5. This woman wore more than 120,000 shell beads, shell disks, a bangle, and ear ornaments. She was also interred with superb pottery vessels, and her tools for fashioning pots.

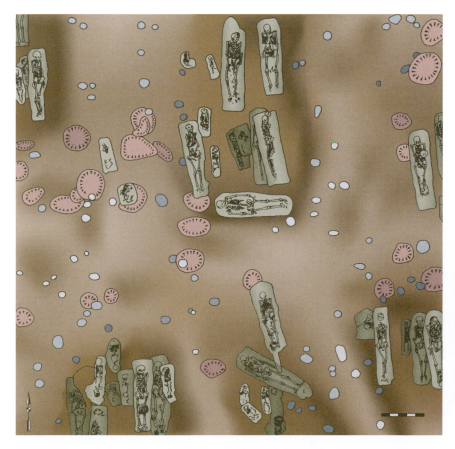

The biological and artifactual evidence indicates that rice farming was practiced for only a few generations, when conditions were favorable. The excavators believe that Khok Phanom Di initially documents interaction between indigenous sedentary hunter-fishers and intrusive rice farmers; before the new settlers dominated and embraced marine hunting and gathering, they continued the practice of rice farming when possible.

COMPLEX HUNTER-GATHERERS: JŌMON JAPAN, 14,000–1000 BCE

From around 14,000 to 800 BCE, the Japanese archipelago was occupied by the Jōmon culture. Jōmon means cord-pattern, a characteristic of their pottery. It is often seen as one of the most complex and enduring hunter-gatherer traditions in the world. Their pottery is probably among the earliest anywhere, and a very clear example that ceramics are not only associated with farming communities.

Whereas in many other regions pottery was first used in early settled agricultural communities, in Japan it was developed for the processing of aquatic resources. Many Jōmon sites on the island of Honshu have yielded evidence for sea fishing, the haul including tuna and mackerel, dolphins, and turtles. Pottery forms became increasingly elaborate, with some designed for ceremonial use and others for food processing or cooking [**9.18**, **9.19**]. Sites, such as Nishida (Late Jōmon, *c.* 1500–1000 BCE) in northern Honshu, demonstrate a layout and size that suggests long-term sedentary occupation. Ringed by rectangular houses, the center of Nishida was reserved for burying the dead in rectangular graves, of which 192 were excavated. The ingredients of preserved biscuits reveal how well the Jōmon people lived: they included a flour made from ground walnuts and chestnuts, meat and blood, and birds' eggs.

The Jōmon are a classic example of sedentism without agriculture: developing permanent settlements with complex material culture without depending upon farming for their subsistence. Instead, Jōmon societies made careful use of the forest and marine resources available to them. Their artifacts included not only elaborate pottery but also figurines, cemeteries, stone circles, and (where waterlogging has preserved them) colored lacquerware vessels.

9.18, **9.19 Jōmon pottery.** Some of the Jōmon pottery of Japan reached levels of sophistication rarely encountered elsewhere in hunter-gatherer societies. The Middle Jōmon vessel (right) is from Kamiina county, Nagano and is 61 centimeters (24 inches) high, and the Late Jōmon vessel (far right) is from Horinouchi shell mound, Ichikawa, and is 42.5 cm (16.8 in.) high.

The flotation of archaeological deposits (using water to process soil samples and recover tiny artifacts) has recently retrieved plant remains that demonstrate the tending and, in some cases, the domestication of several plants. The Jōmon culture has been intensively studied, and recent research has shown that, although generally regarded as a complex society of hunter-gatherers, there is enormous chronological and cultural diversity and strong evidence for Jōmon people exploiting and modifying the habitats of a wide range of plants before the adoption of rice cultivation. These include beans, seen during the Early Jōmon at Sannai-Maruyama by 4000 BCE, the bottle gourd, and the beefsteak plant. Jōmon foragers modified their environment through managing such wild plants and pigs, so that when rice cultivation was introduced into Japan, it fitted readily into their patterned subsistence. Moreover, some plants reveal morphological changes consistent with domestication. Foremost is a species known as barnyard millet, found as early as 7000 BCE. The Jōmon culture therefore offers us a strong example of a complex hunter-gatherer community, which integrated new cultivating practices into a way of life that already involved the manipulating of wild animals and plants.

EXPANSION OF DOMESTICATION: KOREA AND JAPAN

Adoption of Agriculture: Korea

The Korean Peninsula sustained a long and vigorous hunter-gatherer tradition that inevitably encountered and integrated with expansionary millet farmers [**9.20**]. There was also a later introduction of domestic rice, and both stimulated the growth of dominant social elites. Korean riverine and coastal settlements incorporating pit houses stretch from the Yalu and Tumen rivers in the north to the southern coast; they have been given the name **Chulmun** (comb ware) culture, after the pottery found there.

The early Chulmun settlements have traditionally been seen as principally coastal or riverine hunter-gatherers. Numerous stone fishhooks and weights, which probably represent net fishing, indicate a maritime orientation. Sopohang, on the Tumen River near Russian Siberia, is a large mound consisting predominantly of oyster shells, the superimposed house floors indicating a degree of permanence in settlement.

It was during the Middle Chulmun (c. 3500–2000 BCE) that broomcorn and foxtail millets were integrated into the pre-existing hunter-gatherer subsistence system. The recovery of the remains of millet, as at Chitamni, as well as slate hoes, suggests that agriculture was introduced into the region from northeastern China. This appears to have stimulated major population changes, for the number of Chulmun sites increased from the mid-fourth millennium BCE, and new settlements penetrated the hill country of the interior in an easterly direction. Millet contributed to a diet still dominated by fish, shellfish, and hunted mammals.

9.20 Korea and Japan. Map showing the major sites mentioned in the text.

9.21 Korean dolmen tombs. The dead were buried in dolmens of considerable size in Korea after the establishment of rice farming. This one is from Kangwha Island, west of Seoul, and dates to about 1000 BCE.

Rice came to Korea much later than millet, and the reason for this is easily resolved: Korean rice belongs to the *japonica* variety, which underwent a long process of selective adaptation to the cold conditions of the Korean peninsula compared with its subtropical origins. A pollen core from the Kimpo swamp has produced rice pollen dated to around 2000 BCE, while at Kumgokdong rice phytoliths have been identified in Mumun (undecorated) pottery, the dominant pottery in Korea between about 500 and 300 BCE. Since rice is not native to Korea, it must have been introduced from China, but the conjunction of rice with distinctively local ceramics is a strong indication that it was incorporated into pre-existing agricultural communities during the second millennium BCE.

The fine redware pottery vessels, dated to the early first millennium BCE, match ones found in **dolmen** tombs [**9.21**], which were comprised of huge upright stones and a capstone, and associated with rice-farming villages. The considerable size of these tombs (one capstone weighs more than 160 metric tons or 176 US tons), and the fine ceramics and jade grave goods within, suggest that the surplus provided by rice agriculture was associated with the rise of a social elite and a society that was now involved in the intensive cultivation of rice in managed and irrigated rice fields.

dolmen a megalithic tomb, usually consisting of upright stone slabs, on which rests a large capstone or capstones

Adoption of Agriculture: Japan

As we have seen, by the beginning of the second millennium BCE the knowledge and practice of rice cultivation was spreading into Korea, and it was only a matter of time before it crossed into the Japanese islands. The fundamental question is whether rice farming was introduced, along with bronze and iron metallurgy, into northern Kyushu by a wave of immigrant groups, such as the Yayoi (see below), or if it was brought more gradually into Jōmon communities, which integrated rice farming into their long-established economy.

Yayoi Rice Farmers. The Jōmon culture was long-lived, but around 800 BCE the Japan archipelago began to undergo substantial changes, with the incursion of rice-farming communities called the Yayoi. Rice dominated the new economy and appeared fully formed in the Japanese islands. At Itazuke, for example, the remains of irrigated rice fields have been found associated with a village settlement surrounded by a moat. It occupied an area of about 100 × 80 meters (330 × 260 feet), where archaeologists have uncovered storage pits, and burials in jars and pits. Beyond, on an adjacent low terrace, embanked rice fields were fed by irrigation canals. Such sophistication surely indicates contact with established rice-farming communities in Korea or even mainland China, probably involving settlement by immigrants. This interpretation relies not only on the archaeological record of new subsistence activities and types of artifact but also on human remains: the Yayoi were taller than their Jōmon counterparts, and their heads were of a different shape.

The establishment of intrusive rice-farming communities on the island of Kyushu from about 800 BCE was followed by a progressive expansion to the northeast into Honshu, the central and largest of the Japanese islands. The extreme climatic conditions of Hokkaido Island further north, on the other hand, favored the persistence of hunter-gatherers, whose descendants, in all probability, constitute the Ainu people of today.

Tantalizing information on the Late Yayoi period comes from a Chinese historic text known as the *Wei Zhi* ("History of the Kingdom of Wei"), which dates to the late third century CE. It describes the Wa people of the Japanese islands as possessing a social hierarchy in which women shaman leaders were interred in large mounded graves. Some passages appear to

KEY THEME: SOCIAL INEQUALITY The Role of Agriculture and Metallurgy

Why should some individuals and families be richer and more powerful than others? How did this arise? The origins of social inequality have attracted scholarly interest for centuries. If there is one constant in all early communities it is social inequality, with privileged rulers at the apex and lesser orders below. We can see this most clearly in the energy expended on the pyramids of Giza in Egypt, or the tomb of Qin Shi Huangdi in China.

Look around your own community to see how social inequality is expressed. How you dress, where you live, the size of your house, the quality of your car, where you holiday, and, ultimately, the expense of your funeral, all signal social status. It is exactly the same in the remote past. As the climate warmed more than 10,000 years ago in East Asia, the inhabitants lived by hunting and gathering. It is hard to find any evidence for social distinctions. Of course, good hunters might have had more prestige than their peers, but this was not necessarily inherited, and need not have been reflected in a larger house or the ownership of

exotic ornaments. As reliance on food production increased, however, excavations have uncovered hints that social inequality was on the rise. We find that village settlements included a few unusually large houses. Some individuals were buried with status symbols, such as jade ornaments, or many sacrificed pigs. Human beings are intrigued by new discoveries and new products, among them smelting copper and tin, mixing them into a bronze alloy, and then casting new tools, weapons, ceremonial vessels, and ornaments. At Ban Non Wat in northeast Thailand, for example, there is a point in the prehistoric sequence when copper made its first appearance. Within a generation or two, we find a remarkable surge in the mortuary wealth placed with a group of men, women, and infants. Offerings now included superb ceramic vessels, multiple exotic marine-shell and marble ornaments, and copper axes and jewelry. A group in that community had achieved high status through controlling the ownership of valuables.

have been confirmed by archaeology. At Yoshinogari on Kyushu, for example, excavations have revealed a settlement that covered 25 hectares (62 acres) by Late Yayoi times, demarcated by a sizable defensive ditch supplemented with watchtowers. The presence of a huge mounded tomb covering an area of 40 × 26 meters (130 × 85 feet), associated with ritual pottery deposits, suggests the presence of elites.

The adoption of rice cultivation coincided with changes in technology. Pottery vessels had been a major aspect of Jōmon material culture, but forms and decorative techniques changed with the Yayoi, and a set comprising cooking, serving, and storage vessels became the norm; these forms probably mirror the needs of rice farmers. The same can be said for stone tools, particularly the arrival of pestles, mortars, and reaping knives. The form of these knives is widespread on the Chinese mainland, where they had been in use for millennia; wear on the blades proves their use in rice harvesting. Waterlogged conditions at sites, such as Toro, have preserved wooden hoes, spades, rakes, and forks. Weaving was also introduced into Japan, evidenced by many circular spindle whorls, and silk came to Kyushu from southern China.

SUMMARY AND CONCLUSIONS

We began this chapter with the indigenous hunter-gatherer societies of the Yellow and Yangzi river valleys, and discussed the evidence for the development of agriculture in these two crucial areas: the cultivation of millet in the colder Yellow River Valley, and the farming of rice in the warmer, wetter regions of the Yangzi River further south. This involved a long process of transition from foraging to farming, rice becoming the dominant domesticated plant only in the fourth millennium BCE. Substantial agricultural communities eventually grew up in both areas, with attendant developments in material culture, social differentiation, trade, and political rivalry.

From this crucible of agricultural development in central and southeast China, rice and millet farmers spread to Southeast Asia, Korea, Japan, and beyond by the second millennium BCE. The emerging pattern reveals the widespread settlement of Southeast Asia by farming communities. The appearance of such groups may be seen in the archaeology, where, in contrast to the slowly developing domestication of grains in northern China, agricultural practices and associated material culture appear fully fledged. The expansive first farmers did not always move into empty lands. Many would have initially encountered long-established hunter-gatherer groups, some of them sedentary, such as those at Man Bac and Khok Phanom Di. While some of these groups would have been displaced, others would have been involved in close contact and exchange, leading to the adoption and integration of new subsistence practices. The expansion of farming communities into Korea and Japan followed a rather different pattern. In Korea, millet cultivation preceded rice by millennia, and again involved a mixing of different ethnic groups. In Japan, the relationship between the Jōmon and incursive Yayoi was complex.

In discussing the various ways in which millet and rice cultivation dominated the region, and the associated appearance and expansion of permanent settlements and social stratification, this chapter has described the solid cultural foundations for East Asian society that were provided by its pioneering farmers, without which the communities of this region could not have developed as they did. The further growth of East Asian agricultural societies and the rise of the first East and Southeast Asian states are traced in Chapter 10.

FURTHER READING

Useful introductions to the archaeology of East and Southeast Asia can be found in:

Barnes, G. 2015. *Archaeology of East Asia: The Rise of Civilization in China, Korea and Japan.* Oxford: Oxbow Books.

Bellina, B. *et al.* (eds.). 2010. *Fifty Years of Archaeology in Southeast Asia: Essays in Honour of Ian Glover.* Bangkok: River Books.

Bellwood, P. 2004. *First Farmers: The Origins of Agricultural Societies.* Oxford: Blackwell.

Fuller, D. Q. *et al.* 2007. Presumed domestication? Evidence for wild rice cultivation and domestication in the fifth millennium BC of the lower Yangzi region. *Antiquity* 81, 316–31.

Higham, C. F. W. 2014. *Early Southeast Asia: From the First Humans to the Civilization of Angkor.* Bangkok: River Books.

Higham, C. F. W. and Thosarat, R. 2011. *Early Thailand: From Prehistory to Sukhothai.* Bangkok: River Books.

Liu, L. 2004. *The Chinese Neolithic.* Cambridge: Cambridge University Press.

Liu, L. and Chen, X. 2012. *The Archaeology of China: From the Late Palaeolithic to the Early Bronze Age.* Cambridge: Cambridge University Press.

Mizoguchi, K. 2013. *The Archaeology of Japan: From the Earliest Rice Farming Villages to the Rise of the State.* Cambridge: Cambridge University Press.

Underhill, A., ed. 2013. *A Companion to Chinese Archaeology.* Chichester: Wiley-Blackwell.

www.seaa-web.org Website of the Society for East Asian Archaeology.

East Asia: Cities and States

10

Charles Higham

Transitions to States: China, *c.* 3500–200 BCE 210

KEY SITE Sanxingdui 218

KEY DISCOVERY The Origins of Chinese Writing 222

Transitions to States: Korea, 108 BCE**–900** CE 225

Transitions to States: Japan, 250–650 CE 228

Expansion and Integration: Early States in Southeast Asia 229

KEY THEME: SOCIAL INEQUALITY Social Status and the Built Environment 234

Summary and Conclusions 234

Further Reading 235

Ta Prohm temple, part of the vast low-density city of ancient Angkor in Cambodia, which reached the height of its power in the twelfth and thirteenth centuries CE.

From 5000 BCE, agricultural surpluses were sufficiently predictable to sustain larger communities. Social inequality increased, which we can see from the walls that ringed major settlements and cemeteries that contained individuals interred with exotic and rare objects. This initial emergence of an elite class developed into the formation of early states and the rise and fall of dynasties.

The first part of this chapter covers the formation of the first states in China and the Shang and Zhou dynasties that followed, culminating in the establishment of the Qin and Han empires that united the whole of China under a single system of government in the third century BCE. The second part of the chapter describes the rise of state societies in adjacent regions—Japan and Korea, and mainland Southeast Asia—and how many of these states were influenced by interregional connections, above all with their powerful neighbor China.

- The building works and exotic materials of the first cities in Shang and Zhou China depended on agricultural surplus, such as millet and rice.

- Early signs of social inequality appear in the form of walled settlements, large construction works, and burials with exotic and rare artifacts.

- China was ruled by a series of dynasties—Xia, Shang, Western Zhou, Eastern Zhou—mainly centered in the Central Plains.

- The breakdown of central authority in the later Zhou period was followed by the formation of the Qin empire, and then the Han empire, contemporary with the Roman empire in western Eurasia.

- The societies of China, Korea, and Japan were closely connected. The conquest of northern Korea by the Han empire led to the rise of independent states there, which in turn influenced the development of the Yamato state in Japan.

- Further south, maritime connections through trade and exchange led to the formation of states in mainland Southeast Asia, the most famous being the kingdom of Angkor in Cambodia from the tenth to fifteenth centuries CE.

TRANSITIONS TO STATES: CHINA, *c.* 3500–200 BCE

Traditional historical records divide the early history of China [10.1, p. 212] into a succession of dynasties: Xia and Shang between *c.* 2070 and 1046 BCE, followed by the Western and Eastern Zhou. The Eastern Zhou was characterized by warring states that were eventually united under the Qin dynasty. This road to successive dynasties began from 3500 BCE with the **Liangzhu** and the **Longshan** cultures, which include the first signs of the rise of an elite social group.

Liangzhu and the Longshan Culture, c. 3500–1900 BCE

The earliest major walled settlement in China was established at Liangzhu, in the marshy lowlands of the Yangzi delta, around 3500 BCE. This was a settlement bigger than any that had been seen previously, enclosed within an earthen wall 20 meters (66 feet) thick at the base, and encircled by a series of moats and canals that allowed entry into the city by a series of water gates. At the center of the site was a large artificial mound supporting three compounds

TIMELINE East Asia: Cities and States

Years BCE | Years CE

CHINA

Hunter-gatherers — Neolithic — Xia Dynasty — Shang — Western Zhou — Western Han — Eastern Han

Early Neolithic Pengtoushan — Middle Neolithic Yangshao — Longshan Culture — Spring and Autumn — Warring States — Qin Dynasty

KOREA

Hunter-gatherers — Neolithic — Bronze Age — Iron Age

Koguryo, Paekche, Silla — Great Silla

SOUTHEAST ASIA

Hunter-gatherers — Neolithic — Bronze Age — Iron Age — Angkor

Pyu

JAPAN

Hunter-gatherers — Yayoi — Kofun

Yamato

Legend: ▬ Period ▬ People ▬ Site

interpreted as elite residences. The status of the ruling group is illustrated further by cemeteries of powerful individuals that were furnished with elaborate jade ornaments. Other jade items include flat polished rings (*bi*) and rectangular tubes with square facets along their corners (*cong*). These were important symbols of heaven and earth in later Chinese societies.

The landscape around Liangzhu was transformed by the construction of dams and embankments, the longest of them extending over 8 kilometers (5 miles), to control run-off from the neighboring mountains. These enormous undertakings also point to the power of the Liangzhu elite.

Further north in the Yellow River basin, the late Neolithic Longshan culture is crucial in tracing the course toward early state formation. It developed seamlessly from the Yangshao and Dawenkou cultures (see Chapter 9), witnessing a surge in population seen in the foundation of many new settlements. Before long, sites covered the Yellow River Valley.

Though showing a clear development from the Yangshao and Dawenkou cultures, the Longshan period displays signs of turbulence. For example, north of the Yellow River,

10.1 China and Southeast Asia. Map showing major sites and places mentioned in the text.

populations were confined on all sides by uplands, and as the number of people grew, the basin became a hothouse of rivalry and strife that stimulated rapid social change. Taosi, dating to *c.* 2100–2000 BCE, was the dominant center here, lying behind a thick wall enclosing four quadrants. One of these contained the elite palace area; another an observatory and a temple to venerate the ancestors; a third quadrant contained ceramic and stone craft workshops; and commoners occupied the fourth. The royal cemetery included richly furnished graves, such as a boat-shaped coffin containing turquoise ornaments and cowrie shells, while the side niches yielded jade ritual offerings and weapons. Ten pigs had been halved and placed in the grave, which also included a lacquer-handled jade vessel interpreted as symbolizing the power of the royal individual.

Other sites were growing in power, however, and bows and bone arrowheads from Taosi make it clear that warfare was part of the social scene. The city was sacked between *c.* 2000 and 1900 BCE: the palace was razed, walls were flattened, elite graves ransacked, and commoner dwellings were built over the old palace. Significantly, the observatory was also destroyed and a mutilated skeleton buried in its center. The lesson to be learned is that the growth of social inequality and the rise and fall of elites involved intense competition and warfare.

The forces that overran Taosi may have come from Shimao, towards the northern frontier of China, where excavations have uncovered a major walled settlement. The stone-built city walls enclose a total area of 400 hectares (988 acres), making it the largest city of its period.

As is seen in virtually all later centers in northern China, there were craft workshops and cemeteries. The central palace complex, atop a stepped pyramid 70 meters (230 feet) high and with an inner wall around it enclosing 210 hectares (519 acres), was founded around 2300 BCE. Two centuries later, an outer wall was added almost doubling the area of the city, the walls incorporating closely spaced towers up to 18 × 16 meters (59 × 52 feet) and standing to a height of 4 meters (13 feet). Gateways into the city were also heavily defended, and their construction was associated with rituals, evidenced by sacrificial pits containing twenty-four human skulls, most of them of young women.

Shimao belongs to a period when large, walled centers began to dominate the settlement patterns across much of the Yellow River Valley, as well further south in the broad plains that flank the Yangzi. The competitive conflict between these growing centers resulted in the emergence of a dominant state based at the city of **Erlitou**, in the Yiluo basin south of the Yellow River. This site, with a focus on its palace and elite burials, is widely seen as the capital of the Xia Dynasty, long regarded as the first dynasty of China.

The Xia Dynasty, c. 2000–1500 BCE

For a long time, the Xia Dynasty was only known through early historic texts, and thought by many to be entirely mythical. This changed with the archaeological discovery of the city of Erlitou, situated in the right area and dated to the time shown in historical records as belonging to the Xia.

Over a period of four centuries from about 1850 BCE, Erlitou grew as the central city of the Xia Dynasty. It has revealed wealthy burials, workshops for turquoise, ceramics, and bronzes, as well as poorer residential areas and graves. The walled palace precinct covered 10.8 hectares (27 acres), requiring a huge amount of rammed earth in its construction. One palace contained burials accompanied by bronze, jade, ceramic, cowrie shell, and lacquer-ware offerings. These items came from dedicated royally maintained workshops and were all signs of elite status. Sumptuous vessels and weaponry were also cast here, and fired ceramic **piece-molds** have been recovered. A dragon formed from turquoise and jade tablets, together with a bronze bell, covered one skeleton [**10.2**].

piece-mold a mold used in a bronze-casting technique whereby a complex object was cast in sections, which were then joined with mortises and tenons

10.2 An elite leader at Erlitou, capital of the Xia Dynasty, was interred under this remarkable model of a dragon made of more than 2,000 pieces of turquoise.

The reach that Erlitou needed to acquire the raw materials necessary to equip elite people and project their status led to the foundation of dependent settlements as far south as the mid-Yangzi Valley, where there are rich sources of copper. Cowrie shells were imported probably from the Indian Ocean or the Andaman Sea. The most important product was millet, followed by rice, pigs, cattle, and sheep. Surpluses in these commodities made possible the labor and energy needed to maintain this level of building, craft, and trade. Its controlling reach to other settlements and surrounding lands, and the evidence of a highly organized elite class, lend Erlitou the description of an early state.

The Xia Dynasty was not alone, and the rise and fall of other states may well account for its decline. Only 6 kilometers (3.7 miles) away, a competing walled city, Yanshi, was founded, and seems to have been part of an intrusive movement into the heart of Erlitou territory. To the west, however, the new city **Zhengzhou** heralded the beginning of the Shang Dynasty, which is the first in China known from contemporary written records.

The Shang Dynasty, c. 1500–1045 BCE

The Shang Dynasty holds center stage in any consideration of early China because of the long and intensive study of its physical remains. These are found in the cities of Zhengzhou and Anyang in particular, but there are now many other well-known sites. Intensive archaeological and historical research has illuminated the energy and power of the Shang through its massive royal tombs, outstanding bronze [**10.3**] and jade industries, chariot burials, and its social structure.

Zhengzhou. The earlier history of the Shang is seen at Zhengzhou, a capital city that had an inner walled area covering 300 hectares (740 acres) and an outer rammed-earth wall that probably enclosed as much as 2,500 hectares (6,200 acres). This city represents a quantum leap over what went before. Excavations within the walls have uncovered the stamped-earth foundations of a probable palace precinct, represented by large postholes to receive columns. This same area included pits filled with dog skeletons and human skulls. Dogs were often sacrificed to the ancestors, whereas human beings were slaughtered when major new buildings were

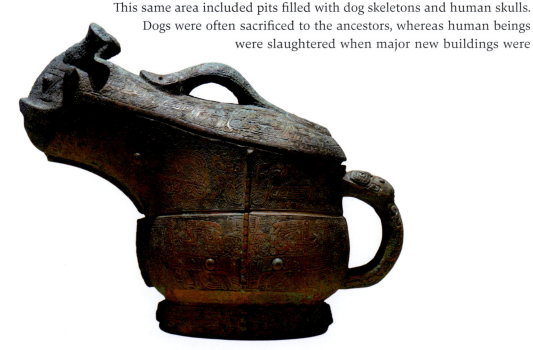

10.3 The tomb of Fu Hao, Anyang. This bronze ritual wine vessel (*gong*) was discovered in the grave of Lady Fu Hao at Anyang, the last Shang capital, and illustrates the sophistication of early Chinese bronzeworking.

constructed. Opulent graves with fine mortuary offerings in this part of the ancient city also offer evidence for the presence of an elite, probably royal, presence.

The area outside the palace precinct incorporated a series of specialist manufacturing areas. One workshop was for casting ceremonial bronze vessels and weapons; the skill of the bronze-casters, who surely worked under royal control and patronage, can be judged from one recovered vessel known as a *ding*, which weighed 86.4 kilograms (190 pounds). Another area was used for shaping and firing ceramics, the homes of the specialists being located nearby. There were workshops for bone workers, whose output included hairpins and arrowheads. Four cemeteries for the non-elite Shang populace have been investigated; mortuary offerings include ceramics, bronzes, and jade ornaments. Similarly to so many of its successors, Shang royal rulers ensured that they exercised control over the specialists who produced not only the necessities for the court life, but also the tools and weapons for the peasantry and the army.

The need to import raw materials involved the maintenance of communication routes. This demand in turn stimulated the rise of elites at such sites as Panlongcheng in the Yangzi Valley, where copper and tin ingots were sent north to Zhengzhou, probably in exchange for agricultural surplus. The Shang-style walled center at Panlongcheng and the outstandingly rich burials of the leaders at this site have suggested that there was a rapid expansion of Shang political control. With this came the spread of bronze technology and military conquest.

Anyang. Zhengzhou was succeeded by the last Shang capital, at Anyang. With the foundation of the royal city of Yinxu at Anyang in about 1250 BCE, we enter a vital period of Chinese history when written records provide the closest insight into the structure of society and the preoccupations of its rulers. Anyang incorporated a palace area, a royal **necropolis**, chariot burials, specialized workshops for the production of bronzes, bone artifacts, and ceramics, as well as extensive cemeteries for the populace.

The royal necropolis contained twelve massive tombs, and although looted in antiquity for their doubtless vast wealth of offerings, enough survives to reveal the practice of human sacrifice, with hundreds of individuals, often buried alive, in associated pits. Birds, pigs, and elephants were also sacrificed. Although no ruler's tomb has survived looting, that of Fu Hao, a consort of King Wu Ding mentioned in his oracle bone texts, was found intact with a wealth of mortuary offerings [**10.4**] (see also **10.3**). In her wood-lined burial chamber were nested and lacquered wooden coffins. Sixteen individuals accompanied the primary burial, including men, women, and children. Some were placed in the wall niches on either side of the tomb, others within the grave fill, which comprised layers of stamped earth. Mortuary offerings included 468 bronzes, incorporating ritual wine and food vessels.

Oracle Bones. Oracle bones were the shoulder blades of oxen or the plastrons (the underside of the shell) of turtles, which were used for divination. The diviners would apply a heated metal rod to the surface of the bone while asking a question. The bone would then crack in the heat, and the shape of those cracks would be interpreted as the answer. In some cases, inscriptions were carved onto the bone to record the question that was asked, the answer that was given, and the subsequent outcome. The oracle bone texts reveal that the rulers of Anyang were principally concerned with the weather as it related to a successful harvest, whether or not it was auspicious to attack

necropolis (pl. necropoleis) a cemetery; literally meaning city of the dead

10.4 The tomb of Fu Hao, Anyang. This phoenix was one of 755 jade items, along with a wealth of other grave goods, found in the tomb of Fu Hao, a consort of King Wu Ding (*c.* 1250–1192 BCE).

a particular enemy, and the portents for successful hunting [**10.5**]. Critical to the divination procedure was communication with the gods and the ancestors. This meant that a successful harvest provided spiritual enhancement for the ruler, but failure implied the contrary. Sacrifices were also made, of animals and captives, to seek the favor of deities and illustrious ancestors. In these ceremonies, we see the ruler performing an intermediary role with the supernatural. Gods and ancestors had a formative function in the success of the kingdom, and it was necessary to consult and placate them to replenish and confirm royal prestige.

The Anyang oracle bones have been used to build up a picture of the geography and extent of the Shang state, but it is clear that its cultural influence spread far beyond that area of direct control. The Shang realm was clearly much smaller than its cultural sphere, which is defined by characteristic bronze ritual vessels, used both by the Shang themselves and several of their rivals.

The charisma of the divine ruler and his ancestors was a key to the continuity of the state, but could not survive superior force from rivals, a fate that befell the Shang when the armies of its great rival, the Western Zhou, overwhelmed it.

Southern Rivals to Shang Culture

Many other states existed in the periphery of the Shang domain. Research in the south, where rice rather than millet was cultivated, has provided a new view of early China. The discovery of **Sanxingdui**, a walled city in Sichuan Province in western China and assigned to the Changjiang culture, demonstrates the equal importance of the Yangzi Valley (see Key Site box: Sanxingdui, p. 218).

Additional evidence comes from a second Changjiang cultural center at **Jinsha**. Extensive excavations revealed palace foundations and a cemetery that included at least 800 graves. Few of the dead lived beyond about thirty years of age, and most were buried with ceramic vessels and jade ornaments [**10.6**]. This site was first occupied in about 1000 BCE and, similarly to Sanxingdui, had sacrificial pits, but at Jinsha these contained elephant tusks and fine jade axes, chisels, disks, and bracelets. A remarkable number of animals were ceremonially sacrificed, and placed in one of the pits: the evidence points to about 500 elephants, 1,500 pigs, and 1,000 deer.

10.5 An oracle bone. Oracle bones are a vital source of documentary information of the Shang Dynasty. This turtle plastron (the underside of the shell) was used to divine the success of hunting expeditions by Prince You. The faint incisions are early Chinese writing.

10.6 Jinsha. This major site of the Changjiang culture of Sichuan Province was discovered in 2001, and extensive excavations have revealed the presence of a 3,000-year-old city in the suburbs of the modern center of Chengdu. Among the finds is this remarkable depiction in jade of a crouching tiger.

The Western Zhou Dynasty, 1045–771 BCE

It was a rival state that led to the end of the Shang Dynasty. Historical texts describe how in 1045 BCE the powerful king of Zhou, based in the Wei Valley, sent his chariots and the Tiger Warrior infantry north to defeat the Shang at the Battle of Muye. The new rulers wielded power from a succession of capitals in the Wei river valley, close to the modern city of Xi'an. With the establishment of the Zhou Dynasty, we enter a period well documented both in terms of texts and in the archaeological record.

One of the key points to emerge from recent archaeological research involves the early Zhou adoption of ritual and mortuary practices from the Shang. We find, for example, the casting of typically Shang forms of bronze ritual vessels, used in banquets to feast the ancestors. Many such vessels contain inscriptions willing their use for generations lasting 10,000 years. During later times of danger, these types of vessel were accumulated and placed in underground hoards, such as the exceptionally rich one unearthed at Zhuangbai [10.7]. The interment of chariots, horses, and charioteers in pits associated with the nobility was also a Shang practice, while the form of the chariots themselves is a clear link between the two dynasties. Nevertheless, the Zhou expressed their own preferences in their bronzes, with distinctive regional styles.

Early Western Zhou emperors adopted an expansive policy under which peripheral states were conquered and ruled by members of the royal clan. Jin, with its capital at Tianma Qucun in Shanxi Province, was one of these conquered states. Excavations of 600 burials have revealed varying degrees of wealth, with some tombs incorporating remarkable jade facial images [10.8] and pits containing horses and chariots. The cemetery of Fangshan, near Beijing, contained extremely rich burials and was probably associated with another of these provincial states. Bronze vessels were of the highest quality, and there were also multiple chariot burials and horse interments. It is worth considering the great cost in labor and materials of a chariot that was then buried with its owner to advertise high status.

10.7 Inscribed bronze vessel. The history of the Western Zhou dynasty has been greatly enriched through the recovery of texts cast into bronze vessels. This Shi Qiang pan from Zhuangbai is part of a hoard of bronzes, and its inscription records the succession of the first seven Western Zhou rulers. It dates to the end of the tenth century BCE. Height 16.2 cm (6.4 in.).

10.8 Jade facial images. The Western Zhou cemetery of Tianma Qucun contained very rich burials, with elite mortuary offerings that included a human head carved from jade.

KEY SITE Sanxingdui

Sanxingdui was contemporary with the Shang Dynasty of the Central Plains. It was a walled city of about 450 hectares (1,112 acres), with occupation and industrial areas covering at least 15 square kilometers (6 square miles). It incorporated specialist workshops for the manufacture of bronzes, lacquerware, ceramics, and jade. Excavations of the walls, which had a maximum width of 47 meters (154 feet), reveal that they were constructed c. 1400–1200 BCE. The site is best known for two ritual pits found in 1986 [**10.9**, **10.10**], and a further six uncovered in 2021.

The Two Ritual Pits

One pit contained layers of animal bones together with 13 elephant tusks, ceremonial jade *yazhang* blades and *ge* daggers. Lower layers included 178 items of bronze, 4 gold artifacts, 129 jades, and other objects of stone and pottery, together with many cowrie shells.

Another pit contained further items of bronze, jade, gold, and stone, including bronze castings of trees, and diamond-shaped fittings. The next layer comprised a gigantic bronze statue of a man, 44 bronze heads [**10.11**], bronze masks, a bronze tree, and bronze vessels containing jades and cowrie shells. This layer was capped by 60 elephant tusks. The final count totaled 735 bronze items, 61 gold, 486 jades, turquoise ornaments, tiger's teeth, ivory, and cowrie shells. All of the material had been burned, and much of it intentionally broken, before being buried carefully in these pits.

The bronzes are of a size and form unparalleled in China. The statue of a man stands 2.6 m (8.6 ft.) high and weighs 180 kilograms (397 pounds) [**10.12**]. He wears a crown and a tunic richly embellished with images of dragons, animal heads, and crowns. His hands in a position suggestive of holding something curved and heavy, such as an elephant's tusk. The bronze tree, complete with leaves, fruit, and buds, and birds perched on its branches, stood nearly 4 m (13 ft.) high. A series of huge human heads with mask-like features, some of gold, stand apart from any other bronzes of this period in China; one mask with eyes protruding on stalks was 1.4 m (4.6 ft.) wide.

10.9, **10.10** Two ritual pits at Sanxingdui contained items of unprecedented grandeur for this period in China—huge bronze masks, splendid jades, and ivory— and were probably ritually associated with the royal Shu Dynasty.

Western Zhou Bronzeworking. The location of bronze foundries in a major settlement with a palace precinct recalls the layout of earlier Shang cities, such as Anyang. Despite a number of new styles and forms, the Zhou bronze industry was a development from the foregoing Shang tradition, both in terms of the types of vessels and weapons cast and the techniques of manufacture [**10.13**, p. 220].

Excavations at Luoyang in Henan Province have uncovered a bronzeworking area that produced clay molds and furnaces used to bring bronze to melting point. Production, which lasted from early in the dynasty until the second half of the tenth century BCE, was intensive. The clay piece-molds could be decorated or incised with texts prior to being fired. As many

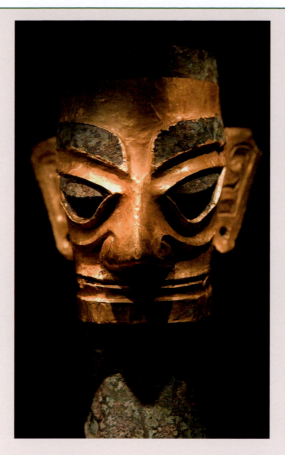

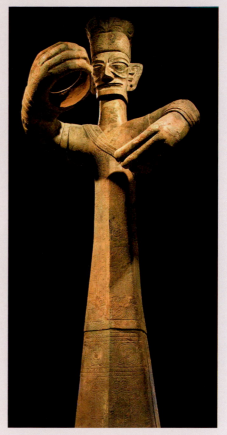

10.11 RIGHT The massive bronze heads found in the sacrificial pits at Sanxingdui probably represent deified ancestors of the ruling elite. No comparable masked heads have been found in China.

10.12 FAR RIGHT This statue of a man from Sanxingdui probably once held a curved object, such as an elephant tusk. A remarkable 2.6 meters (8.6 feet) high, it weighs 180 kilograms (397 pounds).

Interpretation

These pits may have been connected with the burials of the kings of Shu, but as yet no royal tombs have been uncovered. The burning of the contents, despite their value, rarity, and beauty, suggests a sacrificial or ritual purpose.

The quality of the offerings indicates great wealth, and some of the smaller objects provide clues to the use of items deposited in the pits. The function of the fifty-seven *yazhang* jade blades, for example, is represented by a small bronze figure who holds one of these blades, shown in a kneeling posture indicating a form of worship or sacrifice. The massive bronze human heads were probably the components of one or more ritual structures similar to those depicted on a model altar, while the numerous jades would also have had a ritual role.

The rulers of Sanxingdui supported a distinct bronze-casting tradition dedicated to the gigantic. There are few, if any, parallels in the ancient world for the size of the freestanding statue of a man, the trees, or the masks with animal features and eyes on stalks.

as ten separate pieces were necessary in the case of complex vessels, fitted together using mortise and tenon joints. There is evidence in other foundry areas for specialized production—vessels were cast by one group and chariot fittings or weapons by another. Such bronze workshops were established both in the royal domain and in the vassal states, enabling the latter to cast their own important ritual vessels, as well as weaponry that would in due course lead to competition and civil friction.

It is in part through the analysis of the bronzes that social transformation, described by the art historian Jessica Rawson as a "ritual revolution," can be traced. This widespread change dates to the first half of the ninth century BCE and is best documented in the mortuary record,

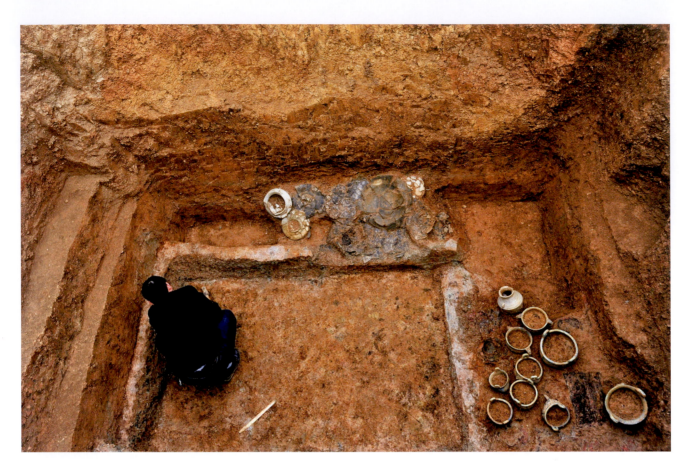

10.13 Western Zhou bronze vessels. An archaeologist at work in an elite tomb containing bronze vessels, in a cemetery of sixty-five tombs of the Western Zhou Dynasty in Jiangzhai, Hubei Province. More than 300 bronze vessels were excavated from the cemetery, many of them inscribed.

the way that chariots were interred, the increasing importance of jade grave goods and, most significantly, in ritual bronzes and the forms of the vessels being cast. Where previously there had been a range of containers to serve food or wine, now sets of virtually identical styles were cast, much heavier, and with longer and similar, or even identical, inscriptions. A series of new designs was introduced. Well-tried vessel types, formerly rendered in clay, were now cast in bronze, and individual rank could be indicated by the number of practically identical items that an individual possessed. Such a move encouraged the mass production, and the commercialization, of a bronze industry that had before been dedicated to the provision of specific items for court ritual purposes. It seems that identical sets of bronzes, which could be added to in number if resources permitted, were a means of exhibiting the status and achievements of particular lineages. Such a change in the use of bronze vessels reflects the rise of competing regional lords, who would weaken and eventually overpower the Western Zhou king.

The Eastern Zhou Dynasty, 770–221 BCE

By the eighth century BCE, the Zhou court faced mounting external pressures from the steppes, and in 771 BCE the capital was moved eastward to Luoyang, marking the transition to the Eastern Zhou. The kings at Luoyang were ultimately too weak to control the power of the regional lords, and in place of a central authority, large and potent regional states became established. The states themselves were also subject to factionalism and splintering, depending on the strength of the ruler of the day.

The Eastern Zhou Dynasty is divided into the periods of the Spring and Autumn Annals (770–481 BCE), and the Warring States (481–221 BCE), both named after contemporary historical documents that recount the period in question. During both, the Eastern Zhou court was virtually shorn of power after its move to Luoyang, and relied on the support of the major states. As feudal ties broke, it became accepted practice for states to expand through naked power lacking morality or the bonds of kinship. It was in this milieu that the philosopher Confucius arose to rail against such perceived immorality from his eastern base, the state of Lu. At the same time, southern states beyond the pale of the Eastern Zhou empire rose in power, particularly the Chu of the middle Yangzi basin, the Wu and the Yue of the lower Yangzi, and the Shu of Sichuan. Adapting to this situation led to the development of the *Ba* system, in which the predominance of the ruler of one major state was accepted by the others.

Technological and Social Changes. This period witnessed major advances in military strategy, and wars of increasing intensity led to the annihilation of states and their ruling houses. These events were fueled by the spread of a new metallurgical technology, involving the casting of molten iron into molds. This technical achievement required the control of very high temperatures, not matched in the West for centuries to come. Furthermore, rapid advances in agriculture meant that permanent armies could be raised.

This competitive milieu encouraged art, architecture, warfare, and industry. Trade and the accumulation of wealth were enhanced by the development of a form of currency. Intriguingly, the first money took the form of cowrie shells, which for a long time had been used as a form of wealth. The first coins took the form of knives or spades before the familiar round coins with a central hole were cast. New cities sprang up, and their internal layout changed. The state of Zhang, for example, had three capitals between 425 and 386 BCE. The city became an anchor for the social elite in times of political stress, and civic plans therefore required strong defenses. Moreover, increases in trade and the rise of the mercantile classes led to wholesale changes in the nature of the city. Formerly a royal administrative center, it became a metropolis of many classes and occupations, with the royal palace as the centerpiece.

Successful states were led by rulers with powerful ministers, whose status was indicated in their grave goods, and in particular by finely crafted bronze vessels [**10.14**]. These states had well-organized social and economic systems but their governance tended increasingly toward totalitarianism. Ultimately, no power could resist the state of Qin, which, under its ruler Qin Shi Huangdi, brought the Eastern Zhou Dynasty to an end in 221 BCE.

10.14 Bronzeworking. This remarkable set of bronzes comes from the tomb of the Marquis of Zeng, Leigudun. It comprises a *zun* or wine vessel on a *pan*, or plate. It was cast by the piece-mold technique and embellished with decorative pieces produced by the lost-wax method of casting, which were soldered on.

KEY DISCOVERY The Origins of Chinese Writing

Chinese writing has very early roots (**Table 10.1**). The earliest evidence for symbolic communication comes from Jiahu, a Neolithic site in the Huai River valley in Henan Province, dated to *c.* 6500 BCE. It has yielded turtle carapaces that were pitted and inscribed with symbols. The Longshan site of Chengziyai in Shandong Province has produced fragments of inscribed bones used to divine the future, dating to *c.* 2500–1900 BCE, and symbols on pottery vessels from Dinggong are thought to be an early form of writing. Those of a similar nature have also been found on pottery sherds from the Liangzhu culture in the lower Yangzi Valley.

Shang Dynasty Pictograms

By the time of the Shang Dynasty, these symbols had developed into a fully fledged system of writing that used pictograms to represent objects and ideas. Since this early script is ancestral to modern Chinese written forms it can be translated, enabling scholars not only to produce a king list and to date specific events but also to probe issues that concerned the court.

One of the foremost of these issues was the making of sacrifices to appease the ancestors, frequently by killing an animal in the ancestral temple. Another concern involved military campaigns. Other texts reveal the king's worry over a consort's pregnancy, whether or not to go hunting, and how to cure the royal toothache. Much thought was also devoted to the success of the millet harvest and the amount of rainfall.

More than 100,000 oracle bones have been recovered, mainly from Anyang, but these were not the only Shang use of texts. Vermilion-colored writing has been detected on some oracle bones prior to their being traced with incisions, and one image took the form of vertical strokes joined by wavy lines. These represent bamboo slips, joined sequentially with threads to form a scroll that could be opened

Table 10.1 The Evolution of Chinese Writing	Oracle bone inscriptions *c.* 1400–1200 BCE	Bronze inscriptions *c.* 1500–700 BCE	Small seal script standardized after 221 BCE	Chancery script *c.* 200 BCE–200 CE	Standard script *c.* 200 CE onward	Standard printed style *c.* 1400 CE onward
Pictograph						
Differentiated pictograph						
Pictographic compound						
Phonetic compound						

The Qin Dynasty, 221–207 BCE

In 221 BCE, the head of the state of Qin, who had conquered all rival states, took the name Qin Shi Huangdi (august emperor of Qin) and became the First Emperor of China. (The name China derives from Qin, pronounced "chin.")

Qin Shi Huangdi created thirty-six commanderies (provinces), each subdivided into counties. These commanderies were placed under a centrally appointed governor, who was a military commander and an inspector who ensured compliance with the emperor's wishes. Qin Shi Huangdi ordered the adoption of a uniform system of writing known as the ***xiaozhuan***. Uniformity was also applied to weights and measures, the gauge of wheeled

xiaozhuan a small seal script, a form of standardized writing instituted under the Qin Dynasty in China

to be read, and then folded to be stored away. Common in later periods, none has survived from the Shang Dynasty, but they clearly existed.

Bamboo Slips

Texts on bamboo slips have been recovered from tombs dating from the period of the Warring States (*c.* 481–221 BCE) [**10.15**]; most derive from southern China, where conditions for the use and survival of bamboo are more favorable than in the north. The tomb of Shao Tuo at Baoshan has yielded a series of such texts, found together with his brush for writing and knife for erasing errors. The texts were largely concerned with legal issues, although there was also an inventory of the tomb contents, and divinations.

Another set of early texts comes from the tomb of Xi, an archivist who lived during the reign of the first emperor of Qin, Qin Shi Huangdi. He was buried in Tomb 11 at Shuihudi, and was accompanied by about 1,200 bamboo slips bearing historic texts, which Xi might well have written himself.

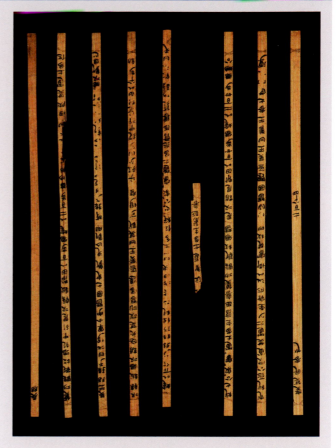

10.15 Annals written on bamboo slips, from Yunmeng County, Qin Dynasty. A total of fifty-three slips were found, written in ink, mostly recording accounts of wars by the Qin to unify the country.

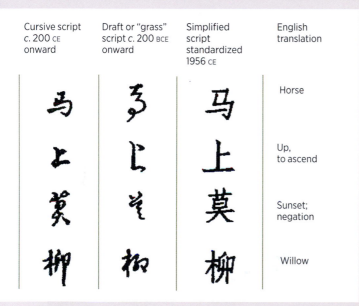

Cursive script *c.* 200 CE onward	Draft or "grass" script *c.* 200 BCE onward	Simplified script standardized 1956 CE	English translation
马	马	马	Horse
上	上	上	Up, to ascend
莫	莫	莫	Sunset; negation
柳	柳	柳	Willow

vehicles, and the currency. The legal system was applied equally across the empire, based on the basic tenet of mutual responsibility. The state controlled huge resources of labor that were deployed on new roads that radiated out from the capital, and on the creation of a canal system. Some 300,000 men were set to work on expanding the Great Wall, which ran along the borders of northern China to keep out the marauding Xiongnu, powerful steppe horsemen. More than 600,000 were engaged on the emperor's tomb at **Lintong**, near modern Xi'an (ancient Chang'an) [**10.16**, p. 224]. Whole communities were uprooted and sent into thinly populated regions, or dispatched to strengthen defenses and increase agricultural production.

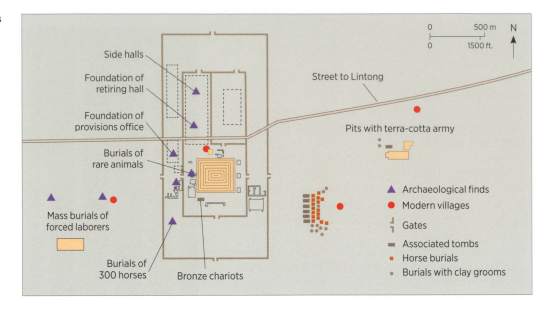

10.16 The tomb of China's first emperor. The tomb complex of Qin Shi Huangdi is one of the largest the world has seen. The emperor took with him to the afterlife all his possessions and followers. The former were buried in pits or placed inside his mausoleum. The latter, represented in bronze or terra-cotta, were interred in huge underground chambers.

Qin Shi Huangdi died in 210 BCE at the age of forty-nine, during a provincial tour of inspection. His body was interred in his massive mortuary complex at Lintong. The subterranean chambers that surrounded the central pyramid of the tomb were filled with the famous life-sized terra-cotta replicas of the emperor's armies (see **1.1**, p. 15), including infantry, chariots, cavalry, and a command center. Each soldier, mass-produced but then individually modeled, was painted and armed. Chambers also contained a replica of the imperial zoological garden, figures of musicians, acrobats, and wrestlers, and a half-sized copy in bronze of the royal chariot, resplendent with four horses and the charioteer [**10.17**].

The Han Dynasty (206 BCE–220 CE) inherited from Qin Huangdi's relatively brief reign the notion of a unified state. Under the reign of Emperor Wudi (r. 140–87 BCE), the empire expanded, an effort requiring a strong army. Military force was deployed to take new territory, particularly in the northwest. To the south, the Han extended as far as the rich Red River basin in Vietnam, and to the east, into the Korean peninsula.

10.17 The emperor's royal chariot. Excavations have still barely scratched the surface of this gigantic complex. This half-size bronze carriage, drawn by four horses, is one of the finest bronzes ever discovered in China.

TRANSITIONS TO STATES: KOREA, 108 BCE–900 CE

In 108 BCE, Han armies occupied the northern part of Korea and divided it into a series of provinces [**10.18**]. They encountered an already established society, versed in intensive rice agriculture and dominated by its elite leaders for centuries. The Han controlled parts of northern Korea for several centuries, but, in response, new states independent from China arose in the rest of the peninsula. These were Koguryo, Paekche, and Silla, occupying a period known as the Three Kingdoms (57 BCE–668 CE). These early Korean kingdoms emphasize several key issues in the history of early Asia. The first is the direct impact of Chinese imperial expansion, which triggered first the foundation of colonial provinces, and then the rise of independent states as central influence waned. The second is the impact of warfare between rival states competing for power.

According to textual tradition, the first state, Koguryo, was founded in 37 BCE, and it survived until its defeat at the hands of its southern rival, Silla, in 668 CE. The early Koguryo capital at **Jian** is surrounded by impressive stone walls and a moat. A reservoir lay within the walled precinct, together with a royal palace. Elite Koguryo burials comprised mounds raised over stone chambers. Although all have been looted, wall frescoes survive [**10.19**, p. 226]. The tombs at Jian include many lively scenes, such as the Tomb of the Dancers, which features images of festive activities, some decorated with gold inlay and jeweled ornaments.

10.18 Map of Korea showing major sites mentioned in the text.

The second state, Paekche, was located in southwestern Korea. Archaeological research has uncovered many sites belonging to this state, including Mongchon, where the walls and moat enclosed a palace and a reservoir. Imported Chinese ceramics show how Mongchon was occupied by the Han during the late third and early fourth centuries CE.

The third state, Silla, was located in the southeastern part of the peninsula. With Chinese help it overcame Koguryo, Paekche, and other smaller states during the sixth and seventh centuries CE. The initial prowess of Silla may have been based on the rich iron-ore deposits that lie near the capital of Kyongju. The earliest phases of this state's formation might well be represented at Choyangdong. Dating to the first to second centuries CE, the pit graves from this site have furnished Han-style bronze mirrors and exotic glass beads.

Later examples of Silla mortuary remains include the rich royal graves at Kyongju dating to c. 300–550 CE. One of these, the Tomb of the Heavenly Horse [**10.20**, p. 226], included a lacquered wooden coffin that was placed within the chamber, with the head pointed to the east. A wooden container for mortuary offerings lay adjacent. This room was then covered by a massive **tumulus** comprising thousands of heavy river boulders, rising to a height of 7.5 meters (25 feet), with a diameter of 23.5 meters (77 feet).

The contents of such royal graves reveal a rich elite. Foremost among the objects are the golden crowns, with tree- or antler-like projections [**10.21**, p. 226]. Jade and gold ornaments were attached to the trees, some in the form of leaves; other gold attachments fell as tassels from the ring of the crown. The royal dead also wore elaborate gold belts, with that from the Tomb of the Golden Crown attaining a length of 2 meters (6.6 feet). They, too, were embellished

tumulus (pl. tumuli) an earthen or stone mound, usually covering a burial or burials

10.19 ABOVE LEFT **Koguryo fresco.** Wall painting from Tomb 3, Anak, showing a nobleman being served by his wife.

10.20 RIGHT **The Tomb of the Heavenly Horse.** This painting on birch bark gives the tomb at Kyongju its name. It belongs to the Silla kingdom of the fifth to sixth centuries CE. Height 53 cm (21 in.).

10.21 ABOVE **Silla gold crown.** The Silla kingdom was renowned for its goldwork. This crown comes from the Tomb of the Gold Crown at Kyongju, fifth to sixth centuries CE. Height 27.5 cm (11 in.).

with dangling gold ornaments, including a model of a fish and a basket. Gold finger and toe rings, bracelets, and heavily ornamented earrings are also regularly encountered. The rulers wore bronze shoes with gold attachments on the soles. Male burials included much armor—iron swords, arrowheads, and helmets—as well as accoutrements for horse riding, such as saddles, harnesses, and stirrups.

Great Silla, 668–918 CE

When Silla defeated Paekche and Koguryo, Korea was unified under one state in 668 CE and the period known as Great Silla began. This state was at its height in the eighth century CE, and was in regular contact with China. Excavations at Kyongju have provided a rare glimpse of palace life, particularly the restoration of the Anapchi Lake, with its ornamental pavilions and bank depicting the outline of Korea, Japan, and Taiwan.

Buddhism flourished under Great Silla, and many temples with statues of the Buddha made of granite, bronze, gold, and iron spread across the landscape. A specific Silla style of architecture and associated sculpture developed by the eighth century CE, the most prominent example being the **Sokkuram cave temple** at Mount Toham, near Kyongju. This famous site comprises three chambers constructed of granite blocks; the circular shrine room, with a diameter of 8 meters (26 feet), contains the finest of the Silla Buddha sculptures, standing 3.3 meters (11 feet) high [**10.22**].

The story of early Korean states therefore mirrors many elements seen in that of China. Not only is it one of opulent social elite groups and competition, but also of conquest and, later, expansionism. Just as China influenced Korea, so Korean states exerted their own influence on the rise of those over the water in Japan.

10.22 The Sokkuram Buddha. Carved in granite, this sculpture dates to the eighth century CE. Buddhism flourished under Great Silla. Height 3.3 m (11 ft.).

10.23 Map of Japan showing major sites mentioned in the text.

TRANSITIONS TO STATES: JAPAN, 250–650 CE

The Japanese kingdom of Yamato, centered in western Honshu, arose from the Late Yayoi culture (see Chapter 9) in the third century CE [**10.23**]. The Yamato kingdom did not develop from outside colonization, but its trajectory was heavily influenced by trade and exchange with Korea and China. The Korea Strait is only 200 kilometers (125 miles) wide, and the rice-growing Yayoi chiefdoms in Japan were well aware of the rise of new kingdoms, religion, and militarism on their doorstep. From 250 CE, the chiefdoms had grown into a militarist society known for their large, distinctive burial mounds known as ***kofun***. The size of the *kofun* was graded by social rank, and particular emphasis in Japan has been given to the huge mounded tombs in the Nara basin, southeast of Osaka. That the period was one of competition and militarism is documented archaeologically in the finds of iron weapons, armor, and horses in elite tombs. These weapons were derived through contacts with the early kingdoms of the Korean peninsula.

By 400 CE, the power base had moved from Nara and onto the Osaka plains near the shore of the Inland Sea. The fifth-century CE Yamato rulers commanded considerable military power and controlled labor in order to construct their massive tombs and excavate irrigation works. Their tombs included the biggest earth-mounded examples ever constructed, up to 486 meters (1,595 feet) in length. Where permission has been granted—for imperial tombs are not to be touched—investigation of these huge mounds has uncovered coffins formed by joining together large stone slabs. The grave offerings featured huge caches of iron weaponry and armor, as well as tools. One interment contained seventy-seven iron swords. From *c.* 450 CE, gold and silver ornaments of Korean inspiration were also found. Elite tombs were now surrounded by moats and ringed by terra-cotta representations of houses, people [**10.24**], and animals. Tomb chambers were lined with massive stones and coated with clay to counter damp; charcoal and pebble-based drains were used for the same purpose.

kofun the burial mounds of the Yamato kings of Japan, also the name of the period when they were built

10.24 Terra-cotta *haniwa*. Figures from Japanese mounded tombs portray the dress and activities of the elite of the period. This example shows a seated female, possibly a shaman, from Ōizumi-machi, Ōra county, *c.* sixth century CE. Height 94 cm (37 in.).

The political situation in Japan was increasingly influenced by its much larger and more powerful neighbor China, as well as by trade and travel. It was these contacts that led to three crucial changes in the sixth century CE that marked the beginning of the historical Japanese state. One was the introduction of Buddhism to Japan. New temples were constructed [10.25], employing immigrant craftsmen, and the earlier tradition of massive mounded burials was abandoned. Another was the construction of a new purpose-built capital city at **Asuka**, designed on a gridded plan borrowed from Chinese capital cities, with a grand imperial palace complex. The third change was the development of a system of writing based on the Chinese script.

While receiving much influence in terms of ideas and goods from Korea and China, Yamato still displayed a specific Japanese ideology. So, while accepting Buddhism, the local *kami* spirits retained their importance, as they do to this day. The rulers developed increasingly efficient forms of rice cultivation, essential to support the imperial capital cities, and had sufficient disposable wealth to deploy a fleet and armed forces across the Tsushima Strait in support of their Korean ally, Paekche, in its struggle with neighboring Silla. Large cities, palaces, and temples were built, again on continental models. Japan can look back at Yamato as its seminal period of development.

10.25 Asuka roof tiles. Tile from the end of an eave, from Asuka-dera at Asuka, *c.* 596 CE. Diameter 15.1 cm (6 in.). The Asuka-dera seemed to have been the first temple to have had roof tiles, but examples have since been found at a number of Asuka-period sites.

EXPANSION AND INTEGRATION: EARLY STATES IN SOUTHEAST ASIA

East Asia, India, and the Mediterranean were linked by a trade route that is widely known as the Silk Road. This was, in essence, a network of trackways, which began with the Gansu corridor (gateway to China) and extended through India and Afghanistan to the Mediterranean world. Ideas, armies, new religions, migrants, merchants, and their precious goods all traveled along it.

The Silk Road that linked China with India and Rome had its roots deep in antiquity [10.26]. With the western expansion of Han domination in China, trade flourished as never before. Merchants plied the maze of routes skirting the Taklamakan Desert, journeying across Central Asia to the Caspian and Mediterranean seas. Many states—some ephemeral, others extensive and powerful—developed through the control of trade along these routes, the potential of irrigated agriculture, and the exploitation of natural resources, such as jade and lapis lazuli.

10.26 The Silk Road was a series of routes linking east and west, traversed by merchant caravans. It brought great wealth to the merchants involved, although also much danger and hardship. In addition to the carriage of goods, it also facilitated the transmission of ideas, not least the spread of Buddhism from its home in India to China.

stupa a domed building often containing Buddhist relics

The Central Asian Silk Road had its maritime counterpart, known as the maritime Silk Road, which ran along the coast of southern China, south to Vietnam, and on to the ports of Thailand, Burma (present-day Myanmar), and India before reaching Africa and the Mediterranean. This became very important following the fall of the Han Dynasty in 220 CE when China was divided into three independent states (220–280 CE). The emperor of the southern Chinese state, cut off from the Central Asia Silk Road to the north, sent emissaries south to seek out an alternative, maritime route to trading partners in the West. In connecting with long-established Indian and Southeast Asian trade networks, the imperial Chinese agents, to their surprise, encountered in Southeast Asia kings and their palaces, cities, intensive rice cultivation, systems of taxation, and writing.

The maritime Silk Road also influenced the rise of societies in Burma. We find this in the adoption of Buddhism, writing, and the wide range of Indian imports. The Pyu state developed in the dry zone of central Burma between about 200 BCE and 900 CE and is best known from three large walled cities: **Beikthano**, Sri Ksetra, and **Halin**. There is compelling evidence at Beikthano for a pre-Buddhist mortuary tradition involving big brick and timber halls containing the cremated remains of high-status individuals. By the fourth or fifth century CE, however, Buddhism had taken root, and many large public buildings were constructed for this faith, including **stupas** and monasteries.

Angkor, Cambodia

In Cambodia, the most prominent and well-known Southeast Asian state is that of Angkor. This is the modern name given to a complex of cities, temples, and reservoirs [**10.27**] located in the northwest of the country. It was first encountered by Europeans in the sixteenth century, when Portuguese missionaries visited and described a gigantic, abandoned stone city, invaded by the jungle. The Angkorian inscriptions were written in Sanskrit and archaic Khmer, leaving no doubt that the people responsible for this state were the ancestors of the present population of Cambodia.

10.27 Angkor. The site reached its greatest extent during the reign of King Jayavarman VII (r. 1181–1219 CE). His rectangular walled city of Angkor Thom housed a substantial urban population, and was dominated by his temple-mausoleum, known as the Bayon. The city was flanked by several huge reservoirs. An earlier center, known as Hariharalaya, lies to the southeast.

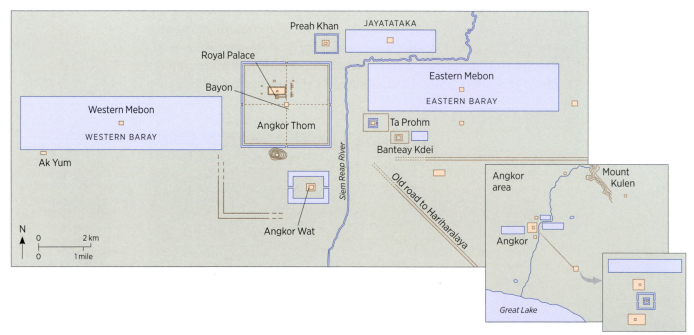

10.28 The temple of Preah Ko at Hariharalaya. This was a monument dedicated to the ancestors of King Indravarman I (r. 877–889 CE). It was formerly covered in brightly painted stucco. The name means sacred ox, after the sandstone oxen that guard its entrance.

The location of Angkor provides easy access to the bountiful resources of the region's Great Lake and access via the Mekong River to the sea. Small, perennial rivers issuing from the Kulen Hills to the north provided the city with fresh water. Prehistoric settlement dates back to the Bronze Age. Several temples predating the foundation of Angkor in 802 CE indicate continuity of human settlement, but the first major Angkorian center is **Hariharalaya**. Its temples lie south of the Indratataka, a reservoir of unprecedented size up to that time. Most buildings were constructed in the late ninth century CE. The royal center incorporated two major temples [**10.28**], while recent excavations have also encountered the foundations of a palace.

From the late ninth to the mid-tenth century CE, capitals moved across the Angkor region, until in about 1080 Angkor attained its present layout. **Angkor Wat**, one of the largest religious monuments known [**10.29**, p. 232], is a temple that incorporates some of the finest and longest bas-relief sculptures in the world, and the scenes do much to illuminate the religious and court life of Angkor during the twelfth century. One shows the king in council, another reveals the Angkorian army on the march, while a third illustrates graphic depictions of heaven and hell. The main temple incorporates five towers, representing the peaks of Mount Meru.

The most powerful of all Angkorian kings was Jayavarman VII (r. 1181–1219 CE), and his reign marks the apogee of Angkorian power. A Buddhist, he was responsible for the construction

10.29 Angkor Wat.
One of the largest religious monuments known, Angkor Wat was the temple-mausoleum of King Suryavarman II.

of Angkor Thom, the walled city that today dominates Angkor. It centers on the Bayon, a temple-mausoleum embellished with gigantic stone heads thought to represent the king [**10.30, 10.31**]. A LiDAR survey has now traced the plan of the city, showing it was laid out on a grid with roads and canals, as well as ponds in residential quarters. These surround the walled palace precinct north of the central Bayon. Jayavarman VII also ordered the construction of the northern reservoir and the central island temple of Neak Pean. According to contemporary inscriptions, visitors here would wash away their sins in the water that gushed from four fountains in the form of human and animal heads.

Most early research at Angkor involved the translation of inscriptions to identify the dynastic sequence, and to conserve monuments suffering through forest encroachment. Now, intensive fieldwork aided by remote sensing and LiDAR are revealing the remarkable extent to which the center grew along the northern margin of the Great Lake. There has also been much debate over the purpose of the reservoirs. Were they, for example, symbolic projections of royal power, or did they also serve as water storage for irrigated rice fields? The discovery of sluice gates to distribute water through an extensive canal system to the fields has helped to answer this. Indeed, the pattern of rice fields demarcated by low banks has been mapped.

10.30 ABOVE **The Bayon, Angkor.** The huge heads that dominate the Bayon temple-mausoleum at Angkor are thought to represent the king, Jayavarman VII, as a *bodhisattva*, a follower of the Buddha who chooses not to attain nirvana, but to stay on earth and help others. His ashes would have been placed below the central tower after cremation rituals.

10.31 LEFT **The Bayon, Angkor.** This section of the reliefs on the Bayon shows a ferocious battle between the army of Jayavarman VII and Cham forces. Note the war elephant in the background.

It is possible that a sharp climatic deterioration involving intermittent aridity and intense rains, linked with the delicacy of the water distribution system and its exposure to silting as deforestation took place in the upper catchment, contributed to the final abandonment of the city. By the fourteenth and fifteenth centuries, the Angkor state was under further stress from the encroaching Thais. It was abandoned in the middle years of the fifteenth century.

KEY THEME: SOCIAL INEQUALITY Social Status and the Built Environment

In the absence of written records, buildings provide the clearest evidence for a fully functioning state society. The palaces where royalty lived represent, in essence, the frozen energy of the many people who would have labored in the construction of such monuments. Walls, likewise, not only demarcate territory and assist in defending key places, but also reflect social organization. The Great Wall of China, with its forts and many watchtowers, stretched for hundreds of kilometers along the northern borders of the Han and Qin dynasties. The first emperor of China, Qin Shi Huangdi, sent tens of thousands of workers north from his capital to work on its construction. His tomb complex has few rivals anywhere for grandeur and complexity. It would have called on specialists in ceramics and bronze and an army of workers to raise up the pyramid over the tomb itself.

Further south, the energy demanded to construct the many temple mausolea, the walls, and the reservoirs of Angkor in Cambodia was colossal (see p. 232). Many quarries were exploited for the sandstone blocks required. Barges were needed to transport them to the city, and elephants to haul them, once cut and carved, to their resting places. At Angkor, the royal capital of King Jayavarman IV, inscriptions are still in place, or are lying on the ground, that record the names and the home bases of the workers brought in during the dry season, when the rice harvest was in, to work on construction projects.

Much research has been dedicated to understanding how societies similar to these originated. Less time has been spent explaining how all this effort so often ended with collapse and abandonment. Climate change and warfare may have played a role in different cases. At Angkor, new information has identified climatic change as a major contributing factor. The failure of the monsoon rains, punctuated by occasional intense storms, slackened central control over the labor force and led to the failure of the irrigation system. In the case of the Shang Dynasty, by contrast, it was conquest by the emerging power of the Zhou that led to its demise. Early Asian societies in their heyday were powerful organizations, but we should be aware that they were also unstable and prone to collapse.

SUMMARY AND CONCLUSIONS

The archaeological record in the central plain of the Yellow River and along the Yangzi River during the second millennium BCE reveals the hard evidence for the rise of social inequality. This is particularly clearly seen in the size and complexity of the walled cities, and the great wealth of the elite.

The royal tombs of Shang and major archaeological discoveries, such as the Shang city of Anyang, reveal a powerful royal dynasty, responsible for the maintenance of craft specialists, a bureaucracy, and far-flung trade relationships. Much stress was placed on the sanctity and the social power of the royal ancestors, and oracular messages were sent and received between rulers present and past. Warfare was endemic, and the two-wheeled chariot was deployed in battle. In 1045 BCE, the Shang Dynasty was defeated by the Zhou, a dynasty that ruled for longer than any other in Chinese history, although during the second half of its existence, from 770 to 221 BCE, it was overshadowed by the growing power of other states. Centuries of warfare ensued, during which the rival states constructed defensive walls, and outbid each other in innovative weaponry and military tactics. The leader of one such state, known as Qin, defeated all rivals, and in 221 BCE established the first unified Chinese state under its emperor, Qin Shi Huangdi. His monumental tomb, associated with the subterranean pits containing his army in terra-cotta, ranks with the largest mortuary complexes on earth. He implemented wholesale changes in the running of the new imperial state. Roads were built, a uniform currency minted, a powerful central bureaucracy was formed, and massive armies were raised. The deployment of labor saw the expansion of the Great Wall on the northern borderland. The death of this emperor brought a period of civil strife that resulted in the establishment of the Han Dynasty in 206 BCE.

To the northwest, Han interest in international trade led to the birth of many small states along the Silk Road. To the east, Han colonialism in Korea was followed by the creation of indigenous states, while the rise of societies in Japan took place in the context of Korean and Chinese trade and influence. Further south, the establishment of a maritime link with India and Rome played a part in the development of many Southeast Asian states.

FURTHER READING

The following provide good introductions to the early state societies of East and Southeast Asia:

Bagley, R., ed. 2001. *Ancient Sichuan*. Seattle and Princeton: Seattle Art Museum.

Barnes, G. 2001. *State Formation in Korea*. London: Curzon Press.

Brown, D. M. 1993. *The Cambridge History of Japan*. Cambridge: Cambridge University Press.

Higham, C. F. W. 2001. *The Civilization of Angkor*. London: Weidenfeld & Nicolson.

Li Liu and Xingcan Chen. 2012. *The Archaeology of China. From the Late Palaeolithic to the Early Bronze Age*. Cambridge: Cambridge University Press.

Li Xueqin. 1985. *Eastern Zhou and Qin Civilizations*. New Haven: Yale University Press.

Loewe, M. and Shaughnessy, E. L. (eds.). 1999. *The Cambridge History of Ancient China*. Cambridge: Cambridge University Press.

Rawson, J. 1989. Statesmen or barbarians? The Western Zhou as seen through their bronzes. *Proceedings of the British Academy* 75, 71–95.

Rawson, J., ed. 1992. *The British Museum Book of Chinese Art*. London: British Museum Press.

Shaugnessy, E. C., ed. 2000. *China: Empire and Civilization*. Oxford: Oxford University Press.

Underhill, A. P., ed. 2013. *A Companion to Chinese Archaeology*. Chichester: Wiley-Blackwell.

Xiaoneng Yang, ed. 2004. *New Perspectives on China's Past. Chinese Archaeology in the Twentieth Century*. New Haven: Yale University Press.

Australia and the Pacific Islands

11

Peter Bellwood and Peter Hiscock

Environments and Landscapes: Australia 240

Hunter-Gatherer Trajectories, *c.* 5000 BCE–1700 CE 242

Environments and Landscapes: The Islands of Southeast Asia 245

Transitions to Agriculture: New Guinea 245

Expansion of Domestication: The Austronesian Dispersal 247

KEY SITE Beinan and the Jade Trade 250

Expansion of Domestication: Oceania and Lapita 251

KEY CONTROVERSY The Origins of Lapita 252

KEY CONTROVERSY Expert Navigation or Sheer Good Luck? 254

Farming Communities: The Austronesian World after Migration, 1100–1500 CE 255

KEY CONTROVERSY Indigenous Archaeology in Hawai'i 259

KEY THEME: CLIMATE CHANGE Human Impact, Environmental Change, and Migration 260

Seaborne Trade and Contact in Southeast Asia 261

Summary and Conclusions 263

Further Reading 263

Massive stone statues (*moai*) on Rapa Nui (Easter Island), located at the southeasternmost point of the Polynesian triangle.

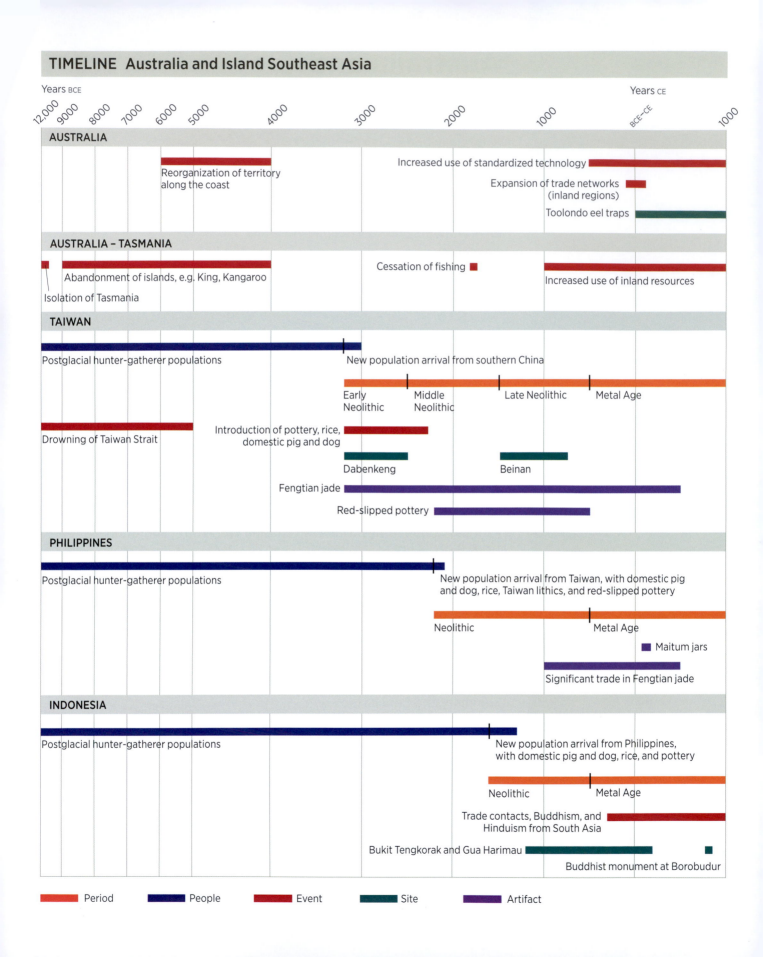

TIMELINE Australia and Island Southeast Asia

Years BCE   Years CE

12,000 9000 8000 7000 6000 5000 4000   3000   2000   1000   BCE–CE   1000

AUSTRALIA

Reorganization of territory along the coast

Increased use of standardized technology

Expansion of trade networks (inland regions)

Toolondo eel traps

AUSTRALIA – TASMANIA

Isolation of Tasmania

Abandonment of islands, e.g. King, Kangaroo

Cessation of fishing

Increased use of inland resources

TAIWAN

Postglacial hunter-gatherer populations

New population arrival from southern China

Early Neolithic   Middle Neolithic   Late Neolithic   Metal Age

Drowning of Taiwan Strait

Introduction of pottery, rice, domestic pig and dog

Dabenkeng   Beinan

Fengtian jade

Red-slipped pottery

PHILIPPINES

Postglacial hunter-gatherer populations

New population arrival from Taiwan, with domestic pig and dog, rice, Taiwan lithics, and red-slipped pottery

Neolithic   Metal Age

Maitum jars

Significant trade in Fengtian jade

INDONESIA

Postglacial hunter-gatherer populations

New population arrival from Philippines, with domestic pig and dog, rice, and pottery

Neolithic   Metal Age

Trade contacts, Buddhism, and Hinduism from South Asia

Bukit Tengkorak and Gua Harimau

Buddhist monument at Borobudur

Period   People   Event   Site   Artifact

TIMELINE Pacific Islands

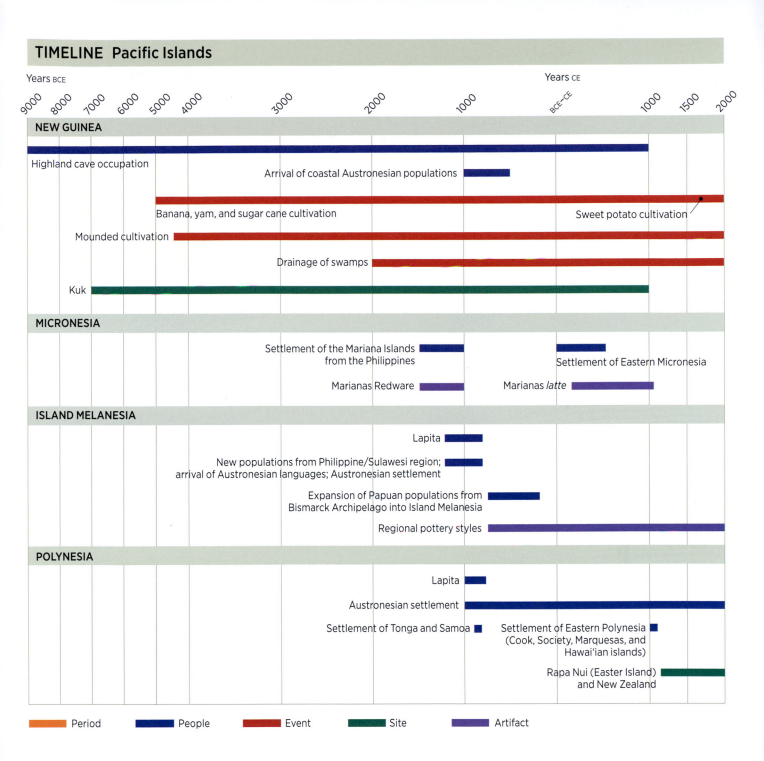

Years BCE

Years CE

9000 8000 7000 6000 5000 4000 3000 2000 1000 BCE–CE 1000 1500 2000

NEW GUINEA

Highland cave occupation

Arrival of coastal Austronesian populations

Banana, yam, and sugar cane cultivation

Sweet potato cultivation

Mounded cultivation

Drainage of swamps

Kuk

MICRONESIA

Settlement of the Mariana Islands from the Philippines

Settlement of Eastern Micronesia

Marianas Redware

Marianas *latte*

ISLAND MELANESIA

Lapita

New populations from Philippine/Sulawesi region; arrival of Austronesian languages; Austronesian settlement

Expansion of Papuan populations from Bismarck Archipelago into Island Melanesia

Regional pottery styles

POLYNESIA

Lapita

Austronesian settlement

Settlement of Tonga and Samoa

Settlement of Eastern Polynesia (Cook, Society, Marquesas, and Hawai'ian islands)

Rapa Nui (Easter Island) and New Zealand

■ Period   ■ People   ■ Event   ■ Site   ■ Artifact

The major regions of Australia, Island Southeast Asia (including East Malaysia, Indonesia, and the Philippines), and Oceania (the islands of Polynesia, Melanesia, and Micronesia) [11.1] together reveal a remarkable narrative of human migration, cultural change, and adaptation to environmental challenge.

In Australia, hunter-gather communities responded to and managed a changing landscape, producing complex cosmologies including the Rainbow Serpent and Dreamtime. In New Guinea, management of the environment led to an independent development of agriculture, far from other origins of domestication in Southwest Asia and East Asia. The Pacific Islands witnessed one of the most remarkable human migrations in human prehistory, across 13,000 kilometers (8,078 miles) of ocean. This chapter follows each of these narratives in turn, offering further examples of human response to climate change, the development and spread of food production, and migration.

- Australia was populated by humans between 60,000 and 55,000 years ago, making these the first long-distance maritime crossings over open sea.

- Indigenous Australian communities developed a symbolic understanding of their landscapes, which was exemplified by a rich tradition of rock art.

- New Guinea provides evidence of the independent development of agriculture and plant cultivation in the highlands dating from *c.* 5000 BCE. The species domesticated were different from those found in China (Chapter 9) and India (Chapter 8), resulting in very different settlement patterns.

- Sailors and colonists from China, Taiwan, and Island Southeast Asia settled the Pacific Islands in a series of impressive long-distance voyages between 1300 and 1000 BCE. Unlike early migrations into Europe (Chapter 12) and the Americas (Chapter 14), these ocean-going settlers depended on a mix of horticultural products, domesticated animals, and maritime resources.

ENVIRONMENTS AND LANDSCAPES: AUSTRALIA

Modern humans had arrived in Australia during the last Ice Age by at least 60,000–55,000 years ago. At this time, the continental landmass was nearly 50 percent larger than today, and the climate was substantially cooler and drier. Some of the earliest sites are found in the Willandra Lakes area in the southeast of the country. Although dry now, during the Pleistocene this area contained a series of interconnected lakes, the most famous of which is Lake Mungo. Early human settlement in the area dates to 50,000 years ago, and the region continued to be occupied throughout the Pleistocene, providing a rich record of life. Burials, including a cremation, are present as early as 42,000 years ago. Camp sites represented by hearths and middens demonstrate a diverse diet dependent on fish, mussels, seeds, and extinct megafauna.

The end of the Ice Age at around 9600 BCE changed the environment dramatically. The massive continental shelf of northern and southern Australia, which had become home to many indigenous groups, was submerged under the ocean [11.2], and continuous environmental changes throughout the last 10,000 years triggered a series of economic and social transformations across Australia.

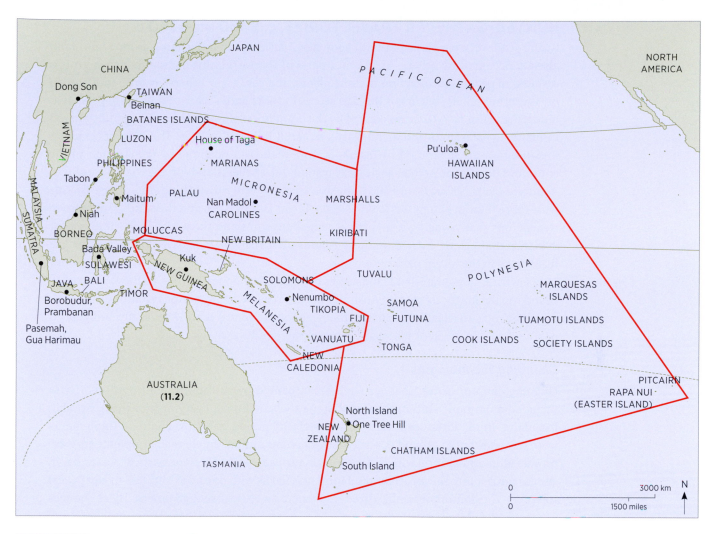

11.1 ABOVE **Map of Southeast Asia, Australasia, and the Pacific,** showing the major areas and sites mentioned and illustrated in the text.

11.2 LEFT **Rising sea levels.** Map of Australia, showing the late Pleistocene coastline and archaeological sites discussed in the text.

HUNTER-GATHERER TRAJECTORIES, *c.* 5000 BCE–1700 CE

Rising sea levels, which lasted until 5000 BCE, forced many indigenous groups onto land already occupied by others. As in other parts of the world, this contact between groups resulted in peaceful interaction in some places, and conflict in others. In Arnhem Land, in northern Australia, rock art of this age seems to show battle scenes [**11.3**], perhaps a vivid rendering of the social dramas created by the inundation of coastal land. Geography altered in many areas; islands and archipelagos replaced hills and valleys. The most spectacular instance was the separation of Tasmania from mainland Australia by the creation of the enormous Bass Strait. Archaeological excavations on smaller islands off the coast of southern Australia, such as King Island and Kangaroo Island, reveal a disturbing story. These islands were more than 10 kilometers (6 miles) from larger landmasses, and the water gaps were so treacherous that voyaging to and fro became dangerous and risky. Although there is clear evidence that people existed on these islands after rising seas isolated them, no one has lived there in the recent past.

Elsewhere, changing island landscapes provided new opportunities. In the Whitsunday Islands on the northeast coast of Australia, people exploited new marine resources, transporting stone tools to islands to enhance their capacity to forage there. Eventually, Indigenous people occupied much of the island group permanently.

Changing Technologies

Ongoing environmental changes were accompanied by cultural transformations. These included a dramatic shift in the use of stone tools in almost every area of the Australian mainland. In the Pleistocene and early postglacial period, the most common implements were scrapers, but at around 500 BCE–1000 CE, standardized finely made implements were produced in abundance, with different forms appearing in different parts of Australia. In the east and south, the most common form was flakes with one edge blunted. In Northwest Australia, the dominant standardized implements were leaf-shaped points. These changes occurred at different moments in each region, and represent local alterations to social practices and foraging strategies. The production of smaller tools was a way to moderate economic and social uncertainty. With these artifacts, people could conserve material while producing reliable tools.

11.3 Scenes of warfare. Rock art from Arnhem Land (Australia) showing humans with spears is perhaps a reflection of increased social tensions caused by rising sea levels inundating coastal lands after the end of the Ice Age. This forced some Indigenous groups onto areas already occupied by others.

After 2000 BCE, the environment of Australia shifted to cooler, drier, more variable conditions and this led to a number of further changes in settlement, foraging, and social patterns. This can be seen very clearly in Tasmania, the island off the south coast of mainland Australia. The most famous change there was the complete cessation of fishing in around 1800 BCE as people expanded the range of resources and environments they exploited: diving to obtain subtidal mollusks and crustaceans, and spending more time hunting terrestrial game, such as the wallabies found in upland areas. As open forests and grassland replaced closed forests, there was a greater emphasis on the exploitation of inland resources in valleys higher than 1,000 meters (3,300 feet) above sea level. Many isolated Bass Strait islands were abandoned, while the use of some less remote islands increased.

These dramatic modifications to the nature of foraging activities involved alterations to territory size and residential locations, as well as social and political organization and ritual activity. For example, the impressive site at Mount Cameron West, where sandstone walls were covered in deeply carved circles, was abandoned in the late postglacial period.

Around the margins of Lake Eyre in the desert of Central Australia, large and dense concentrations of stone artifacts cluster at natural mound springs. These are places where people sought refuge during prolonged drought, until they had either exhausted the food at that location or until rain could be seen in the distance. The length of time spent at each location was perhaps only a few weeks or months.

Changes in Settlement

From around 2000 BCE, Australian archaeological sites become bigger and more abundant, which may have meant populations were increasing. In the past, some archaeologists believed that during this period Aboriginal groups became more sedentary, occupying one location permanently or semi-permanently. This was based on evidence of earth mounds (for example, McArthur Creek in Victoria) and low stone walls (for example, High Cliffy Island on the northwest coast) that have sometimes been interpreted as house foundations. A variety of functions were carried out at these features, including cooking and ceremonial activities. While this is not enough evidence to state permanent settlement, the existence of these structures is indication of repeated visitation to specific areas.

The abundance of potential foodstuffs can be a factor in developing permanent settlements. One possible example is the eel traps of **Toolondo**. In this well-watered area of southeastern Australia, excavations revealed artificial drainage channels up to 1 meter (3 feet) deep, running between small swamps and creeks. Some archaeologists have suggested these channels were used to breed and harvest eels, which would have required a substantial investment of labor and provided a long-term source of food. Other examples are fish traps along the coast or in inland waterways. Targeting abundant food resources through construction of these harvesting and storage facilities would have reduced the size of foraging territories and lowered the frequency of residential moves, but for both eel traps and fish traps, probably did not create conditions suitable for permanent village life.

Changes to Perceptions of the Landscape: The Rainbow Serpent

As the landscape changed, so did conceptualizations of place. In some instances, this included the production of stories about powerful creative beings, such as the Rainbow Serpent. In western Arnhem Land, Rainbow Serpent rock-art imagery can be traced back to a time of marine encroachment in the mid-postglacial, when rising sea levels converted the region

11.4 Rainbow Serpent imagery, western Arnhem Land. The emergence of Rainbow Serpent imagery in rock art can be traced back to the major environmental changes in the mid-postglacial period. The notion of this powerful creative being may well have been formulated at a time of rising sea levels, and was at first a depiction of a pipefish before gradually morphing into an imaginary, composite beast.

from woodland to a diverse coastal landscape. Massive mangrove swamps appeared, and eventually extensive freshwater lagoons were established. The being was at first a depiction of a marine animal, the pipefish, before gradually being transformed into an imaginary, composite beast in more recent art [**11.4**]. These innovations in the iconography indicate significant alterations of older postglacial belief systems.

Rock art may also reveal alterations in social life and territoriality. In the Western Desert, the presence of very localized style regions during the last 1,500 years indicates greater territorial boundedness than in earlier periods.

The Effects of Historic Foreign Contacts

It was only in 1606 CE that Europeans documented their first landing on the continent. Many archaeological assumptions on prehistoric life are based on historical observations of Indigenous people near early colonial outposts. Europeans saw examples of high levels of sedentism, and organized exchange between neighboring groups, including bartering at formal markets and reciprocal gift giving before and after ceremonial events. In arid South Australia, for example, people received narcotic drugs from 400 kilometers (250 miles) to the northeast, stone axes from the Mount Isa region 1,200 kilometers (750 miles) to the north, and pearl shell pendants from the northwest of the continent, more than 2,000 kilometers (1,250 miles) away.

But, in many instances, these historical records describe Indigenous social and economic systems that had already been drastically changed by European contact. The historical lifestyles of Indigenous people may have only a superficial resemblance to pre-contact foraging societies.

The spread of smallpox and other rapidly transmitted diseases in the late eighteenth and early nineteenth centuries killed and injured many Indigenous people. In some regions, the majority of elderly, socially senior people may have perished. By effectively creating power and knowledge vacuums, this process assisted social and political change, perhaps exaggerated by the potential gains in political status that could be acquired by individuals or groups with privileged access to valuable new resources through negotiations with non-Indigenous visitors and colonizers. One way this was manifested was through the development of more extensive and intensive trading systems, probably stimulated by the desire for valuable introduced goods, such as metal knives and axes.

Historical foreign contacts transformed many aspects of Aboriginal life. Technological introductions, such as metal and canoes, altered how and where food was collected. Along the coast, the ability to transport foods in more reliable watercraft probably reduced the frequency of group movement, and the addition of metal to toolkits enhanced the range of foods available (e.g. metal fishhooks or harpoons) through expanded hunting options. Economic and social changes were magnified not only by introduced diseases but also, in the nineteenth century, by competition with expanding European occupiers over territory. There is even abundant evidence for transformations of belief systems as missionary doctrine was spread and Indigeneous religions were modified in response to altered economic and social life.

These transformations represent an intellectual challenge for researchers and a social and ideological challenge for Aboriginal groups working to maintain their heritage. How thoroughly were society and belief altered by cultural contact in historic times, and what elements of continuity and reliance can be identified? There is currently considerable difference of opinion, reflecting the intractability of evidence and different visions of Aboriginal society. This debate is a diverse one, with significant contributions from Aboriginal communities, as well as from new archaeological and environmental studies. And the debate is significant for social and political discussions in Australia.

ENVIRONMENTS AND LANDSCAPES: THE ISLANDS OF SOUTHEAST ASIA

The islands of Southeast Asia cover a region including Brunei, Indonesia, Malaysia, the Philippines, Singapore, and Timor-Leste. During the Pleistocene, many of these present-day islands were not islands at all, but part of a vast dry-land extension to the Asian continent called Sundaland. The present islands of Sumatra, Java, Borneo, and Bali were once part of this continent, which is why they have essentially Asian floras and mammal faunas.

The islands of the Philippines and eastern Indonesia (Sulawesi, the Moluccas, and the Lesser Sundas) were never connected to either Asia or Greater Australia (Australia plus New Guinea and Tasmania) by land bridges, though the distances between them were sometimes much reduced by low Ice Age sea levels. Many of these islands—including New Guinea and eastward to the Solomons in western Melanesia—were sufficiently close together that Paleolithic populations of hunters and gatherers were able to reach many of them before 35,000 years ago. Indeed, early hominins had been able to reach Flores, Sulawesi, and the Philippines by at least the middle Pleistocene. But *Homo sapiens* was probably the first to reach Australia and New Guinea. Beyond the Solomon Islands, the islands of Remote Oceania, from the Santa Cruz Islands eastward, including all of Micronesia and Polynesia, were accessible only to canoe-borne Austronesians after 1500 BCE. [**11.5**, p. 246].

TRANSITIONS TO AGRICULTURE: NEW GUINEA

Humans arrived in New Guinea as early as 60,000–50,000 years ago. Aside from being one of the earliest land masses occupied by *Homo sapiens* in Greater Australia, it was also one of the regions of the world where agriculture developed independently. Two of the most important foods grown during the postglacial period were taro and bananas, together with some varieties of sugar cane and yams.

The New Guinea highland valleys are environmentally unique in this region—broad, fertile, mostly located 1,500–1,700 meters (4,900–5,600 feet) above sea level and, as such, malaria-free. The **cordillera** that supports these valleys is also **geomorphologically** unique, being unparalleled in any of the volcanic islands of Southeast Asia or Borneo. In this way, early postglacial populations in New Guinea were able to enter a highland world with a climate suitable for tropical crops to grow, but also close to the altitudinal limits of the crops. This high altitude perhaps caused fluctuations in food resources due to frost or drought, of a kind that in some other parts of the world are believed to have triggered early agriculture as a way of maintaining short-term supplies of desirable foods under stressful conditions.

cordillera a system of mountain ranges, often consisting of more or less parallel chains; used often to refer to the Andean range

geomorphology the study of the development of land forms

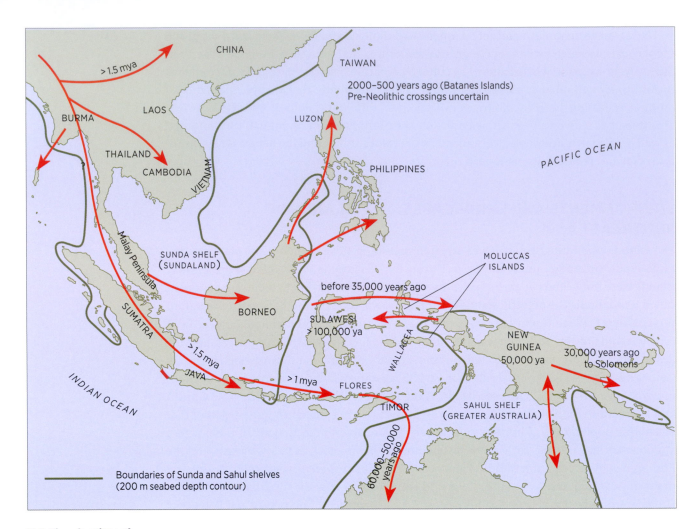

11.5 The migrations of early human populations into Island Southeast Asia and western Oceania during the Pleistocene.
Archaic hominin populations reached Flores, Sulawesi, and the Philippines, whereas early modern humans crossed wider sea gaps to reach Australia and western Melanesia.

The most significant site to reveal evidence for this transition to agriculture is **Kuk**, where a series of drainage ditches cut into the swampy valley floor, presumably to control water flow for agricultural purposes, were found together with well-preserved wooden digging sticks.

The first evidence for human impact at Kuk is in the form of forest clearance, dating to about 7000 BCE. By about 5000 BCE, soil mounds were being constructed for cultivation, and rectilinear grid-like ditching appeared by 2000 BCE, associated with archaeobotanical evidence for taro and banana cultivation.

The absence of cereals and domesticated animals in New Guinea meant that early farming populations were generally small and scattered. Pigs were not introduced to the island from Indonesia by coastal Austronesian populations until after 1000 BCE, and the American sweet potato, which is a major highland food source today, probably did not appear until after 1550 CE.

The deeper significance of Kuk and the New Guinea highlands transition to agriculture is that it can help to explain why New Guinea never experienced major settlement in its interior by incoming populations of Austronesians (see below). The New Guinea highlands today are entirely occupied by Papuan-speaking communities who show no signs of any significant early contact with Austronesians. Given Austronesian success in the complete settlement of the Southeast Asian island of Borneo by moving up the major rivers, one has to ask why nothing similar ever occurred in New Guinea. The answer, apart from sheer remoteness, is surely that the New Guinea continuous cordillera (a landform absent in Borneo) was conducive to an independent development of early agriculture, and that New Guinea highlanders were therefore sufficiently numerous and sedentary by 1000 BCE to make any incursion by Austronesians very difficult.

EXPANSION OF DOMESTICATION: THE AUSTRONESIAN DISPERSAL

The dispersal of Austronesian-speaking farmer-voyagers into Island Southeast Asia and out into the Pacific is one of the great narratives of global history. The migration began around 4,500 years ago, beginning in Taiwan where the oldest reconstructible ancestors of the present-day Austronesian languages developed [**11.6**]. There are more than 1,000 Austronesian languages spoken today, and where Austronesians settled, few other populations have successfully overlain or replaced the Austronesian cultural and linguistic foundations.

Taiwan and the Philippines

The Austronesian language family first developed in Taiwan, after the region was inhabited by migrating communities from China. Reconstructions of ancestral lexical items and meanings through comparison of living and historical Austronesian languages can offer clues to the way of life of the earliest Austronesians. The originators of this language family were rice and millet agriculturalists who made boats and lived in timber houses. They kept pigs and dogs, and used bows and arrows, looms for weaving, and pottery. They did not cast copper or smelt iron. In archaeological terms, they appear to have belonged to fairly typical East Asian Neolithic societies.

The oldest Neolithic complex on Taiwan was the **Dabenkeng,** named after a coastal site in the northern part of the island. Dabenkeng sites date between 3000 and 2500 BCE

11.6 The distribution of the Austronesian languages. These cover 210 degrees of longitude from Madagascar to Rapa Nui, and 70 degrees of latitude (Taipei to southern New Zealand). The map shows the distributions of the major Formosan, Malayo-Polynesian, and Oceanic subgroups.

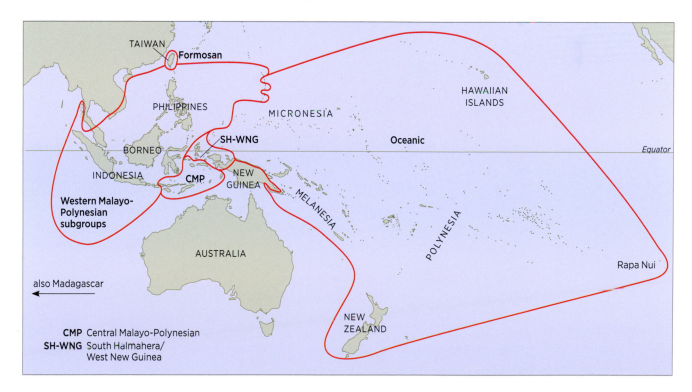

11.7 Dabenkeng sherd.
Dabenkeng-style pottery is found right around the coastal regions of Taiwan and in the Penghu Islands after about 3000 BCE. This incised and painted rim sherd is from Nanguanli.

and occur all around the coastal regions of Taiwan. Their incised and cord-marked pottery [11.7] is very homogeneous in its shape and decoration, which is itself a clear indication that the Dabenkeng people belonged to a relatively unified culture and were perhaps immigrants into Taiwan from Fujian or Guangdong in south China, where similar pottery occurs at around the same time.

A millennium after the colonization of Taiwan, the language ancestral to all the Malayo-Polynesian languages (Proto-Malayo-Polynesian) was carried by a seaborne migration to adjacent areas of Island Southeast Asia. We can trace the Austronesian expansion through the spread of red-slipped and stamped pottery, shell artifacts, polished stone adzes, evidence for rice, and bones of domestic pigs and dogs. In the Batanes Islands, immediately south of Taiwan itself, fine cord-marked pottery dates from 2200 BCE, with plain red-slipped (non-corded) ceramics dating from 2000 BCE onward. By 2000 BCE evidence of rice agriculture and red-slipped pottery is present in the Philippines. The ceramic sequence in these areas follows the same order of stylistic change as in southeastern Taiwan, and suggests the movement of a coherent material culture from Taiwan into the Philippines, and continued interaction between the areas.

11.8 Important Neolithic sites in Island Southeast Asia, with findings of rice remains and red-slipped pottery. The route taken to reach the Mariana Islands is disputed, but Spanish galleons followed the one shown here.

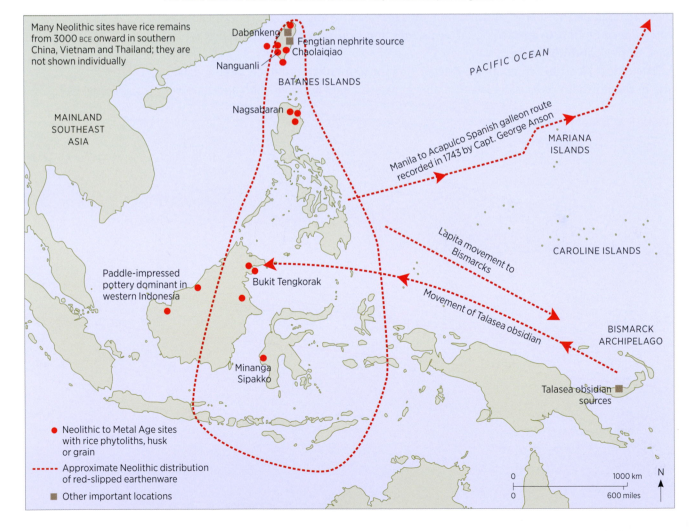

Further into Island Southeast Asia and to Madagascar

After the move to the northern Philippines, a tide of Malayo-Polynesian language dispersal seems to have occurred, moving through the Philippines into Borneo, Sulawesi, and the Sunda Islands of Indonesia, eastward to the Mariana Islands in Micronesia, through the Bismarck Archipelago to Island Melanesia (but not through the interior of New Guinea), and onward to Tonga and Samoa in western Polynesia [**11.8**].

Some long-distance connections at this time are very striking. Taiwan jade from the Fengtian source near Hualian was imported into Luzon (Philippine archipelago) and a little later to Palawan and Central Vietnam (see Key Site box: Beinan and the Jade Trade, p. 250). Red-slipped pottery at the site of Bukit Tengkorak in Sabah, Malaysia (1300 BCE onward) was found with **obsidian** imported from sources in New Britain (east of New Guinea), located more than 3,500 kilometers (2,175 miles) to the east, demonstrating the presence of a robust trade network. This obsidian probably represents one of the longest-distance transfers of any Neolithic commodity in the world.

There seem to have been several pauses prior to further dispersals to Vietnam and the Malay Peninsula. The Malay Peninsula was probably first settled in coastal areas by Austronesians around 2,500 years ago. These new arrivals would have found Neolithic agriculturalists already present, with strong cultural links with Neolithic populations in southern Thailand. Austronesians arriving in Central Vietnam, perhaps before 2,500 years ago, would also have encountered existing Austroasiatic-speaking agricultural populations.

Colonists also sailed to Madagascar *c.* 500 CE, forming the first human population to reach that island. The long-distance passage across the Indian Ocean to Madagascar and the Comoro Islands was one of the most extraordinary feats of Austronesian colonization, but much more was to come. At around 1000 CE, Austronesian populations continued into eastern Polynesia beyond Tonga and Samoa, in the process settling all the islands in the huge triangle formed by Hawai'i, New Zealand, and Rapa Nui (see **11.1**, p. 241) [**11.9**].

obsidian a natural volcanic glass, very hard, used to make tools

11.9 A single-outrigger traveling canoe from Satawal in the Caroline Islands: from François Edmund Pâris, *Essai sur la Construction Navale des Peuples Extra-Européens*, Plate 107, Paris: Bertrand 1841. The balancing outrigger can be seen emerging from the wave on the far side of the canoe, and a raised platform with a thatched roof on the near side.

KEY SITE Beinan and the Jade Trade

The village site of **Beinan**, near Taidong in southeast Taiwan, is one of the most remarkable archaeological discoveries ever made on the island because of its excellent state of preservation. The excavations yielded remains of fifty drystone house foundations and more than 1,500 slate cist burials, dating mainly between 1500 and 800 BCE. The houses were laid out in rows, with adjacent lines of drystone-walled storehouses. Some of the rows were separated by walls of boulders, suggesting possible lineage divisions of some kind within the village plan. The floors of the dwelling houses and the open spaces between them sealed slate-lined burial cists, an arrangement indicating an interest in ancestor veneration. The graves, many of them with multiple interments, revealed a high rate of infant and fetal death, for reasons at present unknown, but perhaps related to malaria. Most importantly, the burials contained some remarkable items of Taiwan jade from an east-coast Fengtian source, including long tubular beads, bracelets, penannular earrings with circumferential projections, anthropomorphic earrings, and perforated projectile points.

Recent excavations at the site of Anaro in the Batanes Islands have uncovered remarkable evidence for the working of Fengtian (Taiwan) jade into a specific type of earring with three circumferential projections, called a *lingling-o* by Philippine archaeologists. *Lingling-o* of this shape were especially popular between 500 BCE and 1 CE, and were distributed over a huge area incorporating the Philippines, Sarawak, central and southern Vietnam, and southern Thailand. Itinerant artisans appear to have traveled these regions with supplies of Taiwan jade, often in the form of recycled Neolithic artifacts, making them into both *lingling-o* and related double-animal headed ear ornaments [**11.10 b** and **f**]. It therefore appears that many Austronesian-speaking communities after the initial migration period continued to be related by shared ornament styles and traditions of jade working, using mostly the Fengtian jade source [**11.10 a–g**].

11.10 a: *lingling-o* manufacture, reconstructed from fragments of Fengtian (Taiwan) jade from Anaro (outer bracelet fragment from Taiwan);
b & **c:** two *lingling-o* of Fengtian jade from the Tabon Caves, Palawan, Philippines (**b** is an Early Metal Age form, **c** is older);
d & **e:** two New Zealand Maori nephrite *kaka poria* (parrot rings);
f & **g:** an animal-headed pendant of Fengtian nephrite from the Tabon Caves and a similar *pekapeka* ornament of New Zealand nephrite.

Such New Zealand Maori ornaments, which resemble the Philippine forms so closely, perhaps reflect late contacts between Island Southeast Asia and Polynesia.

EXPANSION OF DOMESTICATION: OCEANIA AND LAPITA

dentate tooth-like

punctate a pattern of studded dots or points

In the islands east of New Guinea (Melanesia), between 1200 and 750 BCE, a specific group of Austronesian colonists spread what is known as the Lapita culture across about 6,500 kilometers (4,000 miles) of ocean and islands, from the Admiralty Islands north of New Guinea to as far east as Samoa in western Polynesia. This far-reaching migration was accompanied by the spread of Proto-Oceanic, the ancestral dialect of the Oceanic subgroup of languages spoken today in the Pacific Islands from the Admiralty Islands and coastal New Guinea eastward (see **11.6**, p. 247).

Lapita sites are generally well dated and well studied in terms of artifacts and economy. Pottery vessel surfaces were often red-slipped, and the decoration included an intricate range of incised and **dentate**-stamped rectilinear and curvilinear motifs, even including anthropomorphic faces, the latter perhaps indicating the concern with ancestors that was common to all Austronesian populations. Apart from pottery, other items of Lapita material culture included stone or shell adzes, stone chisels, a range of shell ornaments (including beads and arm rings similar to those found in contemporary sites in the Philippines and eastern Indonesia), and fishhooks (see Key Controversy box: The Origins of Lapita, p. 252). Lapita pottery decoration was in decline by 750 BCE, to be replaced by plainware in western Polynesia.

The Mariana Islands of western Micronesia were settled by 1500 BCE, a slightly earlier movement than that indicated for Lapita, by makers of a red-slipped and **punctate**-stamped style of pottery [**11.11 a–h**]. The first settlers appear to have taken rice with them, the only occasion this crop was transported into Oceania. The open-sea crossing to the Marianas from the Philippines, at least 2,300 kilometers (1,429 miles), justifiably could rank as the first great voyage known to us in Austronesian cultural history.

Lapita Economy

Economically, the Lapita culture was based on a mix of horticultural and maritime subsistence. Islands were mostly self-sufficient, despite the strong likelihood that some inter-island contact occurred after initial settlement took place. Pigs, fowl, and dogs are all present in the Lapita record, although not all sites or island groups have yielded them, and it is clear

11.11 a–h Punctate-stamped pottery from Island Southeast Asia and Lapita sites in Melanesia.
a: Xiantouling, Guandong coast, China (pre-3000 BCE?);
b & c: Nagsabaran, Cagayan Valley (1500 BCE);
d: Yuanshan, Taipei, Taiwan (1000 BCE);
e: Batungan Cave, Masbate, central Philippines (800 BCE);
f: Kamgot, Anir Islands, Bismarck Archipelago (Lapita, 1200 BCE);
g: Lapita (Site 13), New Caledonia (1000 BCE);
h: Achugao, Saipan, Mariana Islands (1400 BCE).
All apart from **a** are red-slipped and have lime or white clay infill in the decoration.

Archaeologists working in Melanesia have long debated the origins of the Lapita culture (1200–750 BCE). Many favor a direct connection with the spread of Austronesians from Island Southeast Asia, while others prefer a local Melanesian origin, with only occasional interaction with groups living to the west of New Guinea. The accumulation of archaeological evidence from Taiwan, the Philippines, and eastern Indonesia makes a completely isolationist Melanesian origin for Lapita increasingly untenable.

Tattooed Pottery

One important clue to Lapita origins lies in the chronological development of the distinctive dentate- or punctate-stamped decoration in different areas. Discoveries of similar, contemporary pottery have been made in many sites in China and Island Southeast Asia (see **11.11**, p. 251). Such stamping reflects the Austronesian cultural tradition of body tattooing; Lapita potters incised or tattooed their pots with complex designs, some of which might represent ancestors in human form.

In the northern Philippines, the stamped pottery was preceded for at least 500 years by red-slipped plain pottery. In the Mariana Islands and Melanesia, however, the punctate and dentate stamping appeared with the first human settlement. In both locations, the oldest Lapita sites have not only the first pottery but also the most elaborate dentate decoration, suggesting its introduction by colonization [**11.12**], after initial development out of a tradition of unstamped red-slipped pottery in the Philippines. Similar stamping dating between 1500 and 1000 BCE is also reported from Mansiri in Sulawesi, and one wonders here if any of the remarkable stone statues in the Bada Valley of central Sulawesi (see **11.23**, p. 263) might be of Neolithic date, given the Lapita parallels in the human face carving on the Bulili

11.12 Illustration of a pottery sherd with a dentate-stamped schematic human-face motif from Nenumbo, Santa Cruz Islands, Melanesia, c. 800 BCE.

stone burial-jar lid located there. These Sulawesi carvings are currently undated and some major surprises might be in store for future researchers.

Overview

The Lapita populations of Island Melanesia created the most complex ceramic art form ever to develop in the Pacific, and surely did it in part out of local initiative. As the founder populations of modern island Melanesians and Polynesians, their prehistory involved both migration and interaction, not simply one or the other. Migration did not occur in just one direction out of Southeast Asia. But interaction and secondary movements alone are insufficient to explain the fundamental Lapita cultural and biological patterns with their strong Taiwan and Philippine links, as well as their links to later Polynesian populations. A primary migration is required to explain the whole phenomenon.

that Lapita settlers, for a while at least, would have been distracted from their domesticated food supplies by prolific wild (especially maritime) resources in the areas they colonized, until these became reduced by extinction and local eradication.

Lapita village settlements often included stilt houses over shallow lagoons located in coastal and small offshore island locations. Remains of such villages are recorded over areas of up to 7–8 hectares (18–20 acres) in the Mussau Islands.

The Settlement of Polynesia

Lapita colonists reached Tonga and Samoa in western Polynesia by about 900 BCE. As in Melanesia, the decorated forms of Lapita pottery lasted for only a few centuries, with continuing simplification, before the eventual demise of pottery in Samoa and southern

Micronesia *c.* 300 CE. Together with the losses of rice, millet, and loom-weaving prior to their entry into Oceania, this disappearance of pottery suggests that early Austronesian societies underwent **bottleneck** losses as groups adapted to varied conditions on the islands they settled. Although some inter-island contact was probably present, the further out small groups pushed into Polynesia, the less common those contacts became. The combination of differing island resources with increasing remoteness of the islands resulted in some divergence in economy and cultural practices.

bottleneck a sharp decline in population, generally tied to a need to adapt rapidly to new situations

The Austronesian migration process therefore encouraged increasing cultural diversity as populations adapted to geographical variations in resources and opportunities. Examples of such variations are those characterized as "the wet and the dry" by the American archaeologist Patrick Kirch in his discussion of the agriculturally influenced rises and falls of Polynesian chiefdoms. In Futuna and the Hawaiian islands, the most aggressive and expansive chiefdoms appear to have originated in risk-dominated situations in which agriculture depended purely on seasonal rainfall (the "dry"). These chiefdoms ultimately dominated those societies that held the most fertile alluvial soils (the "wet"), suitable for irrigated taro cultivation. In other words, the poor conquered the rich, presumably because the rich controlled highly fertile regions of agricultural land. The ultimate conquest of the Hawaiian islands by the paramount chief Kamehameha (the Great) in 1810, an achievement aided by the acquisition of firearms, is an excellent example of this. Kamehameha's homeland on the west coast of Hawai'i Island was one of the driest and most risk-prone regions in the whole archipelago.

Eastern Polynesia. The linguistic evidence described above suggests that the settlement of the islands in central and eastern Polynesia that lay beyond the Lapita zone—the Marquesas, Societies, Cooks, Australs, Tuamotus, Hawai'i, Rapa Nui, New Zealand, and many others—occurred after a long period during which population dispersal paused in western Polynesia. The archaeological record supports this. Current interpretations of radiocarbon dates from archaeological sites implies that none of these island groups was settled before 900 CE, and some not until several centuries later. During this migration standstill, Proto-Polynesian society and culture developed in western Polynesia out of its Lapita roots—the basic configuration ancestral to all the ethnographic societies of Polynesia, and one subsequently modified in each island group by differing processes involving chance, environmental variation, and interaction.

Beyond the Lapita settlements in Samoa, the first settlers in eastern Polynesia appear to have traveled via certain atolls in the Solomon Islands, eventually to become aceramic in their technology (atolls lack suitable potting clay). The main components of the oldest eastern Polynesian assemblages are shell fishhooks, bone harpoons, bone imitation whale-tooth pendants, and stone adzes. Recent research has shown that early central and eastern Polynesian cultures were connected over thousands of kilometers by the long-distance transport of basalt. Basalt from Samoa has been found widely in Tonga and the Cook Islands, and that from the Marquesas was taken to the Societies, southern Cooks, Tuamotus, Mangareva, and Fanning Island (see Key Controversy box: Expert Navigation or Sheer Good Luck?, p. 254).

We know from European explorers' and ethnographic records, and from comparisons of late prehistoric artifact styles (especially stone adzes), that some inter-island contact was still occurring in the eighteenth century, and, indeed, into the twentieth century, using traditional canoes and sailing methods in the Caroline Islands of Micronesia (see **11.9**, p. 249).

Expert Navigation or Sheer Good Luck?

At European contact, written records and drawings were made of the kinds of seacraft that might have been used much earlier in time. Most Austronesians at this point used sewn-plank sailing canoes with outriggers that were either single and kept to windward in Oceania, or double (one on each side of the canoe) in much of Island Southeast Asia. The contact-period single outrigger canoes of the Caroline Islands, in particular, were very rapid tacking vessels with reversible ends and lateen (triangular) sails of pandanus matting, which were able to carry both crew and cargo on a platform amid ships (see **11.9**, p. 249).

Double Canoes in Historical Times

While single hollowed-log canoes existed by at least 6000 BCE in Central China, and outriggers and sails by at least 2000 BCE, the double canoe appears to have been an invention of the Malayo-Polynesians prior to their long journeys, at the end of the first millennium CE, toward the distant archipelagos of eastern Polynesia. By the eighteenth century, double canoes were being used in warfare in the Society Islands, the warriors fighting on raised platforms. Johann Reinhold Forster recorded in 1778:

The large war canoes cost the natives infinite labor, and afford the best specimens of their genius...[On Huahine Island] I observed a double war canoe, which required 144 paddles, and eight or ten steersmen to move it forward; the stage for fighting was roomy, and could contain about 30 men. [The stage was] raised on six or eight pillars about four feet high...

The English artist William Hodges painted for posterity a scene of war canoes assembled in Tahiti in 1774 for an attack on Mo'orea [**11.13**]. About 160 such canoes were assembled, with an estimated total crew of 7,760 men, according to the British explorer Captain James Cook.

Partial prehistoric canoe hulls have been excavated on Huahine in the Society Islands and at Anaweka on the northeastern South Island of New Zealand. Distributional facts imply that the pioneer voyagers understood the use of the sail and the outrigger by the time they reached the Philippines, although the first voyages off the coast of Asia, including those during the Pleistocene to Australia, were probably tentative affairs with bamboo rafts and paddles.

Questions of Navigation

More contentious debate has centered on two questions of navigation. First, could Austronesians have navigated regularly between distant, previously known islands? The answer here is yes, but only to a degree. European voyagers, such as Cook and Andia y Varela (in the 1770s), recorded the islanders' use of stars and the sun, ocean swells, and other indicators of distance, speed, and direction, all described in greater ethnographic detail by the researcher and sailor David Lewis, but there are no records of regular voyaging over open-sea distances greater than a few hundred kilometers.

The second question is more difficult to answer: were early Austronesians, Polynesians in particular, able to navigate through unknown waters to find new land, and then return home to mount a full voyage of colonization? The New Zealand

Why Migrate?

Why did all this island migration come about? Simply looking for new islands for agricultural land or other resources does not explain everything, given the huge sizes of many of the islands of Southeast Asia, which even now are only thinly populated in some remote equatorial locations. It has been suggested that periodic increases in the frequencies of westerly winds due to El Niño-Southern Oscillation (ENSO) climatic cycles would have encouraged sailing to the east, but there must also have been cultural factors, including advances in navigation and canoe construction, as well as the development of agricultural economies with domesticated plants and animals that could easily be transported to and reproduced in new island environments.

A further suggestion is that, similar to the youth of today, so the youth of millennia ago needed outlets for their energies, ways to gain self-esteem, success, and peer recognition. In tribal agricultural societies with established forms of land ownership, where status and rights to land were to some degree determined by ancestry, gender, and birth order, there would always have been situations in which younger sons, able to found only lineages of junior rank at home, would have sought to establish a new senior line by the colonization

historian Andrew Sharp concluded that voyages of long-distance discovery could have been only one-way, without hope of a return home. There is actually nothing in the archaeological record that refutes this—the small quantities of pearl shell and basalt transported across Polynesia could just as well reflect one-way voyages by the first settlers as return ones. But as noted by Geoffrey Irwin and Ben Finney, both scholars with practical sailing experience, sensible would-be explorers would have waited for summer westerlies in the tropics or winter westerlies on the edge of the tropics to blow them eastward. Sailing downwind on such westerlies, which

11.13 *Double canoes with stages for hand-to-hand fighting preparing for war in Tahiti*, 1774, painted by William Hodges on Cook's second voyage. The elite individual on the stage at left is wearing a tall headdress of radiating tropic-bird feathers and a crescent-shaped gorget of coir, feathers, hair, and shark teeth on a cane foundation.

would have been enhanced in El Niño climatic conditions, would have given them the chance to return home later using the easterly trade winds that prevail during most of the year.

of new territory. If such desires are institutionalized and given formal social approval (for instance, the New Zealand Maori named many of their tribes after their founder figures), then a very powerful motivating force for active colonization will be unleashed. In the case of the Austronesians, this force appears to have become more significant as populations moved further and further east toward Polynesia.

FARMING COMMUNITIES: THE AUSTRONESIAN WORLD AFTER MIGRATION, 1100–1500 CE

How did Austronesian societies develop after arriving on the islands of Polynesia and those to the west of New Guinea? Some in the Pacific Islands maintained Neolithic cultural traditions representing variations on a shared cultural base until European contact, whereas societies west of New Guinea gradually became metal-using after 500 BCE, and received Indian traders after about 200 BCE and subsequent Hindu–Buddhist religious influences, followed by Islam after 1250 CE.

moai massive stone statues characteristic of Rapa Nui (Easter Island)

marae Polynesian shrine/temple platforms

latte a stone pillar foundation for a chiefly house with a raised floor, built in the Mariana Islands, Micronesia

heiau Hawaiian religious structures comprising terraced platforms and walled enclosures

Monumental Construction: Sculptures and Buildings

The Austronesians of the more fertile Oceanic islands developed large and relatively complex societies, with chiefs, social ranking, and frequent warfare. The most famous of these is that of Rapa Nui (Easter Island), populated by around 1200 CE. The massive stone statues (**moai**) of Rapa Nui, made of volcanic agglomerate, were carved initially in quarries in the steep inner and outer crater walls of the extinct volcano of Rano Raraku. They were then transported and erected in rows facing inland along the tops of raised stone platforms [**11.14**, **11.15**]. Eastern Polynesian shrine/temple platforms, **marae**, as constructed by the major chiefdoms of the densely populated and fertile Hawaiian, Society, Cook, Austral, and Marquesas islands, were often also major feats of construction, involving the use of huge basalt blocks and sometimes erected in pyramidal forms. The Micronesians of the Caroline Islands constructed remarkable enclosures, platforms, and tombs of prismatic columnar basalt at Nan Madol on Pohnpei and at Leluh on Kosrae. The people of the Mariana Islands carved massive stone pillar foundations (**latte**) for their raised-floor chiefly houses [**11.16**].

11.14 ABOVE **Rapa Nui statues (moai).** *Moai* re-erected, one with its red tuff topknot, on an *ahu* (stone platform). Note the positions of the hands and the long fingers, also the distended and perforated earlobes, which carried ornamental disks. Each statue has a stone plinth, aligned above the sloping cobbled ramp.

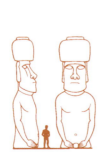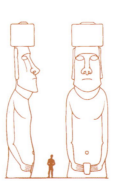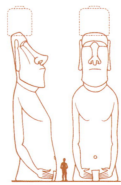

11.15 LEFT **Size and scale of Rapa Nui statues.** Drawings of *moai* of different sizes and body forms. All are busts above the midriff, and all have hands meeting at the navel. The largest statue to be erected successfully on an *ahu* was 11.5 meters (38 feet) high and weighed almost 100 metric tons (110 US tons).

The Hawaiian islands, lush and tropical, were first settled around 1100 CE by people who brought domesticated plants and animals. These communities formed large chiefdoms, and by at least the fifteenth century CE the Hawaiians were building massive religious structures (**heiau**) of uncut volcanic rock. Contemporary hamlet-like clusters of house terraces, enclosures, and platforms indicate a settlement pattern that was spread in small nodes throughout all the cultivable areas of the islands, rather than being strongly nucleated. Field systems for the growing of taro, sweet potato, and gourd consisted of parallel stone boundary lines running along or across contours, and extensive panels of rock carving occur on flat lava surfaces [**11.17**]. Traces of ancient human activity are also found in some remarkable places, including adze quarries in the basalts of Mauna Kea at 3,780 meters (12,400 feet) above sea level, and house and shrine foundations at 3,000 meters (9,850 feet) around the summit of Haleakala on Maui.

New Zealand, by contrast, is temperate in climate and much bigger than the Hawaiian islands. Large chiefdoms emerged as in the Hawaiian islands, but without the tendency to such a marked degree of social stratification. The first Maori, arriving around 1200 CE, adopted a partial hunter-gatherer existence among the numerous seals and flightless moa, but they were soon forced by dwindling

11.16 ABOVE **Stone monuments.** Coral capstones and pillars of a 5.5-meter-high (18 feet) *latte* monument, House of Taga, Tinian Island, Marianas, constructed at an unknown date prior to 1740–44, when a drawing was made showing it still standing, on the voyage of the English navigator George Anson.

11.17 Petroglyphs. These examples, comprising dots, circles, and lines, were carved in pillow lava at Pu'uloa, Hawai'i.

11.18 Maori *pa*.
This example was constructed by terracing the extinct volcanic cone of One Tree Hill in Auckland City, northern New Zealand. The earthern terraces would probably have been palisaded, and used for housing or small plantations.

resources to focus more on cultivation of the only available domesticated plant that would grow well in a temperate climate—the American sweet potato or kumara. Even this would flourish only in the North Island and northern South Island. The dog was the only domesticated animal to be introduced successfully to New Zealand. As a result of this straddling of the climatic limit for Polynesian agriculture, the more southerly Maori remained hunter-gatherers until the nineteenth century.

The result was a series of warlike northern chiefdoms, competitive in terms of rights to the use of cultivable land, but uninterested in the forms of competitive stone monument construction so prominent on the Hawaiian islands and Rapa Nui. They turned instead, after 1500 CE, to an intense preoccupation with the construction of fortified earthwork enclosures termed ***pa***. Some of these fortifications, particularly the terraced volcanic cones of the Auckland Isthmus, have dramatic visual impact even today [**11.18**]. New Zealand is one of the best examples in world prehistory of short parallel trajectories out of a common cultural ancestry, beginning around 800 years ago, into a warlike agricultural society of about 100,000 people in the north, and into a thinly populated hunter-gatherer society in the south.

The Chiefdoms of Polynesia: Comparative Ethnographic Perspectives

In terms of sociopolitical complexity, pre-contact Polynesian societies ranged from the internally stratified chiefdoms of large, close-set, and fertile archipelagos, such as the Samoan, Tongan, and Hawaiian islands, through the more gently ranked societies of temperate New Zealand and many of the smaller tropical volcanic islands and atolls, to the strife-torn warring polities of environmentally marginal islands, such as Mangaia (southern Cooks), the Marquesas, and Rapa Nui. These differences in part reflect factors of island size and degree of isolation, and variations in soil fertility and rainfall reliability. They also reflect differing

pa the Maori earthwork enclosures on New Zealand

patterns of origin, with modification, from a Proto-Polynesian society that was already ranked by birth order and genealogical memory extending back over many generations to remote founders.

Polynesians defined rank in terms of closeness of descent from the founding ancestor of a tribal group, utilizing elder–younger distinctions and stressing patrilineality for inheritance of major status positions. Chiefs functioned as ritually sanctioned stewards of land and food production, and as managers of community affairs and labor projects, such as the construction of *marae*. By virtue of their genealogical rank, chiefs inherited supernaturally charged status (*mana*). They ruled using personal or family names in most central and eastern Polynesian island groups, but high-ranking individuals in Samoa and Tonga were elected to specific trans-generational chiefly titles.

Samoa developed the most complex system of titled office in Polynesia, with a hierarchy of local and regional councils. The titled chiefs of Tongatapu (Tonga's main island) headed the only pre-contact Polynesian polity to rule a whole archipelago through conquest and the imposition of tribute, and exercised prestige exchange relations with eastern Fiji and Samoa. Other archipelagos supported several late prehistoric polities, most maintained by strategic alliances until Europeans introduced firearms and unleashed the prospect of conquest-based total hegemony. The Hawaiians, in particular, achieved a level of true statehood before Europeans arrived (see Key Controversy box: Indigenous Archaeology in Hawai'i).

Theories of Social Evolution. Polynesia has long served as a major anthropological laboratory for reconstructing courses of social evolution through ethnographic comparison. Marshall Sahlins, the American cultural anthropologist, ordered Polynesian societies in terms of intensity of social stratification, with Tonga, Tahiti, Samoa, and the Hawaiian islands at the top, grading down through four divisions to the least stratified societies on small atolls, where Sahlins felt that the multiple social ties required to ensure survival argued against centralized control of resources. Sahlins's ranking reflected differing levels of food production and

---

KEY CONTROVERSY Indigenous Archaeology in Hawai'i

Following almost two centuries of colonial history, Hawaiian communities are working to reshape the role archaeology takes on their islands, calling for a more involved practice that acknowledges the living culture of Hawai'i, past and present. Accounts and opinions of archaeological work by Indigenous Hawaiians has been effectively documented by Kathleen Kawelu, an anthropologist from Hawai'i, who collated conversations from individuals of various backgrounds, including Indigenous activists, non-activist community members, and Indigenous and non-Indigenous archaeologists. Kawelu highlighted two major narratives through these interviews. The first was recognition of a growing Native Hawaiian voice, insisting that archaeologists recognize a living Hawaiian culture that is relevant to archaeological practice. The second is the need for archaeologists to increase their engagement with Hawaiian descendants. This is especially so when concerning contract archaeology as part of development projects, where time and money are seen to conflict with sincere interest and concern with local values.

The relationship between archaeologists and local communities is improving. For example, since the 1990s, archaeologists from the University of Hawai'i–West O'ahu have been engaging high-school students with hands-on archaeology and history, helping them to position themselves for jobs in heritage. Archaeologists work also with a nonprofit organization, Nā Pali Coast 'Ohana, which strives to preserve the natural and cultural resources of the Nāpali Coast State Park in Kaua'i. Such ongoing projects and collaborations, along with the growing number of Indigenous Hawaiians entering the discipline of archaeology, lays a groundwork for using the subject as a further way to advocate Hawaiian culture and people.

CS and TS

That humans impacted quite heavily upon the environments of small Pacific islands is not in doubt. Bird extinction occurred on a dramatic scale—of flightless moas in New Zealand and of hundreds of species in the tropical Pacific Islands. Infilling of coastal flats and valley bottoms with alluvial soil released by forest clearance has been demonstrated for Tikopia in the Solomon Islands and for many other islands in Melanesia and Polynesia. Whether human impact affected the large islands of Island Southeast Asia in such ways is not so clear at present, but we might expect that it did, particularly in such a situation as the apparent abandonment of the dry and sandy Penghu Islands, between Taiwan and the Chinese mainland, between 1500 BCE and 1000 CE.

Whether human or natural, factors of environmental degradation and food resource instability must have acted from time to time to stimulate inter-island movement in Polynesia, particularly in the later periods of prehistory. For instance, the account by the US naval officer David Porter of the Marquesas in 1813 records that there was frequent traffic at that time in double canoes sailing in search of new land, apparently as a result of a famine that appears to have struck the islands around 1806–10. Homelands characterized by great resource unreliability are far more likely to spawn colonizing movements than those where food resources are secure. Both the Austronesian dispersal and the recent diaspora that took Chinese settlers into Southeast Asia and the Pacific Islands originated ultimately from one of the most drought-prone and stressed regions of coastal China—central and southern Fujian and northern Guangdong provinces.

frequencies of feasting, so relating social complexity fairly directly to variations in island ecology. The anthropologist Irving Goldman presented a similar ranking, based in this case on intensity of status rivalry and on the degree to which a traditional system of ascribed ranking based on kinship and birth order (as in New Zealand, for instance), without marked social strata, had been broken down either by warfare (Mangaia, Rapa Nui), or by stratification of an aristocracy above a dominated and sometimes exploited stratum of commoners (Tahiti, Tonga, Hawai'i). These rankings still receive strong support from archaeology in that the biggest stone monuments, whether for religious or burial functions, were associated with the largest and most centralized chiefdoms.

Was there a role for consensus, as well as competition, in the rise of paramount chiefs? At the ancestral Polynesian level, it is quite possible that people rallied around individuals of high descent in order to achieve ritually sanctioned well-being and protection from competitors, particularly during the early phases of island settlement. With population growth and heavy human impact on fragile island ecosystems (see Key Theme box: Climate Change: Human Impact, Environmental Change, and Migration), however, human ingenuity turned ever more toward war, as the thousands of late prehistoric earthwork fortifications in New Zealand's North Island testify. The massive Tahitian war fleet painted by William Hodges on Cook's second voyage is one of the most evocative images of latent power on record from ancient Polynesia (see **11.13**, p. 255). Conquest was much easier and more attractive if islands were close together, and if there were major variations in food-producing capacities. The Hawaiian and Tongan islands were far better placed in these respects, at least from the viewpoints of would-be conquerors, than the small and far-flung Cooks and Marquesas. In this way, differing island ecologies certainly did influence long-term social outcomes, but so too did the threads of common ancestry and interaction.

In recent decades, a number of careful reconstructions of late prehistoric social decline and collapse in Polynesia have also been published. For example, by the time of European contact, environmental poverty, drought, and overpopulation had reduced the chiefdoms of the Marquesas to warring polities dominated by inspirational priests (shamans). Rapa Nui underwent a related form of political change during the nineteenth century, involving the toppling of the ancestor *moai* from their platforms. In such circumstances, hereditary chiefs were replaced by non-aristocratic inspirational priests perceived by the general population to be able to communicate with a higher world through trance, or to have been chosen by the gods.

SEABORNE TRADE AND CONTACT IN SOUTHEAST ASIA

In the islands of Southeast Asia, contact with evolving societies in India, the Mediterranean, and China eventually had an enormous social and religious impact. The expansion of both Hinduism and Buddhism sprang in part from seaborne trading activities between 300 BCE and 500 CE involving both Indonesian and Indian sailors. At this time, much of Southeast Asia experienced a rapid spread of iron, and both iron and bronze artifacts were used as far east as West Papua. In Indonesia, new dates for burials in Gua Harimau in southern Sumatra indicate a presence of bronze-socketed axes and bracelets as grave goods by 600 BCE.

This proliferation of metallurgy occurred, surely not by chance, at approximately the same time as the appearance of major empires in China (the Qin and Han; see Chapter 10), South Asia, and in the Mediterranean and West Asia. These empires exploited iron for tools and weapons and continued trading in exotics, including tropical commodities, such as Southeast Asian spices and aromatics. Cloves and nutmegs from the Moluccas as well as sandalwood from Timor doubtless attracted many early traders, just as they drew the Portuguese to commence the colonial era in Island Southeast Asia around 1,500 years later.

Once seasonal monsoon sailing across or around the Bay of Bengal became a regular occurrence during the last few centuries BCE, trade linked the coastlines of India and Indonesia into a vast network, through which spread the beliefs and philosophies of Hinduism, Buddhism, and later Islam. The massive Buddhist monument known as **Borobudur** (760–830 CE) [**11.19**] in central Java is liberally decorated with scenes of large sailing ships at sea.

11.19 Borobudur.
The terraced Buddhist stupa of Borobudur, central Java, 760–830 CE, from the air.

11.20 Prambanan. The Hindu temple complex of Candi Loro Jonggrang, dating from the ninth to tenth centuries CE, central Java.

11.21 BELOW **The Batu Gajah (Elephant Stone) on the Pasemah Plateau.** Relief carving of a man—wearing anklets, a sheathed dagger, and carrying a Vietnamese-style Dong Son drum on his back—flanking an elephant. Probably first millennium CE, Pasemah Plateau, southeastern Sumatra.

The terraced mountain shape of Borobudur, interestingly, is an Austronesian form, paralleled in prehistoric stone constructions in Java, the Lesser Sundas, and in many Polynesian *marae*. More formally Indian in its inspiration is the Hindu temple complex at Prambanan [**11.20**], constructed about a century after Borobudur.

Not all Island Southeast Asian societies were drawn immediately into inexorable globalism, however. Local cultures with local styles continued to evolve in much of the region, just as they did in the Pacific until European exploration began. These styles can be witnessed in remarkable first-millennium CE phenomena, for example, the bronze-casting traditions of Java, Bali, and the Lesser Sundas; the stone carvings of the Pasemah Plateau in southern Sumatra [**11.21**]; and the anthropomorphic burial jar covers of Maitum on Mindanao Island in the Philippines [**11.22**]. The remarkable stone statues of central Sulawesi could even be Neolithic in age [**11.23**], given the existence of the Bulili carving with its Lapita parallels (see Key Controversy box: The Origins of Lapita, p. 252).

11.22 RIGHT **A Metal Age (early centuries CE) anthropomorphic jar** cover for a secondary human burial. It has a faintly painted necklace of spherical red beads, presumably of carnelian, and measures *c.* 15 cm (6 in.) between the ears, so is roughly life-sized. Compare the eyebrows on the Neolithic face in **11.12** (p. 252). Courtesy National Museum of the Philippines, Manila.

SUMMARY AND CONCLUSIONS

The prehistory of Australia and the Southeast Asian and Pacific Islands involved diverse human activities, including the colonization of some of the most remote places on earth, the establishment of elaborate and socially important trade networks, the developments of food production and maritime transport, and major increases in the sizes and densities of human populations and settlements. Symbolic and **ideational** systems may even have been modified in response to external contacts. Yet, it is clear that many possible introductions were not adopted, from projectile technology to domesticated plants and animals, and major changes to Indigenous economy and society were responses to environmental, demographic, and cultural circumstances. Change was ongoing, and some aspects of Indigenous economy and social life were thoroughly transformed even as late as the last 500 years, as disease and cultural interactions altered technology and trade, procurement and politics.

In the islands that lie between Australia and Asia, postglacial prehistory commenced in a culture similar to that of Australia, then diverged through two seemingly independent processes. One was the generation of an agricultural lifestyle in the New Guinea highlands. The other was the dispersal of Austronesian-speaking agriculturalists. Looking at the whole of Austronesian development, we can observe that a common point of origin can give rise to some remarkably different ultimate outcomes: compare the southern Maori hunter-gatherers, the Hawaiian states, and the spread of Hindu and Buddhist religions. Unraveling these threads of common ancestry and subsequent differentiation is one of the most challenging tasks for modern prehistorians of this region.

FURTHER READING

Useful introductions to the archaeology of Australia and the Pacific Islands can be found in:

Bellwood, P. 2017. *First Islanders: Prehistory and Human Migration in Island Southeast Asia*. Chichester and Boston: Wiley-Blackwell.

Bellwood, P. *et al.* (eds.). 2006. *The Austronesians: Historical and Comparative Perspectives*. Canberra: ANU Press.

Glover, I. and Bellwood, P. (eds.). 2005. *Southeast Asia: From Prehistory to History*. London: Routledge Curzon.

Hiscock, P. 2008. *Archaeology of Ancient Australia*. London: Routledge.

Hiscock, P. 2019. Mysticism and reality in Aboriginal myth: evolution and dynamism in Australian Aboriginal religion. *Religion, Brain & Behavior* 10(3): 321–44.

Kirch, P. 1994. *The Wet and the Dry*. Chicago: University of Chicago Press.

Kirch, P. 1997. *The Lapita Peoples*. Oxford: Blackwell.

Kirch, P. 2017. *On the Road of the Winds*. Revised Edition. Berkeley: University of California Press.

Lilley, I., ed. 2006. *Archaeology of Oceania: Australia and the Pacific Islands*. Malden and Oxford: Blackwell.

Lourandos, H. 1996. *Continent of Hunter-Gatherers: New Perspectives in Australian Prehistory*. Cambridge: Cambridge University Press.

Morwood, M. J. 2002. *Visions from the Past: The Archaeology of Australian Aboriginal Art*. Sydney: Allen & Unwin.

Mulvaney, J. and Kamminga, J. 1999. *Prehistory of Australia*. Sydney: Allen & Unwin.

Spriggs, M. 1997. *The Island Melanesians*. Oxford: Blackwell.

Thomas, N., Guest, H., and Dettelbach, M. (eds). 1996. *Observations Made During a Voyage Round the World* (by Johann Reinhold Forster). 280–81. Honolulu: University of Hawai'i Press.

11.23 A stone statue (Langke Bulawa) from the Bada Valley, central Sulawesi. Note how the arm and hand positions resemble those on the Rapa Nui *moai* (**11.14**, p. 256), and how both this and the *moai* are busts without legs. These Bada Valley statues are undated, but could be Neolithic.

ideational concerned with meaning or the representation of ideas or beliefs

Europe

12

Chris Scarre
with Susan E. Alcock and John F. Cherry

Environments and Landscapes 267

**Hunter-Gatherer Trajectories: Mesolithic Communities in Europe,
c. 9000–6000** BCE 268

Early Farming Communities: Southeastern Europe, *c*. 6900–3000 BCE 269

KEY THEME: MIGRATION The Spread of Farming to Europe 270

KEY SITE The Varna Cemetery 272

**Early Farming Communities: The Mediterranean Zone,
c. 6000–2500** BCE 274

Early Farming Communities: Central Europe, *c*. 5600–3000 BCE 275

KEY DISCOVERY The Iceman 276

KEY DISCOVERY The Talheim Death Pit 278

Early Farming Communities: Atlantic Europe, *c*. 5000–2000 BCE 279

Hunter-Gatherer Trajectories: Northern Europe, 9600–4000 BCE 281

KEY CONTROVERSY Stonehenge: Symbolism and Ceremony 282

Early Farming Communities: Northern Europe, 4000–2000 BCE 284

KEY THEME: MIGRATION Migration from the Steppes? 284

Later Farming Communities: Bronze Age Europe, 2300–800 BCE 285

Transitions to States: The Aegean, *c*. 3000–1000 BCE 290

KEY DISCOVERY Linear B 292

Summary and Conclusions 293

Further Reading 293

A panel of rock-art images from Tanum in Sweden, including boat motifs and human figures, that may illustrate cosmological beliefs, legends, or aspects of everyday life in northern Europe during the Bronze Age. (The red coloring is modern.)

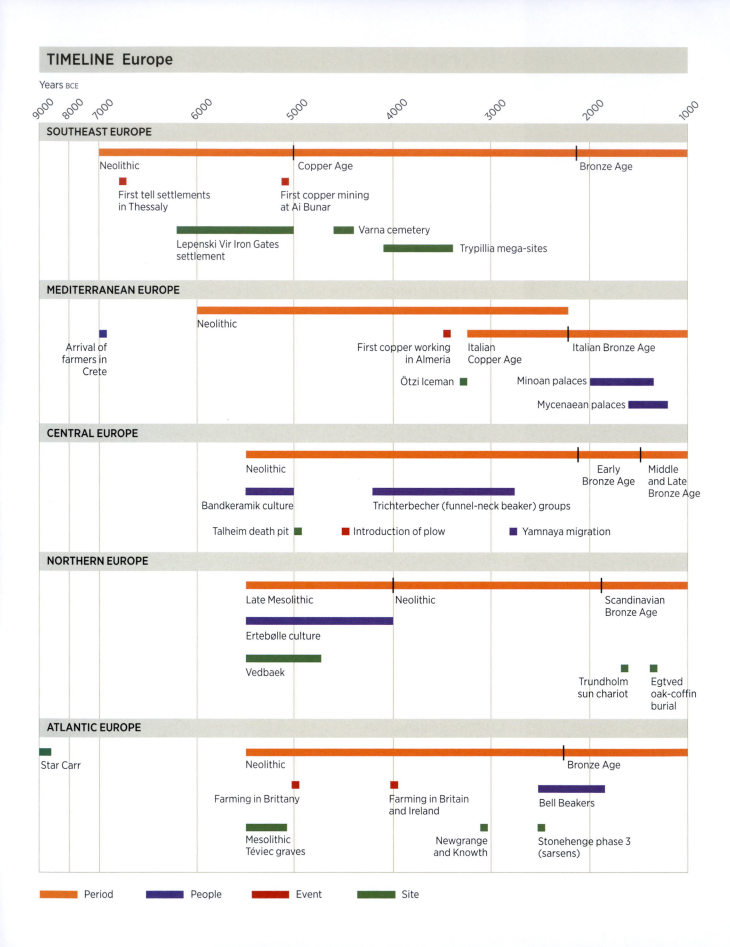

TIMELINE Europe

Years BCE

9000 8000 7000 6000 5000 4000 3000 2000 1000

SOUTHEAST EUROPE

Neolithic   Copper Age   Bronze Age

First tell settlements in Thessaly

First copper mining at Ai Bunar

Lepenski Vir Iron Gates settlement

Varna cemetery

Trypillia mega-sites

MEDITERRANEAN EUROPE

Neolithic

Arrival of farmers in Crete

First copper working in Almeria

Italian Copper Age

Italian Bronze Age

Ötzi Iceman

Minoan palaces

Mycenaean palaces

CENTRAL EUROPE

Neolithic

Early Bronze Age

Middle and Late Bronze Age

Bandkeramik culture

Trichterbecher (funnel-neck beaker) groups

Talheim death pit   Introduction of plow   Yamnaya migration

NORTHERN EUROPE

Late Mesolithic   Neolithic   Scandinavian Bronze Age

Ertebølle culture

Vedbaek

Trundholm sun chariot

Egtved oak-coffin burial

ATLANTIC EUROPE

Star Carr

Neolithic   Bronze Age

Farming in Brittany

Farming in Britain and Ireland

Bell Beakers

Mesolithic Téviec graves

Newgrange and Knowth

Stonehenge phase 3 (sarsens)

Period   People   Event   Site

In this chapter we follow the development of human societies in Europe from the end of the last Ice Age. Mesolithic (Middle Stone Age) communities flourished in the warmer conditions and expanded into the new terrain made available by the melting of the ice sheets in the north. This expansion was followed by the appearance of the first farming communities in the southeast of the continent, the region closest to Southwest Asia, in around 7000 BCE. Agriculture spread from there across Europe primarily as the consequence of farming communities migrating into new territories, ultimately absorbing the indigenous hunter-gatherers. The chapter ends with coverage of metal-using societies of the Bronze Age, and the development of greater social differentiation in the Aegean.

- Mesolithic hunter-gatherer communities expanded across northern and central Europe as the ice sheets retreated.

- Agriculture was brought into Europe by farmers from Southwest Asia, who first arrived in southeastern Europe around 7000 BCE and reached northwest Europe 3,000 years later.

- In western and northern Europe, early farming communities built large ceremonial and funerary monuments, including megalithic graves and (in Britain) stone circles, such as Stonehenge.

- The introduction of copper, gold, and bronze metallurgy was linked to increased social inequality and long-distance exchange that reached across the entire continent.

- In the Aegean, palace-based societies with centralized administrations and writing emerged in the second millennium BCE.

ENVIRONMENTS AND LANDSCAPES

The landscape of prehistoric Europe ranged from the Arctic in the north to the Mediterranean in the south, and from the steppes and forests of the east to the warm ocean currents and rocky outcrops of the Atlantic coast in the west [**12.1**, p. 268]. Substantial areas of Europe lay beyond the limits of human settlement during the last Ice Age, when a massive ice sheet covered the northern part of the continent, with smaller ice caps in the Alps and the Pyrenees. As temperatures began to rise, the ice sheets retreated, and climate and topography became similar to today.

The earlier postglacial was a period of significant environmental change, as the climate warmed and plants and animals recolonized areas that had been too cold and dry during the last Ice Age. The whole shape of the European continent was altered, as rising sea levels flooded the coastal lowlands. In northern areas—which had been covered by the ice sheets—shorelines actually receded, as the surface of the land bounced back as the weight of the ice was removed (see **12.18**, p. 281). Rainfall increased, and western Europe benefited from the re-established Gulf Stream that brought warm tropical water to northern latitudes. As forests spread, the open-country megafauna of the last Ice Age (mammoth, woolly rhinoceros, giant deer) died out, and reindeer retreated to the north. In their place came forest-adapted species—aurochs (wild cattle), red deer, and wild pig—and new lifestyles for hunters and gatherers.

12.1 Map of Europe. At the height of the last Ice Age some 20,000 years ago, the sea level was significantly lower than today's. As the sea level rose with the melting of the ice sheets, extensive areas of low-lying coastal plain were flooded (shown here in darker green). It was only in the seventh millennium BCE that Britain became separated from the European mainland, and the Black Sea was joined to the Mediterranean.

12.2 BELOW **Elk antler macehead from Oleniy Ostrov.** This is the oldest and largest Mesolithic cemetery in northern Europe, with 170 excavated burials out of an estimated total of more than 400. Some have rich grave assemblages, including zoomorphic figures, maceheads, and axes. The graves illustrate the social and cultural complexity of Mesolithic communities, and the iconography of the carved figures may refer to a northern cosmology that has survived into recent centuries.

HUNTER-GATHERER TRAJECTORIES: MESOLITHIC COMMUNITIES IN EUROPE, *c.* 9000–6000 BCE

It was in this context that Mesolithic communities began to appear across Europe, directly descended from the Upper Paleolithic communities of the last Ice Age. Many chose to found their settlements near coasts, lakes, and wetlands, which offered a wide range of fishing and foraging opportunities. Population levels rose across Europe as more resources became available, yet settlements remained small and seasonal for the most part. One such was the lakeside settlement of **Star Carr** in northern England, a seasonal hunting camp *c.* 9000 BCE, with hunting and fishing equipment including microliths (small flint tools) and barbed antler points. To the east, the whole of the area now occupied by the North Sea was a marshy lowland, home to hunters, fishers, and foragers. In recent years, sizable areas of the submerged Mesolithic landscape beneath the North Sea have begun to be mapped and studied.

Mesolithic Social Organization. In some areas, communities were developing larger and more complex forms of social organization. This can be inferred from the emergence of the first cemeteries. The earliest are in northern and eastern Europe and date to *c.* 10,000–9000 BCE. One at **Oleniy Ostrov** in Karelia, Russia contained probably more than 400 burials. Some of the individuals were buried with elk effigies carved in antler [**12.2**], testimony perhaps to their social status or affiliation within the wider community. From 6500 BCE, cemeteries also appear at European Mesolithic sites in southern Scandinavia, northwest France, and Portugal. These are associated with substantial middens of shell debris, testifying to the importance of marine resources to these late Mesolithic coastal communities.

Cemeteries may mark significant changes in social organization, with the formation of larger social groups and greater levels of differentiation in the individual treatment of the dead. There is also evidence that some of these settlements may have been occupied for longer periods of the year, and in the Baltic, pottery vessels were adopted in the sixth millennium BCE, perhaps specifically for the processing of seafoods. Small carvings of bone, antler, and amber also exist from this and earlier periods of the Mesolithic, and testify to the importance of the symbolic and spiritual dimension.

EARLY FARMING COMMUNITIES: SOUTHEASTERN EUROPE, *c.* 6900–3000 BCE

Farming came to Europe from Southwest Asia, brought by settlers from Anatolia. Radiocarbon dates show that it then spread westward from southeast Europe both along the Mediterranean coasts to Italy and Iberia, and northward through the Balkans to central, western, and northern Europe [**12.3**]. Analysis of ancient DNA indicates little continuity between hunter-gatherer and early farming populations, suggesting that farmers themselves must have spread across Europe. This marked the beginning of the Neolithic in Europe (see Key Theme box: Migration—The Spread of Farming to Europe, p. 270).

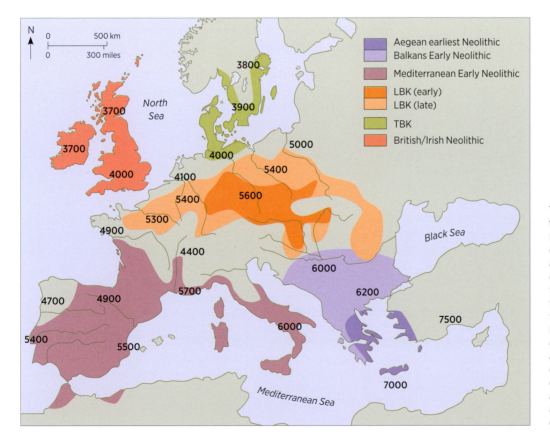

12.3 The spread of farming. Expansion and migration of farming communities carried agriculture across much of central Europe, and travelling by sea led to the establishment of farming enclaves on the Mediterranean coasts of France and Spain, and the Atlantic coasts of Portugal. Farming eventually reached Britain and southern Scandinavia around 4000 BCE. All dates on map BCE.

The first farming settlements in mainland Europe were established around 6800 BCE on the fertile alluvial plains of Thessaly in east-central Greece. This was an area with little evidence for indigenous hunter-gatherers, suggesting that their population levels had been relatively low and communities small and mobile. The most prominent of the early farming communities are those that formed settlement mounds, or tells.

Farming had spread to Thessaly along the north coast of the Aegean, although many of the early sites there have since been drowned by sea-level rise. Other journeys could have been by sea, crossing the Aegean from island to island. Evidence for maritime traffic across the Aegean reaches back to at least 12,000–11,000 BCE, when obsidian from volcanic sources on the island of Melos was left at Franchthi Cave in southeastern Greece. Early farmers from Anatolia reached Crete *c.* 6900 BCE, establishing a settlement on the site of the later Minoan palace of Knossos.

The First Neolithic Settlements, c. 6800–6000 BCE

Greek Neolithic houses were built of mud brick, similar to those of Southwest Asia, but settlements consisted of separate, small rectangular buildings, contrasting with the agglomerated architecture of south-central Anatolia. Miniature clay models portray houses with painted walls, steeply pitched roofs, and rectangular openings for doors and windows.

The use of clay (either mud brick or daub) for building the houses themselves, coupled with the stability and clustering of settlement, led to the formation of tells. These are a feature of Neolithic communities in Greece and the Balkans. As houses decayed or were demolished, the mud-brick or clay daub accumulated to form the mound, a process that was repeated

KEY THEME: MIGRATION The Spread of Farming to Europe

Ancient DNA extracted from skeletal remains provides direct evidence of the relationship between specific prehistoric populations. Analysis of the resulting patterns at the broad geographical scale also offers insights into population movements and the replacement or absorption of one people by another, which can be compared with the artifactual evidence traditionally studied by archaeologists.

From the end of the Ice Age, the hunter-gatherer population of Europe was directly descended from the previous Upper Paleolithic populations. From the seventh millennium BCE, the genetic map of Europe was transformed by the expansion of farmers from Southwest Asia. Recent studies of ancient DNA from early farming communities in Greece have shown that their origin lay in Anatolia. They subsequently spread northwestward into central Europe, where they formed the basis of the Linearbandkeramik (LBK) communities, and separately in a westward movement along the Mediterranean to Spain. The DNA signature of Anatolian immigrants is very clear. There is a sharp discontinuity in DNA profiles between the postglacial hunter-gatherer communities and European populations following the spread of farmers.

It should not be imagined that all of the previous populations disappeared. Stable isotope analyses in the Rhineland have shown that early farming communities there incorporated people from other areas, who may have been indigenous hunter-gatherers. Furthermore, incoming farmers would have targeted the most suitable arable lands for settlement, and hunter-gatherers continued to populate areas less immediately attractive for agriculture. Indeed, the initial wave of farming expansion into central Europe appears to have been followed by a process in which early farmers mixed with the indigenous hunter-gatherer groups. In the Middle Elbe/Saale region of central Germany, for example, one study showed an 80 percent contribution of Anatolian DNA among the earliest farming communities *c.* 5500 BCE, declining to under 50 percent two millennia later. By 2500 BCE, the early farming communities that had initially been clustered in the river valleys had expanded into the intervening regions, and northward into Scandinavia. In the process, hunter-gatherer groups were absorbed into farming communities through intermarriage, while others adopted domesticated plants and animals from their neighbors and became sedentary farmers themselves.

12.4 Karanovo. This tell in southern Bulgaria, standing 12 meters (40 feet) high, is one of the most impressive settlement mounds established by the early farmers of southeastern Europe. The tells were produced through continuous occupation stretching over several thousand years, when buildings would be demolished and new structures built on top.

as new houses were built on the sites of those destroyed. In their earliest stages, many such tells were of relatively modest dimensions; the Neolithic tell of Karanovo in southern Bulgaria [**12.4**] measured only 1.5 meters (5 feet) in height, though in later millennia it grew to a height of 12 meters (40 feet) and spread over 4 hectares (10 acres). Such mounds are not accidental creations but are the result of particular decisions by communities that chose to remain at the same location over successive generations. The prominence of the tells may ultimately have made them visual symbols showing the importance (certainly the longevity) of the community who lived there, and tells must have incorporated a memory of previous generations. This is in striking contrast to other regions of Europe, where prehistoric settlements were generally insubstantial and shifting in character.

Developing Societies, c. 6000–3200 BCE

From 6000 BCE, societies grew in size and organization. Tell settlements appeared in new areas, such as eastern Hungary, Bosnia, northern Croatia, and the lower Danube Valley. More complex houses were built, which were divided internally into several rooms.

Miniature clay models from this period show something of the internal arrangements of domestic buildings, including furniture and pottery. The majority of clay models, however, were figures of humans and animals. Excavations at Achilleion in northern Greece yielded fragments of 200 miniature zoomorphic and anthropomorphic figurines, the earliest dating from c. 6300 BCE. Many of the human figurines have no indication of gender, but where it is shown it is predominantly female, with bodily emphasis on hips, breasts, and belly. A tiny minority were placed in graves; most of them are found in fragments within settlements, showing that the predominant association was with the domain of the living.

KEY SITE The Varna Cemetery

The cemetery at Varna, on the Black Sea coast of Bulgaria, was discovered accidentally in 1972, and the abundance of metal found in some of the graves quickly attracted attention. The large quantity of gold, along with copper and other prestige materials, suggests that Varna was the burial place of an important community [**12.5**, **12.6**]. It also demonstrates how, by the fifth millennium BCE, societies in southeastern Europe were using elaborate material culture to signify differences between individuals, marking an important change from the relatively egalitarian burial practices of the earlier Neolithic. Gold is a particularly suitable material for status display, as it is rare, has a shiny

appearance, is relatively soft—therefore easily worked and shaped—and does not tarnish like most other metals. It has few practical uses, however, and its prominence and sought-after quality illustrate the social role of metal.

The association of the metals with the body in a grave is particularly significant: these were all objects to be displayed on or about the person, whether held in the hand or attached to clothing. Some, perhaps many, of them may have been produced specifically for burial, and their placement in the grave would have made the interment ceremony itself a setting for impressive visual displays of objects that most people would have very rarely seen.

12.5, **12.6** Gold and rich objects from Varna. The appearance of gold and copper was in response to the growing demand for new symbols of social display and differentiation.

From 5000 BCE, evidence of craft specialization appears at a number of settlements in southeast Europe. High-temperature kilns were introduced for the production of thin-walled pottery, which was either painted or graphite-decorated. In some parts of the Balkans, burials were moved outside the settlement area and began to be grouped into cemeteries. The grave goods placed with the dead indicate the increasingly varied social roles that were developing at this period. This is seen most dramatically in the cemetery of **Varna** on the shores of the

Black Sea, where some 280 graves were equipped with rich offerings of gold, copper, pottery, and stone (see Key Site box: The Varna Cemetery).

Fertile lowland basins remained the principal population centers, supported by their rich primary agricultural productivity, but many of the special materials used in status displays came from the surrounding uplands, including metals and stone for axes. It is in these upland zones that the oldest recorded European copper mines are found, as at Ai Bunar in Bulgaria, where copper ore was mined in trenches up to 80 meters long, 10 meters wide, and 20 meters deep (260 × 33 × 66 feet) from as early as 5100 BCE. The products can be traced by metal analysis and suggest complex networks of exchange.

The introduction of these metals does not mark a sharp break in the evolution of southeastern European societies. It does, however, note a stage in the development of ever-growing social differentiation. It is also part of increasing complexity of technology, when there was also an expansion of human settlement and activity across the landscape, associated with the plow and wheeled transport.

Further change came in around 4500 BCE, when tell settlements were abandoned and a new pattern of dispersed farmstead dominated the landscapes of southeast Europe. In the Ukraine, the period *c.* 4100–3400 BCE saw a dramatic development in the establishment of impressive settlements belonging to the Trypillia culture. The largest of these is estimated to have had as many as 3,000 houses arranged in concentric rings and capable of accommodating several thousand inhabitants, although it is possible that not all the houses were occupied at the same time [**12.7**]. The Trypillia settlements

12.7 a, b Trypillia settlement of Nebelivka, Ukraine.
These settlements included as many as 3,000 houses, often containing clay figurines and miniature vessels, usually about 6 to 9 centimeters (2.3 to 3.5 inches) in height (below). The houses (right, shown in red) were arranged in distinct sectors (indicated by the dotted lines) around an open central area. Most of the houses were burned at the end of their occupation.

0 _____ 500 m
0 _____ 1500 ft.

have been labeled mega-sites and dubbed Europe's first towns, although they did not give rise to a lasting tradition of large-scale settlement in this region. Their demise has been linked to environmental changes, a greater emphasis on pastoralism, and the expansion of the Yamnaya steppe communities (see Key Theme box: Migration—Migration from the Steppes?, p. 284).

EARLY FARMING COMMUNITIES: THE MEDITERRANEAN ZONE, *c.* 6000–2500 BCE

Within the Mediterranean basin, the domesticated crops from Southwest Asia were relatively easy to transplant and cultivate since climates were broadly similar. As with other regions of Europe, recent DNA analyses have shown that agriculture was carried by migrating farmers. It spread early from the Balkans to southern Italy where domestic plants and animals were in use by 6000 BCE. There are no tell settlements in southern Italy; the key Early Neolithic sites take the form of ditched enclosures containing numerous smaller C-shaped enclosures, as well as traces of houses and cobbled areas that were possibly hearths for feasting.

In southern France, the first Neolithic settlements with cereals and domestic animals appear in the archaeological record around 5700 BCE, although they remain relatively rare and spread beyond the coastal zone only after 5500 BCE.

In southern Iberia (modern Spain and Portugal), several enclaves of early farming settlement were established by 5400 BCE. The expansion of these settlements led within a few centuries to a significant increase in population, supported by the new mixed farming economy, but a few centuries later, after 5150 BCE, populations appear to fall again. This same pattern of an initial boom in the Early Neolithic followed by a subsequent slowdown has been observed for several other regions of western and central Europe.

Social Distinctions in Mediterranean Europe, c. 3500–2500 BCE

12.8 Exotic materials. Valencina de la Concepción in southern Spain is a mega-site extending over more than 400 hectares (1,000 acres) with a complex pattern of pits and graves. One of the tomb chambers contained two layers of burials and exotic imported materials including amber, cinnabar, and ivory from both African and Asian elephants. The ivory featured a carved elephant tusk and a number of carefully crafted items, such as a dagger hilt and sheath, the blade made of translucent rock crystal.

By 3000 BCE, new levels of social complexity become visible in the Mediterranean zone, especially in southern Spain. Large and complex mega-sites appear in southwest Iberia, the biggest of all being **Valencina de la Concepción** near Seville, covering an area of more than 400 hectares (1,000 acres) and incorporating pits and elaborate **chambered tombs**. It was founded *c.* 3200 BCE and occupied for almost 1,000 years, becoming an important center of copper metallurgy. Exotic materials, such as ivory and amber, appear in the graves, indicating both the emergence of elite groups and the extent of the community's maritime connections. The ivory came not only from North African but also Syrian elephants, while the origin of the amber has been sourced to Sicily [**12.8**].

Small farming settlements are known from this period, some on the shores of the Alpine lakes, where the waterlogging of the remains has preserved details of timber houses. The most vivid single insight into life in this part of Europe shortly before 3000 BCE is provided by the freeze-dried body of the Iceman, found in the high Alps (see Key Discovery box: The Iceman, p. 276).

EARLY FARMING COMMUNITIES: CENTRAL EUROPE, c. 5600–3000 BCE

While one axis of farming spread westward from southeastern Europe to Italy and Iberia, another expansion took the new domesticates north into the Danube Valley and central Europe. Here the growing farming populations encountered Mesolithic communities settled in the Iron Gates region of the Danube Valley (where the river cuts through the Carpathian Mountains on its way to the Black Sea). Some fifty Mesolithic sites are known, spanning the period c. 9500–5500 BCE, the latest and most famous being **Lepenski Vir** [12.9]. Distinctive trapezoidal houses at this site have stone-carved fish sculptures next to their central hearths, and many burials beneath their floors. These Mesolithic sites were finally abandoned c. 5500 BCE.

The Bandkeramik Culture, c. 5600–5000 BCE

From around 5600 BCE, a distinctive culture developed in western Hungary and subsequently spread across the whole of central Europe (see **12.3**, p. 269). It is called **Linearbandkeramik** (**LBK**) (often abbreviated to Bandkeramik), named after a distinctive banded decoration found on its pottery vessels. It spread relatively rapidly across Europe from 5400 BCE, reaching the Rhineland by 5300 BCE, and the Paris basin a century or so later.

The key feature of Bandkeramik settlements were the massively built longhouses [12.10] grouped in clusters in forest clearings on gravel river terraces, with access to water and easily tilled soil. Successive generations of houses shifted over time, but they never developed settlement mounds similar to the tells of southeastern Europe. Patterns of radiocarbon dates

12.9 Lepenski Vir. Fish played a major role in the economy and ideology of Lepenski Vir, a Late Mesolithic settlement on the banks of the River Danube in Serbia.

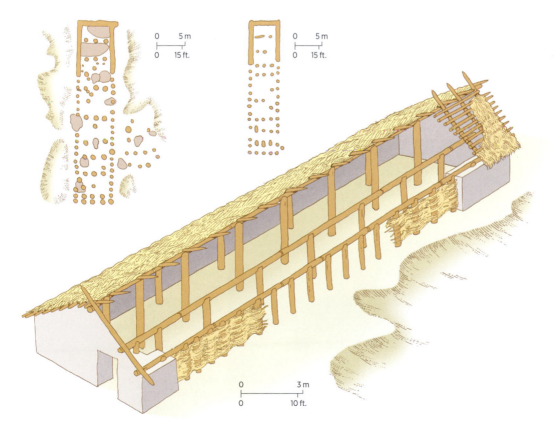

12.10 Bandkeramik longhouses. Of fairly standardized construction, these survive as patterns of postholes flanked by the long lateral pits from which the daub (adobe) for the wattle walls was extracted. Internal groups of massive timber posts supported the pitched roof (covered in thatch), which rested on and overhung the side walls. The northern end of these houses was often more massively built of split timber planks in a bedding trench; occasionally the whole of the outer wall was of timber plank construction. The extravagant use of such large timbers may be a response to the forested settings where these houses were built.

KEY DISCOVERY The Iceman

On September 19, 1991, two German mountaineers came upon the oldest preserved human body ever recorded in modern times [**12.11**]. The site of the discovery was the Italian South Tyrol, close to the main ridge of the Alps and only a little more than 90 meters (300 feet) from the international frontier between Italy and Austria. This section of the Alps is known as the Ötztal Alps, taking its name from the long, narrow Ötztal Valley, and the body is commonly known today by the nickname Ötzi; many, however, simply refer to the corpse as the Iceman.

The Finds

The body proved to be that of a man aged around forty-five years old. It was in an excellent state of preservation, which has allowed detailed analyses to be undertaken, including the sequencing of his complete genome. The reason for this unusual preservation lay in the pattern of events that led to and followed his death. It was thought at first that the man had died after being overcome by an early autumn blizzard. Then, in 2001, an X-ray of the body revealed that a flint arrowhead was lodged immediately below the left shoulder: he had been shot in the back. The thin covering of autumn snow was the medium of preservation, preventing attack from insect larvae as the corpse was gradually desiccated by autumn winds. In essence, what occurred was a natural freeze-drying. The condition of the corpse was already largely stabilized when the heavy winter snows covered it. Radiocarbon dating of tissues from the body, undertaken separately in four different laboratories for greater reliability, indicated that these events took place between 3300 and 3200 BCE. The corpse lay buried for more than 5,000 years before the melting of the ice, accelerated by wind-borne Saharan dust in July 1991, exposed it to view again.

Lying around the body in the ice hollow were a copper axe hafted in a yew handle, an unfinished bow, also of yew, a backpack of larch planks and animal hide, a flint knife and leather scabbard, a deerskin quiver with two flint-tipped arrows and twelve unfinished arrow shafts, and a calfskin pouch that hung from a belt. The remains of his clothing included fur leggings and cap, a fur outer garment of poncho type, leather shoes stuffed with grass for warmth, and a grass cape that could have doubled as a groundsheet or blanket. This was a set of clothing well able to cope with the harsh Alpine climate, at least outside the winter months [**12.12**, **12.13**].

The unfinished nature of his bow and the majority of his arrows suggest, however, that he was not well prepared for his journey. Furthermore, he was not in the peak of health. Analysis of one of his fingernails revealed that he suffered from serious illnesses (resulting in interruptions to fingernail growth) at least three times during the six months before he died. He also bore tattoos on his lower back, left leg, and right ankle and knee. These may have been decorative but more probably had a therapeutic function, since the Iceman suffered from arthritis. Analysis of his colon contents has indicated that he also suffered from an intestinal infestation that could have given him chronic diarrhea. Most serious of all, however, was evidence that his right hand had been seriously injured, perhaps in a knife fight, shortly before his death. A deep cut 4 centimeters (1.6 inches) long across the palm of the hand would have almost immobilized two of his fingers.

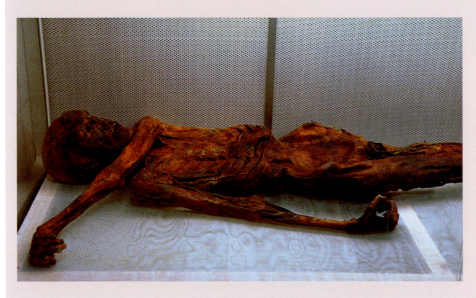

12.11 The body discovered in the Similaun glacier in September 1991 had been preserved by a natural process of freeze-drying. Lengthy and detailed scientific analyses have since established that the man died more than 5,000 years ago after he was shot in the shoulder. A CT scan later revealed that the arrowhead had severed his subclavical artery and caused heavy bleeding.

Yew long bow, unfinished

Deerskin quiver

Grass cape

Backpack of larch planks and hide

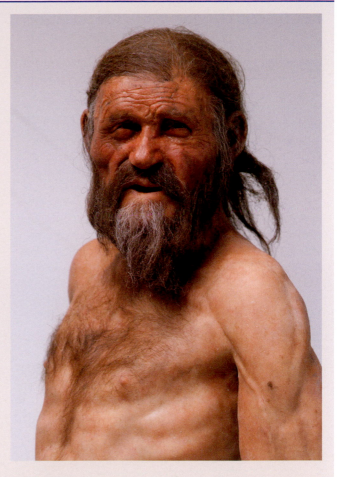

12.12, 12.13 The ice had preserved not only the body of the Iceman but also his clothing, which included leather shoes and loincloth, fur leggings and cloak, and an outer cape, open at the front, made from plaited grasses more than 1 meter (3.3 feet) in length. Capes of this kind, woven from straw or reeds, were still worn in parts of northern Italy in the eighteenth century. Detailed analyses and the excellent preservation of the physical remains have allowed a reconstruction of the Iceman, who was aged around forty-five when he died.

The Interpretation

Analysis of the pollen residues in his gut has allowed a remarkable reconstruction of his last meals, and reveals that in the last thirty-three hours or so before his death he had moved from the high Alps close to the timber line (2,500 m/8,200 ft.) down to a lower wooded valley (1200 m/3,900 ft.), before returning above the snow line where he died.

Examination of moss from the body showed that it had come from the south side of the Alps, quite possibly from the Vinschgau Valley, only 20 kilometers (12.5 miles) due south of the place where he met his end. Isotope studies of the Iceman's bones, teeth, and stomach contents indicate that he spent his childhood in the Eisack Valley in the lowest Vinschgau, and as an adult migrated to slightly higher altitudes or a few kilometers upstream, or was perhaps engaged in transhumance. Pollen suggests that his death occurred in the early autumn.

A CT scan (using X-rays and a computer to create detailed images of the inside of the body) undertaken in 2005 revealed that the flint arrowhead had lacerated his subclavical artery, producing a large hematoma in the surrounding soft tissue and inducing heavy bleeding and cardiac shock, which would have caused his death. The cut on his hand suggests he was engaged in a struggle at close quarters a day or so before he was shot in the back. There is also evidence of blunt-force trauma to the back and a depressed fracture on the front of his skull, suggesting he may have been struck on the head or have hit his head on a rock as he fell.

With the unique nature of the discovery, and the exceptional conditions of preservation, the Iceman presents us with a striking image of a violent encounter more than 5,000 years ago. He may have been returning to his home community after a period in the mountains when he was met by enemies and had to flee for his life back to the mountains, only to be pursued there and killed. It is becoming increasingly clear that violence was more frequent in prehistoric European societies than some earlier scholars have supposed, as evidenced by the mass grave at Talheim in Bavaria (see Key Discovery box: The Talheim Death Pit, p. 278), from a millennium before the Iceman.

KEY DISCOVERY The Talheim Death Pit

The archaeology demonstrates that farming communities in Europe were not peaceful, but subject to large-scale conflict. One of the best-known examples is the mass grave at Talheim in Germany.

Death at Talheim

Talheim is a Bandkeramik settlement site dating to around 5000 BCE. In a pit among the houses, archaeologists found the remains of thirty-four individuals: sixteen children and adolescents as well as eighteen adults, of whom at least seven were female [**12.14**]. Most of the bodies bore traces of violence. At least eighteen had received blows from polished stone adzes. The absence of any evidence of resistance (no injuries to the arms), and the position of the majority of head wounds on the rear of the skulls, suggests that these people were killed while attempting to flee.

The most convincing interpretation is that these were inhabitants of the Talheim settlement who had been killed by raiders from a neighboring Bandkeramik community.

What the Talheim evidence does reveal is that the polished stone adzes of shoe-last form, a characteristic feature of Bandkeramik material culture, are not to be interpreted merely as carpentry tools: they had (or were capable of assuming) a much more aggressive role. This throws new light on the discovery of shoe-last adzes in the graves of older males; they doubled as weapons of war and were evidently male status symbols.

Evidence for Violence Elsewhere

Talheim is not the only Bandkeramik site to show evidence of violent death. At Halberstadt, a pit contained nine skeletons, mostly male, who had been killed by blows to the back of the head. At Schletz in Austria, skeletons had been thrown haphazardly into the ditch of a Bandkeramik enclosure, and of sixty-seven that have so far been studied, all but one showed traces of violence—mainly, once again, blows to the head from shoe-last adzes. In this instance, the enclosure itself may have been a defensive structure, and the discovery of further skeletons in the well within the settlement suggests that it was finally overrun and destroyed.

Violence of a rather different kind has been documented at the Bandkeramik enclosure site of Herxheim in the Rhineland. Excavation revealed eighty deposits of human remains in the enclosure ditches, with up to 2,000 bones in each, representing an estimated 500 individuals. Detailed study of one deposit with remains of ten individuals (adults and children) revealed traces of skinning and defleshing, and the fracturing of long bones to extract the marrow. This may be an instance of large-scale cannibalism, probably sacrificial or ceremonial in character. Some have attributed it, along with Talheim, to a crisis that arose toward the end of the Bandkeramik.

12.14 Excavation of the Talheim death pit in southwest Germany. The shape of the wounds in many of the skulls indicates that the attackers were members of another Bandkeramik community, wielding characteristic Bandkeramik polished stone adzes, rather than (for example) neighboring hunter-gatherers.

---

show a substantial increase in population size during this time. Just as in Iberia, a period of population growth appears to have been followed by a population fall after only a few centuries, until more stable farming strategies were developed. There may indeed have been a crisis at the end of the Bandkeramik period, marked by evidence for violence between neighboring Bandkeramik communities (see Key Discovery box: The Talheim Death Pit).

Analysis of ancient DNA extracted from Bandkeramik skeletons suggests that these settlers spread steadily across central Europe, following the river valleys, planting small fields of cereals and legumes and pasturing cattle along the forest margins. Inevitably, they came into contact with hunter-gatherer groups, and the DNA evidence indicates that while hunter-gatherer populations survived alongside farming communities in some areas, they were ultimately absorbed by the growing agricultural societies from 5000 to 3000 BCE.

Regional Diversification, c. 5000–3000 BCE

By c. 5000 BCE, the relative uniformity of the Bandkeramik had begun to be replaced by more regionally differentiated communities. At first, those of central Europe continued to live in longhouses while beginning to occupy more diverse environments, including the lowlands of the north European plain. Toward the end of the fifth millennium BCE, a new type of pottery appears in northern and central Europe, characterized by beakers with a bulbous body and flaring out-turned rim known as the **Trichterbecher** (funnel-necked beaker), the name also given to its makers. This culture is divided into a series of regional groups among whom ideas, materials, and artifacts circulated widely. It was in this context that copper made its appearance in central Europe, first in the form of imported objects from southeastern Europe, then (from c. 4000 BCE) as products of a local central European metallurgy [**12.15**].

Neolithic farming communities of central Europe underwent other important changes between 5000 and 3000 BCE. The introduction of the plow, probably around 5000–4000 BCE, made it possible to bring new areas into cultivation, and the presence of wheeled vehicles is attested by finds of wooden wheels in wetland areas (for instance in Switzerland and Slovenia) and by ceramic models of wheeled vehicles from graves in Hungary.

12.15 The Bygholm hoard. This hoard of copper objects was discovered in 1924 at Bygholm, Denmark. The objects date to around 3500 BCE and comprise three arm-rings, four axes, and a dagger blade. The arm-rings testify to the demand for personal ornaments, which was a major stimulus to the adoption and spread of metallurgy.

EARLY FARMING COMMUNITIES: ATLANTIC EUROPE, c. 5000–2000 BCE

In central and southeastern Europe, migrating farming communities appear to have moved into regions with relatively low densities of previous Mesolithic settlement. In Atlantic Europe to the west (from Britain and Ireland through western France to Iberia), and northern Europe, however, evidence of Mesolithic occupation is significantly more conspicuous.

Mesolithic settlement is best documented in favored coastal locations of Atlantic Europe where marine as well as terrestrial resources could be exploited. Human remains are found at some of these sites, suggesting that feasting and mortuary rituals may both have been practiced. One grave (Téviec K in Brittany) contained the remains of six individuals, the product not of simultaneous but of successive inhumations. Several of the Téviec graves had a lining of stone slabs, creating a rudimentary cist (box-like container), with a covering slab on which a fire had burned; this has been interpreted as evidence for funerary feasts. These groups of hunter-gatherers had specialized foraging strategies, semi-sedentary settlements, and evidence of social competition. Eventually, they were absorbed into the expanding farming societies. By 5000 BCE, farming communities were established across the region, and shortly after 4000 BCE they reached Britain and Ireland.

Trichterbecher (TBK) culture in northern and central Europe in the late fifth and fourth millennium BCE, defined by a new type of pottery: *Trichterbecher* or funnel-necked beakers

megalith meaning big stone; applied to monuments and structures built with large stones weighing several tons, including dolmens, passage graves, and menhirs

menhir a single standing stone found in Neolithic Europe, sometimes decorated with carvings

passage grave a type of chambered tomb where the burial chamber is reached via a long passage from the edge of the covering mound

Within a few centuries of farming communities entering Atlantic Europe, the construction of monuments began, some of timber and earth, others **megalithic** structures together with mounds and cairns. Megalithic monuments vary widely in scale and construction, but despite the co-ordinated effort that would have been required to build the larger examples, there is rarely evidence for marked social hierarchy in the burials themselves. The monuments take a number of forms. These include stone settings, such as the circles and avenues of Britain and Brittany, or oval settings of standing stones in Portugal. The most famous of the stone circles is that of **Stonehenge** in southern Britain, oriented (at least in its final phase) on midwinter sunset (see Key Controversy box: Stonehenge: Symbolism and Ceremony, p. 282). More numerous still are the single standing stones known as **menhirs**, some of them carved with symbols of crooks, polished stone axes, and other motifs often difficult to identify.

Chambered tombs are one major category of Neolithic monument: chambers or cists of timber or stone, usually, if not invariably, covered by a mound, and associated with the deposition of human remains. Many were places for collective burial, and some contain the remains of hundreds of individuals. Associated mortuary practices frequently involved the removal, manipulation, and sorting of the skeletal elements. The tombs take a variety of forms: mounds or cairns may be circular or quadrangular, and may contain either a single chamber or a whole series; chambers were usually accessible by a door or portal, or by a more formal entrance passage in the classic **passage grave**. Among the most elaborate passage graves are those of Gavrinis in Brittany, and Newgrange [**12.16**] and Knowth in Ireland, where the megalithic blocks are carved with spirals, circles, and lozenges. Decorated stones mark special points within the tombs—curbs, thresholds, and chambers. Some of them are recycled slabs that had originally been free-standing decorated menhirs. An overlapping collection of motifs is found in the rock art of many regions of Atlantic Europe, some of which dates to this period.

12.16 Newgrange. The entrance to this passage grave in the Boyne Valley, Ireland, is blocked by an elaborately decorated curb stone, one of ninety-seven that fringe this impressive burial mound. The concentric patterns of running spirals and lozenge shapes are characteristic of megalithic art, a body of pecked and engraved motifs found especially in Ireland, northwest France, and Iberia, with examples also in adjacent regions. In the background is the vertical tomb facade, built of quartz, granite, and granodiorite blocks, which has been heavily reconstructed.

12.17 RIGHT **Jadeitite axe heads.** These examples are from Cunzierton and Greenlawdean in Scotland. The enormous distances traveled by these axe heads, together with their highly polished finish and sometimes exaggerated size, are evidence of the value and social prestige attached to them. One axe head found at Dunfermline in Scotland has been shown to have been taken from the same parent block of Alpine jadeitite as three axe heads from northern Germany.

Polished stone axes, some from known quarry sites, were extensively traded among the Neolithic communities of western Europe, and often origin and appearance seem more important than practical qualities [**12.17**]. Their patterns of circulation echo those of copper axes further east. Often, it was the appearance of the material that was at least as important as its technical properties, an observation confirmed by the widespread popularity and distribution of copper-colored flint from western France around 2500 BCE, just as copper was being introduced and achieving wide circulation as a material of value.

Jadeitite axes from sources in the western Alps play an important part in this story, journeying northward across France, Germany, and Britain, parallel to contemporary copper axe distributions in eastern Europe. The lustrous, highly polished jadeitite (a variety of jade) was reshaped into regionally preferred forms as it traveled and must have carried a powerful symbolic significance. The movement of the axes is brought sharply into focus by recent spectroradiometric (light measurement) analyses, which have shown, for example, that one from Scotland was probably derived from the same block of Alpine jadeitite as three axe heads found in northern Germany.

The development of monuments of earth and stone sets the Neolithic communities of western Europe apart from those of regions to the east and south, and the circulation of prized raw materials illustrates the networks that connected them. The scarcity of settlement remains, however, suggests that this was not the most populous area of Neolithic Europe, despite the evidence of impressive structures, such as Stonehenge or Newgrange.

12.18 BELOW **Changing shorelines.** Much of the evidence concerning Mesolithic communities around the coasts of Europe has been submerged by sea-level rise. In northern Europe, however, the isostatic rebound of the land following the melting of the ice sheets raised Mesolithic shorelines, and many Ertebølle coastal middens survive on such beaches. The edge of the rebound is marked by a line through Jutland and the Danish islands.

HUNTER-GATHERER TRAJECTORIES: NORTHERN EUROPE, 9600–4000 BCE

In northern Europe, as in parts of Atlantic Europe, the spread of farming came up against well-established Mesolithic coastal communities. In the early postglacial, the retreating ice sheets had reopened this area for human colonization, and hunter-gatherers had settled along lakes, marshes, and rivers in a broad band of territory from Karelia (northwest Russia) in the east to Britain in the west, at a time when the North Sea was yet to be formed.

The latest of these Mesolithic communities were the complex hunter-gatherers of the Ertebølle-Ellerbek. Their living sites include both large coastal settlements, perhaps permanently occupied, such as Ertebølle, and smaller, seasonally occupied camps [**12.18**]. Coastal sites in northern Denmark are dominated by shell middens, while special-purpose sites were devoted to the hunting of seals or swans. The social complexity of Ertebølle communities is revealed by cemeteries, such as those at Skateholm and Vedbaek, where differential treatment of the dead may indicate social ranking. One grave at Vedbaek held the body of

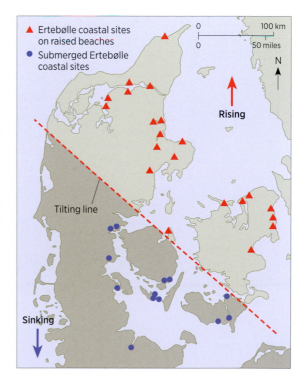

▲ Ertebølle coastal sites on raised beaches

● Submerged Ertebølle coastal sites

0   100 km
0   50 miles
N

Rising

Tilting line

Sinking

KEY CONTROVERSY Stonehenge: Symbolism and Ceremony

Stonehenge is probably the most famous megalithic monument in western Europe, and has been the subject of antiquarian and archaeological inquiry since the seventeenth century. The site is best known for its stone structures, notably the five massive trilithons, each formed of two uprights supporting a horizontal stone slab, at the heart of the monument, and the linteled ring that surrounds them and gives Stonehenge its characteristic appearance [**12.19**].

Preseli: The Magic Mountain?

The earliest stone structures at Stonehenge were not the large sarsen (silicified sandstone) trilithons and linteled ring, with individual stones up to 9 meters (29.5 feet) tall and 36 metric tons (40 US tons) in weight, but the more modest bluestones. Some of these may originally have been set up in the fifty-six Aubrey Holes around the perimeter of the enclosing bank, and others in a small stone circle (Bluestonehenge) on the banks of the River Avon. The bluestones measure around 2 meters (6.6 feet) in height and weigh on average between 2 and 4 metric tons (2.2–5.5 US tons), yet what they lack in size they make up for in provenance. Petrological study in the 1920s showed that they had come from southwest Wales, a distance of 230 kilometers (143 miles) as the crow flies. They were moved from the Aubrey Holes and Bluestonehenge to form a double stone circle at the center of Stonehenge, but when the sarsen structures were built they were moved again, and later re-erected in a circle and horseshoe among the central sarsen structures, echoing their plan.

The modest dimensions and unremarkable appearance of the bluestones make it difficult to understand why they were brought from such a distance, but the answer probably lies in the significance of the place from which they were derived: the Preseli Hills in south Wales [**12.20**].

12.19 OPPOSITE Stonehenge began as a circular enclosure with a bank and ditch, with a ring of stones (probably the bluestones) around its inner edge (Stonehenge 1, *c*. 2950 BCE). The central stone structures built of large sarsens (local sandstone blocks) were added several centuries later (*c*. 2500–2400 BCE).

12.20 RIGHT The rocky spur of Craig Rhos-y-felin in the Preseli Hills of southwest Wales has been identified as one of the sources of the Stonehenge bluestones.

Death and the Ancestors

Stonehenge does not stand isolated and alone, but is at the heart of a dense cluster of monuments. Conspicuous among these are Early Bronze Age round barrows, some furnished with elaborate grave goods, testimony to the powerful attraction of Stonehenge in later centuries. Being buried within sight of the monument was evidently considered especially desirable. Somewhat earlier in date, and contemporary with the sarsen structures at Stonehenge, is the site of Durrington Walls. This vast earthwork enclosure, almost 400 meters (1,312 feet) across with a bank and a ditch up to 6 meters (20 feet) deep, was excavated in the 1960s and shown to enclose at least two structures of concentric timber posts.

A short distance to the south of Durrington Walls, the smaller enclosure of Woodhenge (one of the first sites to be discovered by aerial photography, in the 1920s) also contained concentric circles of timber posts. Drawing on Madagascan ethnography, archaeologists have proposed that the timber circles of Woodhenge and Durrington Walls were ceremonial centers for the living, whereas the stone structures of Stonehenge were designed for the ancestors and the dead.

The southern entrance at Durrington was linked to the River Avon by a formal roadway; a short journey downstream would have brought travelers to the end of the double-banked avenue leading up to Stonehenge. Furthermore, analysis of butchered animal bones (predominantly pig) from Durrington Walls has revealed that these were culled around midwinter, suggesting that this was a place of midwinter feasting. Analysis of stable isotopes in the animal bones has shown that some of the cattle and pigs had been brought here from considerable distances, perhaps as far afield as Scotland. The well-known alignment of Stonehenge on the midsummer solstice sunrise should be reversed, since the same axis also lines up with midwinter sunset in the opposite direction.

Another remarkable discovery from excavations at Durrington Walls has been traces of circular Neolithic houses sited both within and outside the enclosure, and beneath the earthwork's bank. The more elaborate of these may have been residences of ritual specialists; others may have been the dwellings of people congregating for seasonal ceremonies at Durrington Walls and Stonehenge, or even perhaps to participate in the construction of Stonehenge.

If Stonehenge was an ancestral place, then it was also a locus for burial from the thirtieth century BCE down to the twenty-third century BCE, when inhumation replaced cremation at the site. The Aubrey Holes inside the perimeter bank and ditch contained cremated remains of an estimated 150 people, perhaps the successive burials of a single powerful family or lineage.

a young woman with a newborn baby laid on a swan's wing to her right, a reminder that burial practices reflect emotive ties and not just the social status of the deceased.

The Late Mesolithic communities had been for several centuries living alongside farming neighbors to the south, and contact between the two is shown by numerous imports of polished stone axes by Ertebølle communities. But shortly before 4000 BCE, the Ertebølle culture disappeared and was replaced by Early Neolithic groups belonging to the Trichterbecher culture. Genetic analyses reveal that this Neolithic population consisted largely of incoming farmers, presumably moving into the region from the south.

EARLY FARMING COMMUNITIES: NORTHERN EUROPE, 4000–2000 BCE

The Neolithic of south Scandinavia shared many features found in other areas of western Europe, such as long earthen mounds covering timber mortuary houses that can be paralleled in Britain and northern France. These long mounds may have been modeled on the longhouses that were a characteristic feature of the Bandkeramik settlements of central Europe. Megalithic tombs were also built in large numbers in southern Scandinavia and northern Germany from 3650–3000 BCE. Some of the greatest densities of megalithic tombs in Neolithic Europe were found in this region.

An important feature of north European ritual practices was the deposition of pottery and other offerings in wetland or marshy locations, probably as tributes to gods or ancestors. This may owe something to previous Mesolithic practices, despite the break in cultural continuity that the Neolithic transition seems to represent. These dedications include a number of human skeletons with marks or other signs of violence, such as the two Boldkilde bodies (c. 3400 BCE), one of them with a rope round his neck. Offerings were also made at dry-land locations, such as megalithic tombs, and in enclosures formed of multiple circuits of ditches and banks with frequent interruptions or entrances. At Büdelsdorf in northern Germany, a ritual earthwork enclosure founded around 3750 BCE was replaced by a settlement, before that in turn was replaced by another enclosure, in c. 3300 BCE. In southern Scandinavia, enclosures of the period c. 3400–3150 BCE show characteristic evidence of frequent modification. It may be that the construction of these enclosures was itself the key aspect of ritual practice, although pottery, animal bones, and human remains from the interior indicate that feasting and mortuary rituals may also have been carried out there. One suggestion is that bodies of the dead were buried in the enclosure ditches and then exhumed after they had

KEY THEME: MIGRATION Migration from the Steppes?

Recent genetic evidence suggests that eastern and central Europe experienced major population change c. 2800 BCE with the arrival of new groups from the Eurasian steppes. These were the Yamnaya people, herding communities with a distinctive burial practice in which the graves, usually containing a single individual, were covered by a mound and, in the case of males, the dead man was equipped with a battle axe. The practice can be traced across Europe from the Black Sea to Scandinavia and northern Germany, where it is represented in the Corded Ware or Single Grave culture of the north European plain. It has been suggested that these newcomers spoke an Indo-European language, ancestral to those spoken in Europe today. Indo-European languages include most living European languages (French, Spanish, English, German, Greek, Russian, etc.) and also some dead languages (for example Latin).

decomposed, the bones being placed in neighboring megalithic tombs. The fragmentation of bodies after death, and the circulation of bones as relics, appear to have been widespread practices in European prehistory.

Polished stone axes were a prominent feature of northern Europe, and the circulation of axe blades of Alpine jadeitite, common at the time in western Europe, extends into southern Scandinavia. Axe heads of exotic materials, such as these, were here again connected with display and prestige, as well as more practical tasks. Between 2900 and 2350 BCE, elaborate stone axes with shaft holes for hafting became common. Usually referred to as battle-axes, they are associated with a shift in burial practice to individual graves beneath circular mounds. This indicates a growing concern with the expression of status. A new kind of drinking vessel, the Corded Ware beaker (named for its cord-impressed decoration), also features in these graves. The appearance of Corded Ware and battle-axes in northern and central Europe *c.* 2800 BCE may mark an event of major significance: the arrival of Yamnaya groups from the Eurasia steppes, north of the Black Sea (see Key Theme box: Migration—Migration from the Steppes?).

LATER FARMING COMMUNITIES: BRONZE AGE EUROPE, 2300–800 BCE

By 3000 BCE, the continent of Europe, save for the Arctic fringes and the high mountains, was peopled by farming communities practicing plow agriculture and the raising of cattle, pig, sheep, and goat. It was at this point that Yamnaya immigrants from the Eurasian steppe zone appeared in northern and central Europe, bringing with them a new ideology. Social change was felt not only in these regions, however, but also in western Europe, where the expansion of Beakers and related artifact sets represents the spread of a similar dominant ideology. Single graves under circular mounds also become a key feature of the archaeological record.

Over the following 2,000 years, European societies underwent a series of technological and social changes. Among the most important was the adoption of bronze metallurgy. Copper, as we have seen, was already being worked in the fifth millennium BCE in southeastern Europe. The introduction of bronze, involving the alloying of copper with the much rarer tin, at the end of the third millennium BCE forced a realignment and extension of exchange networks far beyond what had been present during the Neolithic. Of the two constituent elements of bronze—copper and tin—the copper (some 90 percent of the bronze alloy) came from a number of sources in mountainous regions. The second element of bronze, tin (10 percent of the alloy), is much less widely available, and the principal European sources exploited in prehistory were in northern Bohemia and the Atlantic zone, especially Cornwall in Britain. The demand for tin from limited and distant sources set up a series of exchange networks across Europe, along which other prized materials, such as Baltic amber, also circulated. The result gave a certain international character to the metalwork traditions of the European Bronze Age, where similar forms of artifact are found across wide areas.

Central and Western Europe and Bell Beakers

Central and western Europe from 2500 BCE witnessed the appearance of what is known as the Bell Beaker tradition, defined by the appearance of a distinctive kind of pottery vessel, the bell beaker, which came into widespread use from Spain to Scandinavia and inland as far as what is now the Czech Republic. These vessels, which frequently accompanied their owners in death as grave offerings, represent the spread of a fashion or a drinking tradition, and are associated with a range of other luxury items: copper daggers, gold ornaments, and fine stone perforated plaques interpreted as archers' wristguards.

The origin of the Beaker vessel itself may lie in western Iberia, but it was soon taken up and reproduced in numerous regional variants. Study of the contents, where these have been preserved, has suggested that the beakers may have held a honey-based (probably fermented) drink, or possibly beer. The importance of Beaker pottery is its wide expansion across western and central Europe, and evidence for long-distance connections, especially along the Atlantic seaways and the river routes, such as the Rhine, leading into the European interior. The new metallurgy of copper and bronze soon spread along these same routes.

Beakers in graves are associated primarily with individual interments; usually covered by a circular mound. The Amesbury Archer grave [**12.21**] in south-central England near Stonehenge contained the skeleton of a man aged thirty-five to forty-five years old, accompanied by an archer's equipment (fifteen finely flaked barbed-and-tanged arrowheads of flint, and two polished stone wristguards), plus five decorated Beaker vessels, three copper knives, a pair of gold hair ornaments, and a black cushion stone for metalworking. Metallurgical knowledge, then, may have been directly connected to social status. The Amesbury burial also demonstrates the interregional contacts characteristic of the Beaker phenomenon in another way, since oxygen isotope analysis of the man's teeth indicated that he had lived as a child in mainland Europe. Therefore new skills and technologies may have been spread by the movement of individuals as much as by the transfer of knowledge. This was part of a much broader pattern of movement into Britain from continental Europe: DNA studies indicate a great influx of migrants from across the North Sea bringing with them Beaker pottery and other features, although contacts along the Atlantic seaways were also important.

The single grave under a modest circular mound became a feature of northern and northwestern Europe during the early second millennium BCE. The Beaker vessel disappears from the graves, but individual wealth and status are indicated by metal objects, now of bronze or gold. Male prestige is marked by finely crafted bronze daggers, and by plaques or other ornaments of gold. Bronze objects also occur in metal hoards, especially in central Germany. A particularly flamboyant metalworking tradition developed in Denmark, rather unexpectedly given the lack of local copper ores. Danish Bronze Age societies did, however, have access to the highly prized Baltic amber, which was used extensively in necklaces and ornaments and was traded as far afield as Italy, Greece, and Syria.

12.21 The Amesbury Archer. This burial, excavated in 2002, is the most richly furnished Beaker grave yet to have been found in Britain. The grave pit (which may have been timber-lined and covered by a small turf mound) contained the skeleton of a thirty-five- to forty-five-year-old man accompanied by archer's equipment.

The bronze that was obtained in exchange was cast into axes and daggers and fashioned into special objects, such as the sun chariot from Trundholm (*c.* 1650 BCE) [**12.22**]. Cult activities are also represented in rock art of the period from both south Scandinavia (see pp. 264–65) and northern Italy. Both bronzes and rock art show an emphasis on ships, solar imagery, and the male warrior.

Social Hierarchies. In central and northern Europe, new kinds of elite social groups arose from 2000 BCE, their wealth and power based on cattle herds and supported by bands of warrior retainers. At the same time, entire sceneries of burial mounds were created, and bronze axes and other objects deposited in marginal and watery locations. These were landscapes structured in entirely new ways.

In southern Scandinavia, a few very large longhouses surrounded by cleared forest and farmsteads are known, which probably represent chiefly residences [**12.23**]. On the higher ridges visible from the farmsteads, thousands of barrows (tumuli) were built, some of them 9 meters (29.5 feet) tall, others 3 to 4 meters (10 to 13 feet). The most striking evidence of social hierarchies are the oak-coffin burials dating to 1300 BCE, where the structure and materials of the burial mound led to the preservation of tree-trunk coffins, bodies, and clothing, along with wooden furniture.

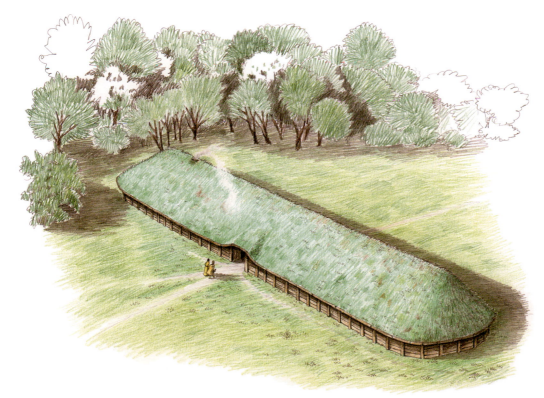

12.22 The Trundholm sun chariot. This bronze wheeled model of a horse pulling a large disk was discovered in a peat bog on the Danish island of Zealand in 1902. It has been dated to around 1650 BCE and was probably buried as a ritual offering. One face of the disk is covered with gold leaf, representing the sun, while it has been suggested that the other face, left plain, represents the moon.

12.23 Danish longhouses. Reconstruction of an Early Bronze Age longhouse from western Denmark.

12.24 The oak-coffin burial from Egtved in Denmark and its contents, c. 1370 BCE. The burial mound covered the grave of a teenage girl who had spent her childhood in southwest Germany and had come to Denmark perhaps through a marriage alliance. The waterlogged conditions led to the survival of many of the organic elements, including the oak coffin iself and the clothing she was buried in, but not her skeletal remains.

Best known of the tree-trunk coffin burials is that of **Egtved**, Denmark, where a woman aged sixteen to eighteen years was laid to rest around 1370 BCE [**12.24**]. Analysis of teeth, fingernails, hair, and preserved woollen clothing all indicate an origin most probably in the Black Forest region of southern Germany. Tooth enamel showed that she had passed her childhood outside Denmark. Strontium analysis of hair samples was particularly revealing, indicating that she had been away from Denmark for two periods during the last two years of her life, returning only a short time before her death.

Eastern Europe, c. 2300–700 BCE

In western Europe, the wide distribution of Beaker vessels points to the existence of international networks around 2500 BCE. In eastern Europe, similar long-distance fashions and contacts are shown most strikingly by the distribution of bronzes. The extensive metal deposits of the Carpathian Mountains gave rise to a flourishing Bronze Age characterized by elaborately cast and decorated swords, axes, and metal vessels. These suggest that individuals were now able to set themselves apart by the possession and display of high-quality metalwork, a trend that ultimately resulted in the rise of a warrior elite.

The widely shared traditions of bronze artifacts—especially swords—may be interpreted as the movement not only of objects, but also possibly of people. Swords were costly to produce and were copied over wide areas. The great amounts of metalwork in Denmark suggest that the region played a particularly important part in these networks, perhaps as the source of the highly prized Baltic amber found as far away as Mycenae in Greece and Qatna in Syria. Traveling in the opposite direction, glass beads from Egypt and Mesopotamia have been found in Danish graves dating to 1300 BCE.

Social hierarchy was expressed not only in material wealth and long-distance contacts but also in settlements. The fact that many became fortified could be further evidence of the impact that the accumulation of portable wealth had on the societies of the time. Some of this wealth found its way into hoards of metal objects. These societies had connections eastward onto the Russian steppes and northward into Poland and Denmark. Horse-drawn chariots appear in eastern Europe at this period, and horses, first domesticated on the steppes between 4000–2000 BCE but not yet used for riding, were another indicator of wealth and status.

12.25 Tell settlements in Hungary. Reconstruction of the Bronze Age tell settlement of Százhalombatta-Földvár in Hungary. The houses were carefully arranged and the whole settlement was surrounded by a fortified perimeter.

In Hungary, a pronounced settlement hierarchy is found, with villages forming tells. Houses and streets were carefully arranged, the former frequently rebuilt, and the villages were defended by a fortified perimeter [**12.25**]. By 2000 BCE, large and densely occupied tells had developed along the major rivers of Hungary.

Urnfields, c. 1300–700 BCE. The fortification of settlements continued in eastern Europe into the later part of the Bronze Age, after 1300 BCE. There were also important changes in burial ritual, beginning in the east and then spreading through central and western Europe. Cremation became the norm, with the ashes of the deceased collected and buried in pottery urns. These burials usually have few grave offerings, although they are sometimes accompanied by metalwork or sets of tableware. A key feature is the size of the cemeteries, called Urnfields, where the cremation burials were often grouped. Burials may number several thousand, suggesting that for the first time the bulk of the population is represented in the archaeological record. Most of these individuals received very similar treatment, with little indication of status differences. Wholly exceptional are the large mounded burials, such as Seddin in Germany, with a stone vaulted tomb chamber and a rich display of pottery and metal objects. These are the graves of the newly emergent elites.

Urnfield-period bronzeworkers were adept at the working of sheet metal; helmets and breastplates with elaborate chased and incised ornamentation were produced for highly ranked people. The development of longer bronze slashing swords, with the weight concentrated toward the end of the blade, is further evidence of serious conflict. In many areas, the threat of violence is also evident in the systematic fortification of settlements with ditches and ramparts or substantial timber stockades.

Among the most impressive of these fortified settlements was the waterlogged timber township of **Biskupin** in northern Poland. Set on a low marshy island on the edge of a lake, the settlement was surrounded by a timber rampart 463 meters (1,519 feet) long and originally some 6 meters (20 feet) high. Along the top was a walkway for the defenders, protected by a timber screen or stockade along its outer edge, while a timber tower may have stood over the single gateway with double-leaf door. The regularity and order of the Biskupin settlement strongly suggests the operation of a powerful central authority. The scale of the project may be judged from the estimated 80,000 trees that were felled to construct it.

The degree of communal organization required by projects, such as Biskupin or other hill and marsh forts of the early first millennium BCE, suggests that societies in this region were becoming more centralized, though still relatively small in scale when compared with the polities of the Mediterranean zone.

TRANSITIONS TO STATES: THE AEGEAN, *c.* 3000–1000 BCE

From 3000 BCE, the Aegean began to follow a different development from that of the rest of Europe. The Minoan and Mycenaean cultures of Crete and the Greek mainland rose and fell between 2000 and 1000 BCE. Although metallurgy spread rapidly throughout regions of Europe and the Mediterranean that had earlier adopted agriculture, within these areas it is in the Aegean that complex societies first developed in the Bronze Age, followed by other islands, such as Cyprus, in 2000 BCE.

Crete. In the period between around 3500 and 2000 BCE, which is called the Early Minoan, clear evidence of emerging social complexity is remarkably slight. Distinctive circular **tholos tombs** were built and used throughout the entire period as communal places of burial, but already they often contained hundreds of corpses. The fact that these were deposited over many centuries indicates that the social groups who used them were quite small in scale. A handful of cemeteries, such as the one at Mochlos in eastern Crete, provide plausible evidence of significant disparities of wealth between graves or family plots.

An important development unique to Crete around 2500 BCE is the indication of contact with Egypt and the Levant, either directly or indirectly. A century or more before the first palaces appear in Crete (see below), there are imports of Egyptian scarabs and stone vessels, **faience**, ivory, lapis lazuli, seals, and several types of semi-precious stones. It is probable that the emergent Cretan elite used these imports to help establish their identity, based on their associations with foreign powers, and to legitimize their authority by controlling exotic materials.

From *c.* 2000–1700 BCE, complexes, such as Knossos and Mallia on the north coast of Crete, and Phaistos in the south, rise in what is known as the First Palace period. These complexes or palaces were remodeled following the destructive earthquakes in what is known as the Second Palace period (*c.* 1700–1490 BCE). While far from identical, the palaces share many features. They are both monumental, but without defensive walls, and with large open-air central courts, residential quarters, and various spaces for performances, adorned with brightly frescoed walls. Various systems of seals and sealings, and two forms of script (hieroglyphic and Linear A, the language of which is unknown) emerged as administrative technologies.

At the end of the Second Palace period, all but one of the palaces were destroyed. Knossos survived, but a new administration was put in place, one employing certain new styles of material culture and, more strikingly, the Linear B script—a version of the Linear A writing that had been used in palaces but was now employed to express the Greek language of the

tholos tomb (pl. tholoi) a circular tomb with a domed or conical roof, also called a beehive tomb

faience a type of ceramic with a glass-like appearance

mainland (see Key Discovery box: Linear B, p. 292). What happened is not known. Arguments range from invasion to peaceful annexation. Some have argued that Crete had been weakened through the effects of a major volcanic eruption on the Cycladic island of Thera (Santorini) early in the Late Bronze Age, though this has been dated as much earlier (*c.* 1600 BCE) than the first signs of destabilization. Whatever the explanation, Crete and the Minoans passed into the political control of a new regional power, Mycenae.

Mycenaean Greece. In the late seventeenth and sixteenth centuries BCE, a series of palace-based, territorial kingdoms rose throughout the southern and central Greek mainland. We know a good deal about several of these polities from the evidence preserved in Linear B tablets.

The site of Mycenae lies in the northeast corner of the Peloponnese. Homeric legends led archaeologists to work here, including Heinrich Schliemann in the 1870s who discovered a grave circle containing rich burials of bodies furnished with golden masks [**12.26**]. The site sits on a commanding hill, and in contrast to Minoan centers, was strongly fortified with massive walls of masonry. Another key feature of the site is the megaron: a three-roomed rectangular structure with a porch leading to an antechamber, and then to a columned hall with central hearth. This was assumed to have been the seat of power of the Mycenaean ruler.

Mycenaean influence overseas is most readily traceable in the spread of fine pottery, or imitations of it, which is very widely found around the shores of the eastern Mediterranean in Egypt, the Levant, Cyprus, Crete, and many of the Aegean islands, as well as in Italy, Sicily, and Sardinia. Trade seems to have been the principal mechanism involved in this, and the acquisition of metal resources necessary for bronzeworking may have been one of the motives for it.

The End of the Aegean Bronze Age. During the thirteenth century BCE, the citadel of Mycenae and neighboring sites reveal signs of renewed or enhanced fortification. Despite such efforts the Mycenaean palaces were destroyed or abandoned over the course of several decades toward *c.* 1200 BCE. What caused this remains a source of scholarly controversy. Troubles local to the Mycenaean world, such as warfare between kingdoms, internal unrest, and crop failure, seem the most plausible explanations, although more complex scenarios involving external raiders have also been envisaged. By 1050 BCE, the craft production, rich burials, great fortifications, and the use of the Linear B script were over, and the Mycenaean monuments began to pass into memory and myth.

12.26 Gold mask.
The most famous of the golden masks, dating to the sixteenth century BCE, discovered by Heinrich Schliemann in Grave Circle A at Mycenae in 1876. Schliemann, who relied heavily on myth in his interpretations, believed he was gazing upon the face of King Agamemnon.

KEY DISCOVERY Linear B

In his first excavation season at Knossos, Crete, in 1900, Sir Arthur Evans, the British archaeologist, discovered large numbers of inscribed clay tablets, the language of which was then unknown [**12.27 a–d**]. Exploration soon afterward at other major Minoan sites also yielded small quantities of tablets with inscriptions, but in a writing system related to, yet distinct from, that at Knossos. Both scripts seemed more highly developed than the arrangements of small pictures of objects sometimes found on engraved sealstones, clay bars, and other prehistoric objects.

As we now appreciate, these are the three main categories of Minoan script, which Evans termed, respectively, Linear B, Linear A, and hieroglyphic (from its generic resemblances to Egyptian writing). Hieroglyphic emerged *c.* 2000 BCE, around the time of the first palaces, whereas Linear A was the principal script in use, mainly in administrative and ritual contexts, from the eighteenth century BCE until the end of the Second Palace era, a little after 1500 BCE. Linear B clearly developed from Linear A, and was in widespread use throughout much of the fourteenth and thirteenth centuries BCE on the Greek mainland, at such sites as Mycenae.

Decipherment and Content

The tablets remained undeciphered for more than fifty years until in 1951 the young British architect Michael Ventris collated an adequate supply of material for a decipherment of Linear B as an early form of Greek. Mindful of the range of subject matter encountered in the immense archives of Mesopotamian palaces, there were those who had hoped that the Linear B documents would reveal Mycenaean legal and business records, letters, annals, royal inscriptions, perhaps even an early version of Homeric poetry. Even prior to their decipherment, however, their brevity, layout, and easily recognizable ideograms made it obvious that these documents dealt mostly with the mundane administrative concerns of the palaces. Nevertheless, during the six decades since the decipherment, impressive amounts of information have been teased out of the several thousand tablets published.

We now know a great deal about the detailed workings of palace-controlled industries concerned with textiles, flax, and perfumed oil, including the distribution of rations

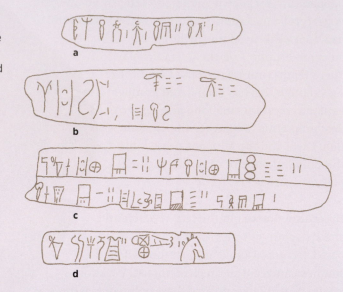

12.27 a–d Linear B tablets from Knossos showing ideograms representing:
a: a man, woman, two girls, and one boy;
b: 50 rams and 50 ewes;
c: different kinds of cloth;
d: a horse, chariot, and tunic.
Examples of leaf-shaped tablets, they were created by forming a clay cylinder, which was then squashed to provide a smooth writing surface.

to different categories of female and male workers. There are sets of tablets dealing (enigmatically) with landholding; others provide powerful evidence that a number of Classical Greek deities (Athena, Poseidon, and Zeus, for instance) were worshiped already in Mycenaean times; and studies of place names have given some sense of the political geography of Mycenaean kingdoms on the mainland and in Crete. Most recently, tablets and sealings from Thebes in Boeotia appear to reveal evidence of state-sponsored feasting. Considering how brief and fragmentary most Linear B texts are, and how routine and commonplace their subject matter, it is remarkable how much valuable information has been extracted from them about Mycenaean society as a whole.

SUMMARY AND CONCLUSIONS

This chapter has described the development of societies in Europe from the end of the last Ice Age to the end of the Bronze Age. A number of key themes have been identified. The first concerns the transformation of the European environment during the earlier postglacial period. This process had begun several millennia earlier as the ice sheets began to retreat, but reached its peak around 10,000 years ago, as sea levels rose steeply. Human communities responded to the new opportunities offered by the warmer climate, recolonizing northern latitudes.

A second theme of this chapter has been the spread of farming, beginning earliest in the southeast and progressively supplanting hunting and gathering across the continent. The origins of the domesticated plants and animals that were adopted lay in Southwest Asia, and analysis of ancient DNA indicates that movement of colonist farmers from Anatolia was primarily responsible for introducing the new economy into southeastern Europe, and further expansion and migration carried it across central Europe and the Mediterranean zone. As farming spread to Iberia, Britain, and Scandinavia, indigenous hunter-gatherer populations were steadily absorbed into the new Neolithic communities.

The key theme of the later prehistoric period is the development of social complexity. The adoption of copper and gold may not only have been significant in itself, but also a marker of other changes, notably the increasing differentiation of individuals and elites. The growing circulation of materials during the second millennium BCE created and reinforced connections between different regions, which are also reflected in the wide distribution of certain artifact types and burial practices. In the eastern Mediterranean, these exchange networks fueled the rise of palace-based polities in the Aegean.

FURTHER READING

The following provide useful general introductions to European prehistory:

Broodbank, C. 2013. *The Making of the Middle Sea: A History of the Mediterranean from the Beginning to the Emergence of the Classical World*. London: Thames & Hudson.

Cunliffe, B. 2001. *Facing the Ocean: The Atlantic and Its Peoples*. Oxford: Oxford University Press.

Cunliffe, B. 2008. *Europe between the Oceans: 9000 BC to AD 1000*. London and New Haven: Yale University Press.

Earle, T. and Kristiansen, K. (eds.). 2010. *Organizing Bronze Age Societies*. Cambridge: Cambridge University Press.

Fokkens, H. and Harding, A. F. (eds.). 2013. *The Oxford Handbook of the European Bronze Age*. Oxford: Oxford University Press.

Fowler, C. *et al.* (eds.). 2015. *The Oxford Handbook of Neolithic Europe*. Oxford: Oxford University Press.

Harding, A. F. 2000. *European Societies in the Bronze Age*. Cambridge: Cambridge University Press.

Shennan, S. 2018. *The First Farmers of Crete. An Evolutionary Perspective*. Cambridge: Cambridge University Press.

Africa

13

Graham Connah

Environments and Landscapes 297

Hunter-Gatherer Trajectories: Intensified Hunting, Gathering, and Fishing, *c*. 9000–5000 BCE 297

KEY CONTROVERSY Symbolism in Southern African Rock Art 298

Transitions to Agriculture: From Cattle Domestication to the Bantu Expansion, 7000 BCE**–500** CE 301

Early States: Ancient Egypt, 3500–1070 BCE 304

KEY DISCOVERY Insights from the Pyramids 307

KEY THEME: URBANIZATION The Concept of Urbanization in Africa 308

Early States: Nubia and Ethiopia, 1500 BCE**–700** CE 310

KEY SITE Ethiopia's Rock-Cut Churches 312

Early Farming Communities: Ironworking Farmers in Central, Western, and Southern Africa, 1000 BCE**–1900** CE 313

KEY CONTROVERSY The Origins of African Ironworking 314

KEY DISCOVERY Nok: Unique Sculptures by Iron-Using Farmers 315

Early States: The Sahara and West Africa, 500–1500 CE 315

Early States: Eastern, Southern, and Central Africa, 1000–1900 CE 316

KEY CONTROVERSY Postcolonial Archaeology in Africa 318

Summary and Conclusions 320

Further Reading 321

Aerial view of the Hill Complex at the site of Great Zimbabwe, dated to the thirteenth to fifteenth centuries CE.

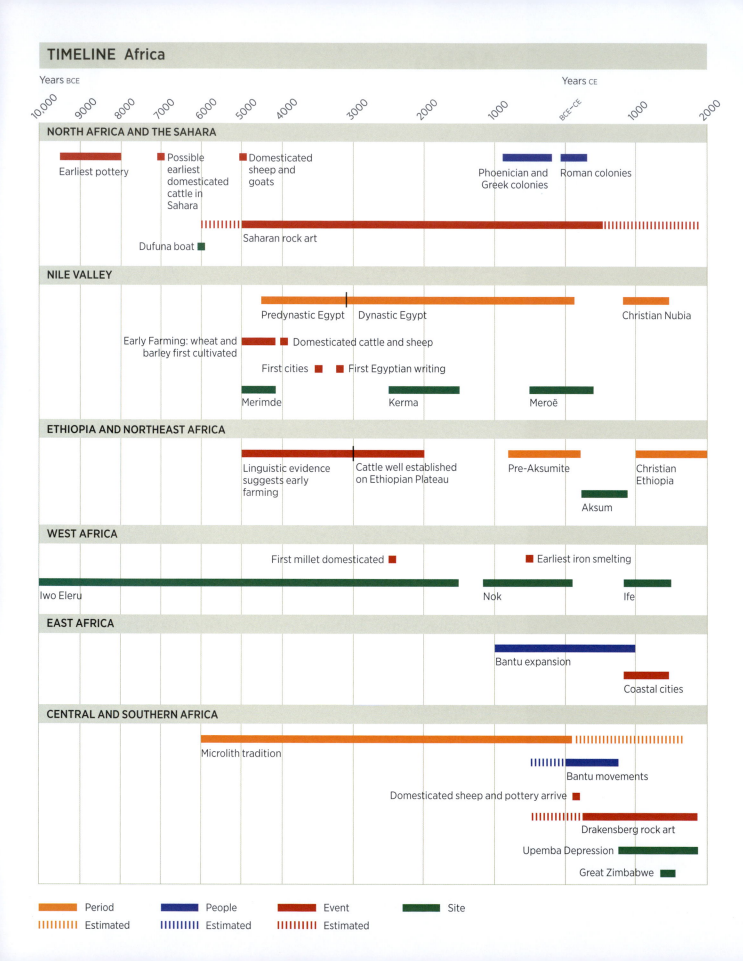

TIMELINE Africa

Years BCE
Years CE

10,000 9000 8000 7000 6000 5000 4000 3000 2000 1000 BCE–CE 1000 2000

NORTH AFRICA AND THE SAHARA

Earliest pottery

Possible earliest domesticated cattle in Sahara

Domesticated sheep and goats

Phoenician and Greek colonies

Roman colonies

Dufuna boat

Saharan rock art

NILE VALLEY

Predynastic Egypt   Dynastic Egypt

Christian Nubia

Early Farming: wheat and barley first cultivated

Domesticated cattle and sheep

First cities

First Egyptian writing

Merimde

Kerma

Meroë

ETHIOPIA AND NORTHEAST AFRICA

Linguistic evidence suggests early farming

Cattle well established on Ethiopian Plateau

Pre-Aksumite

Christian Ethiopia

Aksum

WEST AFRICA

First millet domesticated

Earliest iron smelting

Iwo Eleru

Nok

Ife

EAST AFRICA

Bantu expansion

Coastal cities

CENTRAL AND SOUTHERN AFRICA

Microlith tradition

Bantu movements

Domesticated sheep and pottery arrive

Drakensberg rock art

Upemba Depression

Great Zimbabwe

Period   People   Event   Site

Estimated   Estimated   Estimated

Previous chapters have described origins and development of the earliest humans in Africa, up to the end of the Ice Age. The present chapter takes up the story from the beginning of the postglacial period, around 9600 BCE.

Hunting and gathering were the mainstays of human communities in Africa at the beginning of the postglacial period and continued to be important down to recent times in the south, where they are associated with a vibrant rock-art tradition. Further north, hunter-gatherer communities developed or adopted agriculture, notably cattle-rearing in a then-verdant Sahara. Subsequently, states developed in a number of regions—Egypt in the north, Great Zimbabwe in the south, and Ife and Benin in the west. One of the most profound changes was the expansion of the Bantu societies and languages from an origin in West Africa to much of eastern and southern Africa, replacing or absorbing previous populations.

- Cattle-herding was the first form of domestication in Africa, and may have begun as early as 7000 BCE.

- The earliest state in Africa, Egypt, was made possible by rich agricultural land confined to a narrow band along the Nile.

- Other early states in Africa include Kerma and Meroë in Sudan; Ghana, Songhai, Ife, and Benin in West Africa; and Great Zimbabwe in the south.

- In Africa south of the Sahara, iron was the first metal used for tools, c. 500 BCE.

ENVIRONMENTS AND LANDSCAPES

Africa is larger than the United States, China, and Australia combined. In places, it has some of the world's highest temperatures, but in others they can fall below freezing point, and rainfall varies from more than 4,000 millimeters (156 inches) a year to virtually nothing. For much of the continent, the seasons consist of a hot, dry season and a cool, wet one, occupying opposing parts of the year north and south of the Equator.

The early postglacial in Africa, from 9600 BCE, saw climatic changes that altered the extent and location of vegetation zones [13.1, p. 298], with deserts, savannas, and rainforests alternately expanding and contracting, forcing societies to adapt.

HUNTER-GATHERER TRAJECTORIES: INTENSIFIED HUNTING, GATHERING, AND FISHING, c. 9000–5000 BCE

Lifestyles dependent on hunting and gathering were developed by early modern humans in Africa (see Chapter 4), but it was only later hunting, gathering, and fishing groups (see 13.4, p. 300) (and some early farming societies) that adopted the use of microliths. These were tiny blades and flakes of stone, of which one edge was blunted to make them easier to handle or to mount in a composite tool. The microliths indicate a more efficient use of stone as people on the African continent began to exploit the environment more intensively.

Southern and Central Africa

In much of southern Africa, postglacial hunter-gatherers are best known archaeologically from microlith assemblages from about 6000 BCE onward. These appear to have been made

13.1 Map showing African vegetation.
The vegetation of Africa is characterized by a series of east–west zones each side of the Equator and a more complex pattern in the high country of East Africa. The vegetation ranges from rainforest through increasingly dry savanna and steppe to desert, with Mediterranean vegetation at the northern and southern extremes of the continent and montane vegetation in parts of East Africa.

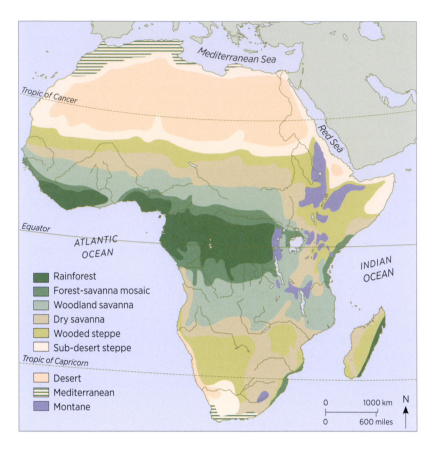

Legend:
- Rainforest
- Forest-savanna mosaic
- Woodland savanna
- Dry savanna
- Wooded steppe
- Sub-desert steppe
- Desert
- Mediterranean
- Montane

KEY CONTROVERSY Symbolism in Southern African Rock Art

Prehistoric rock art offers an intimate document of past societies, but it has frequently frustrated archaeologists because it can be read in different ways and is often difficult to date. Research in southern Africa suggests that more recent rock art has deep symbolic meaning. The South African archaeologist Patricia Vinnicombe showed that the paintings of the Drakensberg Mountains, in southeastern South Africa, included more depictions of the antelope known as the eland than of other animals, although the eland was not a major dietary element of the people who made the art, contradicting the assumption that rock art only betrayed preoccupations with hunting. Ethnohistorical sources showed that a strong ritual relationship had existed between the people and the eland, the animal serving as a link between the material and the spiritual worlds; the idealized paintings provided ritual symbols that were thought of as a source of power [**13.2**]. It remains unclear, however, how far back in time Vinnicombe's interpretations can be applied. Some of the Drakensberg art dates only from recent centuries, making the use of the ethnohistorical sources justifiable, but it is less certain that they are relevant to much older art.

13.2 The eland, a type of antelope, was frequently depicted by hunter-gatherer artists in South Africa. It is thought that there was a strong ritual relationship between people and the eland, the animal serving as a link with the spiritual world and therefore its representation providing a powerful ritual symbol.

by people belonging to the Khoisan language family, spoken today by the Khoekhoen and San groups, who continued their foraging lifestyle in some parts of southern Africa until recent times. Organic remains recovered from dry cave deposits in southernmost Africa, and from waterlogged sites, such as the prehistoric settlements at Gwisho hot springs in southern Zambia, show that these communities used wooden bows, arrows, and digging sticks, made bark into trays, and sewed leather into bags and clothing. The dead were buried accompanied by tools, personal ornaments, and other items, sometimes including painted stones, perhaps indicating a belief in an afterlife. People also adorned themselves with beads and pendants of bone, ostrich eggshell, or freshwater shell.

Rock Art. These communities also created rock art. The hunter-gatherer rock art of southern Africa extends as far north as Zimbabwe, Zambia, Malawi, and Tanzania. Because rock paintings are usually situated in relatively exposed locations, in shallow caves or on stony outcrops, it is thought that many date to only the last few thousand years, although engravings could be much older. At Apollo 11 cave in southern Namibia, however, naturalistic paintings of animals have been found on loose stone slabs in contexts dated to as early as 26,000 years ago.

Frequent depictions of the eland, an animal that was important in San beliefs, and of people apparently in a state of trance, a practice known from the southern San, have been used to reconstruct aspects of prehistoric belief systems (see Key Controversy box: Symbolism in Southern African Rock Art). Rock art appears to be rare in much of Central Africa, where climatic conditions and limited research restrict the archaeological record of later hunter-gatherers mainly to stone artifacts.

13.3 Illustration of a rock painting of a trance dance. A southern African depiction showing five men in a characteristic bent-forward position, who are supporting themselves on dancing sticks. To the left and right women are clapping the rhythm of a ritual song, which intensifies the altered state of consciousness that the men are entering.

There is a similar problem with the research in the same area by the archaeologist David Lewis-Williams. A central ritual for hunter-gatherers has been the trance dance, which is still practiced in the Kalahari. While women clap and sing songs about sources of supernatural power, such as the eland or giraffe, some men are able to dance themselves into a trance or, as they believe, to enter the spirit world. Acting as shamans, they are said to be able to cure the sick, resolve social conflict, and sometimes control game animals, including those that are thought to bring rain. Drawing on nineteenth-century ethnohistorical sources, Lewis-Williams argued that both the trance dance and the altered states of consciousness that it induced were depicted in the rock art of southern Africa [**13.3**]. Figures in a characteristic bent-forward position with blood pouring from the nose, and representations of fantastic creatures—part human, part animal—appear to relate directly to the trance dance and its experiences. The art, he argued, was not merely a record of such rituals but a stored source of potency that made contact with the spirit world possible. This approach has also influenced researchers in other parts of the world, leading some to claim that visionary imagery is widespread in such art, while others doubt this.

Although some of this art is known to be relatively recent, painted stones from the southern Cape with similar depictions might be 2,000 years old, while the date of much of the rest is unknown. Some of it seems to depict more mundane activities than trance dancing, and the question arises of the applicability of this symbolic approach to older rock art in southern Africa and to that in other parts of the continent. Clearly, rock-art interpretation raises fundamental questions about the use of information from recent or near-recent societies to interpret the remote past.

13.4 Intensified hunting, gathering, and fishing sites. These sites have been found in a wide range of environments and consist of both cave- or rock-shelter locations and open sites. In the south of the continent, this economy survived until recent times, meaning that ethnographic observations can assist in the interpretation of the archaeological evidence.

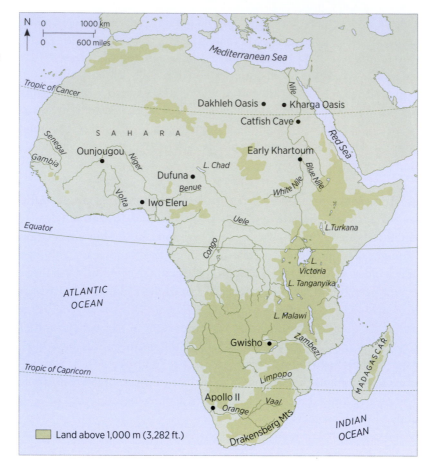

Northern, Eastern, and Western Africa

During the late Pleistocene and early postglacial, changes took place in hunter-gatherer societies in northern, eastern, and western Africa [**13.4**] that became the basis for later transitions to herding or cultivation or both.

North Africa and the Sahara. Before the postglacial period, there were already indications of economic intensification and perhaps the beginnings of sedentism among some hunter-gatherer communities in the Nile Valley, a relatively favorable but confined environment that contrasted with the generally uninhabitable Sahara.

At some sites in the Nile Valley, wild grasses were being gathered by about 8000 BCE. Far to the south, harpoons appeared by about 6000 BCE at Early Khartoum, where they were associated with microliths, decorated pottery and the remains of structures that suggest the adoption of a more sedentary life. And bone harpoons from Catfish Cave in southern Egypt suggest fishing by about 5000 BCE, although they could also have been used in hunting or human conflict.

In North Africa and the Sahara, the climate had become moister and cooler by about 9000 BCE, making parts of the desert that had not been occupied during the previous dry period habitable. Lakes, marshes, and rivers existed in some places where there have been none since. The impact on human settlement was complex: hunter-gatherers expanded into regions where they then became vulnerable to short-term climatic fluctuations, requiring a variety of adaptions. By around 7000–6500 BCE, evidence of stone-based huts at Dakhleh Oasis indicates a partly sedentary way of life, while about 6000 BCE, occupants of sites in the eastern Sahara, such as Kharga Oasis, appear to have been harvesting wild cereals.

Another feature of the occupation of the central and southern Sahara was sites on the shores of rivers and lakes; although hunting and grain-gathering were also practiced, fishing was important. A dugout canoe from Dufuna in northeast Nigeria dated to about 6000 BCE is the oldest known boat in Africa.

West Africa. Hunting and gathering intensified also in many parts of West Africa. One of the most important sites is Iwo Eleru, a rock shelter in the forest zone of southern Nigeria, where a mainly microlithic quartz industry dated to 10,000–1500 BCE increasingly used finer material, chalcedony, as time went on. Both ground-stone axes and pottery first appeared from 4000 BCE, and after about 2500 BCE some of the microliths had sheen on their edges, as if used for cutting plant material, accompanied by an increase in grindstones.

TRANSITIONS TO AGRICULTURE: FROM CATTLE DOMESTICATION TO THE BANTU EXPANSION, 7000 BCE–500 CE

The first African farming communities developed out of these intensifications of hunting and gathering, and of increasing sedentism. This change occurred at different times in different parts of Africa and in different ways. Farming was based on both indigenous and introduced animals and plants, and practiced by both partly mobile and increasingly sedentary societies.

Farming, especially in resource-rich areas, usually resulted in population increase and involved sociopolitical changes, such as the formation of urban communities. A powerful ruler could extend political and economic control over several larger settlements and their surroundings, leading to the emergence of African states, of which Egypt was the earliest. Almost all the earliest evidence of farming comes from north of the Equator.

The Sahara

The earliest farming seems to have been based on domesticated animals in the eastern Sahara. Pastoralism was probably the most reliable adaptation in marginal and fluctuating environments, where plant cultivation was less dependable. Wild cattle, a source of food for some hunter-gatherers, might have been herded as early as 9000–8000 BCE at Bir Kiseiba in the far south of Egypt. Nabta Playa, in the same area, had traces of huts, suggesting seasonal settlement and cattle-herding by about 7000 BCE. By 4800 BCE, these cattle-herding communities had built a monumental stone circle at Nabta Playa, which archaeologists have been able to associate with astronomical phenomena [**13.5**, p. 302].

The earliest pottery in the Sahara comes from Ounjougou in Mali, at the southern edge of the present desert, and dates from before 9400 BCE. This is the oldest pottery found in Africa and predates that from Southwest Asia. Only in Japan, Siberia, and China have earlier ceramics been found, dating from between 15,000 and 10,000 BCE. The reason why pottery appeared at this point may be due to a shift in diet. At this time, the savanna and lakes of the Sahara provided wild grass seeds, which might have been boiled into porridge, as well as fish that could be stewed into soup. Pots were most convenient for either process.

There has been considerable discussion concerning the earliest cattle-herding in Africa but it now seems probable that it was introduced from outside the continent, with possible

13.5 The stone circle at Nabta Playa. Some research suggests that it may have been a prehistoric calendar that accurately marked the summer solstice.

contributions from indigenous animals in the area presently occupied by the Sahara Desert. The main problem is the uncertain origin of the humpless, long-horned, taurine cattle that were the earliest African domesticates; were they indigenous or brought into Africa from Southwest Asia? Some support for the African domestication of native cattle has come from mitochondrial DNA evidence. Nevertheless, the osteological evidence for their differentiation from wild cattle is inconclusive. If Bir Kiseiba and Nabta Playa do represent the beginnings of cattle domestication in Africa, then its date of about 7000 BCE would make it at least as early as the first cattle domestication outside the continent. At all events, there is general agreement that domesticated cattle were present in the central Sahara by 5000 BCE.

Conditions in the desert deteriorated from 3000 BCE onward, and so cattle herds were taken south into areas of West and East Africa. These regions would have been unsuitable in previous periods when the environment was moister, because of the diseases transmitted by tsetse flies. This changed with climate. Whether or not cattle were domesticated in the Sahara, it was from there that the practice of cattle-herding spread into much of the rest of Africa.

The Nile Valley and West Africa

Farming began later in the Nile Valley than in the Sahara, but included cultivation as well as pastoralism. At **Merimde** on the western side of the Nile Delta, village dwellers were making pottery, cultivating barley, emmer wheat, and flax, and keeping cattle, sheep, goats, pigs, and dogs from about 5000 BCE. The settlement was occupied for almost a millennium. Such developments along the lower Nile appear to have been relatively sudden, and to have been brought about partly by the introduction of plants and animals from Southwest Asia.

In the West African savanna, pastoralists were present in Mali around 3000 BCE, and Lake Chad by 2000 BCE. As in the Sahara, there are indications that cultivation developed later than pastoralism. The important crops in the savanna zone were all indigenous to Africa, including pearl millet, West African rice (*Oryza glaberrima*), and sorghum. According to botanical and linguistic evidence, it was in the rainforest and its margins where indigenous yams and oil palms were first domesticated. Banana phytoliths have been recovered from Nkang, Cameroon, dated to *c.* 1000 BCE. Bananas are not indigenous to Africa and must have been introduced from Southeast Asia via the East African coast.

Northeast and East Africa

There is little archaeological evidence for early farming in northeast and East Africa. Almost certainly this lack is the result of limited research, because both botanical and linguistic evidence suggest an early date for farming in Ethiopia. Introduced wheat and barley have been grown there long enough for a number of varieties to develop, some of which are exclusive to the region.

In Eritrea, Ethiopia, and Somalia, numerous rock paintings illustrate the herding of cattle [**13.6**]. At Mahal Teglinos (in Sudan, close to the Eritrean border) there were cattle and sheep or goats by about 3000 BCE, and in Djibouti, domesticated cattle were present by 1500 BCE. In northern Kenya, domesticated sheep or goats and cattle were present close to the eastern shore of Lake Turkana by about 2000 BCE.

The expansion of pastoralism seems to have stopped moving southward for some time, halting at northern Tanzania. The probable reason for this is again the tsetse fly as well as trypanosomiasis (sleeping sickness), to which many domestic animals were vulnerable. It was probably only about 2,000 years ago that climatic changes and consequential changes in vegetation and wildlife opened up tsetse-free corridors to the south. By then, many communities had access to iron tools and weapons, and cultivation was becoming well established and by clearing woodland was helping to reduce the extent of the tsetse-infested areas.

13.6 Rock paintings of Laas Geel, Somaliland. These well-preserved paintings record early pastoralism. The oldest depictions could be dated to between the mid-third and the second millennium BCE and are characterized by humpless cows (visible here), sheep, and goats, as well as wild animals.

Movements of Bantu-Speaking Groups

One of the major events in the later prehistory of Africa was the expansion of Bantu groups across the center, east, and south of the continent, beginning probably before 1000 BCE and continuing into the first millennium BCE and the first millennium CE. Bantu-speaking communities not only introduced new languages in the areas into which they spread but also new lifestyles, where pottery-making and the use of large stone tools played an important role, as farming and metallurgy did subsequently. This major migration transformed human societies in Africa south of the Sahara.

On the basis of linguistic evidence, the Bantu migration began in the grassfields of Cameroon and gradually extended to the east through the savanna until it reached the region of East-Central Africa. From there people moved southward and westward into the savanna south of the equatorial forest. Migrations might also have taken place along the Atlantic coast, along grassy corridors opened up through the forest during a dry phase, or along the many rivers of equatorial Africa. Probably a complex series of small movements was involved, beginning perhaps as early as 2000 BCE and continuing until late in the first millennium CE.

13.7 Agricultural productivity, the economic basis of ancient Egypt. Painting in the Nineteenth Dynasty tomb of Sennedjem, Deir el-Medina, showing wheat and flax harvesting, plowing, and date and dom palms.

EARLY STATES: ANCIENT EGYPT, 3500–1070 BCE

Unlike pastoralism, farming appears to have encouraged both a growth in overall population and an increase in population density. The earliest example of this process in Africa occurred on the lower Nile in what is now Egypt. The Nile flooded annually, enriching the land with both water and fertile silt from the African interior, which, unlike Egypt, was well provided with seasonal rain. The floods supported a narrow strip of extraordinarily productive

farmland virtually surrounded by desert. This allowed for the growth of a large population and the rapid social, economic and political change that became the Egyptian state [**13.7**].

The Predynastic Period

With abundant agricultural resources came trading contacts with Southwest Asia—from where the working of copper, gold, and silver was probably introduced—and the growth of social hierarchies. Numerous villages were clustered along the Nile, and by about 3500 BCE there were large settlements at Hierakonpolis, Koptos, Naqada, and Abydos, all in Upper (southern) Egypt [**13.8**]. These seem to have been low-density settlements, in contrast to the later walled, brick-built ones that held larger populations.

Ancient Egyptian towns and cities appear to have developed as administrative, cult, and craft centers, military bases, or a combination of these. Inevitably, they competed with one another and by c. 3200 BCE there were a number of focal points of power, controlling limited areas and headed by elite figures with a combination of secular and sacred authority. It was out of their continuing and apparently violent rivalry that the Egyptian Dynastic state emerged about 3100 BCE at Hierakonpolis, where a ceremonial cosmetic palette of slate called the Narmer Palette appears to record the early kingship that united Upper and Lower Egypt [**13.9**]. Crucial to the emergence of the pharaonic state was the development of writing, which predated political unification.

13.8 Map of ancient Egypt and Nubia showing sites mentioned in the text.

13.9 The Narmer Palette. Found at Hierakonpolis and dating to about 3000 BCE, this ceremonial cosmetic slate palette appears to record the early kingship that brought together Upper and Lower Egypt. It is carved on both sides, this side showing King Narmer smiting a captive foreigner. Height 63.5 cm (2 ft. 1 in.).

13.10 The Step Pyramid at Saqqara. This was built for Djoser, the first king of the Third Dynasty, and is the oldest stone building of its size in the world. It inaugurated the practice of pyramid building, a distinctive feature of the earlier phases of ancient Egypt.

The Early Dynastic Period and the Old Kingdom, c. 3000–2150 BCE

The Egyptian state survived for some 3,000 years, punctuated by spells of regionalism and disunity known as the First, Second, and Third Intermediate Periods. The beginning of the Early Dynastic Period was marked by an increase in the use of writing and by the founding of Memphis (near modern Cairo), which during subsequent phases was at times the administrative and economic center of the state.

Most remarkable of the rulers during this period was Djoser, the first king of the Old Kingdom, 2686–2150 BCE, who built the Step Pyramid at **Saqqara**, the oldest stone building of its size in the world [**13.10**]. Earlier royal tombs at Abydos and those of high officials at Saqqara had been impressive, but the Step Pyramid was an architectural innovation that began the practice of pyramid building. It was a structure of six steps, unlike the smooth-sided pyramids of later times, with a height of 60 meters (197 feet). The king's body was buried in a chamber beneath the pyramid. The building indicates great technical skill, as well as considerable economic power and administrative organization.

The Old Kingdom was a time of economic prosperity and political stability. The state was organized around the pharaoh, who had both secular and sacred powers. He was regarded as a manifestation of Horus, the hawk god, and later as the son of Ra, the sun god. He also became associated with Osiris, the god of the dead and of the afterlife. It was the pharaoh's task to mediate between the gods and his people, and so guarantee the regular change of seasons, the annual Nile floods, and safety from natural dangers and external enemies.

It is in this context that the massive expenditure of resources on public works that characterized the period is best understood. Usually these involved the construction of royal tombs or temples, and this is the era to which most of the pyramids of ancient Egypt belong. Most remarkable were those built by the pharaohs of the Fourth Dynasty at **Giza**. The Pyramid of Khufu is the largest, with each side measuring 230 meters (755 feet) at the base and with a height of 146.5 meters (481 feet); it has been estimated that it contains 2,300,000 blocks of stone, averaging about 2.5 metric tons (2.75 US tons) each.

KEY DISCOVERY Insights from the Pyramids

Although primarily a place of royal burial and therefore a product of a powerful cosmology, the pyramids are also informative on many other aspects of Egyptian life. The earliest of them (particularly the giant examples at Giza [**13.11**]) functioned as an economic engine that drove the pharaonic state. The sheer size of each monumental building project involved the collection and redistribution of resources on a massive scale in order to support the necessary workforce and specialists associated with construction. Investigations of the pyramids' structures have also shed considerable light on Egyptian astronomical and mathematical knowledge, and on ancient surveying, quarrying, transport systems, engineering, architecture, building methods, and stone masonry.

The pyramids may even help to refine the accepted chronology for the Old Kingdom. They were oriented to true north with extraordinary precision; it seems probable that their alignment was based on observations of a selected pair of stars in the northern sky. This conclusion is supported by the progressive but slight deviations from true north of the pyramid alignments as time went on, reflecting, it is thought, the Earth's extremely slow precession around its axis, of which the ancient Egyptians would not have been aware. Calculations have indicated that the Pyramid of Khufu, for example, could date to 2480 BCE ± 5, a date later than that of 2554 BCE, which is currently accepted.

13.11 Aerial view of the Giza pyramids. Situated at the edge of the Nile Valley and built about 4,500 years ago, their enormous size dwarfs the buildings of the encroaching modern city of Cairo. Although intended for royal burials, they provide insights into many areas of ancient Egyptian life.

The archaeological evidence for pyramid and temple building, together with inscriptions on stone and texts on papyrus, tells us much about on the sociopolitical and economic organization of the Old Kingdom (see Key Discovery box: Insights from the Pyramids). A well-organized system of taxation existed, mainly in the form of agricultural products and labor. To acquire these resources and to make use of them in major state projects required a complex infrastructure and the involvement of a host of government officials, workers, artists, surveyors, architects, and scribes. The pharaoh initially controlled this administrative machine and appointed family to its highest positions. The incumbents were also, in many cases, members of the priesthood. In a non-monetary economy, reward for their services consisted of granting royal estates and their produce, in theory until the official's term of office expired. The ruler's control over such appointments weakened as time went on, however, and their possession, along with the estates, tended to become hereditary. In a situation where productive land was limited but formed the basis of the economy, it was inevitable that the resources at the ruler's disposal were gradually reduced, and power consequently weakened, as that of high officials and of the priesthood increased. The truly gigantic stone pyramids were built during only three generations of rulers; later pyramids were much smaller, their reduction in scale suggesting a state whose control gradually lessened as it depleted its economic base.

The Old Kingdom provided the foundation for much that followed, establishing many of the characteristic institutional, socio-economic, religious, and artistic traditions. During this period the Egyptian state extended its authority as far south as Buhen, far up the Nile at the Second Cataract (area of rapids), from where mining and trading expeditions were able to penetrate even further into the African interior. Nevertheless, the period ended with a weakening of state control, possibly brought on by a catastrophic climatic episode, but more probably because wealth and power had become dispersed rather than being concentrated in the pharaoh.

The First Intermediate Period, 2150–1975 BCE, and the Middle Kingdom, 1974–1640 BCE

The first period of disunion is known as the First Intermediate Period and was characterized by rival rulers in **Thebes** in the south and Herakleopolis in the north. King Mentuhotep (variously given as I or II) of the Theban dynasty eventually reunited the Egyptian state, introducing the era known as the Middle Kingdom, which seems to have been one of general stability. During this time the state maintained control by means of less despotic pharaohs and a substantial bureaucracy. Pyramid building was resumed, but on a relatively small

---

KEY THEME: URBANIZATION The Concept of Urbanization in Africa

African archaeology provides evidence for major settlements in ancient Egypt, Roman North Africa, the Ethiopian highlands, the Swahili coast, the West African savanna and rainforest, the Zimbabwe plateau, and the South African Highveld. They varied greatly in character, some occupied continuously, others only briefly, and increasing or shrinking in size depending on changing environmental conditions, economic circumstances, institutional stability, cultural practices, and regional conflict. In addition, they could be nucleated and even enclosed by walls, or be dispersed collections of houses. The origins of large settlements in Africa can be traced to the fourth millennium BCE in Egypt and the second millennium BCE in Sudan, but elsewhere in the continent they appeared from the first millennium BCE to the second millennium CE. Previous definitions of urbanization, city, and town are of limited relevance in Africa. Fundamental in the African case was the development of locations of denser settlement, places where greater numbers of people decided to live together, attracted by the advantages they offered or coerced by powerful leaders, and supported by mixed agriculture of various types. Characteristic of such larger settlements have been hierarchical social structures controlled by an elite group, but examples where authority was distributed horizontally rather than vertically seem to have existed in some cases. Functional specialization has also been a significant factor, as have religious ideology and trading networks, both regional and long-distance.

scale, and virtually died out by the end of the Middle Kingdom. The period was, however, marked by other major building programs, including the construction of a series of powerful forts in the Second Cataract region. There was an increase in both military campaigning and long-distance trade, in Nubia to the south and Palestine to the northeast, and large numbers of people from Southwest Asia settled in the eastern Nile delta.

Some of these populations, known as the Hyksos, took over the rule of northern Egypt around 1630 BCE, while Theban kings continued to rule in the south from about 1630 to 1540 BCE. This phase of political division is known as the Second Intermediate Period. Although this appears to have been a time of political and economic disintegration, foreign influences introduced several innovations, such as bronzeworking, new crops, the horse and chariot, composite bows, and even new musical instruments.

The New Kingdom and After

The New Kingdom began when the southern pharaoh Ahmose drove the Hyksos rulers from the northern delta in around 1540 BCE. A series of powerful pharaohs not only held the state together, but at times also extended its control further up the Nile and further into Southwest Asia. For a time, Egypt became an imperial power, one made wealthy by its access to Nubian gold resources. The period also saw the growth of an increasingly powerful army and priesthood. Many temples and other buildings were constructed, and numerous rock-cut tombs for royal and other privileged burials were created in the Valley of the Kings, on the west bank of the Nile at Thebes. Ideas about an existence after death resulted in great care and expense being devoted to mummification and burial, for many ordinary people as well as for rulers and elites, during the New Kingdom, continuing a practice that had been present from the foundation of the Egyptian state and persisted into the Roman period.

The New Kingdom was also remarkable for the attempt by Amenhotep IV to replace traditional beliefs with a new religion based on the worship of one god: the sun disk, or Aten. During his reign he changed his name to Akhenaten, which means Beloved of Aten. His successors, including his son Tutankhamun [**13.12**], speedily reverted to previous practices, but of great value for the study of ancient Egyptian

13.12 Detail of one of the gold coffins of Tutankhamun.
The tomb of this short-lived Eighteenth Dynasty pharaoh (c. 1332–1322 BCE) was found in the Valley of the Kings, near Thebes, in 1922. Its contents have provided much information about ancient Egyptian beliefs, rituals, technology, art, and other aspects of society.

13.13 Reconstruction of part of the city of Amarna. This was the new capital created by Akhenaten, which was abandoned after his death. Because it was occupied for only sixteen to seventeen years and not subsequently altered, excavations have provided a considerable insight into ancient Egyptian urban life at that time.

urbanization is Akhenaten's new capital city of **Amarna**, known as Akhetaten, abandoned at Akhenaten's death. Excavations there have provided an insight into an ordered urban life [**13.13**]. The population can be estimated at between 20,000 and 50,000, and house sizes indicate a society grading from poor to rich without any major gaps, the great gulf being between the residents as a whole and the royal family.

Ancient Egypt has sometimes been romanticized, but this was not a golden age for everyone. At the bottom of society was a very large peasant class, mostly of subsistence farmers who supplied the state with food, in the form of taxes, and provided labor for government mining, quarrying, and construction projects. In addition, there were enslaved people, captives from foreign wars. The bulk of the Egyptian population probably had a lifespan of about thirty-five years, were afflicted by diseases, and were kept in a state of poverty—usually overtaxed and often underfed.

EARLY STATES: NUBIA AND ETHIOPIA, *c.* 1500 BCE–700 CE

The process of urban development observed in ancient Egypt also took place in many other parts of the continent, although its form varied markedly. Aggregations of population sometimes resulted in densely occupied centers that continued for long periods, fluctuated seasonally, or shifted every few years. Factors, such as environment, economy, material culture, sociopolitical organization, religion, and trading contacts, influenced the configuration, size, density, and degree of mobility of settlements.

Kerma. The people of Nubia on the middle Nile experienced changes similar to those in Egypt, but more slowly, probably because of a less productive environment. Contact with Egypt during the Old and Middle Kingdoms might have stimulated growing social complexity.

13.14 The Western Deffufa, Kerma. This monumental mud-brick temple, probably much higher than the surviving remains, was solid, with no internal chambers and only a narrow winding stair that must have led to its top. Excavations showed that originally there were rooms that were later filled with brickwork.

Before its abandonment in *c.* 1500 BCE, there was a flourishing urban center on the Dongola Reach of the Nile, south of Egypt, known as the city of Kerma (see **13.8**, p. 305). Excavations have uncovered an elaborate fortification consisting of a ditch and a mud wall with projecting rectangular towers. The economy appears to have been based on mixed agriculture; cattle, sheep, and goats played a major role, and hunting and fishing contributed.

Kerma was probably the most important of a number of related urban settlements in its region, and possibly the center of tropical Africa's first identifiable state. Within the city, there was a large circular building of wood and mud brick, at least 10 meters (33 feet) high and isolated from neighboring houses by a large enclosure, suggesting it was a structure for elite people. The site also included a monumental mud-brick temple, known as the Western Deffufa, its height probably far exceeding the 19 meters (62 feet) that survives [**13.14**]. The city's cemetery contained two monumental mud-brick structures and a substantial number of burial mounds. The excavator of one of the mounds found a principal burial and 322 human sacrifices. Collectively, the evidence from Kerma suggests the existence of a centralized political and spiritual authority.

Meroë. Kerma was followed by other urban and state developments further south in what is now Sudan. From *c.* 800 BCE to 350 CE the city of Meroë and the Meroitic state of which it formed the capital were of major significance in northeast Africa. Meroë was the most important of a number of large settlements, and at its peak had a population that has been estimated at 20,000 people. Its principal buildings included a central walled complex interpreted as a royal precinct, as well as a number of temples dedicated to Egyptian and Meroitic deities. Large mounds of iron slag suggest industrial metallurgical activities. Outside the settlement, six cemeteries contain a range of burials from common citizens to rulers and their families, the tombs of many of the latter being marked by small stone pyramids.

KEY SITE Ethiopia's Rock-Cut Churches

Christian churches in Ethiopia have a long history, commencing in the fourth to seventh centuries CE during the Aksumite period and continuing until the fifteenth century and later. Many churches were built of stone in a conventional fashion, but many others were hewn from solid rock, often with both external and internal details skillfully carved. The most famous of these are eleven churches at Lalibela, some 650 kilometers (404 miles) from the Ethiopian capital Addis Ababa, which have been quarried into relatively soft basaltic rock [**13.15**].

The rock-cut churches have appeared to have little potential for the archaeological excavation that might establish a chronological sequence. In addition, the Lalibela churches, similarly to many ancient churches in Ethiopia, usually lack settlement context, being apparently isolated features in a landscape of shifting settlement. It is probable that they had political, economic, and social roles as well as religious ones, but these have been insufficiently investigated.

Two research approaches are addressing these problems. First, the physical interrelationship of the churches, and their individual morphology and developmental stages, have been used to suggest a five-part chronological sequence beginning in the seventh/eighth centuries CE and continuing to the thirteenth century or later. Another investigation has used standing-structure analysis to identify four phases of quarrying, but without converting these into an absolute chronology. A long development is indicated, beginning with undated pre-church work and ending in either the thirteenth or the fifteenth century.

These investigations have also recognized the excavation potential of huge spoil heaps of debris from the creation of the churches, usually dumped nearby. It is also apparent that surface and subsurface archaeological survey of the surrounding area, followed by selective excavation, could throw light on the settlement context of the churches. Quite apart from the substantial labor force needed to quarry massive quantities of rock, priests and others must have lived in the vicinity. In addition, it is probable that the mobile capitals of early second-millennium Ethiopia were at times situated in the same area, with the Lalibela churches providing an element of stability and authority for the prevailing regime.

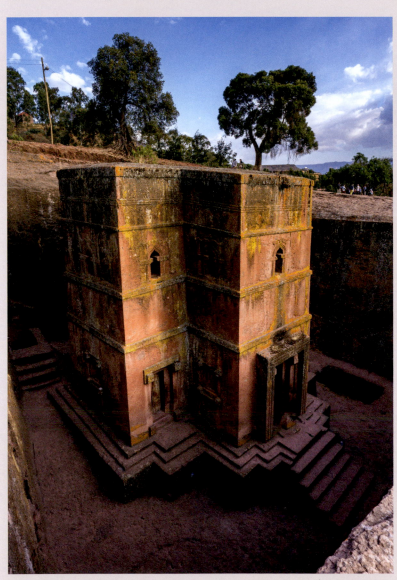

13.15 Beta Giyorgis, one of the Lalibela rock-cut churches, Ethiopia. It is located within a pit quarried into bedrock.

Meroitic society was supported by mixed farming and pastoralism. The material culture was sophisticated, and numerous imports of luxury items, such as fine glassware and metalwork, indicate close trading relations with Ptolemaic and Roman Egypt. The Meroitic state was partly literate, at first using Egyptian **hieroglyphs** for inscriptions but subsequently developing its own alphabet. Unfortunately, although the Meroitic script can be read, the language cannot be fully understood.

Aksum. The Meroitic state disintegrated in the fourth century CE, although the middle Nile Valley was the location of a succession of later urban centers and state developments, first Christian and subsequently Islamic. More immediately, Meroë's role in northeast Africa seems to have been assumed by the state of **Aksum** and the city of the same name, located high on the Ethiopian plateau. Aksum flourished until about the seventh century CE, with urban centers in northeast Ethiopia and Eritrea. For a while it even controlled part of southwestern Arabia, with which it had ancestral cultural connections.

Aksum's affluence seems to have resulted from its successful participation in the trade of the Red Sea, and its political and economic accomplishments were reflected in its material culture. Carved stelae marking burials are justifiably famous [**13.16**], the largest, now fallen, being nearly 33 meters (108 feet) in height and weighing about 517 metric tons (570 US tons). Aksum was the first state in tropical Africa to mint its own coinage, in gold, silver, and bronze, and developed its own form of writing. It was also one of the first states in the world to adopt Christianity as an official religion (see Key Site box: Ethiopia's Rock-Cut Churches).

13.16 One of the larger stelae at Aksum, Ethiopia. These pieces of stone marked the locations of burials, some probably royal. The biggest were carved to represent multi-storied buildings. The one shown is 21 meters (c. 69 feet) in height and weighs about 150 metric tons (165 US tons).

EARLY FARMING COMMUNITIES: IRONWORKING FARMERS IN CENTRAL, WESTERN, AND SOUTHERN AFRICA, 1000 BCE–1900 CE

The Bantu expansion to Central and Southern Africa in the first millennium BCE and the first millennium CE (see p. 304) led to the establishment of successful farming communities across large areas of the continent. In the centuries that followed, these communities developed new technological innovations and, in more complex societies in some regions, this led to the formation of cities and states, often associated with trade and long-distance exchange (see below). Much more widespread was the main technological innovation—the introduction of iron tools and weapons (see Key Controversy box: The Origins of African Ironworking, p. 314).

Iron appears to have been used at first for ceremonial and decorative artifacts, and the speed and extent of its adoption varied greatly. Nevertheless, it had important economic and sociopolitical consequences. It provided tools and weapons of greater efficiency than those of stone, bone, or wood, and its first use in the central and southern parts of the continent took place at about the same time as the later stages of the Bantu expansion.

hieroglyph a stylized picture representing a word or sound, found in early writing systems of ancient Egypt and Mesoamerica

13.17 Terra-cotta head from Lydenburg, Limpopo Province, South Africa, late first millennium CE.

Bantu-speaking people are thought to have taken farming into most of Africa south of the Equator, prior to the advent of iron technology.

In West and West-Central Africa, the earliest ironworking evidence belongs to *c.* 500 BCE. Iron seems to have been widely known north of the Equator by 100 BCE, although in most of Africa south of the Equator it was not adopted until the first millennium CE.

An early iron-using society in West Africa was that of **Nok**, centered on the Jos Plateau in Nigeria. Numerous terra-cottas found in this area, mostly of humans, some of which are life-size, display considerable technical and artistic ability and a unique style (see Key Discovery box: Nok: Unique Sculptures by Iron-Using Farmers).

Ironworking and farming appear to have spread quickly as far as Limpopo Province and KwaZulu-Natal in South Africa as part of a culture called the Chifumbaze complex. Its economy seems to have centered on cereal cultivation with cattle taking a greater role in some regions. For many southern African societies, cattle became of major significance by *c.* 800 CE. These animals made possible the exploitation of some of the drier environments of southern Africa, where the earliest farmers in the region had not penetrated. In southeastern Africa, they also provided a medium for the accumulation of wealth, whereas to the west, metal came to fill this role.

Pearl millet was cultivated in South Africa by the fourth century CE. In the southern Waterberg, a mixed farming economy was well established by the middle of the first millennium CE, and iron, tin, copper, and bronze were produced in this part of southern Africa during the second millennium CE. The stability of these settlements is reflected in a series of life-size terra-cotta human heads found at Lydenburg [**13.17**].

KEY CONTROVERSY The Origins of African Ironworking

Ironworking was the first large-scale metalworking in sub-Saharan Africa. Smelting iron by the bloomery process, which was used in Africa and neighboring parts of the world, involves the achievement of a chemical reaction, not the melting of the metal from an ore. Iron melts at temperatures above 1,540°C (2,804°F), but the result is cast iron, which is unsuitable for blacksmithing. To produce metallic iron that can be shaped in a forge, it is necessary to reduce the iron oxide ore in a furnace environment that has a low level of carbon dioxide and a high level of carbon monoxide, a process that starts at 1,150–1,200°C (2,102–2,192°F). This entails maintaining a balance between oxidation and reduction: oxygen is needed to burn the charcoal fuel used to reach the necessary temperature, but too much oxygen will stop or reverse the reduction of the ore. Therefore the smelting of iron is more complex than that of some copper ores, and it has been thought unlikely that iron smelting could have been developed independently in tropical Africa without a prior knowledge of copper metallurgy.

The earliest dates for iron smelting in tropical Africa are increasingly suggesting that it was developed independently in several parts of the continent. Evidence of smelting excavated at Do Dimmi in Niger, Walaldé in Senegal, Taruga and Opi in Nigeria, and Otumbi in Gabon all date from the first millennium BCE and seem at least as early as the earliest ironworking at Meroë in Sudan, a place long favored by diffusionists (who hold the view that cultural characteristics are always transmitted from one culture to another) as a staging point in the hypothesized spread of ironworking into tropical Africa. Nevertheless, the smelting of iron in Niger and Nigeria by the first millennium BCE suggests that the introduction of the relevant technology from Carthage in Tunisia, another source proposed by the diffusionists, is unlikely, because the earliest iron smelting there is only a little earlier in date. In addition, the variety of furnaces and bellows, as well as the existence of both forced draft and natural draft processes, suggests multiple indigenous origins within different parts of tropical Africa.

Terra-cottas first found near Nok on the Jos Plateau in northern Nigeria have attracted worldwide interest because of their unique art style and technical quality. Iron-using farmers who practiced shifting agriculture in the woodland savanna, mainly growing pearl millet and cowpeas, made them during the late second millennium BCE and the first centuries CE. The terra-cottas are usually of people, some showing symptoms of disease. Although some animals are represented, the sculptures do not appear to include domestic livestock. The origins of this sculptural tradition are unknown and the reason for its eventual disappearance uncertain, although climatic deterioration during the late first millennium BCE might have resulted in droughts that undermined the farming economy.

Nok sculptures have been found over a wide area of northern Nigeria, but their purpose remains the subject of debate [**13.18**, **13.19**]. They are usually fragmentary, deliberately smashed and buried in pits, suggesting that they might have been ritually disposed of at the death of the individual represented. Complete sculptures are very rarely found (most discoveries are separate heads and limbs), and most intact examples are almost certainly fakes, manufactured to deceive international art dealers, whose activities have encouraged so much looting of Nok sites that many have been irreparably damaged.

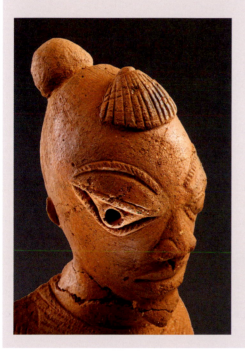

13.18 LEFT Upper part of a Nok terra-cotta of a male figure from Pangwari E., Nigeria, excavated in 2013. There is a representation of a seashell on its head. The rendering of the eyes is a distinctive feature of Nok terra-cottas. Height 31 cm (12 in.).

13.19 RIGHT Nok terra-cotta of a male figure from Daji Gwana 1, Nigeria, brilliantly restored to show it half-kneeling on an upturned vessel. Excavated in 2011, it is a unique piece that is almost complete, standing 73 cm (29 in.) in height. Most other Nok terra-cottas are only heads, limbs, or body parts, and other complete examples are probably forgeries.

EARLY STATES: THE SAHARA AND WEST AFRICA, 500–1500 CE

African states owed their origins (as in other regions) in part to successful farming economies and in part to growing patterns of interconnection that supported expanding networks of trade and exchange. In North Africa, the stimulus to urbanization was provided by Greek and Phoenician colonial settlement during the first millennium BCE, with the establishment of major centers such as Cyrene and Carthage on the Mediterranean coast. By the first century CE, Africa north of the Sahara was under Roman control. During the second half of that millennium, the region became part of the Islamic Arab world.

Small-scale trading contacts between North and West Africa already existed in the first millennium BCE. **Old Jarma**, the desert city in the oases of the Fazzān, participated in these.

13.21 Brass head from Ife, southwestern Nigeria. From the first half of the second millennium CE, near-life-size heads, of either brass or terra-cotta, appear to be representations of rulers and members of their families. Holes above the forehead were probably for the attachment of hair and the lines on the face represent scarification. Height 24 cm (9.5 in.).

13.20 Brass head from Benin City, southern Nigeria. A near-life-size depiction of the mother of a king of Benin in the sixteenth century CE. She wears a beaded headdress and a choker of beads around her neck. Above the eyes is scarification. Height 41 cm (16 in.).

By the late first millennium CE, both urban centers and state systems had appeared in parts of the West African savanna. Ancient Ghana, with its capital at Koumbi Saleh, seems to have originated by 500 CE. There followed a succession of other states in the region between 1–1400 CE, including Mali, Songhai, Kanem, and Borno. Undoubtedly, the growth of trans-Saharan Arab trade stimulated such developments, but did not initiate them. A number of important urban centers grew up on or near the desert margins as participants in this trade, as camel caravans from North Africa and parts of the desert brought salt, copper, manufactured products, dates, cowrie shells, and horses. Going north in exchange were enslaved people, gold, ivory, spices, pepper, alum, and fine leather. The desert trade imported ideas as well as commodities to the West African savanna, and introduced both Islam and the Arabic script.

To the south, in the rainforest and on its margins, indigenous urbanization was in progress by 1100 CE. State development included the Akan states in Ghana, the Yoruba state of Old Oyo, and the Edo state, centered on Benin City. Some of these developments expressed themselves in state-sponsored art—the copper-alloy figures from Benin City [**13.20**] and the copper-alloy and terra-cotta ones from Ife [**13.21**] have become famous. Both of these cities were surrounded by protective earthworks, which in the case of Benin City were part of an extensive regional network.

EARLY STATES: EASTERN, SOUTHERN, AND CENTRAL AFRICA, 1000–1900 CE

The Swahili Coast. Large settlements grew up along the Indian Ocean coast from Somalia to Mozambique (including the Comoro Islands and northern Madagascar) from around 900 CE. Archaeological excavations at Gedi [**13.22**] and Shanga, in Kenya, and at Kilwa in Tanzania, have shed valuable light on this process. The origins of these urban centers were clearly indigenous, but their growth during the first half of the second millennium CE owed much to their participation in the Indian Ocean trade, which brought fine ceramics and other

13.22 The entrance to the palace in Gedi, Kenya. Lime-mortared stone buildings indicate the economic success of the coastal trading communities along the East African coast, which tapped the resources of the African interior and participated in the Indian Ocean trade.

manufactured goods from as far away as China, introduced the Islamic faith, and stimulated the construction of stone buildings. The search for exportable commodities, such as ivory, gold, rhinoceros horn, tortoiseshell, ambergris, copper, iron, rock crystal, frankincense, myrrh, mangrove poles, ebony, and enslaved people, stimulated the growth of trading networks along the coast, among its islands, and deep into the hinterland. This brought the coastal traders into contact with gold producers on the Zimbabwe plateau, adding to the wealth of many in the coastal communities. Subsequently, some of the larger settlements appear to have become the centers of states. As time went on, coastal society developed its own common culture and language (Swahili) that combined indigenous and exotic elements.

The Zimbabwe Plateau. The Zimbabwe plateau, bounded by the Zambezi River to its north and the Limpopo to its south, also experienced urban and state development from around 1000 CE. More than 1,000 meters (3,282 feet) above sea level and therefore not infested by tsetse fly, a suitable climate and areas of fertile soil allowed the cultivation of sorghum, finger millet, pearl millet, beans, and other vegetables. Natural resources included gold, iron, copper, and tin. The use of drystone masonry was widespread in much of Africa but reached its most sophisticated form in the many walled enclosures of this region, most famously at **Great Zimbabwe**.

The site of Great Zimbabwe, from which the modern state of Zimbabwe takes its name, has been known to the outside world since the late nineteenth century CE, but colonial era narratives long obstructed a full understanding of its origins, status, and regional significance (See Key Controversy box: Postcolonial Archaeology in Africa, p. 318). It is only relatively recently that its dating, from the thirteenth to the fifteenth centuries CE, has been established. It is even more recently that its character has begun to be understood. The impressive drystone

KEY CONTROVERSY Postcolonial Archaeology in Africa

The legacy of colonialism is still felt in archaeological practice, from the interpretation of evidence and the weight given to different materials and events, to the forming of research questions. A common trend in the recent history of archaeology in Africa is to rethink past narratives and present updated histories that emphasize local processes in the emergence of cultures and technologies, rather than assuming change occurred due to external influence. Below are three examples.

Great Zimbabwe

The monumental enclosure of Great Zimbabwe has been the object of intense debate since the nineteenth century. Early explorers attributed the building of the monument to Phoenicians or other groups from Southwest Asia, drawing on the tradition, widespread at the time, of assigning innovation in sub-Saharan Africa to colonists from outside the continent. Gertrude Caton-Thompson excavated the site in 1931 and demonstrated that Great Zimbabwe was of local Bantu origin. Older colonialist interpretations continued to circulate for some time, but it is now accepted that it was built by ancestors of the modern Shona, and through the recent research of leading African archaeologists Innocent Pikirayi and Shadreck Chirikure, we have begun to understand more about the chronology and structure of this impressive site.

Swahili Urban States

Along the Swahili Coast and Indian Ocean islands and Madagascar, over 400 sites have been discovered consisting of stone structures, enclosing walls, mosques, or tombs. Some sites contain only wells and fragments of locally made ceramics and pottery imported from India, the Middle East, and China. These Indian Ocean contacts initially led to the view that the stone ruins were built by Persian and Arab colonists, following a traditional assumption that Africa was the receptor of new ideas, rather than an innovator. This interpretation resonated with the colonial climate of the time and persisted until after the Second World War. In subsequent years, with the development of stronger African national identity, interpretations began to incorporate local knowledge of the sites, and appreciate the local Bantu contribution to the origins and growth of these cities and the societies that supported them. The local nature of development is demonstrated through continuity in ritual in ancestor worship and burial practice, as well as house shrines. Archaeologists, such as Chap Kusimba, argue that this need not be a polarizing argument, and that the Swahili culture had its local origins as well as its external influences.

Metallurgy

The question of whether iron metallurgy developed independently in sub-Saharan Africa or as the result of the influence or movement of an outside culture is another example of re-evaluating past assumptions (see Key Controversy box: The Origins of African Ironworking, p. 314). By the second half of the first millennium BCE. and possibly much earlier, communities in the southern savanna zone of West Africa were smelting iron, at sites such as Nsukka in eastern Nigeria and Obobogo in Cameroon, and within a few centuries there was a flourishing iron industry both here and in northwest Tanzania. From the 1900s, scholars have argued that the technology traveled to sub-Saharan Africa from the Mediterranean coastal city of Phoenician Carthage, or from the Romans through the city of Meroë. This was part of a diffusionist interpretation of the human past, widely accepted in the early twentieth century, that considered Egypt and Southwest Asia to be the home of many key innovations, which spread to Europe and Africa via the Mediterranean. It is only in recent decades that the evidence for indigenous African metallurgy has received fuller attention, with new fieldwork and better dating evidence. This has confirmed sub-Sahara as being home to the independent invention of iron metallurgy. With more and more numerous dates pushing back the beginning of iron production in Africa, it is close to becoming one of the world's oldest metallurgies.

structures are now thought to have been elite features in the center of an extensive urban settlement, with a population possibly as high as 18,000. Spatial analysis of this and comparable sites on the Zimbabwe plateau also suggests that Great Zimbabwe was the capital of an early state in the region, which preceded historically documented states, including that of the Mwene Mutapa, known to Portuguese traders in the sixteenth to seventeenth centuries, and Torwa, with its capital at the fifteenth to seventeenth-century site of Khami. The building of Great Zimbabwe was the work of the ancestors of the Shona, who still live in the area.

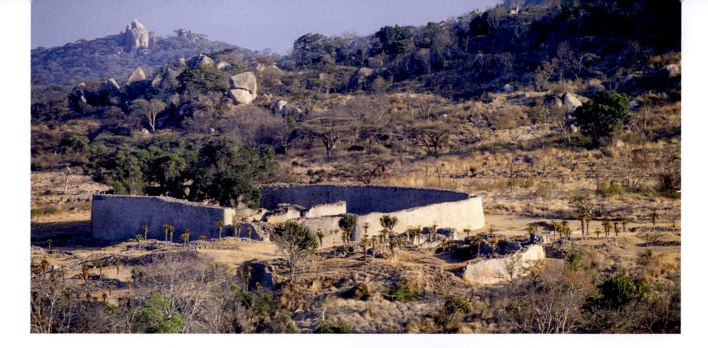

The stone walls appear to have formed enclosures for the dwellings of the ruling family and their supporters, and other stone structures seem to have been for ritual purposes. The site consists of two areas of ruins, around which lay the rest of the settlement; one group of enclosures clustered around boulders at the top of a precipitous granite hill, and another on the far slope of an adjacent valley.

The principal structures were clearly intended to impress: they are monumental both in appearance and in the implied expenditure of resources. The main enclosure in the valley, for instance, consists of a beautifully constructed granite wall 244 meters long, up to 5 meters thick, and 10 meters high (801 × 16 × 33 feet) [**13.23**]. Among the features within this enclosure is a unique conical tower of solid drystone masonry about 5.5 meters (18 feet) in diameter and more than 9 meters (30 feet) high [**13.24**].

13.23, **13.24 Ruins and Tower at Great Zimbabwe.** The tower is about 5.5 meters (18 feet) in diameter and more than 9 meters (30 feet) high, built of solid drystone masonry. It is regarded as one of Africa's most remarkable precolonial structures.

Almost certainly, the successful mixed agriculture of the region was important to Great Zimbabwe, and its elite class, with secular and sacred power, had probably gained control of cattle, fertile soils, and gold sources. There was a flourishing internal trade in iron, copper, salt, and other commodities, particularly gold and ivory, which brought Great Zimbabwe into contact with the trading cities of the East African coast. Persian and Chinese ceramics and Southwest Asian glass have been found at Great Zimbabwe, with glass beads, cowrie shells, and a coin minted in Kilwa, an Indian Ocean trading port on the coast of Tanzania.

The main period of stone-building at Great Zimbabwe was at the same time as the greatest prosperity in the coastal settlements, and both areas eventually declined at the same date, perhaps because of falling world gold prices. In Great Zimbabwe's case, however, environmental deterioration might have been another factor, the result of heavy demands made on the surrounding area by such a large population.

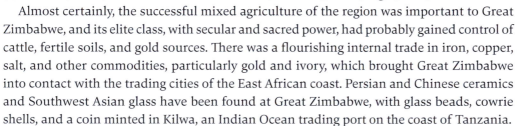

Central Africa. By 1500 CE both urbanization and state formation were also in progress in other parts of Central Africa. Indeed, by the nineteenth century, much of the African interior seems to have become a complex network of states and cities. Control of production and trade in iron, salt, copper, and other commodities was probably the most common means by which power was acquired. The accumulation of wealth in the form of cattle in some areas, or tradable food resources, such as dried fish, in others, must also have been important. Archaeological evidence from southeastern Democratic Congo is significant. There, in the Upemba Depression, along the upper Lualaba River, it has been possible to trace the emergence of the Luba kingdom, of which little is otherwise known before about 1700 CE.

Excavation at the cemetery sites of Sanga, Katongo, Kamilamba, Kikulu, and Malemba Nkulu have allowed the construction of a cultural sequence from the fifth century CE to the beginning of the nineteenth century. The burials indicate the gradual development of functional specialization, social stratification, and political organization. In particular, the eleventh-century CE Classic Kisalian tradition was characterized by sophisticated pottery and metalwork, the latter making considerable use of copper, probably from the rich deposits to the southeast. Apparently important as an indicator of wealth, prestige, and status, after the end of the fourteenth century copper was also used as a currency, in the form of distinctive crosses.

The Far South. The growth of large population clusters and the emergence of states occurred even at the southern end of Africa, although at later dates than further north. For about the last 500 years, mixed farming, and livestock herding or hunter-gathering or a combination of the two, supported the growth of numerous stone-built settlements. Their relatively recent date means that oral traditions, historical documentation, and linguistic data can all help in the interpretation of their archaeological evidence. A little after 300 years ago, some Tswana settlements began to grow to a remarkable size, culminating in populations of 10,000 people or more. Kaditshwene appears to have been one of the greatest, with a population, almost 200 years ago, of 20,000, making it the same size as contemporary Cape Town. Molokwane was even bigger, a settlement 3 kilometers (1.9 miles) in length, averaging 1.5 kilometers (0.9 miles) in width, and with an area of approximately 4–5 square kilometers (2.5–4 square miles). Considered as a whole, this huge settlement and others like it indicate an increasing centralization of economic and political power by local rulers. Out of this emerged the Zulu state, but for the settlements of the area the period has been remembered as the *Difaqane*, meaning the scattering, because the Sotho and Tswana people scattered and others scattered before them. As European settlers moved north they found only deserted stone ruins, not the thriving communities of people that had formerly existed.

SUMMARY AND CONCLUSIONS

During the postglacial period Africa experienced important transformations in human societies. Prior to 10,000 years ago, some hunter-gatherers and fishers in northern and eastern Africa had begun to intensify their exploitation of particular animals and plants, as they experienced climatic variability. For some human groups this intensification led eventually to the development of pastoralism. For others, intensive gathering of wild grasses and other vegetable food resulted in the cultivation of wheat and barley, from Southwest Asia, or of pearl millet and other African plants. Such cultivation made possible a greater degree of sedentism.

The adoption of farming in Central and southern Africa appears to have been the result of a process of diffusion, as pottery-making Bantu-speaking farmers expanded eastward and southward across a huge area of the continent during the first millennium BCE. By the late first millennium BCE they were acquiring a knowledge of ironworking, which had previously become established in parts of West, West-Central, and East Africa. By the early second millennium CE, farming, along with iron technology, had spread over most of the continent south of the Equator, except for some parts of eastern and southern Africa where stone-using hunter-gatherers persisted.

In many parts of the continent, the adoption of metallurgy probably encouraged a continued increase in both population and settlement size, leading in some more bountiful environments to the growth of substantial centers. The need to maintain order within larger groups, and the emergence of elite classes that were able to control the means of production, sometimes led to the growth of states. They seem to have resulted from complex adjustments in socio-economic and political relationships within areas of dense human settlement, rather than from any external influences, although such influences did contribute to their ongoing development, particularly when long-distance trade provided African rulers with both wealth and prestige.

Finally, this chapter presents an essentially external view of Africa's archaeological past. That reflects prevailing interpretations in most of the published literature and is necessary for the chapter to contribute to the global perspective of this book. More work to decolonize archaeology is underway that will undoubtedly cause further changes in accepted perceptions of Africa's past.

FURTHER READING

The following provide good introductions to the formation of states and societies in ancient Africa, and the archaeological evidence for this:

Bard, K. A. 2015. *An Introduction to the Archaeology of Ancient Egypt.* 2nd edn. Oxford: Wiley Blackwell.

Breunig, P., ed. 2014. *Nok: African Sculpture in Archaeological Context.* Frankfurt am Main: Africa Magna Verlag.

Connah, G. 2016. *African Civilizations: An Archaeological Perspective.* 3rd edn. Cambridge: Cambridge University Press.

Kusimba, C. M. 1999. *The Rise and Fall of Swahili States.* Walnut Creek: AltaMira Press.

Lewis-Williams, J. D. and Challis, S. 2011. *Deciphering Ancient Minds. The Mystery of San Bushmen Rock Art.* London and New York: Thames & Hudson.

Maisels, C. 2010. *The Archaeology of Politics and Power: Where, When and Why the First States Formed.* Oxford: Oxbow Books.

Mitchell, P. and Lane, P. (eds.). 2013. *The Oxford Handbook of African Archaeology.* Oxford: Oxford University Press.

Phillipson, D. W. 2012. *Foundations of an African Civilisation: Aksum and the Northern Horn 1000 BC–AD 1300.* Woodbridge, Suffolk, UK: James Currey (Boydell and Brewer).

Vinnicombe, P. 1976. *People of the Eland: Rock Paintings of the Drakensberg Bushmen as a Reflection of Their Life and Thought.* Pietermaritzburg: University of Natal Press.

http://safarchaeology.org Website of the Society of Africanist Archaeologists.

Early Americas

14

David J. Meltzer

Environments and Landscapes 324

Peopling the Landscape: Earliest Occupation in the Americas 327

KEY THEME: MIGRATION Methods and Motives 327

KEY DISCOVERY Genetics and the First Americans 328

KEY CONTROVERSY Genomic Research and Indigenous Communities 330

KEY SITES Earliest Sites 332

Hunter-Gatherer Trajectories: The Clovis Occupation of North America, *c.* 11,400–10,600 BCE 334

KEY SITES Folsom and Clovis 336

Regionalization: North America after Clovis 337

KEY CONTROVERSY Pleistocene Extinctions 340

KEY THEME: CLIMATE CHANGE The Effects of Climate Change on the Earliest Native Americans 342

Peopling the Landscape: The Earliest South Americans 342

Summary and Conclusions 344

Further Reading 345

Clovis fluted projectile points are distinctive stone tools that were used by Ice Age people in many parts of North America. The stone used to manufacture these specimens, from the Drake cache in Colorado, came from a source in Texas.

The Americas were the last major habitable landmass to be peopled in early human history. The Americas were first populated during the Late Pleistocene, sometime before 15,000 years ago, by anatomically modern humans, whose ancestry traces to North Eurasian and East Asian populations. Their jumping-off point for the migration to the Americas was far northeast Siberia, probably across the now-submerged Bering land bridge. These were hunter-gatherers who proved highly successful at adapting to a vast, ecologically diverse landscape in the midst of geologically rapid climate change.

- The American continent was first peopled by hunter-gatherers from Siberia migrating over the Bering land bridge, probably taking a coastal route south.

- The end of the Ice Age involved the extinction of the largest animals, or megafauna, in the Americas.

- Humans reached southern South America by around 15,000 years ago, as demonstrated by the settlement of Monte Verde in Chile.

- The Clovis culture spread across the North American continent, but by around 12,000 years ago communities began to become regionally distinct.

ENVIRONMENTS AND LANDSCAPES

Around 21,000 years ago, the North American continent was covered by two vast ice sheets, the Cordilleran and Laurentide, which had buried much of present-day Canada [14.1]. Water frozen on land around the world could not return to the oceans, and as a result the average global sea level had fallen around 134 meters (440 feet) [14.2]. When that occurred, the shallow continental shelf beneath the Bering Sea (the sea between Alaska and Siberia) was exposed as dry land, creating a land bridge, Beringia, which existed up to 12,500 years ago.

Crossing the land bridge was only the first leg of the journey to the Americas, as the Cordilleran and Laurentide ice sheets would have formed a barrier blocking eastern Beringia (Alaska) to the rest of the American continent further south. A key question is how people got south from Alaska. Once the massive glaciers began to recede, two possible routes opened, but not at the same time. Which route they may have taken depends on when they first reached Beringia.

The Archaeology of Beringia

Beringia was a landmass that bridged northeast Asia to Alaska. The earliest site in this part of Siberia is Yana, dated to 32,000 years ago. A glimpse into this period is provided by DNA, both from ancient skeletal remains and from modern individuals (see Key Discovery box: Genetics and the First Americans, p. 328). Based on this genetic evidence it is estimated that *c.* 23,000 years ago a human population split off from other groups in northeastern Asia. This may have been due to climatic conditions that isolated them in the vastness of Siberia as, over the millennia that followed, there was limited **gene flow** between this population and other Asian and Siberian groups.

Following Yana, the next oldest site in northeast Siberia is Diuktai Cave, first occupied 16,800 years ago. This location includes **microblades**, burins, and bifacial knives, along with animal remains including mammoth, horse, and bison. Diuktai and other western Beringia sites contain artifact types and technologies—including the distinctive bifacial

gene flow the transfer of genetic material from one population to another

microblade a small stone blade, often made of flint, obsidian, or quartz; generally less than 50 mm (1.9 in.) long

14.1 LEFT **Map of the Americas** toward the end of the Ice Age showing sites discussed in this chapter and the approximate location of the two major ice sheets, the Cordilleran and Laurentide, and the ice-free corridor that emerged c. 14,000 years ago as the ice sheets retreated. The beige areas denote the portions of the continental shelf that were exposed as dry land during this time of lowered sea level. The ages of the archaeological sites vary, as noted in the text.

Map labels:
Beringia
Swan Point
Laurentide ice sheet
Cordilleran ice sheet
ice-free corridor
modern coastline
Kennewick
Paisley Caves
Colby
Anzick
Jones-Miller
Olsen-Chubbuck
Meadowcroft
Folsom
Clovis
Sloan
Murray Springs
Aubrey
El Fin del Mondo
Peñon
ancient coastline
Las Vegas
Pedra Pintada
Huaca Prieta
Pedra Furada
Quebrada Jaguay
Lagoa Santa
Monte Verde

14.2 BELOW **The confluence of the Silverthrone and Klinaklini glaciers in southwest British Columbia.** Today, little remains of the vast glaciers that once covered northern North America, save for smaller glaciers at high latitudes and in some mountain ranges. The glaciers are flowing from left to right in the image, until they reach their terminus and melt, forming the source of the Klinaklini River.

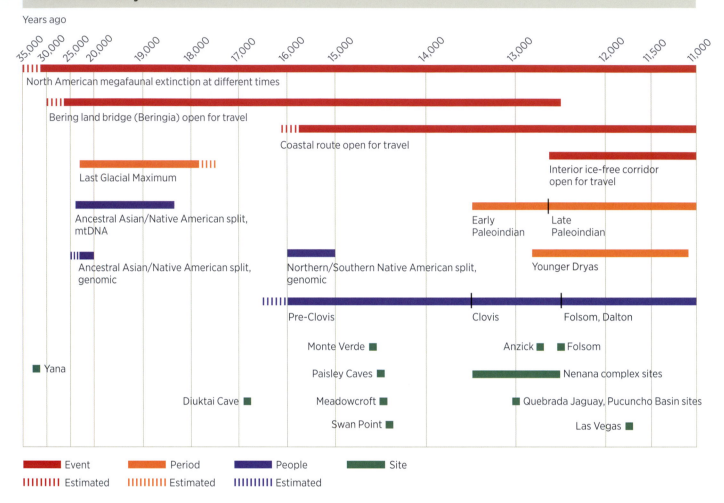

Years ago

North American megafaunal extinction at different times	Event
Bering land bridge (Beringia) open for travel	
Coastal route open for travel	
Interior ice-free corridor open for travel	
Last Glacial Maximum	
Ancestral Asian/Native American split, mtDNA	
Early Paleoindian / Late Paleoindian	
Ancestral Asian/Native American split, genomic	
Northern/Southern Native American split, genomic	
Younger Dryas	
Pre-Clovis	Clovis	Folsom, Dalton
Monte Verde	Anzick	Folsom
Yana	
Paisley Caves	Nenana complex sites
Diuktai Cave	Meadowcroft	Quebrada Jaguay, Pucuncho Basin sites
Swan Point	Las Vegas

Event — Estimated
Period — Estimated
People — Estimated
Site

Chindadn point a type of stone tool characteristic of the Nenana complex in Alaska

Chindadn points—which are later found in eastern Beringia (Alaska) [**14.3**]. Here, the first human presence is found at **Swan Point** in central Alaska, which dates to 14,400 years ago. The earliest artifacts found there include microblades and burins reminiscent of ones found at Diuktai Cave in Siberia. Artifacts dated later, about 12,500 years ago, include Chindadn points along with microblades, though ones made by a different technique than seen earlier. The close similarities between the points and microblades found in the two regions build an archaeological connection between Siberia and Alaska.

0 ——————————— 5 cm
0 ——————————— 2 in.

14.3 Chindadn points, characteristic of the Nenana complex in Alaska.

PEOPLING THE LANDSCAPE: EARLIEST OCCUPATION IN THE AMERICAS

What is puzzling is that neither microblades nor Chindadn points found in Alaska are seen elsewhere in the Americas. Similarly, Clovis fluted points, associated with the first widespread complex in North America south of the ice sheets around 13,400 years ago (see below), are not found in the far north, nor are the types of artifacts discovered at the few known pre-Clovis age sites, though the ancestors of these groups must also have made the trek from Siberia. Archaeologists continue to address questions about these first populations (See Key Theme box: Migration–Methods and Motives). When did they first arrive? Did they do so in one population wave or several, and which route(s) did they take? Both archaeological and genetic evidence has been used to answer these questions.

One Wave of Migration or Multiple?

Did the first populations move into the Americas in one wave or many through time? Genetic research of modern North American populations and ancient remains can address this question (see Key Controversy box: Genomic Research and Indigenous Communities, p. 330). The genomes of all ancient and modern Indigenous communities in the Americas fall into one of two deep branches: one distinctive to northern North America and another to portions of North as well as South America. The two populations initially arrived as one group, but are estimated to have diverged c. 16,000–15,000 years ago, possibly en route south from Alaska. If this pattern holds, it suggests there was initially the migration of a single population from northeast Asia, but one that split into different groups once in the Americas.

There is some anatomical evidence suggesting more than one migration event. Most notable are the so-called Paleoamerican skeletons—including those from Kennewick in Washington and Lagoa Santa in Brazil, and that of Peñon Woman III from Mexico—that date to the Late Pleistocene and early postglacial period, and are said to represent a population separate from

---

KEY THEME: MIGRATION Methods and Motives

We will probably never know what trigger(s) prompted individuals living in Siberia to make their way steadily east until they were in a land never before visited by our species. History records many reasons why groups venture from their homeland, and these can be broadly divided into two categories: negative factors in the home region that *push* a people out, and positive attractions in a distant area that *pull* them in. Certain push factors common in recent centuries and millennia seem unlikely to apply here. It is doubtful, for example, that in Pleistocene Siberia there was overpopulation, strife, or warfare that might have driven groups out of the region. On the other hand, harsh Ice Age conditions may have caused, or at the least led to, the separation and isolation of the group(s) that ultimately did depart for the Americas. On the pull side, those headed east might have hoped—but could not have known—they would find prized resources. For that matter, one should never downplay curiosity, wanderlust, the joy of discovery,

and the like, even though such motivations are impossible to see in the archaeological record.

As to how they occupied the vast, trackless, and increasingly exotic and highly diverse landscape of the Americas, the answer is in the myriad details. But if there was one key element underpinning the process, it appears to have been *flexibility*, both in social organization and adaptive strategies. There seems little other way to explain how hunter-gatherers were able, within a thousand years or so of their arrival, to spread from Alaska to Patagonia, and successfully occupy settings from coasts to continental interiors, from open grasslands to dense temperate and tropical forests, and from sea level to oxygen-starved high-elevation habitats. And this success should be emphasized: so far, at least, the DNA evidence we have points to population-scale continuity between the first communities and their descendants who were living in the Americas when Europeans arrived.

the ancestors of present-day Indigenous populations. Statistical analyses of the shape and size of these and other early skulls show that they differ from those of modern Indigenous populations, and are thought to derive from a source population that shares more affinities to Southeast Asians than Northeast Asians. There is, however, only a small sample of ancient skeletal remains (for example, ones predating 8,000 years ago), which are often fragmentary, and little is known of the variability within these populations, making it difficult to say whether the appearance of the Kennewick and Lagoa Santa skeletons is representative of anatomically distinctive populations. DNA evidence is relevant here too: no Paleoamerican remains sequenced to date proves to be from any group other than Indigenous people of the Americas, indicating that all descend from the same Northeast Asian population.

The Coastal Route and Glacial Corridor

When did the first populations arrive in the Americas south of the massive ice sheets, and what route did they take? As noted, geneticists estimate that a specific group diverged from Asian populations about 23,000 years ago. Assuming this is correct, then or thereafter a population that was to become the Indigenous people of the Americas began its journey to the American continent [**14.4**]. This is a *maximum* age for the peopling of the Americas. Archaeology, in turn, provides a *minimum* age, since human occupation must precede the oldest known site in the Americas—after all, the oldest site known is only the oldest site found. So far, some of the oldest sites discovered are Cooper's Ferry in Idaho, dated to around 16,000 years ago, Gault and Friedkin in Texas, which appear to be at least 15,500 years old, Meadowcroft in Pennsylvania, dating to at least 14,500 years ago, and Monte Verde—arguably the first pre-Clovis age site to be widely accepted—in southern Chile and dated to 14,600 years ago.

How did ancestral Indigenous populations make it south from Alaska? Two possible routes became available as the Pleistocene came to an end and ice sheets melted back: a coastal route on the land between the Pacific Ocean and the western edge of the Cordilleran ice sheet, and the roughly 1,500-kilometer-long (950 miles) interior ice-free corridor, which opened between the Cordilleran and Laurentide ice sheets along the eastern flank of the Canadian Rocky Mountains.

KEY DISCOVERY Genetics and the First Americans

In the early 1990s, geneticists began to reconstruct Indigenous population histories, initially using mitochondrial DNA (inherited by genetic males and females from a maternal ancestor), and Y chromosome DNA (NRY, non-recombining portion of the Y chromosome inherited in males from a paternal ancestor). Later developments made it possible to sequence autosomal DNA (inherited from non-sex chromosomes), which is a mix from both parents so is broadly inherited from many more ancestors. Differences in DNA that accumulated over time as populations diverged make it possible to tell the timing of migrations using the concept of the molecular clock (Chapter 1).

By the late 1990s, it was apparent that Indigenous people in the Americas and many (though not all) Asian groups were members of one of five maternal mtDNA lineages or haplogroups, and two paternal Y-chromosome haplogroups.

Within those haplogroups are variants found largely—or entirely—in Indigenous communities in the Americas. The mtDNA haplogroups diverged from a common ancestor shared with most Asian groups all about the same time, with an estimated most recent common ancestor dated from between 24,900 and 18,400 years ago. This similar range of ages suggests Indigenous Americans originated from the same source population. The two Y-chromosome haplogroups diverged at roughly the same time as the mtDNA haplogroups.

After around 16,000 years ago, the diversity of both Y-chromosome and mtDNA lineages increased rapidly as groups moved into the hemisphere, followed by an estimated sixty-fold increase in the population. After the initial and seemingly rapid expansion of the major haplogroups across the Americas, there was a proliferation of sub-lineages or haplotypes, a result of dispersal that led to isolation

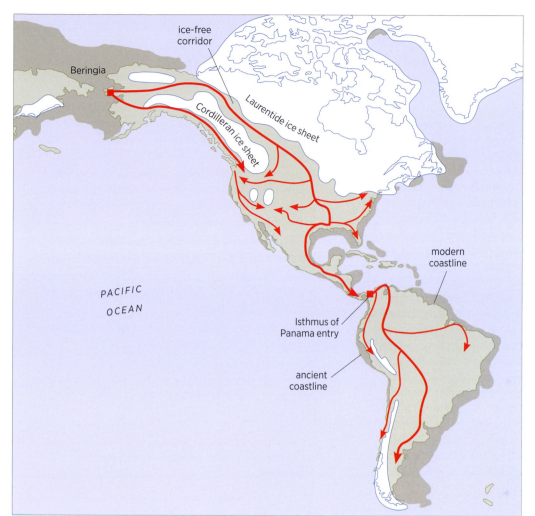

14.4 Map showing possible migration routes into the Americas. The first people in the Americas came via Beringia and from there could have journeyed south either down the Pacific coast or via an ice-free corridor on the eastern flank of the Rocky Mountains. Which route they took would have depended on when they arrived and which was viable for travel at that time; the coastal route was open earlier than the ice-free corridor. Movement into South America was via the Isthmus of Panama, from which point groups could have split and taken several possible pathways into the remainder of the continent.

Labels on map: ice-free corridor · Beringia · Laurentide ice sheet · Cordilleran ice sheet · PACIFIC OCEAN · modern coastline · Isthmus of Panama entry · ancient coastline

and genetic drift (random variations or mutations in gene frequency due to the separation of populations rather than natural selection), resulting in a complex genetic geographic structure within these populations.

MtDNA and NRY are susceptible to lineage loss, particularly if populations experience sharp reductions in size or bottlenecks. The most drastic of these happened in the centuries after 1492, when Western infectious diseases introduced to Native Americans and other Indigenous groups in the Americas triggered massive demographic collapse.

By 2010, it was possible to obtain genomic sequences, which, based on autosomal DNA, represent a multitude of ancestors, not just a single maternal or paternal ancestor. Genomes, both ancient and modern, revealed an ancient population split, creating what is known as northern and southern Native American (NNA and SNA) branches, the former including ancestors of present-day Athabascans and such northern groups as Chipewyan, Cree, and Ojibwa, the

latter including Anzick and Kennewick, and present-day Native Americans from southern North America and Central and South America. The branches appear to have diverged from one another around 16,000–15,000 years ago, having apparently arrived in North America as a single group. A strong population structure (subgroups within each branch) later emerged, probably a function in part of both geographic and social barriers to gene flow.

Even as we discuss these genetic results, it is important to remember that Indigenous societies of North and South America may object to both the excavation and destructive analysis of ancestral skeletal remains. It is important for archaeologists and geneticists to balance the concerns of descendant populations with the quest for knowledge of the past. By working together through consultation, that knowledge can continue to expand while at the same time respecting the traditions and religious beliefs of Indigenous groups.

KEY CONTROVERSY Genomic Research and Indigenous Communities

Genetic studies of human population history allow archaeologists to further the story of how ancient and present-day societies are biologically related, and how they migrated, diversified, and admixed across the world. Early DNA research in the Americas (as well as other places with colonial histories, such as South Africa and Australia), however, often failed to engage with Indigenous communities in any significantly inclusive way, lacked transparency, and mistreated human remains, leading to severe mistrust and conflict. The lack of co-operation between non-Indigenous archaeologists and Indigenous communities in genomic research has been a lasting source of controversy, but stakeholders of both positions are now working to create a more collaborative field of study.

In recent years, archaeologists have been more likely to run ancient DNA projects that seek feedback from Indigenous groups linked to ancestral individuals analyzed in their study, and many Indigenous communities are developing their own policies to promote responsible conduct in research. For example, the Navajo Nation in the United States has developed a strong culturally informed genetic-research code in place of a long-term ban on modern genetic research. These policies were drawn up through frequent communication between researchers (including Indigenous researchers) and Indigenous communities. In 2018, the genetic scientist Katrina G. Claw and colleagues proposed six principles for engaging Indigenous communities in genomic research, which have been used to guide the actions of archaeological projects in the United States.

1. *Understand the sovereignty of Indigenous communities in research regulation* Local council research policies and regulations are important to consider in Indigenous communities.

2. *Engage and collaborate with Indigenous communities* Involve the community in all aspects of the research process from the initial research to question development to the final dissemination of results.

3. *Build cultural competency* Listen and learn from the community about their cultural perspectives.

4. *Improve transparency of research practices* Make research goals and processes clear and understandable through frequent communication.

5. *Build community research capacity* Train and support community members in the research process.

6. *Disseminate findings in a community-accessible format* Collaborate with community partners to use culturally appropriate methods of disseminating and applying the findings.

Work continues to ensure archaeological DNA projects in the Americas are more inclusive, representative, and respectful.

The ice-free corridor was long thought to be the sole entry route used, until it was shown people were at Monte Verde long before it opened. Then it was supposed it might have been the route taken by later arrivals, assuming they represented different groups. Yet it is now apparent that could not have been the case either. Although retreating glacial ice had physically opened the corridor by Clovis times, it was only several centuries later, around or after 13,000 years ago, that the plants and animals necessary to the survival of hunter-gatherers had established themselves in that passage.

In contrast, by 15,000 years ago, if not earlier, a coastal route was open for travel. It has been proposed that the earliest populations exploited sea mammals, shellfish, seaweed, and other marine resources, and because these were available along the length of the coast they would have been able to move rapidly south. Although there is no direct archaeological evidence to support that supposition, a coastal entry seems the only option to get around and south of the continental ice sheets in time for people to reach such sites as Monte Verde and others of that antiquity.

Learning New Landscapes

The earliest sites in the Americas, such as Cooper's Ferry in Idaho, the Paisley Caves in Oregon, Meadowcroft Rockshelter in Pennsylvania [**14.5**], Monte Verde in Chile, and Huaca Prieta in Peru, are few, widely scattered, and unalike (see Key Sites box: Earliest Sites, p. 332). We do not have many clues to the adaptive strategies of the very first people making their way into what was then a land where no humans had ever been; it was a place that would have become increasingly unfamiliar as these groups moved south from the Arctic region into the temperate zone and tropical regions, and from coastal areas into continental interiors.

These early populations were probably flexible in their social organization to make certain they could readily renew ties with other communities they encountered, enabling them to exchange information and mates to ensure that the relatively few people spread thinly across a landscape would survive and thrive.

Communities face the greatest risk of failure early on, when their numbers are low and the terrain and its resources are unknown and unpredictable. In the short term, they had to find food, water, shelter, fuel, and material to make and maintain their tools. But to be successful over the long term they had to learn the landscape. Insurance for hunter-gatherers is not just knowing their immediate surroundings; it is knowing where to go when conditions deteriorate where they are. There would have been a distinct advantage and strong incentive for people to range widely and perhaps rapidly.

There were costs to moving too far too fast, if it meant moving away from other people. Communities had to maintain contact with other dispersing groups, to maintain a critical mass of population, and to prevent inbreeding or extinction. This would have been more or less difficult depending on a group's size, growth rates, kin structure, the age and sex of individuals within the group, and how rapidly and far it was moving away from other groups and population densities.

The scarcity of the very earliest sites makes this process of migration difficult to see, but by Clovis times, when there is a fuller archaeological record, we start to glimpse what dispersing across a new land looked like archaeologically.

14.5 Excavation at Meadowcroft Rockshelter, Pennsylvania. The walls of the more than 5-meter-deep (16 feet) excavation are marked with white tags of various sizes that designate the depositional strata at the site; locate such features as hearths, storage pits, and work areas; and identify points where samples were taken for specialized analyses.

KEY SITES Earliest Sites

There was a time when the idea of archaeological sites dated before Clovis, 13,400 years ago, seemed impossible. The status quo was that the Clovis people, with their fluted points, were the first to people the Americas. It was only with the discovery of sites, such as Monte Verde, and the eventual acceptance of their far earlier dates that archaeologists began to discuss populations that existed before Clovis on the continent. The number of sites dated before this culture (traditionally called pre-Clovis) continues to grow, and some remain hotly debated, especially those with very early dates, such as the recently reported discoveries at Chiquihuite Cave in Mexico, with remains claimed to push human occupation of the Americas as early as 33,000–31,000 years ago. Here is only a sample of the earliest sites in the Americas.

14.6 Remarkable preservation of organic materials in the MV II layer at Monte Verde, Chile, which include wooden beams that formed the base of a structure, covered by mastodon hide tied down with juncus reeds to wooden stakes pounded into the ground.

Monte Verde

Located in Chile along Chinchihuapi Creek and excavated from 1977 to 1985 [**14.6**, **14.7**], Monte Verde is exceptional for its preservation, and was one of the first sites designated as pre-Clovis to be widely accepted. Sometime after the site's inhabitants departed, the creek was obstructed, which led to the formation of peat that preserved the remains in an anaerobic environment. Around seventy-five preserved species of plants were found, some from the coast around 30 kilometers (19 miles) away, and others from high in the Andes. Some plants were charred from cooking, while others were in the form of artifacts, such as wooden mortars and spears. Still others were used as construction materials including wooden planks and pegs from a structure. Found as well were bones, teeth, tusks, and hide fragments of mastodon, and the remains of fish, shellfish, birds, and eggshells. Multiple radiocarbon dates on wood, charcoal, tusk, and bone conducted by independent laboratories returned an average age of around 14,600 years ago.

Although only about 1,000 years older than the Clovis period, Monte Verde's distance from Beringia—roughly

14.7 Foundations of a wishbone-shaped structure in the MV II layer at Monte Verde. Mastodon hide, meat, and the remains of various medicinal plants were recovered from inside the structure.

14.8 Entrance to Paisley Caves, Oregon.

16,000 kilometers (10,000 miles)—and its decidedly non-Clovis appearance, raised many questions about who the earliest people in the Americas were, where they came from, when they crossed Beringia, how they made it south past the continental ice sheets, and why one of the oldest sites in the Americas is so far from the land bridge.

Meadowcroft Rockshelter

Described by some as the longest-occupied site in the Americas, Meadowcroft is located in Washington County, Pennsylvania and is thought to have been first occupied soon after the Last Glacial Maximum; its latest inhabitation was in the eighteenth century CE. The site's oldest artifact-bearing layers date to about 14,500 years ago. The numerous occupation layers contained many thousands of stone flakes (principally from resharpening dulled tools and weapons) along with numerous tools including small blades, knives, and engraving tools, some 150 fire pits, dozens of storage and roasting pits, and almost 1 million animal bone fragments and 1.4 million plant fragments. The earliest levels contained some 700 items of stone (including a lanceolate point) and bone, with the stone for the artifacts having come from both local sources, and sources up to 300 kilometers (186 miles) away.

Some archaeologists questioned the earliest dates, arguing that samples could have been contaminated by coal particles, or by carbon dissolved in the groundwater, resulting in older dates for the specimens. The dates are in stratigraphic order (that is, youngest at the top, oldest at the bottom), however, which would not be the case if contamination had occurred. In addition, a microscopic study of the sediments failed to detect evidence of coal contamination or groundwater activity.

Paisley Caves

Located in central Oregon, the Paisley Caves are a series of hollows in the low basalt hills on the margin of a now-vanished Pleistocene lake [**14.8**]. Dry conditions in the caves have preserved an array of otherwise perishable fragments of baskets, rope, hides, and hair, along with what is perhaps the most unusual evidence of an ancient human presence: coprolites (ancient feces). Apparently this site was used at times as a latrine. The oldest of the coprolites have been dated to around 14,500 years ago and, more striking, have yielded ancient human mitochondrial DNA that matches Native American haplogroups.

Critics asked whether the human DNA had seeped down into and contaminated non-human coprolites, but multiple laboratories have confirmed they are human, and human DNA has not been found in either sediment or non-human coprolites (including of mountain sheep, bobcat, Pleistocene lion, and camel) at the site. The site has also yielded artifacts and features, such as hearths with burned bone and stone tools. But overall there are few artifacts with the coprolites.

HUNTER-GATHERER TRAJECTORIES: THE CLOVIS OCCUPATION OF NORTH AMERICA, *c.* 11,400–10,600 BCE

The Clovis archaeological culture first appears around 13,400 years ago, and within 300 to 500 years its traces are found throughout unglaciated North America as far south as Panama (see Key Sites box: Folsom and Clovis, p. 336). The most iconic aspect of the Clovis is its fluted bifacial projectile points, which were hafted or attached to spears, and used principally as weapons—possibly propelled by an atlatl or spear thrower. They also occasionally served as knives. Although they vary stylistically, Clovis points are readily recognized variations on a theme [**14.9**].

The rapid expansion of Clovis points appears to represent the movement of people, as opposed to the diffusion of a distinctive technology across a population already in place. How and why Clovis groups moved so far so fast remains obscure.

Clovis remains are most abundant in eastern and especially southeastern North America, in what were then species-rich, complex forests. Yet the oldest of these sites are further west and south, including the Aubrey site, Texas, and El Fin del Mundo, Mexico. The unevenness of the Clovis distribution in space and time is partly a function of archaeological visibility resulting from modern land-use practices and geological processes: widespread farming in eastern North America, for example, readily brings up Clovis artifacts from shallowly buried Pleistocene-age surfaces. Overall, their distribution appears broad rather than deep and slips through time, with Clovis-like forms dating as late as around 12,600 years ago in far northeastern North America (Debert site, Nova Scotia).

Broadly speaking, the Clovis toolkit was portable, readily resharpened, and functionally flexible. Their knappers also produced prismatic blades, and these as well as flakes were used as they were or further modified into more formal tools, such as end and side scrapers, gravers, or drills. Artifacts of bone and ivory, including notched or beveled cylindrical rods, occur in Clovis sites but are few in number. Rare, too, are instances of art objects [**14.10**]. The scarcity of artifacts made of perishable, organic materials is almost certainly a result of poor preservation rather than their lack of use in Clovis times.

One unusual aspect of Clovis tools is that some are found as caches. There are more than twelve known, which often comprise dozens of newly made projectile points, bifaces, preforms, blades, flakes, and occasionally bone and ivory rods. Several hypotheses have been offered to explain their occurrence, including that they served as supply depots for living people or as ritual deposits with the deceased. Both possibilities seem reasonable, the latter especially for caches associated with human skeletal remains, as at the site of Anzick, Montana.

In manufacturing their stone tools, Clovis people relied almost exclusively on **cryptocrystalline** chert, jasper, chalcedony, and obsidian (volcanic glass). Because these stone types

14.9 Clovis points
from the Drake Cache, northeastern Colorado. The stone used in their manufacture, Alibates agatized dolomite, outcrops in the Texas Panhandle, a straight-line distance of *c.* 650 kilometers (*c.* 400 miles). Such caches may have served as supply depots for colonizers as they moved out across the landscape. The specimens in the cache range from 8.9–16.5 centimeters (3.5–6.5 inches) in length.

can be distinctive in color, fossils, and chemistry, it is often possible to identify the geological sources where they were obtained. It is usually assumed the stone was acquired as a byproduct of a group's visit to the source, rather than via exchange, an assumption that may not be warranted. But if it is, then the distance from the source to the site where an artifact was discarded provides a gauge of how far foragers moved across the landscape. By this measure, groups on the treeless western Plains and the parkland of northeastern North America routinely traveled 300–400 kilometers (180–250 miles), while those occupying the forests of eastern North America moved shorter distances. This may be a function of the patchiness of resources being exploited, and of how much farther groups in open settings had to travel to encounter them.

14.10 Possible examples of Clovis art include incisions on stones, such as these from the Gault site in Texas.

As to what those resources might have been, there has long been debate regarding the importance of **megafauna**, such as mammoth, mastodon, or giant ground sloth, in the Clovis diet [**14.11**, **14.12**]. At one extreme is the claim that Clovis people and their South American counterparts were wide-ranging, fast-moving hunters whose wanton slaughter of big game caused the extinction of thirty-eight genera of megafauna in North America, and of another fifty-two genera in South America. This claim fails for multiple reasons, not least a lack of archaeological kill sites (see Key Controversy box: Pleistocene Extinctions, p. 340). Others offer a more nuanced view, namely that large prey were an important resource, and were taken in disproportionate frequency to other, smaller prey.

14.11, 14.12 Examples of megafauna during the time of the Clovis people. Skeletons of mastodon (below left) and giant ground sloth (below right). Hunting of such large game may have been for prestige rather than for regular subsistence.

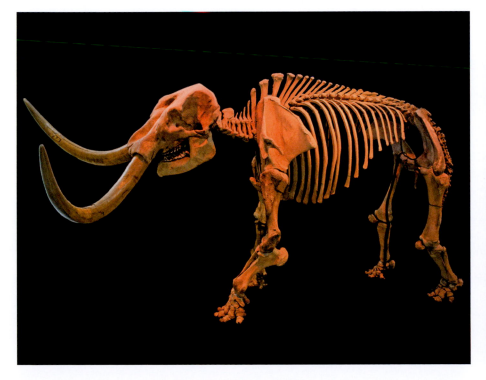

It is true that some very large animals—including mammoth—were on the menu at such Clovis sites as Colby, Wyoming, and Murray Springs, Arizona. Yet of the fifteen sites where human traces were compellingly associated with the remains of extinct megafauna, some may be instances of opportunistic scavenging rather than the deliberate hunting of big, dangerous prey. In fact, given the risk and low success rate associated with big-game hunting, and the apparent underutilization of their carcasses, it has been argued that such hunting may have been conducted more for prestige than provisioning.

Megafauna aside, Clovis groups exploited a range of mammals from large (bison, caribou) to small (rabbits, rodents), as well as reptiles (turtles), birds, and fish, with diet breadth varying across regions. Subsistence strategies of groups in the forests of eastern North America, for example, were more varied and less dominated by large mammals than those of their counterparts occupying the open grassland habitats of the Plains and far western North America. It is important to acknowledge, however, that large mammal bones are highly visible in the archaeological record, and may lead us to overestimate their importance in the Clovis diet, and underestimate the importance of smaller game and plants, which are less visible and often missed without careful field recovery methods.

KEY SITES Folsom and Clovis

In the last century two locations have played pivotal roles in the history of our understanding of the peopling of the Americas.

Folsom

The site of **Folsom**, New Mexico, was excavated from 1926–28 following decades of often bitter dispute over whether humans were in the Americas during the Ice Age or whether they arrived in North America much more recently.

Folsom changed that: in 1927, distinctive fluted spear points—known as Folsom points—were found in unambiguous association with bones of an extinct bison, *Bison antiquus*, which on paleontological and geological grounds dated to at least the Late Pleistocene (an estimate later affirmed by radiocarbon dating, which puts the age of this site at around 12,500 years ago). Folsom established that early groups—termed Paleoindian on the assumption they were ancestors of current Indigenous populations—had arrived in the Americas in Ice Age times.

Folsom was a kill site where hunters maneuvered thirty-two bison into a cul-de-sac within a steep-sided arroyo (rocky ravine or dry watercourse), slaughtered the animals, butchered the carcasses, and then transported off-site large, meaty portions, leaving behind more than two dozen projectile points. Importantly, it taught archaeologists how to find more sites like it: search for the more easily spotted bones of large animals, and then examine the remains closely for associated stone artifacts. This strategy worked. In the two decades that followed the Folsom discovery nearly three dozen large mammal kills were found. Of course, how archaeologists searched for those sites predisposed what they found, and that repeated pattern of kill sites led naturally to the inference that the first people were big-game hunters. These ideas lasted long after it was clear that big-game kill sites were the exception and not the rule.

Clovis

One of the most important discoveries made in the initial decades after Folsom was the site of **Clovis**, New Mexico, a large one-time spring-fed pond rich in animal fossils and artifacts. Here in 1933, fluted projectile points larger and less delicately made than Folsom points—later called Clovis points—were found associated with mammoth bones. Over the course of excavations at the site, it was shown that the Clovis points and mammoth remains occurred stratigraphically below the layer containing Folsom points and bison bones. Clovis culture obviously predated Folsom.

Because the appearance of Clovis appeared to parallel the opening of the ice-free corridor between the Cordilleran and Laurentide glaciers, archaeologists assumed Clovis were the first culture in the Americas. No Clovis remains were found in Beringia, however. One possible explanation for their absence was that Clovis ancestors came through Alaska and the corridor and invented their distinctive spear points only after their arrival. Alternatively, it has been argued that Clovis originated south of the continental ice sheets from a pre-Clovis age population that was already present in this hemisphere before the corridor opened.

Regardless of their foraging strategies and how far they moved, there is little evidence people stayed for long in any one place, or built significant structures, or returned repeatedly to specific locales. With a continent still mostly to themselves, there was little incentive to linger in one place or revisit a spot, unless it offered a prized or predictable resource, for example a known source of stone. Such is the advantage to populations in a landscape with few other people and no apparent territorial boundaries.

REGIONALIZATION: NORTH AMERICA AFTER CLOVIS

The Clovis period marks the first and last time in North American archaeology that there was a broad, almost continent-wide similarity in artifact assemblages. This may have been the result of wide-ranging mobility and social mechanisms aimed at enabling small groups of people to renew ties readily. Clovis points are broadly similar stylistically, technologically, and typologically across a vast area of North America, and may have served as a currency (a term not to be taken too literally) for an extensive social network that maintained recognition and helped check the attenuating effects of distance and time. Gradually, however, the archaeological record changes. Although the timing varies in different areas, post-Clovis projectile point forms began to appear sometime after 12,600 years ago, and by 12,000 years ago the once pan-North American Clovis form has been replaced by a variety of regionally distinctive point types.

The shift from a single broad and relatively homogeneous form to multiple regional styles can be interpreted in a number of ways: as adaptation to specific areas and their food sources; as a relaxation in the pressure to maintain contact with distant kin (populations by then having increased in number); and as a reduction in the spatial scale and openness of the social systems. They are more restricted geographically, are part of new and sometime prey- or region-specific foraging strategies (occasionally involving newly invented technologies), and in places are made of stone obtained from nearby sources, indicating less extensive movement.

The Great Plains. The earliest replacement of Clovis occurred on the Great Plains and Rocky Mountains, and is marked by a succession of archaeological complexes known by their distinctive projectile points (Folsom, Plainview, Goshen, Agate Basin, Hell Gap, Cody) [**14.13**], all of which nevertheless share common elements in their adaptive strategies: most notably, bison hunting.

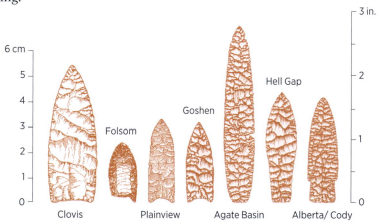

14.13 Select North American early projectile point forms found on the Plains. The bottom edges of these points were intentionally ground from their base to about their mid-portion. The Folsom point shown was heavily resharpened before being discarded. Points were probably ground along their lower edges for several reasons, not least because this is where it was bound by sinew or plant fibers to a bone or wooden spearshaft, and the grinding served to dull the edges so they would not cut their bindings when under the stress of use as projectiles or cutting tools. These points are generally older to younger, from left to right.

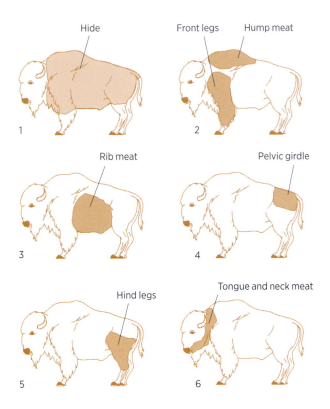

14.14 The river of bison bones at Olsen-Chubbuck. The base of the lower portion of the long, narrow, V-shaped arroyo, into which some 190 bison had been stampeded and killed. The bison in the front of the stampede tumbled into the arroyo and were then fallen upon by the remainder of the herd. Ultimately the arroyo was choked to the brim with bison heaped two to three animals deep. The hunters butchered most of the bison accessible at the top of the pile, but the carcasses at the base were left largely untouched, the hunters by then perhaps having acquired all the meat they could readily eat and transport.

14.15 Generalized butchering pattern of the bison at the Olsen-Chubbuck site. The diagram is based on archaeological evidence, supplemented by observations of bison butchering by historic Plains bison hunters: **1**, the bison carcass was rolled onto its belly and the hide was cut down the back and pulled to both sides to form a blanket of flesh on which the meat could be piled; **2**, the front legs and hump meat were removed; **3**, the rib meat was removed, sometimes with ribs still attached, exposing the inner organs, which were then extracted and perhaps eaten on the spot; **4**, the carcass was then severed just behind the rib cage to remove the pelvic girdle and attached meat; **5**, the meat from the hind legs was then cut away; followed by **6**, severing of the neck and skull, and removal of the tongue and neck meat.

Bison are large, gregarious herd animals, which have poor eyesight (though a keen sense of smell) and tend to stampede when frightened. Folsom and later groups exploited these aspects of bison physiology and behavior by maneuvering and trapping the animals in box canyons or high-walled sand dunes, or running them into stream channels or arroyos. The oft-envisioned image of bison hurtling down artificial drive lines and then over a cliff to their deaths was not part of the Paleoindian hunting repertoire, but occurred only in much later times.

These early bison kills commonly involved relatively few animals, probably being made by small task groups of hunters. There are a small number of spectacularly huge communal kills, however, such as at Olsen-Chubbuck [**14.14**] and Jones-Miller (both in eastern Colorado), in which hundreds of bison were slaughtered in a single episode. The difficult-to-control nature of these incidences meant that oftentimes more animals were killed than could be utilized. At Olsen-Chubbuck, for example, archaeologists found that 16 percent of the 190 animals killed were only partially butchered, and at least 10 percent of the animals at the bottom of the pile showed no evidence of butchering at all.

In fact, Paleoindian groups rarely fully exploited the food potential of their prey, whether in large kills or small. Described as gourmet butchering, carcass processing was often limited to the removal of select cuts of meat [14.15], which were eaten on the spot, or prepared by drying or freezing for transport and later consumption. At some sites, bones were broken open for marrow.

The end of the Paleoindian period on the Plains around 9,000 years ago is marked by a long, severe episode of aridity and drought (the Altithermal), during which bison populations were markedly diminished, and human foragers focused their subsistence on a variety of other food resources (see Key Controversy box: Pleistocene Extinctions, p. 340). That shift away from a bison-dominated diet was not altogether revolutionary, for these groups had always exploited other game species, and perhaps also plants, although the evidence for the latter is admittedly meager.

Western North America. We have only limited evidence of the diet of people in far western North America, including the Great Basin. What does exist indicates that many resources were used, and that these varied by region. Plants were eaten, as well as a wide variety of small mammals and, where available, fish, frogs, and waterfowl.

The toolkits of these foragers were not unlike those of other contemporary groups: they were made to travel and consisted of generalized pieces, such as knives, scrapers, incising tools (burins and gravers) , and projectile points [14.16, 14.17]. The materials for these were often obtained from distant sources. Though mobility decreased from earlier times, the seasonal round still encompassed considerable areas. Later, as the climate warmed still further and wetlands shrank (after around 10,800 years ago) (see Key Theme box: Climate Change–The Effects of Climate Change on the Earliest Native Americans, p. 342), ground-stone tools appear with increasing frequency, presumably for use in more intensive plant and seed processing.

14.16 BELOW LEFT
A montage of Late Paleoindian stone tools from the central Rio Grande Valley of New Mexico. Included are scrapers (left side and top row), finely tipped gravers (center), spokeshaves (concave-edged tools in the upper center), and less formally prepared flake-cutting and scraping tools.

14.17 BELOW RIGHT
New artifacts. A Dalton projectile point **a**, and a Dalton adze **b**. The original specimens are from the Sloan site, Arkansas. The adze appears to have been a woodworking tool.

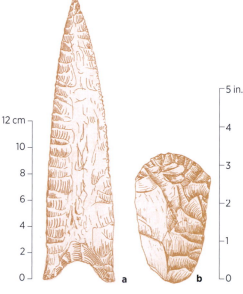

KEY CONTROVERSY Pleistocene Extinctions

The end of the Pleistocene saw the extinction of thirty-eight genera of mammals in North America, and fifty-two mammalian genera in South America [**14.18**]. Most, though not all, of these were large animals, megafauna that weighed more than 44 kilograms (about 100 pounds); some, such as the proboscideans (mammoths and mastodons), tipped the scales at upward of about 4.5 metric tons (5 US tons). The cause of their demise has been debated for more than 150 years, and because their extinction appears to coincide with both the arrival of humans and the end of the Ice Age, there are two principal suspects: human overkill and climate/environmental change. Yet the former fails multiple empirical tests and the latter is poorly understood, with the result that resolution has long been stymied. Fortunately, the advent of ancient DNA may finally move us past this impasse.

Overkill is based on several assumptions: that extinction occurred simultaneously across genera; that it coincided with the spread of Clovis big-game hunters; that hunters moved rapidly; and that the animals, never having encountered human hunters, were naive to this new danger and so vulnerable to predation.

It cannot be demonstrated, however, that all these genera met their demise at the same time. Moreover, only seventeen of those thirty-eight genera can be shown to have been contemporaries of Clovis. A similar pattern appears to hold for South America. In other regions of the world, extinctions were staggered over time and occurred in the absence of people; it would seem this was true in the Americas as well.

A Scarcity of Victims for Human Hunters
There is little compelling evidence that the genera that shared the landscape with humans were hunted in significant numbers. Of the more than ninety sites said to testify to big-game hunting in North America, only fifteen provide secure evidence that humans were responsible for the death of the animals, and four of the sites are in relatively close proximity in Arizona's San Pedro Valley, and may have been the work of just one group. Moreover, only five genera were targeted: mammoth, mastodon, gomphothere, horse, and camel. There are no kill sites of the other thirty-three North American genera that went extinct, and no uncontested evidence of hunting of any of the fifty-two genera that went extinct in South America.

The scarcity of evidence for the hunting of now-extinct megafauna is particularly striking when compared to the rich archaeological record of bison hunting. Bison were first targeted in Clovis times, and preyed upon more or less continuously over the next 11,000 years; nearly 1,000 bison kill sites are known, some in which hundreds of animals were slain at once. This was followed by the relentless slaughter of bison by nineteenth-century commercial hide hunters. And yet, bison survive. It is doubtful Clovis hunters could destroy in a few centuries an entire hemisphere's megafauna, estimated at 100 million animals, yet leave so few traces of the carnage.

Other Causes of Extinction
Given the dearth of kill sites and that different genera disappeared at different times, it suggests extinctions resulted from more complicated causes than the arrival of human hunters at a specific moment in time, notably the complex climatic and environmental changes that took place at the end of the Pleistocene. If such changes were responsible, we expect to see impacts on other taxa beyond megafauna, as indeed we do. In North America, some twenty genera of birds, multiple reptile genera, and a species of spruce tree went extinct, while throughout the continent animals and plants underwent sometimes extensive range shifts in response to fluctuating climatic and ecological patterns, as well as local die-outs, marking the inability of a species to cope with changes in one region, but able to survive elsewhere. Several surviving species also decreased in size, a new species of bison arose, and there was substantial loss of genetic diversity in many taxa (groups), indicative of strong selective pressures in the environment.

The recent application of ancient DNA studies to these now-extinct Late Pleistocene animals may hold the key to understanding the crucial details of their population histories. Efforts in this realm have only just begun, but already have

---

Because of the occasionally spectacular preservation of organic materials in the dry caves of the Great Basin, we also can see how these groups used plant fibers to fabricate baskets, nets, line, and cordage for a variety of purposes.

Eastern North America. In general, adaptations in the late Pleistocene forests of eastern North America involved the exploitation of a wide variety of animal and plant resources, ranging from large to small mammals, birds, fish, and many nut and fruit trees. Among the

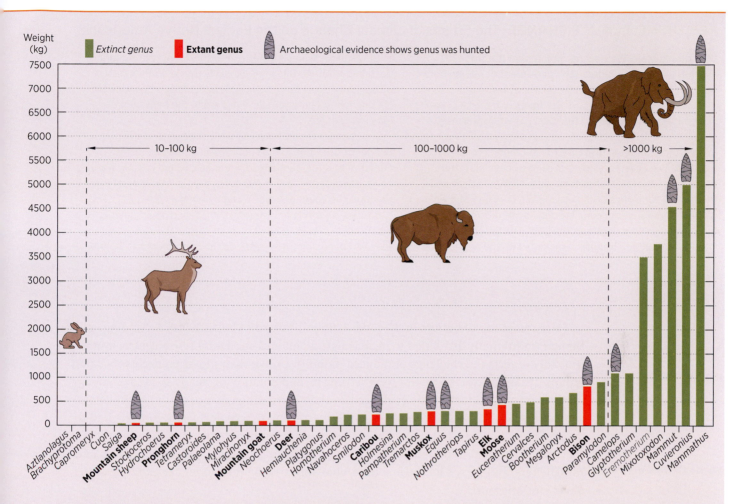

Weight (kg)

■ *Extinct genus* ■ **Extant genus** ◗ Archaeological evidence shows genus was hunted

10–100 kg   100–1000 kg   >1000 kg

Aztlanolagus, Brachyprotoma, Capromeryx, Cuon, Saiga, **Mountain sheep**, Stockoceros, Hydrochoerus, **Pronghorn**, Tetrameryx, Castoroides, Palaeolama, Mylohyus, Miracinonyx, **Mountain goat**, Neochoerus, **Deer**, Hemiauchenia, Platygonus, Homotherium, Navahoceros, Smilodon, **Caribou**, Holmesina, Pampatherium, Tremarctos, **Muskox**, Equus, Nothrotheriops, Tapirus, **Elk**, **Moose**, Euceratherium, Cervalces, Bootherium, Megalonyx, Arctodus, **Bison**, Paramylodon, Camelops, Glyptotherium, Eremotherium, Mixotoxodon, Mammut, Cuvieronius, Mammathus

revealed demographic fluctuations, bottlenecks, and local extirpations in many taxa over the Late Pleistocene, although the scale and timing of these varies. These have shown, as well, that there was a progressive loss of genetic diversity toward the end of the Pleistocene in both extinct and extant (surviving) species, with the overall losses more pronounced in some taxa (bison, lion, muskox, wolf) than others (horse, mammoth, saiga). These changes mostly occurred before humans arrived and are therefore attributable to non-anthropogenic (resulting from human activity, or caused by humans) causes.

14.18 Extinct and extant North American genera ordered by their estimated body weight, and indicating where there is evidence of human predation between 12,000 and 10,000 radiocarbon years ago. Columns in green color are extinct species; those in red are extant genera.

latter were acorns, which to be made palatable require the removal of their tannic acid by leaching. Although no baskets are preserved from this period and place, sites of this age have grinding tools that would have served the mashing purpose. Evidently, experimentation by around 12,500 years ago had shown eastern Paleoindians how to make acorns suitable as food, perhaps as a bread flour. The wide variety of foods consumed in these areas indicates a broad-based utilization of resources from closed forest to relatively open settings to the **ecotones** in between.

ecotone an area forming the boundary between contrasting environmental regions

Eating from top to bottom in the food chain indicates diet breadth was expanding, and though traditionally attributed to increasingly adept and successful resource use, it more probably reflects the challenge of reduced mobility. Unlike their Clovis predecessors, later groups in eastern North America were settling in, and not moving nearly so far and so regularly across the landscape, as evidenced by their increasing reliance on more local stone sources. As populations increased while their territorial ranges decreased, foragers had to expand their diet to include more lower-ranked foods. As a part of their settling-in process, they made frequent and repeated use of fixed spots in the landscape, notably caves and rockshelters, and we see for the first time what appear to be cemeteries, for example at the Sloan site, Missouri.

Although we see use of plant foods in North America at the end of the Pleistocene, their more intensive use as a food source and, ultimately, the purposeful cultivation and domestication of plants come much later in time (see Chapter 15). This contrasts significantly with the South American archaeological record, which probably speaks to differences in the way the early South Americans met the challenges of a new landscape, and the fact that there was no single solution to solving that equation of moving to learn and staying to observe.

PEOPLING THE LANDSCAPE: THE EARLIEST SOUTH AMERICANS

The first groups in the southern hemisphere had ancestors who came via North America and, given the evidence from Monte Verde in Chile, this must have been well before 14,600 years ago. Monte Verde is located near, though not on, the Pleistocene coast and has yielded evidence of the use of coastal resources, including seaweed, which is seen as affirmation that the first South Americans came via the Pacific Coast. Here and at Huaca Prieta and Arroyo Seco (Argentina), the earliest sites on the continent, terrestrial resources from the interior and highlands were also exploited, suggesting that the initial groups foraged widely.

From a geographic point of view, in fact, people poised at the junction of the Panamanian Isthmus and northernmost South America had multiple options to enter the continent: they could have moved south down the Pacific Coast, or eastward around the Caribbean arc, or down the Andean Highlands, from which they could have traveled inland, perhaps along major river valleys into the Amazon Basin, or onto Pampa and Patagonian grasslands.

But just how they entered—and whether movement was along multiple tracks rather than a single pathway or from the outside (coast) inward—is unclear, for as was the case in North America, there are only a few, widely scattered and securely dated South American sites that predate 13,000 years ago. This pattern may partly result from limited sampling: large portions of South America, especially the extensive, now heavily forested Amazon Basin, where archaeological visibility and preservation are poor, have not been thoroughly searched.

As in North America, too, there is a sharp increase in the number of sites after *c.* 13,000 years ago across much of South America, though here it is marked by evidence of human settlement in multiple habitats including high in the Andes, along with evidence of pronounced interregional cultural diversity.

The temporal pattern hemisphere-wide is probably the result of an initially small and mobile population dispersed discontinuously across a vast continent not leaving much of an archaeological record behind. In effect, there were simply too few people on the landscape before 13,000 years ago to have made much of an imprint in North or South America. After 13,000 years ago, there were. But there the similarities between North and South America mostly end.

Adaptation in a Diverse Environment

The adaptations of the first South Americans are distinct in multiple ways from those seen in North America, not least in the absence of a comparable, continent-wide stone tool style similar to Clovis. Instead, there is regional cultural diversification very early on, expressed in differences in artifact types and technology, subsistence patterns, mobility, and other aspects of adaptive strategies.

The biface and blade technology and heavy reliance on fine cryptocrystalline stone so distinctive of early North Americans is uncommon in South America. In the latter, bifaces tend to be rare (and limited to projectile point types), and assemblages are routinely dominated by expediently made unifacial tools made of locally derived stone, which is often relatively coarse-grained and not of particularly good quality, suggesting that the purpose to which these tools were to be put did not demand the finest cryptocrystalline stone. Being able to make use of a wide range of stone tools would have had the incidental benefit of increasing the number of potential sources for raw material, so reducing the need to track great distances across the landscape to a favored rock outcrop. Not having to move far or often to procure vital resources helped to set the stage for early sedentary lifestyles.

Some long-distance movement of stone did occur: obsidian used in tools at the Peruvian coastal site of Quebrada Jaguay, dated to almost 13,000 years ago, came from 150 kilometers (93 miles) away from a source nearly 4,500 meters (14,800 feet) high in the Andes.

That was the start of what became, over the next 10,000 years in Peru, Chile, and Argentina, an increasing use of high-elevation areas in the Andes. Because of the physiological challenges and selective pressure of life at high elevation (more than 3,000 meters, or 10,000 feet)—especially low-oxygen availability—these populations ultimately developed adaptations both biological (for example, higher haemoglobin concentration) and cultural, which eased life at that altitude.

The evidence from the Pucuncho Basin indicates that groups on the western side of the Andes were exploiting multiple elevations, moving higher or lower seasonally to take advantage of both terrestrial and marine resources. Early sites located close to the Pacific Coast at the time have yielded evidence of marine fish (anchovies, shad, herring), shellfish (wedge clams), and birds (cormorants and boobies), along with possible evidence of net fragments used to capture some of these foods. These sites also reveal the use of terrestrial resources that must have been obtained in interior areas, just as interior sites have produced marine resources. In effect, there is no single subsistence specialization; rather, groups exploited a wide range of supply options.

Those resources included plants as well. In fact, there is compelling evidence that plants played a key role in the settling of forest and even more open environments of South America, a role first glimpsed at Monte Verde, with its unmistakable use of plants as a food source, but also as medicine and a construction material. In the Amazonian lowlands of Brazil, the site of Pedra Pintada yielded remains of roughly a dozen species of nut- and fruit-bearing trees and plants. Plant use in several places involved the active manipulation of the environment, as in northwestern South America, where there is evidence for the clearing of forests, the maintenance of those clearings by the use of fire, and the tending and possible transport of wild plants, such as palm nuts, squash, and grass species. Such manipulation of resources would ultimately lead to the comparatively early development of cultigens and domesticated forms. At the Ecuadorian site of Las Vegas, for example, analysis of phytoliths (microscopic plant remains) has shown that groups here 11,750 years ago were cultivating the squash *Cucurbita*.

Reflecting the broad range of resources being exploited, artifact assemblages associated with these various complexes include a variety of hunting and animal-processing implements, notably stone points, scrapers and knives, bone tools, and more specialized hunting implements (sling stones and bola stones). There were, as well, plant-processing tools, such as pestles, mortars, and grinding stones, for processing nuts, seeds, tubers, and other foods.

SUMMARY AND CONCLUSIONS

The Americas were the last habitable continent to be reached by modern humans in ancient times, but people did not arrive there until the end of the Pleistocene, tens of thousands of years after their ancestors departed from Africa. That it took so long was not merely due to the great distance to be traveled; it was also a matter of adapting to life in the Arctic.

But we can further narrow that time window. Genetic evidence reveals that a split between the earliest Americans and Asian populations occurred around 23,000 years ago, indicating these two groups had by then become isolated from one another.

The oldest sites so far known in the Americas date to *c.* 16,000–15,000 years ago. In order to reach these sites in those millennia, people who made it across the land bridge would have had to skirt the still-formidable barrier to the south formed by the continental ice sheets. One route, along the Pacific Coast, was open after at least around 16,000 years ago. The alternative, an ice-free corridor between the Laurentide and Cordilleran ice sheets, did not become biologically viable until about 12,600 years ago, too late for people to have made it to these early sites.

That one of the oldest accepted sites in the Americas, Monte Verde, is also the farthest from Beringia indicates there must be older ones closer to the land bridge. The search for these sites will no doubt continue. So too will genetic investigations, which—despite how few ancient genomes have been sequenced to date—have already provided key insights into earliest American populations, revealing their complex Eurasian ancestry, and showing that the initial population diverged into the northern and southern branches evident among Indigenous communities today. Much more will surely come from such studies, along with greater collaboration between the scientific and Indigenous communities.

By the last millennia of the Pleistocene, people had dispersed throughout the hemisphere. Not surprisingly, given the differences in the habitats they occupied—which ranged from coastal settings to interior grasslands to mountain environments—there was considerable variation in subsistence strategies, technologies, and adaptation, variations that are particularly evident between North and South America. Differences were evident within each of the continents during the early period of dispersal as well. Claims that the first people in the Americas were predominantly big-game hunters fail for lack of archaeological evidence—simultaneously discrediting the claim that human hunting drove to extinction several dozen genera of large mammals in North America, and more than fifty genera in South America. After the end of the Pleistocene, modern animal and plant communities begin to be established; this represents the postglacial, the current era. As this happened, populations became even more regionally different as they adapted to changes in the landscape. This period of differentiation and adaptation is known as the Archaic period and is discussed in Chapter 15.

FURTHER READING

The following provide useful introductions to the archaeology of the early Americas:

Claw, K. G. *et al.* 2018. A framework for enhancing ethical genomic research with Indigenous communities. Nat Commun 9 (1), 2957. doi:10.1038/s41467-018-05188-3.

Gillespie, A. *et al.* (eds.). 2004. *The Quaternary Period in the United States*. New York: Elsevier Science.

Graf, K. *et al.* (eds.). 2014. *Paleoamerican Odyssey*. College Station: Texas A&M University Press.

Huckell, B. and Kilby, D. (eds.). 2004. *Readings in Late Pleistocene and Early Holocene Paleoindians: Selections from American Antiquity*. Washington, D.C.: Society for American Archaeology.

Madsen, D., ed. 2004. *Entering America: Northeast Asia and Beringia before the Last Glacial Maximum*. Salt Lake City: University of Utah Press.

Meltzer, D. J. 2021. *First Peoples in a New World: Populating Ice Age America*. 2nd edn. Cambridge: Cambridge University Press.

Moreno-Mayar, J. V. *et al.* 2018. Early human dispersals within the Americas. Science 362 (6419). doi:10.1126/science.aav2621.

Morrow, J. and Gnecco, C. (eds.). 2006. *Paleoindian Archaeology: A Hemispheric Perspective*. Gainesville: University Press of Florida.

Smallwood, A. M. and Jennings, T. A. (eds.). 2015. *Clovis: On the Edge of a New Understanding*. College Station: Texas A&M University Press.

North America

15

George R. Milner and W. H. Wills, with
David L. Browman, Gayle J. Fritz, and BrieAnna S. Langlie

Environments and Landscapes 349

Hunter-Gatherer Trajectories: Eastern North America, Archaic Period, *c*. 9500–1000 BCE 350

Transitions to Agriculture: Eastern North America, Early and Middle Woodland Periods, *c*. 1000 BCE**–400** CE 352

KEY SITE Hopewell 354

Expansion of Domestication: Late Woodland Period, *c*. 400–1000 CE 355

Early Farming Communities: Mississippian Period, *c*. 1000–1700 CE 356

KEY CONTROVERSY The Size and Influence of Cahokia 358

Transitions to Agriculture: Southwest North America, 2100–1100 BCE 359

Early Farming Communities: Preclassic and Classic Hohokam, *c*. 700–1450 CE 360

KEY DISCOVERY Hohokam Ball Courts 361

KEY THEME: SOCIAL INEQUALITY Identifying Social Distinctions in North America 362

Early Farming Communities: Pueblo Villages on the Colorado Plateau 362

KEY DISCOVERY Chocolate at Pueblo Bonito 365

Hunter-Gatherer Trajectories: Great Plains, Archaic Period, 6500–1000 BCE 368

Transitions to Agriculture: Great Plains 369

Hunter-Gatherer Trajectories: Pacific Northwest 370

KEY SITE Ozette 371

Hunter-Gatherer Trajectories: Arctic and Subarctic 372

Native Americans and European Colonialism 374

Summary and Conclusions 376

Further Reading 377

Cliff Palace, Mesa Verde, Colorado: the largest cliff dwelling in North America, with an estimated population of around one hundred people in the thirteenth century CE.

TIMELINE North America

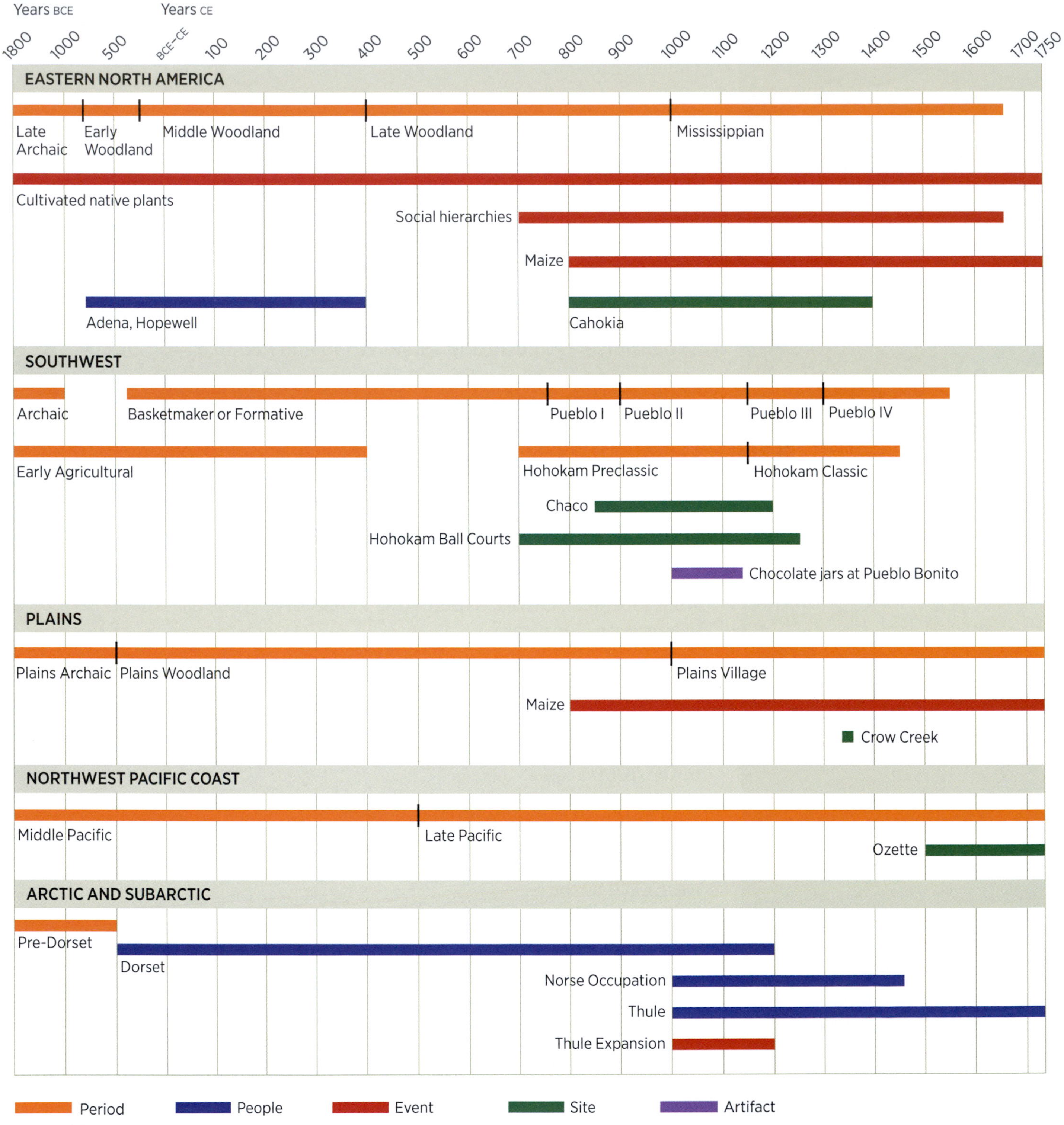

Years BCE   Years CE

1800 1000 500 BCE-CE 100 200 300 400 500 600 700 800 900 1000 1100 1200 1300 1400 1500 1600 1700 1750

EASTERN NORTH AMERICA

Late Archaic | Early Woodland | Middle Woodland | Late Woodland | Mississippian

Cultivated native plants

Social hierarchies

Maize

Adena, Hopewell

Cahokia

SOUTHWEST

Archaic | Basketmaker or Formative | Pueblo I | Pueblo II | Pueblo III | Pueblo IV

Early Agricultural

Hohokam Preclassic | Hohokam Classic

Chaco

Hohokam Ball Courts

Chocolate jars at Pueblo Bonito

PLAINS

Plains Archaic | Plains Woodland | Plains Village

Maize

Crow Creek

NORTHWEST PACIFIC COAST

Middle Pacific | Late Pacific

Ozette

ARCTIC AND SUBARCTIC

Pre-Dorset

Dorset

Norse Occupation

Thule

Thule Expansion

— Period   — People   — Event   — Site   — Artifact

Chapter 14 covered the early postglacial period, from the demise of megafauna through the development of regionally specific societies. By 2000 BCE, some of these societies had domesticated several local plant species, though everywhere hunting and gathering remained important. At about that time, the cultivation of maize began to spread from Mesoamerica into parts of the Southwest, only much later reaching the Plains and Eastern Woodlands. Farther north, in the forests and tundra of Canada and Alaska, and along the Pacific Coast, hunting and gathering remained the primary way of life. In this chapter we follow these developments region by region.

- Early societies of eastern North America engaged in monument building before developing a reliance on agriculture. Compare to Göbekli Tepe in Southwest Asia (Chapter 6).

- In the Southwest, Puebloan communities had to contend with an arid environment, including times of severe droughts. Compare to other adaptations to dry environments elsewhere in the world.

- Maize was introduced to the Southwest from Mexico, and later to the Great Plains and eastern North America where it was grown along with several native plants.

- The Pacific Northwest provides an example of social hierarchies that developed within what were principally hunter-gatherer economies. Compare to the Jōmon in Japan (Chapters 5 and 9).

ENVIRONMENTS AND LANDSCAPES

The people in what are now the United States, Canada, and Greenland adapted successfully to very different environmental settings [**15.1**, p. 350]. The environmentally diverse continent of North America is commonly divided into several cultural areas, among them the Eastern Woodlands, the Plains, the Southwest, California, the Northwest Coast, and the Arctic. Coastlines and river valleys, especially wetlands teeming with edible animals and plants, were among the most productive places for humans to settle. Thick forests blanketed the eastern United States and southeast Canada (the Eastern Woodlands), gradually giving way to vast grasslands west of the Mississippi River. High mountains form the western spine of the continent, and beyond lies the Pacific Coast, with dense, wet forests extending from northern California into southeastern Alaska. The southwestern corner of the United States and adjacent Mexico is a desert, although one with agricultural potential in places. To the north, much of Canada is covered by pine and spruce forests, beyond which is tundra extending to the Arctic Ocean and Greenland. Yet within these broadly defined areas there was considerable regional and local variation in natural resources, differences that had a profound effect on the distribution and density of human populations, and the nature of their cultures.

The full range of North American societies is not covered in this chapter, although those that are discussed are sufficient to illustrate the great variation in how people lived and the challenges they faced. Societies in Mesoamerica and South America are covered in Chapters 16 and 17. The largest and most organizationally complex societies developed in the Eastern Woodlands. Distinctive Southwestern **pueblos**, communal buildings housing many families, are part of a tradition that continues today. The hunters of the north are of particular

pueblo a general term for Indigenous communities of the Southwest USA, distinctive in their use of collective dwellings, often accessible through ladders

15.1 North America showing major sites mentioned in the text.

interest because of their sophisticated adaptations to a harsh environment. They were the first to meet Europeans—small groups of Norse who sailed to Greenland and beyond 1,000 years ago. Several centuries would pass before the continent's other Indigenous societies would have firsthand encounters with Europeans, an experience that left them reeling from devastating population loss, cultural disintegration, and forced migration. But these communities adapted to rapidly changing natural, social, and demographic landscapes, and many continue today.

By the mid-postglacial period (Holocene), people in North America were beginning to find it necessary to increase their food security by domesticating a few plants. But in all the societies covered in this chapter, domesticated plants were integrated into long-standing hunting, fishing, and gathering ways of life. Unlike much of Asia and Europe, there was no suite of early founder crops making up an agricultural package that was spread by colonizing village farmers. Instead, each geographic region in North America had its own independent cultural trajectory.

HUNTER-GATHERER TRAJECTORIES: EASTERN NORTH AMERICA, ARCHAIC PERIOD, *c.* 9500–1000 BCE

As the ice receded during the terminal Pleistocene, the landscape of eastern North America changed, including shifts in the distributions of plants and animals that changed an Ice Age vegetation mosaic into the temperate forests of today. Human responses to this new environment mark the beginning of the Archaic Period. During the early postglacial epoch, people of the Early Archaic period continued their well-established mobile way of life. There were, relatively speaking, few of them, and they were well spread out.

The earliest known domesticated dogs in North America date to this period. Dogs, such as those intentionally buried in Early Archaic contexts in the Illinois River valley, were presumably useful on foraging trips and provided company for the members of small mobile groups. The sample of measurable skeletons is small, but it is sufficient to show that the dogs varied in size and appearance, which is consistent with what is known from bones found elsewhere. Recent genetic analyses indicate that dogs originated in Eurasia. It is not known exactly when they were introduced to the Americas, but it happened relatively early, as indicated by these skeletons.

By the Middle Archaic, population growth had slowed, only to pick up again about four millennia ago, once a few native plants had been domesticated. Eastern North America offers important examples of monument-building undertaken by hunter-gatherer communities. These came in the form of mounds, the first dating to the Middle and Late Archaic periods. One of the earliest mound complexes is Watson Brake, Louisiana [**15.2**]. Here, eleven mounds are connected by a low ridge about 1 meter (3.5 feet) high, and together they form an oval about 280 meters (919 feet) in diameter. Watson Brake has been known about for a long time, but its significance was recognized only when calibrated radiocarbon dates showed that mound construction began as early as 3500 BCE, and took place for about half a millennium afterward. The site is an important example for how large-scale works, such as earth mounds, do not require an agricultural economy.

The mound building tradition seen at Watson Brake continued from that time onward through the prehistoric occupation of the Eastern Woodlands. A remarkable Late Archaic example of mound construction is Poverty Point in Louisiana (1700–1200 BCE). Poverty Point consisted of a series of low earthen ridges accompanied by mounds. Though hunter-gatherer-fishers, the people at Poverty Point maintained connections with others in distant places, as shown by the presence of many unusual artifacts made of non-local materials. The nature

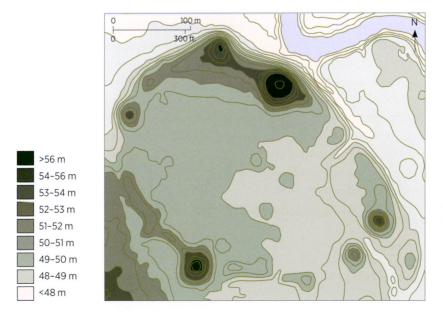

>56 m
54–56 m
53–54 m
52–53 m
51–52 m
50–51 m
49–50 m
48–49 m
<48 m

15.2 Map of Watson Brake. An early example of impressive mound building is Watson Brake, which consists of an oval arrangement of mounds connected by a ridge of soil.

of these relationships, including why more fancy objects arrived at Poverty Point than left it, is presently unknown. Nevertheless, the pattern first seen here—important places marked by mounds and connections with far-flung groups—is one that repeats itself in the Eastern Woodlands throughout prehistory.

Another important innovation of the Archaic period was the development of new kinds of containers for storing and cooking food. Domesticated squash and bottle gourds came first, and at the outset they were quite possibly more valued as containers or net floats than as food. They date back as early as 5000 BCE in the midcontinent, and an equally old gourd has been found with a burial in Florida. Recent genetic analyses of modern and ancient specimens indicate that the wild bottle gourd originated in Africa, floated across the Atlantic, and was subsequently cultivated. This marks the earliest examples of plant domestication in North America.

Gourds were often used as vessels, but starting around 2000 BCE, in the Late Archaic, people began to carve tub-like vessels out of soft stone. Presumably these were used for stone boiling, where water is heated by dropping hot rocks into a container.

The earliest pottery in eastern North America dates to c. 2500 BCE, and it was tempered with plant fibers. The first ceramic traditions of this region are not associated with intensive seed-crop production (in contrast to many other regions of the world), but occur where hunter-gatherers were becoming more efficient harvesters and processors of wild plants. Although ceramic technology is commonly associated with sedentary agricultural societies, early invention and use here of pottery by foragers rather than farmers parallel developments in some other parts of the world.

TRANSITIONS TO AGRICULTURE: EASTERN NORTH AMERICA, EARLY AND MIDDLE WOODLAND PERIODS, c. 1000 BCE–400 CE

By around 1000 BCE, a suite of domesticated plants, including squash, chenopod, and sunflower, all native crops, were in use across much of the Midwest and mid-South. This, along with other social changes, marked the beginning of the Woodland period. Early Woodland groups impacted forests, primarily by cutting and burning down trees and scrub to promote the growth of plants useful to those communities. These included nut masts and plants that provided medicine, fiber, and other desired commodities, in addition to food.

Domesticated native plants would later be accompanied by maize, which in many, but not all, places became a major part of diets between 800 and 1000 CE. Maize was introduced to the Eastern Woodlands, after being exchanged among groups in the Great Plains and Southwest where, in turn, it came from Mexico.

Cultivation in the Eastern Woodlands has received attention with regard to the role of women in the domestication process. The archaeologist Patty Jo Watson remarked that researchers often assign the tending of plants to women, and the domestication of such tended plants is often described as occurring gradually, unconsciously, with very little innovation, as if the plants virtually domesticated themselves. Watson challenges this argument, especially when it is applied to later strains of maize that probably needed to be carefully encouraged to grow in new regions. Watson stresses that if women were responsible for the growth of plants such as sumpweed and sunflower in eastern North America, this process was similar to any other human activity insofar as it involved care, action, and innovation.

The change in diet was presumably related to the widespread adoption of pottery. Ceramic vessels began to be commonly used by many Eastern Woodlands groups in the early part of the first millennium BCE. Pottery is, in fact, used by archaeologists as a convenient marker for the Early Woodland period.

Adena and Hopewell c. 800 BCE–400 CE

As well in shifts in diet and food production, the Early Woodland period involved changes in social relationships, the most conspicuous of which is the dramatic increase in the number of mounds constructed, from the Great Lakes southward into the Southeast. These mounds were a critical component of a rich ceremonial life that featured elaborate burials, graveside rituals, and artifacts often made from widely traded materials. Some of the largest and most elaborate Early Woodland mounds are found in the middle Ohio Valley. Dating between *c.* 800 and 200 BCE, the groups responsible for building them are referred to as **Adena**.

Adena mounds were often built in ritually significant places, where wooden structures or enclosures had earlier stood [**15.3**, **15.4**]. Graves, including log-lined tombs for one or more

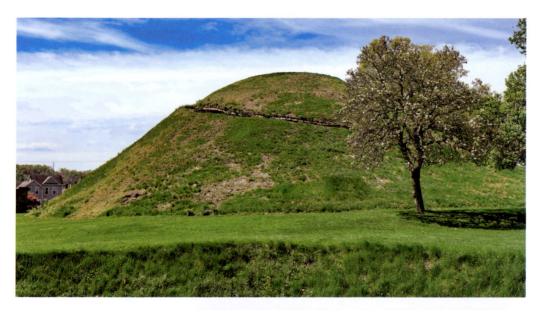

15.3 Grave Creek, West Virginia is one of the largest Adena mounds. This mound, in aptly named Moundsville, has long been of interest; it was visited by the American explorer Meriwether Lewis early in his journey to the Pacific Ocean, in the first decade of the nineteenth century.

15.4 Crigler Mound, Kentucky. Adena mounds were often built near, or over, the former locations of large wooden structures of ritual and social significance, as shown here by postholes defining a circular building, along with an unexcavated part of the mound.

KEY SITE Hopewell

Some of the most extraordinary artifacts ever found in eastern North America were uncovered at the Middle Woodland Hopewell site in Ohio.

The site consists of a square embankment adjacent to a more substantial and roughly rectangular enclosure encompassing over 40 hectares (100 acres), along with more than forty mounds. Within this larger enclosure were two additional embankments, one surrounding the biggest mound at the site, Mound 25. It was about 6.4 meters (21 feet) high, with a base measuring as much as 58 × 168 meters (189 × 550 feet).

Remarkable artifacts, often many buried together in single deposits, were found at Hopewell [**15.5**]. Among the objects from Mound 25 were more than one hundred obsidian bifaces and a cache of copper artifacts, including axes and breastplates. The obsidian points were intended for ceremonial purposes. Many were so large—30 centimeters (12 inches) or more long—that they would not have been used for everyday cutting, and they were often curiously shaped. Other impressive hoards from the site's mounds included 136 kilograms (300 pounds) of obsidian debris, several thousand sheets of mica, and more than 8,000 oval chert bifaces. The biface deposit consisted of small clusters of artifacts, each covered by a little soil, which were seemingly laid down in separate bundles.

15.5 This hand was one of a number of mica cutouts that have been found at Hopewell. Mica is only one of the non-local materials found at this site. Height 29 cm (11.4 in.).

people, were added to growing heaps of earth, and layers of soil were sometimes laid down to cap cemetery surfaces. This emphasis on continuity and renewal was also expressed in the ritual practices of many later Eastern Woodlands groups.

Mounds became more common and widespread during Middle Woodland, or **Hopewell**, times (between around 200 BCE and 400 CE). Conical mounds in Illinois often held centrally located log-lined tombs for a few important people, accompanied by rare objects. Immediately surrounding these central tombs were simple graves, which usually held single individuals with rather plain burial offerings. The most elaborate Middle Woodland mounds were located mostly in Ohio. They covered wooden structures that might contain the remains of more than one hundred people along with great quantities of elaborate artifacts. Rituals involved taking artifacts out of general circulation by burning or burying them.

Long-Distance Exchange. Contacts among communities, which can be seen in finely crafted artifacts buried at the mound sites, broadened and deepened during the Middle Woodland period. These remarkable artifacts are sometimes found in huge numbers, and were made from materials from far afield, for example, copper from the Great Lakes; mica from the southern Appalachians; colorful chert and pipestone from the Midwest; and marine shells, including whelks, from the south Atlantic and Gulf coasts. Most remarkable of all is obsidian from Yellowstone in Wyoming; the straight-line distance between the source and the Hopewell site, where most of the obsidian east of the Mississippi River has been found, is about 2,300 kilometers (1,430 miles) (see Key Site box: Hopewell). Many more Middle Woodland objects made from non-local materials occur in Ohio than elsewhere, and the great majority are from mounds.

Local leaders in Middle Woodland times appear to have maintained contacts, largely ceremonial in nature, among neighboring communities and, at least occasionally, people from distant places. Such events would account for the effort spent on building mounds, constructing elaborate mortuary facilities, and collecting the food consumed and objects destroyed during ceremonial events.

Key community members and families were singled out for special burial treatment with the finest objects. The most important mortuary facilities in Middle Woodland mounds in Illinois and Ohio, and Adena sites in Kentucky, contained individuals of both sexes. Apparently, social-group affiliation was critical in securing access to elaborate mortuary areas. Some of these people held special ritual roles in their communities, such as being a shaman. They wore ceremonial paraphernalia including masks, which are represented archaeologically by cut carnivore **maxillae** and **mandibles**. A small figurine from Newark in Ohio shows one such person, who was wrapped in a bearskin complete with head [**15.6**].

This time interval, especially the Middle Woodland period, for which there are many skeletons, was characterized by little serious intergroup conflict. Compared to the preceding Middle to Late Archaic and subsequent Late Woodland periods, relatively few skeletons show signs of warfare-related injuries. Generally low intergroup tensions are consistent with what were likely to have been permeable social boundaries that permitted the movement of considerable amounts of non-local items of great symbolic value, perhaps carried by people who attended ritual events.

Reliance on Cultivation. One of the most important changes to take place in the mid-continent about 2,000 years ago was a dramatic increase in the use of cultivated plants. By this time, the move toward a more sedentary existence, and diets based partly on native cultigens, had already spanned several thousand years, but the Middle Woodland shift to a greater reliance on cultivated plants was more abrupt than gradual. A point was reached when changes in the way people lived, including modifications of social organization, mobility, and technology, were needed for further increases in reliable yields to ensure survival.

New agricultural practices were presumably linked to ostentatious ceremonies, the exchange of high-value objects, and harmonious relations that characterize Middle Woodland societies. A heavier reliance on cultivated plants resulted in greater food surpluses, at least during good years, blunting the worst effects of shortfalls in wild foods, lessening uncertainty about the future, and reducing the need to extend foraging trips into land claimed by neighboring groups.

EXPANSION OF DOMESTICATION: LATE WOODLAND PERIOD, *c.* 400–1000 CE

By *c.* 400 CE, the beginning of the Late Woodland period in the Midwest and Southeast, erecting elaborate burial mounds and exchanging non-local objects had virtually ceased in most places. Skeletal evidence also shows worsening relations between groups, and by the late first millennium CE defensive works were constructed around some communities.

15.6 Figurine in ceremonial trappings. This stone figurine from the Newark earthworks in Ohio depicts an individual, perhaps a shaman, covered by a bear robe. Height 16 cm (6.3 in.).

maxilla (pl. maxillae) the upper bone of the jaw

mandible the lower bone of the jaw

15.7 Toltec in central Arkansas. With its mounds and plazas, this is one of the most impressive sites of the late first millennium CE.

By that time—toward the end of the Late Woodland period in the Midwest and Southeast—increased tensions contributed to the formation of organizationally complex and militarily formidable groups.

Settlements in most places consisted of isolated buildings or small groups of them. Villages were usually inhabited for only several years by no more than a few dozen people. By this time, once-dense forests in long-occupied places had been transformed into vegetation mosaics of actively cultivated gardens, patches of shrubby growth, and mature stands of trees.

Although at the beginning of the Late Woodland period communities tended to be of similar size, that situation began to change a few centuries before 1000 CE, along the central and lower Mississippi River and its principal tributaries. Here, locally dominant centers developed, surrounded by smaller villages and isolated houses. Marked differences in site size and internal layout indicate the emergence of social hierarchies and inequality. Of particular importance are mounds at lower Mississippi Valley sites collectively referred to as Coles Creek. These mounds were integral parts of site layouts that included both ceremonial precincts and residential areas in close juxtaposition.

The Mississippi Valley was not the only place where mound centers appeared. The single most impressive site is Toltec, in the heart of Arkansas [**15.7**]. Eighteen mounds, two plazas, and habitation areas were spread across 42 hectares (104 acres). They were enclosed on one side by an abandoned Arkansas River channel, and on the others by a defensive embankment and ditch. The two largest mounds, despite years of erosion, are 15 meters (49 feet) and 11.5 meters (37.5 feet) high. They tower over the others, which include rectangular platforms used in feasts at which large numbers of white-tailed deer were eaten. An integration of mounds for important people, public spaces, and residential areas within locally important centers was a distinguishing feature of communities in the Eastern Woodlands from that point onward.

EARLY FARMING COMMUNITIES: MISSISSIPPIAN PERIOD, *c.* 1000–1700 CE

Changes in agricultural practices, population, and inter-group relations were associated with the emergence of new forms of social organization characterized by inequality in many places after 1000 CE. These systems were organized along the lines of ranked lineages that featured powerful leaders. A patchy distribution of the most productive land gave the principal members of strong lineages in especially favorable locations an opportunity to expand their influence. During hard times, desperate people inevitably became indebted to situationally advantaged leaders, who were therefore able to recruit and retain many supporters over lengthy periods of time.

Mounds were central features of major Mississippian settlements. The largest, Monks Mound at **Cahokia** in Illinois, reaches a height of 30.5 meters (100 feet) and towers over the site (see Key Controversy Box: The Size and Influence of Cahokia, p. 358). Many mounds were rectangular, flat-topped platforms that supported wooden buildings, including houses for leaders and their families, community buildings, such as council houses, and charnel structures that held the bones of important ancestors. These elevated buildings, typically more spacious than normal residential structures, raised high-ranking people, literally and figuratively, above other community members.

Mounds were often built in stages. When raising them to new heights, existing wooden buildings on them were leveled, more soil was laid down, and new structures were erected. Adding earth to an existing mound yielded a more impressive platform that maintained a tangible connection with the past, in this way legitimizing the high social position claimed by leading members of these societies.

Charnel houses, bone deposits, and other burials are often found within the mounds. Although some held as many as one hundred or more individuals, burial in them was the prerogative of only a small fraction of local Mississippian populations. People of all ages and both sexes were interred in burial contexts associated with high-ranking members of Mississippian societies, although adults are more frequently represented than juveniles. Occasionally, the mounds held the remains of people sacrificed on special occasions, such as at Cahokia's Mound 72, presumably as part of ritually and politically important events orchestrated by highly ranked people. So while mounds often hold human remains, they were much more than mere burial places.

The mounds occupied prominent positions in major sites, but easy access was occasionally prevented by rows of posts around their bases or summits. These barriers were clear warnings that sacred places should be approached only by the proper people on appropriate occasions. Poles topped with skulls, for example, surrounded a charnel house built by the early historic Taënsa of the lower Mississippi Valley.

Items fashioned from precious materials, including marine shell and copper, regularly ended up in mounds, often with burials. They were frequently decorated with ritually and socially charged symbols, such as weeping eyes, bird designs, and crosses within circles. While there is sufficient stylistic variation to identify places of origin, the objects and what is depicted on them indicate widely shared beliefs. They highlighted the roles of leaders, distanced important people from the rest, reinforced the legitimacy of the existing social order, and depicted supernatural beings or mythical heroes. A few themes received disproportionate attention, particularly ancestors and war. Human figurines of wood and stone [**15.8**] have been found in mound contexts, as have whelk shells and copper plates decorated with warrior and bird-of-prey composites, some clutching maces and severed heads. Many objects would have been exchanged among leading members when shoring up their bases of local support, sealing alliances with neighboring groups, and establishing peace during troubled times.

15.8 Stone figurine.
Human figurines carved from stone, such as this one from Georgia, have been found at a number of major Mississippian sites, often in mounds. Height 61 cm (24 in.).

KEY CONTROVERSY The Size and Influence of Cahokia

A direct connection is commonly drawn between sizable mounds, huge populations, and societies featuring considerable political centralization and coercive power. That line of reasoning is nowhere more evident than at Cahokia, which, with more than one hundred mounds, including massive Monks Mound, is by far the largest prehistoric site in the Eastern Woodlands [15.9]. While a straightforward link between mounds and both population size and societal complexity has been assumed since the early nineteenth century, it is no longer tenable.

Wildly divergent estimates for Cahokia at its peak of development have been proposed, with the high end of the range around 40,000 people. A larger and more representative sample of excavations indicate the site's population was much smaller, perhaps numbering as few as several thousand people. In addition to the site itself there is an extensive hinterland with a lower population density but with strong ties to the center. Taken together, the big and small communities centered on Cahokia made it the most substantial single Mississippian-period society. Cahokia also stands out from the rest in terms of the number and size of its mounds. But the amount of earth moved was well within the capacity of even the lowest population estimates for Cahokia, assuming the work was spread out over the several-century occupation of the area.

The issue of political power is more difficult to address because archaeological data are only indirect measures of social and political organization. Cahokia has been characterized as a powerful center featuring considerable economic specialization and political centralization. Others have argued that any specialization in the production of goods extended no further than fashioning highly valued objects, many of which were ornaments of social and ritual significance that were mainly used by people of high rank. Distinctions between leading figures and the rest of the population were surely present, but a great gulf did not separate leaders and their close kin from other people. The most influential people enjoyed more and better artifacts, as well as larger buildings sometimes placed on mounds. But for the most part, their possessions were not fundamentally different from what other people had.

There is still much to be learned about precisely how the Cahokia system was organized. The site was certainly much larger, and the size of its supporting area far greater, than those of other Mississippian societies. But it is not known whether Cahokia's society was structured along lines fundamentally different from those of its smaller contemporaries. At this point, it is clear that Cahokia was much larger than the rest, but not that it was structurally all that much different from them.

15.9 The central part of Cahokia consisted of a plaza flanked by mounds, including Monks Mound, which is immediately adjacent to swampy ground (lower right), and, at the opposite end, two paired mounds. A wooden palisade surrounded this area for part of the site's history.

How People Lived. Settlements at this time ranged from isolated farmsteads to villages and major mound centers. A few hundred to several thousand people lived in the regionally prominent settlements. Most of the big sites usually had no more than a few mounds, often only one, that fronted plazas used for community-related events. Although the plazas were swept clean, they were not empty. At large mound centers, including Cahokia, nearby Mitchell, and Moundville in Alabama, they contained smaller mounds and posts. Ordinary people lived in houses that surrounded the plazas and associated mounds, and palisades were often erected to protect settlements.

Maize was central to many diets, but it was not grown everywhere. It was not adopted in the lower Mississippi Valley until well after mound centers were established. Little or no maize was eaten in much of peninsular Florida, where organizationally complex societies, which are not classified as Mississippian, developed at about the same time. The Calusa of southern Florida lived where marsh and near-shore resources were abundant, dependable, and concentrated. Agriculture was not, therefore, a necessary prerequisite for the emergence of social inequality in the Eastern Woodlands.

TRANSITIONS TO AGRICULTURE: SOUTHWEST NORTH AMERICA, 2100–1100 BCE

Several million people live today in the Phoenix, Arizona, metropolitan area, which sprawls across a vast inland basin of the Sonoran Desert. The city flourishes there because huge reservoirs in distant, wetter montane zones feed it water through massive aqueducts. The prehistoric farmers of the Sonoran Desert also managed the flow of water that originated in faraway mountains. Indeed, the name Phoenix was chosen by pioneering Mormon settlers because their earliest farms were irrigated from abandoned canals originally constructed a thousand or more years before.

The great variability in temperature, soil, and moisture in the Southwest meant that agriculture, with or without irrigation, was possible in some places, but not in others. Over time, environmental changes affected the potential of local areas for settlement, and there were accordingly periods of population movement across the landscape.

Crops in the region, notably maize, date as far back as 2100 BCE. Quite early on, agricultural practices in the dry Southwest involved land modification beyond the mere preparation of fields to do what was possible to ensure good yields. Irrigation canals have been discovered at Las Capas, in the Tucson basin, that date back as far as 1700 BCE. At Cerro Juanaqueña and other sites in Chihuahua, where early farming relied on rainfall, rock-lined terraces on hillsides supported houses and storage facilities. The terraces overlook the fertile Casas Grandes River valley, where crops, including maize as early as perhaps 1300 BCE, were grown.

It was once commonly thought that the transition to agriculture was gradual in the Southwest, but more recent evidence suggests it may have been more abrupt. As with the study of many other regions of the world, the question over whether agriculture was introduced by a migrating population or adopted through exchange among hunter-gatherer groups has caused much debate, but its origins are clear. DNA studies of both archaeological and modern maize demonstrate it originally spread from Mexico into the American Southwest.

Early agricultural sites were at favorable locations for growing maize, which were occupied repeatedly from one year to the next, though probably only during the growing season. Investigations reveal that crop irrigation in small settlements preceded the development of large, permanent villages in the Phoenix basin. This technological innovation was followed by the emergence of the Hohokam cultural tradition after 700 CE, characterized by a coherent regional system of iconography, ritual, cremation mortuary programs, trade in exotics, and the creation of public architecture.

EARLY FARMING COMMUNITIES: PRECLASSIC AND CLASSIC HOHOKAM, *c.* 700–1450 CE

The relationship between irrigation management and the hallmarks of Hohokam society came together during the Preclassic period (*c.* 700–1150 CE). Excavations at the large site of **Snaketown** on the Gila River valley provide some of the best insights into this period [**15.10**]. Houses here were single-room structures constructed of *jacal* with thatch roofs. Three or four were arranged around small courtyards or plazas. Courtyard clusters were distributed around yet larger central plazas containing ball courts—oval, unroofed, semi-subterranean structures indicative of some degree of political integration among nearby descent groups (see Key Discovery box: Hohokam Ball Courts). Some settlements were occupied by as many as 1,000–2,000 people.

Conditions in the Gila River valley were favorable for the development of irrigation systems during the Preclassic. Flow was perennial in a narrow channel that coursed through a broad floodplain, and regular seasonal flooding deposited fertile silt in fields. Water was diverted into feeder canals for the fields. Between *c.* 1020 and 1160 CE, the main channel of the Gila deepened and widened naturally, presumably due to lowered water tables and intensified

15.10 Snaketown. Aerial view of excavations at Snaketown during the 1960s. Numerous superimposed houses reflect a long occupation between *c.* 200 and 1200 CE.

KEY DISCOVERY Hohokam Ball Courts

Excavations at Snaketown, Arizona, directed by Emil Haury in 1934–35, uncovered a large, oval, earthen depression with high, banked sides and a smooth, flat floor [**15.11**]. Haury described this structure as a ball court, analogous to similar masonry structures found throughout Mesoamerica, which were associated with a ritual game involving rubber balls. There are more than 200 known ball courts at 166 sites in Arizona.

Hohokam ball courts were very similar to earthen ball courts found in the northern Mexican state of Chihuahua. The extent to which these features mimicked the social and ritual contexts of Mesoamerican ball courts is debated.

The earliest Hohokam ball courts date to about 700 CE, and the last versions fell into disuse by 1250 CE. They range from about 20 to 85 meters (65 to 280 feet) in length, but most were between 30 and 40 meters (100 to 130 feet). Opinions vary as to the nature of the ritual uses of ball courts. Whatever their function, most researchers agree with the scholar David Wilcox, who argued that ball-court sites were placed at fixed locations within the region to promote solidarity among nearby dispersed communities.

15.11 The ball court at Snaketown was constructed between 700 and 1000 CE. This unroofed structure measured 63 meters (207 feet) in length and 32 meters (105 feet) in width.

by irregular episodes of extreme and destructive flooding. Hohokam farmers consequently found it increasingly difficult to channel water from the Gila into the canals. Solving the problem of capturing streams for irrigation might have encouraged populations to form big communal labor groups and hierarchical organizations to manage the work that we see in the later Classic period.

The Classic period (c. 1150–1450 CE) is one of socio-economic reorganization. It was marked by the abandonment of many settlements in peripheral areas, and the compression of regional populations into the core portions of the Salt River. **Adobe** construction techniques became widespread and were used to build large walled enclosures, or compounds. Cremation was principally replaced by inhumation, and platform mounds succeeded ball courts as the primary expression of public architecture. Compounds built on top of platform mounds were probably the residences of high-ranked kin groups. At larger villages, Classic-period ritual and political events became increasingly centralized and inaccessible to the overall Hohokam population—indeed, political, social, and ritual influence was consolidated in the hands of fewer people (see Key Theme box: Social Inequality—Identifying Social Distinctions in North America, p. 362).

jacal wattle and daub, used in the construction of buildings in the Southwest United States

adobe dried mud, often mixed with straw to form mud architecture

KEY THEME: SOCIAL INEQUALITY Identifying Social Distinctions in North America

No matter how one goes about classifying human societies, their great diversity means that no single set of categories adequately captures the often bewildering sociopolitical and economic variation that has existed among ethnographically, historically, and archaeologically documented groups. Social inequality is just one, albeit important, dimension of that variability. But it is difficult to pin down.

In eastern North America, archaeologically clear-cut distinctions among people are commonly seen in both Middle Woodland (Hopewell) and Mississippian societies. Only the latter, however, feature readily apparent differences in how people lived, as distinct from how they were buried. In the Mississippian societies, leaders and their families were distinguishable from everyone else in terms of the artifacts and architecture associated with daily life, and presumably much else besides that is not observable archaeologically.

Turning to the Southwest, a few individuals at some sites were buried with disproportionately fine objects, but it is not clear whether that reflected the social status of those people or the importance of the group they belonged to. In other words, are we seeing individual or group identity, including social standing, being expressed in the burial proceedings? Among modern Pueblo people, a strong sense of egalitarianism is coupled with a clear political hierarchy among corporate groups, such as clans and religious societies. That may have been true of their ancestors as well.

These examples show that social inequality encompasses several archaeologically measurable distinctions in how people regarded one another and the perquisites they enjoyed. Readily apparent differences in housing, dress, and commonly used objects do not automatically translate into equally pronounced disparities in diet, morbidity, and mortality.

15.12 Hohokam crafts. Shells (below) used as ornaments were imported into the Hohokam area from the Gulf of California and etched with naturalistic designs. Fired clay figurines (right) are a hallmark of the Hohokam tradition and may have had ritual functions.

The Hohokam were skilled in a variety of crafts [**15.12**], including making elaborately etched shell ornaments. But it does not appear that they were prestige goods in the sense of signifying elevated wealth or political status. Instead, unusual and imported objects, which were widely dispersed among settlements, were probably used in rituals controlled by religious leaders. Many of these items were obtained through long-distance exchange: shell from the Pacific Coast, and copper bells and parrots from Mesoamerica. As in the case of Hopewell societies in the eastern United States, rare items from distant places played a prominent role in ceremonial life.

The end of the Classic period, around 1450 CE, is marked by a shift to more dispersed villages rather than large centers, and a possible decline in regional population. Explanations for this shift vary, but most archaeologists look to systemic problems in agricultural production stemming from regional changes in climate or the effects of prolonged human impact on local environments, such as a salinization of fields.

EARLY FARMING COMMUNITIES: PUEBLO VILLAGES ON THE COLORADO PLATEAU

The Colorado Plateau is a vast region of canyons and tablelands interspersed with rugged mountain ranges, occupying a substantial portion of the northern Southwest. Aridity is the dominant environmental factor in plateau country, but different elevations create distinctive vegetation zones over relatively short distances. For example, in most parts of the Colorado Plateau it is possible to move upward from grasslands through open woodlands and into heavily forested zones in no more than a few dozen kilometers. Higher elevations are wetter, which is good for agriculture, although they are also colder, which is not. Lower, warmer elevations have longer growing seasons but also higher evaporation rates, which hinder plant cultivation. So prehistoric farmers on the Colorado Plateau and adjacent portions of the northern Southwest had to find the right balance of temperature and moisture. Because of changing climatic regimes, there was a seemingly continual ebb and flow of human populations across the region.

Agricultural Foundations. Maize was introduced to the Colorado Plateau from Mexico by at least 2000 BCE, and perhaps as early as 2500 BCE. The first two millennia of farming mostly involved family groups cultivating small plots in frequently changing and loosely integrated residential locales. Shifting agriculture implies relatively low population densities and groups that were able to adjust quickly to environmental change.

Such versatile farming was characteristic of agricultural adaptations on the Colorado Plateau throughout the prehistoric period, although investigations in west-central New Mexico have identified small water-control systems associated with agricultural plots as early as 1000 BCE. Rather than employing one type of production system, farmers altered their strategies to suit local ecological and demographic conditions. Switching back and forth between farming and foraging was probably an economic option for many groups.

The archaeological markers of household development appear shortly after the adoption of pottery between 100 and 400 CE, and include a dramatic increase in the size of domestic structures (pithouses); a shift to storage features located inside dwellings rather than outside in public areas; and technological innovations in food processing that reflect labor intensification, such as larger milling stones and ceramic cooking and storage vessels. The emergence of household organization was probably linked to regional demographic and social factors promoting competition between incipient farmers, rather than simply greater reliance on domesticated plants.

Pueblo I, c. 750–900 CE

Starting around 750 CE, architecture changed from semi-subterranean pithouses to aboveground pueblos. Settlements continued to consist mostly of dispersed households while, occasionally, larger villages formed.

The Great Kiva. Some early villages included an exceptionally sized building that archaeologists refer to as a "great **kiva**," which was probably an important focus of village life. In modern Pueblo villages, a kiva is a multi-purpose room used for religious, political, and social functions, and there seems to be continuity in kiva architecture over the past 1,500 years. The largest known great kiva in the northern Southwest is at **Grass Mesa Pueblo**, a settlement of perhaps 200 or more inhabitants located on the Dolores River in southwestern Colorado; it was occupied between *c.* 700 and 920 CE. Here, it was a circular structure 22.5 meters (74 feet) in diameter. This great kiva undoubtedly served as a focal point in community politics and religion. Since large kivas are relatively rare in the Pueblo I period, researchers generally assume they served social groups spread out among several settlements.

Thanks to the chronological resolution afforded by tree-ring dating in the northern Southwest, we know that the Pueblo I period was a time when villages formed, broke up, and reformed in new locations as people adjusted to an increasing reliance on agriculture. Regional variation in ceramic designs may signify the existence or increased importance of group boundaries.

kiva a multi-purpose room used for religious, political, and social functions in Pueblo villages in the American Southwest

Pueblo II, c. 900–1150 CE

Geographic shifts in regional population concentrations continued during the Pueblo II period (*c*. 900–1150 CE), as small farming settlements expanded over an increasingly larger portion of the Colorado Plateau. Population growth rates during the tenth century seem to have been unusually high in the San Juan basin of northwestern New Mexico, due in part to emigration from other areas.

The Chaco Phenomenon. A truly remarkable transformation in settlement patterns occurred in the San Juan basin in the midst of these late tenth- and early eleventh-century CE population shifts. Small household farmsteads gave way to aggregated communities centered on communal masonry buildings now called "great houses." These structures are found throughout the basin but are concentrated in **Chaco** Canyon, where several examples contained hundreds of rooms and reached four stories in height. The largest great house is **Pueblo Bonito,** which had more than 600 rooms covering 0.8 hectares (2 acres) [**15.13**]. The entire episode of great-house construction in Chaco, the Bonito phase (*c*. 850–1200 CE), was a time of immense cooperative effort. At least 200,000 wooden beams averaging 5 meters (15 feet) long and 20 centimeters (8 inches) in diameter were used in buildings, some obtained from distances of between 40 and 100 kilometers (25–62 miles), signifying a huge labor investment and a complex production process [**15.14**].

Current research focuses on the position of Chaco Canyon within a regional network of agricultural communities. There are formal trails connecting many Chaco great houses, as

15.13 Pueblo Bonito.
This is the largest great house in Chaco Canyon, with more than 600 rooms. Its present form was reached in the middle 1100s CE. The occupation of Pueblo Bonito continued through the thirteenth century, before it was completely abandoned.

well as linking the canyon to smaller great houses (outliers) distributed throughout the San Juan basin.

Archaeologists now describe Chaco Canyon as a pilgrimage center in the middle of a ritual network. These descriptions emphasize aspects of the archaeological record presumed to be associated with ritual activity, including caches of turquoise beads and pendants, unusual ceramic vessels and wooden objects, several rooms with multiple human burials (some accompanied by extraordinary numbers of ornaments), and especially many kivas found in great houses (see Key Discovery box: Chocolate at Pueblo Bonito).

KEY DISCOVERY Chocolate at Pueblo Bonito

Cacao (chocolate) residue was discovered by the archaeologists Patricia Crown and Jeffrey Hurst in fragments of cylinder jars from Pueblo Bonito dating between *c.* 1000 and 1125 CE. Analysis using High-Performance Liquid Chromotography revealed the presence of theobromine, a marker for *Theobroma cacao* (the plant used to make chocolate). The nearest source of cacao is 2,400 kilometers (1,490 miles) to the south in coastal Mexico, which is testimony to long-distance trade linking Chaco to a much wider geographic and cultural region. Chaco cylinder jars are very rare (fewer than 200 are known), and almost all come from Pueblo Bonito [**15.15**]. In size and form, they are similar to specialized ceramic vessels used by the Maya for chocolate drinks. Cacao residue was recovered from the interior paste of the Chaco ceramics, indicating that it was consumed as a beverage, probably during ritual events.

Crown and Hurst argue that the development of social complexity in Chaco was related to the ability of some individuals to gain access to exotic materials and knowledge from Mesoamerica, also including copper bells and macaws. The acquisition and preparation of chocolate would have

15.15 Cylindrical vessels ornamented in the style characteristic of later period occupancy at Pueblo Bonito.

been a high-cost endeavor requiring specialized knowledge and equipment, so its consumption was almost certainly limited to small, possibly elite, segments of Chaco society.

Biometric analyses (statistical analyses of size and shape) of human skeletons and DNA studies indicate that at least two genetically distinct groups were interred at Pueblo Bonito. This is supported by variation in architectural style in the canyon. The presence of different social groups in Chaco during the Bonito phase is consistent with regional patterns of demographic fluidity in the tenth and eleventh centuries.

Pueblo III, c. 1150–1300 CE

Whatever forces led to great-house construction in Chaco and the widespread emulation of great houses at smaller outlying communities, they apparently dissipated by the mid-twelfth century, when building ceased in the canyon. Political and social influence, as well as population concentration, shifted northward, first to a cluster of Chaco-like great houses along the Animas and La Plata rivers, then further north to settlements in the Mesa Verde region of southwestern Colorado. Although great houses initially were similar to those in Chaco Canyon, the farming communities established during the thirteenth century in the northern portions of the San Juan River drainage adopted very different kinds of residential architecture than what is found in Chaco. These developments define the Pueblo III period.

The population of southwestern Colorado increased slightly during the twelfth and thirteenth centuries. Large settlements (in excess of fifty rooms) in the Mesa Verde region during the 1200s were usually situated in defensible locations, which also provided control over local water sources. The large villages included the famous cliff dwellings on Mesa Verde proper, situated along the rims of deep canyons [**15.16**], and pueblos in lowland settings, such as Sand Canyon Pueblo at a canyon headspring.

15.16 Cliff Palace. The largest cliff dwelling at Mesa Verde, Colorado, with more than 200 rooms, which were much smaller than those at earlier Chaco great houses and there was no great kiva. The settlement was built and abandoned during the thirteenth century.

Cliff dwellings were usually quite small, rarely more than one hundred rooms. They lack communal great kivas or large, enclosed plazas, and only a small portion of the regional population resided in them. The densest concentrations of Pueblo III villages were in the McElmo Creek watershed northwest of Mesa Verde, where average village sizes ranged between 200 and 400 inhabitants.

There was economic competition between groups, and indications of violence in the Mesa Verde area. Head and limb trauma consistent with battering and arrow wounds is widespread after 1000 CE. This probably reflects low-level conflict, such as ambushing isolated individuals. By the thirteenth century, however, mass killings were taking place that produced distinctive archaeological deposits of disarticulated and intentionally fragmented human remains, some seemingly byproducts of cannibalism. At Castle Rock Pueblo in southern Colorado, at least forty-one people were killed in a single event that took place around 1280 CE.

Pueblo IV, c. 1300–1550 CE: Migrations from the Colorado Plateau

By 1300 CE, many farming groups moved out of the Mesa Verde region toward the better-watered areas around the Rio Grande, where their descendants still live. The reasons for this move are many and include drought, incursion of groups from adjacent areas, and increasing trade relations to the east. Other areas of the Colorado Plateau (the Hopi Mesas and Zuni) continued to be occupied, though village locations concentrated on permanent water.

Pottery Innovations and Group Expression. In the early fourteenth century along the Rio Grande, a series of technological innovations made it possible for potters to create polychrome designs on ceramic vessels, some of which included lead glazing [**15.17**]. Glaze-ware production was confined to a limited number of villages, which may have specialized in manufacturing pottery for exchange. Some researchers have suggested that glaze wares were markers of status or were coveted for use in ritual, and that demand for these types was driven by social rather than utilitarian needs.

In the western pueblos, Salado polychrome pottery appeared around 1275 CE, and by the late fourteenth century became the most widely distributed ceramic style in Southwestern prehistory, cutting across traditional archaeological culture traditions. Patricia Crown studied hundreds of whole Salado polychrome vessels and discovered that these pots were manufactured locally, with little variation in design composition. She interprets them as one expression of a religious movement that emerged during the regional population relocations of the fourteenth and fifteenth centuries. This was a pan-regional religious ideology tied to water control and agricultural fertility, with an emphasis on social inclusiveness. Therefore it would have lessened social tensions caused during the formation of new villages, which were quite possibly made up of mixed ethnic and linguistic groups.

Population Decline. Pueblo IV was a period of widespread regional population movement by farming groups and the establishment of very large villages. The factors behind these changes are unclear, but some villages were intentionally destroyed, and the overall population of farmers in the Southwest dropped precipitously, perhaps as much as 70 percent between 1300 and 1500 CE. Rock art, which was profuse across the Southwest, began prominently to feature scenes of warfare. There was no shortage of agricultural land, or extreme climate conditions, that would explain such a widespread failure of farming economies, so scholars have found this severe population decline baffling.

By the fifteenth century, Athabaskan groups originating in western Canada entered areas of the Colorado Plateau abandoned by Pueblo farmers. Uto-Aztecan speakers from the Great Basin were also arriving from the west, and various Plains tribes occupied the eastern margins of the Southwest following a shift after 1450 CE from mixed farming economies to more mobile, hunting adaptations focused on bison.

Spanish expeditions and colonizing groups arrived in the sixteenth century. This period is often characterized as something utterly new—an unprecedented clash between different cultures—but Pueblo people were already contending with a tangled crush of new competitors and rapidly changing social networks. It is clear from the archaeological record that by the sixteenth century the Southwest had already witnessed centuries of demographic flux.

15.17 Polychrome ceramic vessel. Painted jar (Four Mile polychrome) from west-central New Mexico, c. 1325–1400 CE.

HUNTER-GATHERER TRAJECTORIES: GREAT PLAINS, ARCHAIC PERIOD, 6500–1000 BCE

The Great Plains of North America once consisted of a vast grassland that extended across the middle of the continent from Texas northward into Canada. This sea of grass was occasionally broken by strips of deciduous forest in river and stream bottomlands. The best places to live for long periods were along these rivers, with their fertile soils and diverse mix of wild animals and plants.

Popular images of life on the Great Plains are far removed from reality. Nomadic horse-riding bison hunters, for example, were a historic-period development. It took until the early eighteenth century before large numbers of Spanish horses from the Southwest spread northward onto the Great Plains. Prior to that time, bison were hunted on foot, and dogs were used as beasts of burden.

Sustained hunting of American bison on the Great Plains was in place by the early post-glacial, if not before (Chapter 14). Early bison hunters focused on provisioning small bands of people for the winter season; most large-scale kills, therefore, seem to have occurred in the autumn. The climate at that time was colder and wetter than today, and the Great Plains had much harsher winters, not only necessitating a good winter food supply but also, serendipitously, providing the conditions for natural storage of the meat. The great number of animals ambushed in arroyos or driven off cliffs appear to have been quickly frozen and covered with snow, leaving a deep-freeze storage of bison that could be dug out and butchered throughout the winter as needed.

By the mid-postglacial, as the climate became generally hotter and drier, grasses died back dramatically and bison numbers dropped. Communities depending on bison for survival were forced to come up with new options. They possibly included movement to better areas

15.18 Head-Smashed-In bison jump site. At this communal, ambush-hunting bison jump, on the high plains of Alberta, great numbers of bison were driven over the cliffs, typically in the autumn for winter provisions.

and the development of new hunting strategies. Those who stayed on the Plains expanded their diet to incorporate more drought-tolerant species.

Several millennia ago, the climate shifted back, bison populations rebounded, and people returned to communal bison hunting. This was the time of elaborate bison jumps, such as **Head-Smashed-In**, Alberta [15.18], where more than 125,000 bison remains, from innumerable hunts spanning more than 5,000 years, have so far been recorded. The sophisticated organization of the many hunters required to kill such huge numbers of bison indicates the cooperation of many hunting groups. A new type of housing, the tipi or tepee, was also developed at this time, and large cobble constructions known as medicine wheels began to be created. The latter were stones placed in large geometric shapes of varying complexity that had some astronomical, religious, or other purpose. In later times some may also have been the sites of the Lakota Indian sun dances.

TRANSITIONS TO AGRICULTURE: GREAT PLAINS

The first millennium CE was a time of change for Plains societies. Hunter-gatherer groups were showing a growing tendency for a more settled existence, as indicated by houses, burial mounds, and occasionally cultivated plants.

Maize was present in the Plains for several centuries before it became a significant component of diets in some regions late in the first millennium CE. From about 1000 CE onward, agricultural societies in the central and eastern Plains, referred to as Plains Village, featured settlements consisting of structures, often earth-covered lodges, accompanied by commodious storage pits. These farmers worked their fields with bison-scapula hoes. They also sought out wild plants and animals, particularly from nearby forested bottomlands, and many groups engaged in long hunting trips for bison.

Villages might be occupied by as many as several hundred people, an example being the fourteenth-century **Crow Creek** site along the Missouri River in South Dakota, where there were fifty or more houses. Movement from one place to another was undoubtedly caused by environmental and social concerns, including the need to forge alliances, aggregate for protection, and flee from enemy groups. Conflicts are indicated archaeologically by skeletal injuries and settlements protected by ditches and palisades.

Connections to Eastern North America and the Southwest

As in all parts of North America, people in different regions maintained some contact, however indirect, with one another. About 2,000 years ago, some Plains groups had at least irregular contact with communities east of the Mississippi River, particularly those in western Illinois. Clusters of sites near Kansas City on the Missouri River, in northeastern Oklahoma, and mounds along the Missouri near the North Dakota and South Dakota border are examples. The Missouri River mounds contained tombs that mostly held disarticulated bones along with artifacts fashioned from marine shell, obsidian, and cut human, bear, canid (wolf/coyote/dog), and beaver maxillae and mandibles. These finds indicate the exchange of ideas, as well as the occasional prized object.

Much later, but also in the Kansas City area, connections to Mississippian societies to the east, specifically Cahokia, are indicated by distinctive forms of pottery. Elsewhere in the Great Plains, wide-ranging exchange networks that reached not only the Eastern Woodlands but the Southwest and Pacific Coast are indicated by non-local pottery and seashells.

HUNTER-GATHERER TRAJECTORIES: PACIFIC NORTHWEST

Societies along the Pacific Coast from northern California to southeastern Alaska are undoubtedly the best-known North American examples of complex societies of hunter-gatherer-fishers. Here, late eighteenth-century explorers, including Captain James Cook, found permanent villages consisting of substantial plank houses and a rich artistic tradition, which in many places included tall totem poles [**15.19**]. The preservation of ancient objects can be excellent, as shown by those from the mudslide-covered **Ozette** site in northwest Washington (see Key Site box: Ozette). Archaeological materials dating back several thousand years demonstrate a strong continuity between prehistoric people and those of modern times.

Organization

The basic outline of Northwest Coast life in historic times—plank houses, permanent villages, and social distinctions—had begun to emerge around 1800 BCE to as late as 500 CE. Rectangular buildings consisting of sturdy post frameworks covered by planks provided housing for large households and storage space for food. Salmon were hung overhead to dry, and other items were kept in watertight bentwood boxes. Net weights, toggle harpoons, and weirs underscore the critical role of fishing. By the first millennium CE, these social and technological changes indicate that societies had begun to resemble those of just a few centuries ago.

Predictable access to river and sea resources, from whales in the open ocean to spawning salmon in rivers, was critical. Of special importance were salmon runs up coastal streams—a plentiful and reliable source of food. Fishing for salmon, however, could be done only for a short period, required coordinated labor, and resulted in an abundant catch that had to be preserved before it spoiled. So, much like agricultural societies elsewhere in North America, the Northwest Coast people had fixed territories, focused much of their attention on highly localized but productive resources, and lived in villages where food could be stored and sufficient labor periodically marshalled for tasks essential for survival.

15.19 Totem poles.
A village with totem poles and plank houses in the Queen Charlotte Islands, British Columbia, as they appeared in 1878.

KEY SITE Ozette

A most remarkable excavation came about when parts of houses and other artifacts washed out of a bank after a storm struck Washington's Olympic Peninsula coast in 1970 [**15.20**]. Somewhere between 250 and 500 years ago, part of a village was destroyed by a mudslide that simultaneously preserved it for the future. This village—one of several built at this particular spot over many centuries—belonged to the ancestors of the present-day Makah, who still occupy the same area.

Up to 3 meters (10 feet) of soil had to be laboriously removed by water pumped through hoses to reach the house remnants and artifacts. The suddenness of the disaster and the depth of burial meant that many everyday objects were left behind and survived to modern times. Among the artifacts were wooden tools, clubs [**15.21**], bowls, and boxes, along with basketry containers, hats, and cords. These discoveries show just how much is missed at Northwest Coast sites because items made from plant materials are normally poorly preserved.

House planks were fashioned from western red cedar, a good choice because of its resistance to decay. Shellfish, along with the bones of fish and sea mammals—especially northern fur seals but also whales—indicate a heavy reliance on what the ocean could provide. The largest of three completely excavated houses had several carved panels and was cleaner than the others. There were also some differences in the proportions of the animal bones in refuse associated with these buildings. Such variation, along with the distance of houses to the shore, reflects the social standing of different households in the community.

15.20, 15.21 Excavations at Ozette (left) were remarkable for the abundance of materials preserved by mud that deeply covered the village, including wooden objects that normally decay in archaeological sites. Among them were elaborately carved clubs (above).

Households were buffered from hardship by access to neighboring territories and exchange networks. Trade among communities is indicated by finds of copper, obsidian, nephrite (a type of stone) for **celts**, and dentalium shell from distant places. Even iron from Asia, obtained through trade or from debris that washed ashore, occurs occasionally in archaeological contexts. Artifacts and debris scattered across house floors show that part-time specialization by household members who focused on various activities extended deep into the past.

celt a stone axe-like tool

Some people were marked by artificially deformed crania or plugs, known as labrets, which pierced lips or cheeks. These practices were in existence for a considerable amount of time, extending into the historic period. Mortuary customs varied geographically and temporally, but also according to an individual's social standing. Archaeologically detectable differences, therefore, existed among people in life as well as in death, underscoring the pervasive nature of social rank for these people.

By the first millennium CE, hilltop fortifications had appeared in many places, as did the bow and arrow. A skeletal collection from Prince Rupert Harbour in British Columbia provides an indication of the difficulties people faced. About one-third of the men and half as many women experienced some form of cranial fracture, many of which had healed. While some of these injuries could have been from accidents, others would have happened in fighting among communities or from altercations within them.

The region's population may have peaked 1,000 years ago, and it plummeted rapidly in the nineteenth century. This precipitous decline, coupled with unprecedented economic opportunities and an abundance of newly introduced goods, resulted in many cultural changes. They included an elaboration of the **potlatch**, during which many items were distributed and destroyed to enhance the prestige of the sponsoring individuals.

HUNTER-GATHERER TRAJECTORIES: ARCTIC AND SUBARCTIC

Life in the far north required a special set of skills, but people nevertheless proved adept at occupying dense pine and spruce forests, open tundra, and coastlines where good use was made of offshore resources. The inhabitants of Greenland, Labrador, and Newfoundland were the first to set eyes on Europeans. They did so around 1,000 years ago when the Norse, who were then spreading westward across the North Atlantic, reached Greenland and the North American mainland. Norse settlements in Greenland were abandoned less than a century before Columbus's so-called discovery of the Americas.

Dorset and Thule Cultures

When the Norse arrived, small groups of people were spread thinly across the breadth of the Arctic, as they had been for 3,000 or more years. The inhabitants of the eastern Arctic at that time are known as Dorset [**15.22**, **15.23**], a term referring to a way of life that had emerged by 500 BCE. Diets varied from one place to another, although musk ox, caribou, and sea mammals were often hunted. Dorset winter settlements each consisted of a handful of small houses heated by oil burned in soapstone lamps. These sites were located in especially favorable places for hunting sea mammals, such as seals and walrus, from the shore or the sea-ice edge. Dwellings are thought to have included snow-block houses, perhaps similar to later igloos, based on discoveries of long snow knives fashioned from bone and antler. Late Dorset sites occasionally feature elongated enclosures of stones, which can be up to several tens of meters long, and nearby hearths. They must have held some ritual or social significance for the people who gathered together in these resource-rich places.

A later Thule expansion eastward across the treeless Arctic perhaps began around 1000 CE, although ancestral cultures in eastern Siberia and Alaska date back as much as 2,000 years. The Thule originated as one of the cultures that focused on rich marine resources along the North Pacific Rim. These skillful hunters of sea mammals possessed a sophisticated technology, which included specialized harpoons and skin-covered boats. A capacity for

15.22, 15.23 Dorset culture. The people of the Arctic made heavy use of elaborately carved tools, such as these Dorset harpoons and needles (far left), which were often aesthetically pleasing as well as functional. A small soapstone carving (left) depicts someone wearing a parka with a high collar.

15.24 Thule houses. Whale bones were used as roof supports for Thule houses, as seen in this reconstruction; other materials used included stone, sod, and driftwood.

open-water whale hunting became increasingly important as the ice pack receded during a comparatively warm interval often referred to as the Medieval Warm Period. Bones at Thule sites show that small bowhead whales were targeted, especially yearlings, wherever whales were abundant. Thule winter communities consisted of houses built of stone, sod, driftwood, and whale bones [**15.24**], with specific house-construction techniques varying across the Arctic. Sometimes there were also buildings for special ritual and social purposes.

At one settlement, and presumably others as well, a nearby freshwater pond and the immediately surrounding area were enriched by enough nutrients from decaying whale carcasses to promote greater moss growth. In this way, even hunter-gatherers in the thinly populated Arctic altered their immediate surroundings.

Sources of food were often widely and unpredictably distributed, and available for only short periods of time. Severe shortages must have frequently resulted in the reduction or extinction of families, even entire communities. One such event took place at Ukkuqsi in Alaska, where a young girl's frozen body was found eroding out of an empty meat-cache pit. Already weakened by chronic illness, she had died of starvation, and before her death she had been reduced to eating gravel, sand, and animal hair, all found in her gastrointestinal tract.

Despite problems related to life in harsh conditions, a specialized technology for hunting whales enhanced the availability of critical resources for larger groups. The Thule, therefore, gained a demographic edge over thinly scattered Dorset people. Bows in the hands of Thule hunters also put them in an advantageous position in any fighting that broke out between these two groups of people, who were competing for many of the same resources in a land characterized by scarcity.

Within a few hundred years of the Thule arrival in the eastern Arctic islands, during the eleventh or twelfth centuries, the Dorset groups and Norse colonies had disappeared for ever. Climatic deterioration surely played a part in the demise of the Greenland Norse, as farming became increasingly difficult when the North Atlantic slipped into the colder and more unpredictable weather of the Little Ice Age. The abandonment of their settlements, which were never large to begin with, need not have involved anything more mysterious than a return to Iceland or Scandinavia of a trickle of people over several generations. Such movement, prompted by climatic change, might also have been related to opportunities to access land following Black Death-related population declines in the islands of the North Atlantic and in Scandinavia.

Physical traces of Norse contact are limited to a small number of artifacts at Dorset and Thule sites. The objects are consistent with Norse sagas that tell of sporadic encounters and uneasy relations with Indigenous groups. This contact had no lasting effect on the native societies of Greenland southward to Newfoundland. That would change, however, starting in the sixteenth century when Europeans returned to the Arctic to search for a sea passage to Asia. Their global economic interests were very different to the local concerns of Norse settlers.

NATIVE AMERICANS AND EUROPEAN COLONIALISM

Native cultures were irrevocably changed following the arrival of Europeans in North America half a millennium ago. Some communities disappeared entirely within a few centuries of the sixteenth-century establishment of a permanent European presence. Native American societies have persevered to the present day, however, despite the tumultuous events of the past few centuries. In some regions—notably along coastlines and in the arid Southwest—it is possible to trace direct connections from archaeological sequences to historically documented communities.

Europeans began to explore North America's coastline in earnest shortly after Columbus's arrival in the Caribbean in 1492 CE. It was not long before expeditions penetrated deep into the continental interior. Two of the best known and most ambitious were undertaken simultaneously by the Spanish in the mid-sixteenth century: Hernando de Soto's in the Southeast, and Francisco Vasquez de Coronado's through the Southwest into the central Plains. They, and others, failed to enrich themselves with gold, as their counterparts did in Mesoamerica and Peru. But by the end of the century, Spanish colonies had been established in Florida and far to the west in New Mexico. By the early seventeenth century, the English had successfully colonized parts of the eastern seaboard, and the French did the same in eastern Canada. In the eighteenth and nineteenth centuries, the Spanish established missions in California; the Americans, first from the colonies and later the United States, pushed their way westward across the continent; the British moved deep into Canada; and the Russians made inroads into Alaska and the Pacific Northwest. Relations with Indigenous groups varied greatly. The Spanish organized native labor for their various enterprises and to protect their interests from other Europeans; the French and Russians were principally intent on establishing trading relationships, notably for furs; and the English and Americans wanted land above all else, which meant pushing the original inhabitants off it.

Indigenous people suffered greatly from wars, mistreatment, and forced relocations; even natural settings were altered by newly introduced plants and animals. But the greatest declines in their populations—which set the stage for the loss of their continent—were surely caused by newly introduced diseases, aggravated by the social and economic disruptions that followed in their wake. The major culprits were acute, highly contagious, fever-producing diseases including smallpox, measles, and influenza. Records are poor, but the reduction in population began in some places, such as around England's Lost Colony at Roanoke, immediately upon the Europeans' arrival in the late sixteenth century [**15.25**].

The plight of surviving Indigenous groups became a matter of widespread discussion only during the late nineteenth century, when most communities were already confined to the poorest land. Indigenous populations increased once again in the twentieth century, despite great problems with health, education, and economic opportunities. Today, tribal communities, such as those involved in the Canadian First Nations Idle No More movement, continue to work to maintain their right to land, their culture, and language. A recent example of an effort to protect the natural environment is the protest against the Dakota Access Pipeline, which highlighted the hazards posed by potential oil spills, as well as the pipeline's impact on archaeological sites and sacred places.

15.25 Watercolor of coastal North Carolina Native Americans. Late sixteenth-century English settlers at Roanoke, North Carolina, reported that the newly contacted inhabitants began to die very quickly and in great numbers; they were surely suffering heavily from pathogens inadvertently introduced by the new arrivals from England. This particular colonizing attempt itself would soon fail.

SUMMARY AND CONCLUSIONS

Over the past few thousand years, people began to settle in villages across much of this vast and environmentally diverse continent. Some areas, however, were never home to people who lived in permanent settlements, including parts of the arid west and the frigid Arctic. Far-flung groups maintained intermittent contact with one another, as indicated by a few objects that ended up a long way from their points of origin. Yet each major cultural area, such as the Southwest, experienced its own cultural trajectory. To understand what happened in any particular part of North America, we must look to local and regional environmental settings and cultural histories.

Agricultural villages scattered across North America relied on a variable mix of native and introduced crops, notably maize. People proved adept at farming even in the arid Southwest, where their cultural achievements include such impressive sites as Chaco. Yet nowhere on the continent did farmers move entirely away from their hunting-and-gathering roots.

In some parts of North America, ranked households or larger descent groups with fixed leadership positions eventually emerged within the context of village-based societies. Archaeologists sometimes focus on the development of agricultural economies to understand the development of organizationally complex societies. But this emphasis is somewhat misplaced. What is of importance is the productivity and reliability of geographically fixed and unevenly distributed resources, regardless of what form they took. Complex sedentary societies arose in several parts of North America where people could make use of highly productive freshwater wetlands, shallow coastal lagoons, or the open sea. They include, among others, the late prehistoric people of southern peninsular Florida, the Pacific Northwest, and the lower Mississippi River valley. The contributions of coastal, riverine, and wetland resources to the subsistence economies of organizationally complex societies in North America deserve as much attention as agriculture has traditionally received.

It is abundantly clear that new technologies and diets, greater sedentism, and more conspicuous differences among burials, houses, and settlements did not appear in lockstep, or change at the same rate. In the Eastern Woodlands, for example, archaeologically visible distinctions among people in Middle Woodland societies are mostly confined to burials. In Mississippian societies, such distinctions are especially noticeable in major centers, both in residential and mortuary contexts. Moreover, there was neither a unidirectional shift toward more elaborate burials nor an ever-increasing difference between the richest and plainest graves. Populations, likewise, did not increase steadily in various parts of North America, as shown clearly by the abundant and tightly dated Southwestern sites.

An emergence of larger and more complex societies often took place in the context of increasing conflicts among communities that relied on spatially fixed resources. That is true of Mississippian societies, as well as those of the Pacific Northwest and elsewhere.

Long-established ways of life were forever changed across the continent in the several centuries following the first sustained contact with Europeans in the sixteenth century. Over just a few centuries, there were precipitous population declines, great changes in cultures and ways of life, and groups disappeared and moved, often to distinctly different natural settings.

Turning to archaeology, a welcome recent development in many places is a greater involvement of Indigenous people in the management and study of their past. Many groups operate their own archaeological and historic preservation programs. For example, their contributions to defining research questions and interpreting archaeological materials are now felt at every level of fieldwork in the Southwest. Native perspectives greatly increase our understanding and appreciation of these societies. There is no question that archaeology's future will involve an increasingly collaborative process among Indigenous groups, scientists, and historians in North America and elsewhere.

FURTHER READING

Good introductions to the archaeology of the early societies of North America can be found in:

Ames, K. M. and Maschner, H. D. G. 1999. *Peoples of the Northwest Coast: Their Archaeology and Prehistory*. London and New York: Thames & Hudson.

Fagan, B. M. 2011. *The First North Americans*. London and New York: Thames & Hudson.

McGhee, R. 1996. *Ancient People of the Arctic*. Vancouver: University of British Columbia.

Milner, G. R. 2021. *The Moundbuilders*. 2nd edn. London and New York: Thames & Hudson.

Plog, S. 2008. *Ancient Peoples of the American Southwest*. 2nd edn. London and New York: Thames & Hudson.

Townsend, R. F. and Sharp, R. V. (eds.). 2004. *Hero, Hawk, and Open Hand*. New Haven: Yale University Press.

Wood, W. R., ed. 1998. *Archaeology on the Great Plains*. Lawrence: University Press of Kansas.

http://cahokiamounds.org The website of the Cahokia Mounds State Historic Site, with events, visitor information, related links, and other features.

https://www.nps.gov/seac/index.htm The National Park Service Southeast Archaeological Center website provides an overview of Southeastern prehistory.

http://historicjamestowne.org Website covering all aspects of the remarkable excavations at Jamestown.

Mesoamerica

16

David Webster and Susan Toby Evans

Environments and Landscapes 381

Transitions to Agriculture 382

KEY THEME: DOMESTICATION Social Consequences of Agriculture 382

Early Farming Communities 383

KEY DISCOVERY The Mesoamerican Ball Game 384

The Olmecs and the Early to Middle Preclassic, *c.* 1200–400 BCE 384

Cities, States, and Empires: Late Preclassic Mesoamerica, *c.* 400 BCE **–250** CE 386

KEY DISCOVERY The Mesoamerican Calendar 388

Expansion and Integration: The Classic Period: Teotihuacán and Its Neighbors, *c.* 100–550 CE 391

KEY SITE Teotihuacán 392

KEY SITE Classic Monte Albán 395

Collapse and Reorganization: Epiclassic Mesoamerica, *c.* 600–900 CE 396

Cities, States, and Empires: The Classic Maya, 250–900 CE 396

KEY DISCOVERY Maya Discoveries with LiDAR 399

KEY SITE Tikal 400

KEY CONTROVERSY How Sudden Was the Maya Collapse? 401

Collapse and Reorganization: Postclassic Mesoamerica, 900–1521 CE 402

Cities, States, and Empires: What the Spaniards Found 403

KEY SITE Tenochtitlán: The Aztec Capital 406

Summary and Conclusions 409

Further Reading 409

The Castillo Pyramid dominating the Postclassic Maya site of Chichén Itzá, a sophisticated urban center, trade hub, and ceremonial and religious focus.

TIMELINE Mesoamerica

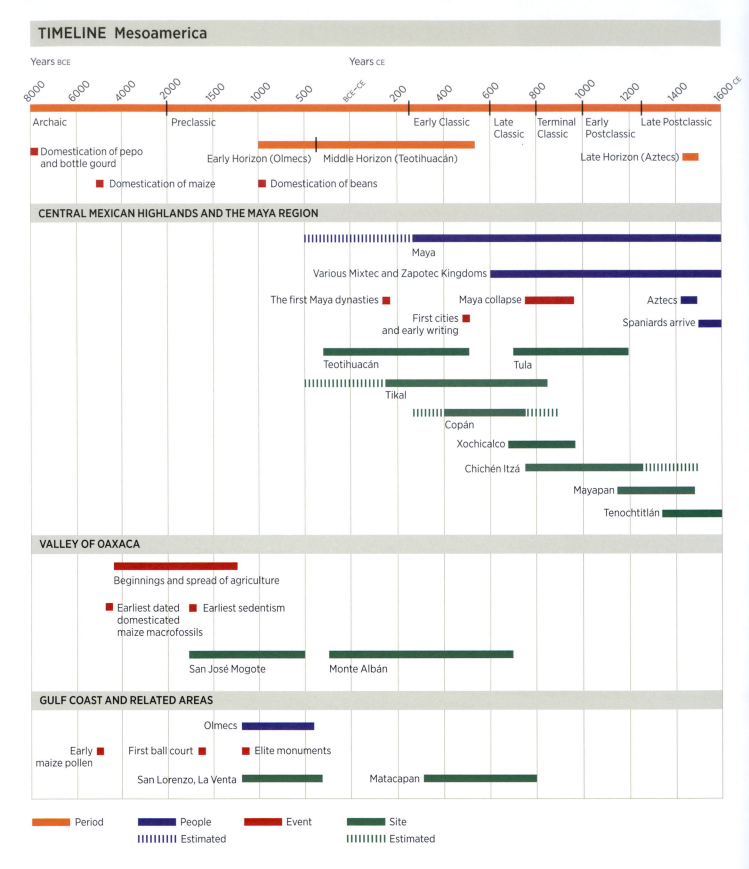

Years BCE
Years CE

8000 6000 4000 2000 1500 1000 500 BCE–CE 200 400 600 800 1000 1200 1400 1600 CE

Archaic

Preclassic

Early Classic

Late Classic

Terminal Classic

Early Postclassic

Late Postclassic

■ Domestication of pepo and bottle gourd

Early Horizon (Olmecs) Middle Horizon (Teotihuacán)

Late Horizon (Aztecs)

■ Domestication of maize

■ Domestication of beans

CENTRAL MEXICAN HIGHLANDS AND THE MAYA REGION

Maya

Various Mixtec and Zapotec Kingdoms

The first Maya dynasties ■

Maya collapse

Aztecs

First cities and early writing ■

Spaniards arrive

Teotihuacán

Tula

Tikal

Copán

Xochicalco

Chichén Itzá

Mayapan

Tenochtitlán

VALLEY OF OAXACA

Beginnings and spread of agriculture

■ Earliest dated domesticated maize macrofossils

■ Earliest sedentism

San José Mogote

Monte Albán

GULF COAST AND RELATED AREAS

Olmecs

Early ■ maize pollen

First ball court ■

■ Elite monuments

San Lorenzo, La Venta

Matacapan

■ Period   ■ People   ■ Event   ■ Site
||||||||| Estimated ||||||||| Estimated

P eople in Mesoamerica (Mexico, Guatemala, Belize, Honduras, and El Salvador) developed a distinctive set of settlement and farming practices, intellectual and aesthetic masterworks, and ideological beliefs. But despite common features, Mesoamerican ethnic diversity was striking, with about 260 separate languages spoken in the sixteenth century. Today, more than eighty are still in use. Mesoamerica was never politically unified, not even by the expanding Aztec empire encountered by the Spaniards in 1519. Yet there were long periods, conventionally called horizons, when vigorous regional cultures exerted strong cultural, ideological, economic, or political influence over this part of the world.

- Mesoamerica shows how social change can be mostly unrelated to technological innovation. Compare to links between technology (bronzeworking) and social change in Europe (Chapter 12).

- Sedentary villages appeared thousands of years after the first development of domestication. Contrast to rapid development of settlements after domestication in Southwest Asia (Chapter 6).

- Teotihuacán was the largest city in the Americas, from *c.* 100 BCE to *c.* 500 CE. Compare with other cities, such as Harappa in South Asia (Chapter 8).

- While many Maya urban centers were abandoned, the Maya persisted, and their descendants live on today. Compare to other examples of abandonment, such as the Puebloan migration (Chapter 15).

- By the 1300s CE, city states began to merge, with the Aztec empire rising in *c.* 1430.

ENVIRONMENTS AND LANDSCAPES

Mesoamerica, a culture in southern North America, covers a set of adjacent yet ecologically diverse regions [16.1]; all can support reliable maize (corn) crops. In countless valleys sheltered among the ridges of two great mountain ranges, local populations developed distinctive ethnic identities while sharing a set of fundamental practices. They used the same essential set of tool types, and a material culture made from stone, wood, basketry, fiber, ceramics,

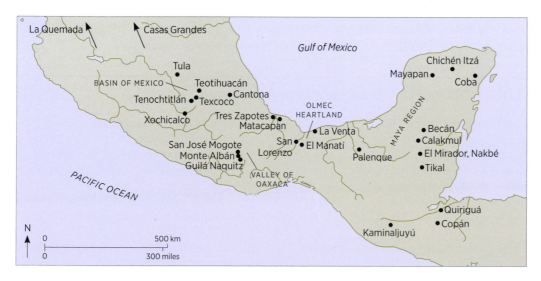

16.1 Major sites and cultural regions of Mesoamerica.

and metal. Elements of their belief systems, methods of governance and styles of social ranking were broadly similar. Over many centuries, populations grew and socioeconomic strategies bcame more complicated.

Productive crops domesticated in Mesoamerica include beans, tomatoes, chiles, agave, chocolate, and vanilla. The dog was their biggest domesticated animal, and so there were no large domesticated animals to save human energy by hauling plows and carts. They made wheels for practical applications (such as spindle whorls for thread production) and for ritual use, to enliven figurines of animals. Metallurgy appeared late—after about 600–800 CE—possibly stimulated by contacts with South America. Gold, silver, copper, and alloys (but not iron) were used to create brilliant objects for ritual and social display, but seldom used to make utilitarian tools or weapons.

TRANSITIONS TO AGRICULTURE

The Mexican Archaic, c. 9500–2500 BCE

Between *c.* 9500–2500 BCE most Mesoamerican people were nomadic foragers, some of whom domesticated plants that became economic mainstays for Mesoamerica, and for many cultures in North and South America. People were highly mobile at this time, and population density was low, even as more plants were being domesticated. Domestication is a form of natural selection in which humans alter characteristics of local plant and animal populations, and this is often accompanied by major changes in culture and the environment.

In the Americas, there were multiple independent occurrences of domestication, but unlike many other regions, sedentary agricultural villages did not become a common feature of the Mesoamerican landscape until 1600 BCE.

Maize, Gourds, and Squash

While more than one hundred domestic plant species were exploited in Mesoamerica, only a few contributed heavily to the diet, and maize was by far the most important. This was not just a plant that was a central source of food, but also one that had ideological and spiritual significance. Seasonal rituals of sacrifice and renewal followed the life cycle of the maize plant, and maize deities ranked high in the pantheon of Mesoamerican gods. Cultivating this crop was an annual act of consecration for farmers, and a family that could not grow its own was not quite respectable—an attitude surviving in many parts of Mesoamerica today (see Key Theme box: Domestication—Social Consequences of Agriculture).

KEY THEME: DOMESTICATION Social Consequences of Agriculture

Mesoamerican culture was based on effective agriculture. The first cobs, or macrobotanical evidence of maize, date to 4300 BCE at Guilá Naquitz Cave (Oaxaca Valley). It was probably grown in lowland zones somewhat earlier. Its wild ancestor, teosinte, showed little promise (many small hard seeds, difficult to process into usable form, and not very palatable), and the process of taming it took thousands of years.

Maize is a grass; plants were often interspersed with other native crops, especially beans, squash, amaranth, and chia, sometimes in fields edged by maguey (*Agave*), the sap of which was another dietary staple. Other natively domesticated staples included avocado, chili peppers, prickly pear cactus, cacao (commonly known as chocolate), and the root plants manioc and sweet potatoes. Such mixed cropping ensured food security for populations of Mesoamerica. While these groups relied on human labor, rather than the work of the large domestic herd animals as in other parts of the world, they were quite sophisticated and sustainable farmers. Mesoamerican agrarian systems eventually became very productive, capable of supporting dense populations and the large cities that so impressed the Spaniards in 1519.

Much research has been devoted to asking when and how maize was transformed from a wild plant (**teosinte**) to its domesticated state. Yet maize was not the earliest cultigen. This position is given to the bottle gourd (*Lagenaria sicereria*) and a squash (*Cucurbita pepo* ssp. *pepo*). Recent DNA evidence shows that the American gourds are most closely related to African varieties, arriving by 8000 BCE. Ocean-current modeling shows that wild African gourds could have simply floated across the Atlantic during the Late Pleistocene. The squash *Cucurbita pepo* ssp. *pepo* is native to the Americas and was domesticated by 8000 BCE. Fruits could have been used as net floats, rattles, or containers, and their roasted seeds are edible and nutritious. These domesticated fruits were tended by hunter-gatherers and did not necessitate a shift towards sedentism or agricultural dependence, similar to dogs. They are therefore excellent examples of crops complementing a mostly hunter-gatherer way of life.

Maize domestication was underway by 5000 BCE, with the earliest cobs directly dated to 4300 BCE. Its cultivation spread across Mesoamerica, though stable carbon isotopes from human bones, plant macrofossils, and phytoliths indicate that early on it was most often used as a supplementary food rather than as a staple.

Maize was adapted to an array of ecological and climatological circumstances fairly rapidly, but it took a long time for domesticated plants to trigger the kinds of changes that we commonly associate with the full commitment to agriculture, such as sedentism and the use of pottery. The first pottery appears at about 2000 BCE at sites on the Pacific Coast of Mexico. Many of these early examples are rather crude, and some of their basic shapes seem to mimic earlier vessels made from gourds or carved from stone. Over the next few hundred years, ceramic assemblages increasingly included vessels carved or painted with complex designs.

teosinte wild maize, from which the domesticated species evolved

EARLY FARMING COMMUNITIES

Around 1600 BCE, sedentary communities became widespread. They typically consisted of small clusters of simple houses with earthen floors, walls of wattle (poles) and daub (mud plaster), and thatched roofs. Often, as at **San José Mogote** in the Valley of Oaxaca [**16.2**], the spaces between houses were used for gardens, producing herbs and vegetables eaten alongside wild deer, rabbits, and quail. Slightly larger structures probably had specialized communal purposes. Remains of imported macaw feathers and oyster and turtle shells hint at differences in wealth, but there were no unusually large residences or elaborate burials.

In the tropical Maya lowlands (see below), there is substantial evidence for farming communities in about 1000 BCE, although forest disturbance typical of cultivation appears at least 2,000 years earlier. Elsewhere in the lowland tropics, farming villages were well established by about 1600 BCE, with some showing the first glimmerings of the great social changes that follow. Ball game courts are early features at some sites (see Key Discovery box: The Mesoamerican Ball Game, p. 384).

16.2 The Valley of Oaxaca. San José Mogote was a large dispersed village, but other early agricultural communities in the Oaxaca Valley were smaller and seem to have been politically autonomous.

KEY DISCOVERY The Mesoamerican Ball Game

The Mesoamerican ball game is somewhat similar to modern soccer [**16.3**]. Formal games were played on a special-purpose ball court: a long rectangular playing surface flanked by embankments with vertical or sloping sides [**16.4**]. Scoring involved striking a rubber ball (without using the hands or feet) through an end zone or, more rarely, through a stone ring set high up on the side wall of the court.

The ball court itself was conceived as a connecting place between the surface of the earth and the underworld; some versions of the game had great cosmological significance, and appear to have been associated with human sacrifice. Some ball games also functioned as events where powerful chiefs or kings hosted emissaries from other polities, with great political significance. Others seem to have been purely recreational, especially during Postclassic times (1000–1519 CE), when gamblers staked their wealth and even their lives on games.

16.3 ABOVE The ball game, depicted here on a Maya vase of *c.* 600–800 CE, had great symbolic significance, and the losers of the contest on the court sometimes also lost their lives.

16.4 LEFT The site of Copán has one of the largest ball courts in the Classic Maya Lowlands, built in the characteristic I-shape with sloping sides.

THE OLMECS AND THE EARLY TO MIDDLE PRECLASSIC, *c.* 1200–400 BCE

During the early 1900s, archaeologists and art collectors began to recognize a distinct style in materials newly excavated from sites in the Mexican Gulf Coast lowlands. Beautifully worked objects of pottery, jade, and other materials were quite unlike those that had been found in other parts of Mesoamerica, and in 1862 a huge stone head in this same style was found in the lowlands at Tres Zapotes. Surveys and excavations beginning in the 1920s confirmed that the style was associated with large lowlands sites, such as **San Lorenzo** and **La Venta**, and the culture and art style were labeled Olmec.

Radiocarbon dating set Olmec culture between 1200 and 400 BCE. Olmec influences were especially pronounced and widespread during the Middle Preclassic (1000–400 BCE), creating what has been called Mesoamerica's Early Horizon—a time when art and symbols, and the ideologies behind them, were widely shared. It is during the Early Horizon that many, though not all, of the hallmarks of later Mesoamerican states first develop, including monumental architecture and impressive ritual precincts, and possibly the ball game.

San Lorenzo and La Venta

Impressive Olmec polities arose in the Gulf Coast lowlands, where rivers meander through dense tropical forests. The earliest of these was San Lorenzo, *c.* 1200–900 BCE, where the Olmecs leveled the top of a natural plateau rising about 50 meters (165 feet) above the surrounding countryside. On its summit stood an impressive building (named the Red Palace), which was probably an elite residence that had an elaborate system of ponds and drains. Water had great ritual significance, which can be seen at another Olmec site called El Manatí, where a spring-fed pond contained spectacular offerings, including carved wooden effigies, large rubber balls, and human sacrifices.

Archaeologists have recovered scores of large basalt sculptures at San Lorenzo, including ten of the trademark colossal stone heads [**16.5**]. All were probably originally set up in public places on the plateau top. Olmec artisans also made mirrors from iron minerals brought from the Mexican highlands to use in displays of wealth, status, and shamanistic power. Other imports included obsidian. Olmec carvings of blue-green jade are particularly distinctive, the raw material transported from the upper reaches of Guatemala.

Around 1000–900 BCE, San Lorenzo declined. This coincided with the rise of La Venta, another large, sprawling center to the northeast. La Venta's abundant domestic refuse and house remains indicate a permanent population, which probably included rulers and their families as well as commoners. Its most impressive feature is an earthen pyramid more than 33 meters (108 feet) high, surrounded by platforms and courtyards. Colossal heads, stelae, and huge rectangular thrones [**16.6**] were set up in the settlement's plazas. During La Venta times, maize symbolism became prominent in Olmec art. Certain notables were interred in richly carved sarcophagi. Two infant burials in an elaborate tomb with rich mortuary offerings indicate the emerging power of inherited rank and social position.

Around San Lorenzo and La Venta lie constellations of smaller sites: some represent tiny hamlets or rural households, others well established villages. Houses were of a style still found in this region: wattle-and-daub walls and steep-pitched thatch roofs. A few of the bigger Olmec settlements have their own large earthen platforms and carved monuments. Some archaeologists believe that centers such as La Venta were complex urban places serving as focal points for rituals and elite residences. Powerful leaders resided in these centers,

16.5 BELOW LEFT **Colossal head.** This example is from San Lorenzo. All the images wear a distinctive cap similar to those sometimes later worn by ball-players.

16.6 BELOW RIGHT **Olmec throne, La Venta.** The carvings on the side of the throne show gorgeously dressed adults holding naked, baby-like figures with fanged, snarling mouths (the mouths are not visible here).

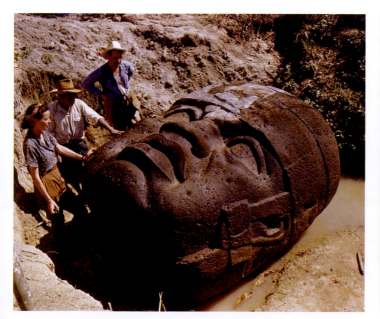

16.7 Drawing of a sculpture from Teopantecuanitlán, in west Mexico, with characteristic Olmec elements, including the snarling, downturned mouth.

supported by outlying populations numbering in the thousands. There may have been other similar capitals, as yet unexplored, in the Olmec heartland.

Olmec's Wider Influence

The Olmec area was the center of a widespread stylistic and ritual network that extended to many areas of Mesoamerica. For example, Olmec-style sculptures are present in Chalchuapa in El Salvador and cave paintings with Olmec iconography are found in west Mexican caves. Teopantecuanitlán in the highlands of western Mexico has Olmec-style zoomorphic monuments and a series of sunken ritual courts and terraces reminiscent of those at La Venta. Smaller, portable sculptures are found throughout the Gulf lowlands [**16.7**].

West Mexico, c. 1500 BCE–400 CE

Despite all this interactive dynamism, some regional societies of Mesoamerica developed distinctively during the Early and Middle Preclassic, and remained for centuries somewhat peripheral to the evolving tradition of Mesoamerican culture. Conspicuous among them are groups in western Mexico, where between about 1500 BCE and 400 CE, individual societies emerged, the center of the tradition encompassing the modern Mexican states of Colima, Nayarit, and especially Jalisco. Because early western Mexican sites often lack monumental buildings and sculpture, and show few indications of calendrical signs, the area has been unfairly characterized as provincial.

Western Mexico societies share the tradition of vertical **shaft tombs**. Some included only single interments, while others were ossuaries serving large groups for generations. Weapons, tools, ornaments, and elaborate pottery accompanied the dead. Most impressive of all the mortuary goods (and the principal target of modern looters) are large, hollow ceramic figurines of dogs, warriors, rulers, and religious practitioners. Other sculptures depict daily life: house parties, rituals, ball games, and concerts. The complexity of west Mexico's material culture seems to reflect a politically fragmented landscape and rivalry among elite factions.

CITIES, STATES, AND EMPIRES: LATE PRECLASSIC MESOAMERICA, c. 400 BCE–250 CE

As Olmec influence declined, other areas rose in regional prominence in the Late Preclassic period (*c.* 400 BCE–250 CE). Large polities with impressive centers became more common. Some were the regal-ritual capitals of rulers, but at least two of them—**Monte Albán** in Oaxaca and **Teotihuacán** in the Basin of Mexico—developed into the earliest true cities in Mesoamerica. Before turning to these political and urban transformations, we examine the development of Mesoamerican writing, calendars, and art, all emerging rapidly during the several centuries following the demise of the Olmecs.

Writing and Calendars

Writing seems to have originated in more than one time and place in Mesoamerica. Its roots and spread were associated with several major groups of languages ancestral to those still spoken today. In the early 1500s CE, the Nahuatl, Mixteca, and Mayan languages retained writing. The earliest writing may have been used to present limited kinds of information, and may not have been as closely linked to speech.

shaft tomb a deep, rectangular burial space

codex (pl. codices) hand-written manuscripts; in Mesoamerican societies they are accordion-fold books, while in Europe they are pages bound into volumes

16.8, 16.9 Early calendrical inscriptions. Modern drawing of a fragment of a monument from Tres Zapotes (right), which has one of the oldest Long Count dates—corresponding to 31 BCE. Monument 3 from San José Mogote (far right) shows a mutilated victim with the calendrical sign for One Earthquake between his legs—a very early Zapotec inscription.

All Mesoamerican scripts were carved, painted, woven, and so on, onto three types of artifacts: stone monuments (stelae, altars, thrones, tombs, building facades, and other architectural elements), small, portable objects (ceramic vessels, jewelry, bones, shells, cloth, and wood), and, with the longest inscriptions, accordion-fold books called **codices**, made of bark paper or parchment pages treated with washes of lime plaster and enclosed in wooden covers. All the legible surviving Mesoamerican books were made shortly before the arrival of the Spaniards with almost no earlier examples demonstrating the evolution of writing methods. Archaeologists must rely, therefore, on the other kinds of inscribed materials to trace the origins of writing.

Calendrical glyphs appear slightly later than script. Working back from their knowledge of Classic Maya calendars, archaeologists long ago documented the Late Preclassic origins of the Long Count (see Key Discovery box: The Mesoamerican Calendar, p. 388). A monument discovered in 1939 at Tres Zapotes, deep in the Olmec heartland, yielded a Long Count date corresponding to 31 BCE, with the characteristic bar-and-dot signs common on later Classic monuments [**16.8**]. Both the 260-day ritual and the 365-day vague year calendars are probably much older [**16.9**].

Rulers, Courts, and Cities

Writing, calendars, and art decorating buildings, ceramics and monuments, such as carved stelae, signal two fundamental and closely related transformations in Late Preclassic Mesoamerica: the rise of rulers and the emergence of the first great urban centers and territorial states. There had been powerful rulers in earlier times, but only in the Late Preclassic does a constellation of traits emerge that later came to characterize the institution of kingship.

Maya Rulers. The best evidence of early royalty anywhere in Mesoamerica comes from the Maya lowlands, where large carved monuments exhibit royal portraits and dated inscriptions—our first certain glimpses of historical individuals. The Hauberg Stela [**16.10**], dedicated in 197 CE, depicts a king, nicknamed by scholars as Bone Rabbit, dressed as a rain god impersonator, and its general themes include bloodletting, agricultural fertility, world renewal, and human sacrifice, all closely associated with later Maya rule and warfare.

16.10 The Hauberg Stela. This carved stone slab has an early inscription (197 CE) and its themes, including sacrifice, agricultural fertility, and world renewal, prefigure those of later Classic Maya monuments. Height 83.8 cm (33 in.).

KEY DISCOVERY   The Mesoamerican Calendar

The most widely shared of all Mesoamerican calendars tracked cycles of 260 days and 365 days. While the latter closely approximates the solar year, the former, the 260-day divinatory almanac, does not correspond directly to any astronomical cycle. It is close to the human gestation period and might also reflect the permutation of the number twenty (the Mesoamerican counting system was twenty-based) and the thirteen levels thought to comprise the heavens.

Calendrical notations were made using dots and bars to signify, respectively, the numbers one and five. These signs could be combined to represent larger numbers. The lowland Maya also had a symbol for zero and placement of the symbol was meaningful in interpreting the number. Combined, these aspects allowed them to express and manipulate very large numbers. There were many regional variations of the two calendars, but in general they worked as follows:

260-day calendar (divinatory almanac). Each day was designated by a number from one to thirteen, and by one of twenty day names [**16.11**]. The same unique designation therefore repeated itself every 260 days (13 × 20), and each day indicated specific fates. In many Mesoamerican societies, divinatory almanacs were interpreted by trained wise ones for guidance about any critical events, such as births, marriages, and illness. In some societies individuals were known by the day name of their birth.

365¼-day calendar. Solar-cycle days were designated by one of twenty day names and eighteen month names, for a total of 360 days (20 × 18). To this was added a period of five days to bring the total close to the solar year, which averages 365¼ days. The Aztecs, and probably many other Mesoamerican societies, intercalated an extra day every four years to correct the calendar.

Calendar Round. Meshing both calendars created a count of uniquely named days extending for fifty-two years. The beginning of a new cycle was of great cosmological and ritual import, a time of dramatic ceremonies and great feasts. The cusp of a fifty-two-year Calendar Round repetition was thought by the Aztecs to herald a moment of potential crisis, ritually marked by their New Fire Ceremony.

The Long Count. A third calendar, the Long Count (also called the Initial Series), tracked such a very long cycle that for all practical purposes it functioned as a linear count of time. Each day therefore had a unique date, not one that repeated itself cyclically as in the other calendars. Although invented elsewhere, by Classic times (250–800 CE) it was used only by the lowland Maya, who perfected it.

Similar to the Gregorian calendar in the West, the Long Count began on a specific day: on or about August 11, 3114 BCE. The Maya often wrote dates far earlier than 3114 BCE, but events since that date are most important here.

The progression of units is always by a factor of twenty except for the *tun*, which is not 400 as expected (20 × 20), but rather 360 (20 × 18), an accommodation Maya mathematicians probably introduced to fit this unit better to the length of the solar year. Full Long Count dates recorded on ancient Maya monuments consist of a sequence of numbers. For example May 1, 738 CE in our calendar would be written 9.15.6.14.6, and the Maya would often have appended the corresponding Calendar Round date as well.

Specific days had great divinatory significance and governed the fate of individuals. Important events were dated in historical or genealogical records.

Such monuments became increasingly common after about 250 CE, which archaeologists mark as the beginning of the Classic period.

While Late Preclassic texts are rare and often ambiguous, those of the Classic Maya frequently reported history, recounting the names, titles, and deeds of much earlier rulers. Along with supporting archaeological evidence, these texts enable epigraphists to trace the historical founders of several royal lines, most conspicuously **Tikal**'s, back to about 100 CE. Judging from the archaeological record, these well-documented founders were not the first Maya rulers, although they may have been singled out because of their subsequent dynastic significance. Even more suggestive of royalty are two huge centers that emerged in northern Guatemala in Late Preclassic times. One center called **Nakbé** was settled *c.* 1000 BCE by simple farmers, but an astonishing burst of construction *c.* 400–200 BCE produced buildings as high as 30–45 meters (98–148 feet). Nakbé's sculptors created some of the first lowland Maya carvings,

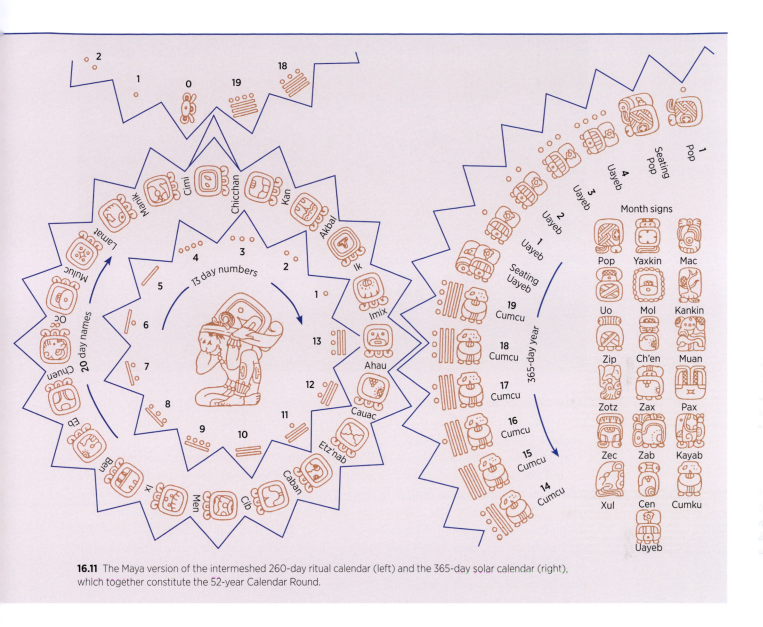

16.11 The Maya version of the intermeshed 260-day ritual calendar (left) and the 365-day solar calendar (right), which together constitute the 52-year Calendar Round.

showing gorgeously attired human figures that could possibly be rulers. Eclipsing Nakbé between about 200 BCE and 150 CE was an even grander center nearby, **El Mirador**, where a vigorous tradition of sculpture arose by 200 BCE, with stela-like monuments bearing possible glyphs and carved building facades, one with figures from the Maya epic, the Popol Vuh.

The scale and complexity of construction at these sites—elite residences, temples, ball courts, causeways, and other buildings—suggest centralization of authority and an impressive capacity to organize communal labor.

Classic Maya rulership was closely associated with warfare. The ritual sacrifice of war captives that later features so prominently in Classic Maya art is supported by examinations of the skeletons of buried individuals, and some early monuments seem to portray trophy heads. War is probably implied by the three severed bodies shown on the Hauberg Stela, and possibly by mass Late Preclassic Maya sacrifices found in northern Belize.

16.12 The Danzante figures from Building L, Monte Albán. These figures, remnants of a much larger frieze, were once thought to be dancers but are now interpreted as dead or sacrificed enemies of Monte Albán. They are accompanied by glyphs that might name them or their polities.

Monte Albán Urban Center. Striking transformations took place in the Valley of Oaxaca and the Basin of Mexico, where the first great cities emerged in Late Preclassic times (see Key Site box: Classic Monte Albán, p. 395).

In the Oaxaca Valley, San José Mogote was for centuries the largest center, until abandoned around 500 BCE by all but a few farmers. By then there were several nearby independent polities. At this time, newly built defensive systems appear in the southern arm of the valley, while in the valley center, the Zapotec city of Monte Albán rapidly developed on a previously uninhabited high, flat-topped hill. The settlement was a defensible center for a powerful confederation of communities embarking on the unification of the entire region. Shortly afterwards, the so-called Danzante warrior frieze was installed, depicting slain enemy captives [**16.12**], adding to the sense that this was a time of prolonged conflict.

By 200 BCE, Monte Albán's summit was crowned with a complex set of acropolis buildings. The surrounding terraced hillsides were packed with more than 17,000 people. A century later, Monte Albán had a ball court, about twenty temples where offerings were made to sky gods and other deities, and huge palace-like residences built over elite chamber tombs housing family ancestors. At this time, the entire population of the Oaxaca Valley totaled some 41,000 people, living in about 500 settlements.

The Monte Albán urban state might have controlled far more distant areas at this time as well. More than forty so-called conquest slabs found in the great plaza are carved with what may be place glyphs or political toponyms. Some think they represent distant polities conquered or otherwise subject to Monte Albán. In any case, by the end of the Preclassic, a centralized and expansive Zapotec state flourished.

Teotihuacán Urban Center. The Basin of Mexico had an extensive lake system and fertile volcanic soils. That would have been attractive to early agriculturalists. Nevertheless, farmers colonized the region fairly late—about 1600 BCE—partly because they had to adapt their tropical crops to the high altitude and cold environment. By c. 400 BCE, the basin's population had reached around 80,000.

Between 300 and 100 BCE, Teotihuacán emerged as a substantial urban center with perhaps 20,000 people. Within a few centuries, the city held possibly 85,000 people, living in an area covering 15–20 square kilometers (6–8 square miles). This remarkable growth was partly accomplished by immigration into the city of 80–90 percent of the basin's entire population, as other polities were abandoned. This centralization of population may have been prompted by volcanic activity during these centuries, where people displaced by these catastrophes migrated to Teotihuacán.

The city became the largest in the Americas, with an immense construction program that started at the beginning of the first millennium CE and created the ceremonial core of Teotihuacán over the next 350 years, including the imposing pyramids of the Sun and the Moon (see Key Site box: Teotihuacán, p. 392).

Most unusual are the commoner neighborhoods, consisting of well-organized apartment compounds distributed over a grid of streets and drainage channels. Families living in these compounds were farmer-artisans, practicing various crafts while cultivating fields in the adjacent alluvial plain. The city depended heavily on irrigation systems watered by the Teotihuacán valley's copious local springs and seasonal streams.

EXPANSION AND INTEGRATION: THE CLASSIC PERIOD: TEOTIHUACÁN AND ITS NEIGHBORS, c. 100–550 CE

During its initial rise to power, Teotihuacán directly controlled the Basin of Mexico. Some scholars believe it also governed a much larger region of about 25,000 square kilometers (9,653 square miles) in the neighboring highlands to the east and south. But whatever the level of actual control, the influence of the city reached far beyond Central Mexico, especially between the fourth and sixth centuries CE. Many archaeologists call this interval the Middle Horizon because Teotihuacán's contacts were so pervasive throughout Mesoamerica.

At this time, apartment compounds at Teotihuacán combined residences and workshops to produce items, such as obsidian tools, intended both for export and for local use. Two of Mesoamerica's major obsidian deposits are near Teotihuacán, including the source of the widely traded, greenish-gold Pachuca obsidian. Other workshops made ceramic vessels, grinding stones, shell objects, jewelry, and pottery, and no doubt numerous perishable items of wood, fiber, basketry, and feathers that have left few traces.

We know little about the social and political structure of Classic Teotihuacán, mainly because of the lack of comprehensible inscriptions. Murals here do not emphasize royalty as individuals; instead they mainly depict processions of costumed officials and priests, deities, fantastic animals, and abstract and repetitive designs. Moreover, virtually all the murals postdate the vast reorganization, around 250 CE, of the city's residential plan and so do not reveal much about the early period of rapid urban growth and monument construction.

For a long time it seemed that Teotihuacán lacked big tombs, but in the 1990s several important discoveries revealed mortuary remains within the pyramids. Beneath the Pyramid of the Feathered Serpent are the looted remains of at least one major tomb, immediately associated with about forty sacrificial victims. Scores of other victims were placed in shallow trenches beneath and around the pyramid as it was completed. They were mostly men of military age accompanied by weapons and war regalia, along with some women. Skeletal

KEY SITE Teotihuacán

Teotihuacán reached the peak of its power and influence between the fourth and sixth centuries CE, following a long sequence of earlier development. Its population of at least 80,000 made it one of the largest urban centers anywhere in the world before it suffered a precipitous decline in the sixth century CE, as evidenced by widespread destruction and burning in the city's ceremonial core. The site was never completely abandoned, nor were its remains buried or heavily destroyed, and they are therefore very accessible to archaeologists.

The Ceremonial Core

Late Preclassic occupation was probably concentrated in the northwest sector of the site, but Classic Teotihuacán grew to cover about 20 square kilometers (8 square miles). Its ceremonial backbone is the Street of the Dead, oriented around 15.5 degrees east of north, which set the alignment

for the site as its grid expanded [**16.13**]. The northern Street of the Dead was laid out around the beginning of the first millennium CE, along with the first stage of the Pyramid of the Moon, which stands at the northern terminus. Roughly a century later, construction started on the immense, west-facing (but on the eastern side of the street) Pyramid of the Sun, erected over an artificial sacred cave. Completed in two main stages over the next fifty years, its base was as large as that of the Great Pyramid of Khufu in Egypt (Chapter 13), and even without its summit temple it stands 63 meters (207 feet) high.

16.13 View of the ceremonial core of Teotihuacán. The view is from the Pyramid of the Moon looking south down the Street of the Dead, with the Pyramid of the Sun on the left. Unlike most archaeological sites, Teotihuacán was not buried or destroyed in subsequent ages.

analysis reveals that most were born far away, or lived elsewhere for long periods. The Feathered Serpent tomb was looted sometime after 250 CE. Most of the pyramid's sculpture was stripped away, and its front facade was hidden behind an addition, perhaps signaling internal troubles in the city and the decline of the the Feathered Serpent cult while a new regime emphasized more collective and impersonal leadership.

Since 2000, several other rich burials have been excavated from the later construction stages of the Pyramid of the Moon (150–350 CE). These may indicate the presence of powerful rulers, although most of the interred individuals appear to be sacrifices.

16.14 ABOVE The Temple of the Feathered Serpent is one of the few buildings at Teotihuacán with impressive façade sculpture.

16.15 RIGHT This example of Teotihuacán mural art shows an elaborately attired female deity, with water dripping from her hands.

The Street of the Dead was later extended farther south, and along its eastern side was erected an immense enclosure, 440 meters (1,444 feet) on a side, called the Ciudadela (Citadel). Within it sits the Pyramid of the Feathered Serpent, famous for the many sacrificial victims buried beneath it. On the other side of the street is the even larger complex called the Great Compound, which was probably the principal marketplace. Today these grand streets and buildings strike visitors as rather plain, because, with the exception of the Pyramid of the Feathered Serpent [**16.14**], architectural sculpture was not emphasized at Teotihuacán. Mural art was the city's great artistic expression, and plastered walls were brightly painted with polychrome murals, only fragments of which remain [**16.15**]. Surprisingly, no ball court has been found on the site, although murals show the game being played, probably in some suitable but informal open space.

Apartment Compounds

More than 2,000 apartment compounds have been mapped in the city, and a few have been excavated. Most were complexes of residential rooms around patios, with kitchens, storerooms, shrines, dense deposits of domestic refuse, and numerous sub-floor burials. A few have elaborate courtyard shrines overlying rich burials of adult males, who were possibly revered ancestors. Each compound housed about sixty people, and even the smaller ones had facilities for four to six families. Some have spacious and comfortable layouts, while others are cramped and barracks-like. Most were solidly built of plastered masonry, roofed with wooden beams, and had well-engineered drains. A few compounds are so elaborate and beautifully decorated that they deserve to be called palaces; at the other extreme are shoddy adobe residences.

All this variation among the internal features of the compounds indicates differences in rank and organization among families, and many structures included artisanal workshops. Clearly, however, many Teotihuacános lived in social groups larger than the nuclear family, and just as clearly there was great variation in status and wealth among the inhabitants.

Teotihuacán's Wider Influence

On January 15, 378 CE, a foreign lord named Siyaj K'ak arrived, from Teotihuacán, at the Classic Maya center of Tikal (northern Guatemala), some 1,000 kilometers (621 miles) east of Teotihuacán. He appeared just days after the death of the incumbent Tikal king. Siyaj K'ak's name is recorded on monuments at other centers, suggesting the spread of a new political order.

The following year, the son of one of Siyaj K'ak's entourage was enthroned as Tikal's king. Half a century later, a similar intrusion happened on the southeastern frontier of the

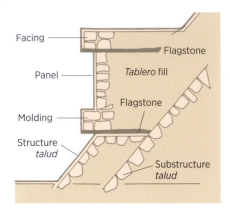

16.16 Teotihuacán architectural elements.
Large Teotihuacán buildings feature combinations of rectangular vertical (*tablero*) and sloping (*talud*) elements. Murals are often painted on the inset panels. These architectural elements also frequently appear at sites far from Teotihuacán.

Maya lowlands at **Copán**. Teotihuacán therefore exerted strong political and military influence, which was also seen in the art and architecture of the region [**16.16**].

Many more examples demonstrate Teotihuacán's influence, but it is unlikely that Teotihuacán had a conquest empire similar to that of the later Aztecs. Quasi-military intrusions at such places as Tikal might instead reflect the opportunistic activities of noble Teotihuacán factions detached from their homeland by political events—a process evident in later Mesoamerican ethnohistoric accounts. Undoubtedly, trade and commerce were fundamental to much of this Middle Horizon interaction. Outright colonization of strategic locales seems probable, and we cannot discount less tangible kinds of cultural influence, as reflected in the adoption of Teotihuacán dress, weapons, political and military imagery, and ritual. Teotihuacán's importance as a pilgrimage center persisted throughout the Postclassic period.

Cantona and the Teuchitlan Cultural Tradition—Independent Polities?

Teotihuacán's influence was not present everywhere, nor did it lack competitors. Nearly 200 kilometers (118 miles) due east of Teotihuacán, **Cantona** is a Classic period center close to fertile valleys and several major obsidian sources. It boasts many workshops and an astounding twenty-five ball courts, some of which are parts of larger complexes that include extensive plazas and possible palaces, such as at Monte Albán (see Key Site box: Classic Monte Albán).

Cantona shares remarkably few architectural features with Teotihuacán and has its own distinctive ceramic tradition. Unlike other centers of comparable size, it lacks monumental sculpture or other surviving symbolic statements of ritual or political power (ball courts aside). Well situated to dominate trade between the central Mexican highlands and the Gulf Coast, Cantona probably exchanged obsidian and other commodities.

Far to the west of Teotihuacán, western Mexico continued to develop in a distinctive fashion, as exemplified by remains of the Teuchitlan cultural tradition. Between 400 and 700 CE, clusters of elaborate shaft tombs here were associated with local polities dominated by hierarchies of impressive centers.

The Demise of Teotihuacán

The collapse of Teotihuacán as a major power was marked by extensive burning and deliberate destruction of temples and other buildings along the Street of the Dead, in the Ciudadela, and elsewhere around 550 CE, signaling the termination of the city's great power. Who was responsible? No neighboring polities seem strong enough to have mounted an attack, nor is there evidence of a foreign culture. Possibly, an internal, factional conflict destroyed the major symbols and facilities of traditional rule. On at least two earlier occasions Teotihuacán had experienced internal crises: around 250 CE, when the city's residential layout was dramatically reorganized, and slightly later, when the Pyramid of the Feathered Serpent was looted and its tombs despoiled. Whatever the scenario, the decline of Teotihuacán caused widespread political and social upheaval, and the disappearance of a religious and ideological order that had long integrated much of Mesoamerica.

By the mid-500s, Teotihuacán was a spent force, although its powerful reputation haunted the Mesoamerican imagination long thereafter and some 30,000–40,000 people continued to live in enclaves around it, in towns that are occupied to this day.

KEY SITE Classic Monte Albán

Monte Albán is a Spanish name for this major site, the original Zapotec name of which is unknown. The city peaked during the Late Preclassic (see p. 386); its urban population subsequently declined slightly, and other communities in the Valley of Oaxaca asserted more autonomy. Actual conflict is suggested by a series of impressive defensive walls protecting vulnerable points around the lower slopes of the hills.

Yet, Monte Albán's rulers continued to control distant areas to the north, and the city as we know it today assumed its basic form in Classic times, between 300 and 700 CE. Some 2,000 terraces were constructed on the slopes of the hill to accommodate the city's growing population. Nearly 3,000 separate residences have been mapped on these terraces, most of them quite simple, consisting of several adobe structures arranged around a courtyard. Some fifty-seven others, unusually elaborate, might be elite houses. Ceramic kilns are found with some houses but overall there is less evidence for basic commodity production than at Teotihuacán.

Monte Albán's rulers and highest elites occupied the hill's summit, the Main Plaza, which was difficult to access and rather isolated from the rest of the community [**16.17**].

At the northern and southern ends of this huge space (around 300 meters, 984 feet, long) were two enormous platforms, and smaller temples and a compact ball court lined its east and west sides. The North Platform was a gigantic palace complex where Monte Albán's royal family lived amid the administrative and ritual facilities essential to their rule; elaborate tombs with carved and painted chambers lay beneath the floors. These, and monuments in the Main Plaza, have inscriptions, but except for some names and dates they have not been deciphered. Paintings show rulers, their accessions to power, their military victories, and royal ancestors or relatives.

By 700 CE, Monte Albán's population had probably reached 25,000 people. About that time, a severe decline is signaled by the cessation of large-scale construction and much reduced ritual activity in the Main Plaza. As with Teotihuacán, the city was not permanently deserted, and thousands of people continued to live on the residential terraces. Nevertheless, it never again dominated the Oaxaca Valley.

16.17 A view of the summit of the Monte Albán, looking south, showing the palace (center) and the Main Plaza and the South Compound beyond it.

16.18 Epiclassic Xochicalco. Carvings on the Pyramid of the Plumed Serpent depicted warriors and toponyms of towns.

COLLAPSE AND REORGANIZATION: EPICLASSIC MESOAMERICA, *c.* 600–900 CE

Well-established communities elsewhere in the Basin of Mexico continued to thrive, but none filled the political vacuum created by Teotihuacán's collapse. In Oaxaca, Monte Albán was also in decline. A new Mesoamerican political pattern arose in what is called the Epiclassic period, a chronological label mainly applied to Mesoamerica west of the Isthmus of Tehuantepec and dated there to *c.* 600–900 CE. Instead of great capitals, a series of local centers and polities rose to become regional powers.

The best known of all Epiclassic sites is **Xochicalco**, which comprises five separate hills, each crowned with architectural complexes. Such hilltop locations suggest defensive functions, and the community core was heavily protected by earthworks, ramparts, and terraces. Carvings on the Pyramid of the Plumed Serpent show warriors with what appear to be toponyms (place names representing local topographical features) identifying outlying towns tributary to Xochicalco [**16.18**]. Several stelae are incised with name glyphs of kings—among the earliest known for Central Mexico. Sometime around 900 CE, the site was suddenly and violently destroyed by unknown enemies, and never subsequently reoccupied.

Farther north, but within the geographical limits of Mesoamerica, lies **La Quemada**, another hilltop center of Epiclassic date. The main community was small but complex, with artificial terraces, numerous residential patio complexes, temple and palace-like structures, and ball courts, all within a defensive wall. Archaeologists have unearthed unusual concentrations of cut, broken, and burned human bones, and evidence that human skeletons were displayed in some buildings, perhaps as war trophies.

The greatest beneficiary of the decline of Teotihuacán was Tula, founded after 700 CE some 80 kilometers (50 miles) to the northwest; it was destined to become a major city in the Early Postclassic period.

CITIES, STATES, AND EMPIRES: THE CLASSIC MAYA, 250–900 CE

The Maya are the best known of all Mesoamerican cultures, dominating the Yucatán Peninsula. The first Maya centers were established during the Preclassic, before 250 CE, and some (for example, Tikal and Kaminaljuyú) interacted with Teotihuacán before the city's abandonment. The Classic Maya has attracted an inordinate amount of scholarly attention, from archaeological excavations and surveys (see Key Discovery box: Maya Discoveries with LiDAR, p. 399) to decipherment and interpretation of complex calendars and texts (see Key Discovery box: The Mesoamerican Calendar, p. 388). The Maya developed in the lowlands region in the Yucatán Peninsula. Most of this landscape is flatter, hotter, and more humid than the Mesoamerican highlands. There are marked wet and dry seasons, natural vegetation is distinctly trop-

16.19 Maya art.
A dramatic set of murals was discovered at the site of Calakmul. The unusual imagery might depict a market scene.

ical, with few streams, large rivers, or lakes. After the end of the Late Preclassic period, distinctive markers of the Classic Maya tradition spread widely in the southern Maya lowlands, including the practice of erecting altars and stelae carved with royal and ritual statements. From these texts, scholars have charted a network of interacting kingdoms.

By the early 500s CE, Tikal was a Maya superpower, and head of a coalition embroiled in protracted struggles with another great alliance led by the rulers of Calakmul. All this mayhem ushered in a period of disruption and political crisis. For long intervals, no royal monuments were erected in previously vigorous centers, such as Piedras Negras and Tikal. But other polities, including Caracol and Copán, continued to prosper, so the crisis was not universal. Nevertheless, it stimulated considerable reorganization of Maya society and culture. Monuments erected after 600 CE presented rulers in highly personalized ways, attributed new titles to them and subsidiary lords, and increasingly emphasized warfare.

All this elite self-promotion foreshadowed the great flowering of Late Classic Maya society between around 650 and 800 CE, a richly documented period. About 20,000 texts have been recovered, some carved or painted on monuments or buildings, but most recorded on smaller objects, such as pottery vessels, which were used in palaces or elite residences, or placed in tombs; no Classic books have survived intact. In combination with associated architecture and art [**16.19**], these texts reveal the lives of Maya: the names and titles of rulers and nobles and their births, deaths, accessions, wars, rituals, and alliances; gods and ancestors; emblems of dynasties and polities.

Late Classic Maya culture matured just after Teotihuacán declined, c. 550 CE. Teotihuacán's early influence on the Maya was dramatic and direct, but it was probably inconsequential by the seventh century.

Kingdoms and Capitals

Far from being imperialists, the Late Classic Maya were never politically unified. At least forty-five to fifty separate kingdoms are indicated by their emblem glyphs, although many of them were periodically drawn into the great hegemonies centered on Tikal and Calakmul (see Key Site box: Tikal, p. 400). Beneath the veneer of similar art, writing, and architecture, these kingdoms varied greatly. Polities, or more properly their dynasties, were identified with different sets of patron gods. Several Mayan languages and dialects were spoken, and pottery and tools in use differed from one region to another. Some polities, such as Tikal, were very ancient, while others were newcomers. Some had large populations and hinterlands, while many could be walked across in a day or a few hours.

16.20 Palenque.
The buildings in the core of Palenque were all built during an interval of about one century. King Pakal was buried beneath the Temple of the Inscriptions, the pyramid in the center of the photograph, wearing a jade mask. Just to the right is the great palace occupied by successive Palenque rulers.

Political and social arrangements varied among kingdoms as well. Yet an underlying Maya-ness clearly united all these kingdoms, reinforced by trade, military alliances, intermarriage among elite families, common rituals, shared religious beliefs, and the periodic movement of people.

In each major Late Classic kingdom, a central precinct was dominated by large masonry pyramid-temples, palatial residences of kings and lords, spacious public plazas with altars and stelae, and ball courts. Often these complexes grew by accretion, and in the process incorporated the elaborate tombs of rulers and other elites. Despite their impressive appearance, however, some Maya centers were extremely short-lived. All the large buildings at King Pakal's capital of Palenque, for example, were erected in about a century [**16.20**]. Elsewhere, as at Tikal, settlement thinned out gradually with distance, increasingly dominated by the rural residences of the farmers who formed 80–90 percent of the population. Maya centers, with a few exceptions, are best envisioned as enormous courtly and ritual places, the sources of royal rule. Commoners were sometimes densely settled around the edges of these centers, and in other places their dwellings were more dispersed.

Maya Society

Royalty. The strong hierarchy of Maya social and political organization centered on the institution of rulership. Rulers were sacrosanct, hedged about with ritual and sacred duties. Their role was to ensure balance and stability in the cosmos, and particularly agricultural fertility. Rulers impersonated gods at royal ceremonies and were custodians of sacred god bundles. Some rulers, such as Palenque's Pakal, were believed to have been resurrected as gods themselves. Deceased royal ancestors were thought to influence the living world powerfully.

From very early times, some rulers seem more exalted than others. Copán's dynasty, for example, oversaw the founding of Quiriguá's line of succession, which might have constituted a cadet lineage. Conflict could overturn such relationships, however: Quiriguá asserted its independence when Copán's ruler was killed there in 738 CE.

KEY DISCOVERY Maya Discoveries with LiDAR

Much of the Maya heartland is in the rainforest, meaning that for a long time archaeological research tended to be restricted to excavation and small-scale survey. These methods tended to lead to the interpretation that Maya cities were relatively small and disconnected in the jungle, and many questions about landscape use and their form of agriculture remained unanswered. Clearing the rainforest for farming and logging has revealed more remains, and recent aerial surveys using LiDAR (light detection and ranging) are helping to change this narrative. LiDAR's laser scanning is able to penetrate the forest canopy and ground surface vegetation to pick up archaeological features.

In 2016, an extensive LiDAR survey was launched, covering 2,144 square kilometers of the rainforest. The survey discovered more than 60,000 new structures, including settlements, temples, causeways, and fortifications. New data continues to be accumulated.

New Interpretations

Large-scale LiDAR surveys enable archaeologists to detect new patterns across wide landscapes [16.21]. They have revealed that communities were sometimes more densely occupied and populous than first thought, suggesting the Maya area may have held between 2 and 11 million people at its height. LiDAR also revealed causeways or paths leading from temples within settlements, possibly for ritual processions. Causeways also linked settlements and temple complexes across large distances.

LiDAR surveys also indicate that swampy areas thought to be mostly untouched by the Maya may have had canals to drain land for agricultural field systems, although this needs to be confirmed with ground surveys. Such discoveries help archaeologists answer questions about how the Maya were able to feed such large populations in the jungle.

16.21 Laser technology known as LiDAR digitally removes the forest canopy to reveal ancient ruins below, showing that Maya cities, such as Tikal, were larger than ground-based research had suggested.

Succession focused on suitable males in royal patrilineages, but in the absence of acceptable male heirs, women served as regents and queens in their own right. Male kings were expected to be powerful warriors, and their monuments often boast of the capture and sacrifice of enemies. Other members of royal lineages administered the polity and the royal household, and some elites were artisans. Some of the most talented sculptors and painters were apparently loaned among kingdoms. Other elites were scholars who had mastered the highest levels of literacy and calendrical lore. Royal courts were places of elegance, indulgence, and conspicuous display, and, as elsewhere, centers of production of elaborate textiles and royal children to become high-status marital partners for other ruling families.

KEY SITE Tikal

Tikal is one of the largest Classic centers in the Maya lowlands, and many conceptions of the ancient Maya derive from research done there since the late 1950s. Major episodes of construction were especially concentrated in the Late Preclassic/Early Classic and in the Late Classic, especially the eighth century. During Late Preclassic and Early Classic times, Tikal's kings were buried in the imposing North Acropolis. A series of temples with astronomical orientations was built in the nearby Lost World (Mundo Perdido) complex, with a 30-meter (98 feet) pyramid that was the tallest building at Tikal until the eighth century. In the fourth century CE, the great king Jaguar Paw I built the first royal palace, which grew to accommodate his many successors.

Despite the foreign disruption in 378 CE, when Siyaj K'ak' arrived (from Teotihuacán, see p. 393), Tikal continued to prosper, while Teotihuacán architectural elements were incorporated into some buildings. A vast set of Early Classic earthworks, at least 25 kilometers (15.6 miles) long was built to enclose the center and the immediately surrounding territory that formed the core of the polity.

Long assumed to have been fortifications, many sections of the earthworks make little defensive sense and the dating is uncertain. Nevertheless, they signify boundary features, revealing how the inhabitants of Tikal thought about formal delineation of their landscape.

The heavily reconstructed core of Tikal as visible today, sprawling over an area of about 4 square kilometers (1.5 square miles), represents the mature site as it looked around 800 CE [**16.22**]. The most imposing set of buildings is around the Great Plaza. Across from the North Acropolis, burial place of Tikal's kings, is the Central Acropolis, with its hundreds of rooms and courtyards, which housed living kings, their families, and retainers. Temples 1 and 2 are on the east and west, and altars and stelae are in the plaza.

Other imposing sets of buildings are attached to the Great Plaza by wide causeways. On the hilly terrain around Tikal are hundreds of smaller clusters of buildings, most of them residential compounds on well-drained high ground. Artificial reservoirs were constructed to capture water. Population density declines with distance from major palaces and temples, and about 60,000 people probably lived within 10–12 kilometers (6–8 miles) of the site core.

Tikal began to decline after about 800 CE, and its last royal monument is dated to 869 CE. Most of its population disappeared around 830–950 CE, although the larger region was never completely abandoned.

16.22 The temple pyramids of Tikal rise steeply out of the surrounding forest. Temple 1, at lower left, is about 47 meters (154 ft.) high, including its roofcomb (a structure, usually with important iconography).

The Elite and Officials. Ranked below royalty were other great members of the elite as well as officials. Some of the most exalted had titles identifying them as subordinate rulers and courtiers who kept the royal books. Inscriptions suggest that titles were bestowed by rulers and inherited in family lines. Women sometimes bore them as well as men, and some titled officials were royal relatives. Texts often characterize these people as owned or possessed by rulers. Living in their own palaces, they attended royal courts and served various governmental and ritual functions. Rulers and elites were leaders in ritual, war, tax collection, diplomacy, and construction projects, but whether Maya kingdoms had bureaucracies in the modern sense is unknown.

Commoners. Supporting all this complexity were commoners, mostly farmers, who made up the vast bulk of the population, and paid taxes in food, goods, or service (work or warfare). They are known mainly from the remains of their modest households. Where population densities were low, they practiced various forms of **swidden** (slash-and-burn) agriculture, augmented in other regions by more intensive systems of cultivation utilizing terraces and drained fields.

Warfare. Wars were fought among the Classic Maya to capture sacrificial victims, avenge past defeats, acquire titles and prestige, neutralize enemies, exact tribute, and perhaps to annex territory. Conflict could be extremely violent, as seen at several sites where entire elite families were killed. No particular polity or coalition, however, became powerful enough to unite any appreciable part of the Maya lowlands for long. By the late 700s, there were more kingdoms than ever before, and populations reached unprecedented densities over large areas. Many spectacular building projects were initiated at this time, but all this apparent vitality and prosperity masked underlying stresses, which soon brought down one kingdom after another (see Key Controversy box: How Sudden Was the Maya Collapse?).

swidden land made cultivable by cutting and/or burning off the vegetable cover

---

KEY CONTROVERSY How Sudden Was the Maya Collapse?

According to popular belief, Classic Maya culture collapsed rather suddenly. Kingdom after kingdom failed in the southern Maya lowlands, an area of about 150,000 square kilometers (58,000 square miles, roughly the size of Florida). Eventually most of the population, several million people, also disappeared. In contrast, the whole northern half of the Yucatán Peninsula was comparatively well populated until the Spanish conquest.

The Maya collapse was first perceived by scholars studying dated royal monuments. They saw how the rate of monument erection lessened until eventually it disappeared altogether. The decline began about 760 CE in the western kingdoms and accelerated during the next century. A few centers still dedicated monuments with Long Count dates as late as 909 CE or slightly later. Fewer and fewer royal construction projects were undertaken, and some were left unfinished. No more kings or nobles were buried in elaborate tombs.

The collapse was clearly not a sudden event, but a decline that occurred over about 150 years. The worst effects of this decline, as well as many subsequent cultural readjustments, are notably apparent between 800 and 1000 CE, a period sometimes called the Terminal Classic. Elite artistic traditions were abandoned, and the old polychrome pottery tradition disappeared, along with the monumental art.

Such a protracted and variable process of decline does not lend itself to simple explanations. Many archaeologists agree that a complex set of interacting factors was responsible, and that the most important elements in this mix were overpopulation and a deteriorating agricultural landscape. These stresses, perhaps aggravated by drought, triggered more savage warfare, population movements, famine, disease, and loss of confidence in the pretensions of rulers.

COLLAPSE AND REORGANIZATION: POSTCLASSIC MESOAMERICA, 900–1521 CE

Between 800 and 1000 CE, Maya Long Count dates disappear, indicating a crisis; the Postclassic period for all of Mesoamerica starts at this point. Postclassic Mesoamerica is well understood because this era is known from reliable traditional histories, surviving Indigenous books, and, ultimately, documentation by natives and Europeans of life in the early sixteenth century.

The Rise of the Toltecs

Among Early Postclassic Mesoamerican kingdoms, the most celebrated in myth and history is Tula (de Hidalgo, Mexico), the great successor to Teotihuacán, located 80 kilometers (50 miles) to the northwest.

Tula was established around 700 CE with a modest group of civic structures. In Classic times, the surrounding area, about 1,000 square kilometers (386 square miles), was heavily colonized by people with strong ties to Teotihuacán, who produced lime (calcium oxide) for making plaster.

Ceramics and other artifacts at Tula show affinities with areas to the north and west. Following a slight relocation of its ceremonial core, Tula matured into a city between 900 and 1200 CE with a population as large as 60,000 people concentrated in an area of about 16 square kilometers (6 square miles). Many of its inhabitants may have been new migrants from southern parts of the Basin of Mexico, and Tula's culture represents a fusion of Central Mexican and northern influences. Other influences (especially religious), and perhaps migrants, came from the Huasteca in the northern Gulf lowlands. Clearly, the city was cosmopolitan.

The city's sacred precinct had large pyramids, ball courts, and spacious colonnaded halls [16.23]. Building facades are decorated with panels showing processions of jaguars and deities, and pillars depict warrior figures. Above their heads are undeciphered glyphs resembling later Aztec writing, possibly representing names. In general arrangement and specific architectural elements, Tula's monumental buildings show similarities with Teotihuacán.

A typical city house had a central courtyard surrounded by sets of rooms. Such compounds probably housed several related nuclear families. Many city dwellers farmed nearby irrigated

16.23 The sacred precinct of Tula. Pyramid B, with pillars in the form of warrior figures, overlooks the *Palacio Quemado* (Burned Palace), a vast colonnaded set of buildings.

land or perhaps cultivated the plant maguey. As at Teotihuacán, many workshops manufactured special products, such as obsidian tools, mold-made pottery, and stone vessels. Tula's hinterland included numerous outlying rural communities, especially to the east, where 30–40 percent of the population resided.

Tula forged strong links with other parts of Mesoamerica, importing marine shell from the Pacific and Gulf of Mexico, and pottery from as far away as Central America (to the south of Mexico). What may be Toltec trading colonies have been identified as far south as El Salvador. Equally important were exchanges with outlying groups far beyond the northern Mesoamerican frontier, for example Casas Grandes in northern Mexico.

While not as powerful as Teotihuacán, Tula dominated sizable territories. Populations remained in outlying settlements after its collapse around 1150–1200 CE, and the urban zone was later reoccupied, surviving as a small city subject to the Aztecs in the early 1500s. The Aztecs copied Toltec carved and painted motifs in their own capital, and looted some sculpture from Tula.

The Postclassic Maya

Maya polities in the northern Yucatán Peninsula weathered the collapse of the great southern kingdoms and in some ways might even have benefited from it. According to Maya chronicles, **Chichén Itzá** was the greatest of all Postclassic capitals. It began its rise during the 700s CE on the flat northern Yucatán plains near a huge **cenote** that became a major pilgrimage center. At the core of this immense site are the Castillo Pyramid, the Monjas Palace, a gigantic ball court, and other impressive structures with architecture and motifs that are central Mexican—and more specifically Toltec—in character.

Details of Chichén Itzá's cultural history are obscure because inscriptions and dates are limited, confined to the 800s CE. Warrior imagery celebrates conquest and sacrifice, and Chichén Itzá was undoubtedly embroiled in many conflicts. After about 900 CE, it eclipsed its major Maya rival, Cobá, a large site in northeastern Yucatán. For the next several centuries, Chichén was the capital of an expansive state, as well as a mercantile emporium, benefiting from the trade in salt, among many other commodities. Sometime around 1200 or 1250 CE, it rapidly declined as a regional power. The city itself was never completely abandoned, however, and remained a famous pilgrimage center where sacrifices were made even after the Spaniards arrived.

Native Maya histories say that Chichén Itzá's successor was **Mayapan**, a city surrounded by a low stone defensive wall that protected more than 4,000 structures, mostly residential, and a diminutive replica of Chichén's Castillo Pyramid. Several Maya accounts say that Mayapan fell around 1441 CE, beset by drought, famine, and a rebellion. Signs of burning have been found in the ruins of some elite households, and the city was mostly abandoned two or three generations before the Spaniards came.

CITIES, STATES, AND EMPIRES: WHAT THE SPANIARDS FOUND

The first Spanish colonies in the Americas were in the Caribbean. From this base, they expanded to other areas. In 1519, the Spaniard Hernan Cortés sailed with a small fleet from the Caribbean to the Yucatán. Best known for his conquest of the Aztec empire, Cortés also left accounts of the sixteenth-century Maya, who were the first Mesoamerican people he encountered.

cenote a sacred or ritual well, especially natural sinkholes in the limestone landscapes of Mesoamerica, as at Chichén Itzá

The Maya of the Early Sixteenth Century

In northern Yucatán, no great power replaced Chichén Itzá and Mayapan. Instead, the landscape held scores of small polities ruled by hereditary leaders, most with only a few thousand subjects. Coalitions shared the same lineage, or made alliances for mutual benefit, but war was common. Occasionally, powerful leaders managed to dominate, creating petty kingdoms that might number as many as 60,000 people.

The Spaniards were impressed by the large towns organized around temple pyramids, public plazas, and elaborate houses. After conflict with the Maya there and along the Gulf Coast, Cortés moved on to confront the Aztecs, leaving the Maya free for two more decades.

The Aztecs and the Late Horizon: History and Myth

Back in late Toltec times, climate change and political instability prompted migrations south from the northern fringes of Mesoamerica, some migrants claiming origin in a mythical homeland called Aztlán. By the early 1500s, many in the Central Highlands of Mexico claimed descent from Aztlán migrants and we know these ethnic groups as Aztecs.

Language is an important marker of ethnicity, and in 1519, Nahuatl (Aztecan) was the dominant tongue in the Basin of Mexico and the Central Highlands, and the international language of Mesoamerican trade. Scholars disagree about the time depth of Nahuatl in the Basin of Mexico. Some believe Early Postclassic migrants first introduced it, others believe it was spoken at Classic Teotihuacán, if not before.

Scholars also disagree about the truth of the migration accounts. Did such journeys take place, or are they reconstructed history to mythologize local origins? The accounts are largely plausible, substantiated by archaeological and skeletal studies and by the complicated ethnic relations and language distributions in the Central Highlands. They are also corroborated by population increases that prompted expansion over good farmland until all was claimed, and ethnic boundaries were drawn.

The most famous Aztecs were the Mexica (pronounced may*shee*kah), after whom the modern Mexican nation and capital are named. History casts them as a typical group of tribal farmer-migrants who arrived in the Basin of Mexico after the best agricultural land there had been taken. They became vassals of the Tepanec Aztecs, who allowed them to settle on small islands in the west lagoon of Lake Texcoco. There, in about 1325, the Mexica formally founded Tenochtitlán, which later became Mexico City (see Key Site box: Tenochtitlán: The Aztec Capital, p. 406).

By the late 1300s, the basin's several dozen independent, warring city states began to coalesce into political confederations. The Mexica were part of the Tepanec confederation, and Mexica warriors conquered towns for the Tepanecs and shared the tribute from their victories. In about 1375, the Mexica married into the Culhua dynasty, descended from Toltec kings. Thereafter the Tenochca (centered at Tenochtitlán) would be the Culhua Mexica (a name the Spaniards heard all over Mexico). They began their Aztec empire in response to a falling out with the Tepanecs around 1430. Aided by two other states (Texcoco and Tlacopan), the Culhua Mexica led this Triple Alliance to take over the Tepanec confederation. Victory promoted the power of the Mexica king Itzcóatl and the Mexica tribal god Huitzilopochtli, and created a dominant class of nobles and a tradition of powerful rulers. Mexica lords also reduced their commoners to a subservient class by burning the sacred books and rewriting history to formalize social stratification. All this set the stage for the dramatic explosion of empire under the Triple Alliance during the next ninety years. This short interval of less than a century represents the third and last of the episodes of relative cultural unity in Mesoamerica—the so-called Late Horizon.

The Aztec Empire in 1519

By 1519, the Aztec empire dominated some 400 previously independent polities over an area of about 200,000 square kilometers (77,226 square miles), including the Gulf Coast, the Oaxaca Valley, parts of western Mexico, and places as distant as the Pacific Coast of Guatemala. Its subjects numbered somewhere between 6 and 10 million people, and about a million of them lived in the Basin of Mexico, giving it a demographic advantage over any outlying region.

The basin's landscape was heavily transformed by terracing, irrigation systems, and artificially drained fields, and represented the most productive agrarian region of Mesoamerica in the early 1500s. Abundant wild resources included deer and rabbits, as well as lake products, such as fish, waterfowl, and blue-green algae, which was made into high-protein cakes.

The Aztec empire was assembled through intimidation, alliance, and outright conquest. Many conquered polities were grouped into more than forty allied provinces, many providing tribute that flowed into the Basin of Mexico [**16.24**]. All this wealth disproportionately enriched the king of Tenochtitlán and his nobles, who dominated the Triple Alliance. Other provinces were military allies, paying only nominal tribute, but essential to expanding and maintaining the empire because of the logistical problems in moving and feeding large armies without effective transport. These allies supplied loyal soldiers and staging areas for military operations.

Enemies close to the Aztecs were the Tlaxcalan confederation, east of the Basin of Mexico, whose people were culturally similar to the Aztecs. Although surrounded by Aztec empire territory and allies, the Tlaxcalans retained their independence and ultimately became staunch supporters of the Spaniards.

The Triple Alliance states administered their provinces quite effectively, notwithstanding the occasional rebellion. The Aztecs preferred to rule through the cheap expedients of intimidation and the frequent appearance of tax collectors. Pliant local rulers were left in place, and their offspring married into the royal families of the Triple Alliance. Sometimes, mainly in the imperial core territory, the Basin of Mexico, rebellious local dynasties were extinguished and their lands and people directly absorbed by the great rulers, who governed through their stewards.

Outside the basin, in about twenty places including the Oaxaca Valley and along the border of the western Mexican Tarascan empire, the Aztecs also arranged more direct control through imperial governors and garrisons. On occasion they used harshly punitive measures against local communities, enslaving everyone and taking them to Tenochtitlán and replacing them with groups of commoners from the basin who served as military colonists for sensitive frontier posts.

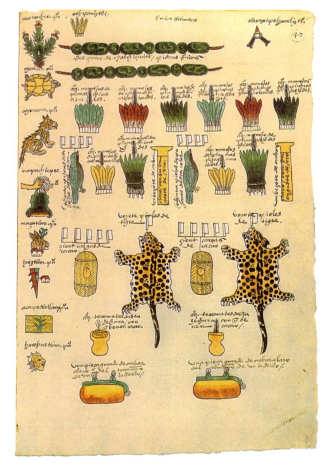

16.24 Aztec tribute.
This tribute list shows jaguar skins, gold, feathers, and other costly items that the Aztecs collected from tributary polities. It is a page from the *Codex Mendoza*, which was commissioned by the Spaniards but largely painted in pre-Columbian style.

KEY SITE Tenochtitlán: The Aztec Capital

From its formal foundation around 1325, by the early 1500s Tenochtitlán was the largest and most complex city in the Americas—a worthy successor to Teotihuacán and Tula. The core of the city—originally a swampy island that was transformed into an urban center by draining and infilling the surrounding reclaimed area—covered a 12–15-square kilometer (4.6–5.8 square miles) area near the western edge of Lake Texcoco [16.25]. When Cortés and his soldiers first explored it in 1519 it reminded them of Venice, with its network of canals; causeways (totaling 60 kilometers, 37 miles) linked it to the mainland.

Perhaps 50,000 or more people lived in the city, most of them in single-story adobe houses aligned along streets, alleyways, and canals. The edges of the city were farmstead plots on *chinampas*, gardens or fields constructed from reclaimed land in a shallow lake bed, where flowers and fresh vegetables were grown.

At the center of Tenochtitlán was a great enclosure, the Templo Mayor Precinct. Its perimeter comprised a wide platform topped by smaller temples. The enclosure held about eighty structures, including temples, dormitories for priests, schools, dance platforms, ball courts, skull racks, and clubhouses for warrior societies. Dominating all was the 30-meter-high (98 feet) Templo Mayor (Great Temple) [16.26], with its twin sanctuaries dedicated to Tlaloc, the rain god, and Huitzilopochtli, the god of war and the sun. The Templo Mayor was rebuilt and enlarged seven times and archaeologists have recovered from the fill about 7,000 offerings, along with many human sacrifices.

This vast complex of buildings was an architectural cosmogram—a model of the world, or at least the important elements of it. At the Templo Mayor the most extravagant human sacrifices took place to ensure rain, energize the sun, and guarantee military success. Many other gods of the Aztec pantheon were honored at lesser temples in the sacred enclosure. As among the Maya, the primary concern of ritual

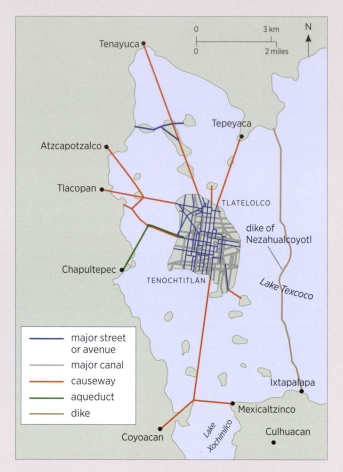

16.25 Tenochtitlán, the island capital of the Mexica (Aztecs), was linked to the mainland by a system of causeways and an aqueduct. The shallow lake to the west and south of the capital was transformed into a vast zone of *chinampas* and canals.

Aztec Society. No matter what their ranks in the imperial hierarchy, city states in the Basin of Mexico shared many common features, such as language, diet, technology, religion, and customs as well as sociopolitical organization. Each was ruled by one or more hereditary dynasties. Dynastic families, along with other high nobles, comprised the upper class, the primary beneficiaries of the tribute of empire. Rulers and noble households were polygynous, and the many wives and concubines produced valuable textiles and noble children. The elite class grew rapidly, necessitating further resources and therefore additional conquests. Nobles owned private lands, estates rewarded for military or governmental service, and while

16.26 This 12-metric-ton (13 US tons) monolithic sculpture, now broken, represents Tlaltecuhtli, a goddess of beginnings and endings, and was found in 2006 buried near a stairway of the Templo Mayor. Mexican archaeologists believe it was made in the reign of Ahuitzotl (*c.* 1502 CE) and may cover a royal tomb.

was to maintain balance in the universe and to suppress the forces of disorder that might destroy the world.

South of the Templo Mayor was—and is—the city's great plaza, known by its Spanish name, the Zócalo (derived from the Arabic *souk*, meaning marketplace). Around the Zócalo were the palaces of the highest nobles and officials, and, grandest of all, the palaces of the emperor. Motecuzóma II's palace, located on the east side of the Zócalo, was a labyrinthine complex of several hundred conjoined rooms leading off a main entry courtyard.

Markets were held in the Zócalo, but the largest marketplace was about 1 kilometer (0.62 miles) north of the sacred precinct, in Tlatelolco. Attended by thousands of people each day, it featured food and goods from all over the Aztec world,

brought to Tenochtitlán through tribute or trade, particularly by the *pochteca*, professional long-distance merchants.

Tenochtitlán's destruction in the Spanish siege of 1521 and subsequent rebuilding has deeply buried the Aztec city under the modern streets and houses of Mexico City, but strong similarities between the two exist. Tenochtitlán's layout established that of Mexico City, and the Zócalo remains the pivot of the capital's culture. The Metropolitan Cathedral stands within the former Templo Mayor Precinct, and the National Palace rises from the foundations of Motecuzóma II's palace. The Aztecs established a pleasure park at Chapultepec 600 years ago, and to this day it remains a vital green space for the city.

exempted from paying taxes they were expected to serve the state as special attendants to the ruler. After receiving special education, the elite monopolized the highest political and religious offices and led the army, which was otherwise conscripted. Two of the most prestigious military classes were the Eagle and the Jaguar warriors [**16.27**, p. 408].

Most commoners were farmer-artisans, living together in communities or neighborhoods organized into collectives headed by local leaders. Each collective had its own school and temple, and owed the state corvée (unpaid) labor and military service. Successful commoner warriors occasionally achieved quasi-noble rank and were rewarded with gifts, titles, and land. Many talented artisans, such as goldsmiths, gained high prestige from their close associations with nobles. Women at all levels of society wove cloth, and luxury textiles were produced in the palaces.

Below free commoners in rank were the *mayéque*, who were tied to the estates of kings and nobles, and paid taxes only to their immediate lords. Many *mayéque* were originally free commoners whose land had been conquered, reducing them to serfdom. At the bottom of society were the enslaved people. Some were war captives, while others fell into this condition through debt or criminal acts. They could buy their freedom, and their children were born free, but their owners could sell them to be sacrificed as someone's offering to the gods.

The Spanish Conquest

In 1519, the Aztec empire showed no signs of serious weakness but had ceased to expand. Motecuzóma II, the reigning Mexica emperor, had sent emissaries into the highlands of Guatemala to demand gifts, usually a prelude to conquest. We can never know if the Aztecs would have conquered the highland Maya. A new and unexpected threat appeared in the form of Hernan Cortés and his small armed force, initially numbering only about 500 men.

Upon landing in the Gulf lowlands due east of Tenochtitlán, in a province of Motecuzóma's wealthy empire, Cortés exploited the discontent of the conquered Aztec subjects, forming alliances with the natives. The Spaniards marched inland in August of 1519, accumulating allies, including the Tlaxcalans. Backed by their native partners, the Spaniards entered Tenochtitlán in early November. They were received amicably, if reluctantly, by Motecuzóma, whom they immediately took under a form of custody, living with him in one of his palaces. For six peaceable months, this hybrid court consolidated Spanish control and allowed the Spaniards to observe many details of Aztec life. Cortés and Motecuzóma went on hunting trips together, and Spanish soldiers played games of chance with the Aztec monarch.

But in May 1520, hostilities broke out, and Motecuzóma was killed. In the most damaging defection, Texcoco (one state of the Triple Alliance) turned on its former imperial partner. Tenochtitlán fell to the Spaniards and their allies in August 1521. Most of Mesoamerica was firmly in Spanish hands by 1550, but in the forests of northern Guatemala the Itzá Maya held out for another 150 years.

The Maya Today

The Maya are often considered in relation to their distant past, but there are more than six million still living today in Mesoamerica and across the world, and self-identity and self-determination remain important to the descendant communities of ancient Mesoamerica. The Maya are not a single community, nor a single ethnic group. They speak many languages, including Mayan languages (Yucatec, Quiche, Kekchi, and Mopan), Spanish, and English. The future of the Maya is not based solely upon their past, but is organized around their desire for cultural and economic self-determination.

After centuries of oppression from Spanish colonialists and later nation-states, the Maya are reclaiming their social and political freedom. In Guatemala, for example, they make up a majority of the population. Maya men and women have been elected to governorships

16.27 Ceramic statue of an Eagle Man, 1.8 meters (*c.* 6 feet) tall, found in the Hall of the Eagle Warriors, a cult meeting house near the Templo Mayor in Tenochtitlán. Eagles were an important symbol of status and power for the Aztecs, tied to the founding of the site of Tenochtitlán.

and other official political positions within the Mexican states in the Yucatán Peninsula the National Assembly of Belize.

In 2007, the Maya people of southern Belize won a landmark legal case when the Supreme Court of Belize affirmed their rights to control traditional lands and the resources on and below those lands. The Maya people continue to assert their territorial rights.

SUMMARY AND CONCLUSIONS

Societies in the Americas developed independently, without contact from Africa, Asia, or Europe. When Hernan Cortés wrote to the Spanish king Charles V to describe what the Spaniards saw on their march toward Tenochtitlán, he was commenting on aspects he recognized from Europe, Southwest Asia, and North Africa: social hierarchies, urbanization, literacy, scientific knowledge, and sustainable agriculture. But there was much that puzzled the Spaniards. How could Mesoamerican groups be so prosperous without large domestic animals for food and labor, without machines or metal tools (metallurgy being used for ornaments only)? How could merchants and markets thrive without sailing ships, or beasts of burden, or coinage; trading and paying taxes and tribute with goods and labor? Such questions demonstrate just how restricted past colonial views were on the ways in which complex and sophisticated human societies could develop. Over thousands of years, pre-Hispanic Mesoamerica created traditions particular to itself, and many of the region's contemporary cultures, languages, and communities, including those of the Maya, continue these traditions today.

FURTHER READING

The following provide useful introductions to the cultures of Mesoamerica and the archaeological evidence for them:

Coe, M. D. and Houston, S. 2015. *The Maya*. London and New York: Thames & Hudson.

Coe, M. D. and Koontz, R. 2018. *Mexico: From the Olmecs to the Aztecs*. 8th edn. London and New York: Thames & Hudson.

Evans, S. T. 2013. *Ancient Mexico and Central America: Archaeology and Culture History*. 3rd edn. London and New York: Thames & Hudson.

Evans, S. T. and Webster, D. 2010. *Archaeology of Ancient Mexico and Central America: An Encyclopedia*. New York: Routledge.

Lentz, D., Dunning, N., and Scarborough, V. (eds.). 2015. *Tikal: Paleoecology of an Ancient Maya City*. New York: Cambridge University Press.

Lopez Austin, A. and Lopez Lujan, L. 2007. *Mexico's Indigenous Past*. Norman: University of Oklahoma Press.

Martin, S. and Grube, N. 2008. *Chronicle of the Maya Kings and Queens*. 2nd edn. London and New York: Thames & Hudson.

Miller, M. 2019. *The Art of Mesoamerica from Olmec to Aztec*. 6th edn. London and New York: Thames & Hudson.

Nichols, D. and Pool, C. (eds.). 2012. *The Oxford Handbook of Mesoamerican Archaeology*. New York: Oxford University Press.

South America

17

Michael E. Moseley and Michael J. Heckenberger

Environments and Landscapes 413

Hunter-Gatherer Trajectories 415

Transitions to Agriculture, *c.* 9000–2000 BCE 416

Urban Communities: Aceramic Communities, *c.* 3000–1800 BCE 417

Early Farming Communities: Initial Period and the Early Horizon, *c.* 1800–200 BCE 419

Collapse and Reorganization: The Early Intermediate Period, *c.* 200 BCE–650 CE: Andean Confederacies and States 421

KEY SITE Sipán and the Presentation Theme 422

Cities, States, and Empires: The Rise and Fall of the Andean Empires 425

KEY THEME: SOCIAL INEQUALITY Descent and the *Kurakas* 426

KEY SITE The Sacred Valley of the Inkas and Machu Picchu 430

KEY DISCOVERY The *Khipu* 432

Amazonia 434

Transitions to States: The Amazonian Formative Period, *c.* 1000 BCE–500 CE 434

Regionalization: Amazonia, *c.* 1–1500 CE 435

KEY CONTROVERSY Amazonian Mound-Builders 436

KEY CONTROVERSY Amazonian Dark Earths and Anthropogenic Landscapes 439

Summary and Conclusions 440

Further Reading 441

El Paraíso, a monumental site on the central coast of Peru, constructed in the late second millennium BCE.

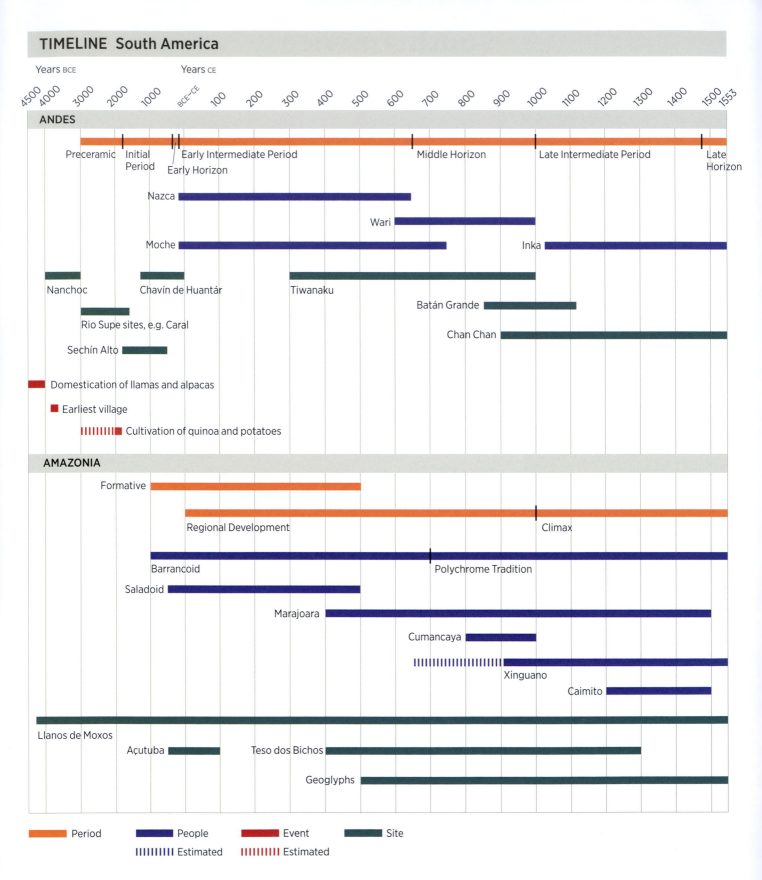

TIMELINE South America

Years BCE   Years CE

4500 4000 3000 2000 1000 BCE–CE 100 200 300 400 500 600 700 800 900 1000 1100 1200 1300 1400 1500 1553

ANDES

Preceramic — Initial Period — Early Horizon — Early Intermediate Period — Middle Horizon — Late Intermediate Period — Late Horizon

Nazca

Wari

Moche

Inka

Nanchoc

Chavín de Huantár

Tiwanaku

Batán Grande

Rio Supe sites, e.g. Caral

Chan Chan

Sechín Alto

Domestication of llamas and alpacas

Earliest village

Cultivation of quinoa and potatoes

AMAZONIA

Formative

Regional Development

Climax

Barrancoid

Polychrome Tradition

Saladoid

Marajoara

Cumancaya

Xinguano

Caimito

Llanos de Moxos

Açutuba

Teso dos Bichos

Geoglyphs

Period | **People** | **Event** | **Site**
IIIIIIIIII Estimated | IIIIIIIIII Estimated

In this chapter, we review the development of societies in South America from 3000 BCE up to European contact in the sixteenth century CE, focusing on two major regions: the Andes and Amazonia. The Andean mountain range is well known for its monumental stone architecture and elaborate terracing and irrigation systems. When Europeans first arrived, the whole of this region had recently been brought under the control of the Inka empire, but that was only the final phase in a long process of formation, coalescence, and collapse of the Andean states. Amazonia is, in contrast, much less well studied, but there is now evidence that thriving communities and earthwork builders also existed here during recent millennia.

- In the Andes, urban centers arose before major reliance on domestication or pottery. Contrast with East Asia (Chapter 9) or Southwest Asia (Chapter 6).

- Competition between major elite-led confederacies ended with the supremacy of the Inkas in 1476 CE.

- The Amazon is not a pristine forest, but has been altered by human activity for more than 2,000 years.

- By *c.* 500–1000 CE, large regional polities were established along major rivers in Amazonia.

ENVIRONMENTS AND LANDSCAPES

South America is home to one of the world's biggest rivers, largest tropical forest, driest desert, and longest mountain range, second only to the Himalayas in height and harshness. These dramatically contrasting highlands and lowlands inevitably influenced the human societies that developed in South America [**17.1**, p. 414].

The Andean Highlands

The Andes mountain range runs along the west of South America. From the Caribbean coast to Ecuador, the range is low, moist, and well vegetated. Conditions change dramatically as the mountains move down to northern Peru, rising and dividing into parallel eastern and western branches. These arms bracket a series of sierra basins, culminating in a vast mountain trough that holds Lake Titicaca, which straddles Peru and Bolivia at an altitude of 3,805 meters (12,500 feet). As the parallel ranges grow progressively higher, wider, and drier, they split the continental climate. The mountain slopes of the eastern range are well watered, in contrast to the dry western slopes of the western chain, which are crossed by a series of short, steep river valleys. The richest fishery in the southern hemisphere stretches along this Pacific coastland, which is parched desert, and in Chile arid conditions push up into the highlands, creating the driest region on earth. The dry mountain chain is also extremely sensitive to climatic dynamics and to El Niño–Southern Oscillation (ENSO) events. Above about 2,700 meters (9,000 feet), hypoxia (deprivation of oxygen due to high elevation) and cold conditions are a major source of stress on all life.

Amazonian Lowlands

Dominated by the Amazon, Orinoco, and other large rivers, Amazonia is predominantly high, tropical rainforest, interspersed with diverse other forest types, varied savannas and

17.1 Map of South America showing the main regions and sites mentioned in the text.

parklands, and a wide range of riverbank settings and other wetlands [**17.2**]. The Amazon environment harbors the greatest biodiversity of any similar-sized geographic area in the world, which researchers now recognize is in part due to an equally complex and varied history of human culture.

Coasts. Coastal areas include the Caribbean, the mainland coasts, and the island of Marajó, which dominates the massive estuary at the mouth of the Amazon. Human coastal adaptations were diverse and long-lived, and the entire littoral was densely populated by large, regional polities, including so-called circum-Caribbean chiefdoms, such as the Arawak-speaking Taino and the coastal Tupi.

17.2 The Amazonion region is dominated by tropical forest and varied waterways. While in the past the Amazon has been seen as pristine and untouched, humans have been affecting its environment for thousands of years.

Floodplains. Major floodplains occur along the Amazon and many of its principal tributaries, as well as along much of the Orinoco River. These have come to signify the vast, seasonally flooded bottomlands of the Amazon and its primary Andean-derived tributaries, the white-water rivers.

Uplands. The uplands constitute more than 95 percent of Amazonia and are highly variable between and within regions, characterized by savannas, parkland, or scrub forests, and closed and gallery (riverbank) tropical forests. True uplands, associated with the Guiana and Brazilian highlands and the Andean foothills, ring the Amazon basin and flank the Orinoco River, but a great deal of Amazonia is essentially flat. Human occupation throughout much of the region was on smaller rivers between major ones. The highland forests of Brazil and Guiana and the sub-Andean foothills and plains show pronounced seasonal change. All these upland areas have supported a variety of cultural developments, including large, settled communities in many areas.

HUNTER-GATHERER TRAJECTORIES

The South American Pacific coastal lowlands appear to have been the pathway for the earliest hunter-gatherers entering the continent. This coast runs for thousands of miles and includes tropical and desert environments as well as sub-arctic conditions at Tierra del Fuego. On the north coast of Peru, Early Archaic (*c.* 9500–7000 BCE) communities relied on collecting shellfish, fishing, and hunting coastal terrestrial fauna. The earliest evidence of these communities, called the Paijan complex, is dated to 11,800 BCE and continues to 7000 BCE.

Along the southern Peruvian coast there is solid evidence for the beginnings of a maritime industry of fishing, gathering shellfish, and hunting birds by at least 10,000 BCE. This strategy seems to have expanded after relative stabilization of sea levels around 6000 BCE, when net fishing became a dominant technique.

Along the northern Pacific Coast are areas of inland tropical forests. There is very little evidence of an Early Archaic occupation of these regions. By the Middle Archaic (*c.* 8000–4500 BCE), the resource base was rich enough to support the inhabitants of the **Las Vegas** site, a semi-sedentary village of about fifty people on the Guayaquil peninsula of Ecuador. Residents here relied on a mixture of deer hunting, fishing, and gathering cactus fruits and algarroba (mesquite) pods. There is phytolith evidence that Middle Archaic residents of the region used leren, squash, bottle gourds, and possible maize. Las Vegas was eventually abandoned during a long dry period.

During the Late Archaic (*c.* 4500–2000 BCE), there was a rapid development of more sedentary villages along the Colombian and Ecuadorian coasts. In some cases, these villages were occupied or re-occupied over hundreds of years. There may have been an agricultural component as well as a strong maritime focus (in particular shellfish-collecting and fishing), especially as the earliest ceramics appear at this time, ranging from 4500 to 3500 BCE and coming from coastal sites in Colombia and Ecuador.

TRANSITIONS TO AGRICULTURE, *c.* 9000–2000 BCE

In the Americas, there was only a small number of varieties of indigenous domesticated animals. South America was limited to llama, alpaca, guinea pig, muscovy duck, and dog. The llama was initially important to prehistoric groups for its meat and hides, and llama dung later became a critical fertilizing component of agriculture. By the time of the Inkas and late prehistoric societies, llamas were the primary transport and cargo animals for Andean people. The alpaca was another animal initially utilized for meat and hides, but later was most valued for its soft wool. Textiles were among the most important wealth items for Andean societies, and wool (and the cotton plant) became a very important fiber. Ancient DNA analyses, archaeozoological studies, and fiber analyses indicate the separate domestication of alpacas in central Peru and llamas in central Bolivia and northwest Argentina by 4000 BCE.

Guinea pigs were raised primarily for food. They were an important source of meat, as well as for religious rituals. Although guinea pigs were extensively managed in some sites as early as 8000 BCE, the best current evidence of domestication is between 6000 and 2000 BCE.

The best-known lowland Pacific and highland Andean domestic plants include quinoa, lima bean, peanut, bottle gourd, tomato, and potato. Based on direct radiocarbon analysis of crops, potato and ullucu date to *c.* 5500 BCE and three species of beans, cotton, and possibly tomato were indirectly dated to *c.* 3000–2200 BCE in the central highlands of Peru. All molecular studies on the common bean support how domestication occurred independently from Central America, with well-dated samples from the Andes currently predating any from Mesoamerica.

The shift in subsistence strategy to managing domestic plants was accompanied by very rapid development in social and political complexity, including constructing mounds (locally called pyramids) for religious and political purposes, particularly in the Pacific lowlands.

Some of the earliest examples of agriculture in South America are from Peru at the site of **Nanchoc** in the Zaña Valley, dating to the Middle Archaic period. This community shows a form of fishing–farming symbiosis. Nanchoc has a pair of small, flat-topped mounds that measure about 30–35 meters (100–115 feet) long and 1.2–1.5 meters (4–5 feet) high. These are associated with a small hut, an area of lime processing (presumably for use in coca chewing), and nearby agricultural field furrows. In the Nanchoc side valley, evidence of moschata squash, manioc, beans, pacae, and a peanut-like plant were AMS dated to 6500 BCE, with coca leaf by 6000 BCE and cotton by 4000 BCE. On this basis, the excavators argue for an early occurrence of farming villages by 6500–6000 BCE.

An intriguing question is why this apparent early appearance of cultivation and manipulation of plants in the Nanchoc side valley did not expand into the rest of the valley, and why farming in general did not result in development of similar pockets of cultivated plants on the north coast of Peru at this time. Groups of farmers living in some areas of the Nanchoc Valley flourished during most of the early to middle postglacial period while other groups survived on a mixed foraging subsistence strategy. Archaeologists argue that small pockets of early agriculturalists popped up in suitable locales, such as the Las Vegas area of the Guayaquil peninsula and the Nanchoc side valley, but the conditions were not favorable for wider adoption of agriculture until later.

URBAN COMMUNITIES: ACERAMIC COMMUNITIES, *c.* 3000–1800 BCE

In the Andes, urban centers with large temple mounds and attendant elite quarters arose long before people made pottery, wove cloth, or relied principally on domesticated plants and animals for subsistence. This remarkable experiment flourished in the wake of a pervasive environmental turning point. Around 3800 BCE, glaciers ceased melting and sea levels stopped rising, so allowing marine, meteorological, and ecological conditions to assume their modern patterns.

The largest prepottery monuments in the hemisphere were erected along a 600-kilometer stretch (370 miles) of Peru's desert, where the near-shore Andean fishery is richest and easily accessible by rafts and small watercraft. Fishing required terrestrial resources, including reeds for watercraft, cotton for fishing line and net, fruit trees for wood and edibles, and gourds for floats and containers. Aceramic remains of these cultigens are common in comparison to the less frequent remains of chili peppers, beans, squash, tubers, and occasional specimens of maize at a few sites. In theory, managerial elites first arose to facilitate the mix and integration of these two separate, but interdependent, economies.

Temple Mounds and Sunken Courts

Between 3000 and 2000 BCE, the very largest architectural monuments in the Americas were being erected in Peru. These were stone-faced platforms that consisted of superimposed floors atop artificial layers of fill that gradually added height to the structures. This kind of episodic construction was an important means of reaffirming corporate identity by bringing people together, and later, architectural fill often consisted of coarse reed satchels that each held about 11 kilograms (25 pounds) of rocks, apparently reflecting a labor tax.

The sides of masonry mounds were plastered and steep, but often rose in terraces that could support courts and compartments, as did the flat-topped summits. Broad central staircases were emphasized as processional display stages for the audiences of commoners, who assembled in ground-level forecourts but were not allowed access to the elevated inner sanctums. Ceremonial architecture occurs at many sites with little refuse, which suggests they were pilgrimage centers rather than sedentary residential centers. The platforms are considered temples and civic-ceremonial facilities, where governance transpired in the names of the gods.

17.3 Pyramide Mayor, Caral. A large circular sunken court controlling access to the platform mound behind via a narrow doorway with stairs; in the distance, further stairs lead up to the summit of the mound itself.

Indigenous cosmology holds that high mountain rainfall descends to fertilize Mother Earth, from whose caves and springs humans first emerged to settle this world. This origin myth seemingly underlies an enduring Andean concern with semi-subterranean ritual structures. Stone-lined circular sunken courts [**17.3**] with moderate-sized subterranean chambers were commonly constructed centrally in front of larger platforms. In later times, circular and rectangular sunken courts were built at **Chavín de Huántar**, and rectangular forms became common in the Lake Titicaca region.

The largest of these prepottery monuments were erected along the coast between Ríos Chicama and Chillon. Other than **El Paraíso** (see below), the coastal monuments can be assigned to the Supe tradition, named after a valley containing seventeen aceramic mounds. This included the Caral complex, which covers 66 hectares (163 acres). Here, six major platforms began as idiosyncratic structures, but by 2400 BCE a central authority had emerged and induced a reconfiguration of the temples so that each faced and framed a grand nodal plaza. This sweeping transformation is read as increased sociopolitical integration that led to Caral becoming the Rio Supe capital and a regional center. Elite functionaries staffing each temple lived in immediately adjacent palatial quarters.

Around 1800 BCE, fishing and farming in the Supe region were permanently devastated by an exceptionally severe earthquake and ensuing El Niño rainfall and flooding that choked the sea floor with landslide debris. This cleared the way for the construction of El Paraíso, marking the arrival of the Initial Period and of farming and ceramic use. Near Lima and overlooking the easily farmed Rio Chillon floodplain 2 kilometers (1.25 miles) from the sea, El Paraíso [**17.4**] (see also pp. 410–11) is unique in its exceptional monumentality. More than 100,000 metric tons (110,000 US tons) of quarried stone

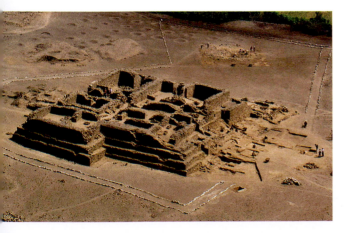

17.4 El Paraíso. A small, restored section of the prepottery masonry complex of El Paraíso is more than two stories high and about half the size of a football field.

were used to erect nine grand architectural complexes, three stories high, which sprawl over 58 hectares (143 acres). There is little evidence that the multitudes that erected El Paraíso resided there, but analysis of the scant refuse indicates that protein consumed there came entirely from the sea—they were certainly inheritors of long-lasting maritime adaptations.

EARLY FARMING COMMUNITIES: INITIAL PERIOD AND THE EARLY HORIZON, *c.* 1800–200 BCE

The Initial Period, c. 1800–400 BCE

The Initial Period is marked by significant transformations, which began about 1800 BCE in northern Peru and spread south gradually, reaching the Titicaca basin four centuries later. People began to use pottery and weave cloth, and relied on agricultural staples and domesticated animals. Innovative economic adaptations opened up new inland habitats for use, enabling the growth of populations along the coast and in the highlands. The Initial Period also saw a widespread spate of collaborative work and corporate construction, as each community seems to have erected its own temples and civic-ceremonial facilities. There is mortuary evidence of Initial Period elites at La Galgada, but elsewhere graves of those in power are less obvious. Yet times were not entirely peaceful. In the Casma Valley, the modest-sized rectangular temple mound of **Cerro Sechín** is enclosed by a megalithic mosaic wall with bas-relief carvings that depict individuals with axe-like clubs parading among dismembered heads and other human body parts [**17.5**, **17.6**].

More monuments and mounds were erected in coastal valleys during the Initial Period than at any other time. The numbers suggest each community had facilities housing a local patron god, while multitudes of communities toiled together to build and sustain enormous civic-ceremonial facilities

17.5, **17.6 Cerro Sechín.** A monumental mosaic wall at the site depicts men carrying arms (right), parading among dismembered body parts (not visible here). Processions along each side of the wall converged at the entrance, framed by tall monolithic stelae, each with a carved banner (below).

serving regional deities. The most distinctive temples are U-shaped complexes with a high rear platform fronted by two lower wing mounds, which frame a spacious central court. Many were ornamented with monumental adobe friezes of supernatural beings. The largest is the vast monument of **Sechín Alto** in the Casma Valley. The epoch of prosperity commemorated by Sechín Alto and its contemporary monuments ended unexpectedly between 900 and 800 BCE, when persistent drought induced a drastic turning point in human development.

The Early Horizon, c. 400–200 BCE

A long drought induced the abandonment of almost every U-shaped center, with the notable exception of Chavín de Huántar, situated high in the northern sierra between two streams that feed into the distant Amazon. Chavín's main complex, called the Castillo, comprises two conjoined U-shaped platform mounds framing a circular sunken court and fronted by a second, smaller, U-shaped plaza containing a sunken court and flanked by buildings [**17.7**].

The Castillo was ornamented with splendid stone carvings [**17.8**], including three-dimensional mounted heads of humans, birds, and felines, as well as numerous engraved wall plaques of felines, serpents, and supernatural composite beings. The art drew inspiration from the Amazonian tropics in its prominent featuring of the jungle's top predators, including harpy eagles and spotted jaguars. The paramount Chavín deity, known as the Staff God, is depicted on a 4.5-meter-tall (15 feet) stela mounted in the West Temple as a finely attired standing figure with a cat-like face and claws. Curled lips expose two tusk-like canine teeth, while eyebrows and hair are rendered as snakes. This god is emblematic of the Early Horizon; its iconography spread over much of northern and central Peru between

17.7, 17.8 Chavín de Huántar. The West Temple section of Chavín de Huántar held a circular sunken court ornamented with stone-carved depictions of fanged deities, including this one carrying a cactus (below right). The contemporary U-shaped East Temple section framed a rectangular sunken courtyard (below left).

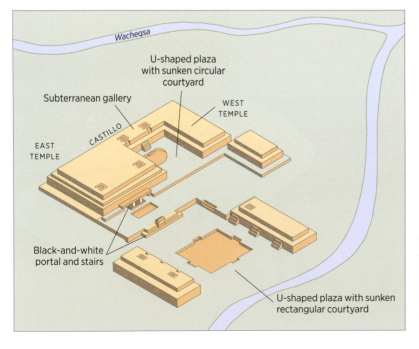

400 and 200 BCE as Chavín religious beliefs cut across old social boundaries in the northern sphere of the Andean region. The Early Horizon was also marked by the spread of innovative technologies. Cloth production was revolutionized as tapestry came into use, along with complex techniques of tie-dyeing and batik. Metallurgical innovations included soldering, **sweat welding**, **repoussé**, and alloying gold with silver or copper.

Paracas. The necropolis of Paracas offers special insight into the world of the newly arising elites of the Early Horizon. Large paired platform mounds, one at each end of a thick, high-walled rectangular enclosure, formed distinctive civic–ceremonial architecture. In an elite necropolis, rulers and their relatives were interred in subterranean vaults in the form of large bell-shaped pits and rectangular masonry crypts that were used over generations; some contained up to forty mummy bundles. Nude corpses were prepared for burial by being placed in a flexed, seated position, wrapped in textiles in a large shallow basket containing garments and other offerings. Then the basket, accompaniments, and corpse were swathed together in many layers of plain cotton cloth to create the final mummy bundle [**17.9**]. Grave goods include exquisite fabrics in dazzling colors. Intricately embroidered mantles, tunics, and headgear depict mythical creatures and ornately garbed humans who wear gold decorations resembling cat whiskers, and carry human trophy heads and ornamental staves. A preference for polychrome embellishment extends to Paracas ceramics, and aligns the arts of this coastal society with southern traditions of highly colorful adornment.

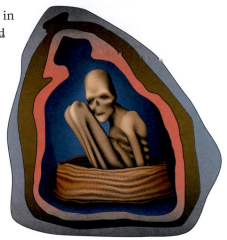

17.9 Mummy bundle.
Placed in a large basket in a seated position, Paracas elites were accompanied by finely embroidered garments and headgear, and ornaments of gold and shell. The basket, body, and grave goods were then wrapped in multiple layers of plain cloth to form a large mummy bundle.

COLLAPSE AND REORGANIZATION: THE EARLY INTERMEDIATE PERIOD, *c.* 200 BCE–650 CE: ANDEAN CONFEDERACIES AND STATES

A marked change in Andean life took hold during the Early Intermediate period. By now, exploited habitats were full of communities, and hostilities arose as recurrent long droughts sparked fierce competition over resources. Earlier sites, including Chavín, Pukara, and Paracas, were abandoned. Locations with monumental structures increased in size but decreased in frequency, and simple residential communities became the norm. Fortified villages and hilltop bastions point to conflict. Governance was now fully in the hands of a well-established elite class. Noble status was carried to the grave and marked by elaborate mortuary treatment and rich grave goods. The powerful monopolized the production of fine arts, resulting in vibrant corporate styles reflecting the political, religious, and ethnic composition of sponsoring bodies.

The Moche

Some archaeologists describe the Moche as a unified state with its capital at the twin mounds of the **Temple of the Sun** and the **Temple of the Moon** in the Moche Valley, others as a group of loosely confederated principalities. Ongoing research suggests that there was probably variability between regions within the Moche, rather than unity imposed by conquest. Almost every desert valley within the Moche terrain had a dominant court–mound complex wall with murals narrating opulent ceremonies, which are also reflected in its pottery, providing insight into the ideology of Moche nobles. Ritual drinking vessels were made in the form of

sweat welding welding together pieces of metal using solder

repoussé a metalwork technique whereby relief decoration is produced by hammering, usually from the reverse

KEY SITE Sipán and the Presentation Theme

Moche elites justified their rule with stories and myths that provided subject matter for fine arts and narrative iconography, and combat between richly garbed warriors is a frequent topic. The aim of armed engagement was to capture, but not kill, opponents, who were stripped of their armaments, shields, and finery, with the spoils going to the victor. After being paraded about naked, what happened next to the losers is portrayed in the so-called Presentation Theme, which narrates an elaborate ceremony [**17.10**].

It begins with the nude, hands-bound captives having their throats slit by elaborately garbed figures wearing feline or fox masks. The masked sacrificers collect the victims' blood in distinctive chalices with extended flaring bases that serve as handles. They then pass the chalices to much higher-ranking

17.10 Along the bottom of this fine-line drawing of the Presentation Theme, captive warriors have their throats cut and the blood is collected in chalices. At the top, priests and a priestess carry one such chalice to a paramount warrior priest, who, accompanied by a small spotted dog, consumes the contents.

members of a supreme priesthood. The entourage often includes an important individual ornately bedecked as an owl, and it always includes a finely attired priestess adorned with sashes ending in serpent heads, and wearing a distinctive double-plumed headdress. Carefully carrying a chalice, they present it to the paramount celebrant, the warrior priest [**17.11**], who ritually consumes the sacrificial content. Generally accompanied by a spotted dog, the warrior priest is crowned with a double-flared headdress and often carrying a war club.

Although the art and iconography of the Presentation Theme was long considered fanciful, it is now clear that the story reveals ceremonies and social roles that Moche rulers regularly enacted. Tombs of females in priestly attire have been excavated at San Jose de Moro in the Jequetepeque Valley. Most importantly, at Sipán in the Lambayeque Valley, archaeologists have exposed the richly accompanied burial of a warrior priest, replete with his special costume, headgear, sacrificial chalice, and accompanying spotted dog.

17.11 Earspool from Tomb 1 at Sipán, with the miniature figure of a richly attired warrior priest, flanked by attendants. His war club and nose plate are made from separate pieces, and his necklace consists of owl heads.

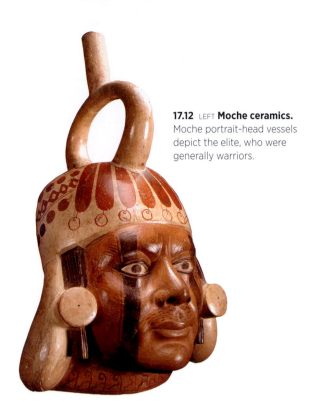

17.12 LEFT **Moche ceramics.** Moche portrait-head vessels depict the elite, who were generally warriors.

17.13 Moche art. This composite of three different fine-line drawing scenes shows fox hunting (top), combat between elite warriors (center), and a deity battling a fish monster (bottom).

spouted globular bottles, some of them three-dimensional depictions of divinities, people [**17.12**], and animals. Others were ornamented with finely painted scenes illustrating particular themes or stories. A common set of scenes depicts ritual combat and human sacrifice [**17.13**] (see Key Site box: Sipán and the Presentation Theme). Warrior combatants are almost always other Moche *elite*. Some portrait vessels depict specific individuals attired for combat, while others show them later stripped, bound, and awaiting ceremonial execution. The shedding of one's blood and life for the good of the gods and society was clearly an honorable demise commemorated in the arts.

The Temples of the Sun and the Moon. Dominating the nexus of the southern Moche realm are two enormous mounds, the Temple of the Sun (Huaca del Sol) and the Temple of the Moon (Huaca de la Luna) [**17.14**, p. 424]. Built on the flanks of a white hill, the smaller Luna complex consists of three platforms interconnected and enclosed by high adobe walls richly ornamented with polychrome friezes and murals. The large central mound had spacious summit courts decorated with huge depictions of the head of a supernatural being. The rayed face gazes forward with curled lips, exposing elongated, interlocking canine teeth. Other polychrome panels depict spider-like creatures, anthropomorphic beings, and the parading of warrior captives. To the south, a small platform was built over the upper side of a rocky outcrop, leaving the high stony face exposed to viewers in an enclosing court below. The outcrop platform was apparently the sacramental stage for rituals depicted in Moche arts that show the mountaintop sacrifice of captive warriors, whose mutilated corpses were then flung downhill. Below the outcrop platform, the dismembered remains of more than twenty executed young males were excavated.

Sovereigns apparently resided in opulent quarters atop the great platform of the Temple of the Sun. Standing more than 40 meters (130 feet) high today, it is one of the largest mounds

17.14 Huaca del Sol and Huaca de la Luna. The heavily looted Huaca de la Luna in the foreground was a teeming city occupying the plains stretching up to the remains of Huaca del Sol in the background, which overlooks the floodplain of the Moche River.

ever erected in South America, though less than half of the original monument survives. It was erected in stages, each phase building over existing summit rooms and courts. Millions of mud bricks were used in the construction, and before drying, many of the bricks had distinctive maker's marks impressed upon them, identifying different communities of workmen assigned to different sections of the project. Originally, the Temple of the Sun took the form of a cross that rose from the north in three successively higher tiers before descending to a fourth level, probably comprising servants' or retainers' quarters.

The Moche realm contracted and waned following devastating El Niño floods, sand dune incursions, and an exceptionally severe drought between 562 and 594 CE. In this harsh climate, the Moche recast its ideology and endured in a smaller form until *c.* 800 CE at Galindo, San Jose de Moro, and Pampa Grande.

Nazca and the South Coast

Partially contemporary with Moche, the Nazca culture flourished *c.* 200 BCE–650 CE in its namesake valley. Known for polychrome decoration, Nazca weavers and potters produced vibrant arts, conveying a rich, often abstract iconography. There are recognizable depictions of plants, animals, people, and supernatural beings, but rarely are they portrayed in scenes that reveal broader stories or rituals. Some supernatural creatures sprout feline-like whiskers [**17.15**] and carry human heads, and some grave accompaniments include whiskered nose ornaments of gold or mummified human trophy skulls.

17.15 Nazca vessel. The Nazca were accomplished potters and produced vessels decorated with a wide range of imagery, often brightly colored. A whiskered feline being is depicted on this polychrome double-spouted Nazca drinking vessel.

Nazca Lines. Nazca is justly famous for its desert ground drawings found on the rocky plains between river tributaries. Called **geoglyphs**, these lines and figures were created by removing the dark upper sun-baked rocks and gravel to expose lower, lighter-colored sediments. Sizable areas can be cleared and large glyphs can be made with relatively little work. While geoglyphs were sporadically created along much of the coastal desert, their greatest concentration is on the Nazca plains [**17.16**]. There are more than 1,000 kilometers (620 miles) of straight lines of varying widths, and some lengths exceed 20 kilometers (12 miles); many lines issue from isolated hills and end at other hills. In addition, there are more than 300 geometric figures, including trapezoids, triangles, zigzags, and spirals. Near the valley in one corner of the plains, some three dozen animal figures were etched in the desert, including numerous birds, several killer whales, a monkey, a spider, a fox or llama, one human, and several plants.

Glyphs on hillsides were similar to billboards, while many on flat land were to be walked on, and others may have served still other purposes. Newer creations cross older ones in amazing profusion, indicating that the works were not integrated in an overall plan; rather, each geoglyph was separately created, used for a time and then forgotten.

CITIES, STATES, AND EMPIRES: THE RISE AND FALL OF THE ANDEAN EMPIRES

The Inka realm, stretching more than 5,000 kilometers (3,100 miles) along the Andes Mountains, was the largest ancient empire (1476–1533 CE) ever to develop south of the Equator, and the largest native state ever to arise in the Americas. It enveloped the most rugged mountain chains in the hemisphere and the greatest biotic and cultural diversity in the continent. The Inkas themselves were a closed ethnic group defined by dual descent (with power passing to one heir and economic wealth retained by others to maintain the ancestors) from a venerated

geoglyph a drawing or image made in the ground surface by removal of earth (e.g. Nazca Lines) or by using banks and mounds (e.g. Serpent Mound)

founder called Manco Capac. Manco's heirs ruled as a great royal family of ten elite lineages, with kinship terminology serving as the idiom of social and political relationships.

Similar kin-based organizations characterized states and societies the Inka conquered, each of which scrupulously maintained its own separate ethnic identity. There is debate about the degrees to which pre-Inka states—Tiwanaku and Wari in the highlands, Chimor on Peru's north coast—were hierarchical and centralized, or heterogeneous and confederated (see Key Theme box: Social Inequality—Descent and the *Kurakas*).

The Middle Horizon, c. 650–1000 CE: Tiwanaku and Wari

Foundations for Inka economic organization were laid during the Middle Horizon times (*c.* 650–1000 CE), when two states held sway over the cordillera: **Wari** ruling in the north and **Tiwanaku** in the south. Characterized as youthful, secular, militant, centralized, and hierarchical, Wari governed almost all of highland and coastal Peru from its upland capital in the sierra of Ayacucho. Portrayed as mature, religious, proselytizing (attempting to convert someone's beliefs), heterogeneous, and more confederated, Tiwanaku dominated the mountains of southern Peru, Bolivia, and northern Chile from its metropolis on the plains of Lake Titicaca.

Although relatively flat, Titicaca's expansive high plains, the **altiplano**, lie above 3,200 meters (10,500 feet), where highland crops thrive, including quinoa and potatoes. The Ayacucho sierra is lower and receives more rain, but the topography is broken and very rugged. Wari increased agricultural production by constructing large irrigated terrace systems on steep mountain slopes, where maize and other crops could be cultivated. Tiwanaku also built terraces and reclaimed flat terrain for farming potatoes and other high-altitude crops, while herding llama and alpaca in marsh pasturelands. Both states employed llama caravans to import resources from colonies and clients in distant provinces.

Great labor was lavished on monumental construction at both capitals, although very different forms of architecture were emphasized. Tiwanaku stressed imposing temple mounds for ritual display visible to large congregations. The Akapana pyramid anchored the capital's monumental core [**17.17**]. Tiwanaku is renowned for its fine stonework, and mounds and courts were faced with well-cut masonry and housed numerous large stelae,

altiplano high-altitude grasslands in the central Andes

17.17 Tiwanaku. Situated on the plains of Lake Titicaca, this site was the capital of a large state and contained the biggest platform mound (pyramid) in the southern Andes. A megalithic stairway leads up to the east entrance of the Kalasasaya (a substantial courtyard to the north of the Akapana pyramid), which frames a tall anthropomorphic stela in the background.

some of anthropomorphic form. Portals were of great ritual significance, and finely carved lintels depicted rows of individuals converging on the mid-point of the door, as if passing through an ornate gate united people. The most ornate is the Gateway of the Sun, with a lintel depicting rows of winged beings moving toward a central figure standing atop a platform mound and holding a vertical staff in each hand.

Gateways, stelae, and temple mounds were avoided by Wari, which employed fine-cut stonework only occasionally. Monumental architecture tended to be cloistered and compartmentalized, stressing grand compounds with high walls and interiors subdivided by clusters of one- and two-story hall-like buildings called galleries, arranged around open patios.

Architectural canons for each capital were followed in the hinterlands. Although provincial centers served different functions, their monumental architecture provided graphic statements about the power of their respective capitals. A buffer zone typically separated the Wari and Tiwanaku empires, except in Peru's Moquegua Valley, where a provincial center of each state lay within distant eyesight of the other. Here, mid-valley, Tiwanaku colonists erected a major temple at Omo, while in the higher sierra a Wari complex was built with walled compounds atop the high, sheer-sided mesa and natural bastion of Cerro Baul.

Three to four centuries of interaction in Moqeugua may explain how Wari came to adopt Tiwanaku's paramount pantheon, depicted on the Gateway of the Sun. Holding two vertical staffs, the richly garbed divinity is a probable revitalization of the Chavín Staff God. Short rays issuing from the head terminate in feline heads or ovals (perhaps potatoes) in Tiwanaku renditions, whereas Wari added terminal corncobs, more appropriate for its maize-based economy. Faith in both religion and government was seemingly undermined after about 1050 CE, when the climate turned drier for centuries. With economic stress exacerbating social tensions, Wari and Tiwanaku dissolved. In many areas people built hilltop forts and resided in defensible settlements.

The Late Intermediate Period, c. 1000–1476 CE: Chimor and Lambayeque

Governed from the Moche Valley metropolis of **Chan Chan**, Chimor was a pre-Inkan empire of the Late Intermediate Period. Its core holdings were the very largest of the irrigated valleys that crossed the northern coast. With massive canals extending laterally to parallel desert drainages, Lambayeque was the biggest and most powerful of Chimor's coastal adversaries.

Chimor and Chan Chan. Ethnohistorical sources say that prosperous Chimor elites resided in spacious walled compounds with interior facilities for receiving their subjects and entertaining other important people. They comprise the dominant monuments of the imperial capital, Chan Chan [**17.18**, **17.19**], a densely packed civic center that covered 6 square kilometers (2.3 square miles). The metropolitan majority, totaling perhaps 29,000, were skilled craftspeople, particularly weavers and metalsmiths who lived and worked in humble quarters built of cane and thatch. Rulers and elites were the urban minority, numbering 6,000 or less. The minor nobility resided in

17.18 ABOVE **Chan Chan.** Adobe decoration on the Temple of the Dragon.

17.19 BELOW **Chan Chan.** An aerial view of metropolitan Chan Chan, capital of Chimor, with vast rectangular compounds reserved for the ruling elite.

thirty modest-sized compounds with relatively low adobe walls, while paramount rulers and their kin held court in enormous *ciudadelas*.

Thick mud-brick walls towering three stories high enclosed the *ciudadelas*. Lacking battlements, the perimeter walls were for social seclusion. Access to the complex was through a single narrow gateway in the north. High curtain walls partitioned the interiors into northern, central, and southern sectors; all contained palatial buildings except for the southern sector, where retainers lived in simple cane quarters. The northern and central sectors each held large, centrally positioned entry courtyards, focal points for pomp and ceremony and often ornamented with carved friezes. Maze-like corridors connected smaller courts with rows of cell-like rectangular rooms for storage of valuable goods.

Situated in spacious courts within the *ciudadelas*, single- or multi-storied burial platforms with numerous interior chambers are the largest buildings within the imperial compounds. The grand sepulchers were commercially looted for treasure and precious metal artifacts in post-conquest times. Excavations produced remains of fine ceramics, ornate textiles, rich artworks, and bones of young women, all apparently accompaniments of the primary royal interment in a centrally positioned T-shaped chamber. The mortuary structures are compatible with propositions that a succession of Chimor's potentates built *ciudadelas* to serve as palaces and then as family mausoleums, as the reins of power passed to subsequent generations. Ancient wooden models of *ciudadela* entry courts portray processions of priests leading llamas and captives to sacrifice in front of cloth-bundled royal mummies occupying the rear of the court.

ciudadela a Spanish term meaning citadel, applied, for example, to the unfortified royal complexes at Chan Chan in Peru

Lambayeque and Batán Grande. After the Moche polities dissolved *c.* 800 CE, the pre-eminent center in the Lambayeque region arose at **Batán Grande** in the northern lateral drainage of the Leche River. By about 1000 CE, the civic core had grown to more than 4 square kilometers (1.5 square miles), and was dominated by a dozen enormous platform mounds surrounded by smaller monuments. Batán Grande was hallowed ground, with more than 10,000 interments. It may have been akin to a Vatican-like religious center, where multitudes from near and far were buried with their richest finery [**17.20**]. Batán Grande was probably one of the many Lambayeque sites that figure in oral traditions recorded by the Spanish. Rains from an exceptionally catastrophic El Niño event around 1100 CE flooded Batán Grande, leading to its abandonment. Prior to Chimor's conquest of the region, a long interregnum followed the flood. Tucume Viejo became Lambayeque's major political center, retaining its importance after the region was conquered first by Chimor and then the Inkas. The Tucume complex has one of the very biggest platform mounds ever erected in the Andes, Huaca Larga.

17.20 Batán Grande goldwork. A product of masterful goldworking, this exquisite headgear accompanied a noble to his death at Batán Grande. The site contained a large civic core and a dozen huge platform mounds as well as smaller monuments. More than 10,000 burials were made here.

The Late Horizon, 1476–1533 CE: Cuzco and the Inkas

The Chimor in the lowlands and the Inka in the highlands were pitted against each other in a struggle for sovereignty over the cordillera. Protracted drought tipped the economic and demographic balance of power, and the Inka of the southern mountains prevailed over

KEY SITE The Sacred Valley of the Inkas and Machu Picchu

The confluence of two revered streams, the Huantanay and Tullumayo, framed Cuzco, the center of the Inka universe. Straightened, canalized, and faced with fine masonry, the waterways converged at the base of the metropolis that they helped drain. Believing the waters to be therapeutic, people bathed in the streams, offered sacrifices to them, and used them to carry away the hallowed remains of numerous ceremonies. Upon subduing the local inhabitants, the lords of Cuzco invested extraordinary resources in transforming the valley into an amazing imperial parkland. Hillsides were expertly terraced with polygonal stone masonry, and the fields irrigated from rock-lined canals.

Audacious engineering and exceptional effort were devoted to canalizing the Urubamba River and then facing its vertical banks with well-cut stone walls, still visible today. A series of stunning sanctuaries and settlements were erected in the valley.

Machu Picchu is a spectacular example of the royal retreats. It is lower and wetter than Cuzco, sitting in a canyon-like valley where the Urubamba enters the upper fringes of the Amazonian rainforest [**17.21**]. Although the forested terrain is exceptionally rugged, the Inkas terraced and farmed the slopes and perched Machu Picchu on a towering promontory overlooking a verdant agricultural landscape.

17.21 With the Sacred Valley below, Machu Picchu is a masterwork of Inka engineering and architecture that began with artificially leveling the hilltop and terracing the hillsides, and culminated in fine-cut stone buildings frequented by the nobility and their retainers.

Chimor of the northern desert. This brought the final political synthesis of the Andes under the Inkas, and the Late Horizon.

The Inka empire consisted of eighty political provinces, each embracing ethnically diverse and linguistically distinct subjects. The plethora of mutually unintelligible tongues compelled the Inkas to impose a lingua franca, called Quechua (also known as Runa Simi), for conducting business of state. The provinces were grouped into four geographical territories. Four conceptual lines creating the grand quadrants radiated out of the capital, Cuzco, as did four splendid all-weather highways uniting the empire, a configuration reinforcing the Inkas' view that their metropolis was truly the navel of the known universe (see Key Site box: The Sacred Valley of the Inkas and Machu Picchu). The opulence of this *axis mundi* amazed the Spanish conquistadors, whose first-hand accounts say that Cuzco's splendor was unmatched in Europe. Cuzco vividly expressed highly distinctive imperial styles of art and architecture, yet these styles were relatively young; radiocarbon dates suggest that uniquely Inka hallmarks of technique and fashion began to crystallize only shortly after 1375 CE.

Origins and Expansion. More than a dozen different ethnic groups lived within a 100-kilometer (62 miles) radius of Cuzco. Some groups allied themselves peacefully with the Inkas, whose rulers often married noble women of other ethnic collectives to establish coalitions. Groups that did not resist Cuzco's early expansion were made Inka by privilege and given minor bureaucratic posts, while still paying tribute to the Inkas by birth. Some groups fiercely defended their independence, however. One of these was the Mohina, who lived upstream from Cuzco in the Lucre basin, where Wari formerly had its largest provincial center. Upon abandonment by the Wari, it was replaced by a local metropolitan center, Chokepukio. Repeated conflict between the Mohina and Inkas led to the creation of a sparsely occupied buffer zone separating the forces of Cuzco and Chokepukio. When the Inkas finally prevailed, many of the Mohina were exiled, and people loyal to the Inkas were settled in the area.

With their homeland consolidated, the lords of Cuzco were well positioned to launch aggressive expansion further afield. Their initial foreign conquests were in the Titicaca basin; securing this high mountain breadbasket in turn fueled northern expansion into the sierra and subjugation along the coast.

Cuzco and the Trappings of Empire. Inka subjects were highland agropastoralists, coastal farmers, and fishermen. The imperial economy was based on extracting labor levies. Commoners of both sexes were required to plow, plant, and harvest both government and state religious lands. Records of taxes were kept using *khipus* (see Key Discovery box: The *Khipu*, p. 432). Goods and military, as well as political edicts and reports of revolt, moved rapidly along road systems that linked imperial installations to outlying areas. Military posts were positioned along the roads. Food tax could be paid at the posts, allowing standing armies to be stationed throughout the empire to ensure payment of tribute and quick suppression of rebellion. Larger forts were built in areas where resistance from local populations was greater. Incomes from tribute supported the Inkas by birth in regal style, not simply in life but also in death. Deceased rulers and important officials were artificially mummified. Venerated as grand ancestors and religious objects, the mummies often continued to reside in their former quarters or in special sanctuaries tended by family members, and were brought forth to attend major ritual events with the living.

khipu in Andean South America, a method of record-keeping expressed by knots and colored strings

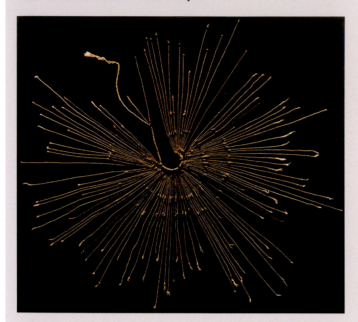

All state-level societies have non-oral means of record-keeping, but it does not necessarily follow that all state societies have writing. The Inka had a record system that differed from the glyphs used by the Maya and Egyptian states: a system based on knotted strings called the *khipu* [**17.22**]. Its origins reach back to the Middle Horizon period.

The *khipu* consists of hundreds of pendent strings hanging from a primary cord. Though archaeologists have not completely translated the system, we know information was coded in a number of ways. For example, the number of pendent strings, their color, and how they were grouped together was important to the code, as was the strings' ply, or the way thinner ones are twisted together. Finally, the size, placement, number, and type of knot present indicate different types of information. The *khipu* was used until the arrival of the Europeans.

17.22 *Khipus* were used to record information about taxes and other economic transactions. The color of the string, placement and type of knot, and twist of the string recorded different types of information.

Women were obliged to weave textiles for the regime, while men were additionally drafted to work on building projects. Reconstructing what people ate during the Inka period by analyzing the isotopes of collagen in skeletons help show how the treatment of women may have changed during this time. While skeletons of the period preceding the Inka show little sign of dietary variation between men and women, in Inka burials men and women appear to have eaten different foods. While women ate similar food to those of the previous period, men ate substantially more maize. This is important as much consumption of maize was in the form of *chicha*, a beer made from fermenting maize, which is associated with ritualized political gatherings. This change in diet could therefore reflect a shift in attitude toward women's roles in ritual events, and a greater restriction of women compared to periods before the Inka hegemony.

Imperial-style buildings employed two notable forms of cut-rock masonry that did not use mortar. One of these, ashlar, employed rectangular stones hewn to the same size and was generally used for the freestanding walls of buildings. The other, polygonal [**17.23**], used for facing terraces and solid structures, employed large, multi-sided rocks, each uniquely faceted and sized to fit the angles of adjoining blocks. A rotating force of 20,000 corvée laborers reputedly worked for decades to erect Cuzco's largest monument, Sacsahuamán, interpreted as either a temple or a fort—a massive acropolis of masonry terraces and summit buildings crowning the heights of the imperial capital [**17.24**]. The metropolis that sprawled out below was composed of high-walled enclosures for royalty, each about the size of a city block, with a single entry. The Coricancha, a great temple, held the gold-bedecked House of the Sun, while another adorned with silver served the moon.

17.23 Inka masonry. At the royal Inka compound of Ollantaytambo in the Sacred Valley, massive polygonal blocks were individually carved into unique shapes to fit with similarly irregular adjacent blocks of stone.

17.24 Sacsahuamán. Crowning the heights of the Inka capital at Cuzco, the fort-like temple of Sacsahuamán had three high ramparts of polygonal masonry with individual cut stones weighing tons, which had been hauled in from great distances.

In 1492, the Inka empire was at its height. This Native American marvel was decimated by a one-two punch of European disease and avarice. First, the unprecedented smallpox pandemic in 1519 killed the emperor and millions of his Andean subjects, triggering a disastrous seven-year civil war between rival claimants to the Inka throne. Then, just as one of them was marching south to claim Cuzco, he was intercepted, kidnapped, ransomed, and killed by Pizarro's forces as they dismembered the apex of Indigenous political achievement and plundered the empire's cities.

Today Peru is home to fifty-one Indigenous communities. Of the 31 million people living in the country, more than 70 percent are of Indigenous heritage. More than fifty distinct languages are also used there, the majority of which are of native origin. The most widely spoken of these is Quechua, which was the unifying tongue of the Inka. With 7 million people speaking a language of the Quechua family, it is the second most spoken in Peru, and Indigenous communities are working to ensure the national government protects and promotes the continuation of this language and others that have been inherited from Peru's past.

AMAZONIA

In the Amazon, European and colonial explorers searched for centuries for the lost cities of legend. Today, regional specialists agree that in parts of Amazonia in 1492 CE, large, hierarchical societies with sophisticated technology and spectacular architectural complexes of earthen mounds and enclosures existed. Population movements and cultural interaction dominated the Amazonian Formative period (*c.* 1000 BCE–500 CE), which was overlapped and followed by the so-called Regional Developmental and Climax periods from 1 to 1500 CE throughout most of the area. These later periods were characterized by internal growth and diversification in technology, culture, and populations. By the time of European contact, *c.* 1500–50 CE, societies ranged from the large polities of the lower and middle Amazon, ranked into regional hierarchies, and the equally large and powerful confederacies that lacked rigid hierarchies (for example, the Tupinamba), to the small, egalitarian groups.

TRANSITIONS TO STATES: THE AMAZONIAN FORMATIVE PERIOD, *c.* 1000 BCE–500 CE

Despite greatly exceeding the size of Europe, Amazonia was long ignored by archaeologists. Because the archaeological record is very poorly sampled, reconstructions of past cultural groups are often made from the much better investigated record of Amazonian languages in order to model the origins and dispersals of ancient societies of eastern South America and the Caribbean.

The Linguistic Evidence

The earliest European expeditions in the Americas encountered groups descended from Amazonian populations. The Taino of the Greater Antilles and the coastal Tupi of Brazil were the endpoints of two great Amazonian linguistic dispersals: the Arawak and Tupiguarani language families. The speakers of both of these languages expanded rapidly across much of the lowlands *c.* 1000–500 BCE.

The Tupian languages began dispersing from somewhere in southwestern Amazonia *c.* 3000–2000 BCE. Tupiguarani groups in eastern Brazil and around the Paraguay River to the west were in place from at least around 2,000 years ago. Occupation of the Amazon basin and the land north of it occurred after about 1500 CE (for example, Kocama/Omagua and northern Amazonian tongues).

Proto-Arawak languages also began to diverge by around 2000 BCE or soon after, although the place of origin is less certain. Proto-Arawak already had words for manioc, ceramics, cayman, and, perhaps, an older/younger sibling distinction, but great linguistic distance between sometimes even neighboring languages suggests that the divergences happened quickly in the remote past.

Technological innovation is often seen as the root cause of both the Arawak and Tupiguarani dispersal, particularly the emergence of a developed system of root-crop agriculture. Manioc and other core crops were well established by *c.* 5000–6000 BCE, and may have been domesticated as early as 8350 BCE. Innovations in the swidden (slash-and-burn) agricultural system may have been at the heart of the early Amazonian dispersal *c.* 1000–500 BCE, but the small size of sites of this period suggests that population pressure was not the principal cause. Changes in social, political, and ideological forces, notably the emergence of hierarchical systems of prestige and value, including hereditary rank, a founder's ideology, and rivalry between high-status individuals, may have been a primary stimulus for village break-up, expansion, and even long-distance migration of Arawak groups.

The Archaeological Evidence

Archaeological work in the Llanos de Moxos indicates agriculture was present as early as 8350 BCE; an area that continued to be occupied through historic times. Between *c.* 1000 and 500 BCE, Arawak societies with ceramics, called the Saladoid and the Barrancoid, were established in the middle Orinoco floodplains and the Caribbean. Early Saladoid sites in the Lesser Antilles place initial occupation at around 500 BCE, slightly later in Puerto Rico. These sites were apparently occupied by people who constructed villages characterized by circular plazas, and who transported their agricultural and fishing technologies, including domesticated and other managed plants (manioc, bananas, etc.) and animals. The colonization of much of the Caribbean seems to have occurred relatively quickly (*c.* 500–200 BCE). Research in the mainland lower Rio Negro basin suggests a correlation between central plaza villages and Barrancoid ceramics.

The Arawak groups of the early diaspora, *c.* 500 BCE–500 CE, most neatly fit the model of Formative people described for other parts of the Americas: agricultural, hierarchical, monument-building, theocratic chiefdoms. These populations lived in large, settled, and sometimes fortified villages organized around central public spaces, elaborations of the circular plazas characteristic of the earlier Caribbean and Orinocan Arawaks, but there is also now a significant body of evidence for various pathways to early social complexity, based on hereditary social hierarchy or meritocracies, and for the probable presence in prehistoric Amazonia of people who chose to live in small communities.

REGIONALIZATION: AMAZONIA, *c.* 1–1500 CE

Around 2,000 years ago, the two great linguistic diasporas of Arawak and Tupiguarani had expanded to nearly their maximum extent. Many of these populations entered a new phase from around 1 to 500 CE, as both immigrants and established groups settled and developed discrete regional social systems. Early examples of emergent social complexity are present, notably in the areas transitional with the central Andes. These small regional polities are characterized by small earth and stone domestic and ceremonial structures that date to as early as the mid-first millennium BCE. By about 500 CE, the era of large-scale population movements was largely over.

By *c.* 500–1000 CE, large, densely populated regional polities became established along many of the primary rivers of Amazonia. These were tied into regional systems of interaction that, although competitive and even occasionally at war, clearly shared great cultural traditions across the broad region. There is evidence of trade in precious stones, metals, ceramics, and other objects. In fact, the late prehistoric period in greater Amazonia is remarkable for the largely shared ceramic tradition—the Polychrome Tradition.

The Lower Amazon

Marajó Island, in the vast Amazon estuary, was dominated by the Marajoara from around 400 to 1400 CE. They are particularly well known for their elaborate polychrome ceramics and their large and spectacular platform mounds. Initial construction of the Marajó mounds, which rise up to 8 meters (26 feet) above the rivers, began about 400 CE. Mound-building

KEY CONTROVERSY Amazonian Mound-Builders

Unlike Mesoamerica and the central Andes, where stone masonry was so critical, earth mound-building societies dominated the Amazon. Proto-Arawak communities of Amazonia lived in villages organized around exclusive centralized sacred and public areas. An essential feature of their settlements is the central plaza, and the monuments and ceremonies attached to it.

Mounds have now been found associated with the Dubali complex in Guyana by 3000 BCE. Other than this, the earliest expression of mound-building comes from Marajó Island. The single occupational mound of Teso dos Bichos, initiated around 400 CE and formed by accretion, ultimately reached a height of some 7 meters (22 feet) by 1100–1300 CE or later. The large Camutins group [**17.25**] contains some forty mounds spread over about 6 kilometers (3.75 miles) of the headwater tributary of the Anajás River. At Camutins, numerous additional small- and medium-sized mounds, generally only a few meters high, are located up- and downstream from the major paired mounds that face one another on either side of the river.

Major earthworks, including domestic or ritual structures and raised fields, are also known from the Orinoco, the Guiana coast, and the Caribbean. Along the Upper Xingu in the southern Amazon, massive and extensive earthworks in the form of banks and ditches that outline the primary features of landscape architecture—plaza enclosures, roads, and moats—create an integrated, even grid-like settlement pattern of broad straight roads and circular plaza nodes. The massive plaza center at Açutuba has sculpted banks some 10 meters (33 feet) above a huge central plaza (450 × 100 meters, or 1,475 × 328 feet) with ramparts and a terminal barricade.

17.25 Artist's reconstruction of the domestic mound complex in the Camutins mound group, Marajó Island.

apparently peaked in the period from around 600 to 800 CE, although the mounds continued to be occupied and used for ceremonial purposes until *c.* 1100–1300 CE or later (see Key Controversy box: Amazonian Mound-Builders). Recent excavations and geophysical survey show that they were occupational mounds, with cemetery features built into them. Burial urns are located in mounds of all sizes, but it appears that burial in the major ones was reserved for elites, an assumption supported by the concentration of highly decorated urns in the large mounds.

Equally impressive is the **Santarém**, or Tapajós, culture; its capital was located some 500 kilometers (310 miles) upstream of Marajó Island, atop a large bluff just east of the mouth of the Tapajós River. It is deservedly famous for its elaborate plastic (sculpted) arts, especially ceramics [**17.26**, **17.27**], suggesting craft specialization and far-flung trade in prestige goods. Unlike Marajoara, the Santarém culture survived well into the European historical period— Friar Gaspar de Carvajal, a priest who chronicled the first expedition down the Amazon in 1541, marveled at the "great white city" that lay just beyond the banks of the river. ***Terra preta*** (dark soil) in the Santarém region has demonstrated fairly dense settlement, with

terra preta in South America, a Portuguese term meaning black earth, referring to occupation-related (settlement) sediments; also includes ancient cultivation areas that lack artifacts; also referred to as dark earth

17.26, 17.27 Tapajônica ceramics associated with the Santarém archaeological culture. A caryatid vessel (height 19 cm, 7.5 in.) and a seated male figure wearing prominent earspools and a headband (height 32 cm, 12.6 in.).

sites commonly separated by only a few kilometers (see Key Controversy box: Amazonian Dark Earths and Anthropogenic Landscapes, p. 439), extending discontinuously over an area of some 25 square kilometers (10 square miles). If actually a reflection of the size of the Santarém capital, it is well within the range of some of the larger pre-Columbian centers.

The Central Amazon

Widespread sharing across large areas of Amazonia resulted in changes in broad regional political economies. In the Central Amazon, at **Açutuba**, which extends more than 30 hectares (about 75 acres), the central plaza is composed of a massive sunken amphitheater the size of four football fields, ramped by a sculpted slope over 10 meters (33 feet) high on three sides and bisected by a linear trench at the western margins of the site.

Trade items are amply documented in the ethnohistoric record, including gold, precious gems, tropical forest woods, bird feathers, animal body parts, and salt, as well as shamanic knowledge, ritual presentation, medicinal plants, pigments, etc. Apart from decorated fine-ware ceramics, however, and occasional ceremonial axe heads, it is often difficult to find concrete archaeological evidence of trade in these types of specialty items, since most were perishable and have not survived. Changes in ceramic technology are clearly documented at Açutuba. Elite ceramics became more elaborated and finer, and their production and distribution more restricted and specialized. This suggests that, in part, the widespread sharing across broad areas of Amazonia is the result of changes in broad regional political economies.

The Upper Amazon

The upper Amazon has one of the better-known cultural sequences in Amazonia. In this region, immigrant tropical forest farmers had settled by around 200 BCE into fixed villages, which grew into large riverbank towns in later periods. These established communities entered into relations with incoming groups, which sometimes involved warfare. As often as not, however, smaller groups within the community maintained their unique cultural identities. The Cumancaya (c. 800–1000 CE), for example, became culturally and geographically intermixed with the Caimito society, bearers of the Polychrome Tradition in this area, giving rise to the modern Shipibo–Conibo style [**17.28**].

17.28 Pottery from modern Shipibo Pano-speaking societies of the Peruvian Amazon. Ceramics, such as this Shipibo vessel, show clear affinities with pre-Columbian ceramics of the Amazonian Polychrome, such as the Caimito sub-tradition—also from the Ucayali River area—where the Shipibo-Conibo live today.

This part of Amazonia, strategically positioned between the Andes and the Amazon, experienced complicated cultural pluralism and subtle historical twists. Indigenous communities reside in the northern Amazon today, such as the Yanomami, who live along the borders of Brazil and Venezuela. Currently, most Indigenous tribes live in reserves called *resguardos*, where they practice a lifestyle that integrates both traditional and modern elements. Few live in complete seclusion from the modern world.

The Orinoco and the Caribbean

The Orinoco is one of the longest rivers in South America at 2,140 kilometers (1,1330 miles). The archaeology of the Orinoco basin is less known than many other parts of South America. Between 1000 and 500 BCE, if not earlier, Saladoid–Barrancoid agriculturalists, apparently Arawak speakers, migrated into and came to dominate the middle and lower parts of Orinoco, as well as the coast of Venezuela. From Venezuela, Arawak speakers moved into the Caribbean, colonizing most of the islands by 200 BCE. As Arawak societies expanded, people began to develop localized traditions, resulting in a variety of cultural elaborations of the pre-existing structures from the early diaspora.

The various Arawak-speaking groups that inhabited the Caribbean in 1492 CE, generally called Taíno, lived in large plaza settlements and were ruled by chiefs. As elsewhere in the Arawak diaspora, major plazas, causeways, and other ceremonial structures characterize the political core. These also included the unique Greater Antillean ball courts, or *bateys*, as at Caguana in Puerto Rico, and circular plazas, such as En Bas Saline, which were centers of power and operated as sacred focal points in regional landscapes.

The Southern Amazon

When Europeans arrived in the southern peripheries of Amazonia in central Brazil and eastern Bolivia in the late seventeenth and early eighteenth centuries, drawn by rumors of gold and precious gems, they remarked on the high level of engineering in the planned plaza villages, with their ceremonial houses—referred to by the Europeans as temples—idols, and an elaborate ritual life. The southern Amazonian societies mostly comprised a related group of Arawak cultures, manioc farmers who supplemented their staple foods—manioc, fish, and fruits—with a wide range of secondary resources. These uniformly show characteristics commonly found in many other polities: a regional, hierarchical organization, staple agricultural and fishing economies, central plaza space, and monumentality, among other things. Archaeological research continues to reveal just how large and complex these southern Amazonian societies really were, perhaps rivaling much better-known areas of the Amazon floodplains, the Caribbean, and even much of the Andes.

The southern Amazon is important because it shows a pattern of complex multi-ethnic social formations, which while rooted in the Arawak diaspora took on an increasingly hybrid character over time. In much of this region, the sedentary societies were often surrounded by smaller, more mobile Tupiguarani- and Gê-speaking societies of the uplands.

The Upper Xingu region is particularly important, since we can see cultural continuity between earlier Arawak polities (*c.* 800 CE onward) and current Xinguano communities. Similarities are visible in basic village organization (circular plaza villages), regional settlement locations, and material culture—notably ceramic technology, a late variant of the Amazonian Barrancoid. The sequence of settlement here recaps in some ways the general chronology of the Arawak diaspora: initial occupations by plaza agriculturalists, rapid and

KEY CONTROVERSY Amazonian Dark Earths and Anthropogenic Landscapes

Traditionally, the Amazon was seen as an untouched tropical forest. Recent research there has discovered, however, widespread archaeological remains in deposits currently forested over as well as earthworks, testimony that much of the region is not in fact pristine forest, but instead represents complicated constructed or domesticated landscapes, created over 2,000 years ago. Thick, continuous deposits of habitation refuse and management activities are known as Amazonian dark earths (ADE) or *terra preta* [**17.29**]. These dark, anthropogenic soils are fertile due to high levels of organic matter and nutrients, such as nitrogen, phosphorus, calcium, and other important elements, incorporated into the often infertile background soils. ADE occur in patches generally smaller than 20 hectares (50 acres), but some large ADE, including areas over 100 hectares (247 acres), have been reported. Studies of forest cover in the Upper Xingu region have also suggested unique semi-intensive strategies of land management in the past, based particularly on patchy forest agriculture, and there is evidence of a complex history of biocultural diversity in this region. Understanding such intensive Indigenous systems is essential to knowledge of land use and cover change in the region, and developing the critical middle ground in the exploitation of the forest.

17.29 Amazonian dark earths (ADE) or *terra preta* at the Açutuba site (Iranduba), Brazil, representing humanly modified soils. Recent research has revealed that much of the Amazonian region shows evidence of human land use, which has implications for conservation and sustainable development today.

large-scale development of settlements, then the extensive, integrated regional polities of late prehistoric times.

Recently, the combination of land clearance for grazing and the availability of images from satellite surveys has revealed a new aspect to our picture of the southwestern Amazon basin. More than 360 large, precise geometric earthworks, or geoglyphs, composed of linear ditches with banks, some connected by straight roads, have been identified over an area

17.30 Amazonian geoglyphs. The complex of Fazenda Colorada is dated to *c.* 1–1400 CE and shows a diversity of enclosures, roads, and small oval mounds, including a circular cluster within the double-ditch U-shaped structure that suggests residential occupation.

kuraka an Andean elite class who claimed descent from sacred ancestors

of 250 kilometers (155 miles) [**17.30**]. Numerous radiocarbon dates show the main period of construction and use extended from the late first millennium CE until late pre-Columbian times, and probably into the European contact period after *c.* 1500 CE. Such sites suggest that a substantial population was living in the area to provide the labor force, with some sort of central organization and planning.

SUMMARY AND CONCLUSIONS

This chapter has illustrated the enormous diversity of South American societies in the later postglacial period, a diversity that arose as people adapted to such environmental extremes as the world's largest river and longest mountain range. Yet there were commonalities and shared patterns of behavior across this vast area. Where fish and wild plant foods were abundant on the Pacific Coast, relatively sedentary societies flourished without agriculture or with low-level use of domesticated plants, such as gourds. The high population density and political complexity of these people demonstrate that sophisticated non-agricultural systems were long-enduring, sustainable strategies in their own right. Independent domestication of plants and animals occurred across different regions of South America and diffusion of crops from one region to another, including from Mesoamerica, further propelled sociopolitical complexity and the rise of cities and states. In addition to grains including quinoa and kañiwa, tuber crops were principal staples, with potatoes prevailing in the highlands and manioc in the lowlands.

South American people organized themselves by kinship and descent, real and fictive. The so-called rank revolution separated commoners from chiefs, and Andean **kurakas** rationalized their privileged position and class by claims of descent from special ancestors and creators; ultimately, the Inkas did nothing less than proclaim special descent from the sun.

With standardized currency all but absent, people relied on labor to render tribute to their social collectives and leaders. This practice underwrote the earthwork enclosures of Amazonia, as well as the monumental masonry of the Andes. Communities also rendered labor by producing arts and crafts that were standardized relative to linguistic, ethnic, and social milieus, culminating in the Amazonian ceramic horizon styles and Andean corporate styles.

We can see that South America, as Africa or South Asia, presents a complex mosaic of technologically sophisticated diverse societies, separate though often interrelated.

FURTHER READING

The following provide useful introductions to the cultures of ancient South America and the archaeological evidence for them:

Bauer, B. *et al.* 2015. *Vilcabamba and the Archaeology of Inca Resistance.* Los Angeles: The Cotsen Institute of Archaeology Press.

Burger, R. and Salazar, L. (eds.). 2008. *Machu Picchu: Unveiling the Mystery of the Incas.* New Haven: Yale University Press.

Conklin, W. J. and Quilter, J. (eds.). 2008. *Chavín: Art, Architecture, and Culture.* Los Angeles: The Cotsen Institute of Archaeology Press.

Donnan, C. B. 2012. *Chotuna and Chornancap: Excavating an Ancient Peruvian Legend.* Los Angeles: The Cotsen Institute of Archaeology Press.

Hirth, K. G. and Pillsbury, J. (eds.). 2013. *Merchants, Markets, and Exchange in the Pre-Columbian World.* Washington, D.C.: Dumbarton Oaks.

Millaire, J-F. and Morlion, M. (eds.). 2009. *Gallinazo: An Early Cultural Tradition on the Peruvian North Coast.* Los Angeles: The Cotsen Institute of Archaeology Press.

Morris, C. and von Hagen, A. 2011. *The Incas. Lords of the Four Quarters.* London and New York: Thames & Hudson.

Moseley, M. E. 2001. *The Incas and Their Ancestors: The Archaeology of Peru.* 2nd edn. London and New York: Thames & Hudson.

Reinhard J. and Constanza Ceruti, M. 2010. *Inca Ritual and Sacred Mountains.* Los Angeles: The Cotsen Institute of Archaeology Press.

Rostworowski de Diez Canseco, M. 1999. *History of the Inca Realm.* Cambridge: Cambridge University Press.

Stanish, C. 2012. *Lake Titicaca: Legend, Myth and Science.* Los Angeles: The Cotsen Institute of Archaeology Press.

Silverman, H. and Isbell, W. H. (eds.). 2008. *Handbook of South American Archaeology.* New York: Springer.

Tantalean, H. and Zapata Benites, C. (2014). *Chaupisawakasi y la formacion del estado Pukara (400 A.C. – 350 D.C.) en la Cuenca norte del Titicaca, Peru.* BAR International Series.

http://www.museocontisuyo.com Website of the Museo Contisuyo, with information on the prehistory of the Moquegua area (Peru), including bibliography and links.

The Human Past: Current Horizons

18

Tammy Stone and Chris Scarre

Migration 444

Domestication and Population Increase 445

Climate Change 447

Urbanization 448

Social Inequality 449

Summary and Conclusions 450

Further Reading 450

Archaeological research into Inka cultivation terraces, such as these in Pisac, Peru, is helping modern local farmers to rebuild terraces and irrigation systems, and reclaim traditional crops and methods of farming as part of efforts to mitigate the effects of climate change.

In this book, we have described the development of human societies over the past 2.8 million years. Throughout these chapters we have examined a number of themes that are important to all people, regardless of when and where they lived: migration, the process and consequences of domestication and population increase, climate change, urbanization, and social inequality. As we have seen, these patterns have been repeated over and over across different locations and through time. The world we inhabit today is situated within these processes, and humans today face many of the same problems in our daily lives as people did in the past. Archaeology can help reveal those patterns in the past, but it can do more than simply disclose what has happened before. Its methods and insights can and do contribute to solutions to the challenges we face today.

As a discipline, archaeology is changing, especially in who is choosing to study and work in the discipline, and that increasing diversity brings more variety to the questions archaeology asks. The greater participation of women and other groups traditionally underrepresented in the field is broadening the scope of archaeology and improving our ability to reconstruct the past.

Using the key themes followed in this book, this final chapter explores how archaeology meets with important issues today, and how its perspective on the past is changing as the discipline itself evolves.

MIGRATION

Early humans were a migrating species, spreading from their African homeland to occupy every habitable continent of the globe. Movement and migration are recurring features of the human story at both the individual level and for entire communities. Migration may be prompted by warfare or political change, by a change in climate, or because populations grow and need to expand into new areas. When a new population displaces another, that can result in conflict, or the new group may be absorbed into the existing society. Migration does not only include the movement of people. The arrival of Europeans in the Americas, for example, led to an exchange of crops and raw materials, but it also brought diseases to the American continent, and the introduction of smallpox, measles, typhus, cholera, bubonic plague, and malaria resulted in demographic crashes of as much as 80–95 percent in some areas.

By documenting the causes, contexts, and consequences of such historical movements, archaeology can cast new light on migration in the modern world. For example, archaeologists have studied and mapped the camp at Koutsochero in Greece, which was built in 2016 to receive refugees fleeing the Syrian civil war and other conflicts. Koutsochero was compared with an earlier refugee camp that had been established in the nearby village of Mandra in 1924, and this comparison made it far more apparent that such camps have been a permanent reality of Greek life for nearly a century. The study also showed how medieval monuments, abandoned industrial buildings, bankrupt markets, and decommissioned army bases were used to house refugees.

Other archaeologists have studied the life vests abandoned by people arriving on the Greek island of Lesvos by sea. One life vest was displayed at Manchester Museum in the UK as a reminder that political concerns about migration to Europe and the United States frequently overlook an individual refugee's real experiences. Archaeologists have also recorded the graffiti art left by those crossing the US border from Mexico into Arizona [18.1].

These images often include political messages and expressions of human experiences; art that has now been preserved for the future.

There are many examples of forced migration in the human past—of communities being forcibly displaced from their homes. We see this in the history of Indigenous people in the Americas (see below), and in examples of war, both in ancient and modern history. In Canada and the United States during World War II, individuals and families of Japanese heritage were subjected to mass relocation and incarceration. Executive Order 9066 in 1942 resulted in individuals of Japanese heritage in the United States, two-thirds of whom were American citizens, being denied their rights and forced into camps that featured barbed-wire fences, guard towers, and machine guns. One example was Idaho's Kooskia Internment Camp, which had been a federal prison before it was repurposed to imprison Japanese Americans [**18.2**].

The archaeologists Mary Farrell and Jeffrey Burton have done much to bring these camps to the public's attention, using documentary and ethnographic and archaeological research to present these histories that were otherwise buried in archives. Farrell and Burton brought together oral histories, interviews, archival research, and archaeology to examine the internment landscapes and the individuals imprisoned there. Some surviving internees and their descendants were involved in the restoration and archaeological work at incarceration camps, and these sites continue to be memorials to the violence perpetrated there.

18.1 Section of the wall mural created by Enrique Chiu's Mural of Brotherhood project on the US Mexican border wall, promoting peace, unity, and hope.

18.2 Hand-carved stone found on the surface of the large trash midden during the 2013 field season at the Kooskia Internment Camp.

DOMESTICATION AND POPULATION INCREASE

At the end of the last Ice Age, world population numbered perhaps only a few million. Today that population stands at 7.5 billion, and is set to increase further. The dramatic growth in human numbers has been the product of a combination of factors, including the relative stability of the climate and the ability of humans as a species to develop various ways to support high population densities. The most important factor, however, was the domestication of plants and animals.

In some areas, the development of increasingly sophisticated strategies of hunting and gathering was sufficient to allow population increase, as in the Jōmon societies of Japan (**Chapters 5 and 10**), the Natufian of Southwest Asia (**Chapter 6**), or the societies of the Northwest Coast of North America (**Chapter 15**). In other areas, a dramatic change in peoples' relationship with the landscape was needed. But those changes had consequences on both humans and the environment. In arid regions, elaborate irrigation systems provided all-important water. In many parts of the world, plowing with draft animals enabled larger areas of land to be cultivated more efficiently to support human population growth, and in the nineteenth century, mechanization took the process a step further, eventually resulting in the industrialized farming we use today.

From archaeology, we know that agriculture also had a downside. Studies have shown that early farming populations had poorer health than their hunter-gatherer predecessors. Population growth provided a much greater reservoir of human hosts for parasites and disease, and crowding people together in bigger communities created ideal conditions for epidemics. For example, at Çatalhöyük (**Chapter 6**) skeletal analysis indicates increased stress on the body from agricultural labor, even in children. Their crowded living conditions, minimal sanitation, and carbohydrate-based diet also led to diminished oral health and increased infection and disease. In the packed working and living conditions of parts of ancient Egypt (**Chapter 13**), the bubonic plague was initially transmitted from rats to humans through the fleas infesting both. The first written reference to the plague is 1500 BCE in Amarna, a workers' community on the Nile, and its origin has been confirmed with recent DNA analysis.

Living in proximity to domestic animals, in particular cattle and pigs, also allowed the mutation of animal diseases into human-related forms. Human tuberculosis may have been derived from bovine tuberculosis in this fashion. This process continues today. The 1918 epidemic of Spanish flu, which may have killed more than 50 million people, probably crossed to humans from poultry, and the specter of a similar devastating outbreak re-emerged in the 1990s with bird flu, the N5N1 variety of influenza. Disease can also cross over from non-domesticated animals living close to human settlements. Both the SARS outbreak in the early 2000s and the COVID-19 pandemic of 2020 are believed to have been transmitted to humans from bats. Recent analysis has shown disease can also cross in the other direction. Big cats in zoos and some domesticated house cats have been diagnosed with COVID-19 caught from their handlers and owners.

Commitment to domestication has also had an impact on the natural environment. Fields are cleared of trees, water tables are reduced by increased agricultural demands for water, and wild resources (for example, nuts and produce from forests) that used to buffer against crop failures are eliminated. In partial response to these environmental consequences, communities and industries are drawing on the past to find more sustainable solutions, using traditional agricultural knowledge.

For example, the Zuni Sustainable Agricultural Project and Zuni Folk Varieties Project have established a successful soil and water conservation program on the Zuni reservation in central New Mexico. The Folk Varieties Project builds in part on the Zuni Traditional Crops Project carried out by Carol Brandt and Jerome Zunie of the Zuni Archaeology Program in 1991, and works to reintroduce traditional farming techniques and plants that are well suited to the arid environment of the northern Southwest of the United States, and less damaging to the environment. These farming practices include spreading fields over different types of landscapes using terracing and small dams, and forms of irrigation near streams, rivers, and springs to ensure crops are watered. These approaches are supplemented with traditional methods of minimizing topsoil loss to wind, such as the use of sagebrush windbreaks, leaving their stalks in the field after harvest. The Zuni Folk Varieties Project has also concentrated on preserving traditional crop varieties as a means of maintaining biological diversity, particularly of crops well adapted to the dry environment.

CLIMATE CHANGE

Over many thousands of years, early human populations became adept at adjusting to the cycle of warm and cold episodes as ice sheets advanced and retreated in northern latitudes, deserts grew or shrank, and sea levels rose and fell. Human groups prospered, decreased in size, or were forced to migrate in response to these changes (**Chapter 5**). The beginning of the postglacial 11,600 years ago ushered in an altogether more benign and stable epoch. Environmental shifts have still impacted human activity, but human actions have also affected the environment, as we have seen in the Amazonian basin (**Chapter 17**), on Rapa Nui (**Chapter 11**), and in the Indus River basin (**Chapter 8**).

Humans have always extracted not only food from the environment but also many other resources for housing, clothing, tools, technology, and fuel. The problem of how to achieve long-term environmental sustainability has haunted societies for more than 4,000 years. By the Roman period, mining increased lead pollution in Europe by a factor of ten, resulting in lead levels in the Greenland ice cores not seen again until the eighteenth century. The twentieth century saw an intensification of pollution, with the burning of fossil fuels on an unprecedented scale, resulting in rising global temperatures. This was accompanied by new factors, such as the proliferation of plastics and the widespread use of nitrogen fertilizers in agriculture, altering the acidity of the oceans. These changes have led to the proposal of a new age called the Anthropocene, a period where human activity is so great that it is the main agent of climate change today.

In addition to providing a long-term perspective on human causes and responses to climate change, archaeology can help educate the public about damage to the environment. Museums especially can play an important role. For example, in 2016, research from Aarhus University and the Saxo Institute in Copenhagen led to an exhibition at the Moesgaard Museum called *Mild Apocalypse* [**18.3**]. The project explored the impact of humans on the landscape of a former coal-extraction site in Søby, Denmark, that left permanent traces in the natural environment. Now abandoned, the coal site is surrounded by acid lakes, moved earth caused by landslides, and abandoned and buried equipment. These changes in the environment have affected the lives of animals, plants, and people in the area.

The exhibition showed archaeologically recovered equipment and environmental samples to explain how Søby was an example of a localized, termed "mild," apocalypse, as a way of illustrating how massive environmental changes seen across the world can be broken down into smaller events. The researchers argued that when seen more locally, people may be more likely to take action and influence policy.

18.3 Poster from the *Mild Apocalypse* exhibition at the Moesgaard Museum in Copenhagen, Denmark.

URBANIZATION

Higher agricultural productivity and larger populations were often accompanied by growing social and economic complexity. Inequality of wealth and status led to the rise of hierarchical societies and the development of cities and state societies that shape the world today. The United Nations estimated that by 2007 more people on earth lived in urban areas than in rural areas.

In cities, high social status and wealth tend to be concentrated in a very small zone, alongside areas of great poverty [**18.4**]. It has been estimated that one-third of city dwellers live in urban slums, while the majority of the most expensive real estate can also be found in cities. Archaeology allows us to view these trends in long-term perspective, but also offers new ways of studying severe inequality in cities, and structural violence (harm caused by how society is organized) today.

A number of archaeologists have studied modern homelessness, combining archaeological methods (survey, mapping, analysis of material culture) with interviews and engagement with homeless populations to dispel inaccurate assumptions sometimes made about them. Interviews with homeless individuals have revealed a complex and heterogeneous population very different from popular portrayals; although drugs and crime are present, many people without homes work, go to school, have families, and contribute to their communities in a variety of ways.

When the information gathered from interviews is combined with the mapping of material culture at camps and the paths of movement between jobs, locations of food resources, and camps or shelters, it is possible to build a deeper understanding of daily life. This has resulted in recommendations to help groups working with homeless communities better serve these populations. For example, camps often contain cached belongings required for daily survival, including medication, clothing, and tools needed to prepare and consume food. Indiscriminate clearing of camps denies homeless people the means of maintaining their health and continuing to work. Hygiene packs that are given out, while well intentioned, are sometimes of little use. Toothpaste is frequently used, but bottles of shampoo are often thrown away without opening because the lack of a reliable water supply makes them impossible to use. Conversely, providing manual can openers is recommended as it allows consumption of lower-cost canned foods; the inability to access canned goods can force people to rely on more expensive fast-food products.

18.4 Urbanization.
Paraisópolis, a favela (informal settlement neighborhood) in São Paulo, Brazil, is home to more than 100,000 residents, many of whom do not have access to secure housing and employment or healthcare. It is surrounded by the high-rise buildings of Morumbi, one of the city's richest districts.

SOCIAL INEQUALITY

The level of inequality between the powerful and disenfranchised has been a source of social tension from the past to today. In modern history, archaeology has itself been used to justify the silencing and unequal treatment of many communities; a colonial legacy that many archaeologists are working to reverse. This research (often driven by the increasing diversity of the archaeologists themselves) aims to understand the political and social problems prevalent in our society today and to impact public policy in positive ways.

A significant example grew out of archaeological efforts by members of Native American, First Nations, Métis, and Inuit communities in the United States and Canada. In the 1970s, many programs were launched to study ancestral Indigenous lands, with the aim to bring their histories, once ignored or disregarded by colonial settlers, to greater light. Today, Indigenous archaeology is applied to many questions archaeologists may ask. It is a multivocal approach that brings together scientific methods and theories with the knowledge and values of Indigenous societies, both in exploring distant pasts, and unearthing and preserving stories of the historically marginalized.

A powerful example is the work that is taking place following the 2015 Truth and Reconciliation Commission of Canada (TRC) report. From 2007, the Commission has gathered witness accounts from more than 6,500 Indigenous individuals who testified their intense suffering under the Residential Schools system, which existed between the mid-1800s and 1996. During this time, children were often removed from their families, sometimes forcibly, with the intent to erase their family languages and their cultures; an act that resonates in the intergenerational trauma of communities today. The final 2015 report concluded that the establishment and operation of residential schools had worked to erase Indigenous people as distinct legal, cultural, and racial entities, in a process of cultural genocide.

A major aim of the TRC report is reconciliation, which to the Commission is about "establishing and maintaining a mutually respectful relationship between Aboriginal and non-Aboriginal peoples in this country. In order for that to happen, there has to be awareness of the past, acknowledgement of the harm that has been inflicted, atonement for the causes, and action to change behaviour." Archaeology has a part to play.

Among its ninety-four calls for action by the Canadian government are demands by the Indigenous communities most affected to document, maintain, and commemorate residential school cemeteries (many of which are unrecorded and abandoned). Archaeologists are now working in Indigenous-led projects to record residential schools and the burials of children as part of the ongoing efforts of reconciliation. One of the most prominent is the Save the Evidence campaign, based at the Mohawk Institute, a residential school that closed in 1970. As well as recovering material from the school, one of the campaign's most important projects has been to restore the building and commemorate the lives and suffering of the children who lived there, so that this dark chapter of Canadian history is not forgotten.

New, diverse directions of archaeology have faced their challenges. Some people have seen multivocal approaches as a rejection of science, and the movement into community engagement and collaboration as an abandonment of the archaeological tradition. Unfortunately, this idea has sometimes manifested itself in discrimination and harassment of archaeologists who are women or members of underrepresented minorities, in ways that are similar to other fields.

Most archaeologists reject both these intolerant actions and the idea that such new approaches are a threat to the field. They recognize that these movements do not dismiss science, and that they strengthen the field rather than weaken it. To make this value more explicit, archaeological professional organizations, such as the Society for American Archaeology (SAA) and the Archaeological Institute of American (AIA), have endorsed statements banning discrimination and harassment as part of the discipline's professional ethics. Recent movements, such as #MeToo, have highlighted the pervasiveness of sexual harassment in academic subjects, and archaeology is no exception. In 2019, more than 2,000 archaeologists and scholars campaigned for the Society for American Archaeology to review its sexual harassment policy, leading the SAA to publish a set of new codes of conduct and safety measures for future conferences. As part of the Black Lives Matter movement, the Association for Black Anthropologists has called for an examination of past contributions to racist and colonial narratives. This call is part of a broader movement in archaeology to embrace the views and concerns of under-represented and marginalized groups in how archaeology is practiced and the questions it asks, and to celebrate the contributions of an increasingly diverse discipline.

SUMMARY AND CONCLUSIONS

By exploring the past, we can learn from what has worked and from what has failed. Its insights can help us develop a more sustainable interaction with the planet, and understand and appreciate the wide diversity of human beings today. Archaeology contributes to addressing histories of oppression by acknowledging its responsibility to ensure the past is accessible and representative of everyone. Archaeology provides understanding of how ancient cultures responded to changes in their environment or developed new methods for feeding their growing populations. Their successes can serve as models for the future. Their failures are a warning to act responsibly, to protect and preserve the planetary ecosystem that has supported us for many thousands of years. That, at the broadest scale, is the story that archaeology has to tell.

FURTHER READING

The following offer interesting examples of archaeology engaging with contemporary issues:

Camp, L. S. 2016. Landscapes of Japanese American Internment. *Historical Archaeology* 50(1): 169–86.

Farrell, M. and Burton, J. F. 2004. Civil rights and moral wrongs: World War II Japanese American Relocation Sites. *SAA Archaeological Record* 4(5): 22–25.

Cleveland, David A., *et al.* 1995. Zuni Farming and United States Goverment Policy: The Politics of Biological and Cultural Diversity in Agriculture. *Agriculture and Human Values* 12(3): 2–18.

The Truth and Reconciliation Commission of Canada. 2015. *What We Have Learned: Principles of Truth and Reconciliation*. Winnipeg: Truth and Reconciliation Committee: 119. http://www.trc.ca/assets/pdf/Principles%20of%20Truth%20and%20Reconciliation.pdf

http://aba.americananthro.org/ Website of the Association of Black Anthropologists.

https://anthropocene.au.dk/exhibitions/mild-apocalypse-2016/ Website of the 2016 *Mild Apocalypse* exhibition at the Moesgaard Museum, Copenhagen.

https://www.saa.org/annual-meeting/submissions/meeting-safety-policy The Society for American Archaeology's Meeting Safety Policy and Code of Conduct at SAA Events.

https://woodlandculturalcentre.ca The Save The Evidence campaign and related resources.

GLOSSARY

absolute chronology determination of chronological sequence with reference to a fixed time scale or calendar date.

aceramic a time or place in which pottery was not created, traded, or used; also known as preceramic, and prepottery.

acropolis the upper part of a city; usually a group of fortified buildings atop of a hill.

adobe dried mud, often mixed with straw to form mud architecture.

altiplano high-altitude grasslands in the central Andes.

AMS dating accelerator mass spectrometer dating, a highly accurate form of **radiocarbon dating**.

ancient DNA (aDNA) extracted from ancient human remains—often many thousands of years old—these molecules provide scientists with the genetic code for long-dead individuals.

anthropology the study of humans, their evolution and culture.

archaeology the study of past human societies through their material remains.

Ardipithecus extinct **genus** of a **hominin** that existed in East Africa between 5.8 and 4.4 million years ago.

artifact any portable object made, used, or modified by humans.

assemblage a group of **artifacts** recurring together at a particular time and place, representing the sum of human activities in that respect.

atlatl a spearthrower.

aurochs a Paleolithic **species** of wild bovine.

Australopithecus extinct **genus** of a **bipedal hominin** that existed in southern and eastern Africa between about 4.2 and 1 million years ago; probably the ancestor of the genus *Homo*, which includes modern humans.

biface a flat cobble flaked over both surfaces to produce a sharp edge around the entire periphery; the earliest example is the Acheulean **handaxe**.

biostratigraphy a dating method that allows the relative placement of a site or strata based on the presence of animal **species** found at sites of known age.

bipedalism walking on two legs.

bottleneck a sharp decline in population, generally tied to a need to adapt rapidly to new situations.

braincase the part of the skull that encases the brain.

broad-spectrum economy a subsistence system that includes multiple food sources rather than a narrow range of resources.

burin a stone flake or blade with chisel-like edges.

cell in a dwelling, a walled space without a doorway; a common example is storage cells under the floors of a building.

celt a stone axe-like tool.

cenote a sacred or ritual well, especially natural sinkholes in the limestone landscapes of Mesoamerica, as at Chichén Itzá.

Chalcolithic the period between the Neolithic and the Bronze Age in Europe and West Asia, marked by the widespread use of copper metallurgy, which probably developed in northern Mesopotamia.

chambered tomb a chamber or **cist** of timber or stone, usually, if not invariably, covered by a mound, and associated with the deposition of human remains.

Chindadn point a type of stone tool characteristic of the Nenana **complex** in Alaska.

cist a box-like container made of stone slabs, often used for burials.

city state an autonomous political unit comprising a city and its supporting hinterland.

ciudadela a Spanish term meaning citadel, applied, for example, to the unfortified royal complexes at Chan Chan in Peru.

coalesce the appearance of specific genotypes in **mitochondrial DNA**.

codex (pl. codices) hand-written manuscripts; in Mesoamerican societies they are accordion-fold books, while in Europe they are pages bound into volumes.

complex a recurring group of **artifacts** and activities that appear together at a particular time and place and are presumed to represent an archaeological culture.

cong a Chinese ceremonial jade tube with a square or circular cross-section, often elaborately carved.

cordillera a system of mountain ranges, often consisting of more or less parallel chains; used often to refer to the Andean range.

core the parent piece of rock from which flakes are detached.

cryptocrystalline rock that has a fine crystalline structure that is desirable for chipped-stone tool manufacture.

cultigen a plant or crop cultivated by humans, as opposed to wild **species**.

cuneiform a form of script used in Southwest Asia during the Bronze Age and Early Iron Age; literally meaning wedge-shaped, from the impressions made in the originally damp clay.

dendrochronology an absolute dating method based on counting the growth rings in trees.

dentate tooth-like.

denticulate a stone flake or blade retouched to produce a saw-tooth edge.

dentition teeth: incisors, canines, and molars.

DNA deoxyribonucleic acid, the molecule that carries genetic instructions from parents to offspring.

dolmen a **megalithic** tomb, usually consisting of upright stone slabs, on which rests a large capstone or capstones.

domestication the human propagation of selected **species**, generally involving change to their genetic make up and physical characteristics as compared with their wild progenitors.

dry farming farming without the use of irrigation, in areas where normal rainfall is sufficient for cultivation.

ecotone an area forming the boundary between contrasting environmental regions.

encephalization enlargement of the brain.

Epipaleolithic a period between the Upper Paleolithic and Neolithic, often marked by the production of small stone bladelets.

ethnography a branch of **anthropology** that studies an individual society, its people and customs.

faience a type of ceramic with a glass-like appearance.

flowstone a sheet-like deposit of calcite or carbonate left by water running over cave walls, sometimes forming stalagmites or stalactites.

foraminifera skeletons of shelled protozoa, also called forams, found in deep-sea cores.

ge a Chinese ceremonial jade halberd, an axe-like weapon.

gene flow the transfer of genetic material from one population to another.

genome complete genetic component of a cell; **nuclear DNA** and **mitochondrial DNA** each comprise a single genome.

genus (pl. genera) a group of closely related **species**.

geoglyph a drawing or image made in the ground surface by removal of earth (e.g. Nazca lines) or using banks and mounds (e.g. Serpent Mound).

geomorphology the study of the development of land forms.

GIS Geographical Information Systems; software-based systems for the collection, storage, retrieval, analysis, and display of spatial data held in different layers, which can be combined or examined separately.

glacial an Ice Age.

GPS Global Positioning System; a worldwide navigation system based on signals received from satellites orbiting Earth, enabling archaeologists to map quickly and accurately locations of sites in the landscape.

hafted furnished with a handle (refers to a tool or a weapon).

half-life the time it takes for half the quantity of a radioactive isotope in a sample to decay.

handaxe a flat cobble flaked over both surfaces to produce a sharp edge around the entire periphery; also called a **biface**.

haplogroup a collection of genetic markers shared by a group of people.

heat treating the heating of stone in a controlled manner to facilitate the process of tool **knapping**.

heiau Hawaiian religious structures comprising terraced platforms and walled enclosures.

hieroglyph a stylized picture representing a word or sound, found in early writing systems of ancient Egypt and Mesoamerica.

hominin species in human evolution that are more closely related to people than to chimpanzees.

iconography a set of artistic representations that have overt religious or ceremonial significance; the study of such images.

ideational concerned with meaning or the representation of ideas or beliefs.

Indigenous archaeology a form of **archaeology** that Indigenous groups participate in directly.

interglacial a period of warmer, wetter climate between two Ice Ages or **glacials**.

isostatic uplift the rising of landmasses once the weight of the ice sheets has been removed.

jacal wattle and daub, used in the construction of buildings in the Southwest United States.

karstic region a limestone region with sinkholes, underground streams, and caverns.

khipu in Andean South America, a method of record-keeping expressed by knots and colored strings.

kiva a multi-purpose room used for religious, political, and social functions in Pueblo villages in the American Southwest.

knapping to work a piece of stone using percussion or pressure to remove flakes.

kofun the burial mounds of the Yamato kings of Japan, also the name of the period when they were built.

kuraka an Andean elite class who claimed descent from sacred ancestors.

latte a stone pillar foundation for a chiefly house with a raised floor, built in the Mariana Islands, Micronesia.

Levallois technique the method of stone flaking associated with Mousterian societies, in which the core was shaped in advance so that when **knapped** it would provide a flake of predetermined size and shape.

LiDAR Light Detection and Ranging, an airborne remote-sensing technique that sends pulses of laser light to the ground and, by measuring the time it takes them to return to the instrument, calculates the distance with extreme accuracy; produces a detailed image of the ground surface, especially since forests and clouds can be filtered out.

Linearbandkeramik (LBK) also called Bandkeramik, a cultural package that began in western Hungary in the middle of the sixth millennium BCE.

loess fine, wind-blown silt.

mandible the lower bone of the jaw.

marae Polynesian shrine/temple platforms.

material culture the physical products of culture; culture is defined as socially transmitted rules for behavior and ways of thinking about the world, and the term is also used by archaeologists to describe a distinctive collection of archaeological remains, which might often be associated with an ancient population.

maxilla (pl. maxillae) the upper bone of the jaw.

megafauna large animals, such as mammoth, mastodon, and giant ground sloths.

megalith meaning big stone; applied to monuments and structures built with large stones weighing several tons, including **dolmens**, **passage graves**, and **menhirs**.

menhir a single standing stone found in Neolithic Europe, sometimes decorated with carvings.

microblade a small stone blade, often made of flint, **obsidian**, or quartz; generally less than 50 mm (1.9 in.) long.

microlith a small, standardized stone blade originally set into a composite tool or weapon.

microwear minute patterns of wear or damage on teeth or on stone tools, which can reveal how they were used.

midden a concentration of cultural debris (**artifacts** and food remains); in places where marine resources are a primary element in subsistence middens are often made up predominantly of shells.

mitochondrial DNA (mtDNA) genetic material inherited through the maternal line.

moai massive stone statues characteristic of Rapa Nui (Easter Island).

molecular clock the estimated rate of evolutionary change that can be measured through the study of fossil and modern DNA.

morphology physical structure or form.

Native American Graves Protection and Repatriation Act (NAGPRA) the law (1990) that requires federally funded institutions and government agencies in the United States to assess the cultural affiliation of Native American and Native Hawaiian **artifacts** held in collections and, where cultural affiliation can be shown, to return the materials to the affiliated group or organization; also dictates how human burials encountered in the future will be treated.

necropolis (pl. necropoleis) a cemetery; literally meaning city of the dead.

notch a **denticulate** tool with a single indentation.

nuclear DNA DNA present within the chromosomes in the nucleus of the cell.

obsidian a natural volcanic glass, very hard, used to make tools.

ocher the iron oxide minerals hematite (for red ocher), limonite and goethite (for brown, yellow, and black ochers), used as pigments for painting and pottery slips.

oxygen isotope analysis analysis of the ratio of two oxygen isotopes (^{18}O and ^{16}O) in ancient materials; in sediments from the deep-sea floor, differences in oxygen isotope ratios correlate with glacial and interglacial intervals recorded on land, enabling archaeology to be dated by extrapolation from the deep-sea record.

pa the Maori earthwork enclosures on New Zealand.

paleoanthropology the study of earliest humans from fossil remains.

paleontology the study of fossils.

palynology the study of pollen and spores.

passage grave a type of chambered tomb where the burial chamber is reached via a long passage from the edge of the covering mound.

pastoralist an individual or society depending primarily on the herding of domestic animals, often associated with a mobile or nomadic lifestyle.

phalange a finger or toe bone.

phytoliths minute particles of silica derived from the cells of plants, able to survive after the organism has decomposed or been burned; common in ash layers, pottery, and even on stone tools.

piece-mold a mold used in a bronze-casting technique whereby a complex object is cast in sections, which are then joined with mortises and tenons.

pisé rammed earth.

potlatch a feasting ceremony common among Indigenous Northwest Coast groups of North America, involving the conspicuous consumption and destruction of food and valuables in a competitive display of wealth.

prehistory the period of human history before the invention of writing.

pseudomorphs the spaces left by decayed organic objects within brecciated sediments.

pueblo a general term for Indigenous communities of the Southwest USA, distinctive in their use of collective dwellings, often accessible through ladders.

punctate a pattern of studded dots or points.

rachis the tiny stalk that connects the cereal grain to the ear in plants, such as maize, wheat, and other cereals.

radiocarbon dating absolute dating method based on the radioactive decay of the isotope carbon-14.

refitting reassembling stone flakes or blades to recreate the original core, in order to determine the sequence in which the flakes had been removed, and give insight into **knapping** technology.

relative chronology determination of chronological sequence without reference to a fixed time scale.

repoussé a metalwork technique whereby relief decoration is produced by hammering, usually from the reverse.

retouched where the edges of stone flakes have been further modified by the striking off of tiny chips to reshape or sharpen the edge.

Sahul the continuous landmass formed by Australia and New Guinea in periods of low sea level.

seal a stone object carved with a design that is impressed into a lump of clay to form a **sealing**; the design might be carved into the flattened surface of the stone (a stamp seal) or around the surface of a cylindrical stone to be rolled over the clay (a cylinder seal).

sealing a lump of clay impressed with a **seal**, used for administrative purposes to seal jars, documents, and other objects.

sedentism a residence pattern of permanent, year-round settlement.

shaft tomb a deep, rectangular burial space.

sherd a fragment, usually of pottery.

species distinct populations of plants or animals that can and do interbreed and produce fertile offspring.

stela (pl. stelae) a free-standing carved stone monument.

stratigraphy the successive deposition of superimposed layers of either natural or cultural material.

stupa a domed building often containing Buddhist relics.

Sundaland the continuous landmass formed by island Indonesia and Borneo during periods of low sea level.

sweat welding welding together pieces of metal using solder.

swidden land made cultivable by cutting and/or burning off the vegetable cover.

technocomplex a group of cultures that share a similar technology or technologies.

tell an artificial mound created by the accumulation of centuries of disintegrated mud-brick walls and domestic debris; characteristic of early cities in Southwest Asia.

temper the material added to clay to improve the firing qualities of pottery, preventing excessive shrinking and cracking.

teosinte wild maize, from which the domesticated **species** evolved.

terra preta in South America, a Portuguese term meaning black earth referring to occupation-related (settlement) sediments; also includes ancient cultivation areas that lack **artifacts**; also referred to as dark earth.

tholos tomb (pl. tholoi) circular tomb with a domed or conical roof, also called a beehive tomb.

Three Age System the classification system for the sequence of technological periods (Stone, Bronze, Iron) identified for the **prehistory** of Africa, Asia, and Europe.

transhumance the seasonal movement of human groups with their livestock, such as sheep, between mountain and lowland pastures.

Trichterbecher (TBK) culture in northern and central Europe in the late fifth and fourth millennium BCE, defined by a new type of pottery: *Trichterbecher* or funnel-necked beakers.

tumulus (pl. tumuli) an earthen or stone mound, usually covering a burial or burials.

type site an archaeological site considered definitively characteristic of a particular culture; the name of the site is often applied to that culture.

world system an economic system articulated by trade networks extending beyond the boundaries of individual political units and linking them together in a larger functioning unit.

xiaozhuan a small seal script, a form of standardized writing instituted under the Qin Dynasty in China.

yazhang a Chinese ceremonial jade blade.

ziggurat in Southwest Asia, a high platform surmounted by a small temple.

zooarchaeology a branch of **archaeology** specializing in the analysis of animal bones and shells; also called archaeozoology.

SOURCES OF ILLUSTRATIONS

p. 1 XYZ Pictures/Alamy Stock Photo; pp. 2-3 adfoto/123RF Stock Photo; pp. 12-13 Photo Joanna Hammond; 1.1 vladj55/123RF Stock Photo; 1.2 iamlukyee/123RF Stock Photo; 1.3 Rowena Alsey; 1.4 Photo Chip Colwell; 1.5 Staatliche Museen zu Berlin; 1.6 Image © DigitalGlobe/U.S. Department of State; 1.7 NASA Earth Observatory; 1.8 Vladyslav Starozhylov/123RF Stock Photo; 1.9 JACK GUEZ/AFP via Getty Images; 1.10 Drazen Tomic; 1.11 Jacopin/Science Photo Library; 1.12 Jada Images/Alamy Stock Photo; 1.13 Damian Evans/Khmer Archaeology LiDAR Consortium; 1.14 Pool DEVILLE/ASFM/Gamma-Rapho via Getty Images; pp. 30-31 Danita Delimont/Alamy Stock Photo; 2.1 Ben Plumridge, after Fagan, B. (2004), *People of the Earth*, p. 38; 2.2 ML Design; 2.3 John Reader/Science Photo Library; 2.4 © John Sibbick; 2.5 Brett Eloff/Lee Berger/University of Witwatersrand; 2.6 John Reader/Science Photo Library; 2.7 University of Missouri Museum of Anthropology; 2.8 Mary Jelliffe/Ancient Art and Architecture Collection; 2.9 Peter Bull Art Studio; 2.10 M. H. Day; 2.11 Schick and Toth; 2.12, 2.13 Michael Rogers; pp. 48-49 W. L. Jungers; 3.1 ML Design; 3.2 Javier Trueba/MSF/Science Photo Library; 3.3 Peter Bull Art Studio; 3.4 Photo RMN; 3.5 Peter Bull Art Studio; 3.6 Photo RMN; 3.7 Drazen Tomic, after Richard Klein; 3.8 Richard Klein; 3.9, 3.10 W. L. Jungers; 3.11 Martin Bates; 3.12 Richard Klein; 3.13 After Galway-Witham, J., Cole, J., & Stringer, C. (2019), *Aspects of human physical and behavioural evolution during the last 1 million years.* Journal of Quaternary Science 34: 355-78, Fig. 2; 3.14 Copyright Peter Pfarr, Niedersächsisches Landesamt für Denkmalpflege; 3.15 Copyright Christa S. Fuchs, Niedersächsisches Landesamt für Denkmalpflege; 3.16 Photo Juraj Lipták, Landesamt für Archäeologie; 3.17 Courtesy Francesco d'Errico, CNRS; 3.18, 3.19, 3.20 Lee Berger; 3.21 Richard Klein; pp. 72-73 © Maxime Aubert; 4.1 Peter Bull and Drazen Tomic; 4.2 Natural History Museum, London/Science Photo Library; 4.3 Richard Klein; 4.4 Pascal Goetgheluck/Science Photo Library; 4.5, 4.6, 4.7 Courtesy Christopher Henshilwood; 4.8 Carles Lalueza-Fox; 4.9 The Natural History Museum/Alamy Stock Photo; 4.10 Ivana Fiore and Matteo Romandini; 4.11 Morning Glory Publishers, Beijing; 4.12 Starlight Child/Creative Commons 3.0 licence; 4.13, 4.14 ML Design; 4.15 Ministère de la culture et de la communication, Direction régionale des affaires culturelles de Rhone-Alpes, Service régionale de l'archéologie; 4.16 Photo Hilde Jensen, Institut für Ur-und Frühgeschichte und Archäologie des Mittelalters, Eberhard-Karls-Universität, Tübingen; 4.17 Courtesy Alberto Broglio, Mirco De Stefani and Fabio Gurioli, University of Ferrara, Italy; 4.18, 4.19 Photo Hilde Jensen, Institut für Ur-und Frühgeschichte und Archäologie des Mittelalters, Eberhard-Karls-Universität, Tübingen; 4.20 © Mietje Germonpré; 4.21 Erich Lessing/akg-images; 4.22 Photo H. Jensen © University of Tübingen; 4.23 Erich Lessing/akg-images; pp. 94-95 Science History Images/Alamy Stock Photo; 5.1 Drazen Tomic, after Simon Fitch and Ben Geary, University of Birmingham. Images derived from USGS NED and ETOPO2; 5.2 Sally Nicholls; 5.3 Chris Scarre; 5.4 Drazen Tomic, after Manning, K. and Timpson, A. (2014), *The demographic response to Holocene climate change in the Sahara.* Quaternary Science Reviews 101: 28-35, Fig. 2; 5.5 aomori-jomon.jp; 5.6 Drazen Tomic; 5.7 PLOS CC BY 4.0; 5.8 Simon Hillsom, University College, London; 5.9 ML Design; 5.10 ML Design, after Sherratt, A. (1997); 5.11 Photo 27727344 © Simon Gurney/Dreamstime.com; pp. 110-11 Photo Nico Becker © DAI; 6.1, 6.2 ML Design; 6.3 Drazen Tomic; 6.4 Philip Edwards, La Trobe University; 6.5 Peter Bull Art Studio; 6.6 Gordon Hillman; 6.7 A. M. T. Moore; 6.8, 6.9, 6.10, 6.11 Danielle Stordeur; 6.12 © 2013 Crassard *et al.* https://doi.org/10.1371/journal.pone.0068061.g011; 6.13 geothea/123RF Stock Photo; 6.14 Rowena Alsey, after Willcox, G. & Stordeur, D. (2012), *Large-scale cereal processing before domestication during the tenth millennium cal BC in northern Syria.* Antiquity 86: 99-114, Fig. 3; 6.15, 6.16 Photo Klaus Schmidt © DAI; 6.17 Photo Nico Becker © DAI; 6.18 ML Design; 6.19 Prof. Harald Hauptmann, Heidelberg University; 6.20 ML Design, after Çatalhöyük Research Project; 6.21, 6.22, 6.23 Çatalhöyük Research Project; 6.24 Photograph Jason Quinlan, Çatalhöyük Research Project; 6.25 Danielle Stordeur; pp. 138-39 Trustees of the British Museum, London; 7.1 Michael Zysman/123RF Stock Photo; 7.2 Peter va Evert/Alamy Stock Photo; 7.3 ML Design; insets (left to right): Peabody Museum of Archaeology and Ethnology, Harvard University; The Art Institute of Chicago; Acropolis Museum, Athens; Staatliche Museum zu Berlin; British Museum, London; National Museum, Karachi; Qin Terracotta Museum, Lintong, Shaanxi Province; 7.4, 7.5 ML Design; 7.6 Baghdad Museum, Iraq; 7.7 Peter Bull Art Studio; 7.8 Courtesy Hassan Fazeli, Nashli, Dept of Archaeology, University of Tehran; 7.9, 7.10 Iraq Museum, Baghdad; 7.11 Tell Brak Project; 7.12 Peter Bull Art Studio; 7.13 Rowena Alsey, after Roaf, M., *Cultural Atlas of Mesopotamia and the Ancient Near East*; 7.14 Iraq Museum, Baghdad; 7.15 Metropolitan Museum of Art, New York; 7.16 Peter Bull Art Studio; 7.17 Iraq Museum, Baghdad; 7.18 ML Design; 7.19 The Trustees of the British Museum; 7.20 University of Pennsylvania Museums, Philadelphia; 7.21 Interfoto/Alamy Stock Photo; 7.22 Philip Winton and Drazen Tomic; 7.23 Paolo Matthiae; 7.24 Photo RMN – Chuzeville; 7.25 Peter Bull Art Studio; 7.26 Universal History Archive/Getty Images; 7.27 akg-images/Eric Lessing; pp. 164-65 Universal Images Group North America LLC/DeAgostini/Alamy Stock Photo; 8.1 ML Design; 8.2, 8.3 © C. Jarrige; 8.4 ML Design; 8.5 Georg Helmes; 8.6 Islamabad Museum, NMP 50.236; 8.7 National Museum, Karachi, NMP 50.852; 8.8 Georg Helmes; 8.9 J. M. Kenoyer, Courtesy Dept. of Archaeology and Museums, Govt. of Pakistan; 8.10 © Taisei Corporation; 8.11 Robin Coningham; pp. 182-83 123RF Stock Photo; 9.1 ML Design; 9.2 Robert Harding Picture Library; 9.3 People's Government of Hunan Province; 9.4 Shanghai Museum; 9.5 Brookhaven National Laboratory; 9.6, 9.7 CPAM of Kaifeng Prefecture; 9.8 akg-images/De Agostini Picture Library; 9.9 Hbcs0084/Dreamstime.com; 9.10 Xinhua News Agency/PA Images; 9.11 Shandong Museum, Jinan; 9.12 Charles Higham; 9.13 Nguyen Kim Dung; 9.14 Lorna Tilley, Australian National University in Canberra; 9.15 Charles Higham; 9.16 Drazen Tomic, after Charles Higham; 9.17 Charles Higham; 9.18 Tokyo National Museum; 9.19 Art Institute of Chicago; 9.20 ML Design, after Charles Higham; 9.21 artaporn/123RF Stock Photo; pp. 208-9 photojeong/123RF Stock Photo; 10.1 ML Design, after Charles Higham; 10.2 Institute of Archaeology, Chinese Academy of Social Sciences; 10.3 Lou-Foto/Alamy Stock Photo; 10.4 Institute of Archaeology, Chinese Academy of Social Sciences; 10.5 Morning Glory Publishers, Beijing; 10.6 Chengdu Museum, Sichuan, China; 10.7 Zhou Yuan Adminisrative Office of Cultural Relics, Fufeng, Shangxi Province; 10.8 Institute of Archaeology, Chinese Academy of Social Sciences; 10.9 Charles Higham; 10.10 Institute of Archaeology, Chinese Academy of Social Sciences; 10.11, 10.12 William Perry/123RF; 10.13 EPA/STR; 10.14 Hubei Provincial Museum, Wuhan; 10.15 Morning Glory Publishers, Beijing; 10.16 ML Design; 10.17 Melvyn Longhurst China/Alamy Stock Photo; 10.18 Drazen Tomic; 10.19 Heritage Image Partnership/Alamy Stock Photo; 10.20 Cultural Heritage Association Korea; 10.21 National Museum of Korea; 10.22 Chad Ehlers/Alamy Stock Photo; 10.23 ML Design; 10.24, 10.25 Tokyo National Museum; 10.26 ML Design; 10.27 Peter Bull Art Studio; 10.28 Charles Higham; 10.29 Rufolf Ernst/123RF Stock Photo; 10.30, 10.31 Charles Higham; pp. 236-37 Jesse Kraft/123RF Stock Photo; 11.1 ML Design; 11.2 ML Design, after Jenny Sheehan in the Cartography Unit, Research School of Pacific and Asian Studies, Australian National University; 11.3 oliophotography/123RF Stock Photo; 11.4 Photo © Tom Till; 11.5 ML Design, after Jenny Sheehan in the Cartography Unit, Research School of Pacific and Asian Studies, Australian National University; 11.6 Cartography Services, Australian National University, Canberra; 11.7 Peter Bellwood;

11.8 Drazen Tomic, after Peter Bellwood; 11.9 From Pâris, François Edmund (1841), *Essai sur la Construction Navales des Peuples Extra-Européens*; 11.10a, 11.10c Photo Hsiao-chun Hung, Academia Sinica, Taipei and National Museum of the Philippines; 11.10b Institute of Archaeology, Hanoi and National Museum of the Philippines; 11.10d Trustees of the British Museum, London; 11.10e Courtesy Glenn Summerhayes; 11.10f Photo Yoshiyuki Iizuka, National Museum of the Philippines; 11.10g Courtesy Stephen Hooper; 11.11a Courtesy Yang Yaolin, Shenzhen Museum; 11.11b National Museum of the Philippines. Photo Hsiao-chun Hung; 11.11c Courtesy Department of Anthropology, Taiwan National University; 11.11d Courtesy Tsang Chengohwa, Academia Sinica, Taipei; 11.11e Courtesy Glenn Summerhayes; 11.11f, 11.11g, 11.11h Courtesy Social Science Research; 11.12 Peter Bull Art Studio; 11.13 Granger Historical Picture Archive/Alamy Stock Photo; 11.14 Alberto Loyo/123RF Stock Photo; 11.15 Drazen Tomic and Annick Boothe; 11.16 Hsiao-chun Heng; 11.17 Peter Bellwood; 11.18 Kevin L. Jones; 11.19 Alexei Kornylyev/123RF Stock Photo; 11.20, 11.21 Peter Bellwood; 11.22 National Museum of the Philippines; 11.23 Ng Sebastien; pp. 264–65 pixsaju/123RF Stock Photo; 12.1 Drazen Tomic, after Simon Fitch and Ben Geary, University of Birmingham. Images derived from USGS NED and ETOPO2; 12.2 Peter the Great Museum of Anthropology and Ethnography (Kuntskamera), Russian Academy of Sciences, St. Petersburg; 12.3 Drazen Tomic; 12.4 Vassia Atanassova – Spiritia; 12.5, 12.6 Archaeological Museum, Varna, Bulgaria; 12.7a Yvonne Beadnell, based upon geophysical survey by Duncan Hale; 12.7b The Nebelivka Project; 12.8 Photo Miguel Angel Blanco de la Rubia; 12.9 Photo Drag. Kazié, Belgrade; 12.10 Peter Bull Art Studio; 12.11 Kenneth Garrett; 12.12 Drazen Tomic and Tracey Wellman; 12.13 Ochsenreiter, South Tyrol Museum of Archaeology, Bolzano; 12.14 Courtesy Landesdenmalamt Baden-Württemberg – Archäeologisches Denkmalpflege; 12.15 The National Museum of Denmark, Copenhagen; 12.16 Michael Jenner; 12.17 The Trustees of the National Museums of Scotland. Edinburgh; 12.18 ML Design, after S. Andersen; 12.19 4kclips/123RF Stock Photo; 12.20 Chris Scarre; 12.21 Drawing by Elizabeth James, Wessex Archaeology; 12.22 Kit Weiss, The National Museum of Denmark, Copenhagen; 12.23 artwork Centro Camuno di Studi Preistorici, Capo di Ponte, Italy; 12.24 National Museum of Denmark, Copenhagen; 12.25 drawing Brigitta Kürtösi. Courtesy Matrica Museum, Százhalombatta; 12.26 Wiliam Perry/123RF Stock Photo; 12.27 After Chadwick, J. (1976), *The Mycenean World*, Fig. 12; pp. 294–95 Christopher Scott/Alamy Stock Photo; 13.1 ML Design, after Iliffe, J. (1995), *Africans: The History of a Continent*, Fig. 1; 13.2, 13.3 Rock Art Research Institute, University of Witwatersrand; 13.4 ML Design, after Iliffe, J. (1995), *Africans: The History of a Continent*, Fig. 1; 13.5 Mike P Shepherd/Alamy Stock Photo; 13.6 Maurice Brand/Dreamstime.com; 13.7 Invictus SARL/Alamy Stock Photo; 13.8 ML Design; 13.9 Egyptian Museum, Cairo; 13.10 davidmontalenti/ 123 RF Stock Photo; 13.11 Tips Images/Tips Italia Srl a socio unico/Alamy; 13.12 Robert Harding Picture Library; 13.13 After Kemp, B. J. (1991), *Ancient Egypt: Anatomy of a Civilization*, Fig. 98; 13.14 Christopher Kean; 13.15 Rudolf Ernst/123RF Stock Photo; 13.16 Graham Connah; 13.17 South African Museum, Cape Town; 13.18, 13.19 Courtesy Institute for Archaeological Sciences, Goethe University, Frankfurt; 13.20 Photo Kevin Tildsley, British Museum, London; 13.21 Museum of Ife Antiquities, Nigeria; 13.22 Graham Connah; 13.23 Giampaolo Cianella/123RF Stock Photo; 13.24 Robert Harding/Alamy Stock Photo; pp. 322–23 Smithsonian Institution, Washington, D.C.; 14.1 ML Design; 14.2 David J. Meltzer; 14.3 University of Alaska Museum of the North; 14.4 ML Design; 14.5 Tom Uhlman/Alamy Stock Photo; 14.6, 14.7 Thomas Dillehay; 14.8 John R. Foster/Science Photo Library; 14.9 Smithsonian Institution, Washington, D.C.; 14.10 The Gault School of Archaeological Research; 14.11 Science Stock Photography/Science Source; 14.12 Millard H. Sharp/Science Source; 14.13 David J. Meltzer; 14.14 Joe Ben Wheat, University of Colorado Museum; 14.15 David J. Meltzer; 14.16 Tony Baker; 14.17 David J. Meltzer; 14.18 Drazen Tomic, after Meltzer, David J., *Pleistocene Overkill and North American Mammalian Extinctions*, Annual Review of Anthropology 44; pp. 346–47 alexeykamenskiy/123RF Stock Photo; 15.1 ML Design; 15.2 ML Design, after Saunders, J. W. *et al.*, *Watson Brake, A Middle Archaic Mound Complex in Northeast Louisiana*, American Antiquity 70 (2005): 631–68, Fig. 2; 15.3 aceshot1/Shutterstock; 15.4 Courtesy the W. S. Webb Museum of Anthropology, University of Kentucky (5622); 15.5 Photo Dirk Bakker © 1985 The Detroit Institute of Arts/Ohio Historical Society; 15.6 J. Cooper after the Ohio Historical Society; 15.7 State Parks, Arkansas; 15.8 Photo G. Milner. Field Museum of Natural History, Chicago, Illinois, 55500; 15.9 Richard Schlecht, National Geographic Society Image Collection; 15.10, 15.11, 15.12 Arizona State Museum, University of Arizona. Photo Helga Teiwes; 15.13 William Silver/123RF; 15.14 W. H. Wills; 15.15 Charles Martin. Courtesy of the National Geographic Society. Neg.#5016-B; 15.16 alexeykamenskiy/123RF Stock Photo; 15.17 Photo Dirk Bakker © 1985 The Detroit Institute of Arts; 15.18 Ken Thomas; 15.19 Photo Collection, Royal Anthropological Institute, London; 15.20, 15.21 Richard D. Daugherty, 15.22, 15.23 Newfoundland Museum, Government of Newfoundland and Labrador, St. John's; 15.24 Bryan and Cherry Alexander; 15.25 Trustees of the British Museum, London; pp.378–79 Kevin Tildsley; 16.1 ML Design; 16.2 Joyce Marcus and Kent V. Flannery; 16.3 Dallas Museum of Art, Gift of Patsy R. and Raymond D. Nasher 1983.148; 16.4 Sergey Strelkov/123RF Stock Photo; 16.5 Richard Hewitt Stewart/National Geographic Stock; 16.6 David Hilbert/Alamy Stock Photo; 16.7 Evans, S. T. & Webster, D. (2001), *Archaeology of Ancient Mexico and Central America: An Encyclopedia*, p. 725; 16.8 After R. Diehl; 16.9 Joyce Marcus and Kent V. Flannery; 16.10 Princeton University Art Museum; 16.11 After Newsome, E. A. (2001), *Trees of Paradise and Pillars of the World: The Serial Stela Cycle of "18-Rabbit-God K," King of Copán*, p. 3; 16.12 iStock/Getty Images; 16.13 Vladimir Korostyshevskiy/123RF Stock Photo; 16.14 Photo Irmgard Groth-Kimball © Thames & Hudson Ltd; 16.15 Gianni Dagli Orti/Shutterstock; 16.16 Drazen Tomic; 16.17, 16.18 ffotograff; 16.19 © Jorge Pérez de Lara; 16.20 Adolfo Francisco Usier Leiter/Dreamstime.com; 16.21 Wild Blue Media; 16.22 © Stephan Gore/Ancient Art & Architecture Collection; 16.23 Martin Schneiter/Dreamstime.com; 16.24 Bodleian Library, University of Oxford; 16.25 ML Design; 16.26 Kenneth Garrett; 16.27 Great Temple Project, Mexico City; pp. 410–11 AFP/Getty Images; 17.1 ML Design; 17.2 Lake Sachavacayoc 10 or 3000ad/Dreamstime.com; 17.3, 17.4 AFP/Getty Images; 17.5, 17.6 © Philip Baird/www.anthroarcheart.org; 17.7 Drazen Tomic; 17.8 DEA/G. Dagli Orti/Getty Images; 17.9 Drazen Tomic; 17.10 Drazen Tomic, after Fowler Museum of Cultural History, University of California, Los Angeles; 17.11 Royal Tombs of Sipán Museum, Lambayeque; 17.12 Museo Rafael Larco Herrera, Lima; 17.13 Drazen Tomic; 17.14 mathess/123RF Stock Photo; 17.15 Fowler Museum of Cultural History, University of California, Los Angeles; 17.16 Jarno Gonzalez Zarraonandia/iStockphoto.com; 17.17 Cezary Wojtkowski/123RF Stock Photo; 17.18 Gary Cook/Alamy Stock Photo; 17.19 Photo Mario Gaubert/Overflightstock; 17.20 Sicán Archaeological Project, Photo Y. Yoshii; 17.21 Mark Green/123RF Stock Photo; 17.22 Sally Anderson/Alamy Stock Photo; 17.23 © Michael Langford 2003; 17.24 Adriana Von Hagen; 17.25 Drawing Alexander Jubran; 17.26, 17.27 Museu de Arqueologia e Etnologia da Universidade de São Paulo, Brazil; 17.28 Vespasian/Alamy Stock Photo; 17.29 Brian Heckenberger; 17.30 Photograph courtesy Martti Pärssinen; pp. 442–43 Erlantz Perez Rodriguez/123RF Stock Photo; 18.1 Courtesy Enrique Chiu; 18.2 Photo Glenn Caldwell/Kooskia Internment Camp Archaeological Project; 18.3 Courtesy Natahlia Sofie Brichet and Felix Riede, photo by Anna Tsing; 18.4 Pulsar Imagens/Alamy Stock Photo.

Page numbers in *italics* refer to illustrations.

Aboriginal Australians 101, 242, 243, 244–45, *242, 244*
Abric Romaní 84
absolute chronology 24, 25, 312
Abu Hureyra 114, 119, 120–21, *114, 115, 120, 121*
Abydos 305, 306, *305*
aceramic Neolithic 114; South America 417–19, *418*; South Asia 170; Southwest Asia 114, 120, 121–35, *121, 124, 125*
Acheulean industry 39, 40, 59, 60, 62–63, 65, 68, 69, 78, *41, 65, 69*; handaxes 53–54, *53, 54*
acropoleis 18, 19, 157, 390, 400, 432
Açutuba 436, 437, *414, 439*
ADE see Amazonian dark earths
Adena 353–55, *353, 355*
adobe 361, 393, 395, 406, 420, 423, 429, *275, 428*
Aegean 290–92, *269, 291, 292*
Africa 297–321; agriculture/ farming 109, 301–4, *108*; environments and landscapes 35, 297, *36, 298*; evolution of language 80; farming communities 313–15, *314*; *Homo sapiens* (modern humans) in 76–79, *76, 77, 78, 79*; human migration from 87, *87*; human origins in 32–47, 52, 82, *34, 36, 37, 38, 40, 52*; hunter-gatherers 297–301, *300*; states 304–13, 315–20, *305*
African Humid Phase 98
Agate Basin points 337, *337*
agriculture/farming 100–4, 107–9, *102, 105, 108*; Africa 109, 301–4, *108*; Australia and the Pacific Islands 245–47; consequences of 106–9, 195, *104, 108*; East Asia 185–87, 191–93, 195, 197–206; Europe 269, 270, *269*; Mesoamerica 382–83; North America 352–55, 359–60, 369; and social inequality 205, 382; South America 416–17; South Asia 168–71, *169, 170*; Southeast Asia 197–202; Southwest Asia 121–22, 135–36, *125*; *see also* farming communities
Ahmose, pharaoh 309
Ai Bunar 273
Aiello, Leslie 43, 44
'Ain Ghazal 128, 136, *114*
Akapana pyramid 426, *427*
Akhenaten (Amenhotep IV) 309–10, *310*
Akkadian empire 154, 156–58, 161, *158*
Akrotiri-Aetokremnos 119–20, *114*
Aksum 313, *313*
alabaster *153*

Aleppo 157, 162, *146*
alpacas 416, 426
Altai Cave 82, 83
Amarna 18, 310, *18, 305, 310*
Amazonia 414–15, 434–40, *414, 415, 436, 437, 439, 440*
Amazonian dark earths (*terra preta*) 436–37, 439, *439*
amber 269, 274, 285, 286, 288, *274*
Amenhotep IV (Akhenaten) 309–10, *310*
Americas 324–45; earliest occupation 327–31, 342–44, *329*; earliest sites 332–33, *332, 333*; environments and landscapes 324–26, *325*; hunter-gatherers 334–37, *334, 335, 337*; regionalization 337–42; *see also* Mesoamerica; North America; South America
Amesbury Archer 286, *286*
Amorite Dynasties 160–61, *160*
AMS dating 24, 25, 417
An (deity) 150
An Son 200, *186, 200*
Anak 225, *226*
Anatolia 113, 119, 130, 135, 136, 155, 156, 160, 161, 269, 270
ancient DNA (aDNA) 26, 161, 269, 270, 278, 293, 330, 340, 416
Andersson, J. G. 58
Andes 413, *414*; confederacies and states 421–25, *422, 423, 424, 425*; descent and the *kurakas* 426, 440; empires 424–33, *427, 428, 429, 430, 432, 433*
Angkor 230–33, 234, *209, 212, 230, 231, 232, 233*
Angkor Thom 232, *230*
Angkor Wat 231, *15, 28, 230, 232*
animal bones 58, 70, 116, 117, 119, 189, 198, 248, 369; Abu Hureyra 121; Acheulean sites 64, 65, 68, *69*; Beringia 324; cut-marked 42–46, 63, 84, *43, 85*; Dinaledi Cave 66; Folsom 336; Jiahu 192; Liang Bua Cave 57; Meadowcroft Rockshelter 333; Mehrgarh 170; Olduvai Gorge 40; Ozette 371; Sanxingdui 218; Stonehenge 283; Tianluoshan 196
Anson, George 248, 257
anthropology 14, 144
Anuradhapura 180, *168*
Anyang 214–16, 222, *212, 214, 215, 216*
Anzick 329, 334, *325*
apes 33–36, *34*
Apollo 11 cave 299, *300*
Arabic script 316, *151*
Arago 64, *50, 55*
Arawak language 434–35, 438
Archaeological Institute of America (AIA) 450
archaeology 14, 444; approaches and techniques 23–29, *25, 26, 27, 28*; current state of 17; key concepts 14–16, *16*; key themes 20–23, 444–50, *21, 22, 445, 447, 448*; responsibilities of 17–20, *17, 19*

Archaic 350–52, 382, 368–69, 415–16, *246*
Arctic/Subarctic 105, 267, 285, 331, 342, 349, 372–74, *350, 373*
ardipithecenes 36; *Ardipithecus* 32, 33, 36, 46
Ariendorf 64, *50*
Arnhem Land 242, 243–44, *241, 242, 244*
arrowheads see points
art: Akkadian 158, 159; Aurignacion 89, *90*; Blombos Cave objects 81, *81*; Çatalhöyük wall paintings 130–32, *132*; Clovis objects 334, *335*; early 65, *65*; Early Horizon 420; Maya 389, 397, *397*; Moche 423, *423*; Olmec 384–85; Tomb of the Heavenly Horse 225, *226*; *see also* figurines; murals; rock art; sculpture
artifacts (defined) 17
Ashur 160, *146, 155*
Asia see East Asia; Eurasia; Island Southeast Asia; South Asia; Southeast Asia; Southwest Asia
assemblages 53–54, 63, 70, 83, 116, 198, 253, 297, 337, 343, 344, 383, *77, 268*
Association for Black Anthropologists 450
Asuka 228, 229
Atacama Desert 102, *102*
Atahualpa, emperor 426
Atapuerca 59, 62, 82, *50, 55*
Aten (sun disk, deity) 309
Athabaskan 367
Athenian Acropolis 18
Atlantic Europe 279–81, *280, 281*
atlatl 90, 92, 334
Attirampakka 54
Aubrey 334, *325*
Aurignacian 87–92, *77, 90, 91*
aurochs 83, 88, 267
Austral Islands 253, 256
Australia 240–63; agriculture 245–47; domestication 247–49, 251–55, *247, 248*; environments and landscapes 240, *241, 246*; farming communities 255–61, *258*; *Homo sapiens* (modern humans) in 85–86, *86, 87*; hunter-gatherers 242–45, *242*; seaborne trade and contact in Southeast Asia 261–62
australopithecines 32, 33, 36–37, 38, 40, 46, *36, 37, 41*; *Australopithecus aethiopicus* 37, *41*; A. *afarensis* 36, 38, *36, 41*; A. *africanus* 37, *41*; A. *boisei* 37, 40, *41*; A. *garhi* 37, *41*; A. *robustus* 37, *41*; A. *sediba* 37, *37, 41*
Austronesian dispersal 247–50, 255–61, *247, 248, 249, 250, 256, 257, 258*
Austronesian languages 247–48, *248*
axes 39, 42, 56, 173, 179, 192, 244, 281, 285, 437; battle 284, 285; bronze 261, 287, 288; celts 371; copper 205, 276, 281, 354, *279*; ground-stone 301; jade 216;

jadeitite 281, 285, *281*; polished stone 107, 169, 171, 191, 244, 273, 280, 281, 284, 285; shaft-hole 179; *see also* Acheulean industry
Aztecs 404–8, *408*; tribute list 405, *405*
Aztlán (mythical land) 404

Ba system 221
Babylon 156, 160, 161, 162, *146*
Bada Valley 241, 263
Bagor 168, 175, *168*
Balakot 171, 179
Bali 245, *241, 246*
Balkans 269, 270, 272, 274, *269*
ball courts 361, 384, *361, 384*
Baluchistan 168, 178, 179
bamboo 63, 189, 190, 191; texts on bamboo slips 223, *223*
Ban Chiang 198, *186*
Ban Non Wat 205, *186*
Bandkeramik see Linearbandkeramik (LBK)
Bangkok Plain 200–2, *201*
Banpo 183, *186, 194*
Bantu 301–4, 313–14, *302, 303*
Baoshan 223, *212*
barley 101, 102; Africa 302, *303*; Asia 113, 121, 122, 125, 168, 170, *125, 169*; depicted in proto-cuneiform 151, *151*
Barrancoid 435, 438
basalt 117, 126, 253, 255, 256–57, 312, 333, 385, *118*
Bashidang 189, *186*
Basin of Mexico 144, 386, 390–91, 396, 402, 404–6, *386*
baskets 99, 147, 170, 190, 333, 340, 341, 371, 381, 391, 421, *421*
Batán Grande 429, *414, 429*
Batanes Islands 248, *241, 248*
Battle Creek *13*
Batu Gajah (Elephant Stone) 262, *262*
beads 78, 88, 107, 299; choker of *316*; copper 135, 175; glass 225, 288, 319; jade 169, 250; malachite 134, 135; nephrite 199; painted red 262; shell 81, 116, 168, 200, 201, 251, *201*; steatite 168, 170; stone 148, 195; turquoise 365
behavior: of early modern humans 78–79, 84–85, *79, 85*; of hominins 44–46, 62–70, *45, 63, 65, 69*
Beikthano 230, *212*
Beinan 250, *241, 251*
Belcher, William 175
beliefs see religion and beliefs
Bell Beakers 285–88, *286*
Benin 316, *316*
Berekhat Ram 65–66, *50, 65*
Beringia (Bering land bridge) 97, 324–26, *325, 329*
bifaces 53, 78, 84, 334, 343, 354, *53*
Bilzingsleben 65, *50, 55, 65*
biostratigraphy 64
bipedalism 32, 33, 34, 35, 36, 38, 41, 52, *34, 36*
Bir Kiseiba 301–2
bird-bone flutes 192, *192*

Biskupin 290–91

bison 83, 90, 324, 336, 337–38, 368–69, *89, 338*; butchering pattern 339, *338*; Pleistocene populations 339, 340, *341*

Blombos cave 79, 81, *81*

Bone Rabbit, king 387, *387*

Borneo 87, 245, 246, 249, *87, 97, 241, 246*

Borobudur 261–62, *261, 241*

Boserup, Ester 103

bottle gourds 203, 352, 383, 416

bottleneck population losses 253

Bowanni, John 17

bows and arrows 90, 92, 116, 247, 286, 372, *124, 286*

Boxgrove 68, *50, 55*

Brahmagiri 180, *181*

Braidwood, Robert 113, 136

brain expansion (encephalization) 43–44, 46, 47

brain size 32, 34, 37, 41, 43, 44, 52, 53, 60, 61, 70, 79

braincases 57, 58, *56, 60*

Brandt, Carol 446

broad-spectrum economy 78–79, 119, 136, 169

Bronze Age 24; Europe 283, 285–91, *265, 285, 286, 287, 288, 289*; South Asia *172, 176, 178*; Southeast Asia 231; Southwest Asia 148, 154–62, *155, 156, 157, 158, 159, 160, 162*

bronze/bronzeworking: Africa 309, 313, 314; axes 261, 287, 288; East Asia 205, 213–21, 224–26, 227, 234, *214, 215, 217, 218, 219, 220, 224*; Europe 261, 262, 287, 291, *287*; Southwest Asia 154, 160

Buddhism 180, 227, 229, 230, 255, 261, *229, 233*; Sokkuram Buddha 227, *225, 227*; stupas 230, *176, 261*

Büdelsdorf 284–85

Buhen 308, *305*

Bukit Tengkorak 249, *248*

burials 16, 18, 19, 449; Africa 307, 309, 311, 313, 318, 320, *307, 313*; Australia and Pacific Islands 240, 250, 252, 260, 261, 262, *262*; cist 180, 250, 279, 280, *180*; coffin 287, 288, *288*; early modern humans 76, 77, 84, 85, 89, 90, 91, *78*; East Asia 189, 191, 192, 194, 197–201, 205, 213–15, 217, 219, 225, 226, 228, 229, *193, 194, 199, 201, 217, 224*; Europe 268, 272, 275, 280, 283–91, *27, 268, 274, 280, 286, 288*; human ancestors 46, *44*; Mesoamerica 383, 385, 392, 393, 400; mounded 228–29, 287, 289, 311, 355, 369, *280, 288*; North America 352, 353, 354, 355, 357, 362, 365, 369, 371; South America 421, 429, 432, 436, *421, 429*; South Asia 170, 173, 174, 179, 180, *180*; Southwest Asia 116, 117, 119, 130–34, 147, 148, 150, *148, 149*; *see also* cemeteries; tombs

burins 90, 324, 326

Burton, Jeffrey 445

Bygholm hoard 279, *279*

cacao 365, 382

Cahokia 357, 358, 359, 369, *350, 358*

Caimito 437, *437*

Calakmul 397, *397, 381*

calendars 386–87, 388, 402, *387, 389*

Callao Cave 85, *246*

cannibalism 278, 366

canoes 254–55, 249, *255*

Cantona 394, *381*

Caral 418, *414, 418*

Caroline Islands 256, *241, 249*

Carpenter's Gap 86

Carthage 314, 315, 318

Casas Grandes 359, 403, *381*

Çatalhöyük 128, 130–33, 151, *104, 114, 130, 131, 132, 133*

Catfish Cave 300, *300*

Caton-Thompson, Gertrude 318

cattle 125, 128, 133, 171, 189, 283, 287, 301–4, 314, 320, 446, *108*; rock art depictions of 303, *95, 303*; wild and zebu 116, 120, 168, 170, 171, 267, 301, *169*; *see also* pastoralism

Cauvin, Jacques 119

cave art *see* rock art

Çayönü Tepesi 129–32, *114*

cells 121, 122, 124, 132, *122*

celts 371

cemeteries 19; Bangkok Plain 200; Bashidang 189; Brahmagiri 180, *181*; Central Africa 320; Crete 290; Dinaledi as 67; Eastern Woodlands 354; European Mesolithic 269; Fangshan 217; Harappa 174; Jiahu 192; Jinsha 216; Kerma 311; at Lake Mungo 86; Man Bac 199, *199*; Mehrgarh 171; Meroë 311; Natufian 117; Olenly Ostrov 268–69, *268*; Peiligang 192, *193*; permanent 197; Qujialing 191; Royal Cemetery of Ur 155–56, *139, 155, 156*; at Sannai-Maruyama 100; Shang Dynasty 215; Shixia 197; Sibri 179; Sloan 342; Songze 190–91; Ubaid 148; Urnfields 289–90; Varna 272, *272*; Vedbaek 281–84; Xipo 194; Zhou 217, 220; *see also* burials; tombs

cenote 403

Central Africa 313–20, *314, 315, 317, 319*

Central Europe 275–79, *275, 276, 277, 278, 279*

ceramic Neolithic 114, 121

ceramics *see* pottery

cereals 21, 28; Africa 301, 314; early human consumption 99, 101–2, 107, *104*; Europe 274, 279; South Asia 147, 170; Southeast Asia 246; Southwest Asia 114, 116, 117, 118, 120, 123, 124, 125, 126, 133, 147, *115, 125*

ceremony *see* ritual and ceremony

Cerro Sechín 419, *419*

Chaco 364–66, 376, *350, 364*

Chalcolithic 146, 148, *130*

chambered tombs 274, 280, *274*

Chan Chan 428–29, *142, 414, 428*

Chang'an 223, *212*

Changjiang 216, *216*

chariots 288, 309, *155, 292*; in burials 214, 215, 217, 220, 224, 287, *15, 224, 287*

Chauvet Cave 88–89, *89*

Chavín de Huantár 418, 420, 421, *414, 420*

Chengtoushan 189, *186, 190*

chicha 432

Chichén Itzá 403–4, *379, 381*

Chifumbaze complex 314

chili pepper 104, 382, 417

Chimor 428–29, *428, 429*

China: agriculture/farming 185–87, 191–93, 195, *192, 193*; early human migration to 85, 87, *87*; environments and landscapes 185, *186*; expansion of farming beyond 197–202; farming communities 187–91, 193–97, *190, 194, 195*; states 210–24, *213, 214, 215, 216, 217, 218, 219, 220, 221, 224*; writing 222–23, *216, 222, 223*

Chindadn points 326, 327, *326*

Chiquihuite Cave 332

Chitamni 203, *203*

Chiu, Enrique, Mural Brotherhood Project 444, *445*

chocolate jars 365, *365*

Christianity 313; Ethiopian rock-cut churches 312, *312*

Chulmun 203

cist burials 180, 250, 279, 280, *180*

cities 141–45, *145*; Mesoamerica 386–91, 396–401, 403–9; South America 425–35; South Asia 173–80, *165, 172, 174, 176, 177, 178*; Southwest Asia 145–49, 154–59, 160–62, *155*

city states 144, 154–59, 404, 406, *155*

ciudadelas 393, 394, 429

Classic Hohokam 360–62

Classic Mesoamerica 391–95, *392, 393, 394, 395*; Maya 396–401, *397, 398, 399, 400*

Claw, Katrina G. 330

Cliff Palace 366, *347, 366*

climate change 20–21, 55, 114, 260, 342, 447, *21, 443, 447*; *see also* environments

clothing 88–89, 91, 117, 276, 288, 299, 421, 277, *288, 355, 421*

Clottes, Jean 88

Clovis 334–42, *87, 325, 335, 338, 339, 341*; points 334, 336, 337, *323, 334, 337*

Côa Valley 88

coalesce 80, 93

Cobá 403, *381*

codex 386, 387; *Codex Mendoza* 405

Cody points 337, *337*

coffin burials 287, 288, *288*

coinage 221, 313, 319

Colby 336, *325*

Colorado Plateau 362–67, *364, 365, 366, 367*

colossal heads 385, *385*

communal buildings 121–25, 129, 150, *149, 364, 366, 383, 123*

Confucius 221

cong 197, 211

Congo, Democratic Republic of 320

Constantini, Lorenzo 170

Cook, James 254, *255*

Cook Islands 253, 256, *241*

cooking 57, 64, 84, 123, 124, 158, 192, 196, 202, 206, 332, *131*

Cooper's Ferry 328, 331

Copán 394, 397, 398, *381, 384*

copper 107, 135, 153, 154, 160, 175, 179, 180, 205, 214, 274, 286, 305, 314, 316, 319, 320, 357, 371, 382; axes 205, 276, 281, 354, *279*; beads 135, 175; bells 362, 365; Bygholm hoard 279, *279*; ingots 170, 215; mining 273; Sargon head 156, *156*; Varna cemetery 272, *272*

Corded Ware 284, 285

cordillera 245, 247, 426, 429

Cordilleran ice sheet 324, 328, *325, 329*

cores 39, 54, 55, 84, *118*

Cortés, Hernan 403, 408

cosmology 307, 384, 388, 418, *265, 268*

Cosquer Cave 88

cotton 170, 416, 417

courts, circular sunken 418, 420, *418, 420*

Cradle of Humankind 66, *66*

crafts/craftspeople 22, 142, 145, 229, 362, 428, 440, 362

crania *see* skulls

Crete 290–92, *292*

Crigler Mound *353*

crocodiles, depictions of *98*

Crow Creek 369, *350*

cryptocrystalline 334, 335, 343

cultigens 104, 344, 355, 383, 417

cultivation 100, 104, 125, 185, *102, 125*

cults 149, 150, 287, 305, 392, *147, 408*

Cumancaya 437

cuneiform 150, 151–52, 154, 161, *151*

Cunzierton *281*

currency 179, 221, 223, 234, 320, 337, 440

cut-marked bones 42, 43, 44, 45, 46, 63, *43, 85*

Cuzco 429–33, *414, 433*

cylinder seals 152–53, 154, *152*

Dabenkeng 247, *248*

Dakhleh Oasis 301, *300*

Dali cranium 85, *85*

Dalton 339, *339*

dance 299, 299

Danzante figures 390, *390*

"dark ages" 180

Darwin, Charles 23–24

dating 24–26, *25*

Dawenkou 193, 195–97, 221, *186, 195*

Daxi 189–90, *186, 190*

death pits 278, *278*

Dederiyeh Cave 83

deities: An 150; Aten (sun disk) 309; Chavín 420, 427, *420*; Enki 147; Enlil 155, 159; fanged 420, *420*;

Greek 292; Horus 306; Inanna 150, 153, 158; Ishtar 161, *162*; Osiris 306; Shamash *160*; *see also* myth
dendrochronology 24, 25, 26
Denisovans 26, 76, 82, 83, *61*, *75*
Denny (girl) 83
dental decay 104, *104*
dentate-stamped motifs 251, 252, *252*
denticulates 84
dentition 36, 37, 57
Dholavira 173, 177–78, *168*, *178*
Dhra' 109
Diaotonghuan 187–88, *186*
diet: Africa 298, 301; Americas 335, 336, 339, 342, 352, 353, 355, 359, 362, 369, 372, 382, 432; Asia 120, 168, 194, 203, 446, *104*; Australia 240; early modern humans 82–83; hominins 37, 41, 42–44, 46, 68–70
Dinaledi Cave 66–67, *50*, *66*, *67*
dings 215
disease 68, 191, 244, 375, 433, 444, 446, *375*
Diuktai Cave 324–26
Djoser, king 306, *306*
Dmanisi 55–56, 59, *50*, *55*
DNA 19, 26–27, 80–82, *26*, *82*
dogs 90, 101, 200, 214, 251, 258, 351, 368, 382, *90*; depictions of 386, 422, *422*
dolmen tombs 204, *204*
Dolní Věstonice 90, *91*
domestication 20, 21, 100, 101–3, *102*; Australia and the Pacific Islands 247–49, 251–55, *247*, *248*; and contemporary archaeology 445–47; East Asia 101, 185, 203–6, *203*; expansion of 105–6, *105*; Mesoamerica 382; North America 355–56; Southwest Asia 125, 133, 135, 128
Dong Son *241*, *262*
Donghulin 191
Dorset 372–74, *373*
dragons, depictions of 213, 218, *213*, *428*
Drake Cache *323*, *334*
Drakensberg Mountains 298, *300*, *298*
dry farming 130, 146, *146*
drystone masonry 250, 317–18, 319, *319*
Dufuna boat 301, *300*
Duinefontein 68, *69*
Dura-Europos 19, *19*
Durrington Walls 283
Dyje River 90

Eagle Man statue 407, *408*
Early Horizon 384, 419–21, *419*, *420*, *421*
Early Intermediate Period 421–25, *422*, *423*, *424*, *425*
Early Khartoum *300*, *300*
Early Preclassic 384–86, *385*
Early Woodland 352–55, *353*, *354*
earspools *422*, *437*

earthworks 258, 260, 283, 284, 316, 400, 436, 439–40, *355*
East Africa 35, 37, 40, 52, 301–4, 316–20, 321, *298*, *303*, *317*, *319*
East Asia 185–207, 210–35; agriculture/farming 185–87, 191–93, 195, 197–206; domestication 101, 185, 203–6, *203*; environments and landscapes 185, *97*, *186*, *203*; expansion and integration into Southeast Asia 229–34, *229*; farming communities 187–91, 193–97, *190*, *194*, *195*; *Homo sapiens* (modern humans) in 85–86, *86*, *87*; hunter-gatherers 99, 187, 195, 202–3, *99*; states 210–29, *212*, *225*, *228*
Easter Island *see* Rapa Nui
Eastern North America 350–55, *351*, *353*, *354*
Eastern Woodlands 349, 351–54, 356, 358, 359, 369, 376, *358*
Ebla 156, 161, 162, *146*, *155*; archive at 157, *157*
ecotones 341
Egtved oak-coffin burials 287–88, *288*
Egypt 18, 304–10, *18*, *300*, *302*, *304*, *305*, *306*, *307*, *309*, *310*; hieroglyphs 173, 290, 292, 313, *292*
El Fin del Mondo 334, *325*
El Manatí 385, *381*
El Mirador 389, *381*
El Paraíso 418–19, *411*, *414*, *418*
El Sidrón Cave 82, *82*
el Wad 117, *114*
Elamites 159, 160, *160*
elephants 53, 57, 65, 83, 216, 218, 234, 274, *65*, *98*, *219*, *233*, *262*, *274*
elites 142, 143, 144; Africa 305, 308, 309, 311, 318, 319; East Asia 189, 190, 193, 196, 197, 203, 204, 206, 210, 211, 212, 213, 214, 215, 221, 225, 227, 228, *195*, *213*, *217*, *219*, *220*, *228*; Europe 274, 287, 288, 289, 290; Mesoamerica 385, 386, 389, 390, 395, 397, 398, 399, 401, 403, 406–7; Pacific Islands 255; South America 417, 418, 419, 421, 422, 423, 426, 428–29, 436, 437, *421*, *423*, *428*; South Asia 173, 174, 179, 180; Southwest Asia 149, 150, 151, 154, 155, 156, 158
elk-antler macehead 268–69, *268*
En Esur 22, *22*
encephalization 43–44, 46, 47
Enheduanna, priestess 158
Enki (deity) 147
Enlil (deity) 155, 159
enslavement 23, 161, 195, 310, 316, 317, 408, *160*
environments: Africa 35, 76, 297, *36*, *75*, *298*; Australasia and Pacific 240, 245, *241*, *246*; early Americas 324–26, *325*; East Asia 185, *97*, *186*, *203*; Europe 267, *268*; Mesoamerica 381–82, *381*; North America 349–50, *350*; South America 413–15, *414*; South Asia

167, *168*; Southwest Asia 113–14, *114*, *115*; *see also* climate change
Epiclassic 396, *396*
Epigravettian 90, 92
Epipaleolithic 114, 115–21, 132, 134, 135, *118*, *120*, *121*, *124*
Erech 149, *150*
Eridu 147–49, *146*, *147*, *148*, *213*
Erlitou 213–14, *212*
Ertebølle-Ellerbek 281–84, *281*
Ethiopia 76, 303, 310–13, *311*, *313*; rock-cut churches 312, *312*
ethnography 22, 42, 104, 283
Euphrates River Valley 119, 120, 122, 124, 125, 129, 133, 144, 145, 147, 153, 154, 157, 161, *114*, *115*, *120*, *146*, *155*
Eurasia 55–56, 61, 64, 70, 93, 105, *55*, *77*, *108*; steppes 220, 267, 284, 288, *115*
Europe 267–93; agriculture/farming 269, 270, *269*; environments and landscapes 267, *268*; farming communities 269–81, 284–90, *287*, *289*; hominins in 59, 79, 80, *59*; *Homo sapiens* (modern humans) in 87–92, *87*, *90*; hunter-gatherers 268–69, 281–84, *281*; migration from the Steppes 284; states 290–91
European colonialism: Mesoamerica 403–9, *405*; North America 374–75, *375*
Evans, Arthur 292
evolution 23–24, 32–35, 55, *34*, *61*
exchange *see* trade and exchange
extinctions 24, 26, 46, 55, 80, 260; Pleistocene 340–41, *341*
Eynan 118, *114*, *118*
Eyre, Lake 243, *241*

faience 290
Fangshan 217, *212*
farming communities: Africa 313–15, *314*; Australia and the Pacific Islands 255–61, *258*; East Asia 187–91, 193–97, *190*, *192*, *193*; Europe 269–81, 284–90, *287*, *289*; Mesoamerica 383, *383*; North America 356–59, 360–67; South America 419–21; South Asia 168–71, *169*, *170*; Southwest Asia 125–35, 145–46, *128*, *146*; *see also* urban communities; village settlements
farming *see* agriculture
Farrell, Mary 445
Fazenda Colorado *440*
Fengtian jade 249, 250, *248*, *250*
Fertile Crescent 99, 113, 114, 121, *105*
fieldwork 27–28, *27*
figurines: animal 89, 195, *90*, *195*; earliest 65, *65*; Eridu clay 148, *148*; female 65, 91, 147, *65*, *91*, *147*; *haniwa* terra-cotta 228, *228*; Hohokam clay 362, *362*; stone carved 355, 357, 372, *355*, *357*, *373*; Tapajônica small 436, *437*; Venus 91, *91*

Fiji 259, *87*, *241*
Finney, Ben 255
fire 45–46, 64, *45*
First Family 38
fish/fishing: Africa 297–301; Americas 344, 370, 371, 413, 415, 416, 417, 418; Asia 148, 175, 192, 199, 202, 203; Australia and Pacific Islands 243, 253, 268; by early modern humans 78, 90; depictions of 244, 275, *244*, *275*, *423*; dried/salted 175, 320; fishhooks 203, 244, 251, 253; harpoons 370, 373, *373*
flaked stone 37, 39, 41, 42, 53–54, 55, 56, 57, 58, 68, 84, 242, 334, *53*, *54*, *339*; *see also* microliths
Flannery, Kent 119, 136
Flores 54, 57, *57*, *246*
flowstone 62
Folsom 336, 338, *325*, *337*
foraging: Africa 299; Americas 335, 337, 339, 342, 351, 352, 363, 382, 417; Asia 115, 120–21, 203; Australia 242, *243*; early modern humans 84; Europe 268, 279; hominins 42, 43, 68
foraminifera 28, 29
Formative Period 434–35
Formosan 247
Forster, Johann Reinhold 254
foxtail millet 191, 203
friezes 179, 390, 420, 423, 429, *390*
Fu Hao, Lady, tomb 215, *214*, *215*
Fuller, Dorian 188
Fumane Cave 84, 89, *85*, *90*
Futuna 253, *241*

Galgenberg 91, *91*
Gamble, Clive 91
Ganga (Ganges) basin 167–71, 180, *168*
Gansu 193, *186*
Ganweriwala 174, 177–78, *168*
Garrod, Dorothy 117, 119
Gaspar de Carvajal, Friar 436
Gaudzinski, Sabine 83
ge 198
Gedi 316, *317*
gene flow 324
genomes 78, 80–82, 330, *82*; genomic research and Indigenous communities 330
genus 32, 33, 35, 37, 40, 41, 46, 80, 335, 340, 345, *341*
geoglyphs 425, 439–40, *425*, *440*
geomorphology 245
Gero, Joan 42
Gesher Benot Ya'aqov 68, *50*, *55*
Ghana, ancient 316
Girsu 160, *146*, *155*
GIS (Geographical Information Systems) 23, 27
Giza pyramids 145, 205, 306, 307, *305*, *307*
glacials/interglacials 28, 29, 35, 55, 59, 64, 87, 92, 99
goats 103, 116, 125, 128, 132, 148, 168, 171, 285, 303, *303*; depictions of *156*

Göbekli Tepe 123, 124–27, 129, *111*, *114*, *123*, *126*, *127*
gold/goldworking 107; Aztec 405, *405*; Batán Grande 429, *429*; inlay 225; mummy ornaments 421, *421*; Mycenaen gold mask 291, *291*; Nubian 309; Royal Cemetery of Ur 155, *155*, *156*; Sanxingdui pits 218; Silla ornaments 225–27, *226*; Trundholm sun chariot 287, *287*; Tutankhamun coffin 309, *309*; Varna cemetery 272, *272*; Zimbabwe plateau 317, 319
Goldman, Irving 260
Gona *36*, *39*
Gorham's Cave 83
Goshen points *337*, *337*
GPS (Global Positioning System) 27
Gran Dolina 59
Grave Creek *350*, *353*
grave goods 46, 90, 91, 156, 174, 189, 193, 201, 204, 220, 221, 228, 261, 272, 283, 286, 289, 421, *201*, *215*, *421*
graves *see* burials; cemeteries; tombs
Gravettian 87, 88–92, *90*, *91*
Great Plains 337–39, 352, 368–69, *368*, *337*, *338*
Great Silla 227, *227*
Great Wall of China 223, 234
Great Zimbabwe 317–19, *295*, *319*
Greater Australia (Sahul Shelf) 57, 85, 245, 87, *86*, *87*, *246*
Greece 18, 270, 292, 315, 444; Minoan and Myceneaean 290–92, *291*, *292*
Greenland 349, 350, 372, 374, 447, *21*, *350*
Greenlawdean *281*
Gua Harimau 261, *241*
Guilá Naquitz 382, *381*, *383*
guinea pigs 416
Gulf Stream 96, 267
Gwisho 299, *300*

Hadar *36*, 38, *36*, *38*
hafted points 83, *84*
Halaf 145–49, *146*, *147*, *148*
Halberstadt 278
half-life 24, 25
Halin 230, *212*
Hammurabi of Babylon 160–61, *160*
Hammurabi's Law Code 160, *160*
Han Dynasty 224–25, 229–30, 234–35
handaxes *see* axes
haniwa figures 228, *228*
haplogroups 26–27, 328, 333
Happisburgh footprints 59, *59*
Harappa 172–75, 177, *168*, *177*
Harappan 171–72, *172*
Hariharalaya 231, *231*
harpoons 370, 373, *373*
Hauberg Stela 387, *387*
Hawai'i 249, 253, 256, 257, 259, 87, *241*, *257*
headdresses/headgear 421, 422, *255*, *316*, *421*, *429*
Head-Smashed-In bison jump 369, *368*

heat treating 78, 92
heiau 256, 257
Hell Gap points 337, *337*
Hemudu 188, *186*
Herakleopolis 308, *305*
Herr, Sarah 17
Herto crania 76
Herxheim 278
Hierakonpolis 305, *305*
hieroglyphs 173, 290, 292, 313, *292*
Hindu Kush 179, *168*
Hindusim 255, 261–62, *15*, *262*
"Hobbit" (*Homo floresiensis*) 57, 75, *57*
Hodder, Ian 119, 130, 132
Hodges, William 254, 260, *255*
hoe agriculture 109, 201, 203, 206, 369, *108*
Hohle Fells Cave 89, 91, *91*
Hohlenstein-Stadel 89, *90*
Hohokam 360–62, *360*, *361*, *362*; ball courts 361, *361*
Hokkaido 104, 205, *203*, *228*
Holocene *see* postglacial
hominins 14, 15; behavior 44–46, 62–70, *45*, *63*, *65*, *69*; dispersal of 50–71, *50*, *55*, *61*; early 24, 25, 35–37, *36*, *37*; food procurement and diet 42–44, *43*; language 80; and the Oldowan 41–42, *41*
Homo antecessor 59, 60, 75
Homo erectus 37, 41, *41*; African 52, *52*; Asian 56–59, *56*; crania and skeletons 40, 76, *76*, *77*, *85*; dispersal of 54–56, 61, *55*, *75*; in Europe 59, *59*
Homo ergaster see Homo erectus
Homo floresiensis ("Hobbit") 57, 75, *57*
Homo habilis 51, 52
Homo heidelbergensis 50, 60, 75, 76, 78, 79, 80, *60*, *76*
Homo naledi 66–67, *61*, *66*, *67*
Homo neanderthalis (Neanderthals) 60, 62, 64, 67, 69–70, 75, 78–85, 87, *75*, *77*, *82*, *85*, *87*
Homo rhodesiensis 76
Homo rudolfensis 37, 41, 51, 52
Homo sapiens (modern humans) 26, 32–33; in Africa 76–79, *76*, *77*, *78*, *79*; climate-driven dispersal 76, *75*; crania and skeletons 76–77, *85*, *76*, *77*, *85*, *86*; and the Denisovans 83; into East Asia and Australia 85–86, 245, *86*, *87*; into Europe and Russia 87–92, *87*, *90*; interbreeding with Neanderthals 82; language 80
Hongshan 197
Honshu 202, 205, 228, *203*, *228*
Hopewell 353, 354–55, 362, *350*, *354*
horses 83, 169, 180, 288, 309, 316, 324, 368; in burials 217, 225, 228, *224*, *226*; depictions of 92, 224, 225, *90*, *224*, *226*, 287, *292*
Horus (deity) 306
House of Taga *241*, *257*
housing 16; Africa 308, 310, 311; cliff occupation 366, *347*, *366*; early 100, 106, 107; East Asia

189, 191, 192, 193, 194, 196, 197, 202, 203, 205, *183*, *196*; Europe 270–71, 273–75, 278, 279, 283, 284, 287, 289, 27, *273*, *275*, *287*, *289*; longhouses 275, 287, *275*, *287*; Mesoamerica 383, 385, 393, 395, 402, 404, 406; North America 349, 356, 357, 359, 360, 363–65, 366, 369, 370, 371, 372, 373, *360*, *364*, *366*, *370*, *373*; Pacific Islands 252, 256, 257; plank 370, *370*; semi-/subterranean 122, 123, 124, 126, 132, 192, 193, 194, 203, 360, 363, *122*; South Asia 169, 171, 176, *178*; Southeast Asia 243, 247, 250; Southwest Asia 118, 120, 121, 122–23, 128–34, *121*, *123*, *129*, *130*, *131*, *132*, *133*; tipis/tepees 369; *see also* wooden and timber construction
Huaca Prieta 331, 342, *325*
Huai River Valley 192, 222
Huleh, Lake 115
human sacrifice: Africa 311; Asia 156, 213, 215, 216; Europe 278; Mesoamerica 384, 385, 387, 389, 391, 392, 393, 399, 401, 406, 408, *387*, *390*; North America 357; South America 422, 423, 429, *423*
hunter-gatherers: Africa 297–301, *300*; Australia 242–45, *242*; earliest 99–100, *99*; early Americas 334–37, *334*, *335*, *337*; East Asia 99, 187, 195, 202–3, *99*; Europe 268–69, 281–84, *281*; New Zealand 257–58; North America 350–52, 368–69, 370–74; South America 415–16; South Asia 167–68; Southeast Asia 245; Southwest Asia 115–21
Hurrians 160, *151*
Hyksos 309

Iberia 92, 269, 274, 275, 278, 279, 286, 280
Ice Age (last) 92, 96, 99, 104, 187, 240, 267, 268, 445, *97*, *268*
ice sheets 324, 328, *325*, *329*; melting 267, 281, *268*, *281*
ice-free corridor 330, *325*, *329*
Iceman (Ötzi) 276–77, *276*, *277*
iconography 158, 244, 386, 420, 422, 424, 268
Ife 316, *316*
Inanna (deity) 150, 153, 158
Indigenous archaeology 17–18, 259, 330, 449, *13*, *17*
Indigenous communities: and genomic research 330; present day 433, 438, 449
Indo-European languages 284
Indravarman I, King 231
Indus cities 173–80, *165*, *172*, *174*, *176*, *177*, *178*
Indus script 173, *173*
Indus Valley 143, 144, 167, 173–78, *168*, *174*, *176*, *177*, *178*
Initial Period 419–21, *419*, *420*, *421*
Inka empire 425–26, 429–33, *414*, *433*, *443*; *khipus* 431, 432, *432*;

Sacred Valley of the Inkas and Machu Picchu 430, *414*, *430*
Inter-Tropical Convergence Zone 98
Iron Age 198, *180*
iron/ironworking 24, 180, 205, 221, 228, 247, 261, 303, 311, 313–15, 371, 385, *314*, *315*
irrigation 21; in early agriculture 101, 107, 108–9; East Asia 190, 205, 228, 229, 234, *190*; Mesoamerica 391, 405; North America 359–61; present day 446, *443*; South America 426, 428, 430; Southwest Asia 145, 146, 147, 149, 154, 161, *29*, *160*; and state formation 142, 144
Irwin, Geoffrey 255
Isaac, Glynn 41–42
Ishtar (deity) 161, *162*
Isin 160, *146*
Islam 255, 261, 316
Island Southeast Asia 245, 247–49, 260, *241*, *246*, *247*, *248*, 261, *262*, *263*; navigation across 254–55, *255*; seaborne trade 261–63
isostatic uplift 97
Isthmus of Panama 329
Itazuke 205, *203*
ivory 88, 89, 90, 91, 92, 180, 274, 319, 334, *90*, *218*, *274*
Iwo Eleru 301, *300*

jacal 360, 361
jade 189, 190–91, 195–96, 197, 204, 211, 212, 225; axes 216; beads 169, 250; *cong* 197, 211; facial images 217, *217*; Fengtian 249–50, *248*, *250*; *ge* 198; Jinsha crouching tiger 216, *216*; Olmec 385; Sanxingdui ritual pits 218–19, *218*, *219*; tomb of Fu Hao Anyang 215, *215*; *yazhang* 198, 218, 219
jadeitite 281, 285, *281*
Jaguar Paw I, king 400
Japan 97, 195, 202–6, 228–29, 97, *186*, *202*, *203*, *228*
Japanese-Americans during WWII 445, *445*
Java 245, 261–62, *241*, *246*, 261, *262*
Jayavarman VII 231–32, *230*, *233*
Jebel Qafzeh 77, 78, 87
Jerf el Ahmar 121, 122–23, 124, 128, *114*, *122*, *123*
Jericho 124, *114*, *124*
jewelry: anklets 262, *262*; arm rings 279, *279*; bone 201, *201*; earrings 250, *250*; necklaces 262, *262*; semi-/precious stones 148, 155, 166, 168, 175, 180, 290, 438; *see also* beads; shells
Jiahu 192, 222, *186*, *192*
Jian 225, *225*
Jinsha 216, *212*, *216*
Jōmon 99, 100, 104, 202–3, *99*, *202*
Jones-Miller 338, *325*

Kabwe cranium 76, *76*
Kaditshwene 320
Kalahari San 103
Kalako-deray 169

Kalambo Falls *50*
Kalibangan 172, 175, 177, *168, 172*
Kamehameha, chief (the Great) 253
Kamgot *251*
kami spirits 229
Kangaroo Island 242, *241*
Kangwha Island 203, *204*
Kapthurin 65, *50*
Karanovo tell 271, *271*
karstic regions 41
Kashmir 169
Kathu Pan 65, *50*
Kattwinkel, Wilhelm 40
Kawelu, Kathleen 259
Kebara Cave 83
Kennewick 327–28, *325*
Kenyon, Kathleen 121–24, 132
Kerma 310–11, *305, 311*
Kharaneh IV 116, *114*
Kharga Oasis 301, *300*
khipu 431, 432, *432*
Khoisan language 299
Khok Phanom Di 201–2, 206, *186, 201*
Khorat Plateau 198, *186*
Khufu Pyramid 306, 307
Kimpo swamp 204, *203*
King Island 242, *241*
Kirch, Patrick 253
Kish 156, 160, *146, 155*
kivas 363, 365, 366, *366*
Klinaklini glacier *325*
knapping 42, 78
KNM-ER 1808 (skeleton) 68
Knossos 270, 290, 292, *292*
Knowth 280
kofun 228
Koguryo 225, *225, 226*
Kokiselei 53, *50*
Koobi Fora 45, 68, *36, 45, 50, 55*
Kooskia Internment Camp 445, *445*
Koptos 305, *305*
Korea 195, 203–6, 225–27, *186, 203, 204, 225*
Kot Diji 171–72, 175, *168, 172*
Koutsochero camp 444
Krapina 82, 84
Kuahuqiao 189, *186*
Kudatini 171, *168*
Kuijt, Ian 133
Kuk 246, *241*
Kumgokdong 204, *203*
!Kung 80
kurakas 426, 440
Kusimba, Chap 318
Kyongju 225, 227, *225, 227*
Kyushu 205–6, *203, 228*

La Cotte de St. Brelade 83
La Ferrassie 84
La Quemada 396, *381*
La Venta 384, 385–86, *381, 385*
Laas Geel 303, *303*
lacquerware 202, 212, 213, 215, 218, 225
Laetoli footprints 36, 38, *36, 38*
Lagoa Santa 327–28, *325*
Lal, B. B. 172

Lalibela churches 312, *312*
Lambayeque 428–29, *429*
language(s): Arawak 434–35, 438; Austronesian 247–48, *248*; and domestication 105; evolution of 80; Indo-European 284; Khoisan 299; Malayo-Polynesian 248, 249, 254, *247*; Nahuatl (Aztecan) 386, 404; Quechua (Runa Simi) 431; Semitic Akkadian 156; Sumerian 154, 156, 158, 159, *151*; Swahili 317; Tupian 434; *see also* scripts; writing
lapis lazuli 148, 155, 175, 180, 229, 290, *155, 156*
Lapita 251–55, *251, 252, 255*
Larsa 154, 160, *146*
Las Vegas 344, 416, *325, 414*
Last Glacial Maximum 92, 114, 119, 342, *115*
Late Horizon 404–5, 429–33, *433*
Late Intermediate Period 428–29, *428, 429*
Late Preclassic 386–91, *387, 389, 390*
Late Woodland 355–56, *356*
latte 256, 257
Laurentide ice sheet 324, 328, *325, 329*
Leakey, Louis 40
Leakey, Mary 39, 38, 40
Lee, Richard 104
Leigudun 212, *221*
Lepenski Vir Iron Gates settlement 275, *275*
Lesser Sundas 245, 262, *246*
Lesvos life vests 444
Levallois technique 54, 84, *54*
Levant 115–21, *118, 120, 121*
Lewis, David 254
Lewis, Meriwether 353
Lewis-Williams, David 299
Liang Bua Cave and Liang Bua (LB) 1 57, *49, 50, 57*
Liangzhu 191, 210–13, 222, *186, 212*
Libby, Willard 25
LiDAR (Light Detection and Ranging) 27–28, 232, 397, 399, *28, 399*
Lieberman, Daniel 85
Linear A script 290, 292
Linear B script 292, *292*
Linearbandkeramik (LBK, or Bandkeramik) 270, 274, 275–79, *269, 275, 278*
lingling-o (earrings) 250, *250*
lions 88, 89, 150, 179, *89, 90*
Liuwan *186, 194*
llamas 416, 426, 429
Llanos de Moxos 435, *414*
loess 55, 185, 193
longhouses 275, 287, *275, 287*
Longshan 210–13, 222
looting 19, 423, *19, 423*
Luba kingdom 320
Lucy 36, 38, *36*
Luoyang 218, 220–21, *212*
Luzon 109, 249, *108, 241, 246*
Lydenburg 314, *314*

McDermott, LeRoy 91
Machang *194*
Machu Picchu 430, *414, 430*
Madagascar 249, *249, 247*
Madjedebe 85, *86*
Magdalenian 91, 92
Mahagara 169, *168*
Maitum 262, *241, 262*
maize 144, *105*; beer (*chicha*) 432; Mesoamerica 381, 382–83, 385; North America 352, 359, 363, 369; preserved cobs 102, *102*; South America 427, 432
Malayo-Polynesian languages 248, 249, 254, *247*
Malaysia 245, 249, *241, 246*
Malthus, Thomas 103–4
mammoth 83, 335–36, 341; ivory 88, 89, 90, 91, 92, *90, 91*
Man Bac 197, 199, *186, 199*
Manco Capac 426
mandibles 38, 55, 57, 58, 62, 355, 369, *66, 133*
Maori 257–58, *258*
marae 256, 259, 262
Marajó Island 415, 435–36, *414, 436*
Marajoara 435–36
Marcus, Joyce 144
Mari 157, 161–62, *146, 162*
Mariana Islands 249, 251, 252, 256, *241, 248, 251, 257*
Marib Dam 29, *29*
Marquesas Islands 253, 256, 260, *87, 241*
masks 218, 219, 291, 355, 422, *218, 219, 291, 398*
Mata Menge *246*
Matacapan *381*
material culture 14, 15, 16; Africa 310, 313; Americas 381, 386, 438; Asia 118, 149, 154, 161, 185, 187, 192, 197, 202, 206, 248; early modern humans 89; early societies 99, 106, 107; Europe 272, 278, 290; human ancestors 36–37, 42, 44; Pacific Islands 251; present day 448
maxillae 355, 369
Maya 383, 396–401, 403, 404, *381, 384, 398, 399, 400*; calendar 388, 389; mural art 397, *397*; present day 408–9; rulers 387–89, *387*
Mayapan 403, 404, *381*
Meadow, Richard 170
Meadowcroft Rockshelter 331, 328, 333, *325, 331*
meat 43–44, 45, 46, 68, 69–70, 83, 116, 118, 121, 128, 368, 416, *332*; butchery 338
Mediterranean Europe 267, 269, 274, *268, 269, 274*; *see also* Aegean
megafauna 334, 335–36, 340–41, *335, 341*
megalithic structures 280, 282, 284–85, 419, *180, 280, 427*
megaron 291
mega-sites 114, 274, *274*
Mehrgarh 170, 171, *168, 169, 170*
Mekong River 198, 231, *186, 212*
Melanesia 245, 252, *241, 246, 251, 252*

Mellaart, James 130, 132
Memphis 306, *305*
Mendel, Gregor 23
menhirs 281
Mentuhotep, King 308
Merimde 302
Meroë 311–13, 314, *305*
Meroitic state 311, 313
Mesa Verde 366–67, *347, 366*
Mesoamerica 381–409; agriculture 382–83; ball game 384, 393, 395, *384*; cities, states, empires 386–91, 396–401, 403–9; collapse and reorganization 396, 402–3; environment and landscapes 381–82, *381*; expansion and integration 391–94; farming communities 383, *383*; Olmecs 384–86, *385, 386*; Spanish in 403–9, *405*
Mesolithic 99, 267, 268–69, 275, 279, 281, 284, *268, 275, 281*
Metal Age 248, *250, 262*
metallurgy 107; Africa 304, 311, 313, 314, 318; Americas 382, 421; Asia 149, 153, 205, 221, 261; Europe 107, 274, 279, 285–86, 288, 289, 290, *279*; *see also* bronze; copper; gold; iron
Mexica 404, 408, *406*
Mexico–US border, wall mural 444, *445*
mica 354, *354*
microblades 324, 326, 327
microliths 99, 116, 117, 119, 121, 170, 297–99, 301, *118, 124, 169*
Micronesia 245, 249, 251, 253, 256, *241, 249*
microwear 68
middens 78, 169, 240, 269, 281, *202, 281, 445*
Middle Horizon 391, 394, 426–27, 432, *427*
Middle Preclassic 384–86, *385*
Middle Stone Age 40, 66, 69, 76, 78, 81
Middle Woodland 352–55, *353, 362, 376, 354*
migration 22–23, 87, 254–55, 269, 270, 284, 327, 444–45, *87, 269*
Miller, Danny 174
millet 100, 101, 103; Africa 302, 314, 315, 317; Asia 171, 175, 185–86, 191–95, 197, 203–4, 214, *247*; Pacific Islands 253
Minoan Greece 270, 290–91, 292
Mississippi River/Valley 349, 356, 357, 359, 369, 376, *350*
Mississippian 356–59, 362, 369, 376, *357, 358*
Missouri River 369, *350*
mitochrondrial DNA (mtDNA) 26, *26*, 62, 78, 85, 199, 302, 328, 329, 333
Mixtec 386
moai 256, *237, 257*
Moche 421–24, *414, 422, 423*
Moesgaard Museum, *Mild Apocalypse* exhibition 447, *447*
Mohenjo-daro 173, 174, 175, 176, 179, *165, 174, 176, 168*

Mohina 431
molecular clock 26, 328
Molokwane 320
Moluccas 245, *241, 246*
Mongchon 225, *225*
Monks Mound 357, 358, *358*
Monte Albán 395, 386, 390, *381, 395*
Monte Verde 328, 330, 331, 332–33, 342, 344, *332, 325*
Mo'orea 254, *255*
morphology 24, 33, 36, 44, 59, 100, 181, 312
mortars and pestles 116, 117, 193, 196, 206, 344, *118*
Motecuzóma II 408
mounds: Adena and Hopewell 353–55, *353, 355*; ash 171, *168*; building 351, 435–36, *351, 436*; burial 228–29, 287, 289, 311, 355, 369, *280, 288*; settlement 126, 198, 210, 275, 270, *271*; temple 417, 419, 426, 427, *418, 419*; see also tells
Moundville 359, *350, 353*
Mount Cameron West 243, *241*
Mousterian 84, *84, 85, 77*
mud-brick construction 106; Africa 311, *311*; Europe 270; South America 424, 429, *142*; South Asia 168–69, 170, 171, 172, 174, 176, 177, 178, *170, 172, 176*; Southwest Asia 122, 128, 132, 147, 150, 154, 161, *121*
Mugharet es-Skhūl 77, *87*
mummy bundles 421, *421*
Mundigak 175, *179*
Mungo, Lake 85–86, 240, *86, 241*
murals: Koguryo fresco 225, *226*; Maya 397, *397*; Moche 421, *423*; Mural of Brotherhood project 444, *445*; Teotihuacán 391, 393, *393, 394*
Murray Springs 336, *325*
music 192, 299, *192*
Must Farm 27, *27*
Muye 217, *212*
Mycenaean Greece 290–92, *291, 292*
myth 15, *161*, 173, 357, 402, 404–5, 418, 421, 422, *15, 162, 291*

Nabta Playa 301–2, *302*
Nagsabaran *248, 251*
Nahuatl (Aztec) language 386, 404
Nakbé 388–89, *381*
Nan Madol 256, *241*
Nanchoc 416–17
Nanzhuangtou 191
Naqada 305, *305*
Nara basin 228, *228*
Naram-Sin 158, *158*
Narmer Palette 305, *305*
Narungga project 17–18
Native American Graves Repatriation Act (NAGPRA) 18
Native Americans 328–29, 330, 342, 374–75, *375*
Natufians 99, 117–18, *118*
Navajo Nation 330
navigation 254–55, *255*
Nazca 424–25, *414, 424, 425*

Neanderthals *see Homo neanderthalis*
necropoleis 215, 421, *421*
Nefertiti, bust of 18, *18*
Nenana complex 326, *326*
Nenumbo *241, 252*
Neolithic: East Asia 192, 197–200, 211, 222, *191, 192, 194, 198*; Europe 269, 270–71, 272, 274, 279, 280, 281, 283, 284, 285, *269*; Island Southeast Asia and Pacific 247, 249, 250, 252, 255, 262, 248, 262, *263*; South Asia 168–69, 170, 171, 180, *169, 170*; Southwest Asia 115, 119, 134, *111*
Neolithic Demographic Tension 106
Neolithic Revolution 119
Nevalı Çori 129, *114, 129*
New Britain 249, *241*
New Caledonia *241, 251*
New Guinea 85, 87, 245–47, 252, *86, 87, 97, 241*
New Zealand 249, 253, 254, 257, 258, 260, *87, 241, 250, 258*
Newark 355, *350, 355*
Newgrange 280, *280*
Ngandong 58, *86*
Niah Cave 85, *86, 241, 246*
Nihewan 58, *50, 55*
Nile Valley 87, 300, 302–3, 313, *307*
Nineveh 160, *146, 155, 156*
Nippur 155, 159, *146, 155*
Nishida 202, *203*
Nok 314, 315, *315*
Norse 350, 372, 374
North Africa 76, 300–301, 308, 315–16, *98*
North America 349–77; agriculture 352–55, 359–60, 369; Clovis occupation 334–37, *334, 335*; domestication 355–56; environments and landscapes 349–50, *350*; farming communities 356–59, 360–67; hunter-gatherers 350–52, 368–69, 370–74; Native Americans and European colonialism 374–75, *375*; regionalization after Clovis 337–42, *337, 338, 339, 341*
Northern Europe 281–85, *281, 282, 283*
notches 84, 192
Nubia 309, 310–13, *305, 311, 312, 313*
nuclear DNA 26, *26*
nuts 37, 82–83, 113, 202

oars 196
Oaxaca Valley 382, 383, 386, 390, 395, 396, 405, *381, 383*
obsidian 133, 134, 135, 146, 161, 249, 270, 343, 354, 385, 391, 394, *248*
Oceania 245, 251–55, 256, *246, 247, 251, 252, 255*
ocher 77, 79, 81, 84, 88, 90, 91, 119, 129, *81*
Ohalo II 116, 135, *114*
Ohio Valley 353, *350*
Ōizumi-machi 228, *228*
Old Jarma 315–16

Oldowan industry 37–42, 44–46, *39, 41, 45*
Olduvai Gorge 37, 40, 41–42, 46, 68, *31, 36, 39, 40, 50, 55*
Oleniy Ostrov 268–69, *268*
Olmecs 384–86, *381, 385, 386*
Olorgesailie Basin 68, 78, *50, 55*
Olsen-Chubbuck 338, *325, 338*
One Tree Hill *241, 258*
oracle bones 215–16, 222, *216, 222*
Orinoco River 415, 435, 436, 438, *414*
Osiris (deity) 306
Ötzi Iceman 276–77, *276, 277*
Ounjougou 301, *300*
Owens Valley Paiute 101
oxygen isotope analysis 28, 286
Ozette 370, 371, *350, 371*

pa 258, *258*
Pääbo, Svante 83
Pacific Islands 240–63; agriculture/farming 245–47; domestication 247–49, 251–55, *247, 248*; environments and landscapes 245, *241, 246*; farming communities 255–61, *258*; hunter-gatherers 242–45, *242*; seaborne trade and contact in Southeast Asia 261–62
Pacific Northwest 370–72, 375, 376, *370, 371*
Paekche 225, 229, *225*
Paisley Caves 331, 333, *333, 325*
Pakal, King 398, *398*
Palenque 398, *381, 398*
Paleoamericans 327–28
paleoanthropology 36, 37, 38, 40
Paleoindians 336, 339, *339*
Paleolithic 62, 75–76, 84, 88–89, 91, 92, 99, 101, 113, *77, 89, 91*
paleontology 32, 40, 62, 88, 336
palynology 28, *29*
Panlongcheng 215, *212*
Paracas 421, *421*
Paraisópolis 448, *448*
Parthenon marbles 18
Pasemah 262, *241, 262*
passage graves 280, *280*
pastoralism 101, 114, 136, 167, 168, 180, 274, 301–3, 313, 431, *95, 303*
Pedra Pintada 344, *325*
Peiligang 192, *186, 193*
Penghu Islands 260, *248*
Pengtoushan 189
Peninsular India 171
Peñon 327, *325*
Peñon Woman III 327
pepo 383
Persian Gulf 147, 149, 155, 160, 162, *146*
perspective, drawn 88, *89*
pestles and mortars 116, 117, 193, 196, 206, 344, *118*
Petermann glacier 20, *21*
Petralona 60, *50, 55, 60*
petroglyphs 257, *257*
phalanges 36, 37, 83
Philippines 109, 245, 247–48, 249, 252, 262, *108, 241, 246, 251, 252, 262*

Phoenicians 315, 318
Phung Nguyen 197–98, *186, 198*
phytoliths 28, 187, 199, 204, 303, 344, 383, 416, *248*
piece-molds 213, 218, *221*
Piggott, Stuart 174
pigments 65, 66, 78, 79, 81, 84, 88, 194, *81*; see also ocher
pigs 103, 446; Africa 302; early Americas 327; East Asia 187, 189, 192, 194, 195, 196, 197, 199, 200, 203, 205, 212, 214, 215, 216; Europe 267, 283, 285; figurines 195, *195*; Island Southeast Asia 246, 248; Pacific Islands 251; Southwest Asia 119, 125, 128, 146, 155
Pikirayi, Innocent 318
Pirak 180, *168*
Pisac *443*
pisé 106
Pizarro, Francisco 426
Plainview points 337, *337*
plaques 123, 286, 420, *123*
plazas 359, 360, 395, 407, 420, 435, 436, 437, 438, *358, 395, 420*
Pleistocene 75, 92, 114, 130, 240, 242, 245, 254, 328, 333, 334, 342, 350, *86, 128, 246*; extinctions 340–41, *341*; Late 97, 187, 300, 327, 336, 340–41, 383, *241*; Upper 87, *87*
plowing 21, 107, 109, 189, 273, 279, 285, 382, 431, 446, *108, 304*
points: Australian 242; bone 78; Chindadn 326, 327, *326*; Clovis 334, 336, 337, *323, 334, 337*; Dalton 339, *339*; Epipaleolithic *118*; Gravettian 90; Great Plains 337, *337*; hafted 83, *84*; Middle Stone Age 78; Neanderthals 84; Neolithic *124*
polychrome: murals 393, *423*; pottery 171, 367, 401, 421, 424, 435–37, *367, 424, 437*
Polychrome Tradition 435–37, *437*
Polynesia 98, 245, 252–56, 258–61, *241, 255*
population size 21–22; Africa 59, 301, 304–5, 310, 311, 318, 319, 320; early Americas 328, 331, 343; early communities 100, 103, 104, 107; East Asia 186, 191, 192, 195, 211, *230*; Europe 268, 270, 274, 278; Mesoamerica 382, 390, 391, 392, 395, 400, 401, 402, 404; North America 350, 351, 358, 362, 363, 364, 366, 367, 372, 374, 375, 376, *347*; Pacific Islands 260; present day 445–46; South America 434, 440; South Asia 169, 176; Southwest Asia 119, 121, 128, 133, 135; and state formation 141, 143, 144
Porter, David 260
Postclassic Mesoamerica 402–3, *402*
postcolonial archaeology 318
potatoes 416, 426, 440
potlatch 372
pottery/ceramics: Dabenkeng style 248, *248*; Early Woodland 353;

Jōmon 99, 202, *99*, *202*; Khok Phanom Di burials 201, *201*; Kot Diji style 172, *172*; Lapita 252, *252*; Melanesian 251, *251*; with Mesoamerican ball game *384*; Metal Age anthropomorphic jar 262, *262*; Moche 423, *423*; Nazca vessel 424, *424*; Phung Nguyen decoration 197, *198*; polychrome 171, 367, 401, 421, 424, 435, *367*, *424*, *437*; Pueblo Bonito chocolate jars 365, *365*; red-slipped/redware 204, 248, 249, 251, 252, *248*, *251*; Shipibo-Conibo style 437, *437*; Songze earthenware jar 191, *191*; stamped 251, 252, *251*; Tapajônica 436, *437*; temper 170, 187, 188, 189, 200; Trypillia vessels 273, *273*; Warka vase 153, *153*; Yangshao vessels 193, 194, *194*; Yayoi 206; *see also* figurines; sculptures/statues

Potts, Rick 55

Poverty Point 100, 351–52

Prambanan 262, *241*, *262*

Preclassic 360–62

Předmostí 90, *90*

Predynastic Egypt 305, *305*

prehistory 20, 24, 29, 40, 55, 75–76, 252, 258, 260, 263, 285, 304, 352, 367; *vs.* history 16, *16*

Preseli Hills bluestones 282, *283*

Presentation Theme 422, *422*

Priest-King statue 174, *174*

primates 15, 34, 43–46, *34*

proto-cuneiform 151, *151*

Proto-Oceanic dialect 251

pseudomorphs 84

Pucuncho Basin 343–44

Pueblo Bonito 364–66, *364*, *365*

Pueblo I 363

Pueblo II 364–66, *364*, *365*

Pueblo III 366, *366*

Pueblo IV 367, *367*

pueblos 349, 362–67, *350*

pulses 103, 113, 116, 117, 118, 121, 155, *115*

punctate-stamped pottery 251, 252, *252*

pyramids: Akapana 426, *427*; Giza 145, 205, 306, 307, *305*, *307*; Palenque 398, *398*; Saqqara 306, *306*; Teotihuacán 392–93, *392*; Tikal 400, *400*; Tula 402, *402*; Xochicalco 396, *396*; *see also* platform mounds

Pyu 230

Qafzeh (Jebel Qafzeh) 77, 78, 87

Qatna 162, 288, *146*

Qazvin Plain 148, *146*

Qesem Cave 69, *50*

Qin Dynasty 210, 222–24, *223*, *224*

Qin Shi Huangdi 221–23; tomb of 223, *15*, *224*

quarries 234, 256, 257, 418

Quebrada Jaguay 343, *325*

Quechua (Runa Simi) language 431

quinoa 416, 426, 440

Quiriguá 399, *381*

Qujialing 191, *186*

rachis 102, *102*

radiocarbon dating 24, 28

Rainbow Serpent 243–44, *244*

rainfall 35, 108, 113, 130, 146, 185, 188, 192, 195, 222, 253, 258, 267, 297, 359, 418, *98*

Rakhigarhi 173, 177–78, *168*

Ram in a Thicket sculpture *156*

Rapa Nui (Easter Island) 247, 249, 253, 260–61, *87*, *241*; *moai* of 256, *237*, *256*

Rawson, Jessica 219

Reck, Hans 40

red-slipped pottery/redware 204, 248, 249, 251, 252, *248*, *251*

refitting 64

Regional Development 434

regionalization: Amazonia 435–40, *436*, *437*, *439*, *440*; early Americas 337–42; Europe 279, *279*; South America 435–40; South Asia 171–72

Rehman Dheri 172, 175, *168*

relative chronology 24, 25

religion and beliefs 15, 16, 18, 20; Africa 299, 308, 309, 312; Australia 244–45; early communities 107; East Asia 228; Europe *265*; Mesoamerica 382, 394, 398, 402, 407; North America 357, 362, 363, 367; Pacific Islands 255, 257; South America 416, 421, 427, 431; South Asia 176, 180; Southeast Asia 231, 261; Southwest Asia 126, 147, 148, 150, 152, 154, 155; and state formation 142; *see also* Buddhism; Christianity; deities; Hinduism; Islam; myth; shamans

Renfrew, Colin 134

repatriation 18–20, *18*, *19*

repoussé 421

retouched tools 39, 40, 46, 63, 78, 191

rice 101, 188, *105*, *188*; Africa 302; East Asia 100, 104, 185–91, 195–97, 203–6, *190*; South Asia 169–71, 175; Southeast Asia 198–202, 248, *108*, *200*, *248*

Rice, Patricia 91

Rio Grande Valley 339, 367, *350*

Rio Supe 418

Rissman, Paul 174

ritual and ceremony: Africa 298–99, 305, 313, 315, 318, 319, *298*, *299*, *305*, *309*; in archaeology 15; Australia and Pacific Islands 243, 244, 259, 260; early Americas 334; early communities 107, 116; East Asia 191, 192, 194, 197, 202, 205, 206, 212, 213, 215, 216, 217, 218, 219–20, *194*, *214*, *218*, *233*; Europe 278, 279, 283, 284–85, 289, 292, 287; hominins 46; Mesoamerica 382, 385, 386, 387, 388, 389, 394, 395, 397, 398, 399, 401, 406–7, *389*; North America 353, 354, 355, 357, 358, 361, 362, 365, 367, 372, 373, *353*, *355*, *361*, *362*; South America 416, 418, 421–23, 426, 427, 431, 432, 437, 438; South Asia 175, 176;

Southwest Asia 117, 118, 119, 125, 126, 132–34, 147, 148, 150

rock art: Aboriginal Australian 242–44, *242*, *244*; of Laas Geel 303, *303*; Newgrange 280, *280*; Pueblo IV 367; Saharan 98, *98*; symbolism in Southern African 298–99, *298*, *299*; Tanum site *265*; Upper Paleolithic 88–89, *89*

rock shelters 84, 85, 92, 119, 301, *330*

rock-cut churches 312, *312*

Roman empire 109, 308, 313, 315, 318, 447, *19*

Royal Cemetery of Ur 155–56, *139*, *155*, *156*

Runa Simi (Quechua) language 431

Sacred Valley of the Inkas 430, *430*, *433*

sacrifice 219, 382, 403, *219*; animal 205, 214, 215, 216, 222; *see also* human sacrifice

Sacsahuamán 432, *433*

Sahara 98, 99, 300–302, 315–16, *98*, *105*, *316*

Sahlins, Marshall 259–60

Sahul Shelf (Greater Australia) 57, 85, 245, *87*, *86*, *87*, *246*

Saint-Acheul 50, 53, 55

Saladoid 435, 438

salt 316, 319, 320, 403, 437

Sambungmacan 58, *50*

Samoa 249, 253, 259, *241*

San 14, 103, 299

San José Mogote 383, 390, *381*

San Lorenzo 384, 385–86, *381*, *385*

Sangiran 50, 55, 56, *246*

Sannai-Maruyama 100, 203, *203*

Santa Cruz Islands 245, *242*

Santarém 436–37, *414*, *437*

Sanxingdui 198, 216, 218–19, *186*, *212*, *218*, *219*

Saqqara 306, *305*, *306*

Sarawak 85, 250

Sarcina, Anna 174

Sargon, king 156–58, *156*

Scandinavia 269, 284–85, 287, 374, *269*

scavenging 42–43, 68–70, 82–84, 336, *43*, *69*

Schletz 278

Schliemann, Heinrich 291, *291*

Schöningen 63, *50*, *55*, *63*

Schug, Gwen Robbins 174

scripts: Arabic 316, *151*; hieroglyphs 173, 290, 292, 313, *292*; Indus 173, *173*; Linear A 290, 292; Linear B 292, *292*; Meroitic 313; *see also* language(s); writing

sculpture/statues: Benin heads 316, *316*; colossal heads 385, *385*; Eagle Man 407, *408*; Jinsha jade tiger 216, *216*; Langke Bulawa 262, *263*; Lydenburg head 314, *314*; Nefertiti bust 18, *18*; Nok terra-cotta 315, *315*; Priest-King 174, *174*; of Rapa Nui (*moai*) 256, *237*, *256*; Royal Cemetery of Ur/Ram in a Thicket 155, *156*; Sanxingdul ritual pits

218–19, *219*; Sokkuram Buddha 227, *227*; Tenochtitlán monolithic 407, *407*; Teopantecuanitlán 386, *386*; Teotihuacán facades 393, *393*; terra-cotta warriors 15; *see also* figurines

seals 146, 147, 173, *173*; cylinder 152–53, 154, *152*

Sechín Alto 420, *414*

sedentism 101, 107, 116, 118, 186, 202, 244, 300, 301, 376, 383

Semitic Akkadian language 156

Sennedjem 304

Seowtewa, Octavius 17

settlement mounds 126, 198, 210, 275, 270, *271*; *see also* tells

settlements *see* farming communities; village settlements; urban communities

Shaffer, Jim 171, 173

shaft tombs 386, 394

Shahr-i Sokhta 175

shamans 117, 205, 260, 299, 355, *194*, *228*, *355*

Shamash (deity) 160

Shandong 193, 222, *186*

Shang Dynasty 192, 195, 210, 214–16, 222–23, 234, *214*, *215*, *216*, *222*

Shangchen 55–56, 58, *50*, *55*

Shangshan 188, *186*

Shanidar Cave 84

Shao Tuo 223

Sharp, Andrew 255

Shea, John 85

sheep 103, 116, 121, 125, 128, 133, 157, 168, 171, 302, 303, *128*, *303*

shellfish 78, 79, 199, 201, 203, 344, 371, 415, 416

shells: beads 81, 116, 168, 200, 201, 251, *201*; as decoration 155, 156, *315*; engraved 65, 79, 119, 362, *362*; jewelry/ornaments 79, 81, 88, 195, 201, 212, 244, 251, 326, 421, *81*, *201*, *362*, *421*; offerings 199, 200, 213; as tools 84, 251; *see also* middens

sherds 180, 187, 200, 222, *248*, *252*

Shijiahe 191, *186*

Shimao 212, 213, *212*

Shimoda shironaya 99

Shipibo-Conibo pottery 437, *437*

Shixia 197, *186*

Shona 318

shrines 107, 155, 159, 161, 227, 256, 257, 318, 393, *17*, *153*, *159*

Shu Dynasty *218*

Shuihudi 223

Siberia 26, 82, 83, 85, 87, 89, 90, 203, 301, 324, 326, 327, 342, 372, *87*

Sibri cemetery 179

sickles 102, 103, 117, 169, 170, 187, 192, 195, *169*

Silk Road 229–30, *229*

Silla 225–26, *225*, *226*

Silverthrone glacier 325

Sima de los Huesos 59, 62, 82, *50*, *55*

Singapore 245, *241*, *246*

Single Grave culture 284

Sipán 422, *414*, *422*

Siyaj K'ak 393
Skeetchestn First Nation 13
skeletons: Hobbit (Liang Bua) 57, 57; Homo erectus 52, 76–77, 52, 77; Homo sapiens 76–77, 78; KNM-ER 1808 68; Lucy 36, 36; Paleoamerican 327–28; see also skulls/crania
Skhūl (Mughâret es-Skhūl) 77, 87
skulls/crania 35; australopithecine 37, 37; curation and caching 134, 134; Dali cranium 85, 85; Deep Skull 85, 86; Dinaledi Cave 66–67, 66; Herto crania 76; Homo erectus 40, 50, 56, 76, 56, 76, 77, 85; Kabwe cranium 76, 76; Petralona 60, 60; wolf 90, 90; Xuchang crania 82; see also skeletons
slavery see enslavement
Sloan 342, 325, 339
Snaketown 360, 361, 350, 360, 361
soapstone 372, 373
Søby 447
social inequality 22, 135, 174, 186, 193, 205, 212, 234, 310, 362, 426, 440, 449–50
social order/organization: Africa 305, 308, 320; early America 331, 337; early communities 106–7; East Asia 193, 195–96, 206, 212, 221, 234, 260, 195; Europe 268–69, 271–74, 287–88; hominins 44; Mesoamerica 385, 391, 398–401, 404, 405, 407–8; North America 356, 361–62; Pacific Islands 260; South America 417, 431, 440; Southwest Asia 148, 152–54, 158, 162; and state formation 141
Society for American Archaeology (SAA) 450
Society Islands 253, 254, 256, 87, 241
sod 373, 373
Sokkuram cave 227, 225, 227
Solomon Islands 245, 253, 260, 246
Solutrean 92
Songze culture 190–91, 191
Sopohang 203, 203
Sotho 67, 320
South America 413–40; agriculture/farming 416–17; cities, states, empires 425–35; collapse and reorganization 421–25; earliest occupation of 342–44, 325, 329; environments and landscapes 413–15, 414; farming communities 419–21; hunter-gatherers 415–16; regionalization 435–40; urban communities 417–19, 418
South Asia 167–81; agriculture/farming 168–71, 169, 170; collapse and localization 178–80; environments and landscapes 167, 168; expansion and integration 180; hunter-gatherers 167–68; states and regionalization 171–72; urban communities 173–78, 176, 177, 178

South Halmahera/West New Guinea language 247
Southeast Asia 241; agriculture/farming 197–202; creation of 97, 97; seaborne trade and contact in 261–62; states 229–34, 229; see also Island Southeast Asia
Southeastern Europe 269–74, 269, 271, 272, 273
Southern Africa 313–20, 314, 315, 317, 319
Southwest Asia 113–37, 141–63; agriculture/farming 121–25, 135–36, 125; city states, cities, kingdoms, empires 145–49, 154–59, 160–62, 155; early humans in 79, 85; environments and landscapes 113–14, 114, 115; farming communities 125–35, 128; hunter-gatherers 115–21; urban communities 149–54, 149, 150
Southwest North America 359–60
Spaniards in Mesoamerica 403–9, 405
spears 99, 152, 196, 334, 124, 242; wooden 63, 83, 84, 332, 63, 337
spearthrowers (atlatl) 90, 92, 334
species 14, 15, 23–24, 26, 32–33
Spring and Autumn Annals 221
squash 344, 352, 382–83
Sri Ksetra 230, 212
Sri Lanka 167–68, 180, 168, 180
stamped pottery 251, 252, 251
Standard of Ur 139, 155
standardization 70, 172, 173, 174, 175, 176, 179, 180, 197, 242, 440, 275
Star Carr 268
states 141–45, 145; Africa 304–13, 315–20, 305; East Asia 210–29, 212, 225, 228; Europe 290–91; Mesoamerica 386–91, 396–401, 403–9, 381; South America 425–35, 414; South Asia 171–72, 168; Southeast Asia 229–34, 229; Southwest Asia 145–49, 146; see also city states
statues see sculpture
Steinheim 62, 50, 55
stelae 159; Aksum 313, 313; Cerro Sechín 419, 419; of Hammurabi 160, 160; Hauberg Stela 387, 387; Tiwanaku 426, 427; Victory Stela of Naram-Sin 158, 158
steppes 220, 267, 284, 288, 115
Stiner, Mary 84
stone circles 180, 202, 280, 282–83, 301, 282, 283, 302
stone tools 15, 24, 32, 34, 37–42, 44, 45, 53, 65, 119, 121, 134, 169, 206, 242, 304, 339, 343, 39, 41, 65, 339; see also axes; points
Stonehenge 280, 282–83, 282, 283
storage of food 101, 115, 121–24, 130, 135, 206, 243, 352, 363, 368, 370, 429, 123, 131; pits and silos 106, 170, 189, 193, 205, 333, 369, 331
stratigraphy 24, 26, 27, 56, 333, 336, 77
stump drawing 88, 89
stupas 230, 176, 261

sub-Saharan Africa 82, 103, 105, 314, 318, 98, 105
Sulawesi 245, 249, 252, 262, 73, 241, 246, 263
Sumatra 245, 261, 262, 97, 241, 246, 262
Sumerian Dynasty 154–56, 158, 157, 159, 155, 156
Sumerian language 154, 156, 158, 159, 151
Sundaland/Sunda Shelf 85, 87, 97, 245, 86, 87, 246
Sungir' 90
Susa 153, 159, 160, 146, 160
Swahili language 317
Swahili coast 308, 316–17, 318, 317
Swan Point 326, 325
Swanscombe 62, 50, 55
Swartkrans Cave 45, 64, 66, 36, 50
Swat Valley 168, 169
sweat welding 421
sweet potato cultivation 246, 257, 258
swidden 401, 434
swords 226, 228, 288, 289
symbolism 81, 99, 118, 119, 126, 132, 298–99, 385, 81, 298, 299
Százhalombatta-Földvár 289, 289

Tabon 241, 246, 250
Tahiti 254, 259, 260, 255
Taiwan 247–48, 252, 241, 247, 251; Fengtian jade 249, 250, 248, 250
Taiwan Strait 196
Talasea obsidian 248
Talheim death pit 278, 278
Tanum 265
Taosi 212, 212
Tapajônica ceramics 436–37, 437
Tapajós 436–37, 414, 437
taro 245, 246, 253, 257
Tasmania 85, 97, 242, 243, 86, 87, 241
Tassili n'Ajjeri 95
Taurus Mountains 113, 114
taxation 159, 230, 307, 310, 401, 405, 407, 408, 417, 431, 432
technocomplexes 90, 92
Tell Abu Salabikh 156, 146
Tell al-Ubaid 146, 155
Tell Aswad 133–34, 134
Tell Brak 149, 146, 149, 155
Tell es-Sultan 132–33
Tell Fara 156, 146, 155
Tell Haloula 133
tells 128, 270–71, 273, 274, 275, 289, 271, 289; see also settlement mounds
temper 170, 187, 188, 189, 200
temple mounds 417, 419, 426, 427, 418, 419
temples: Africa 311, 311; depictions of 152, 152; East Asia 227, 227, 229; Mesoamerica 400, 400; Pacific Islands 256, 262; South America 420, 421, 423–24, 428, 432, 420, 424, 428, 433; Southeast Asia 229, 231–32, 234, 262, 15, 28, 230, 231, 232, 233, 262; Southwest Asia 147–49, 146, 147

Tenochtitlán 406–7, 381, 406, 407, 408
Teopantecuanitlán 386, 386
teosinte 382, 383
Teotihuacán 142, 144, 386, 390–94, 381, 392, 393, 394
Tepanecs 404
Terminal Classic 401
terra preta 436–37, 439, 439
terraces/terracing 109, 117, 122, 142, 150, 188, 258, 262, 359, 390, 395, 401, 405, 417, 426, 430, 432, 446, 108, 258, 261, 430, 443
terra-cotta: Benin heads 316, 316; haniwa 228, 228; Lydenburg head 314, 314; Nok sculptures 315, 315; warriors 15
Teso dos Bichos 436
Teuchitlan 394
Téviec graves 279
Texcoco 408, 381
textiles 128, 149, 157, 158, 161, 292, 399, 406, 408, 416, 429, 432; see also clothing; weaving
Thailand 198–200, 249
Thebes 308–9, 305
Thessaly 270
tholos tombs 290
Three Age System 24
Three Kingdoms 225
Thule 372–74, 373
Tianluoshan 196, 186, 196
Tianma Qucun 217, 212, 217
tigers 196, 218, 216
Tigris river 144, 145, 147, 154, 114, 115, 146, 155
Tikal 388, 393, 397, 400, 143, 381, 399, 400
Tikopia 260, 241
timber see wooden and timber construction
Timor 245, 241, 246
tipis/tepees 369
Titicaca, Lake 413, 418, 419, 426, 431, 414, 427
Tiwanaku 426–27, 414, 427
Tlaxcalans 405, 408
Toltecs 356, 402–3, 404, 350, 356, 402
tombs: chambered 274, 280, 274; dolmen 204, 204; Fu Hao 215, 214, 215; Koguryo 225, 225, 226; megalithic 284–85; Monte Albán 395; Qin Shi Huangdi 223–24, 15, 224; Sennedjem 305, 304; shaft 386, 394; Shao Tuo 223; Sipán 422, 422; Tenochtitlán 407, 407; Teotihuacán 391–92; tholos 290; Tomb of the Dancers 225; Tomb of the Golden Crown 225–26, 226; Tomb of the Heavenly Horse 225, 226; Tutankhamun 309, 309; Xi (archivist) 223; Zeng 221, 221; Zhou 218, 220; see also burials; cemeteries
Tonga 249, 252, 253, 258, 259, 260, 87, 241
Toolondo eel traps 243
Toro 206, 203
totem poles 370, 370

trade and exchange: Africa 309, 313, 315, 316, 317, 318, 319, 320, *317*; Australia and Pacific Islands 244, 249, 250, 255, 259; early Americas 331, 335; early networks of 88; East Asia 195, 196, 206, 214, 215, 221, 228, 229–30, 234; Europe 273, 281, 285, 286, 287, 291; Island Southeast Asia 261–63; Mesoamerica 391, 394, 398, 403, 404, 407, *379*; North America 352, 353, 354–55, 357, 359, 360, 362, 365, 367, 369, 371; South America 435, 436, 437; South Asia 168, 171, 173, 175, 177, 179–80; Southwest Asia 134–35, 147, 148, 149, 153–54, 157, 160, 161, 162, 163; and state formation 141, 142, 143, 145, 151
trance dance 299, *299*
transhumance 167, 169, 277
Tres Zapotes 384, 387, *381, 387*
Trichterbecher (TBK) culture 279, 284
Trinil 58, *50*
Trundholm sun chariot 286–87, *287*
Truth and Reconciliation Commission of Canada (TRC) 449
Trypillia mega-sites 273–74, *273*
Tswana 320
Tuamotu Islands 253, *241*
tubers 45, 68, 99, 171, 344, 417, 440
Tula 396, 402, *381, 402*
tumuli 225, 287
Tupian languages 434
Turkana, Lake 52, 303, *36, 50, 300*
Turkana Boy 52, *52*
turquoise 148, 168, 212, 213, 318, 365, *213*
Tutankhamun 309, *309*
Tuttul 160, *146*
Twin Rivers 65, *50*
type sites 40, 92

Ubaid 145–49, *146, 147, 148*
'Ubeidiya 54, *50, 55*
Ugarit *146, 151*
Umm el Tlel 83
Upemba Depression 320
Upper Mesopotamia 147, 149, 152, 156, 157, 161–62
Upper Paleolithic 75, 84, 88–89, 91, 92, *77, 89, 91*
Upper Pleistocene 87, *87*
Upper Xingu 436, 438, *414*
Ur 154, *146*; Royal Cemetery of 155–56, *139, 155, 156*
Ur III empire 159, *159*
urban communities: Africa 301, 309–11, 313, 316–18, *310*; South America 417–19, *418*; South Asia 173–78, *176, 177, 178*; Southwest Asia 149–54, *149, 150*; *see also* farming communities; village settlements
urbanization 21–22, 142, 149, 151, 154, 173, 179, 308, 315, 316, 320, 448, *448*
Urnfields 289–90
Uruk 142, 149–54, 160, *146, 150, 151, 152, 153*

Valencina de la Concepción 274, *274*
Valley of the Kings 309, *309*
Varela, Andia y 254
Varna cemetery 272–73, *272*
Vedbaek 281–84
Ventris, Michael 292
Venus figurines 91, *91*
Vietnam 197–200, 249, *186, 200, 241*
village settlements 24, 27, 100, 106; Africa 302, 305; East Asia 187–90, 192–93, 197, 204, 205, *183*; Europe 289, *289*; Mesoamerica 382, 383, 385, *383*; North America 350, 356, 359–67, 369, 370, 371, *366, 370*; Pacific Islands 252; South America 416, 417, 421, 435, 436, 437, 438, *436*; South Asia 168, 169, 171, 178; Southwest Asia 118, 120–23, 128, 136, 145, *122*; *see also* farming communities; urban communities
Vindija Cave 82
Vinnicombe, Patricia 298
Vogelherd Cave 89, *90*
vultures 84, 132, *85*

Wadi Feynan 124
Walaldé 314
wall painting *see* art; murals; rock art
Wallacea Strait 85, *86, 246*
walled settlements: Africa 311, 317; East Asia 189, 190, 210, 212, 213, 214, 215, 216, 218, 225, 230, 232, *230*; North America 361; South America 421, 427, 428, 432; South Asia 175, 177, 178, *178*; Southwest Asia 124, *19*
war and conflict: Africa 310; Australia and Pacific Islands 242, 254, 256, 260, *242*, 255; early Americas 327; early humans 105; East Asia 212, 213, 221, 225, 234, *223, 233*; Europe 278, 289, 291; Mesoamerica 387, 389, 390, 391, 394, 395, 396, 397, 398, 401, 403, 404, 408; modern day *19*, 444, 445; North America 355, 357, 366, 367, 369, 376; South America 421, 431, 433, 435, 437; South Asia 174, 175; Southwest Asia 149, *149*; and state formation 143, 144
Wari 426–27, *414*
Warka 149, *150*
Warka Vase 153, *153*
Warring States 221, 223
warriors 217, 254, 287, 288, 399, 404, 407–8, 423; representations of 174, 357, 386, 390, 396, 402, 403, 407, 422, 423, *15, 396, 402, 408, 422, 423*
Watson, Patty Jo 352
Watson Brake 100, 351, *350, 351*
weaving 107, 197, 198, 206, 247, 253
Wei River Valley 217
West Africa 37, 301, 302–3, 308, 315–16, 318, *314, 315, 316*
Western Deffufa 311, *311*

Western Europe 61, 92, 97, 279–83, 285–88, *97, 268, 269, 280, 281, 282, 283, 286*
whale bones 373–74, *373*
wheat 101, 113, 121, 125, 155, 168, 170, 303, 320, *105, 169, 304*; einkorn 125, 126, *125*; emmer 302; wild 99, 126, *115*
Wheeler, Peter 43, 44
Whitsunday Islands 242, *241*
Willandra Lakes 240, *86, 241*
Willcox, George 125
Willendorf 91, *91*
wine vessels 193, 221, *194, 221*
wolves, domesticated 90, *90*
women's roles: in archaeology 42, 449; in cultivating plants, eastern North America 352; in elite Maya society 399, 401; in Inka society 432; in Mesopotamian society 158; in stone toolmaking 42
wooden and timber construction: Americas 332, 353, 354, 357, 364, 365, *332, 353, 358, 365*; early 100, 106; East Asia 189, 196, 157, 230, *196*; Europe 274, 277, 280, 283, 284, 289–90, *27, 275, 286*; South Asia 169; Southeast Asia 247; Southwest Asia 120, 131, 133, 136, 148, 160, 161, *118, 121, 127, 157*
wooden artifacts 63, 84, 189, 190, 196, 206, 215, 225, 256, 278, 299, 371, 429, *63, 155, 156, 371*
Woodhenge 283
wool 149, 157, 160, 163
world system 154
writing 141, 145, 151–53, *151, 152*; Chinese 222–23, *222, 223*; Ebla clay tablets 157, *157*; Mesoamerican 386–87, *387*; *see also* language(s); scripts
Wu Ding, King 215, *215*
Wudi, emperor 224

Xi (archivist) 223
Xia Dynasty 210, 213–14, *213*
xiaozhuan 222
Xinguano 438
Xipo 194, *186, 194*
Xochicalco 396, *381, 396*
Xuchang crania 82

Yamato 228–29, *228*
Yamnaya 274, 284, 285
Yana 324
Yangshao 193–94, 211, *183, 194*
Yangzi River Valley 185, 186–91, 195, 213, 214, 215, *186, 190, 191*
Yanshi 214
Yarim Tepe 147, *146, 147*
Yarim-Lim 162
Yayoi 205–6, 228, *203*
yazhang 198, 218, 219
Yellow River Valley 185, 191–97, 211, 213, *186, 192, 193, 194, 195, 196, 212*
Yilou basin 213
Yinxu 215
Yoshinogari 206, *203*
You, prince *216*

Younger Dryas 96, 114, 119, 120–21, 187, 342, *115*
Yuchanyang 187, *186*
Yuchisi 196, *186*

Zagheh 148, *146, 148*
Zagros Mountains 113, 119, 135, 153, *114, 115, 158*
Zapotec 390, 395, *387*
Zeng, Marquis of 221, *221*
Zeribar, Lake *114, 115*
Zhang 221
Zhengzhou 214–15, *212*
Zhou Dynasty: Eastern 210, 220–21, *221*; Western 210, 217–20, *217, 220*
Zhoukoudian 58, *50, 55, 56*
Zhuangbai 217, *212, 217*
ziggurats 150, 159, *159*
Zimbabwe plateau 317–19, *319*
Zimri-Lim palace 161–62, *162*
zooarchaeology 46, 175
Zulu state 320
Zuni reservation projects 446–47, *17*
Zunie, Jerome 446